Praise for *Advanced Linux Networking*

"An excellent Linux networking book is made available, the rest is now up to you. My recommendation to you is to go out and get it."

—ALEKSANDAR STANCIN, Help Net Security, www.net-security.org

"If you want to take advantage of Linux's strengths in a networked environment, this is the book for you. I highly recommend it."

—MICHAEL J. JORDAN, Linux Online

"At last: an 'advanced' book which truly deserves the title. Most 'advanced' books have breadth; this one also has depth. In under 800 pages, the author packs almost all the knowledge needed to administer a Linux system in a hostile environment."

—ROGER BURTON WEST, DiverseBooks.com

Advanced Linux Networking

Roderick W. Smith

✦✦Addison-Wesley

Boston • San Francisco • New York • Toronto • Montreal
London • Munich • Paris • Madrid
Capetown • Sydney • Tokyo • Singapore • Mexico City

The publisher offers discounts on this book when ordered in quantity for special sales. For more information, please contact:

Pearson Education Corporate Sales Division
201 W. 103rd Street
Indianapolis, IN 46290
(800) 428-5331
corpsales@pearsontechgroup.com

Visit AW on the Web: www.awprofessional.com

Library of Congress Control Number: 2002106713

ISBN 0-201-77423-2
2 3 4 5 6 7 8 9 10—MA—0605040302
Second printing, November 2002

DEDICATION

To all those who donated time, money,
products, or blood after September 11, 2001.
You give hope that humanity's best side
may win out over its worst side.

Contents

CONTENTS

CONTENTS

Preface

Computer networks have changed our lives. They grew slowly, and mostly unnoticed, in the 1970s and 1980s. In the 1990s, though, something happened. Perhaps it was the availability of the World Wide Web (WWW, or Web) and graphical Web browsers, which made computer networks accessible to Grandma Dorothy and Uncle Stan. Maybe it was that the availability of network connections had reached a critical threshold. Perhaps the quality and quantity of network-enabled software passed a critical threshold. Possibly it was two or all three of these things, or something else entirely. In any event, networks became noticeable. Most importantly, *the Internet* became noticeable.

The Internet comprises millions of computers, many of which run *servers*—software packages designed to listen for and respond to data transfer requests from other computers. Because the protocols upon which the Internet was built were designed to work in a cross-platform manner, both Internet clients and the servers they use run on many different platforms. One of the most popular of these is Linux. Coupled with inexpensive *x*86 hardware, Linux makes a very cost-effective server platform for small and mid-sized sites. Indeed, with increasing computer performance and Linux versions working their way up the computer performance hierarchy, Linux is beginning to make inroads into the large server market. Thus, with Linux on everything from tiny network appliances to large servers, knowing how to set up and maintain a Linux server system is an important skill for networking professionals today.

Which servers, though? There are hundreds, if not thousands, of individual server programs. Most general-purpose Linux networking books focus on a handful of popular servers—Web (HTTP) servers like Apache, login servers like Telnet and SSH, file servers like NFS and Samba, and a few others. These books present enough information to get a user up and running, but little more. They also give short shrift to servers that are less visible but that are often extremely important, like DHCP servers, time servers, and Kerberos. This book takes a different approach to Linux networking: I assume that you know at least a minimal amount about Linux and networking in general, and you want to take you skills to a higher level. Although this book does cover the "usual suspects," it spends less time introducing the basics and more time describing advanced or unusual configurations. This book also covers some of the servers and topics that are neglected in most entry-level Linux networking books. The result is the closest thing possible to a book that's both a *general* Linux networking book and an *advanced* Linux networking book.

To be sure, you won't learn everything there is to know about complex packages like Apache or Samba in this book. The relevant chapters provide quick introductions to these tools, a summary of some popular techniques you won't find covered in other introductory Linux networking books, and pointers to additional resources. This book's approach is to be a general-purpose Linux networking book for people who are not novices.

WHO SHOULD BUY THIS BOOK

This book is designed to be an advanced tutorial and reference for those with some Linux networking experience, or at least some Linux and some networking experience. The first few chapters cover low-level configuration, including such factors as getting the network up and running to begin with; but I assume you're already familiar with Linux, or at least UNIX, and with basic networking terminology. If you're not familiar with these things, an introductory Linux system administration book, such as Marcel Gagné's *Linux System Administration: A User's Guide* (Addison-Wesley, 2002) or Vicki Stanfield's and my *Linux System Administration* (Sybex, 2001) should help fill in the gaps.

If you want to learn a bit more about big servers like Apache or Samba but don't want to buy dedicated books for them, or if you want to learn about the small but potentially important servers like xntpd or xfs, then this is the book for you. This book also covers miscellaneous networking topics, like how to start and stop servers, backing up a network, running a server in a chroot jail, and using iptables. Knowing these topics will help fill out your networking knowledge base and make you better able to adapt to new requirements and generally improve the networks you administer.

In writing this book, I imagined the audience to be administrators of small or mid-sized networks. Your network might be dominated by Linux, UNIX, Windows, MacOS, or something even more exotic, but of course you've got at least one Linux system. Most chapters describe the basic principles upon which a tool is built and then describe how to use the tool. You should, therefore, be able to learn a lot about the tools by reading this book, but you can also use this book as a quick reference. I aim for this to be the book you would choose if you could have just one Linux networking book.

LINUX DISTRIBUTIONS

One of the challenges of administering Linux is that Linux isn't a single OS. Instead, it's a collection of OSs, all built around the same kernel. Each of these variant OSs is known as a *distribution*. A distribution consists of a Linux kernel; a distribution-specific installation program; a wide assortment of support tools, user programs, and so on; and a set of default startup and configuration scripts. Different distributions frequently use different versions of the Linux kernel and of support programs. Indeed, they sometimes ship with different programs entirely to fill particular roles, such as sendmail, Exim, or Postfix for a mail server. For these reasons, Linux distributions can vary substantially in overall feel and in many administrative details.

Many books on Linux fail to address the variability among Linux distributions. They intentionally focus on just one distribution, or provide coverage of others in a cursory manner. One of the goals of this book, though, is to cover several of the most popular Linux distributions explicitly. Specifically, I cover Caldera OpenLinux 3.1, Debian GNU/Linux 2.2, Mandrake 8.1, Red Hat 7.2, Slackware 7.0, SuSE 7.3, and TurboLinux 7.0. To be sure, I can't cover every detail for each of these OSs, but I point out where they differ in important ways, such as where each places network startup scripts and what FTP servers each includes. Some chapters—notably those on server startup tools, LPD print servers, SMTP mail servers, and FTP servers—cover multiple servers in order to be applicable to the default configurations for each of these seven major Linux distributions.

HOW THIS BOOK IS ORGANIZED

This book is broken down into four parts of four to thirteen chapters. The structure represents the assumption that your network includes some servers that are used primarily by local users and others that are exposed to the Internet at large, but of course some servers can do double duty, so the placement of some servers may not reflect the configuration on your network. The book's four parts are as follows:

- **Part I: Low-Level Configuration**—This part is the shortest, at only four chapters. It covers kernel network configuration options, basic TCP/IP network configuration, network stacks, and starting servers.
- **Part II: Local Network Servers**—This part covers servers and procedures that are most likely to be used by other computers on your local network. This includes DHCP servers, Kerberos, Samba, NFS servers, printing with LPD, time servers, POP and IMAP mail servers, news servers, remote login servers, X and VNC servers, font servers, remote administration servers, and network backups.
- **Part III: Internet Servers**—These chapters cover servers that are often accessible to the world at large. Topics include DNS servers, SMTP mail servers, Web servers, and FTP servers.
- **Part IV: Network Security and Router Functions**—This part diverges from the emphasis on servers as distinct topics for chapters and focuses on network security. Topics include a general look at network security, using a `chroot` jail, configuring advanced router functions, using `iptables` for firewall and NAT purposes, and setting up a VPN.

CONVENTIONS USED IN THIS BOOK

In discussing computers and software, it's easy to become confused because it's not always clear when a word has its usual meaning and when it refers to a computer, file, program, command, or what have you. For this reason, this book uses certain typographic conventions to help clarify matters. Specifically:

- The bulk of the text appears in a normal, proportionally-spaced font, like this.
- *Italicized text* indicates an important term that's appearing for the first time in a chapter. It's also occasionally used for emphasis.
- `Monospaced text` indicates a filename, computer name, the syntax used by a command, the contents of configuration files, or the output of commands typed at a command prompt. Sometimes program names appear in this way, when these names are really the software's filename.

- *Italicized monospaced text* indicates a variable—information that may differ on your system. For instance, instructions might say to create a file whose name is unimportant or system-specific. The instructions might then refer to this file as *file.txt*.

- **Bold monospaced text** indicates information you should type exactly at a command prompt. When isolated on a line of its own, it's usually preceded by a monospaced but non-bold prompt, such as #, which the computer generates. This type of text may also be italicized, to indicate that what you type will depend upon your configuration or the results you intend to achieve.

When a command you type appears on a line of its own, the command is preceded by a command prompt. A pound sign (#) indicates a root command prompt. Such commands are usually entered by root, not by ordinary users (although there are exceptions to this rule). If the command prompt is a dollar sign ($), ordinary users may, and often do, enter the command. Some unusually long commands use line continuation characters—backslashes (\)—at the ends of all their lines but the first. You can type such commands exactly as they appear, including the backslashes, or you can omit the backslashes and type these commands entirely on one line. The backslashes exist just so that the command can be typeset in a reasonable font size.

This book also uses a number of special text elements that apply to entire paragraphs or larger segments of text. These elements are intended to highlight important or peripheral information. They are:

NOTE   A Note is not critical to the main discussion, but the information it contains is interesting or may be helpful in certain circumstances. For instance, a Note might point out how a feature differed in previous versions of a program.

TIP   A Tip contains information that can help you achieve a goal in a non-obvious way, or that can point you to uses of a system or software that might not have occurred to you.

WARNING A Warning describes a potential pitfall or danger. Warnings include software that could damage your system if used incorrectly, the potential to run afoul of ISP policies that forbid certain behaviors, and configurations that might leave your system vulnerable to outside intruders.

Sidebars

A Sidebar is like a Note, but it's usually longer—typically at least two paragraphs. These components contain extended discussion of issues that don't fit neatly into the overall flow of the chapter, but that are nonetheless related, interesting, or even important.

In discussing networks, it's often necessary to give specific IP addresses as examples. In most cases, I've used IP addresses from the ranges reserved for private networks (192.168.0.0–192.168.255.255, 172.16.0.0–172.31.255.255, and 10.0.0.0-10.255.255.255) even for systems that would normally be on the Internet at large. I've done this to avoid potential confusion or inadvertent offense that might occur if I were to pick random legitimate IP addresses.

CONTACTING ME

If you have questions or comments about this book, I can be reached at rodsmith@rodsbooks.com. I also maintain a Web page about the book at http://www.rodsbooks.com/adv-net/.

ACKNOWLEDGMENTS

I'd like to thank my editor, Karen Gettman, for her careful work shepherding this book through the production process. She was helped in this task by Emily Frey, the project coordinator, who received my chapters and generally saw that things went smoothly. No technical book can reach print without the assistance of technical experts, who help ensure that what the author writes resembles reality as closely as possible. This book's reviewers were Karel Baloun, Amy Fong, Howard Lee Harkness, Harold Hauck, Eric H. Herrin II, David King, Rob Kolstad, Matthew Miller, Ian Redfern, and Alexy Zinin. If any errors remain after the text ran their gauntlet, those errors are, of course, my own. Even aside from his help in technical reviewing, I'd like to thank David King for many helpful discussions about Linux networking. Finally, I'd like to thank my agent, Neil Salkind at Studio B, who helped get this book off the ground, with help from Michael Slaughter at Addison-Wesley.

PART I

LOW-LEVEL CONFIGURATION

Kernel Network Configuration

"All roads lead to Rome," the saying goes. Something similar is true of Linux networking, except that in this case, Rome is the Linux kernel. Sooner or later, all network traffic passes through the kernel. Given that not all computers or networks are identical, the Linux kernel includes several options you can set to optimize a system for your specific needs. You can set some of these options by passing parameters to the kernel, either during the boot process or after the system has booted, and many of these cases are covered in subsequent chapters of this book. In other cases you must recompile your kernel to activate a needed option or to deactivate one that might degrade your system's performance.

This chapter is devoted to discussing these kernel configuration options. First up is a discussion of kernel configuration procedures. Next is information on network protocol options, such as TCP/IP features, network filters, and support for non-TCP/IP protocol stacks. Next comes a discussion of Linux's drivers for various types of network hardware. The chapter concludes with a brief overview of the process of kernel compilation and use.

NOTE This chapter does not attempt to teach you everything you need to know to compile a kernel; instead, it focuses on the networking options in the kernel. The "Starting Kernel Configuration" and "Compiling and Installing a Kernel" sections include some discussion of more general kernel configuration and use, but if you're new to kernel compilation, you may want to consult the Linux Kernel HOWTO (http://www.linuxdoc.org/HOWTO/Kernel-HOWTO.html) or the kernel compilation chapter of an introductory Linux book.

STARTING KERNEL CONFIGURATION

To configure compile-time kernel options, you must begin with the kernel source code. All major distributions ship with this, but it may or may not be installed by default. Many distributions make changes to the standard kernel (say, to add new drivers that aren't yet standard). You may prefer to start with a standard kernel and add only those patches you need (it's possible you won't need any). Check http://www.kernel.org or a major Linux archive site like ftp://sunsite.unc.edu for the latest kernel source code. (You can also obtain kernel source code from your Linux distribution, but many distributions ship with kernels that have been patched to include non-standard drivers. Using a more standard kernel can be beneficial if you run into problems and need help solving them.)

NOTE There are two current branches of kernel development, which are distinguished by the second number in the three-part version number. Those with even second numbers (like 2.4.17) are known as *stable* or *release* kernels. Kernels with odd second numbers (like 2.5.2) are *development* kernels. Stable kernels are best for production environments, because they are, as the name implies, quite reliable. Development kernels, on the other hand, are being actively tinkered with—the kernel developers use this line to add new drivers, change interfaces, and so on. Development kernels are therefore best avoided unless you want to contribute to kernel development or if you really require some new driver. (In the latter case, you can often find a *back-port* of the driver to an older stable kernel.)

Kernel source code normally resides in /usr/src/linux, or in a subdirectory of /usr/src that includes the kernel version number, like /usr/src/linux-2.4.17. In the latter case, it's common practice to create a symbolic link called /usr/src/linux and point it to the true Linux source directory. This allows other programs that assume the source is in /usr/src/linux to function correctly, even if you want to keep multiple versions of the kernel source code; you can simply change the symbolic link as required.

Once you've uncompressed the kernel source code into /usr/src/linux, you should change to that directory in a normal command shell. You can then issue a command to configure the kernel options. Possibilities include the following:

- **make config**—This is the basic configuration tool. It asks you about every kernel option in turn, which can be tedious. If you make a mistake, you must normally go back and redo everything. For this reason, it's seldom used today.

- **make menuconfig**—This configuration procedure uses text-based menus for configuration options, which enables you to look through the options and adjust only those that require changes. This is a common method of configuration in text-mode environments.

- **make xconfig**—This method is similar to **make menuconfig**, except that **make xconfig** uses GUI configuration menus. You can click on a topic to see its options, then click your mouse to select how or if you want to compile any option. This is a popular means of kernel configuration when the X Window System (or X for short) is running.

All of these methods present the same options, which are organized into broad categories. (Some categories also include subcategories.) When you select one category with **make menuconfig** or **make xconfig**, a new menu appears showing the options within that category. (Figure 1.1 shows this for **make xconfig**.) Of particular interest for networking are the Networking Options and Network Device Support categories, which are the subject of the next two sections.

NOTE   This chapter describes the Linux 2.4.x kernel options, and particularly those in the 2.4.17 kernel. Kernel network options have changed in the past, and are likely to do so again in the future. 2.2.x kernels use similar options, but several details differ. A new kernel configuration tool, known as CML2, is under development in the experimental 2.5.x kernels. Check http://tuxedo.org/~esr/cml2/ for more information on it.

Most kernel options use a two- or three-way toggle (the Y, M, and N options shown in Figure 1.1). Y and N refer to the option's presence or absence in the kernel file itself, respectively, and M stands for *modular compilation*—

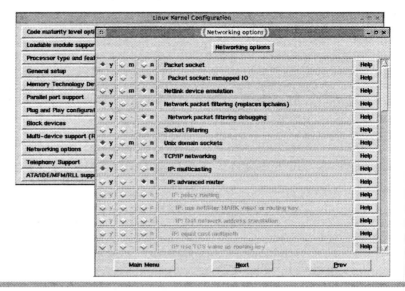

Figure 1.1 Linux kernel compilation options are organized into categories and sub-categories, each with its own menu.

compiling the option as a separate file that can be loaded and unloaded. These options are described in more detail in the upcoming section, "Drivers: Modules or Built-In."

NETWORK PROTOCOL SUPPORT

The Networking Options kernel menu contains options related to network protocols. You can include or exclude support for entire protocol stacks, and for some (particularly TCP/IP), you can fine-tune the support to optimize the kernel for particular roles, such as router options or packet filtering.

PACKET AND SOCKET OPTIONS

At a fairly low level, Linux networking operates by allowing programs to send or receive chunks of data (known as *packets*) via data structures known as *sockets*. In most cases, a program opens a socket in a manner that's similar to the way a program opens a file. The program can then send and receive data via that socket. The network protocol stack (discussed shortly in "Alternative Network Stack Options") processes the data in ways that allow it to reach its destination or to be interpreted by the program after having been received from the sender.

In some cases, it's desirable or even necessary to process network data in some other way, or to modify or extend the standard packet and socket operations. Some of these options are important enough that they have their own sections. A few miscellaneous options include the following:

- **Packet Socket**—This option allows applications to bypass much of the normal protocol stack. Most programs don't need this feature, but some network diagnostic tools and other low-level utilities do need it. For instance, tcpdump, which displays low-level TCP/IP packet information, uses this kernel option. Including this option unnecessarily will slightly increase the size of the kernel and might allow an intruder to use low-level network diagnostics like tcpdump that you'd rather the intruder not be able to use. Omitting this feature will prevent *you* from running these utilities, though.
- **Packet Socket: Mmapped IO**—This is a packet socket suboption that, if enabled, can improve the performance of tools that use packet socket connections.
- **Unix Domain Sockets**—Several common and important Linux programs use networking protocols to communicate with each other when they run on a single computer. Examples include syslogd (which handles log files) and X (X programs use network protocols to communicate with the X server, which displays their windows). The Unix Domain Sockets option allows this within-computer communication even on systems that lack conventional network hardware. When computers have conventional hardware, the domain sockets approach is faster than using the more general-purpose TCP sockets. You should include this option on all normal Linux systems; only specialized embedded devices or the like might lack this option.

These options all have default settings that are reasonable for most installations. You might want to disable packet socket support on some systems, though.

NETWORK FILTER OPTIONS

Network filters are designed to allow the system to block or modify packets that come into or leave a computer. One of these options (packet filtering) is particularly important for constructing firewalls or performing IP masquerading, as discussed in Chapter 25, Configuring `iptables`. A firewall can block certain types of undesirable access to a computer or a network that it protects, and IP masquerading lets you share a single IP address among an entire network. Specific kernel network filter options include the following:

- **Socket Filtering**—Normally, the kernel passes all packets that it receives for a given socket on to the program that created the socket. This option allows the program to point the kernel to a small program (known as a *filter*) that will block some of the packets it receives. Few programs require this facility, but the Dynamic Host Configuration Protocol (DHCP) is an important exception—both recent DHCP servers and some DHCP clients require it. You should therefore enable this option if your network uses DHCP.

- **Network Packet Filtering**—This option is the 2.4.*x* kernel's most important type of filter, because it enables certain firewall and IP masquerading techniques. Because these are so important, it's generally a good idea to include this support. When you do so, the Network Packet Filtering Debugging option becomes available, which you can enable if you experience problems. A later submenu, IP: Netfilter Configuration, also becomes available. Subsequent items in this list appear on this submenu.

- **Connection Tracking**—Enabling this option allows the kernel to track network connections in greater detail than is normal. For instance, a router usually passes packets more-or-less blindly between two network interfaces, but when this option is enabled (both in the kernel and by user-level tools), Linux can match up the source and destination IP addresses and ports for future reference. This feature is required for IP masquerading, so it should be enabled on a computer that is to function in this way. It's not necessary for most other systems. If you enable it, the FTP protocol support option becomes available. FTP requires extra housekeeping, so enable this option if you want to use FTP on an IP masqueraded connection.

- **IP Tables Support**—This option includes kernel support routines for the `iptables` utility, which is used to set up packet filter firewalls and IP masquerading, as discussed in Chapter 25. Activating this option also allows you to select a number of suboptions that fine-tune the features available to you. Many of these options have names of the form *Criterion Type* Match Support, which enables the kernel to match on the specified *Criterion Type*. Of these, Connection State Match Support is particularly important, because it allows the system to perform *stateful packet inspection*, a useful form of firewall operation discussed in Chapter 25. The Packet Filtering, Full NAT, and LOG Target Support options are also very important, as are each of their suboptions. Enable all of these features if you want to use a computer as an IP masquerading router or firewall. You can omit Full NAT for a standalone workstation or server.

- **ipchains (2.2-Style) Support**—If you have an older firewall script that's based on the ipchains utility used by the 2.2.*x* kernels, you can activate support for this utility as long as you don't compile IP Tables Support directly into the kernel. (The ipchains and iptables tools are mutually incompatible methods of doing largely the same things, but iptables is more advanced.) If you're creating a firewall from scratch, you can safely omit ipchains support.

- **ipfwadm (2.0-Style) Support**—The 2.0.*x* kernels used a firewall tool called ipfwadm. If you have an ipfwadm-based firewall script, you can use it by compiling this feature, which is incompatible with both the iptables and ipchains support. Unless you have such a script and lack the inclination to modify it to use iptables, you can safely omit this option.

Between the 2.0.*x* and 2.4.*x* kernels, Linux's network filtering options have become more sophisticated. The 2.4.*x* kernel includes many optional features, and it's important that you activate all those you'll need for the type of firewall you intend to implement. When in doubt about a specific feature in the IP: Netfilter Configuration menu, I recommend you activate it. This will increase the kernel's size slightly, but it will also provide you with greater flexibility in designing firewall rules.

WARNING

You may think that you don't need to implement firewall rules on a Linux computer, particularly if it resides on a network behind a dedicated firewall. Unfortunately, even many allegedly protected networks have security flaws, so it's best to err on the side of caution. To that end, implementing simple firewalls on individual Linux computers is often a good idea.

TCP/IP ROUTING OPTIONS

A *router* (also referred to as a *gateway*) is a computer that transfers data between two or more networks. For instance, a department at a large company or university is likely to have a router to link its own subnetwork with the larger network that belongs to the company or university as a whole. The company or university will then have a router to link all of its computers to the Internet. This topic is important enough that Chapter 24, Advanced Router Options, is devoted to the subject. For now, know that the Linux kernel includes several options that can influence its router operation. These are clustered as suboptions of IP: Advanced Router. Chapter 24 discusses the configuration and use of these options in more detail.

IPv6 Support Options

The Internet is built on TCP/IP protocols, and particularly on version 4 of the IP protocols (*IPv4*). Unfortunately, IPv4 is showing its age in many ways. For instance, it supports IP addresses that are four bytes (32 bits) in length, meaning that there is a theoretical maximum of 2^{32}, or 4,294,967,296, addresses. Because of inefficiencies in the way addresses are assigned, the number of Internet addresses is actually much lower than this. Consequently, the Internet is running out of addresses. IPv4 also has security limitations that allow miscreants to seriously disrupt Internet operation. These problems are not severe in 2002, but they're likely to become critical well before decade's end.

For these reasons, an upgrade to IPv4, known as *IPv6*, is under development. Among other things, IPv6 uses a 128-bit IP address for a theoretical maximum of 2^{128}, or 3.4×10^{38} addresses—enough for 2.2×10^{18} addresses per square millimeter of land surface on the Earth. IPv6 also includes better hooks for certain types of security systems than does IPv4. In 2002, few networks allow the use of IPv6, but if yours is one, or if you want to experiment with IPv6 on a private internal network, you can activate experimental Linux IPv6 support via the IPv6 Protocol (Experimental) option in the Networking Options menu. Once you do this, another option or two may become available, including an entire submenu entitled IPv6: Netfilter Configuration. This submenu includes a subset of options similar to those described earlier, in "Network Filter Options," but geared towards IPv6 rather than IPv4.

NOTE In order to activate IPv6 support, you must select Yes for the Prompt for Development and/or Incomplete Code/Drivers option in the kernel's Code Maturity Level Options menu. This is true of other "experimental" drivers as well. Eventually, IPv6 will become mainstream and nonexperimental. Like other experimental features, you should treat IPv6 support with some caution.

QoS Options

Suppose your Linux system is a router for a busy domain, or is a major server that processes a lot of traffic. In situations like this, it's not uncommon for Linux to find that it has more packets to process than it can send over its network interfaces. Thus, Linux needs some system for scheduling the transmission of outgoing packets. Ordinarily, Linux uses a first-in/first-out (FIFO) strategy, in which each outgoing packet waits in line behind all the others that have already been queued. In some situations, however, you might not want to use this system. You might want to favor certain types of packets, such as those delivered to certain networks or those that involve certain protocols. For instance, you might want to favor packets that carry real-time data, such as Internet telephony protocols. Adjusting packet priorities is the job of the *quality of service (QoS)* options. These options are all available from the QoS and/or Fair Queueing menu off of the Networking Options menu.

In order to implement a QoS system, you must select the QoS and/or Fair Queueing option in the menu of the same name. This action enables many of the options on this menu. A few others rely upon your selection of one or more other specific options. The most basic features are enabled by the various packet scheduler and queue options, such as CBQ Packet Scheduler and SFQ Queue. These options allow the kernel to schedule packets in more complex ways than the default FIFO. The QoS Support and Packet Classifier API options, as well as their individual suboptions, enable the use of Differentiated Services and the Resource Reservation Protocol (RSVP). These both allow routers to communicate QoS priorities to other routers. If all the routers between two sites implement compatible QoS protocols, the end result can be greatly improved performance for time-critical protocols, at the expense of less time-critical protocols.

Most nonrouter systems don't need any QoS options. If you're configuring a Linux computer as a router, though—particularly a heavily used router—you may want to activate these options. If you activate one, it may make sense to activate them all, because without all options activated, the tools you use to specify QoS criteria won't be as flexible. For instance, if you omit the U32 Classifier option, you won't be able to prioritize traffic according to the destination address.

In practice, using QoS features requires the use of advanced routing tools, such as `ip` and `tc`. Chapter 24 touches upon these tools, but they can be extremely complex. The `iproute2` + `tc` Notes (`http://snafu.freedom.org/linux2.2/iproute-notes.html`) and Differentiated Services on Linux (`http://diffserv.sourceforge.net`) Web sites contain additional documentation on these tools.

High-Level Protocol Support

The Linux kernel includes explicit support for several high-level network protocols. Placing this support in the kernel has two principal advantages. First, this code can run more quickly than can an ordinary user-level program. Second, placement in the kernel permits a tighter integration of the features of that protocol with the rest of the system. For instance, kernel-level support for network file-sharing protocols allows Linux to mount remote file exports as if they were local filesystems. The 2.4.*x* kernel includes support for three particularly important high-level protocols: HTTP, NFS, and SMB/CIFS.

NOTE This list of protocols is not comprehensive. Several others (particularly for network file-sharing protocols) are supported.

HTTP Acceleration

The Hypertext Transfer Protocol (HTTP) is at the core of the World Wide Web. Beginning with the 2.4.*x* kernels, Linux includes what is effectively a simple HTTP server in the kernel. This server is included with the Kernel HTTPd Acceleration option and configured and activated by writing specific values to pseudofiles in the `/proc/sys/net/khttpd` directory, as described in Chapter 20, Running Web Servers.

The kernel's HTTP server was created because the work of serving static Web pages (that is, those whose contents are fixed, as opposed to dynamic pages whose contents may be customized for individual users) is essentially just one of copying files from disk to a network address. This operation can be performed much more efficiently in the kernel than in a user-space program. For dynamic content and even some types of static content, the kernel's server falls back on a user-space Web server such as Apache. No special Apache configuration is required; Apache simply doesn't see requests for static Web pages.

NFS Options

Sun developed the Network Filesystem (NFS) as a way to share files among several computers as if those files were local. Linux includes support for NFS, as detailed in Chapter 8, File Sharing via NFS. To mount remote NFS exports, you must include NFS support in the kernel. Most Linux NFS servers also rely on support in the kernel. Both client and server NFS options reside in the Network File Systems submenu off of the File Systems menu, not in the Networking Options menu. Specifically, options you might want to activate include the following:

- **NFS File System Support**—This option enables basic NFS client support (that is, the ability to mount remote NFS exports as if they were local disk partitions). Enable it if you want to mount NFS directories exported by other computers.

- **Provide NFSv3 Client Support**—NFS has undergone various revisions, the latest of which is version 3 (NFSv3). This support must currently be explicitly enabled, because it's not as reliable as is support for older versions of NFS, as activated by NFS File System Support. The NFSv3 support relies on the basic NFS support.

- **Root File System on NFS**—If you select IP: Kernel Level Autoconfiguration in the Networking Options menu, you can select this option, which lets Linux mount its root filesystem from an NFS export. You'll normally only use this option on workstations that lack hard disks.

- **NFS Server Support**—To have Linux function as an NFS server (that is, to make some or all of its directories available to other computers), you need to run an NFS server. This option provides acceleration features for NFS servers that are written to take advantage of it. This option is not strictly required to run an NFS server, but it's generally a good idea to include it, since most Linux NFS servers are written to expect this support.

- **Provide NFSv3 Server Support**—If you want to run a kernel-aware NFS server for clients that understand NFSv3, activate this option. As with NFSv3 client support, this option relies upon the matching generic NFS support.

 NOTE NFS is used mainly by Unix and Linux systems. File sharing between other platforms is usually handled by other tools, one of which is discussed next.

SMB/CIFS Options

NFS isn't the only network file-sharing protocol available. Macintoshes often use AppleTalk, for instance, and Novell's IPX/SPX is a popular protocol stack with associated file-sharing tools. Perhaps the most common file-sharing tool for Linux, aside from NFS, is Samba, which implements the Server Message Block (SMB) protocol, which is also known as the Common Internet Filesystem (CIFS). Chapter 7, File and Printer Sharing via Samba, covers Samba configuration and use.

Samba provides everything needed for Linux to function as an SMB/CIFS server, so there's no kernel configuration required for this function. If you want Linux to be able to mount SMB/CIFS shares, though, you must activate the SMB File System Support option, which is roughly equivalent to NFS File System Support for NFS. Two suboptions (Use a Default NLS and Default Remote NLS Option) let Linux perform filename translations based on National Language Support (NLS) character sets. These options may be important if you use non-Roman alphabets like Cyrillic, or even extensions to the Roman alphabet as used by English, like characters that contain umlauts.

NOTE   It's possible to use Linux as an SMB/CIFS client using the smbclient program, even if you don't activate Linux's SMB/CIFS kernel options. smbclient doesn't actually mount an SMB/CIFS share, though; it gives you access to the share using an FTP-like interface.

ALTERNATIVE NETWORK STACK OPTIONS

Although TCP/IP is the most popular set of network protocols for Linux, and the one upon which the Internet is built, it's not the only choice of network protocol stack. The Networking Options menu includes several others. Most of the options in this menu are actually suboptions of TCP/IP Networking. If you scroll past these, you'll see the alternatives to TCP/IP:

- **Asynchronous Transfer Mode (ATM)**—This is an experimental set of options to support ATM hardware and protocols. ATM is really at least as much of a hardware definition as a network stack, but in the 2.4.x kernels, it's enabled in the Networking Options menu, along with other protocol stacks.

- **The IPX Protocol**—Novell's Internetwork Packet Exchange (IPX) is a protocol stack that's used on many local networks, particularly those running the Netware server OS. To use this stack, you'll need additional software, such as Mars_nwe (documented at http://www.

redhat.com/support/docs/tips/Netware/netware.html). The NCP File System Support option in the Network File Systems submenu of the File Systems menu will let you mount Netware volumes, much as the equivalent NFS and SMB/CIFS options let you mount NFS exports or Windows file shares.

- **AppleTalk Protocol Support**—Apple developed the AppleTalk protocol stack to enable file and printer sharing on its Macintosh computers. Linux supports AppleTalk through a combination of the kernel and the Netatalk package (http://netatalk.sourceforge.net/).

- **DECnet Support**—Digital Equipment Corporation (DEC; since bought out by Compaq) developed a network technology known as DECnet for its computers. Linux includes support for DECnet, but you must have a package of programs to use this protocol stack. Check http://linux-decnet.sourceforge.net for more information.

Linux also includes support for a handful of more obscure network protocols, such as Acorn's Econet. On most systems, TCP/IP and possibly one or two other protocols will be quite sufficient. Because of the success of the Internet, vendors who had previously used proprietary protocol stacks have been converting their tools to use TCP/IP. For instance, although Apple has long used AppleTalk, its file-sharing tools now work both over plain AppleTalk and a TCP/IP-based variant.

NOTE The standard Linux kernel lacks support for one common network stack, NetBEUI. This stack was the default for Windows file sharing via SMB/CIFS in the past, but SMB/CIFS today works equally well over TCP/IP.

Chapter 3, Alternative Network Stacks, covers network stacks and their use in more detail.

NETWORK HARDWARE OPTIONS

The Network Device Support kernel menu contains options related to network hardware. The most important of these options are drivers for specific network cards. The most common types of network cards today are Ethernet devices, but others include traditional local network hardware, long-distance devices, and wireless devices. PC Card devices (for notebook computers) have their own submenu off of the Network Device Support menu. You also select dial-up devices (used to establish connections over telephone modems and some other types of hardware) here.

Most of these devices require that you select the Network Device Support option at the top of the Network Device Support menu. If you fail to do this, other options won't be available.

ETHERNET DEVICES

Ethernet is the most common type of local network hardware in 2002, and it seems likely to retain that status for some time. (Wireless technologies, discussed shortly, are becoming popular in some environments, but they lag behind Ethernet and several other wired technologies in terms of speed.) From the point of view of an OS, the problem with Ethernet's popularity is that it's spawned literally hundreds, if not thousands, of specific Ethernet cards.

Fortunately, most Ethernet cards use one of just a few chipsets, so Linux can support the vast majority of Ethernet cards with about 60 drivers. These drivers are split across two submenus: the Ethernet (10 or 100 Mbit) and Ethernet (1000 Mbit) menus. By far the most drivers appear in the first menu, which as the name implies covers 10 and 100Mbps devices. (The most popular type of Ethernet in 2002 is 100Mbps, although 1000Mbps, or *gigabit Ethernet*, is gaining in popularity, and 10 gigabit Ethernet is being developed.)

NOTE   In addition to three common Ethernet speeds, there are several different types of Ethernet cabling: coaxial (used only with some forms of 10Mbps Ethernet), twisted-pair (used by some types of 10Mbps, all types of 100Mbps, and some forms of gigabit Ethernet), and fiber-optic (used by some forms of gigabit Ethernet). Twisted-pair cabling supports distances of up to 100 meters (m) between devices (one of which is normally a central hub or switch), and fiber-optic cabling permits distances of up to 5 kilometers (km) between devices.

The organization of the 10 or 100Mbps driver menu is less than perfect. The menu begins with listings for several popular or once-popular devices from 3Com, SMC, Racal-Interlan, and a few other companies; proceeds with a grouping of Industry Standard Architecture (ISA) bus cards; continues with a grouping of Extended ISA (EISA), VESA Local Bus (VLB), and Peripheral Component Interconnect (PCI) cards; and concludes with a grouping of parallel-to-Ethernet adapters. You may need to search for your card in two or three places because of this organization.

A few Ethernet devices aren't activated through drivers in the Network Device Support menu or its submenus. Specifically, PC Card devices have their own drivers, as described shortly, and USB-to-Ethernet adapters are activated in the USB Support menu. To use a USB device, you must activate Support for USB; either UHCI Support or OHCI Support, depending upon which type of controller your motherboard uses; and an appropriate USB network driver option, such as USB ADMtek Pegasus-Based Ethernet Device Support.

ALTERNATIVE LOCAL NETWORK DEVICES

Although it's extremely popular, Ethernet isn't the only choice for local network hardware. The Linux kernel includes support for several other types of network, although there aren't as many drivers available for any of these as there are for Ethernet. (There are also fewer models of non-Ethernet network hardware available, so this restricted range of drivers doesn't necessarily mean poor support for the hardware that is available.) Options available in the 2.4.17 kernel's Network Device Support menu include the following:

- **Token Ring**—Historically, Ethernet's most important competitor has been IBM's Token Ring. Ethernet gained momentum in the 1990s, in part at the expense of Token Ring. Most Token Ring cards support a top speed of 16Mbps, although 100Mbps models have now become available. Maximum distances between Token Ring stations vary from 150–300m. Linux includes support for several Token Ring cards, in the Token Ring Devices submenu of the Network Device Support menu.

- **LocalTalk**—Apple developed its own networking technologies, including both hardware (LocalTalk) and software protocols (AppleTalk), for its Macintosh line of computers. A few *x*86 boards for interfacing *x*86 systems to LocalTalk networks were produced, and Linux supports some of these, from the AppleTalk Devices submenu. (Ironically, Linux on Macintosh hardware doesn't support that hardware's own LocalTalk interfaces.) LocalTalk is slow by the standards of 2002, reaching a maximum speed of 2Mbps.

- **ARCnet**—ARCnet is a network technology that's often used for specialized purposes like security cameras and scientific data acquisition systems. These devices support speeds ranging from 19Kbps to 10Mbps over coaxial, twisted-pair, or fiber-optic cabling. Linux's ARCnet support is activated from items in the ARCnet Devices submenu. In addition to drivers for your specific chipset, you'll need to enable a driver for a specific ARCnet packet format (RFC 1051 or RFC 1201).

- **FDDI and CDDI**—*Fiber Distributed Data Interface (FDDI)* and *Copper Distributed Data Interface (CDDI)* are closely related 100Mbps local network technologies that use fiber-optic and copper wiring, respectively. FDDI's primary advantage over 100Mbps Ethernet is that it supports greater cable lengths—theoretically up to 2km, vs. 100m for twisted-pair Ethernet. Gigabit Ethernet with fiber-optic cabling supports distances of up to 5km, though. The 2.4.17 kernel includes support for two lines of FDDI/CDDI products, both selectable from the Network Device Support menu after selecting FDDI Driver Support.

- **HIPPI**—*High-Performance Parallel Interface (HIPPI)* supports speeds of 800Kbps or 1600Kbps, with distances of up to 25m over twisted-pair copper wiring, 300m on multi-mode fiber-optic cabling, or 10km on single-mode fiber-optic cabling. The 2.4.17 kernel supports one HIPPI card, the Essential RoadRunner, but the driver is considered experimental.

- **Fibre Channel**—This type of network interface supports both copper and fiber-optic network media, and provides speeds of 133–1062Mbps. When used over fiber-optic cables, Fibre Channel can be used over a 10km range. The 2.4.17 kernel includes support for one Fibre Channel chipset, the Interphase 5526 Tachyon.

Some of these network media, such as Token Ring, are most often used on local networks, typically contained within a single building or a small cluster of buildings. Others, like FDDI and HIPPI, are more often used to link clusters of computers across greater distances, such as between buildings on corporate or university campuses. Linux's support for these technologies means that Linux can function as a router, linking a local network with Ethernet to a broader network that uses a wider-ranging (and higher-speed) standard.

NOTE Throughout this book, the assumption is that a computer uses Ethernet. The main feature that changes if one or more interfaces use some other networking technology is the name for the network interface. For Ethernet, this is eth0 for the first device, eth1 for the second, and so on. Other devices use other names, such as tr0 for the first Token Ring device or fddi1 for the second FDDI device.

BROADBAND AND WAN DEVICES

Broadband is a term that's commonly applied in a couple of different ways. First, it may refer to a networking technology that allows for the simultaneous transmission of multiple types of information, such as video, audio, and digital data. Second, it may refer to a substitute for ordinary dial-up telephone network connections that permits substantially higher speeds (typically 200Kbps or greater). Although 200Kbps doesn't sound like much compared to technologies like Ethernet, it's a substantial improvement over 56Kbps telephone dial-up speeds.

Residential and small business customers frequently use broadband technologies to link to the Internet through an Internet Service Provider (ISP), or occasionally to link multiple sites without running dedicated cables. Typically, broadband connections link a computer that you own to the Internet as a whole. This contrasts with the other network technologies described here, which normally link together a group of computers that you own or administer. Therefore, broadband connections frequently require that you conform to some requirements of the ISP that provides the connection. Many low-end broadband ISPs require that you not run servers, for instance.

In 2002, the most popular forms of broadband are Digital Subscriber Line (DSL) and cable modems. DSL comes in several varieties, such as Asymmetric DSL (ADSL) and Single-Line (or Symmetric) DSL (SDSL), and operates using high-frequency signals over ordinary telephone lines. Cable modems operate over cable TV networks by occupying the bandwidth of one TV channel (often with some additional bandwidth reserved, as well). Broadband through satellite systems, local radio-frequency transmissions, and fiber-optic cabling are also available in at least some areas.

NOTE For more information on broadband Internet connections, consult my *Broadband Internet Connections: A User's Guide to DSL and Cable* (Addison-Wesley, 2001).

Most broadband connections use an external modem that sports a broadband connector for linking to the broadband network and an Ethernet port for connecting to your computer. You therefore need a supported Ethernet adapter, and you configure that adapter with the standard Linux drivers. The broadband modem itself needs no special drivers, although some ISPs require you to use the Point-to-Point Protocol over Ethernet (PPPoE), which is implemented in Linux via the experimental PPP over Ethernet driver in the Network Device Support menu. (This option requires that you first enable the PPP Support option, discussed shortly in "Dial-Up Devices.") Another PPPoE option is to use the Roaring Penguin PPPoE package, available from http://www.roaringpenguin.com/pppoe/.

Some broadband modems come with USB interfaces rather than Ethernet interfaces. The 2.4.17 Linux kernel supports none of these devices, although Alcatel provides Linux drivers for its Speed Touch USB DSL modem at `http://www.alcatel.com/consumer/dsl/supuser.htm`. Check with the hardware manufacturer or at `http://www.linux-usb.org` for updated information on drivers for other USB products.

Some broadband modems, particularly for low-end ADSL accounts, come as internal PCI cards. As with USB devices, support for these is rare. The 2.4.17 kernel includes support for the General Instruments Surfboard 1000, an old one-way cable modem. (*One-way* means that it only receives data; you must use a conventional telephone modem to send data. One-way broadband services are undesirable and are becoming rare.) Drivers for the Diamond 1MM DSL modem are available from `http://www.rodsbooks.com/network/network-dsl.html`, but these drivers are an unsupported modification of existing Ethernet drivers and may not work on 2.4.*x* or later kernels.

TIP

If your broadband provider doesn't give you the option of an Ethernet-interfaced modem, buy one yourself and sell the modem your ISP provides on an auction site like eBay (`http://www.ebay.com`). Be sure you buy a compatible modem, though, and only sell the one your ISP provides if it's given to you or if you must buy it; don't sell a modem your ISP rents to you!

Another type of long-distance connection is a *Wide-Area Network (WAN)*. This type of technology allows connections over dedicated long-distance circuits, often called *leased lines* because they may be ordinary telephone lines leased from the telephone company. (The phone company doesn't provide a signal on the other end, though; you do.) Such connections often use external devices, known as *WAN routers*, which link to a Linux computer or local network much as do broadband modems. Another option is to use a dedicated WAN interface card. Linux includes support for a range of such devices in the WAN Interfaces submenu of the Network Device Support menu. As with many other submenus, you must select the first option (WAN Interfaces Support), then select the option corresponding to the device you intend to use.

WIRELESS DEVICES

Beginning in the late 1990s, wireless networking technologies rose rapidly in popularity. These technologies allow computers to network even without physical cabling connecting them. Such an arrangement is particularly helpful in existing homes and offices in which running conventional wired network cables would be troublesome, and for users of notebook computers and other portable devices, who might want or need to roam about without plugging the computer into a physical network.

Unfortunately, in 2001 the wireless world still suffers from some drawbacks compared to conventional Ethernet networks. Wireless networks are more expensive than are Ethernet networks, they're slower, and they aren't as well standardized. The most important standards for wireless in 2001 are 802.11 and 802.11b. The former supports speeds of 2Mbps, with a fallback to 1Mbps. (*Fallback* refers to a renegotiation of the connection when signal strength falls, as when there's interference or the computers are far apart from one another.) 802.11b supports speeds of 11Mbps, with fallback speeds of 5.5Mbps, 2Mbps, and 1Mbps. Another wireless technology that's received a lot of press is *Bluetooth*, which supports speeds of up to 1Mbps. Bluetooth-enabled printers, cell phones, and the like will probably begin shipping in volume in 2002. Future developments are likely to increase available speeds. For instance, plans are underway to develop a wireless version of ATM with speeds of up to 155Mbps.

Wireless LANs are typically implemented through wireless PC Cards in notebook computers. These cards may either communicate directly with one another or may require the use of a base station, which may also serve as an interface to a conventional wired network or to a broadband or conventional telephone modem connection to the Internet. There are also wireless ISA and PCI cards, so that desktop systems can participate in wireless networks, or serve as base stations for roaming devices. PC Cards, ISA cards, and PCI cards all require Linux drivers, but base stations require no special support.

Linux support for wireless devices appears under the Wireless LAN (Non-Hamradio) submenu. This menu lists specific drivers by the chipsets or cards for which they're written, not for the technology (such as 802.11b or Bluetooth) those cards use. In addition to kernel drivers, there are two packages known as the Wireless Extensions and Wireless Tools that help you manage a wireless network under Linux. Check `http://www.hpl.hp.com/personal/Jean_Tourrilhes/Linux/Tools.html` for information on these packages, and for additional links to information on wireless networking in Linux.

PC CARD DEVICES

Most notebook computers come with at least one *PC Card* slot. (Much Linux documentation refers to PC Card technology by its old name,

PCMCIA, which stands for the developer of the standards, the *Personal Computer Memory Card International Association.*) PC Card devices can be installed and removed from a computer while it's still running, and the OS has no say over this matter. Because Linux was designed with the assumption that network interfaces would not disappear without warning, a separate package, *Card Services,* helps manage these matters, cleanly starting and stopping kernel features related to PC Card devices when they're inserted or removed. You can find more information on Card Services at `http://pcmcia-cs.sourceforge.net`.

The 2.4.17 kernel includes support for many PC Card network devices in the PCMCIA Network Device Support submenu. Some wireless cards' drivers appear in the Wireless LAN (Non-Hamradio) submenu. When you select such a card and configure it, it functions much like a standard ISA or PCI card. For instance, an Ethernet PC Card appears as `eth0` and is configured with the standard tools, as described in Chapter 2.

Kernels prior to the 2.4.*x* series required a separate package of drivers to use PC Card devices, and in fact many PC Card devices are still not supported in the standard kernel. You may therefore need to check out this package, which is part of the Card Services collection. You're unlikely to need to use special drivers for a PC Card network device if you use a 2.4.*x* or later kernel, but you might need this for a modem, SCSI host adapter, or something else.

DIAL-UP DEVICES

The final class of network devices is the dial-up device. Most typically, this is a conventional telephone modem used in conjunction with the Point-to-Point Protocol (PPP) to establish a connection to the Internet via an ISP. Such connections are established via command-line or GUI tools, as described in Chapter 2. In addition to these tools, though, the Linux kernel requires support for the dial-up connection.

To activate this support, you must select the PPP (Point-to-Point Protocol) Support option in the Network Device Support menu. When you select this option, several suboptions will become available, such as PPP Support for Async Serial Ports and PPP Deflate Compression. These options aren't usually strictly necessary, but sometimes they can improve a connection, such as by automatically compressing highly compressible data like text for higher net throughput. The experimental PPP over Ethernet option is required if you intend to use the kernel's PPPoE features for some DSL connections, but this option is *not* required with some add-on PPPoE packages, like Roaring Penguin.

PPP is sometimes used on connections that don't involve modems. For instance, you can use it to network two computers via their serial ports. Such configurations are seldom worthwhile with desktop systems, because Ethernet cards are inexpensive and provide *much* faster connections. You might want to use this type of link when connecting a desktop system to a palmtop computer, though, or for a temporary connection if you don't want to bother installing network cards.

PPP isn't the only type of dial-up connection that Linux supports. The kernel includes support for the older *Serial Line Internet Protocol (SLIP)*, which serves much the same function as PPP. SLIP has been largely abandoned by ISPs, so it's unlikely you'll need to use it over a modem. A few Linux tools use it locally, though; for instance, some types of *dial-on-demand* utilities (which dial a PPP connection whenever network activity is detected) use SLIP to detect outgoing connection attempts.

Another protocol that's akin to PPP and SLIP is the *Parallel Line Internet Protocol (PLIP)*. As you might guess by the name, this protocol lets you connect two Linux computers via their parallel (printer) ports. Because these ports are much faster than are RS-232 serial ports, PLIP offers a speed advantage over PPP or SLIP for two-computer local networks. Ethernet is still faster, though. To use PLIP, you must select the PLIP (Parallel Port) Support option in the Network Device Support menu. To do this, you must first activate the Parallel Port Support option in the menu of the same name, including the PC-Style Hardware option (if you're using an *x*86 computer). If you need to use PLIP networking, you should consult the PLIP Mini-HOWTO (`http://www.linuxdoc.org/HOWTO/mini/PLIP.html`) for further details, including wiring for the necessary cable, if you can't find a Turbo Laplink cable.

COMPILING AND INSTALLING A KERNEL

The preceding discussion has covered the most important options you'll encounter in configuring a kernel to use the networking protocols on your network, and the hardware you use to connect a computer to that network. The process of compiling the kernel, however, is another matter, and one that's not, strictly speaking, a networking task. Nonetheless, this task is important if you need to recompile your kernel to add or delete support for specific network features, so this section provides an overview of some of the decisions and procedures involved.

WARNING

Don't adjust only the options described earlier in this chapter and then compile your kernel. Although they're beyond the scope of this book, kernel options relating to features like EIDE controllers, SCSI host adapters, and disk filesystems are critically important for a functioning Linux computer. If you incorrectly configure these features, your computer may not boot at all, or it may perform in a substandard way (for instance, with very poor disk speed). These options are discussed in documents such as the Linux Kernel HOWTO at http://www.linuxdoc.org/HOWTO/Kernel-HOWTO.html (among many other places) and many general Linux books.

DRIVERS: MODULES OR BUILT-IN

The preceding discussion made many references to enabling or disabling particular kernel features, such as drivers for your particular Ethernet adapter. If you check Figure 1.1, though, you'll find that many options can be set to more than two values. Consider the Packet Socket option in Figure 1.1. This option can be set to any of three values: Y, M, or N. The Y and N values, as you might expect, stand for *yes* and *no*, respectively, meaning that the code is compiled directly into the main kernel file or not compiled at all. The M option falls in-between these two extremes. If you select M, the feature will be compiled, but it won't be linked into the main kernel file; instead, the code will be available as a kernel module, which can be loaded and unloaded as required. Options that are suboptions of others, such as Packet Socket: Mmapped IO in Figure 1.1, often lack the M option because they're compiled into the kernel or as modules, depending on their parent options' settings. Thus, selecting Y for such an option may place it in the kernel or in a module.

A feature that's compiled into the kernel is always available, and is available early in the boot process. There's no chance that the feature will become unavailable because it's been unloaded. Some features *must* be compiled in this way, or not at all. For instance, the filesystem used for the root directory must be available in the kernel at boot time, and so must be compiled directly into the kernel. If you use the Root File System on NFS option, described earlier, you'll need to compile support for your network hardware into the kernel.

The down side to compiling a feature directly into the kernel is that it consumes RAM at all times. It also increases the size of the kernel on disk, which can complicate certain methods of booting Linux. For these reasons, Linux distributions ship most options that can be compiled as modules in this way. This allows the distribution maintainers to keep their default kernels manageable, while still providing support for a wide array of hardware. Because most network hardware can be compiled as modules, most distributions compile drivers for network cards in this way.

As somebody who's maintaining specific Linux computers, though, you might decide to do otherwise. If you compile a network card driver directly into the kernel, you won't need to configure the system to load the module before you attempt to start networking. (In truth, most distributions come preconfigured to handle this task correctly, so it's seldom a problem.) On the other hand, if you maintain a wide variety of Linux systems, you might want to create a single kernel and set of kernel modules that you can install on all the computers, in which case you might want to compile network drivers as modules.

Features such as network stacks can also be compiled as modules or directly into the kernel. (TCP/IP is an exception; it must be compiled directly into the kernel or not at all, although a few of its suboptions can be compiled as modules.) You might decide to compile, say, NFS client support as a module if the computer only occasionally mounts remote NFS exports. Doing this will save a small amount of RAM when NFS isn't being used, at the cost of greater opportunities for problems and a very small delay when mounting an NFS export.

As you might gather, there's no single correct answer to the question of whether to compile a feature or driver directly into the kernel or as a module, except of course when modular compilation isn't available. As a general rule of thumb, I recommend you consider how often the feature will be in use. If it will be used constantly, compile the feature as part of the kernel; if it will be used only part of the time, compile the feature as a module. You might want to favor modular compilation if your kernel becomes large enough that you can't boot it with LOADLIN (a DOS utility for booting Linux), though, because this can be an important way to boot Linux in some emergency situations.

A TYPICAL KERNEL COMPILATION

After you've configured your kernel with **make xconfig** or some other configuration command, you must issue four commands to compile the kernel and install the kernel modules:

```
# make dep
# make bzImage
# make modules
# make modules_install
```

The first of these commands performs some housekeeping tasks. Specifically, dep is short for *dependency*—**make dep** determines which source code files depend on others, given the options you've chosen. If you omit this step, it's possible that the compilation will go awry because you've added or omitted features, which requires adjusting the dependency information for the features you have.

The second of these commands builds the main kernel file, which will then reside in the /usr/src/linux/arch/i386/boot directory under the name bzImage. There are variants on this command. For instance, for particularly small kernels, **make zImage** works as well (the bzImage form allows a boot loader like LILO to handle larger kernels than does the zImage form). Both zImage and bzImage are compressed forms of the kernel. This is the standard for *x*86 systems, but on some non-*x*86 platforms, you should use **make vmlinux** instead. This command creates an uncompressed kernel. (On non-*x*86 platforms, the directory in which the kernel is built will use a name other than i386, such as ppc for PowerPC systems.)

The **make modules** command, as you might guess, compiles the kernel modules. The **make modules_install** command copies these module files to appropriate locations in /lib/modules. Specifically, a subdirectory named after the kernel version number is created, and holds subdirectories for specific classes of drivers.

NOTE   You can run the make dep, make bzImage (or equivalent), and make modules commands as an ordinary user, provided that the user has full read/write access to all the kernel source directories. You *must* run make modules_install as root, though.

The entire kernel compilation process takes anywhere from a few minutes to several hours, depending on the options you select and the speed of your computer. Typically, building the main kernel file takes more time than does building modules, but this might not be the case if you're building an unusually large number of modules. At each step, you'll see many lines reflecting the compilation of individual source code files. Some of these compilations may show warning messages, which you can usually safely ignore. Error messages, on the other hand, are more serious, and will halt the compilation process.

COMMON KERNEL COMPILATION PROBLEMS

Kernel compilation usually proceeds smoothly if you configured the kernel correctly, but occasionally errors pop up. Common problems include the following:

- **Buggy or incompatible code**—Sometimes you'll find that drivers are buggy or incompatible with other features. This is most common when you try to use a development kernel or a non-standard driver you've added to the kernel. The usual symptom is a compilation that fails with one or more error messages. The usual solution is to upgrade the kernel, or at least the affected driver, or omit it entirely if you don't really need that feature.

- **Unfulfilled dependencies**—If a driver relies upon some other driver, the first driver should only be selectable after the second driver has been selected. Sometimes, though, the configuration scripts miss such a detail, so you can configure a system that won't work. The most common symptom is that the individual modules compile, but they won't combine into a complete kernel file. (If the driver is compiled as a module, it may return an error message when you try to load it.) With any luck, the error message will give you some clue about what you need to add to get a working kernel. Sometimes, typing `make dep` and then recompiling will fix the problem. Occasionally, compiling the feature as a module rather than directly into the kernel (or vice-versa) will overcome such problems.

- **Old object files**—If you compile a kernel, then change the configuration and compile again, the `make` utility that supervises the process should detect what files may be affected by your changes and recompile them. Sometimes this doesn't work correctly, though, with the result being an inability to build a complete kernel, or sometimes a failure when compiling individual files. Typing `make clean` should clear out preexisting object files (the compiled versions of individual source code files), thus fixing this problem.

- **Compiler errors**—The GNU C Compiler (GCC) is normally reliable, but there have been incidents in which it's caused problems. Red Hat 7.0 shipped with a version of GCC that could not compile a 2.2.*x* kernel, but this problem has been overcome with the 2.4.*x* kernel series. (Red Hat 7.0 actually shipped with two versions of GCC; to compile a kernel, you had to use the `kgcc` program rather than `gcc`.)

- **Hardware problems**—GCC stresses a computer's hardware more than many programs, so kernel compilations sometimes turn up hardware problems. These often manifest as *signal 11* errors, so called because that's the error message returned by GCC. Defective or overheated CPUs and bad RAM are two common sources of these problems. `http://www.bitwizard.nl/sig11/` has additional information on this problem.

If you can't resolve a kernel compilation problem yourself, try posting a query to a Linux newsgroup, such as `comp.os.linux.misc`. Be sure to include information on your distribution, the kernel version you're trying to compile, and any error messages you see. (You can omit all the nonerror compilation messages.)

INSTALLING AND USING A NEW KERNEL

Once you've built a new kernel, you'll need to install and use it. As noted earlier, the fresh-built kernel normally resides in `/usr/src/linux/arch/ i386/boot` (or a similar directory with a name matched to your CPU type rather than `i386`). You normally copy or move the kernel file (such as `bzImage`) to the `/boot` directory. I recommend renaming the file to something that indicates its version and any customizations you may have made. For instance, you might call the file `bzImage-2.4.17` or `bzImage-2.4.17-xfs`. You should also type **make modules_install**, if you haven't already, to install your kernel modules in `/lib/modules/x.y.z`, where `x.y.z` is the kernel version number.

Unfortunately, copying the kernel to `/boot` isn't enough to let you use the kernel. You must also modify your boot loader to boot the new kernel. Most Linux distributions use the Linux Loader (LILO) as a boot loader, and you configure LILO by editing `/etc/lilo.conf`. Listing 1.1 shows a short `lilo.conf` file that's configured to boot a single kernel.

NOTE LILO is used on *x86* computers. If you're running Linux on some other type of hardware, you'll have to use some other boot loader. Some of these model themselves after LILO, but some details are likely to differ. Consult your distribution's documentation, or a Web site devoted to Linux on your platform, for more information.

Listing 1.1 A sample `lilo.conf` file

```
boot=/dev/sda
map=/boot/map
install=/boot/boot.b
prompt
default=linux
timeout=50
image=/boot/vmlinuz
        label=linux
        root=/dev/sda6
        read-only
```

To modify LILO to allow you to choose from the old kernel and the new one, follow these steps:

1. Load /etc/lilo.conf in a text editor.

2. Duplicate the lines identifying the current default kernel. These lines begin with an image= line, and typically continue until another image= line, an other= line, or the end of the file. In the case of Listing 1.1, the lines in question are the final four lines.

3. Modify the copied image= line to point to your new kernel file. You might change it from image=/boot/vmlinuz to image=/boot/bzImage-2. 4.17, for instance. (Many Linux distributions call their default kernels vmlinuz.)

4. Change the label= line for the new kernel to something unique, such as mykernel or 2417, so that you can differentiate it at boot time from the old kernel. Ultimately, you'll select the new kernel from a menu or type its name at boot time.

5. Save your changes.

6. Type lilo to install a modified boot loader on your hard disk.

WARNING

The preceding instructions assume that your /etc/lilo.conf file is valid. If it's not, performing Step 6 may damage data on your hard disk. Also, be sure not to modify or delete any other entries from the file.

The next time you boot the computer, LILO should present you with the option of booting your old kernel or the new one, in addition to any other options it may have given you in the past. Depending upon how it's configured, you may see the new name you entered in Step 4 in a menu, or you may be able to type it at a lilo: prompt.

If you can boot the computer and are satisfied with the functioning of your new kernel, you can make it the default by modifying the default= line in /etc/lilo.conf. Change the text after the equal sign to specify the label you gave the new kernel in Step 4, then type lilo again at a command prompt.

There are ways to boot a Linux kernel other than LILO. Some distributions use the Grand Unified Boot Loader (GRUB) instead of LILO. Consult the GRUB documentation for details on how to configure it. You can also use the DOS program LOADLIN to boot Linux. To do this, you need to place a copy of the kernel on a DOS-accessible disk—a DOS partition or a floppy disk. You can then boot Linux by typing a command like the following:

```
C:> LOADLIN BZIMAGE root=/dev/sda6 ro
```

In this example, BZIMAGE is the name of the kernel file, as accessed from DOS, and /dev/sda6 is the Linux identifier for the root partition. The ro option specifies that the kernel should initially mount this partition read-only, which is standard practice. (Linux later remounts it for read-write access.) LOADLIN can be a useful tool for testing new kernels, if you prefer not to adjust your LILO setup initially. It's also a good way to boot Linux in an emergency, should LILO become corrupt. If you don't have a copy of DOS, FreeDOS (http://www.freedos.org) is an open source version that should do the job. LOADLIN ships on most Linux distributions' installation CD-ROMs, usually in a directory called dosutils or something similar.

SUMMARY

The Linux kernel lies at the heart of all input to and output from a Linux computer, including network data transfers. For this reason, it's important that any networked Linux computer have appropriate options selected in the kernel. You can optimize a kernel for a particular task by including options you might not otherwise include, or by omitting options that are unnecessary memory wasters. Most networking options fall under just two kernel configuration menus: Networking Options and Network Device Support. Both menus include many options and several submenus. Once you've selected the options you want, you must compile the Linux kernel by typing a few commands. You can then install the kernel for use by reconfiguring LILO to give you the option of using the new kernel.

TCP/IP Network Configuration 2

Although the Linux kernel lies at the heart of any Linux system and controls all network access, the process of configuring a Linux computer to use a network involves more than the kernel. This chapter covers three popular methods of network connection: the Dynamic Host Configuration Protocol (DHCP), static IP addresses, and the Point-to-Point Protocol (PPP). DHCP and PPP are used to automatically assign an IP address and set other configuration information, but in different contexts. Static IP addresses, by contrast, require that you set up the details manually. In each of these cases, there are a handful of tools with which you must be familiar if you're to get your system working. Before using any of these methods of network configuration, you must load appropriate network drivers. This topic therefore begins this chapter.

LOADING NETWORK DRIVERS

The first step in configuring a network card is to load the appropriate drivers. As described in Chapter 1, Kernel Network Configuration, drivers may reside on your system in one of two forms: as an integral part of your Linux kernel, or as separate kernel module files. In the first case, the task of loading network drivers is easy, because it's done when the kernel loads. For some cards, though, you may need to pass parameters to the driver via kernel boot options. If you use LILO, these can be passed with an append

option in /etc/lilo.conf. For instance, the followi̇
as part of a kernel definition, tells the kernel to look
first Ethernet card) at I/O port 0x240:

```
append="ether=0,0,0x240,eth0"
```

You can include several options within the quote:
arating them with spaces. You can use this trick to
ernet card to link itself to a particular net
multi-interface system by identifying the I/O p
card. In most cases, you won't need to pass any o
into the kernel; the driver should detect the netv
available without further intervention, although
it in some other way.

If your network card drivers are compiled as modu
parameters via the /etc/modules.conf file (which is
ules on some older distributions). For instance, this
like the following:

```
alias eth0 ne
options ne io=0x240
```

This pair of lines tells the system to use the ne driver
to look for the board on I/O port 0x240. In most cases,
will be unnecessary, but you may need to make the
situations. This is especially true if your system ha
interfaces. The GUI configuration tools provided by
can help automate this process; you need only select
card or driver from a list, and the GUI tools m
/etc/modules.conf entries.

When you've created an entry in /etc/modules.con
load the network drivers automatically whenever
start up a network interface. If you should need
any reason, you may use the insmod command to d

```
# insmod ne
```

This command will load the ne module, making it
nel module auto-loading doesn't work reliably, yo
placing such a command in a startup script such as
/etc/rc.d/boot.local.

32

If your connection uses PPP, SLIP, or some other software protocol for communicating over serial, parallel, or other traditionally nonnetwork ports, you must load the drivers for the port itself and for the software protocol in question. You do this in the same way you load drivers for a network card—by building the code into the kernel file proper or by placing it in a module and loading the module. In most cases, you'll need to attend to at least two drivers: one for the low-level hardware and another for the network protocol. Sometimes one or both of these will require additional drivers. For instance, a USB modem may require you to load two or three drivers to access the modem.

USING A DHCP CLIENT

If your local network has a DHCP server, you can configure Linux to obtain its IP address from this server automatically, by using a DHCP client. This client sends a broadcast message on its local network segment to search for a DHCP server. If a DHCP server responds, and if the ensuing negotiation is successful, the result should be a system with an IP address and associated information, fully configured to use the connection.

NOTE If you want your computer to function as a DHCP server so that it can deliver IP addresses to other systems, consult Chapter 5, Configuring Other Computers via DHCP. You'll need to configure the DHCP server with a static IP address.

Most Linux distributions give you the option of using DHCP during installation. You should be able to select a DHCP option when configuring the network settings. If not, or if you need to reconfigure the computer after installation, the easiest way to enable this feature is usually to use a GUI configuration tool, such as Linuxconf (Red Hat or Mandrake), COAS (Caldera), or YaST or YaST2 (SuSE). For instance, Figure 2.1 shows the YaST2 configuration screen in which this option is set. Click Automatic Address Setup (via DHCP), and the system will obtain its IP address via DHCP.

Unfortunately, DHCP configuration isn't always quite this easy. Potential problems include the following:

- **Incompatible DHCP clients**—Four DHCP clients are common on Linux systems: pump, dhclient, dhcpxd, and dhcpcd (don't confuse either of the latter two with dhcpd, the DHCP server). Although all four work properly on many networks, some networks use DHCP servers that don't get along well with one or another Linux DHCP clients. You

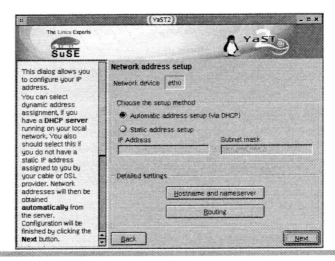

Figure 2.1 GUI configuration tools make it easy to enable DHCP client operation.

might therefore need to replace your DHCP client package with another one.

- **Incompatible DHCP options**—DHCP client options sometimes cause problems. In practice, this situation can be difficult to distinguish from an incompatible DHCP client, but the solution is less radical: You can edit the DHCP startup script to change its options. Unfortunately, you'll need to learn enough about your DHCP client to have some idea of what options to edit. Reading the man page may give you some ideas.

- **Multi-NIC configurations**—If your computer has two or more network interface cards (NICs), you may need to get the DHCP client to obtain an IP address for only some cards, or to disregard some information (such as the gateway address, described in more detail shortly in "Adjusting the Routing Table") for some NICs. Again, editing the DHCP client startup script may be necessary, or you may need to create a custom script to correct an automatic configuration after the fact.

To help you make adjustments, Table 2.1 presents the default DHCP client package, alternative DHCP client packages, locations of DHCP startup scripts, and locations of closely related configuration files for each of several popular Linux distributions. (Debian's ifup tool, unlike similarly named tools in other distributions, is a binary program with the DHCP client package commands hard-coded, which can make modifying those commands tricky. Some limited control can be exerted through the /etc/network/

Table 2.1   DHCP Client Information for Seven Popular Linux Distributions

Distribution	Default DHCP Client	Alternative DHCP Clients	DHCP Client Startup Script	Extra Configuration Files
Caldera OpenLinux Server 3.1	dhclient	none	/etc/sysconfig/ network-scripts/ ifup-dhcp	/etc/sysconfig/ network, /etc/sysconfig/ network-scripts/ ifcfg-eth0, /etc/ dhcp/dhclient.conf
Debian GNU/ Linux 2.2	pump	dhcpcd	/sbin/ifup (binary file)	/etc/network/ interfaces
Linux Mandrake 8.1	dhcpcd	dhclient, dhcpxd	/sbin/ifup	/etc/sysconfig/ network, /etc/ sysconfig/network- scripts/ifcfg-eth0
Red Hat Linux 7.2	pump	dhcpcd	/sbin/ifup	/etc/sysconfig/ network, /etc/ sysconfig/ network-scripts/ ifcfg-eth0
Slackware Linux 8.0	dhcpcd	none	/etc/rc.d/ rc.inet1	none
SuSE Linux 7.3	dhcpcd	dhclient	/etc/init.d/ dhclient	/etc/rc.config
TurboLinux 7	dhclient	none	/sbin/ifup	/etc/sysconfig/ network, /etc/ sysconfig/network- scripts/ifcfg-eth0

interfaces configuration file.) Even if your distribution doesn't officially support your preferred DHCP client, you can install and use it. At worst, you'll need to modify the DHCP client startup script specified in Table 2.1, or create a custom DHCP client startup procedure by modifying some startup script (precisely what script you might modify is partly dependent on your distribution and partly a matter of personal preference).

If you suspect you're encountering problems because of DHCP client options that don't get along well with those of your network's DHCP server, you can try editing the DHCP startup script listed in Table 2.1. Look for the line that calls the DHCP client program and examine its options, using the man page for the DHCP client program for reference. You may need to add or remove options to get the behavior you need. For instance, some DHCP servers require that the client send a hostname, so you may

35

need to add an option like -h *hostname* for dhcpcd. Sometimes these scripts rely on values set in other configuration files, as listed in the Extra Configuration Files column of Table 2.1. More frequently, though, these files tell the system whether to use a static IP address or DHCP.

CONFIGURING A STATIC IP ADDRESS

Although DHCP is a common method of configuration on many networks, it's not used universally. It's awkward to configure some systems (such as DHCP servers) via DHCP, and some networks simply lack DHCP servers. In these situations, you'll need to configure your computer's IP address manually. This section describes how to do this, starting with the tools to do the job a single time. The section entitled "Making Your Changes Permanent" describes how to configure your system to use your settings automatically whenever it reboots.

NOTE Traditionally, server computers have used static IP address assignment, because this ensures that the computer's IP address won't change. This fact is important for mapping hostnames (such as mail.threeroomco.com) to IP addresses (such as 172.23.45.67) via a DNS server, as described in Chapter 18, Administering a Domain via DNS. As described in Chapter 5, though, it's possible to assign the same address to a computer time after time via DHCP. There are also *dynamic DNS* services that permit the mapping of a hostname onto a dynamic IP address.

CONFIGURING NETWORK INTERFACES

Loading a driver, as described earlier in this chapter, is the first step in making a network interface available. To use the interface, you must assign it an IP address and associated information, such as its network mask (also called the subnet mask or netmask). This job is handled by the ifconfig utility, which displays information on an interface or changes its configuration, depending upon how it's called.

Basic ifconfig Syntax and Use

The ifconfig utility's syntax is deceptively simple:

```
ifconfig [interface] [options]
```

The program behaves differently depending upon what parameters it's given. On a broad level, ifconfig can do several different things:

- If used without any parameters, ifconfig returns the status of all currently active network interfaces. Used in this way, ifconfig is a helpful diagnostic tool.

- If given a single interface name (such as eth0 or tr1), ifconfig returns information on that interface only. Again, this is a useful diagnostic tool.

- If fed options in addition to an interface name, ifconfig modifies the interface's operation according to the options' specifications. Most commonly, this means activating or deactivating an interface.

If you're using ifconfig to configure an interface, you'll be most concerned with the options you can pass to the utility. The utility's man page gives a complete listing of options, but the most important are the following:

- **up** *address*—This option activates an interface and associates the specified IP address with the new interface. If the command doesn't also include a netmask option (described shortly), ifconfig assigns a netmask based on the class of the address, as shown in Table 2.2. In many cases, you can actually omit the up keyword; ifconfig assumes this if you give it an interface name and IP address.

- **down**—This option is the opposite of up; it closes down an interface.

- **netmask** *nm*—This option sets the network mask of the interface, which determines which bits of the IP address correspond to a network address and which identify a specific computer on a network. If this option is omitted, ifconfig sets the netmask to a default value, as shown in Table 2.2. You can also provide the netmask as the number of bits of network address in part of the up *address* option, as described shortly.

- **[-]promisc**—Ordinarily, a network card accepts only those packets that are directed at it, or at all systems on its network segment. This option enables (promisc) or disables (-promisc) *promiscuous mode*, in which the card reads *all* network packets that traverse its local network segment. Promiscuous mode is necessary for packet sniffers, which can be used as network diagnostic tools. (Crackers also use packet

Table 2.2 Traditional TCP/IP Classes and Their Network Masks

Class	Address Range	Private Address Range	Netmask
Class A	1.0.0.0–127.255.255.255	10.0.0.0–10.255.255.255	255.0.0.0
Class B	128.0.0.0–191.255.255.255	172.16.0.0–172.31.255.255	255.255.0.0
Class C	192.0.0.0–223.255.255.255	192.168.0.0–192.168.255.255	255.255.255.0

sniffers to acquire passwords that are sent unencrypted.) Some programs can enable promiscuous mode themselves. The default is to bring up an interface in nonpromiscuous mode.

- **mtu** *n*—This option sets the Maximum Transfer Unit (MTU) of an interface, which is the maximum size of low-level data packets. For Ethernet networks, the MTU is normally 1500, but you can set it to something else if you like. (Some routers and protocols use smaller MTUs, which can degrade performance if your system's MTU is set higher, because your larger packets will have to be broken up and sent as multiple packets.)

- **add** *address/prefixlength*—This option is the equivalent of up and netmask, but works with IPv6, the next-generation Internet standard. As described in Chapter 1, IPv6 permits many more IP addresses than does the current IPv4. In 2002, IPv6 is still uncommon, but it's likely to become important in coming years.

- **del** *address/prefixlength*— This option is the opposite of add; it removes an IPv6 address from the interface.

- **media** *type*—Some network cards include two or more media connectors (for instance, connectors for 10Base-2 and 10Base-T cabling). You can specify which connector you want to use with this option, as in media 10baseT. Consult the driver's documentation for details about what *type* values it accepts.

- **hw** *class address*—This option allows you to control the hardware address of the network card. You might want to change this if you've replaced one network card with another but want to use the old hardware address to continue receiving the same IP address from a DHCP server, for instance. Also, manufacturers occasionally slip up and ship a large number of cards with identical hardware addresses, which can wreak havoc if you try to use several such cards on a single network. This option requires two suboptions: the *class* of the network device (such as ether for Ethernet or ARCnet for ARCnet) and the hardware *address*. This function works with many, but not all, network cards.

- **txqueulen** *length*—This option sets the length of the transmit queue, which is the number of packets the interface will attempt to queue together. The default for Ethernet devices is 100, which usually works well. Setting a lower transmit queue length on slow connections may improve interactive performance (say, for a Telnet or SSH session).

In most cases, a simple ifconfig command will suffice to activate an interface. For instance, the following command activates the first Ethernet card with the address 172.23.45.67:

```
# ifconfig eth0 172.23.45.67
```

If you must use a more complex configuration, you may do so by adding parameters to the command, such as:

```
# ifconfig eth0 172.23.45.67 netmask 255.255.255.0 mtu 1420
```

The netmask specifies which parts of an IP address correspond to the network address, and which parts identify a specific computer. A computer uses this information in determining how to address outgoing packets, so setting it incorrectly can result in some computers being inaccessible. When converted to binary, the netmask consists of a series of binary 1 values followed by a series of binary 0 values. For instance, 255.255.255.0 is twenty-four 1 values followed by eight 0 values. A shorthand notation for

IP Address Classes

These examples show activating a network interface in a private address range, as shown in Table 2.2. Private addresses are reserved for use on private networks; no Internet site uses these addresses. In order to avoid accidentally using somebody's IP address, I also use these private addresses in my examples throughout this book. I use the 192.168.*x.x* addresses in my examples as they're intended, but I use addresses in the 172.16.0.0–172.31.255.255 and 10.*x.x.x* ranges as if they were routable Internet addresses.

In addition to Classes A–C shown in Table 2.2, Classes D and E also exist. Class D is used for *multicasts* (traffic destined for multiple hosts), and Class E is reserved for future use.

Although IP address netmasks have traditionally been assigned as shown in Table 2.2, deviations from these standards have become increasingly common in the 1990s and later. This is because the initial allocation scheme had too many huge Class A networks and too few Class C networks. Deviations from the netmasks shown in Table 2.2 rely upon *Classless Inter-Domain Routing (CIDR)*, which allows arbitrary assignment of netmasks to IP address ranges. For instance, an ISP might ask for a couple of Class C networks, and be given addresses that are traditionally part of a Class A network, such as 10.34.56.0/24 and 10.34.57.0/24. By carving up these networks, the existing range of IP addresses is extended further than it could be by strict adherence to the Class A–C designations. The downside is that people who enter IP address information must take care to specify the netmasks for these addresses. If you let ifconfig set the netmask automatically for, say, 10.34.56.78, the netmask will be set to 255.0.0.0, which is wrong. Given its allocation method, the netmask should probably be 255.255.255.0.

the IP address and netmask is to follow the IP address with a slash (/) and the number of bits in the network portion of the address. For instance, 172.23.45.67/24 is equivalent to 172.23.45.67 with a netmask of 255.255.255.0. You can use this notation as part of the up *address* option to ifconfig, instead of specifying a separate netmask *nm* option.

Configuring Multiple Network Interfaces

If a computer has multiple network interfaces, you must issue the ifconfig command once for each interface. For instance, you might issue the following two commands:

```
# ifconfig eth0 up 192.168.1.1
# ifconfig eth1 up 172.23.45.67/24
```

These commands configure eth0 on the 192.168.1.1 address (presumably for a local private network), and eth1 on 172.23.45.67, using a netmask of 255.255.255.0. Both interfaces will then function. How, though, does the computer know to which interface to send any given network packet? For instance, suppose a program tries to contact the computer at 10.9.8.7. Over which interface should Linux send this packet? It's the job of the *routing table* to answer this question. In fact, this question is important even for a single-interface computer, as described shortly.

ADJUSTING THE ROUTING TABLE

The routing table directs traffic in two ways. First, it tells Linux over what interface to send traffic. This may seem obvious in a single-interface computer, but Linux supports a special virtual interface known as the *localhost* or *loopback* interface. This interface uses the 127.0.0.0/8 network, but it's usually addressed using just one IP address: 127.0.0.1. Because this interface exists on all computers, programs can use it when they need to use networking protocols to interface to other local programs. It's also faster than using the computer's regular network interface. Rules must exist to properly direct traffic to the localhost interface or the physical interface (and to a *particular* physical interface, if a computer has more than one). The second job of the routing table is to direct traffic that's destined for other computers on the local network, as opposed to computers that are located on remote networks and thus must be routed. In the case of local network traffic, Linux can use the Address Resolution Protocol (ARP) to communicate directly with the destination system, but remote targets need to be handled by a *router* or *gateway* system—a computer that passes packets from one network to another. Most Linux systems' routing tables list just one gateway computer, but some complex configurations use multiple gateways. Configuring the routing table is the job of the route command.

NOTE The path between two arbitrary computers on the Internet typically includes a dozen or more routers, but your computer needs to know only the address of the first of these, and of the destination system. The first router knows how to reach the next one, and so on until the final destination computer is reached.

Understanding Routing Table Structure

The routing table consists of a series of entries specifying what to do with packets sent to certain ranges of IP addresses. When a program sends an outgoing packet to the kernel, the kernel compares the destination address to the destination address ranges in the routing table, starting with the most specific destination address ranges (that is, those that define the smallest networks). If the packet's destination matches one of these ranges, it's sent in the way specified by the routing table rule. If not, the next rule is checked. Normally, the most general rule in the routing table is known as the *default route*, which matches *any* address. The default route normally directs packets through the local network's gateway computer.

To understand this better, it may help to examine a sample routing table. Figure 2.2 shows the result of the **route -n** command, which displays the routing table, on one system. (The route command is discussed in more detail in the next section, "Basic route Syntax and Use.") Figure 2.2 shows the routing table entries from the most to the least specific. The first entry, for a destination of 255.255.255.255, is for broadcasts. These go out over the eth0 interface and do not involve a gateway. The next two entries, for destinations of 10.92.68.0 and 192.168.1.0, represent local network traffic for networks with netmasks of 255.255.255.0 (as shown in the Genmask column). Network addresses usually end in 0, but the network portion of the address is defined by the netmask, as described earlier. These entries send traffic to the eth1 and eth0 interfaces, respectively; a computer with just one network interface would probably have only one entry of this form. The fourth entry, for 127.0.0.0, is the localhost interface, as described earlier. (Some distributions, such as Debian, don't explicitly show this route, but it still works.) Note its interface device (in the Iface column) is lo. The final entry, for a destination of 0.0.0.0, is the default route. This address, in conjunction with the netmask of 0.0.0.0, matches any traffic that has not already been matched. It sends traffic

```
[rodsmith@speaker rodsmith]$ route -n
Kernel IP routing table
Destination     Gateway         Genmask         Flags Metric Ref    Use Iface
255.255.255.255 0.0.0.0         255.255.255.255 UH    0      0        0 eth0
10.92.68.0      0.0.0.0         255.255.255.0   U     0      0        0 eth1
192.168.1.0     0.0.0.0         255.255.255.0   U     0      0        0 eth0
127.0.0.0       0.0.0.0         255.0.0.0       U     0      0        0 lo
0.0.0.0         10.92.68.1      0.0.0.0         UG    1      0        0 eth1
[rodsmith@speaker rodsmith]$
```

Figure 2.2 You can determine how Linux will route a packet by comparing its destination address to the Destination and Genmask columns of the routing table.

over the eth1 interface, and it's the only route in this sample that uses a gateway—10.92.68.1 in this case.

When you activated an interface with ifconfig, the utility automatically added one entry for the interface to your routing table. This entry corresponds to the local network route for the interface (the routes with netmasks of 255.255.255.0 in Figure 2.2). Default Linux startup scripts automatically add the localhost interface entry. The broadcast entry (for 255.255.255.255) is not required or active on most systems, but some utilities need this entry. In normal operation, the main routing table entry that's left to be defined is the one for the default route.

Basic route Syntax and Use

If it's given without any parameters, or with only certain parameters like -n (which produces numeric output rather than hostnames for entries like the gateway systems), route displays the current routing table. You can also use this tool to add, delete, or change routing table entries. To do this, you use route with additional parameters. The syntax for such use is as follows:

```
route add | del [-net | -host] target [netmask nm] [gateway gw]
[metric m] [mss m] [window W] [[dev] interface]
```

Each of these parameters has a specific meaning:

- **add | del**—Specify add if you want to add a route, or del if you want to delete one. In either case, you must give enough information for route to act on the route. (For deletions, you can usually get away with nothing more than the target.)

- **[-net | -host]**—You can specify a target address as either a network (-net) or a single computer (-host). In most cases, route can figure this out for itself, but sometimes it needs prompting. This is particularly likely if you're adding a route for a second gateway (like a gateway that only handles one small subnet, rather than the default route's gateway).

- **target**—The target address is the computer or network whose packets should be defined by the route. In the case of the default route, this will be 0.0.0.0, or the equivalent keyword, default. This parameter is required when you add or delete a route.

- **[netmask nm]**—If your target network follows the traditional class structure for network addresses, Linux can determine what the netmask should be. If your network doesn't follow this pattern, though, you must include the netmask nm parameter, in which you give route the netmask. (Alternatively, you can include this information with the target address as the number of bits in the network component, as described earlier.)

- **[gateway gw]**—If you're adding a route that doesn't involve a gateway, you can omit this parameter. If you want to specify a gateway system, though, you must include the gateway gw parameter. You'll use this to define the default gateway or any other gateway system.

- **[metric m]**—If you examine Figure 2.2, you'll see a column labeled Metric. This column shows the *routing metric* for a route—its estimated "cost" of delivery, which is normally associated with time. Slow routes should have high metrics, whereas fast routes should have low metrics. You can set this feature with the metric m parameter. This feature is normally only used on router computers, as described in Chapter 24, Advanced Router Options.

- **[mss m]**—The mss m option sets the Maximum Segment Size (MSS). Like the metric m option, this option is useful primarily on routers.

- **[window W]**—The *TCP Window Size* is the amount of data that a computer will send before it requires an acknowledgment from the recipient. If this value is set too small, network transfers may be slowed because the system will end up waiting for acknowledgments before sending new data. If it's set too high, the risk of having to re-send a lot of data because of errors will be increased. As a general rule, Linux's default TCP Window size of 64KB is acceptable. If your system uses a connection that's fast but that has very high latencies, such as a satellite broadband connection, you might consider raising this to 128KB or so.

- **[[dev] interface]**—Usually, Linux can figure out what interface to use from the target IP address or the gateway system's address. This might not always be true, though, and in such cases, you can force the issue by using the [dev] interface parameter. (The dev keyword is optional, and interface is the interface name, such as eth0 or tr1.)

The most common use of route is to add the default route after adding the primary network interface using ifconfig. This use is fairly simple, as illustrated by this example:

```
# route add 0.0.0.0 gw 10.92.68.1
```

If you prefer, you can substitute the keyword default for 0.0.0.0; the two have precisely the same effect. On rare occasions, you must add a -net specification, device name, or some other option.

Multiple Interfaces with One Gateway

As noted earlier, each time you add an interface with ifconfig, that utility automatically adds an entry to your routing table for that interface. This does not extend to adding a gateway, however. As a consequence, the configuration required on many computers with multiple interfaces consists of two types of action:

1. Run ifconfig for each of the computer's interfaces.
2. Run route once to add the computer's default route to the routing table.

This set of steps will be adequate for a small router, such as a Linux computer that functions as a router for a small department in a larger organization. For a router, you'll also have to enable routing by turning on IP forwarding. You can do this by typing the following command:

```
# echo "1" > /proc/sys/net/ipv4/ip_forward
```

NOTE If the computer has two interfaces but should *not* function as a router, you should *not* enable IP forwarding. This might be the case if a computer exists on two networks that should not communicate with each other, or that use some other computer as a router.

NOTE Routing duties shouldn't ordinarily be performed by a computer that does other work. Non-routing tasks can consume CPU time and network bandwidth that can degrade the router's performance. There are also potential security issues; routers today often include firewall features, and running unnecessary software on a firewall leaves an avenue of attack open.

If you have just one external IP address but want to connect several computers to the Internet, you can use a special type of routing known as Network Address Translation (NAT). Chapter 25, Configuring iptables, covers this technology. The basic steps are the same as for a normal router, but NAT requires you to run extra commands to allow the router to translate addresses in order to make your entire network look like a single computer to the outside world.

Multiple Interfaces with Multiple Gateways

A trickier configuration is one in which a computer can use multiple gateways. Most systems use just one gateway, which is associated with the default route. The gateway ties the local network to some other network, and often ultimately to the Internet. There are other configurations possible, however. For instance, consider Figure 2.3. This figure depicts an environment in which an organization has connected two subnetworks via routers. The regular computers in both offices can be configured quite simply—they need only point to their local routers as their gateways. Likewise, the router in Office 2 can point to the router in Office 1 as its sole gateway system, although the Office 2 router has two interfaces, as just discussed. The router

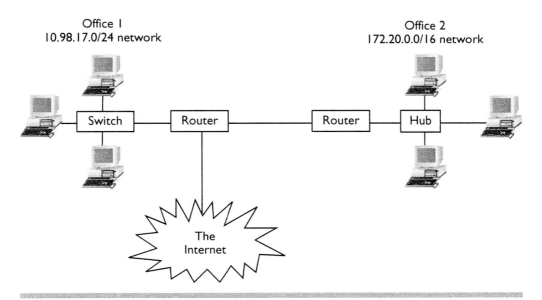

Figure 2.3 Routers with more than two interfaces require at least two gateway definitions in order to function properly.

in Office 1, however, requires a more complex configuration. Its default route leads to the Internet, but it must also configure a route to the Office 2 router for traffic destined for the 172.20.0.0/16 network. You might use a `route` command like the following to accomplish this goal:

```
# route add -net 172.20.0.0 netmask 255.255.0.0 gw 172.21.1.1
```

NOTE A configuration like this makes the most sense when Office 1 and Office 2 are widely separated geographically and are linked by some form of long-distance network protocol. If the offices were located close together, both might be tied into a single hub or switch and served by a single router.

This command assumes that Office 2's router talks to Office 1's router using the 172.21.1.1 address. (Note that this address is not part of the Office 2 network proper; it's on a different network card in Office 2's router.) The end result of issuing this command as well as a normal `route` command to define the default route will be a routing table that includes two gateways: one for the default route and one to handle traffic destined to Room 2's systems. None of the other computers that link to Office 1's router need to know anything about this arrangement; they only need to know that this router is the gateway for the default route.

There are other situations in which a similar configuration might be required. For instance, if Office 1 used a second router to link to the Internet, all of the computers in Office 1 would need to have two gateways defined: one default route pointing to the system that leads to the Internet, and a second route pointing to the router that leads to Office 2. (Alternatively, regular systems could list just one router, which could pass traffic to the other router when appropriate, but this would increase local network traffic.) Because a network with two routers involves more tricky configuration for all computers on the network, it's best to use a single router on any given subnet whenever possible.

CONFIGURING DNS

Once an interface is active and a gateway set, a computer can send and receive network traffic destined for anywhere on its local network or any other network to which the gateway connects, directly or indirectly. Traffic must be addressed by IP address, though, which is tedious at best. It's the job of the *Domain Name System (DNS)* to provide a better user interface by converting the alphanumeric names (such as www.awl.com) used by people to IP addresses used by computers. (DNS can also do the reverse conversion.)

DNS is a globally distributed database, but any given computer needs to know just one IP address to gain entry to that database: the address of a single DNS server. Most organizations and ISPs provide at least one DNS server, and many provide two or three. You should consult your network administrator to learn the addresses of your network's DNS servers. When you've obtained this information, you can enter it into the /etc/resolv.conf file. This file can have up to three lines that begin with the keyword nameserver and end with the IP address of a DNS server. The file can also specify the default domain of the Linux system (using the domain keyword) and an arbitrary number of domains that are to be searched when you omit a domain name (for instance, if you specify mail rather than mail.threeroomco.com) using the search keyword. Listing 2.1 shows an example of an /etc/resolv.conf file illustrating these three keywords.

Listing 2.1   An example /etc/resolv.conf file

```
domain threeroomco.com
search tworoomco.com fourroomco.com
nameserver 10.98.17.34
nameserver 172.20.13.109
```

WARNING

Although the search option makes it possible to reduce typing by omitting the specified domain names when performing network accesses, this option should be used sparingly. The problem is that two domains may have identically named computers, and this could lead to confusion. For instance, if tworoomco.com and fourroomco.com both have Web servers called www, a user who types www in a Web browser on a computer with Listing 2.1's /etc/resolv.conf file may get one Web server and believe it's the other domain's Web server. These searches also take time, so most other name lookups will be slowed down. Normally, even when you specify a complete name, the system searches for that name first in the domains specified by the domain and search lines. For instance, if a user types www.awl.com, Listing 2.1's /etc/resolv.conf causes the system to first search for www.awl.com.threeroomco.com, www.awl.com.tworoomco.com, and www.awl.com.fourroomco.com, and only then to search for www.awl.com. This final (correct) search can be done first by including a period at the end of the domain name, as in www.awl.com..

Once you've edited /etc/resolv.conf to your liking, there's no command needed to activate the changes. Linux will simply begin using the specified name servers and searching the specified domains.

If you want Linux to function as a DNS server for your network, consult Chapter 18. This chapter includes information on running a DNS server, which can be used by other computers on your own network, by computers on the Internet at large, or by both, depending upon the server's configuration.

SETTING THE HOSTNAME

Many TCP/IP protocols require that computers identify themselves by name to each other. To simplify configuration of individual programs, Linux maintains a global hostname setting, which can be viewed or set with the hostname command. Typing the command alone displays the current hostname. Typing the command followed by a hostname (as in **hostname larch.threeroomco.com**) sets the hostname to the specified name. You can store the hostname in a file and pass that file to the hostname command with the -F or --file option, as in **hostname -F /etc/HOSTNAME**. Most distributions do this automatically at boot time, although the location of the hostname varies from one distribution to another. Check /etc/hostname, /etc/HOSTNAME, and the files listed in the Extra Configuration Files column of Table 2.1.

Unfortunately, although the ideal is to set the hostname once, this isn't always possible. Some user-level programs—particularly e-mail clients and Usenet news readers—allow users to override the default hostname setting. You or your users may therefore need to set the hostname in these programs, particularly if you ever change the hostname. You might also want to set the hostname in /etc/hosts. This file exists as a method of name resolution that's an alternative to DNS. It consists of lines that begin with an IP address and continue with a series of hostnames. Most commonly, the first hostname is a *Fully-Qualified Domain Name (FQDN)*—that is, a complete hostname, including the machine name and the domain to which it belongs, as in larch.threeroomco.com. Subsequent names on the same line are "nicknames"—normally shortened forms, such as larch. If your system's DNS settings are correct, and if your computer has appropriate entries in your network's DNS server, it won't be necessary to create an /etc/hosts entry for the computer. If your network's DNS servers, or the network path to those servers, is unreliable, however, creating an /etc/hosts entry for your computer can improve overall reliability. You might also want to ensure that the 127.0.0.1 address is represented, with hostnames of localhost.localdomain and localhost. Examples of both entries might resemble the following:

```
10.92.68.1 larch.threeroomco.com larch
127.0.0.1 localhost.localdomain localhost
```

TIP If the computer pauses for several seconds or even minutes during the boot process, particularly when starting sendmail, chances are you need to set entries such as those mentioned above in your /etc/hosts file, or you need to fix your network's DNS server entries for the computer. Some programs, including sendmail, pause for long periods of time if they can't connect their hostnames and IP addresses via DNS, /etc/hosts, or some other method.

If a computer has multiple network interfaces, you'll set one hostname using the hostname command, but you'll normally create multiple hostnames, one for each interface, in the /etc/hosts file, although this isn't required. (Your network's DNS servers will also normally have two or more names for the computer in this case.)

TIP On a small private network, you can use /etc/hosts to handle all your local hostnames, obviating the need to run a DNS server for local computers only. This practice becomes tedious as a network grows in size, though, so many larger networks use a centralized DNS server.

MAKING YOUR CHANGES PERMANENT

Some of the preceding procedures, such as adjusting hostnames in /etc/hosts and setting up name server addresses in /etc/resolv.conf, involve editing configuration files. These changes are permanent; once you make them, you won't need to make them again unless your configuration files become damaged or you reinstall Linux. Other changes, by contrast, are transient in nature. When you run ifconfig, route, or hostname to adjust a system feature, that change will last only as long as the computer runs or until it's undone by another action. If you reboot, the change will be lost. In order to make such a change permanent, you must adjust a startup script or configuration file, either by editing the file in a text editor or by using a GUI configuration tool.

Using a GUI Configuration Tool

One of the easiest ways to make a permanent change in a network setting is to do it with a GUI configuration tool—at least, if your distribution includes such a tool. (Debian and Slackware both eschew the use of such tools.) Specific options include the following:

- **Red Hat and Mandrake**—These distributions use a GUI configuration tool called Linuxconf, which is also used by some other distributions, such as LinuxPPC. The user interface differs slightly from one distribution to another. You can launch this tool by typing `linuxconf`. It operates in text mode using text-based menus, in GUI mode using GUI menus, and in an optional Web server mode to permit remote administration.

- **SuSE**—SuSE uses Yet Another Setup Tool (YaST) as a menu-driven text-based tool, and YaST2 as a GUI counterpart to YaST. (Figure 2.1 shows YaST2 in operation.) Type `yast` or `yast2` to launch these tools.

- **Caldera**—Caldera uses the Caldera Open Administration System (COAS) as its GUI setup tool. It can be launched by typing `coastool` in an xterm window.

- **TurboLinux**—TurboLinux uses the TurboLinux Configuration Center for a GUI configuration tool. You can launch it by typing `turbocfgcenter`.

- **All Distributions**—The Webmin project (`http://www.webmin.com/webmin/`) is a Web-based administration tool that can be used with many different Linux distributions and non-Linux Unix-like systems. It's not installed by default with most distributions, but if your distribution is supported by Webmin, getting it running shouldn't be too difficult.

The exact details differ from one tool to another, but to configure a system using GUI tools, you must normally locate a network configuration menu, and possibly delve another layer or two into the interface to locate the settings you need to alter. You then enter the configuration options you want to set permanently. For instance, in Figure 2.1, you can click Static Address Setup and enter the IP address and netmask in the fields provided, then click the Hostname and Nameserver button and the Routing button to adjust these features.

One drawback to GUI tools is that they sometimes don't permit more advanced configurations. For instance, there might be no way to adjust a routing table with the precision required for configurations like those discussed earlier, in the section "Multiple Interfaces with Multiple Gateways." These tools are almost always adequate for simpler configurations, though. If you have trouble with the GUI tools, you can resort to directly editing the configuration files.

Editing Configuration Files

Table 2.1 gives the locations of configuration files in which DHCP client commands and extra configuration information are listed. These files also hold commands and configurations for handling static IP addresses. You should peruse these files, looking for calls to `ifconfig`, `route`, `hostname`, or other configuration commands. Some files don't include commands, but instead set environment variables that hold information such as whether the system uses DHCP or a static IP address configuration, and hold the static configuration information in the latter case. A perusal of the scripts and configuration files involved should be enough to let you configure your system.

Should you encounter problems with the normal configuration scripts, one way to force the issue is to create entries in a local startup script that call the configuration commands you want to use. Most distributions use `/etc/rc.d/rc.local` as a local startup script, but SuSE uses `/etc/rc.d/boot.local`. Debian has no single local startup script, but you can create such a file in the `/etc/rc.boot` directory. When you create or edit such a script, you can enter any commands you like, including network commands like `ifconfig` and `route`. These commands will execute after other startup scripts, though, so this isn't the ideal location for most network configuration commands. It might be an acceptable way to get the system to add an unusual route, however, such as a gateway route for a single small subnet, as discussed earlier.

USING A PPP LINK

Most of this book assumes that the network to which the Linux computer is connected is a dedicated one, such as an Ethernet network. In this environment, it's possible to run servers, as discussed in Parts II and III; the security and router issues of Part IV are very important, as well. Some configurations, though, use a less permanent type of network link. These connections use a telephone modem and PPP to create a temporary connection to the Internet, or at least to one other computer. Although you're not likely to run servers over a PPP link, they do have their place. For instance, you might run a small office or home office network, and so use

PPP over Ethernet

Some low-end DSL connections use a variant of PPP, known as PPPoE. The 2.4.x Linux kernel includes PPPoE support, but it's considered experimental. The most common PPPoE tool for Linux in 2002 is the Roaring Penguin PPPoE client (`http://www.roaringpenguin.com/pppoe/`). This package comes in source code form or as RPM packages for a variety of platforms.

After you install Roaring Penguin, type **adsl-setup** or **tkpppoe** to configure the tool. (The latter command requires installation of Roaring Penguin GUI tools; the former is a text-based program.) You'll be asked for information such as your username and password, and the script will store all the information and create a dialing script called `adsl-start`. You can run this script to initiate a PPPoE connection.

It's important to note that Roaring Penguin requires that you have support for your network device. Linux works with all external Ethernet-based DSL modems, provided you have a supported Ethernet card. If your DSL modem is USB-based or internal, though, you'll need to locate drivers for it, and these are rare in 2002.

various local network servers, as discussed in Part II, but use a PPP link to connect that network to the Internet on an as-needed basis. You can even share this connection among all the computers on the network by setting up Network Address Translation (NAT; also called IP masquerading), as discussed in Chapter 25. In order to do these things, though, you'll first have to establish the PPP connection. This section describes how to do this.

USING A GUI DIALER

PPP can be a tricky tool to use; the protocol has many options that, if set incorrectly, can disrupt the PPP connection or even prevent it from coming up initially. For this reason, many people find it easier to use PPP via a GUI dialer than through configuration scripts. In fact, many Linux GUI PPP dialers closely resemble their counterparts in other OSs, such as Windows, so if you're familiar with PPP in another OS, you shouldn't have too much difficulty using a Linux GUI PPP dialer.

Different GUI dialers differ in some details, but they are similar in broad outline. This section presents information on the popular KPPP dialer, which is part of the K Desktop Environment (KDE). You can use KPPP even if you don't use KDE; or you can use GNOME PPP (part of the GNU Network Object Model Environment, or GNOME) or a dialer that's not part of any desktop environment, such as X-ISP (`http://xisp.hellug.gr`).

NOTE   Before using KPPP, you must sign up for a dial-up account and test your modem's functionality in Linux. Check your telephone book for ISPs to obtain an account, or consult an online resource such as The List (http://www.thelist.com) if you've got access through some other computer. To test the modem, connect it and (if it's an external model) turn it on. You should be able to send data to /dev/ttyS0, /dev/ttyS1, or some other port. If you're using the new devfs (http://www.atnf.csiro.au/~rgooch/linux/docs/devfs.html) to automatically create device files, you'll use /dev/tts/0, /dev/tts/1, and so on. You can most easily test this configuration by using a terminal program like the text-based minicom or the GUI Seyon, both of which ship with most Linux distributions. If you can get an AT prompt from the modem, you know that Linux can use the modem.

To start KPPP, you can select it from a menu on your desktop environment, or you can type **kppp** in an xterm. The result should resemble Figure 2.4, except that the first time you launch KPPP, it probably won't include any ISP names in the Connect To list, nor a login ID or password. In order to set the program up to use an account, follow these steps:

1. Click the Setup button. This action will produce the KPPP Configuration dialog box shown in Figure 2.5. From here, you can enter critical account information for future connections.

2. Click New to create a new account. KPPP asks if you want to use a wizard or set up via dialog boxes. Although the wizard is purported to be easier, it begins by asking for your country, and there's no entry for the United States. I therefore present the dialog box procedure, which produces the New Account dialog box shown in Figure 2.6.

3. Type the name of your ISP into the Connection Name field.

Figure 2.4   GUI PPP dialers usually provide some way of selecting an account, entering a username and password, and initiating a connection.

53

Figure 2.5   The KPPP Configuration dialog box controls hardware features associated with a PPP connection, such as what modem device to use, and lets you modify specific accounts using other dialog boxes.

Figure 2.6   The New Account dialog box lets you enter many important account details.

4. Click Add. This action produces a small dialog box in which you may enter a telephone number for your ISP. Be sure to include any digits you need to dial an outside line, or the area code if you need to dial it. When you click OK in this dialog box, the Phone Number field should reflect the addition. You may repeat this step if you want to enter multiple numbers that the dialer will attempt in sequence, should one number be busy.

5. Most ISPs today use the Password Authentication Protocol (PAP) for communicating the username and password, so you should probably leave the Authentication selector in the New Account dialog box set to PAP. You can change this to various other options if required, though. Of particular interest is the Challenge Handshake Authentication Protocol (CHAP), which some ISPs use.

6. If your ISP gave you a list of DNS servers as part of your sign-up process, click the DNS tab of the New Account information and enter each IP address in the DNS IP Address field, clicking Add after entering each address.

7. Click OK in the New Account dialog box. You should see the new entry appear in the list in the KPPP Configuration dialog box (Figure 2.5).

8. Click the Device tab in the KPPP Configuration dialog box. Set the Modem Device to whatever device name your system uses for the modem. This is often /dev/modem (the default), but may be /dev/ttyS0, /dev/ttyS1, or something more exotic. You may also want to adjust the Connection Speed option on this tab. The default is 57,600, but 115,200 provides better speed on most systems. (Higher values don't work on most hardware.) The speed you set here is for communication between your computer and your modem. The connect speed between your modem and your ISP is likely to be lower, but if your modem uses compression, a local connection speed of about twice the modem-to-modem speed is optimal.

9. Click OK in the KPPP Configuration dialog box. You should now be able to select your new account in the main KPPP window (Figure 2.4), if it's not selected by default.

NOTE The KPPP Configuration and New Account dialog boxes both include tabs and options I've not discussed here. In most cases, you won't need to adjust these values, but sometimes they're vital. If you have problems connecting or if you want to enable a feature you've heard about but that's not covered here, check these tabs for options that might help. The PPP HOWTO document (http://www.linuxdoc.org/HOWTO/PPP-HOWTO/) includes additional information on PPP and debugging PPP connections.

Using a GUI PPP dialer is a fairly simple matter; after launching the program, you need only click the Connect button (which may be called something else in some programs). Some dialers will provide you with an indication of their progress during the connection phase, and many modems will echo the sounds of the modem negotiations. In KPPP, clicking the Show Log Window button will provide added details. Some dialers, including KPPP, require you to enter the username (in the Login ID field) and password before clicking Connect. Others will ask for this information after you click Connect. Many let you store your password on disk (the Store Password check box in the KPPP New Account dialog box lets you set this option).

WARNING

Storing your PPP dialup password on the computer is a potential security risk. This risk may be small for an isolated computer that you use to initiate connections, but if the computer has many users, some of whom shouldn't have access to the PPP account, the risk may be greater. At the very least, you should not use your PPP dialup account password for any other purpose, so that if the PPP password is stolen you need not change any other passwords.

Once a connection is initiated, the Connect button changes names so that you can break a connection. (Some dialers may use a different button or present another dialog box to let you end a connection.) If your ISP or telephone company charges by the minute, remember to do this or you'll get an unexpectedly large bill!

ADJUSTING CONFIGURATION SCRIPTS

GUI dialers are a convenient way to get started with PPP, but they aren't ideal for all situations. For instance, if you want to initiate a PPP connection automatically, a GUI dialer won't do the job, because it requires manual intervention to begin the call. For this reason, PPP connection scripts can also initiate connections. You may use these scripts manually or as part of an auto-dialing scheme, as discussed in the next section, "Configuring Dial-on-Demand." Using the scripts requires setting authentication options and configuring the scripts themselves.

Setting PPP Authentication Options

As noted earlier, most ISPs use a protocol called PAP for authenticating dial-in users. In order to use this protocol from a dialing script, you need to edit the file /etc/ppp/pap-secrets. (A similar file, called /etc/ppp/chap-secrets, is used by another protocol that some ISPs use. Both files use the same format, so you can edit both, if you like.) This file consists of a series of lines, one for each PPP account you have. The format of each line is as follows:

```
username    server    password    IP_address
```

Each of these elements is separated by one or more spaces or tabs. Their meanings are as follows:

- *username*—This is the username to be used on the ISP's system. This username is unrelated to your Linux username; it's the one your ISP gave you.
- *server*—This is the name of the computer to which yours communicates. You don't normally know this name, so this field should contain a single asterisk (*), to denote that PPP will accept any hostname.
- *password*—As you might guess, this is the password on the remote system.
- *IP_address*—This is the IP address your system expects to get. Most PPP systems don't guarantee you a specific IP address, so this field is empty (the line has only three fields).

WARNING

! The pap-secrets file must store the password in an unencrypted form. This fact means that the file is extremely sensitive; if an unauthorized party obtains the file, that individual will be able to use your PPP account without your authorization. If possible, you shouldn't use this password for anything other than basic access; try to use a different password for e-mail retrieval or to log on to any other computer or network, for instance. For security, most distributions ship with pap-secrets set to root ownership, and only root has read access to the file. You should leave it this way unless you have a good reason for changing it.

Most systems connect to just one ISP, so the pap-secrets file will have just one line. This line might resemble the following:

```
penguin    *    w8terfowl
```

Configuring Dialing Scripts

Once you've set up the PAP or CHAP authentication file, you can begin adjusting the dialing scripts themselves. Because GUI dialers have become so prevalent, most distributions now hide these scripts in a documentation directory, such as /usr/share/doc/ppp-*version*/scripts, where *version* is the version of PPP your distribution uses, such as 2.4.0. There are three scripts that are of interest:

- **ppp-on**—This script sets important variables, such as your ISP's telephone number, and calls the Linux PPP utility (pppd).
- **ppp-on-dialer**—ppp-on passes this script to pppd, which uses it to control the initial stages of communication with the ISP's system.
- **ppp-off**—This script terminates a PPP session.

You'll need to modify ppp-on, and possibly ppp-on-dialer, in order to connect to an ISP. You'll also probably want to move all three scripts to a convenient location, like /usr/local/bin. In ppp-on, set the following items:

- Locate the TELEPHONE variable and set it to your ISP's telephone number. For instance, the line might read TELEPHONE=555-9876 when it's set correctly.
- Set the values for the ACCOUNT and PASSWORD variables. If your ISP uses PAP, these variables won't actually be used, so you should set them to some dummy values, such as the values they contain by default.
- If your ISP provides you with a fixed IP address or if you know the IP address of the system to which you'll be connecting, you can set the LOCAL_IP and REMOTE_IP variables appropriately. Likewise, you can change the NETMASK variable if you know what your network mask should be. You can usually leave all three of these variables alone.
- Locate the DIALER_SCRIPT variable and set it to point to the location of your ppp-on-dialer script. (Point to the copy you intend to modify, not the original in the documentation directory.) The default value is /etc/ppp/ppp-on-dialer, and you can put your script there if you like.
- The end of the script is a call to pppd. This is Linux's PPP tool, and it supports a large number of options. You should not have to modify most of these, but there are some exceptions. Specifically, you may need to set the device file used by your modem (the default is usually /dev/ttyS0), as well as the connection speed (the default is normally 38400, but 115200 usually works better).

Once you've adjusted your ppp-on script to your needs, you should examine the ppp-on-dialer script. This script controls pppd's interactions with your modem, including sending the commands that cause it to dial, and any interactions required to log in if your ISP doesn't use PAP or CHAP. The script does this by calling a utility known as chat, which handles automated exchanges with tools that expect text-based input. Most of this script is a series of expect/reply strings, arranged in columns. The first column is the value for which the script looks, and the second column is the response that chat sends in response. Some of these, such as an expect value of ABORT, carry special meaning; for instance, ABORT tells chat when to halt because of an error. Most of the lines end in a backslash (\), the common convention for a line continuation. (In reality, chat expects a single line with interspersed expect/reply pairs; they're grouped in columns only for the convenience of humans.) The final line lacks a backslash.

The main feature that may need adjustment is the final three lines of the ppp-on-dialer script. The default script is usually written with the expectation that the ISP is *not* using PAP, so it concludes with two lines that echo your username and password (as entered in the ACCOUNT and PASSWORD variables in ppp-on). You may need to delete these lines or comment them out (by preceding them with pound signs, #). If you do this, you'll also have to remove the backslash from the third-to-last line, which normally begins with an expect string of CONNECT. Removing these final two lines and adjusting the preceding one will cause chat to terminate immediately after connection, whereupon pppd will try to use PAP or CHAP to authenticate the connection. If your ISP does *not* use PAP or CHAP, you may need to modify the expect portions of these lines to match the prompts your ISP uses for your username and password, and possibly add more prompts if you have to enter additional commands yourself, such as a command to explicitly start PPP on the ISP's system.

Using PPP Dialing Scripts

Editing the script files is the most difficult part of initiating a PPP connection via these scripts. When this task is done, you need only type **ppp-on** (preceded by a complete path to the script, if you didn't put it somewhere on your path) to initiate a connection. If your modem is external, you should see its lights blink, and if it's configured to echo sounds to its speaker during dialing, you should hear this process. If all goes well, after a few seconds you should be able to access the Internet using Linux's normal networking tools.

If you encounter problems, you should first check the log file to which pppd logs its actions (normally /var/log/messages). The end of this file should contain information on pppd's actions, including whatever caused it to fail—a timeout waiting for PAP, a failure when running chat, or what have you. If this output is cryptic or doesn't provide you with the clues you need, try searching for keywords related to your problem on http:// groups.google.com. This site hosts archives of recent posts to Usenet newsgroups, where discussions of problems with PPP and other Linux networking tools frequently appear. Searching there will quite possibly turn up an answer, or at least a lead you can follow. The PPP HOWTO document, mentioned earlier, also has PPP debugging tips.

One drawback to connecting via scripts is that most distributions are configured in such a way that only root may initiate a PPP connection. This can be an important security measure on a multi-user system, because you may not want unauthorized personnel making random PPP connections. It can be a nuisance, though. The GUI dialers get around this problem by using the set user ID (SUID) bit to have the GUI dialer run with root privileges. Of course, this opens up the system to the security problems of allowing random users access to the dialer. (You may restrict execute privileges to the GUI dialer by creating a PPP users group, assigning the GUI dialer to that group, and denying world execute privileges on the program.)

Many ISPs communicate the IP addresses of DNS servers along with other information as part of the PPP negotiation. Sometimes, though, you'll need to enter this information in /etc/resolv.conf yourself, as described earlier in this chapter in "Configuring DNS." You should be able to set up your DNS servers permanently.

CONFIGURING DIAL-ON-DEMAND

When your computer is used primarily as a single-user workstation, GUI dialers or manually launched scripts like ppp-on are good methods of initiating PPP connections. In a multi-user environment, though, these tools have their problems. Users could try to initiate connections when they're already up, terminate connections when other users are using them, or accidentally leave connections active for long periods of time. For this reason, Linux supports a procedure known as *dial-on-demand*, which is implemented through a program called diald. This tool detects outgoing network traffic, initiates a PPP connection in response to the traffic, and terminates the connection after a specified period of time with no network activity. The result is that users may use network tools almost as if they were on an always-up network connection; they need take no explicit actions to start or stop the PPP link. There will be a delay, however, between the time when diald detects the outgoing traffic and the time the connection is finished (after all, the system has to dial the modem, and the modem must negotiate the connection). If you program the system to drop a connection too soon after the cessation of network activity, this can result in annoying delays during normal network use—say, a long pause when a user clicks on a link in a Web page, because the connection timed out when the user was reading the first page.

To use dia1d, you must have SLIP support compiled in your kernel, as described in Chapter 1. This is because dia1d uses SLIP to set up a virtual connection, essentially linking your computer to the dia1d program itself. Programs therefore see an always-up network interface, and dia1d receives the network traffic so that it can control when to initiate the real connection.

Unfortunately, most Linux distributions don't ship with dia1d. You can obtain the package from its home Web site, http://dia1d.sourceforge.net, or you can search for a prebuilt binary on http://www.rpmfind.net or http://www.debian.org/distrib/packages for RPM or Debian packages, respectively.

The dia1d program is controlled through three configuration files:

- **/etc/dia1d.conf**—This file sets many of the configuration options that are normally handled by ppp-on, including the modem device filename (device) and connect speed (speed). The local and remote options set the IP addresses used internally by dia1d. You should set both addresses to ones on the same network segment, but neither address should be used on the Internet or your own local network (if you have one). Addresses in the 192.168.*x.x* range are typically good choices.

- **/etc/ppp/dia1d-dialer**—This file is essentially identical to the ppp-on-dialer script described earlier. You should adjust it just as you would ppp-on-dialer.

- **/usr/lib/dia1d/standard.filter**—This file defines the timeout periods that dia1d uses to decide when to drop a connection. You can specify different types of connections by the destination connection type, as shown in /etc/services. In each case, you tell dia1d to remain up for a given number of seconds. The default file should be a reasonable starting point, and you can modify it if you find that dia1d is dropping connections too soon.

In addition to these configuration files, you must edit your /etc/ppp/pap-secrets or /etc/ppp/chap-secrets file if your ISP uses PAP or CHAP, just as for a regular script-based PPP connection. You may also need to enter your ISP's DNS server addresses in /etc/resolv.conf, as described earlier. To use dia1d, type **/usr/sbin/dia1d** as root to start the program. It should then detect outgoing network activity and initiate a connection. Because of the connection delays, though, a first attempt to use a tool may fail; for instance, a Web browser may time out before it can display a page. The second attempt should work, though.

If you want your system to start `diald` automatically when it boots, you can create a SysV startup script, or add an entry to a local startup script, such as `/etc/rc.d/rc.local` or `/etc/rc.d/boot.local`. Whether you start it manually or automatically, `diald` can detect network traffic that originates on a local network if you configure your computer to function as a NAT router, as described in Chapter 25. Thus, you can link a small local network to the Internet via a Linux computer and modem, and configure your local computers as if they were on the Internet at large, using the Linux system as the local gateway.

Summary

Using a network requires that you initiate some form of network connection. Most local networks use Ethernet as a connection medium, and Linux includes excellent support for Ethernet networking. Most such networks require that you either configure your IP address manually or use a DHCP client to do the job. Linux includes support for both methods. Many other local network technologies use these same methods of configuration. One major exception is a PPP connection, which is most commonly used for low-speed network links over telephone lines. These are handled by `pppd`, the Linux PPP daemon. This program may be controlled through GUI configuration tools, simple scripts, or the `diald` dial-on-demand daemon. In any of these cases, a PPP connection creates a network interface that, from a software perspective, is similar to an Ethernet or other local network interface.

Alternative Network Stacks

Computers are very good at following precise instructions, but they're not very good at improvising or dealing with deviations from expectations. For this reason, computer networks rely on a series of very precisely defined protocols—descriptions of how a procedure or transaction is supposed to occur. As described briefly in Chapter 1, these protocols are arranged in a linear fashion to form what's referred to as a *network protocol stack*, or a *network stack* or *protocol stack* for short. The *Transmission Control Protocol/Internet Protocol (TCP/IP)* stack is the most common network stack; it forms the basis of the Internet, as well as of most Linux network tools. Chapter 2 described configuring Linux to use TCP/IP. There are several alternative network stacks, however, and Linux includes support for some of these.

This chapter begins with an overview of what a network stack is, including a brief description of TCP/IP. Next up are discussions of three common alternative network stacks: AppleTalk, IPX, and NetBEUI. These alternative stacks are used mostly on local area networks for file and printer sharing among Macintosh and Windows computers.

UNDERSTANDING NETWORK STACKS

In discussing network stacks, including their relative merits, it's necessary to understand something about how a network stack is organized, how it works, and what it can accomplish. All network stacks are similar on a broad level of analysis, but the details of how they operate determine some of their important differences. Understanding the theory behind network stacks will help you understand each network stack's features.

THE OSI NETWORK STACK MODEL

One common model of network stacks is the *Open System Interconnection (OSI) model*. This model consists of seven *layers,* each of which handles a specific networking task. When a computer sends data, the information originates from a program residing at the top layer of the OSI model (known as the *Application layer*). The program passes data to the next layer (the *Presentation layer*), and so on down the stack. Each layer processes the data in some way. At the bottom of the OSI model is the *Physical layer*, which corresponds to the network hardware, such as cables and hubs. Data pass over the Physical layer from the sending computer to the receiving computer. (This transfer may be simple when both computers are on the same network segment, but it can involve many other systems when the two computers are at disparate points on the Internet.) On the destination system, the data pass *up* the network stack, ultimately reaching the recipient program at the Application layer on that system. This system may then send a reply down its network stack, and that reply passes up the stack of the first system. Figure 3.1 illustrates this process.

NOTE Although the OSI model is frequently used in describing networking generically, use of OSI as a full protocol stack is rare. More common network stacks, such as TCP/IP, AppleTalk, and NetBEUI, can be described in OSI terms, sometimes with a few changes. TCP/IP, for instance, is often described using a four-layer model, rather than the seven-layer OSI model. The principles remain the same, though.

Each layer of the OSI model communicates directly only with the layers immediately above and below it. (In the case of the Application and Physical layers, the chain ends. Applications communicate with users or perform automated network tasks, and the Physical layer links the two computers.) On any given computer, the layers of the network stack must be written to facilitate such communication, using clearly defined interfaces. Sometimes, the components at a given layer must be interchangeable. For instance, the Application layer consists of network applications, such as Web browsers and Web servers. You should be able to swap out one Web browser or Web server for another without causing problems

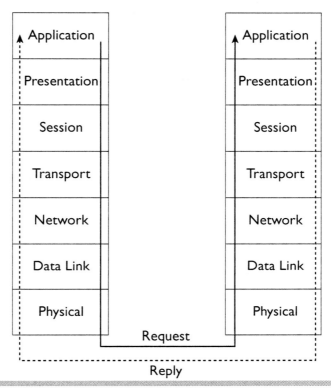

Figure 3.1   A network stack processes data so that it can be transferred to another computer, or "unwraps" data received from another computer.

with the network stack. (Any given Web browser or Web server may lack certain important features, such as the ability to handle Secure Sockets Layer [SSL] encryption; however, this isn't really an issue of network stack integration.) Similarly, you should be able to swap out network cables and hubs at the Physical layer, or even replace a network card and its driver, without impacting higher-up layers.

Each layer of the network stack corresponds to its counterpart on the opposite computer. In some sense, the recipient computer's network stack undoes whatever the sender computer's network stack did. The ultimate goal is to allow Application-layer programs to communicate. Therefore, any layer should receive from the layer below exactly the data sent by its counterpart layer on the sending system. In some sense, any given layer should work as if it were talking to its counterpart on the other system, not another layer of the local protocol stack. For this reason, network stacks must be very standardized across computers, even if those computers run radically different OSs. For instance, the network stacks of such diverse OSs as Linux, Windows XP, MacOS X, and BeOS must all work in almost precisely the same ways, even if they use entirely independent code bases.

WRAPPING AND UNWRAPPING DATA

The network stack is a useful way to envision the passage of data through a computer's network software, but it doesn't clearly describe what happens to data along the way. This can be thought of as *wrapping* and *unwrapping* data. Each layer of the network stack does something to the data it receives. Actions performed during wrapping may include breaking data into chunks (usually called *packets* or *frames*, depending on the level of the stack under discussion), adding information to an existing chunk of data, or modifying existing data (data modification is rare, though). Unwrapping reverses these actions.

For instance, consider data transfer via the File Transfer Protocol (FTP), which uses the TCP/IP network stack, over an Ethernet network. The data being transferred might be a file, but that single file might be much larger than the data packets or frames that TCP/IP or Ethernet are designed to transfer. Therefore, the file will be broken down into many small chunks. Each of these chunks will have *headers* added to it by various portions of the network stack. (Some layers may add *footers*, as well.) Headers and footers begin or end a given chunk of data, and include information to help the system parse and deliver the rest of the data packet. The idealized result of this wrapping is shown in Figure 3.2. In fact, matters can become more complex, because the packets delivered by one layer of the network stack may be even further split by subsequent layers of the stack. For instance, the Ethernet drivers might break down an IP packet into two Ethernet frames. Routers might do the same thing. When this happens, the IP, TCP, and FTP headers of Figure 3.2 are all just part of the data payload; they aren't duplicated in both Ethernet packets, and could wind up in either Ethernet packet. All of this is transparent, though, because each layer of the network stack on the recipient computer reassembles the packets or frames that its counterpart on the sending computer created, even if those packets have been split up *en route*.

The details of Figure 3.2 vary from one network stack to another, and even with details of a single stack. For instance, the FTP Header of Figure 3.2

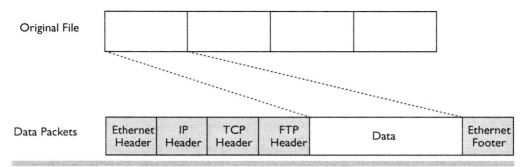

Figure 3.2   A network stack splits up a file into chunks and wraps each chunk in data that help the recipient computer reassemble the original file.

would be a Hypertext Transfer Protocol (HTTP) header for a Web browser data transfer. If the computers used network hardware other than Ethernet, the Ethernet header and footer would be replaced by headers and footers for the particular network hardware used. Indeed, a router that transfers data across network types would, as part of its processing, strip away these headers and footers and replace them with appropriate substitutes. This processing can occur several times during a packet's journey across the Internet, but the goal is to deliver the original data in its original form to the destination.

The headers and footers include critical addressing information, such as the sender's and recipient's IP addresses, the port numbers of the originating and destination programs, numbers identifying the place of a packet in a sequence, and so on. Intervening computers use this information to route individual packets, and the recipient uses it to direct the packet to the appropriate program. This program can then use the sender's address and port number to direct a reply to that system and program.

THE ROLE OF THE TCP/IP STACK

TCP/IP is the most popular network stack. The Internet is built upon TCP/IP, and the stack supports the most popular network protocols, including most of those discussed in this book. In most cases, you can't simply unlink a network application from one stack and tie it to another stack, although a few applications do support multiple network stacks. Part of the reason for TCP/IP's popularity is its flexibility. TCP/IP is a *routable* network stack, meaning that a computer with multiple network interfaces can partially process TCP/IP packets and pass those packets from one network to another. TCP/IP routing is flexible and allows for routing based on decentralized network maps; there's no need for a centralized database for network routing to occur. Furthermore, TCP/IP supports a large network address (32 bits, with 128-bit addresses coming with IPv6, as described in Chapter 2) and a hierarchical naming structure. All these features make TCP/IP well suited to function as a network stack for a globe-spanning network.

On an individual Linux computer, TCP/IP is a good choice because of its support for so many important network protocols. Although many non-Unix platforms developed proprietary protocol stacks in the 1980s, Unix systems helped pioneer TCP/IP, and most Unix network protocols use TCP/IP. Linux has inherited these protocols, and so a Linux-only or Linux/Unix network operates quite well using TCP/IP alone; chances are you won't need to use any other network stack in such an environment.

Common protocols supported by TCP/IP include HTTP, FTP, the Simple Mail Transfer Protocol (SMTP), the Network File System (NFS), Telnet, Secure Shell (SSH), the Network News Transfer Protocol (NNTP), the X Window System, and many others. Because of TCP/IP's popularity, tools that were originally written for other network stacks can also often use TCP/IP. In particular, the Server Message Block (SMB)/Common Internet File System (CIFS) file-sharing protocols used by Windows can link to TCP/IP via the Network Basic Input/Output System (NetBIOS), rather than tying to the NetBIOS Extended User Interface (NetBEUI), which is the native DOS and Windows protocol stack. (All versions of Windows since Windows 95 also support TCP/IP.) Similarly, Apple's file-sharing protocols now operate over TCP/IP as well as over AppleTalk.

Although it's very popular and can fill many network tasks, TCP/IP isn't completely adequate for all networking roles. For instance, your network might contain some systems that continue to use old OSs that don't fully support TCP/IP. An old Macintosh might only support file sharing over AppleTalk, for instance, or you might have DOS or Windows systems configured to use IPX or NetBEUI. In these situations, Linux's support for alternative network stacks can be a great boon.

APPLETALK

Apple developed its AppleTalk protocol stack in conjunction with the LocalTalk networking hardware for some of its earliest Macintoshes in the mid-1980s. (In fact, early on, both the hardware and software went by the name *AppleTalk*, although today this name is reserved for the software side.) As Ethernet grew in popularity, Apple developed a way to use AppleTalk over Ethernet hardware—a variant that's sometimes called *EtherTalk*. Linux supports AppleTalk over either the original LocalTalk hardware (if your system has a supported LocalTalk network card, as described in Chapter 1) or over Ethernet.

NOTE   Ironically, Linux doesn't support the LocalTalk hardware built into Macintosh computers. If you run Linux on such a system, you will *not* be able to use the LocalTalk hardware, although you may still use AppleTalk over Ethernet, if the computer has a built-in Ethernet adapter or a supported Ethernet expansion card.

APPLETALK FEATURES AND CAPABILITIES

Like TCP/IP, AppleTalk uses a 32-bit machine address. Also like TCP/IP, the AppleTalk address is broken down into two components—a network address and a computer address; however, the division of these two components is fixed, with each consuming 16 of the 32 bits available for the address. AppleTalk includes a procedure by which the computers on the network can negotiate their own AppleTalk addresses, so you need not set this address explicitly. (You *can* request a specific address or an address in a specific range if you want to, but this usually isn't necessary.)

Above the AppleTalk numeric addresses lies a two-tiered alphabetic naming system that humans use more directly. Each computer has a name, and resides in a *zone*, which is a logical group of computers. Small networks may be *zoneless*, meaning that the zone name doesn't obtrude itself upon users. When you start Netatalk, the primary AppleTalk package for Linux, the software sets the system's AppleTalk name based upon the TCP/IP hostname, unless you override this setting. For instance, if a computer has the TCP/IP hostname larch.threeroomco.com, the computer's AppleTalk name becomes larch. The domain information is lost, though. (In a zoned network, the computer attempts to set its zone automatically, and the zone name may bear no resemblance to anything in the TCP/IP hostname.) The two-tiered nature of AppleTalk names is an important limiting factor on AppleTalk networks; without more layers of names, creating an AppleTalk network with more than a few hundred computers becomes awkward.

The primary applications for AppleTalk are the file and printer sharing for which the protocols were developed. Many network-enabled printers "speak" AppleTalk natively, and AppleTalk file-sharing protocols are understood by MacOS, Windows NT and 2000, Linux, BeOS, and other systems. There's seldom any reason to use AppleTalk except on a network that contains MacOS systems, though, because most other OSs provide better support for other network protocols. Even in the case of Macintosh-dominated networks, the Unix-based MacOS X supports NFS as well as AppleTalk, so you may prefer to use NFS if your network's Macintoshes run MacOS X. The Netatalk package (see `http://netatalk.sourceforge.net`) is the main program that uses AppleTalk in Linux; it's discussed in the next section.

TIP The fact that AppleTalk packets are seldom routable by typical routers makes AppleTalk a good choice for providing a little extra security. You can disable TCP/IP on a Netatalk server if you want to be absolutely certain that nobody can break into your system from outside your local network by exploiting a flaw in your Netatalk server. Similarly, disabling everything but AppleTalk printing on a network-enabled printer or print server can keep this system from being abused by outsiders, unless they first gain a foothold on another system in your local network. Good security practices, as discussed in Part IV, can help secure a TCP/IP network, though, so AppleTalk isn't the only option for improving security.

USING LINUX APPLETALK SOFTWARE

The Netatalk package, which comes with most Linux distributions, is the primary AppleTalk software for Linux. This package provides three features:

- **An AppleTalk file server**—The `afpd` program allows a Linux computer to operate as a file server for Macintosh systems. The file server supports both native AppleTalk and TCP/IP, so Linux can serve even old Macintoshes, so long as they share a network hardware type. (In the event they don't, LocalTalk-to-Ethernet converter devices are available to bridge the gap.) This server is controlled through a file called `afpd.conf`, typically in `/etc/atalk`. In addition, the `AppleVolumes.default` file controls which directories are shared, and `AppleVolumes.system` maps filename extensions onto Macintosh file and creator types, which are stored directly on MacOS-native filesystems.

- **An AppleTalk print server**—The `papd` program allows a Linux computer to operate as a print server for Macintosh systems. Used in conjunction with Ghostscript (part of Linux's standard print queue), this allows you to share even an inexpensive inkjet printer as if it were a full-featured PostScript device. The print server features work only over the original AppleTalk, not via TCP/IP. The papd server is controlled through papd.conf, which is usually located in /etc/atalk.

- **An AppleTalk print client**—The pap program allows Linux to submit print jobs to AppleTalk-enabled printers or print servers. This can be useful if your Linux computer is on a Macintosh-dominated network that hosts printers that don't understand other protocols. You can even print from one Linux computer to another using this tool, although in most cases Linux's native printing tools, as described in Chapter 9, Printer Sharing via LPD, will be simpler to configure. The pap client has no control file; you specify the printer to which you want to send a file with the -p parameter, as in **pap -p Laser2 sample.ps** to print sample.ps to the printer called Laser2.

The first two of these programs rely upon another one, atalkd, which configures the computer's overall AppleTalk presence—features such as the AppleTalk name and address. This program is controlled through a file called atalkd.conf, which is also typically stored in /etc/atalk.

NOTE   Netatalk doesn't include a file-sharing client program. Therefore, you can't access AppleTalk file shares from Linux using Netatalk. The afpfs package (http://www.panix.com/~dfoster/afpfs/) theoretically provides this capability as of version 1.03b-alpha, but it's very old and unreliable. If you want to access Macintosh files from Linux, you're better off using a Macintosh NFS or SMB/CIFS server, such as MacOS X's native NFS server or DAVE (http://www.thursby.com).

Most default installations of AppleTalk work correctly as soon as they're installed, but they're typically configured to share only the home directory of the user who logs in. You can alter this configuration by editing AppleVolumes.default. For instance, the following lines in this file tell the system to export both the user's home directory (specified by a tilde, ~) and the /mnt directory:

```
~
/mnt "Mount Points" options=noadouble
```

The first of these lines is the default, and includes no special options. The second includes a name to use instead of /mnt for the share as seen on a Macintosh client, as well as an options specification, which sets special options. In this case, the only option set is noadouble, which makes Netatalk not create AppleDouble files (these are special files stored in the `.AppleDouble` subdirectory to hold MacOS-specific data) unless they're absolutely required.

If your Netatalk package shipped with your distribution, it will probably start up automatically when you start the computer. If not, consult Chapter 4, Starting Servers, for general server startup information (a SysV or local startup script are the best options for starting Netatalk). You should start `atalkd` first, then `afpd` and `papd`. One of the quirks of Netatalk, and particularly of `atalkd`, is that this server can take quite some time to start—sometimes over a minute, particularly on older hardware. You can avoid a pause in your system startup procedure by including an ampersand (&) after the program call in your startup script.

IPX/SPX

Internetwork Packet Exchange (IPX) was developed by Novell (based closely on earlier work by Xerox) as a low-level network transport protocol. It's frequently used in conjunction with the Sequenced Packet Exchange (SPX) protocol; the two together form the core of a network stack that's comparable in scope to AppleTalk or NetBEUI. IPX/SPX has historically been used by the NetWare product, but IPX/SPX packages are available for DOS, Windows, and other OSs. One of the most popular uses of this network stack is to support the NetWare Core Protocol (NCP), which is Novell's file- and printer-sharing tool. Linux also supports these protocols, both in the kernel (as described in Chapter 1) and in client and server packages.

IPX/SPX FEATURES AND CAPABILITIES

Like TCP/IP and AppleTalk, IPX/SPX supports a 32-bit address, which is usually expressed in hexadecimal, as in 0x23a91002. This address, however, isn't assigned to a single computer, but to an entire network—usually a network segment that's isolated from others by routers, or completely disconnected from the outside world. An IPX/SPX network is also identified by the underlying hardware's *frame type*, which is how the Ethernet frames are built at a very low level; all computers on a single IPX/SPX network must use the same frame type. To identify individual computers, IPX/SPX relies on the underlying hardware's addressing scheme, such as Ethernet's 48-bit (6-byte) addresses.

As you might guess from the name and addressing scheme, IPX/SPX is designed for internetworking—that is, linking networks together. This is accomplished via IPX routers, which work much like TCP/IP routers in broad detail. (In fact, a single system can function as both a TCP/IP and an IPX router.) A simple network may not require a router, but IPX/SPX does support the option.

IPX/SPX servers use a protocol known as the *Service Advertisement Protocol (SAP)* to periodically announce their names and the services they make available, such as shared directories or printers. Other systems on the local network segment will "hear" these announcements, and IPX routers should echo them to other network segments. This design can help make locating the right server easy, but it can also increase network traffic as the network size increases; with more servers, there will be more SAP broadcasts consuming network bandwidth.

USING LINUX IPX/SPX SOFTWARE

Like most Linux software, Linux's IPX/SPX software is largely open source. (Caldera once licensed NetWare from Novell and made it available for Linux, but Caldera has discontinued this official port of NetWare. A three-user version is still available from `ftp://ftp.calderasystems.com/pub/old-products/netware/`, but it requires an old 2.0.35 kernel.) Other IPX/SPX tools for Linux include the following:

- **Kernel NCPFS support**—The Linux kernel includes support for the NCP filesystem in the Network File Systems submenu of the File Systems menu. This support allows a Linux computer to mount NetWare file shares. You need the `ncpmount` program, which usually ships in a package called `ncpfs`, to accomplish this task.
- **LinWare**—This package provides limited NCP server support. At the time of this writing, however, the current version is 0.95 beta, which was designed for the 1.3.*x* kernels—in other words, the software hasn't been updated since 1996. This might change in the future, though. The package is housed under the name `lwared` at `ftp://sunsite.unc.edu/pub/Linux/system/network/daemons/`.
- **Mars_nwe**—This is another NetWare server package for Linux. This package is hosted at `http://www.compu-art.de/mars_nwe/`, which is largely in German. English documentation is in the Mars_nwe HOWTO document, `http://www.redhat.com/support/docs/tips/Netware/netware.html`. Mars_nwe supports both file and print services. Its primary configuration file is `/etc/nwserv.conf` or `/etc/nwserv/nwserv.conf`, and it can be started by typing **nwserv**, if it's not started automatically by a startup script.

All of these IPX/SPX packages require you to have IPX support compiled into your kernel, as described in Chapter 1. Some distributions also require a separate package, usually called ipxutils, which contains utilities for activating and controlling the IPX/SPX network stack. (Alternatively, some distributions include these tools in the ncpfs package.)

If you intend to run a server for NetWare clients, Mars_nwe configuration is usually not too difficult, because the default configuration works fairly well. The configuration file is also usually very well commented, so you can learn how to configure it by reading its comments. You should pay particular attention to a few details:

- Section 1 of the file defines the volumes that are to be shared. In Linux terms, these are directories. The configuration file that ships with your copy of the server may or may not define volumes that you'd want to share.

- Section 7 controls password encryption options. You may need to enable nonencrypted passwords if your network doesn't have a regular NetWare *bindery* server—a computer that handles authentication.

- Section 13 defines users who are to be allowed access to the server. You may need to add usernames and passwords to this section, duplicating the regular Linux username and password configuration. Passwords are stored in an unencrypted form, which is a potential security flaw. If the network has a bindery, though, you can remove these entries after starting Mars_nwe for the first time, so the security risk may not be as bad as it first appears. Instead of dealing with individual accounts, you can set up Section 15 to do this automatically, but the drawback is that all the accounts will have the same password.

The Mars_nwe package includes the means to automatically enable IPX support on your network interface. This convenience doesn't exist in the case of Linux's NetWare client support as implemented in ncpmount, however. Before you can use this command, you should enable auto-configuration with the ipx_configure command. You can then mount a NetWare volume with ncpmount. The entire procedure might resemble the following:

```
# ipx_configure --auto_interface=on --auto_primary=on
# ncpmount -S NW_SERV -U anne -P p4rtu3a /mnt/nwmount
```

This sequence enables auto-detection of the local network number and mounts volumes stored on NW_SERV associated with the user anne at /mnt/nwmount, using the password p4rtu3a.

NetBEUI

NetBEUI is similar in many ways to AppleTalk and IPX, but it has historically been used primarily by IBM and Microsoft as the basis for networking in DOS, Windows, and OS/2. The Linux kernel does not, as of the 2.4.*x* series, include a standard NetBEUI stack. This omission is offset by two facts, though. First, the common uses of NetBEUI can be served by NetBIOS over TCP/IP (sometimes called *NBT*), which Linux does support. Second, a third-party NetBEUI stack is available, although it's of limited utility.

NetBEUI Features and Capabilities

Like AppleTalk and IPX, NetBEUI was designed with small networks in mind. In fact, NetBEUI is even more limited than its competing small-network protocols, because it's restricted to networks of just 256 computers. NetBEUI uses computer names similar to TCP/IP hostnames, but there is no underlying numeric addressing system, as is true of TCP/IP, AppleTalk, and IPX; NetBEUI uses the computer's name directly. These names are two-tiered in nature, much like AppleTalk's names (which include a computer name and a network zone name). NetBEUI calls its higher-order groupings *workgroups* or *domains*, depending upon whether a centralized computer exists to control logins (domains support this feature, but workgroups leave authentication to individual servers). When it starts up and periodically thereafter, a computer configured to use Net-BEUI makes a broadcast to announce its presence.

NetBEUI can theoretically be used over just about any network medium, but it's most commonly used over Ethernet. Like AppleTalk and IPX, Net-BEUI can coexist on Ethernet with TCP/IP or other network stacks.

NetBEUI is most frequently used in conjunction with the SMB/CIFS file- and printer-sharing protocols. These are comparable in scope to NFS/lpd for Unix and Linux, AppleTalk's equivalent protocols, or NCP. They can also be used over TCP/IP, and in fact this configuration is very common, even on networks that contain Windows computers exclusively. Because it's not easily routed, however, NetBEUI offers some security benefits—a distant attacker is unlikely to be able to launch a successful attack against a NetBEUI server.

Obtaining a NetBEUI Stack for Linux

Few Linux computers participate in NetBEUI communications because the standard kernel lacks a NetBEUI stack. In 2000, Procom Technologies (http://www.procom.com) released an open source NetBEUI stack for Linux, as well as patches to Samba (described in Chapter 7, File and Printer Sharing via Samba), to allow Samba to operate over NetBEUI rather than TCP/IP. These patches have not become commonplace, and in fact they aren't posted directly on Procom's Web site, although you can request the stack from their technical support department. The NetBEUI stack may not work properly with kernels beyond the 2.0.x series (I was unable to get the patches to compile with a 2.2.18 kernel, for instance). The NetBEUI stack was also designed for versions of Samba before 2.0.7, although there's been some talk of adding the NetBEUI support to Samba sometime before Samba 3.0 is released. The support also requires recompiling both your kernel and Samba. For these reasons, you're probably better off foregoing the use of NetBEUI unless you have a very compelling reason to use it, such as a network on which TCP/IP is forbidden. If you really must use NetBEUI, you may need to use it with an older 2.0.x kernel and Samba 2.0.6 or earlier.

In addition to patching the Linux kernel and Samba, the NetBEUI stack comes with a number of tools that let you configure and manipulate it. This configuration tends to be fairly simple, and in most cases you'll use new Samba options to control the computer's NetBEUI behavior, but the separate utilities can be useful for troubleshooting and for learning more about NetBEUI. One utility in particular, netb, is also required to start up the NetBIOS stack, as described shortly.

USING LINUX NETBEUI SOFTWARE

The NetBEUI stack includes a README file with complete installation and use instructions. This file outlines two methods of installation. One requires you to edit the Makefile to point to your Linux kernel and Samba source code trees and set a few other system-specific options. You can then recompile both Linux and Samba with a single command, install your new kernel, and reboot the system. The second procedure also requires you to edit the Makefile, but proceeds to give instructions on performing individual steps in a piecemeal fashion. This second approach is likely to be superior if you run into any difficulties, because you'll be better able to isolate and correct the problem.

Whichever way you do it, you'll need the source code to both the Linux kernel and Samba. You can obtain these from http://www.kernel.org and http://www.samba.org, respectively, or from many common Linux download sites, like ftp://sunsite.unc.edu. Both packages can take several minutes to compile and install, so even if you don't run into problems, installing NetBEUI support is likely to take several minutes.

Once you've installed NetBEUI support, you can use several commands to enable or manipulate this support. These commands, included with the NetBEUI stack, are as follows:

- **netb**—Type this command followed by **start** to start NetBEUI on Linux. To stop NetBEUI, type **netb stop**. You must use this utility before you can use NetBEUI on Linux.
- **nbview**—Use this command if you want to check on the status of the local NetBEUI stack. This command reads the /proc/sys/netbeui file, which contains this information, and formats and parses the information for easier human consumption.
- **nbstatus**—This command displays information on the specified machine or workgroup; for instance, **nbstatus SERVER** displays information on the computer called SERVER.
- **nbadmin**—This command allows you to bind NetBEUI to a specific network interface, unbind NetBEUI from a specific interface, or drop a specific NetBEUI session. It does this using the bind, unbind, and drop commands, respectively, as in **nbadmin bind eth0** or **nbadmin drop 102**. (You can obtain NetBEUI session numbers from nbview.)

For the most part, you'll only need to issue a **netb start** command, then start Samba. The NetBEUI stack adds a parameter to nmbd (the NetBIOS name daemon), smbd (the SMB daemon), and smbclient (the text-mode Samba client) to specify whether to use TCP/IP or NetBEUI. This parameter is -Z <NETBEUI | TCPIP>. For instance, to launch smbd to use NetBEUI, you'd type **smbd -Z NETBEUI**. You can also use the new -S *NAME* parameter to smbd to set the system's NetBEUI name to *NAME*.

To sum up, you can turn Linux into a NetBEUI SMB/CIFS server called *NAME* by recompiling the kernel and Samba with the Procom NetBEUI stack, rebooting, shutting down Samba (if necessary), and typing the following commands:

```
# netb start
# nmbd -Z NETBEUI
# smbd -Z NETBEUI -S NAME
```

You can place these commands in a startup script, or modify your regular Samba startup script to incorporate these changes. Other Samba features, such as the definitions of shares, all function as described in Chapter 7. The advantage of this procedure boils down to two factors. First, it can be used with some older clients that support NetBEUI but not TCP/IP, and it reduces the chance of malicious outside access to the computer via Samba, because NetBEUI isn't normally routed over the Internet. On the downside, NetBEUI support is duplicated in NetBIOS over TCP/IP, which works with all recent Linux kernels and versions of Samba, and doesn't require patching or recompiling the kernel or Samba.

SUMMARY

A network stack provides the foundation upon which common network tools (both client and server programs) are built. Programs like Netscape, sendmail, and many others discussed throughout this book must be mated to one or more network stacks, and two computers need compatible network stacks in order to communicate over a network. At the start of the twenty-first century, TCP/IP is by far the most popular network stack. TCP/IP forms the basis of the Internet, and is the network stack upon which most Linux networking tools are built. There are alternatives, however. In particular, AppleTalk, IPX, and NetBEUI have all been popular in the past on local networks, primarily for file- and printer-sharing tasks. Even today, these stacks all continue to be used on many small networks. Linux can use all three of them, although Linux's support for each is limited. (In the case of NetBEUI, both the Linux kernel and Samba must be patched and recompiled to use the network stack.)

Starting Servers

The bulk of this book (specifically, Parts II and III) deals with the operation of a wide variety of servers. These programs should normally be accessible at all times once a computer has booted, aside from any scheduled downtime or restrictions you might impose for security reasons. It's therefore important that you understand how servers are started. Without this knowledge, you might find yourself unable to start a server once you've installed it, or unable to restart a server after making changes to its configuration.

Fortunately, in many cases Linux configures things so that a server starts automatically after it's installed, or at least once you reboot the computer after installing the server. There are three major methods you can use to start a server on a regular basis: via System V (SysV) startup scripts; via a *super server*, such as inetd or xinetd; or via a local startup script. You can always configure any of these methods by manually editing the appropriate configuration files or scripts. With most distributions, you can also accomplish the task through the use of GUI tools. This chapter covers all these methods of starting servers. Subsequent chapters refer back to this one to convey how a specific server is most commonly started.

USING SYSV STARTUP SCRIPTS

AT&T's System V, or SysV, UNIX set many of the standards used on today's UNIX and Linux systems. One of these was a method of starting system services, including servers. In the SysV scheme, each service comes with a script that can be used to start or stop the service by passing the script the start or stop parameter, respectively. Many of these startup scripts support additional parameters, such as restart to shut down the server and start it up again (say, to implement a changed configuration).

NOTE SysV startup scripts can and do start programs other than network servers. In this book, I use the terms *service* and *daemon* to refer to a program or OS feature that's more-or-less constantly accessible, whether or not it interacts with the network; *server* is used to refer to programs that respond to network requests, or to a computer that runs server programs. Most of the services discussed in this book are servers. Not everybody uses these terms in precisely this way; for instance, some people use *service* to refer exclusively to what I call server programs.

The SysV startup scheme is closely tied to the *runlevel* of the computer. Each runlevel is associated with a specific set of startup scripts, and hence with a specific set of services that the system runs. (SysV scripts can start more than just network servers; they can start system loggers, filesystem handlers, and so on.) Thus, configuring servers to start via SysV scripts is closely related to configuring these runlevels. This is done by altering the names of links to the startup scripts, as stored in directories associated with each runlevel.

STARTUP SCRIPT LOCATIONS AND NAMING CONVENTIONS

Although the basic outline of SysV startup scripts is the same across most distributions, there are differences in many details. Most importantly, different distributions place the startup scripts in different locations. They may also call scripts by different names, although these differences are usually not too extreme. Table 4.1 summarizes these SysV layout differences for several major Linux distributions. Note that distributions differ in where they place the actual scripts, where they place the links to the scripts that are associated with specific runlevels, and where they place local startup scripts (which are discussed in more detail shortly, in the section "Using Local Startup Scripts"). In the case of script links, a ? in the directory name refers to a number from 0 to 6 corresponding to the runlevel.

Table 4.1   Startup Script Locations in Major Linux Distributions

Distribution	Startup control script	SysV script directory	SysV script link directory	Local startup scripts
Caldera OpenLinux Server 3.1	/etc/rc.d/ rc.boot	/etc/rc.d/ init.d	/etc/rc.d/ rc?.d	/etc/rc.d/ rc.local
Debian GNU/ Linux 2.2	/etc/init.d/ rcS	/etc/init.d	/etc/rc?.d	Files in /etc/rc.boot
Linux Mandrake 8.1	/etc/rc.d/ rc.sysinit	/etc/rc.d/ init.d	/etc/rc.d/ rc?.d	/etc/rc.d/ rc.local
Red Hat Linux 7.2	/etc/rc.d/ rc.sysinit	/etc/rc.d/ init.d	/etc/rc.d/ rc?.d	/etc/rc.d/ rc.local
Slackware Linux 8.0	/etc/rc.d/ rc.S	/etc/rc.d	N/A	Various files in /etc/rc.d
SuSE Linux 7.1	/etc/init.d/ boot	/etc/rc.d	/etc/rc.d/ rc?.d	/etc/rc.d/ boot.local
TurboLinux 7.0	/etc/rc.d/ rc.sysinit	/etc/rc.d/ init.d	/etc/rc.d/ rc?.d	/etc/rc.d/ rc.local

NOTE   The runlevel is a number from 0–6 that corresponds to a particular set of running services. It's described in more detail shortly, in the section "Setting and Changing the Runlevel." For now, know that the computer enters a specific runlevel when it starts, which means it runs the SysV startup scripts associated with that runlevel. You can also change runlevels after the computer has booted.

NOTE   Throughout this chapter, I refer to SysV script directories and SysV script link directories. These are the locations outlined in Table 4.1, and it's important that you modify files in the appropriate location if you choose to do so.

Several distributions (notably Red Hat, Mandrake, TurboLinux, and to a lesser extent Caldera) are quite similar to each other, particularly in their placement of SysV scripts (/etc/rc.d/init.d) and the links to those scripts (/etc/rc.d/rc?.d). Others place the scripts in slightly different locations. Slackware is the most unusual in this respect. Rather than running individual scripts in a directory named after a runlevel, Slackware uses a single script for each runlevel. For instance, the /etc/rc.d/rc.4 script controls the startup of runlevel 4.

For most Linux distributions (Slackware being the major exception), the links in the SysV startup script link directories are named in a very particular way. Specifically, the filename takes the form *C##name*, where *C* is a character (S or K), *##* is a two-digit number, and *name* is a name that's traditionally the same as the corresponding script in the SysV script directory. For instance, the link filename might be S10network or K20nfs—filenames that correspond to the network and nfs scripts, respectively. As you might guess, this naming scheme isn't random. The *name* portion of the link filename helps you determine what the script does; it's usually named after the original script. The leading character indicates whether the computer will start or kill (for S and K, respectively) the script upon entering the specified runlevel. Thus, S10network indicates that the system will start whatever the network script starts (basic networking features, in fact), and K20nfs shuts down whatever the nfs script controls (the NFS server, in reality). The numbers indicate the sequence in which these actions are to be performed. Thus, S10network starts networking before S55sshd starts the secure shell (SSH) server. Similar rules apply for shutdown (K) links.

The names and numbers of the startup and shutdown links vary from one distribution to another. For instance, Mandrake uses S10network to start its basic networking features, but Debian uses S35networking for this function. Similar differences may exist for the scripts that launch specific servers. What's important is that all the necessary servers and processes are started in the correct order. Many networking tools must be started after basic networking features are started, for instance. It's generally not wise to change the order in which startup and shutdown scripts execute, unless you understand this sequence and the consequences of your changes.

One additional wrinkle requires mention: SuSE uses the /etc/rc.config file to control the SysV startup process. This file contains sections pertaining to major servers that can be started via the SysV process, and if a server is not listed for startup (via a line of the form START_*SERVERNAME*="yes"), SuSE doesn't start that server, even if its link name begins with S. Caldera uses a similar scheme for a few servers, but uses files in /etc/sysconfig/daemons named after the servers in question. The ONBOOT line in each of these files determines whether the system starts the server. Many startup scripts ignore this option in Caldera, though.

MANUALLY ENABLING OR DISABLING STARTUP SCRIPTS

If you find that you need to enable or disable a server that's started through a SysV startup script, one way to proceed is to adjust the startup scripts or the links to them. One approach to disabling a server is to remove the startup script from the SysV script directory. This is a quick fix that affects all runlevels, but it's rather inelegant. It also doesn't help you if you want to start a server rather than disable one.

A more elegant solution is to rename the link to the startup script in the SysV link directory that corresponds to your current runlevel. For instance, to disable a server, rename it so that it starts with K rather than S; to enable it, reverse this process. The difficulty with this procedure is that the sequence number isn't likely to be the same when killing the server as when starting it. One way around this potential pitfall is to locate all the links to the script in all the runlevels. If any of the other runlevels sport the configuration you want, you've found the sequence number. For instance, the following command finds all the links for the Postfix mail server startup scripts on a Mandrake system:

```
$ find /etc/rc.d -name "*postfix"
/etc/rc.d/rc0.d/K30postfix
/etc/rc.d/rc1.d/K30postfix
/etc/rc.d/rc2.d/S80postfix
/etc/rc.d/rc3.d/S80postfix
/etc/rc.d/rc4.d/S80postfix
/etc/rc.d/rc5.d/S80postfix
/etc/rc.d/rc6.d/K30postfix
/etc/rc.d/init.d/postfix
```

This sequence shows that Postfix is started with a sequence number of 80 in runlevels 2 through 5, and shut down with a sequence number of 30 in runlevels 0, 1, and 6. If you wanted to disable Postfix in runlevel 3, you could do so by renaming S80postfix to K30postfix in that runlevel's directory.

If you want to *temporarily* start or stop a server, or if you want to initiate a change immediately without restarting the computer or adjusting the runlevel, you can do so by running the startup script along with the start or stop parameters. For instance, to stop Postfix immediately, you could type the following command on a Mandrake system:

```
# /etc/rc.d/init.d/postfix stop
```

Most Linux distributions display a message reporting the attempt to shut down the server, and the success of the operation. When starting a SysV script, a message about the startup success appears. (In fact, you may see these messages scroll across your screen after the kernel startup messages when you boot your computer.)

In the case of Slackware, instead of renaming, adding, or deleting startup scripts or their links, you should edit the single startup script file for the runlevel in question. For instance, if you want to change the behavior of runlevel 4, you'd edit /etc/rc.d/rc.4. Most servers, though, aren't started in these runlevel-specific scripts; they're started in /etc/rc.d/rc.inet2, with very basic network tools started in /etc/rc.d/rc.inet1. To change your configuration, you'll have to manually modify these scripts as if they were local startup scripts, as described in the section "Using Local Startup Scripts."

USING STARTUP SCRIPT UTILITIES

Some distributions include utilities that help you control startup scripts. These tools can be very useful because they reduce the chance of misnaming a script. For instance, an automated tool won't mistype S80postfix as s80postfix (using a lowercase s instead of an uppercase S). Unfortunately, not all distributions support these tools—they're most common on Red Hat and its derivatives, such as Mandrake. Installing one of these tools from one distribution for use on another is unlikely to work because of the differences in SysV script locations and startup sequence numbers.

NOTE This section focuses on text-based startup script tools. GUI tools, as described shortly in the section "Using GUI Tools," can also accomplish this task.

Using chkconfig

The SysV startup script tool with the crudest user interface is chkconfig. This program is a non-interactive command—you must provide it with the information it needs to do its job on a single command line. The syntax for the command is as follows:

```
chkconfig <--list|--add|--del> [name]
chkconfig [--level levels] name [on|off|reset]
```

The first format of this command is used to obtain information on the current configuration (using --list) or to add or delete links in the SysV link script directory (using --add or --del, respectively). The second format is used to enable or disable a script in some or all runlevels by changing the name of the SysV link, as described earlier. Some examples will help clarify the use of this command.

Suppose you want to know how Postfix is configured. If you know the Postfix startup script is called postfix, you could enter the following command to check its configuration:

```
# chkconfig --list postfix
postfix    0:off   1:off   2:on    3:on    4:on    5:on    6:off
```

This output shows the status of Postfix in each of the seven runlevels. You can verify this by using the find command described earlier. When chkconfig shows an on value, the startup link filename should start with S, and when chkconfig shows an off value, the startup link filename should start with K.

If you type **chkconfig --list** without specifying a particular startup script filename, chkconfig shows the status for all the startup scripts, and possibly for servers started through xinetd as well, if your system uses xinetd.

The --add and --del options add links if they don't exist or delete them if they do exist, respectively. Both these options require that you specify the name of the original startup script. For instance, **chkconfig --del postfix** removes all the Postfix SysV startup script links. The result is that Linux won't start the server through a SysV startup script, or attempt to change a server's status when changing runlevels. You might do this if you wanted to start a server through a super server or local configuration script. You might use the --add parameter to reverse this change.

You'll probably make most chkconfig changes with the on, off, or reset options. These enable a server, disable a server, or return the server to its default setting for a specified runlevel. (If you omit the --level option, the change applies to *all* runlevels.) For instance, suppose you want to disable Postfix in runlevel 3. You could do so by typing the following command:

```
# chkconfig --level 3 postfix off
```

This command won't return any output, so if you feel the need to verify that it's worked, you should use the --list option or look for a changed filename in the startup script link directory. You can enable a server by using on rather than off. If you want to affect more than one runlevel, you can do so by listing all the runlevels in a single string, as in 345 for runlevels 3, 4, and 5. If you've experimented with settings and want to return them to their defaults, you can use the reset option:

```
# chkconfig postfix reset
```

This command will reset the SysV startup script links for Postfix to their default values. You can reset the default for just one runlevel by including the --level *levels* option as the first parameter to the command.

Although chkconfig is generally thought of as a way to manage SysV startup scripts, it can also work on xinetd configurations on many systems. If chkconfig is configured to treat, say, your FTP server as one that's launched via a super server, you can use it to manipulate this configuration much as if the FTP server were launched through SysV startup scripts. The difference is that the --level *levels* parameter won't work, and the --list option doesn't show runlevel information. Instead, any server started through a super server will run in those runlevels in which xinetd runs. Furthermore, the --add and --del options work just like on and off, respectively; the /etc/xinetd.d configuration files aren't deleted, only disabled, as described in the upcoming section, "Using xinetd."

When you change the SysV configuration with chkconfig, it does *not* automatically alter the servers that are running. For instance, if you reconfigure your system to disable sshd, that server will not be immediately shut down without manual intervention of some sort, such as running the SysV startup script with the stop option to stop the server.

Using ntsysv

The ntsysv program provides a text-based menu environment for manipulating server startup. To run the program, type its name, optionally followed by --level *levels*, where *levels* is one or more runlevels you want to modify. If you omit this parameter, ntsysv modifies the configuration only for the current runlevel. Either way, the result should resemble Figure 4.1.

The ntsysv display shows all the servers that have SysV startup scripts. Some versions also display servers started through xinetd. To enable or disable a server, use the arrow keys on your keyboard to move the cursor to the server you want to adjust, then press the spacebar to toggle the server on or off. An asterisk (*) in the box to the left of the server name indicates that the server is active; an empty box indicates that the server is disabled. When you're done making changes, use the Tab key to highlight the OK button, then press the Enter key to exit from the program and save your changes.

As with chkconfig, you can't adjust the specific runlevels in which servers mediated by a super server are run, except by changing the runlevels for the super server itself. Also, disabling a server won't cause it to shut down

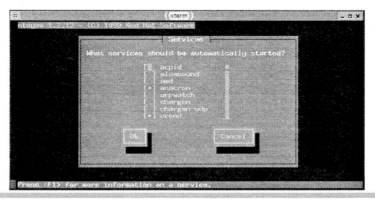

Figure 4.1   The ntsysv program provides an easy-to-use interface for SysV configuration.

immediately; you must do that by manually shutting the server down, as described earlier, or by restarting the super server, if your target server is handled by the super server.

SETTING AND CHANGING THE RUNLEVEL

The preceding discussion has referred to the runlevel, but with only a minimal description of what it is. The runlevel and SysV startup scripts are tied together quite intimately. When the computer boots, it enters a specific runlevel. Ultimately, what this means is that the computer executes the startup scripts to which the links in the SysV script link directories point. More specifically, Linux passes the start parameter to the scripts whose links start with S, and passes the stop parameter to those whose links begin with K.

How does Linux know what runlevel to enter when it boots, though? That's set in the /etc/inittab file, which is the configuration file for init, which is the first process that Linux runs and the progenitor of all other processes. Specifically, /etc/inittab contains a line such as the following:

```
id:5:initdefault:
```

The leading id is the key to identifying this line, but the following number (5 in this example) is what you'll use to *permanently* set the runlevel. If you change this value and reboot, the computer will come up in a different runlevel. Runlevels 0, 1, and 6 have special meanings—they correspond to a system shutdown, a single-user mode, and a system reboot, respectively. Runlevels 2 through 5 are normal runlevels, but their precise meanings vary from one distribution to another. For Caldera, Red Hat, Mandrake, SuSE 7.3, and TurboLinux, runlevel 3 is a normal text-mode startup (X is *not* started), and runlevel 5 is a GUI login mode (X *is* started, and a GUI login program is run). Earlier versions of SuSE use runlevels 2 and 3 instead of 3 and 5, and Slackware uses 3 and 4 for text-mode and GUI logins. By default, Debian doesn't run any SysV scripts differently in different normal operational runlevels, although it runs fewer text-mode login tools in runlevels above 3 (this detail is handled by subsequent lines of /etc/inittab). Most distributions include a series of comments in their /etc/inittab files describing the function of each runlevel, so look for that if you need more information or are using a distribution I don't discuss in this book.

WARNING

> *Do not* set the default runlevel to 0 or 6. These values will cause the computer to immediately shut down or reboot, respectively, upon booting. Either action renders the computer unusable, although you could correct it by using an emergency boot disk or other recovery method or tools, and editing /etc/inittab to correct the error.

If you want to change the runlevel temporarily, you can do so with the telinit command (init also works on most systems). The syntax for this command is as follows:

telinit [-t *seconds*] [*runlevel*]

When you change runlevels, it's possible that certain processes will have to be killed. Linux can do this through either a SIGTERM or a SIGKILL signal. The former is a more polite way of doing the job; it lets the program close its own files and so on. SIGKILL, by contrast, unceremoniously kills the program, which can lead to file corruption. When you change runlevels, telinit first tries to use a SIGTERM. Five seconds later, if a process hasn't quit, telinit sends a SIGKILL. If specified, the -t *seconds* parameter changes this interval. In most cases, the default five seconds is adequate.

The *runlevel* specification is a single-character code for the runlevel. Most obviously, you can provide a runlevel number. There are certain other characters you can pass that have special meaning, however:

- **a, b, or c**—Some entries in /etc/inittab use runlevels of a, b, or c for special purposes. If you specify this option to telinit, the program only handles those /etc/inittab entries; the system's runlevel is not changed.

- **Q or q**—If you pass one of these values as the *runlevel*, telinit reexamines the /etc/inittab file and initiates any changes.
- **S or s**—This option causes the system to change into a single-user mode.
- **U or u**—This option causes the init process to restart itself, without reexamining the /etc/inittab file.

Why would you want to change the runlevel? Changing the default runlevel allows you to control which servers start up by default. On most distributions, the most important of these is the X server. This is usually started by a special line towards the end of /etc/inittab, not through a SysV startup script, although some use a SysV startup script for XDM to do the job. Changing the runlevel while the computer is running allows you to quickly enable or disable a set of servers, or change out of GUI mode if you want to temporarily shut down X when your system is configured to start it automatically.

USING inetd

Normally, a server runs and ties itself to a specific *port* (a resource identified by protocol type and a number between 1 and 65,535). Incoming requests are directed to specific ports associated with particular server types. For instance, Simple Mail Transfer Protocol (SMTP) mail servers conventionally use TCP port 25, and Hypertext Transfer Protocol (HTTP) servers (Web servers) normally use TCP port 80.

The inetd program is one of two common *super servers* for Linux. These are servers that function as intermediaries; instead of running the target server itself, the computer runs the super server, which links itself to the ports used by all of the servers it needs to handle. Then, when a connection is made to one of those ports, the super server launches the target server and lets it handle the data transfer. This has two advantages over running a server directly. First, the memory load is reduced; a super server consumes little RAM compared to the servers it handles, particularly if it handles many servers. Second, the super server can filter incoming requests based on various criteria, which can improve your system's security. The drawback is that it takes time for the super server to launch the target server, so the time to connect to a server may be increased, although usually only by a second or two. As a general rule, it's good to use super servers for small or seldom-used servers, whereas big and frequently used servers should be run directly.

THE /etc/inetd.conf FILE FORMAT

You can configure `inetd` through the `/etc/inetd.conf` file. Aside from comments (lines that begin with a pound sign, #, that `inetd` ignores), `inetd.conf` consists of a series of lines, each of which defines a single server. A sample line resembles the following:

```
telnet  stream  tcp  nowait  root  /usr/sbin/tcpd  in.telnetd
```

Each line consists of a series of fields, which are separated by spaces or tabs. The meaning of each field is as follows:

- **Server name**—The first field is the name of the server protocol, as recorded in `/etc/services`. In the case of the preceding example, the server protocol name is `telnet`, and if you check `/etc/services`, you'll see that this name is associated with `23/tcp`—in other words, TCP port 23. There must be an entry in `/etc/services` in order for `inetd` to handle a server. For this reason, you may need to edit `/etc/services` if you want `inetd` to handle some unusual server. In most cases, though, `/etc/services` has the appropriate entries already.

- **Socket type**—The second field relates the network socket type used by the protocol. Possible values are `stream`, `dgram`, `raw`, `rdm`, and `seqpacket`.

- **Protocol type**—The third field is the name of the protocol type, which in this context means a low-level network stack protocol such as TCP or UDP. Possible protocol values appear in `/etc/protocols`, but the most common values are `tcp` and `udp`.

- **Wait/Nowait**—The fourth field takes just one of two values, `wait` or `nowait`, and is meaningful only for datagram (`dgram`) socket types (other socket types conventionally use a `nowait` value). Most datagram servers connect to a socket and free up `inetd` to handle subsequent connection attempts. These servers are called *multi-threaded*, and they require a `nowait` entry. Servers that connect to a socket, process all input, and then time out are said to be *single-threaded*, and they require `wait` entries. You may optionally add a number to these values, separated by a period, as in `wait.60`. This specifies the maximum number of servers of the given type that `inetd` may launch in one minute. The default value is `40`.

- **Username**—You can tell `inetd` to launch a server with a specific user's privileges. This can be an important security feature, because restricting privileges for servers that don't require extensive access to the system can prevent a bug from causing a security breach. For instance, the

Apache Web server usually doesn't need unusual privileges, so you could launch it as nobody or as some special account intended *only* for Apache. The preceding example shows the username as root because root privileges are needed to launch the login processes required by a Telnet server. If you add a period and a group name, the specified group name is used for the server's group privileges. For instance, nobody.nogroup launches a server with the username nobody and the group nogroup.

- **Server program**—The sixth field specifies the name of the server program that inetd launches when it detects an incoming connection. The preceding example gives /usr/sbin/tcpd as this program name. In reality, tcpd is not a server; it's the program file for the TCP Wrappers program, which is described shortly. Most Linux distributions that use inetd also use TCP Wrappers, and so launch most inetd-mediated servers through tcpd. You can bypass TCP Wrappers for any server you like, although it's generally best to use TCP Wrappers for reasons that are described shortly.

- **Server program arguments**—The final field is optional. When present, it contains any arguments that are to be passed to the server program. These arguments might modify the server's behavior, tell it where its configuration files are, and so on. In the case of servers launched through TCP Wrappers, the argument is the name of the ultimate target server, such as in.telnetd in the preceding example. (You may add the ultimate server's arguments to this list, if it needs any.)

You can edit /etc/inetd.conf using any text editor you like. Be sure that any new entries you create, or existing ones you modify, span a single line. (Long filenames, server arguments, and the like sometimes produce lines long enough that some editors will try to wrap the line onto two lines, which will cause problems.) If you need to add an entry for a server you've installed, consult the server's documentation to learn what its inetd.conf entry should look like. In some cases, you can model an entry after an existing one, but without knowing what values to enter for the server name, socket type, and so on, such an entry might not work.

Most distributions that use inetd ship with an /etc/inetd.conf file that contains entries for many different servers. Many of these entries are commented out, so they're inactive. You can activate a server by uncommenting such a line, if the matching server is installed. Some inetd.conf files include multiple entries for any given service; for instance, a file might have two or three different entries for different FTP servers. If yours is like this, be sure you uncomment only the line corresponding to the specific server you've installed, such as ProFTPd or WU-FTPD.

TIP One of the first things you should do after installing Linux is to go through /etc/inetd.conf (or the xinetd configuration files, as described shortly) and comment out entries related to servers you don't need. A good rule of thumb is to eliminate any entries you don't understand; Linux doesn't need any of the servers listed in inetd.conf to boot, although it may need some to accept network logins. Eliminating unnecessary servers improves your security by limiting avenues of attack available to undesirable outsiders. Unfortunately, you can't do the same thing with SysV startup scripts, because many of these start vital nonnetwork services upon which Linux relies to do useful things.

USING TCP WRAPPERS

As mentioned earlier, TCP Wrappers functions as an intermediary between inetd and the ultimate target server. The reason for doing this is security: TCP Wrappers can apply rules to determine whether or not a given connection should be allowed, thus protecting the server from unwanted accesses. For instance, suppose you want to allow only people on your own local network to access your computer's Telnet server. If you were running the Telnet server directly, it would have to be programmed to reject unwanted accesses, but not all servers include such code. Placing the responsibility for limiting access in TCP Wrappers extends the flexibility of the system without requiring extensive rewriting of all your server programs.

TCP Wrappers is controlled through two files: /etc/hosts.allow and /etc/hosts.deny. These files have identical formats, but they have opposite actions—hosts.allow specifies computers that are to be allowed access to the computer, with all others denied access; hosts.deny specifies computers that are to be denied access, with all others allowed access. When a server is listed in both files, hosts.allow takes precedence. This allows you to set a restrictive policy in hosts.deny but override it to grant access to specific computers. For instance, you could disallow access to *all* computers in hosts.deny, then loosen that restriction in hosts.allow. If a server isn't specified in either file (either explicitly or through a wildcard, as discussed shortly), TCP Wrappers grants access to that server to all systems.

NOTE

In some ways, TCP Wrappers is similar to a local firewall, as discussed in Chapter 25, Configuring `iptables`. A firewall provides broader-based protection, but TCP Wrappers can provide both redundancy in case of a firewall failure and a few features that `iptables` can't provide, such as the ability to filter based on an NIS netgroup name.

As with many other configuration files, a pound sign (#) at the start of a line indicates a comment. Other lines take the following form:

```
daemon-list : client-list
```

The *daemon-list* is a list of one or more servers to which the rule applies. If the list contains more than one server, commas or spaces may separate the server names. The names are those listed in /etc/services. The ALL wildcard is also accepted; if the *daemon-list* is ALL, then the rule applies to all servers controlled by TCP Wrappers.

WARNING

Remember that not all servers are run through TCP Wrappers. Thus, an ALL wildcard for the `daemon-list` may *not* apply to all servers run on the computer. Similarly, listing a server in `daemon-list` won't protect it unless the server is run through `inetd` and TCP Wrappers or uses TCP Wrappers directly.

The *client-list* is a list of computers that are to be allowed or denied. As with the *daemon-list*, the *client-list* can consist of just one entry or a list separated by commas or spaces. You can specify computers in any of several ways:

- **IP addresses**—You can list complete IP addresses, such as 10.102.201.23. Such an entry will match that IP address and that IP address only.
- **IP address range**—There are several ways to specify ranges of IP addresses. The simplest is to provide fewer than four complete bytes followed by a period. For instance, 10.102.201. matches the 10.102.201.0/24 network. You can also use an IP address/netmask pair, such as 10.102.201.0/24. IPv6 addresses are also supported, by a specification of the form [n:n:n:n:n:n:n:n]/len, where the *n* values are the IPv6 address and *len* is the length in bits of the range to be matched.

93

- **Hostname**—You can provide a complete hostname for the computer, such as `badcracker.threeroomco.com`. This will match that computer only. Because this method relies upon a hostname lookup, though, it's subject to problems if your DNS servers go down or if the person who controls the domain modifies its entries.

- **Domain**—You can match an entire domain or subdomain much as you can match a single hostname. The difference is that you must precede the domain name with a period, as in `.threeroomco.com`—this example matches all the computers in the `threeroomco.com` domain.

- **NIS netgroup name**—If a string is preceded by an at symbol (@), the string is treated as a Network Information Services (NIS) netgroup name. This method relies upon your network having a functioning NIS configuration.

In addition, the `client-list` specification supports more wildcards than does the `daemon-list` specification. Specific wildcards you may use include the following:

- **ALL**—This wildcard matches all computers.
- **LOCAL**—This wildcard is intended to match all local computers, based on hostname. If the computer's hostname lacks a period, it's considered local.
- **UNKNOWN**—This wildcard matches computers whose hostnames aren't known by your name resolution system.
- **KNOWN**—This wildcard matches computers whose hostname and IP addresses are both known to the system.
- **PARANOID**—This wildcard matches computers whose names and IP addresses don't match.

These last three options should be used with care, since they usually depend upon proper functioning of DNS, and DNS can be unreliable because of transient network problems. For instance, if a client's own DNS system is down or inaccessible, you might be unable to verify its hostname. As an example of a short but complete `/etc/hosts.allow` file, consider the following:

```
telnet,ftp : 192.168.34. dino.pangaea.edu
ssh : LOCAL .pangaea.edu
```

The first line specifies identical restrictions for the Telnet and FTP servers, allowing access only to the 192.168.34.0/24 network and the host called dino.pangaea.edu. The second line applies to SSH and restricts access to local computers and all those in the pangaea.edu domain. Because no other servers are listed in the *daemon-list* fields, TCP Wrappers doesn't block access to any other server. For instance, if you were to run Apache through inetd and TCP Wrappers, everybody would be granted access to Apache with this configuration.

In addition to matching entire computers, you can use the *user@computer* form to match individual users of the remote system. This form, however, requires that the client computer run an ident (aka auth) server, which returns the name of the user who is using a given network port. Your own server can query the client's ident server about the connection attempt, thus getting the username associated with that attempt. This may cause additional delays, however, and the information often isn't particularly trustworthy, especially from random hosts on the Internet. (You're more likely to want to use this feature to control access from specific users of systems that you control.)

The EXCEPT operator is another special keyword; it specifies exceptions to the rules just laid out. For instance, consider the following /etc/hosts.deny entry:

```
www : badcracker.org EXCEPT goodguy@exception.badcracker.org
```

This example denies access to the Web server to all the computers in the badcracker.org domain, unless the connection is coming from goodguy@exception.badcracker.org. (Because /etc/hosts.allow takes precedence over /etc/hosts.deny, entries in the former can also override those in the latter.)

If your goal is to run a very secure system, you may want to begin with the following /etc/hosts.deny file:

```
ALL : ALL
```

This blocks access to all computers for all servers handled by TCP Wrappers. You must then explicitly open access to other servers in /etc/hosts.allow. You should open access as little as possible. For instance, you might only give access to computers in a specific network block or domain for sensitive servers like Telnet. (Telnet passes all data in an unencrypted form, so it's a poor choice for logins over the Internet as a whole. See Chapter 13, Maintaining Remote Login Servers, for a discussion of this issue.)

USING xinetd

Traditionally, inetd has been the super server used on Linux systems. Since 2000, however, a shift has begun toward the use of an alternative, xinetd (pronounced "zi-net-dee"). As a first approximation, you can think of xinetd as being a combination of inetd and TCP Wrappers. This is only a rough analogy, though; there are things that xinetd can do that inetd with TCP Wrappers can't do, and things that inetd with TCP Wrappers can do that xinetd alone can't do. In the end, though, xinetd is more flexible because it can be combined with TCP Wrappers, if required, to extend its flexibility. In early 2002, Red Hat and Mandrake are the two major distributions that use xinetd by default, but you can add xinetd to other distributions if you like.

THE /etc/xinetd.conf FILE FORMAT

As a new super server with expanded capabilities, xinetd requires a new file format. The /etc/xinetd.conf file controls xinetd, but both Red Hat and Mandrake provide only a minimal xinetd.conf file. This file includes default settings for all servers and a line that causes xinetd to read all the files in /etc/xinetd.d and treat them as supplementary configuration files. Thus, xinetd configuration is something like SysV configuration, in that each server has its own control file named after the server, such as /etc/xinetd.d/telnet to control the Telnet server. You can configure xinetd using just its main xinetd.conf file if you prefer, but server packages for Red Hat and Mandrake often drop their startup files in /etc/xinetd.d.

Whether it's located in /etc/xinetd.conf or a file in /etc/xinetd.d, a xinetd server definition spans several lines; however, a basic definition includes the same information as an inetd.conf entry. For instance, the following xinetd definition is mostly equivalent to the inetd.conf entry presented earlier for a Telnet server:

```
service telnet
{
        socket_type = stream
        protocol    = tcp
        wait        = no
        user        = root
        server      = /usr/sbin/in.telnetd
}
```

This entry provides the same information as an inetd.conf entry. The xinetd configuration file format, however, explicitly labels each entry and splits them across multiple lines. Although this example presents data in the same order as does the inetd configuration, this order isn't required. Also, the xinetd definition doesn't call TCP Wrappers, although it could (you'd list /usr/sbin/tcpd on the server line, then add a server_args line that would list /usr/sbin/in.telnetd to pass the name of the Telnet server to TCP Wrappers).

In addition to the standard inetd features, xinetd provides many configuration options to expand its capabilities. Most of these are items that appear on their own lines between the curly braces in the service definition. The most important of these options include the following:

- **Security features**—As noted earlier, xinetd provides numerous security options, many of which are roughly equivalent to those provided by TCP Wrappers. These are discussed in greater depth in the upcoming section "Setting Access Control Features."

- **Disabling a server**—You can disable an inetd server by commenting out its configuration line. You can accomplish the same goal by adding the disable = yes line to a xinetd server definition. The same effect can be achieved in the main /etc/xinetd.conf file by using the disabled = *server_list* option in the defaults section, where *server_list* is a space-delimited list of server names. Various configuration tools use one of these methods to disable servers, and in fact a disable = no line may be present for servers that are active.

- **Redirection**—If you want to pass a request to another computer, you can use the redirect = *target* option, where *target* is the hostname or IP address of the computer that should receive the request. For instance, if you include the redirect = 192.168.3.78 line in the /etc/xinetd.d/telnet file of dummy.threeroomco.com, attempts to access the Telnet server on dummy.threeroomco.com will be redirected to the internal computer on 192.168.3.78. You might want to use this feature on a NAT router (see Chapter 25) to allow an internal computer to function as a server for the outside world. The iptables utility can accomplish the same goal at a somewhat lower level, but doing it in xinetd allows you to apply xinetd's access control features.

- **Logging**—You can fine-tune xinetd's logging of access attempts using the log_on_success and log_on_failure options, which determine what information xinetd logs on successful and unsuccessful attempts to access a server. These options take values such as PID (the server's process ID, or PID), HOST (the client's address), USERID (the user ID on the client system associated with the access attempt), EXIT (the time and exit status of the access termination), and DURATION (how long the session lasted). When setting these values, you can use a += or -= symbol, rather than =, to add or subtract the features you want to log from the default.

- **Connection load limits**—You can limit the number of connections that xinetd will handle in several ways. One is the per_source option, which specifies how many connections xinetd will accept from any given source at any one time. (UNLIMITED sets xinetd to accept an unlimited number of connections.) The instances option specifies the maximum number of processes xinetd will spawn (this value may be larger than the per_source value). The cps option takes two space-separated values: the number of connections xinetd accepts per second and the number of seconds to pause after this limit is reached before enabling access again. You can adjust the scheduling priority of the servers that xinetd runs using the nice option, which sets a value in much the same way as the nice program. Finally, max_load takes a floating-point value that represents the system load average above which xinetd refuses further connections. Taken together, these options can reduce the chance that your system will experience difficulties because of certain types of denial of service (DoS) attacks or because of a spike in the popularity of your servers.

You can use most of these options directly in the server definition or in the defaults section in the main /etc/xinetd.conf file. If placed in the latter location, the feature applies to all servers handled through xinetd, unless overridden by a competing option in the server definition area.

If you make changes to the /etc/xinetd.conf file or its included files in /etc/xinetd.d, you must restart the xinetd server program. Because xinetd itself is usually started through a SysV startup script, you can do this by typing a command such as **/etc/rc.d/init.d/xinetd restart**, although the startup script may be located somewhere else on some distributions. Alternatively, you can pass xinetd the SIGUSR1 or SIGUSR2 signals via kill. The former tells xinetd to reload its configuration file and begin responding as indicated in the new file. The latter does the same, but also terminates any servers that have been inactivated by changes to the configuration file.

SETTING ACCESS CONTROL FEATURES

Part of the appeal of xinetd is that it combines access control features that closely resemble those of TCP Wrappers in the super server itself. This can simplify configuration. The TCP Wrappers and xinetd access control features aren't exactly identical, though, so there are situations in which one tool or the other is superior. Like other xinetd configuration options, you can set access control features either globally or for specific servers. Major access control options include the following:

- **Host-based restrictions**—The only_from and no_access options are conceptually very similar to the contents of the /etc/hosts.allow and /etc/hosts.deny files for TCP Wrappers, but xinetd sets these features in its main configuration file or server-specific configuration file. Specifically, only_from sets a list of computers that are explicitly allowed access (with all others denied access), whereas no_access specifies computers that are to be blacklisted. If both are set for an address, the one with a more specific rule takes precedence. For both options, addresses may be specified by IP address (for instance, 172.23.45.67), by network address using a trailing .0 (for instance, 172.23.0.0 for 172.23.0.0/16) or with an explicit netmask (as in 127.23.0.0/16), a network name listed in /etc/networks, or a hostname (such as badguy.threeroomco.com). If a hostname is used, xinetd does a single lookup on that hostname at the time the server starts, so if the hostname-to-IP address mapping changes, a hostname may not be very effective.

- **Temporal restrictions**—You can specify a range of times during which the server is available by using the access_times option. This option requires an access time specified as *hour:minute-hour:minute*, such as 08:00-18:00, which restricts access to the server to the hours of 8:00 AM to 6:00 PM. Times are specified in a 24-hour format. Note that this restricts only the initial access to the server. For instance, if the Telnet server is restricted to 8:00 AM to 6:00 PM, somebody could log in at 5:58 PM and stay on indefinitely.

- **Interface restrictions**—You can bind a server to just one network interface using the bind or interface options (they're synonyms), which take the IP address associated with an interface. For instance, if eth1 is linked to 172.19.28.37, bind = 172.19.28.37 links a server *only* to eth1. Any attempt to access the server from eth0 is met with silence, as if the server weren't running at all. This feature is most useful on routers and other computers linked to more than one network, but it's also of interest to those with small internal networks and dial-up links. For instance, you can bind servers like Telnet or FTP to your local Ethernet interface, and they won't be available to the Internet at large via your PPP connection.

Although this and the preceding section outline the most useful xinetd options, there are some less often used options that aren't described here.

You should consult the xinetd man page for further information on additional options.

USING LOCAL STARTUP SCRIPTS

Most Linux distributions start the majority of their standard servers through either SysV startup scripts or a super server. One notable exception to this rule is the X server, which is often started through a line near the end of /etc/inittab, which launches the X server only in a particular runlevel. Slackware also does things a bit differently, using /etc/rc.d/rc.inet2 to start most of its servers. Most distributions provide a "local" startup script, which is intended to be modified by the system administrator to handle starting unusual system-specific servers, running initialization utilities, and so on. Table 4.1 lists the local startup scripts for several common Linux distributions.

The usual reason to use a local startup script is that you're adding a server that you don't want to run via a super server and that doesn't come with an appropriate SysV startup script. Because SysV startup scripts are closely tied to specific distributions, you might not have an appropriate SysV startup script if you obtained a server from a source other than your own distribution. For instance, if you're running Mandrake but install a server intended for SuSE, the SuSE SysV startup script may not work on your Mandrake system. You may also run into this problem if you obtain the server in source code form from the server's author; an original source such as this is unlikely to include customizations for specific Linux distributions. The code may compile and run just fine, but you'll need to start the server yourself.

Of course, it's possible to write your own SysV startup scripts for such servers. You can do this by modifying a working SysV startup script. You might try modifying the startup script for an equivalent tool (such as an earlier version of the server you're installing, if you've resorted to a third-party source because your distribution's official tool is out of date), or some randomly selected startup script. This process can be tricky, though, particularly if you're not familiar with your distribution's startup script format or with shell scripting in general. (SysV startup scripts are written in the bash shell scripting language.) If you run into problems, or if you're in a hurry and don't want to put forth the effort to create or modify a SysV startup script, you can start it in the local startup script.

You can modify the local startup script using your favorite text editor. To start a server, simply include lines in the file that are the same as the commands you'd type at a command prompt to launch the program. For instance, the following line starts a Telnet server:

```
/usr/sbin/in.telnetd
```

If the server doesn't start up in *daemon mode* by default (that is, if it doesn't run in the background, relinquishing control of your shell if you launch it directly), you should use an ampersand (&) at the end of the command line to tell the server to run in the background. Failure to do this will cause the execution of the startup script to halt at the call to the server. This may be acceptable if it's the last line in the script, but if you want to start additional servers, the subsequent servers won't start if you omit the ampersand.

You may, of course, do something more complex than launching a server using a single line. You could use the bash shell's conditional expressions to test that the server file exists, or launch it only under certain circumstances. These are the sorts of tasks that are usually performed in SysV startup scripts, though, so if you want to go to that sort of effort, you might prefer writing your own SysV startup script.

One important point to keep in mind is that different distributions' local startup scripts aren't exactly equivalent to one another. For instance, SuSE runs its boot.local script earlier in the boot process than Red Hat runs its rc.local. Therefore, SuSE's local startup script is more appropriate for bringing up interfaces or doing other early startup tasks, whereas Red Hat's script is better for launching servers that rely on an already-up network connection. If the tasks you want to perform in the startup script are very dependent upon the presence or absence of other servers, you may be forced to create a SysV startup script with a sequence number that's appropriate for the tasks you want to perform.

The usual reason for using a local startup script is to create a quick-and-dirty method of launching a server or running some other program. Once launched, the local startup script provides no easy way to shut down the server (as does the stop parameter to most SysV startup scripts); you'll have to use kill, killall, or a similar tool to stop the server, if you need to do so.

USING GUI TOOLS

Many Linux distributions provide GUI interfaces that permit configuration of basic networking features, common servers, and often other aspects of system operation. These tools vary substantially from one distribution to another, although they do share certain commonalities. They can usually be launched from a menu option in the distribution's default K Desktop Environment (KDE) or GNU Network Object Model Environment (GNOME) desktops, or they can be launched by typing their names in xterms. (You may need to be root to launch these tools, particularly in the latter way.) These tools include Linuxconf (used by Red Hat and many of its derivatives, including Mandrake), YaST and YaST2 (used by SuSE), and ksysv (a GUI variant on ntsysv, discussed earlier).

NOTE   There are also Web-based administration tools, such as Webmin and SWAT. Indeed, Linuxconf can be used remotely via a Web-based interface, as well as locally. Chapter 16, Maintaining a System from a Distance, describes such tools. Although intended primarily for remote administration, they can also be used locally by pointing a Web browser at its local system's Web-based administrative tool.

USING LINUXCONF

The Linuxconf utility is a modular configuration tool; it consists of a framework that accepts configuration modules to handle specific servers and other configuration tasks. You can run Linuxconf in text mode (in which it uses text-based menus), in GUI mode (in which it runs in a separate window), or via a Web-based interface (accessed via a Web browser, as discussed in Chapter 16). The GUI interface requires not just the main linuxconf package, but a separate package typically called gnome-linuxconf or linuxconf-gui. If Linuxconf can use its GUI tools, it does so automatically; otherwise it falls back on its text-based mode. This section emphasizes the local GUI access methods, but the same options are available in text-mode or Web-based access; only the details of the user interface are different. The details of the GUI interface differ somewhat from one distribution to another. In particular, Red Hat uses a single window and displays all the configuration modules in that window, whereas Mandrake uses separate windows for each configuration module.

NOTE The official Linuxconf Web site is http://www.solucorp.qc.ca/linuxconf/. Although it ships with both Red Hat 7.2 and Mandrake 8.1, it is officially deprecated on both, and so may eventually disappear from these distributions. It's unclear in early 2002 if Linuxconf will be replaced in these distributions by another unified tool or by a series of server-specific tools. Although it's most strongly associated with Red Hat and Mandrake, versions of Linuxconf tailored to other distributions are available from the main Linuxconf Web site.

When first launched, Linuxconf presents an expandable list of configuration areas, broken down into three tabs: Config, Control, and Status. Each area has subareas, until you reach specific configuration modules. (In Mandrake's implementation, you click on one area to obtain a separate window showing the options within that area, and so on until you reach the configuration module you want.) Figure 4.2 shows Red Hat's implementation of this model, with the Control ➤ Control Panel ➤ Control Service Activity module selected. This module allows you to control SysV startup scripts and servers started through xinetd. To enable or disable a server, follow these steps:

1. Start Linuxconf and locate the Control ➤ Control Panel ➤ Control Service Activity module, as shown in Figure 4.2.

2. Locate the server you want to control in the list on the right. For instance, to control sendmail, you'd locate the sendmail item and click it. The result is a new tab on the right of the Linuxconf window showing the current status of the server.

3. Click the Run Levels tab. The display should now resemble Figure 4.3. You can enable or disable the server for any of the specified runlevels by clicking the checkboxes next to each runlevel number.

4. Click Accept in the Service tab, then click Dismiss in the Service Control tab.

5. Select File ➤ Act/Changes from the Linuxconf menu bar. The program will display a list of the things it will do. Click Do It to accept these changes.

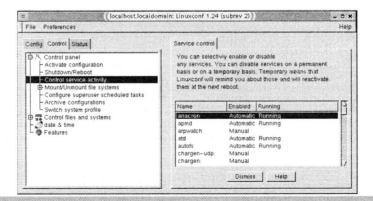

Figure 4.2   You can use linuxconf to control many aspects of a Linux system's operation.

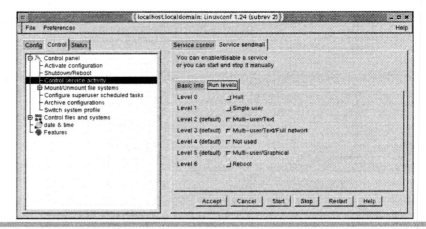

Figure 4.3   You can control servers through Linuxconf by enabling or disabling a server in any of its runlevels.

At this point, your system should be reconfigured to launch the servers in the runlevels you've selected. You can verify this with chkconfig or by examining the filenames in the SysV script link directory.

In addition to enabling or disabling servers, Linuxconf includes the ability to configure some servers. As Red Hat and Mandrake have been moving away from the use of Linuxconf, they have omitted more of these configuration modules with each new version of their distributions. You can locate many of them on the Linuxconf Web site, although they don't always work correctly. The problem is that server configuration file locations, and even the contents of the files, vary from one distribution to another or from one version of a server to another. This makes creating a truly universal configuration module impossible for many servers.

USING YaST AND YaST2

SuSE's Yet Another Setup Tool (YaST) and YaST2 are text-based and GUI configuration tools, respectively. Although they feature different user interfaces, the two tools provide very similar options. This section emphasizes the use of YaST2, but you shouldn't have trouble using YaST if you choose to do so. (For simplicity's sake, I use the word *YaST* to refer to both tools unless the distinction is important.) You can launch the text-mode YaST by typing **yast**, or YaST2 by typing **yast2**. The main YaST2 window resembles the one shown in Figure 4.4. You select broad areas of configu-

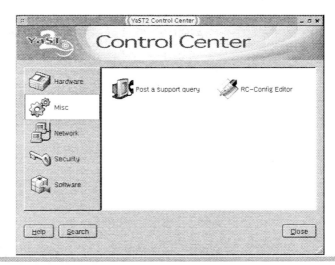

Figure 4.4   YaST provides several specific configuration tools that are grouped into a handful of specific configuration categories.

ration from the list on the left, and specific configuration tools from the options on the right.

Because SuSE uses the /etc/rc.config file to control the startup process, as well as the naming of files in the SysV script link directories, YaST must alter the configuration file to handle server startups. In fact, this is the primary means that YaST uses to control server startup. The naming of the tool to alter these options reflects this fact: It's the RC-Config Editor tool in the Misc section. Click this tool, and YaST2 displays the window shown in Figure 4.5. Most of the network server startup variables are located in the Start-Variables ➤ Start-Network area. Click one of the specific options, as shown in Figure 4.5, and YaST allows you to edit the variable—usually to set it to Yes or No, which causes the server to start or not start, respectively.

YaST can also control many other aspects of network configuration. Indeed, many important variables for specific servers are stored in the /etc/rc.config file, so the same configuration tool you use to control SysV server startup can set these variables. For instance, you can set your hostname (Network ➤ Network-Basics) or tell SuSE whether or not to accept remote root logins (Security ➤ Security-Basics). You may want to browse through the options available in this tool to familiarize yourself with its capabilities.

105

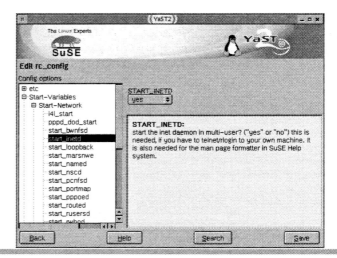

Figure 4.5   Network server startup in YaST involves setting variables to Yes or No.

Other YaST tools, particularly in the Network area, can be used to configure specific servers. For instance, the Network area hosts both an NFS tool and a Sendmail Configuration tool, which are used to configure NFS and sendmail, respectively. (These topics are covered in Chapters 8 and 19, although these chapters don't focus on YaST configuration.)

USING ksysv

Earlier in this chapter, I described the chkconfig and ntsysv tools for managing SysV startup scripts (and sometimes servers launched through a super server). These tools are useful, but if you're a fan of fully GUI administrative tools, they may not be quite enough to suit your tastes. There are some fully GUI alternatives, though, such as ksysv and tksysv. The former is part of the KDE project, but can be used in other environments if you prefer. The latter is not associated with any particular GUI suite. Both are most likely to work smoothly with Red Hat or its derivative distributions. Figure 4.6 shows ksysv in operation.

Both ksysv and tksysv feature a list of available SysV startup scripts in a scrollable list box to the left of the window, and lists of servers that are set to start and stop in various runlevels in the rest of the window. Clicking on an entry in either type of list produces information on the startup script, but the information differs depending upon whether you click in the Available Services list or in a specific runlevel list. In the former case, ksysv pres-

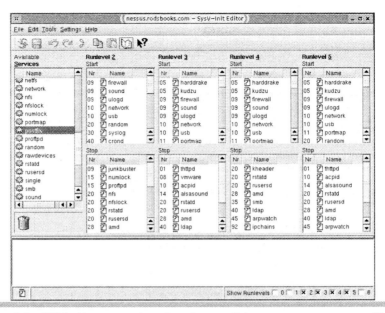

Figure 4.6 GUI SysV startup script editors let you click on a server name to modify its operation.

ents a dialog box that includes a description of the service, and in which you can start, stop, or restart the service or change the permissions or file-name for the script. If you click on a service name in a runlevel list, the dialog box also provides a description of the service (in the Service tab), and you can edit the link's name, the startup script to which it points, and the sequence number, as shown in Figure 4.7.

To change which servers start automatically, click and drag a server name from the Start to the Stop runlevel list, or vice versa. You can also drag a server from the Available Services list to the desired runlevel list. In any of these cases, ksysv will assign the service a default sequence number based on where you drag it. For instance, if you drag a service in between services with sequence numbers of 20 and 30, ksysv will assign a default sequence number of 25. You can change this number by clicking the service name in the runlevel list and editing the Sorting Number field, as shown in Figure 4.7. Unfortunately, ksysv doesn't know what sequences are most appropriate for your system, so you'll have to pay careful attention to this detail. Also, it's possible to configure the system to have a service listed in both the start and stop lists using ksysv, so you should be careful not to do so.

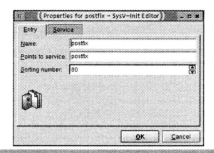

Figure 4.7 You can edit SysV startup script and link features from dialog boxes by clicking the name of a service in `ksysv`.

On the whole, GUI startup script utilities like `ksysv` and `tksysv` are less flexible than tools like Linuxconf or YaST. This is by design; the SysV script tools are intended to do just one job, not the many jobs performed by more general-purpose configuration tools. The SysV script tools can help you tweak your SysV startup scripts, but they aren't a substitute for knowing how the system works. You must understand runlevels and the startup sequence for your scripts, or at least the basic principles of SysV startup script sequencing.

WHEN TO USE EACH STARTUP METHOD

With so many different startup methods available, it's not always easy to decide which one to use. Most servers packaged for specific Linux distributions ship in such a way that they immediately work with one startup method. For instance, the server may ship in a package that includes a SysV startup script or a `xinetd` configuration file in `/etc/xinetd.d`. You need not be bound by the defaults, however; in most cases, you can start a server in any of the ways mentioned. There are a few exceptions, and there are more cases in which servers are almost always run in a particular way because the benefits of that method are overwhelming. Table 4.2 summarizes the pros and cons of each of the three methods of starting servers.

Most distributions start most servers (and many nonserver services, such as sound card configurations) through SysV startup scripts. Many servers are important enough that you don't want to impose delays as a super server launches the server program, and SysV scripts are superior to local startup scripts from a distribution maintainer's point of view because it's easy to add and delete SysV startup scripts as part of a server's package file. Some servers, such as Samba's `nmbd`, tend to be unreliable when run

Table 4.2 Pros and Cons of Server Startup Methods

Startup method	Advantages	Disadvantages
SysV startup script	Custom server sets in different runlevels; fast server responses; server startup configurable by renaming files; easy manual start and stop of servers	Large memory footprint for large servers; fewer outside access controls possible
Super server	Low memory footprint for seldom-used servers; opportunity to add access controls	Slow server responses; some servers don't work well from this environment; servers can't as easily maintain state across calls
Local startup script	Fast server responses; easy to add server if it doesn't include SysV scripts	Poor integration with configuration tools (chkconfig, ksysv, and so on); startup scripts vary across distributions

from a super server. Sometimes this is related to a need of the server to maintain information from one call to another—for instance, nmbd may keep information on the names and addresses of other computers on the network, and that information will be lost if it's run from a super server.

Super servers have their place, though. Many distributions use them by default for small servers that can load and run quickly, such as Telnet and FTP servers. You might also be willing to take the speed hit on large servers like Apache or sendmail if these servers aren't called very often. Some distributions, such as Debian, give you the option of running such servers from SysV startup scripts or via a super server when you install the server. Even if you're not given this choice, though, you can change your configuration after installation by disabling the SysV startup scripts and adding appropriate super server configurations.

In most cases, it's simplest to use the super server that comes with your distribution (either inetd or xinetd). If you find that you need a feature of one particular super server (probably xinetd, since it's more sophisticated), you can replace your distribution's standard super server with the new one. You may need to modify the super server's SysV startup script or launch the new one through a local startup script. After you've done this, you can configure the new super server as described earlier in this chapter.

Local startup scripts are best reserved for cases when you would ordinarily run the server through a SysV script, but you lack a normal SysV startup script or it doesn't work correctly. If you're a new administrator, this is likely to occur when you install a server intended for one distribution on another one. As noted earlier, in the section "Using Local Startup Scripts," it's generally possible to create a custom SysV startup script, but if you're in a hurry or are inexperienced with such matters, adding a simple call to a local startup script can be a faster way to accomplish the goal.

NOTE One additional method of starting servers is by hand; you can usually type the server's name to launch it. This method is useful mainly for testing, though. In most cases, you'll want to configure the server to start automatically, so that's what this chapter has emphasized.

SUMMARY

Knowing how to start a server program is critically important to using Linux as a server computer. Considered broadly, there are three major methods of starting a Linux server: SysV startup scripts, super servers, and local startup scripts. Every Linux distribution is unique in the details of how it starts servers using these methods, so you'll have to study your own distribution's methods in order to adjust your system's configuration. Particularly important are the locations and startup sequence numbers of SysV startup scripts, and whether the computer uses inetd or xinetd as its super server. Once you've learned the methods provided by your distribution for starting servers, you'll be well prepared for setting up both common and uncommon servers and other network tools, as described in the rest of this book.

Part II

LOCAL NETWORK SERVERS

Configuring Other Computers via DHCP

Chapter 2, TCP/IP Network Configuration, covered configuring a computer to function on a TCP/IP network in any of several different ways. One of these ways was to use a Dynamic Host Configuration Protocol (DHCP) server. In this configuration, the computer sends out a broadcast query to locate a DHCP server, which responds by providing the computer with an IP address and other necessary configuration information. This configuration is very convenient for the DHCP client, because it obviates the need to enter the computer's IP address, IP addresses for gateways, and related information. DHCP doesn't work by magic, though. If you're running your own network, it requires that you configure a DHCP *server* computer to answer DHCP client requests. This chapter covers how to do this.

Before configuring a DHCP server, you should ask yourself whether you want to do this. If so, you need to locate the DHCP configuration files. The most basic configuration involves having the DHCP server assign IP addresses that may vary from one client boot to another, but with some more work you can have DHCP assign the same IP address to specific computers time after time. The final topic covered in this chapter concerns integrating a DHCP server with other servers, such as Samba and a Domain Name System (DNS) server.

As with many topics covered in this book, this chapter cannot cover all the details, but it should get you started, and may be enough for many configurations. If you need to create an extremely complex DHCP configuration, you may need to consult a book dedicated to the topic, such as Droms & Lemons' *The DHCP Handbook: Understanding, Deploying, and Managing Automated Configuration Services* (New Riders Publishing, 1999) or Kercheval's *DHCP: A Guide to Dynamic TCP/IP Network Configuration* (Prentice Hall, 1999).

WHEN TO RUN A DHCP SERVER

In some sense, the answer to the question of when you should run a DHCP server is easy: You should run one whenever your network contains clients that are configured via DHCP. When configuring an individual computer, though, you select DHCP only when a DHCP server is available. You can break out of this circular logic by considering the network as a whole: Is it easier to configure individual computers with static IP addresses, or to set up a DHCP server on one computer and use it to configure individual computers?

You can get some idea of how difficult it is to configure individual computers for static IP addresses by reviewing the "Configuring a Static IP Address" section of Chapter 2—but be aware that different OSs may impose different configuration needs. Your Linux DHCP server can deliver IP addresses not just to Linux systems, but to systems that run other UNIX variants, Windows, MacOS, OS/2, BeOS, or just about anything else for which a TCP/IP stack is available. All of these OSs require more-or-less the same information to be configured with static IP addresses, though, so the differences between them relate to user interface details. It's almost always true that a DHCP configuration on the client will be simpler than a static IP address configuration.

NOTE A DHCP client can be a server for other protocols. Sometimes this is inadvisable, because the server should remain accessible at all times and it's usually important that a server's IP address not change. You can assign a server an unchanging IP address via DHCP, though, as described in the upcoming section "Assigning Fixed Addresses." Even so, you may prefer to assign static IP addresses directly to servers to avoid the possibility of problems should the DHCP server become inaccessible at an awkward time.

Configuring a DHCP server is usually more work than is configuring a single computer to use a static IP address. It's therefore seldom worthwhile to configure a DHCP server for the benefit of just one or two DHCP clients. The total effort of DHCP server configuration begins to become worthwhile at perhaps half a dozen clients. (If a computer dual-boots between multiple OSs, its configuration effort rises as if it were multiple computers, which in some sense it is.)

In addition to the total configuration effort on DHCP clients and the server, you should consider the expertise of the people who will be doing the configuring. If ordinary users on your network set up their systems, using DHCP offers great benefits because it becomes much less likely that these users will accidentally enter information incorrectly because they've misunderstood the instructions. If somebody experienced in basic network configuration sets up all the computers, this factor becomes less important.

Although DHCP can simplify network configuration greatly, there is at least one computer that won't be using DHCP to set its basic network options: the DHCP server itself. You'll configure this computer with a static IP address, and set up the DHCP server program so that it doesn't attempt to issue that IP address to any clients.

NOTE   A computer with multiple network interfaces might conceivably function as a DHCP client on one network, but host a DHCP server on the other network.

The DHCP server is extremely important to the normal functioning of your network. If the DHCP server goes down, clients won't be able to obtain IP addresses when they boot, or when they would normally renegotiate the maintenance of their IP addresses with the server. You may want to consider preparing a backup DHCP server computer. This computer's DHCP server shouldn't be active, but you should be prepared to start it should the main DHCP server go down. If possible, you should arrange to keep the backup server constantly supplied with the main server's lease file so that the backup server won't mistakenly issue an IP address that the main server assigned to another computer. You might do this through cron jobs that transfer the lease file, for instance. Such a configuration is probably overkill on a small network, though. Also, long lease times will minimize the risk should a DHCP server go down, because clients that are already booted may not need to contact the DHCP server while it's out of operation.

Finally, you may want to consider non-Linux DHCP options. All major Linux distributions ship with a DHCP server; this isn't true of some other

OSs, so using Linux as a DHCP server platform often makes a great deal of sense. You might, however, be setting up a small network that uses a broadband router—the type of device that links small office and home networks to cable or digital subscriber line (DSL) networks. These devices usually include DHCP servers. If yours does, it's probably simpler to configure than a Linux DHCP server, although broadband router DHCP servers are also usually much less flexible than are Linux DHCP servers. For instance, broadband router DHCP servers seldom give you any way to consistently deliver the same IP address to a client.

DHCP servers are normally run via SysV scripts. This configuration provides for quick responses to clients and allows the server to maintain important configuration information in memory. Chapter 4, Starting Servers, discussed options for starting servers in general.

KERNEL AND NETWORK INTERFACE ISSUES

You may need to adjust your kernel configuration or other aspects of your network to use a DHCP server. In particular, you must enable the Packet Socket and Socket Filtering options in your kernel configuration, as described in Chapter 1, Kernel Network Configuration. (Version 1 of dhcpd doesn't require Socket Filtering, but more recent versions do.)

Some DHCP clients require responses from the DHCP server addressed to 255.255.255.255. Unfortunately for DHCP server operation, Linux defaults to changing such addresses to your local broadcast address (such as 192.168.1.255). If you have problems with some DHCP clients (particularly Windows systems), you may need to correct this by adding an explicit route to your DHCP server computer's routing table. You can do this with the following command:

```
# route add -host 255.255.255.255 dev eth0
```

You may need to change eth0 to whatever value is appropriate for your system. This command may be present in your DHCP startup script. You can check if it's present by typing **route -n** at a command prompt. This command displays all your system's routing table entries, as described in Chapter 2. You'll see the 255.255.255.255 route at the top of the output, if it's present.

DHCP CONFIGURATION FILES

Most Linux distributions ship with the DHCP server written by the Internet Software Consortium (http://www.isc.org/products/DHCP/). ISC released version 3.0 of its DHCP server in late 2001, but as of early 2002, many Linux distributions still ship with the older 2.0 version. Most of the configuration features described here apply to both 2.0 and 3.0 versions of the DHCP server, but 3.0 adds support for some advanced features, including the DNS integration described in the section "Communicating with a DNS Server."

The DHCP server relies on a configuration file called dhcpd.conf. This file usually resides in the /etc or /etc/dhcp directory. Like other Linux configuration files, dhcpd.conf is a plain text file, so you can edit it with your favorite text editor. In addition to this file, dhcpd creates its own status file, dhcp.leases, which usually resides in /var/lib/dhcp. This file contains information on *leases* issued by dhcpd. DHCP operates on the principle that the DHCP server orchestrates the allocation of IP addresses. It does this by telling a DHCP client that it may use a particular IP address for a particular period of time—that is, the DHCP client obtains a lease, which it must periodically *renew*. The dhcp.leases file also contains information on the Ethernet addresses of the clients. The dhcp.leases file isn't a configuration file *per se*, though; you won't edit it, although there are a few circumstances in which you might want to examine it, such as when you are troubleshooting or if you need to locate a client's media access control (MAC) address.

The main dhcpd.conf file, like many configuration files, may contain comments, which begin with the pound sign (#). The file's noncomment lines are known as *statements*, and they fall into two broad categories:

- **Parameters**—Parameters tell the DHCP server whether to do something (such as providing addresses to unknown clients), how to do something (such as how long a lease to offer), or what information to provide to clients (such as the network's gateway address).
- **Declarations**—Declarations describe the topology of the network (what addresses are associated with particular interfaces, for instance), specify IP addresses that can be assigned to clients, or associate a set of parameters with a set of declarations.

Some declarations rely on information described in parameters. When this is the case, the parameter must precede the declaration in the file. As described shortly, most configuration files begin with a series of global parameters, then move on to declarations.

Some declarations span multiple lines, and such declarations may include parameters within the grouping. Such multi-line declarations are indicated by the use of curly braces ({}) surrounding the enclosed lines. For instance, the following lines define an individual computer and the IP address it's to be given, as discussed in the upcoming section "Assigning Fixed Addresses:"

```
host teela {
    hardware Ethernet 00:05:02:a7:76:da;
    fixed-address 192.168.1.2;
}
```

The details of what this declaration does are discussed later. For now, you should note that the host keyword begins the declaration, it's followed by an additional option (the name of the computer, teela), and the curly braces enclose additional configuration lines that define key features needed for this declaration. Such multi-line declarations may be nested within each other in certain circumstances. It's common practice to indent the nested declarations a few spaces in such cases, to help you identify the nested components at a glance. Such indentation isn't required, though; dhcpd ignores extra spaces and lines except when they're enclosed in quotes.

ASSIGNING DYNAMIC ADDRESSES

The simplest configuration for a DHCP server is to assign dynamic IP addresses. In this case, the DHCP server provides whatever IP address is convenient to a computer when that computer connects. No IP addresses are reserved for particular computers, so any given client might receive one IP address one day and another address the next day. A client may request a specific address, and most clients request the last address they received, but the server may ignore this request. In practice, computers are likely to receive the same addresses time after time if they're seldom turned off or if they're powered down only for short periods, but this isn't guaranteed. Dynamic configurations may be useful if your network sports a large number of clients, but it has a drawback: Because client IP addresses may change at unpredictable times, it's difficult to tie them to specific hostnames, because the DNS servers that tie hostnames to IP addresses are typically configured with static IP address mappings. This makes running servers on dynamic DHCP clients problematic. The "Communicating with a DNS Server" section later in this chapter describes one way around this problem, but another is to assign fixed IP addresses to servers, as described in the section "Assigning Fixed Addresses."

SETTING GLOBAL OPTIONS

Listing 5.1 shows a complete dhcpd.conf file that can assign dynamic IP addresses. This file is fairly simple, but it may be suitable for a small network, and it illustrates the basic structure of the file.

Listing 5.1   A sample dhcpd.conf file

```
default-lease-time 7200;
max-lease-time 10800;
option subnet-mask 255.255.255.0;
option routers 192.168.1.1;
option domain-name-servers 192.168.1.1, 172.17.102.200;
option domain-name "threeroomco.com";

subnet 192.168.1.0 netmask 255.255.255.0 {
    range 192.168.1.50 192.168.1.150;
}
```

The first six lines of Listing 5.1 define the global options. These are parameters that define critical aspects of the network or of the server's configuration, and that apply to all the clients served by dhcpd, unless the global option is overridden in a more specific declaration. Specifically, the first two items (default-lease-time and max-lease-time) set the length of leases in seconds. Like a tenant and landlord negotiating the lease to an apartment, the DHCP client and server must negotiate an appropriate lease time for an IP address. The default-lease-time value sets the lease time that the DHCP server prefers. In Listing 5.1, this is 7,200 seconds, or 120 minutes. If the client asks for a longer lease, the max-lease-time value sets the maximum that dhcpd will permit—10,800 seconds (180 minutes) in the case of Listing 5.1. You can adjust these values up or down as you see fit. Setting lease times low increases network bandwidth consumption, as clients must renew their leases regularly, and makes it more likely that the network will be disrupted if the DHCP server crashes. Setting lease times too high makes it more likely that you'll run out of IP addresses if computers connect briefly and then disconnect, because these systems will still have leases on IP addresses they're no longer using. If you want to test a DHCP server, you might set lease times quite low—say, to 60 seconds—so that you can make changes and observe the effect of these changes without undue delay. If a network sees a lot of changes (say, laptops being connected and disconnected regularly), you might set leases at a moderately low value, such as those in Listing 5.1 or a bit lower. On a network dominated by systems that remain connected for days at a time, you might set leases in the hundreds of thousands of seconds (that is, a period of days).

The next four lines in Listing 5.1 set global parameters that are passed on to DHCP clients—specifically, the network's netmask, gateway/router address, DNS server addresses, and domain name. These are the same values you'd enter when configuring a computer to use a static IP address, as described in Chapter 2. Although Listing 5.1 shows IP addresses, you may specify hostnames if name resolution works correctly on the DHCP server. If you do this, dhcpd resolves the hostnames you provide and passes IP addresses on to the clients. The DHCP server or client automatically derives or uses defaults for some values not shown in Listing 5.1, but you can override these defaults. When setting any of these parameters, you must including a trailing semicolon (;) on the line, as shown in Listing 5.1. Some of the values you might want to set include the following:

- **filename "*filename*"**—The dhcpd server can function as a boot server for computers that boot from an OS stored on a network server. When so configured, the DHCP server must be able to provide the name of an initial boot file for the client, and this is done through the filename parameter. The client will then retrieve this file with some other file transfer protocol.

- **next-server "*hostname*"**—This parameter sets the name of the computer on which the boot file (specified by filename) can be found. If you don't include this parameter, the default is the DHCP server itself.

- **server-name "*hostname*"**—This is another network-boot option. It's used to tell the client the name of the server that holds the boot files, aside from the initial boot file specified by filename and next-server.

- **boot-unknown-clients *flag***—Normally, *flag* defaults to true, which makes dhcpd issue an IP address to any computer that requests one. If *flag* is false, the server issues IP addresses only to computers that have explicit host declarations, as described in the section "Assigning Fixed Addresses."

- **option broadcast-address *ip-address***—If your network uses an unusual broadcast address, you can set it with this parameter. Normally, clients can compute this value correctly on their own.

- **get-lease-hostnames *flag***—If *flag* is set to true, dhcpd looks up a hostname via DNS before issuing an IP address, and passes the returned value to the client as its hostname. This results in clients whose hostnames match their IP addresses, which may be important if the clients run programs that incorporate their hostnames in outgoing network traffic (as do some mail servers, for instance). This parameter's default value is `false`.

- **use-host-decl-names** *flag*—This parameter is similar to `get-lease-hostnames`, but if it's set to `true`, it causes `dhcpd` to pass the hostname as set in a `host` declaration (described shortly) to the client, rather than the hostname associated with the IP address obtained from a DNS lookup. The default value is `false`.

NOTE   The `get-lease-hostnames` and `use-host-decl-names` parameters both determine whether or how the DHCP server will set the client's hostname *on the client.* These options do *not* affect hostname lookups performed through DNS from other systems, although `get-lease-hostnames` sets the hostname on the client to match the DNS name for the IP address. If you want to reliably reach a DHCP client by hostname from other computers, consult the upcoming sections, "Assigning Fixed Addresses" and "Communicating with a DNS Server."

There are a wide variety of additional parameters, many of which are options (they use the `option` keyword followed by the name of the option). Many of these options set the locations of various servers on a network, such as X font servers, time servers, and print servers. Others set low-level network interface options like whether the client should enable IP forwarding. Consult the `dhcpd.conf` man page if you need to set any of these options. Many of these options require additional tools on the client to do any good; standard DHCP clients don't automatically reconfigure features such as X font servers.

For the most part, these parameters may be set globally at the start of the file; or as part of a definition for just one set of IP addresses, by placing the parameters within the declaration for an individual subnet or group as described shortly.

DEFINING A SUBNET RANGE

Listing 5.1 demonstrates a very simple DHCP configuration, in which just one range of IP addresses is assigned. This is done through the `subnet` declaration in that listing:

```
subnet 192.168.1.0 netmask 255.255.255.0 {
    range 192.168.1.50 192.168.1.150;
}
```

This declaration specifies that the server operates on the 192.168.1.0/24 network. Consequently, the computer must have an active interface on that network. The DHCP server binds to that network interface and offers DHCP leases to clients that broadcast asking for an address on that network. The `range` declaration defines the range of IP addresses that the server will offer—192.168.1.50 to 192.168.1.150 in this example. You may use other addresses within the 192.168.1.0/24 network but outside of the specified range for computers that require static IP addresses, including the DHCP server itself; *do not* include the DHCP server's IP address within the values specified by the `range` declaration.

A single `dhcpd.conf` file may contain multiple `subnet` declarations. You might do this if the server has two network interfaces, in which case you'd use one `subnet` declaration per interface. You might also do it if there were just one physical interface, but that interface linked to multiple logical subnets. Versions of `dhcpd` prior to 3.0 *require* a separate `subnet` declaration for each physical interface, whether or not the server is to operate on the interface. For instance, if the computer is to function as a DHCP server on the 192.168.1.0/24 network but not on the 172.20.30.0/24 network, you'd still need a `subnet` declaration for the latter interface. This declaration could be empty, thus:

```
subnet 172.20.30.0 netmask 255.255.255.0 {
}
```

This empty declaration causes the server to not respond to DHCP requests on that interface. Version 3.0 of `dhcpd` allows you to omit this empty declaration to achieve the same end.

WARNING

If you're configuring a computer as a DHCP server on one network and another computer functions as the DHCP server on a second network to which the computer is connected, be *positive* you configure your server to *not* respond to DHCP requests on the second network. If not properly configured to work together, two DHCP servers on a single network can be a recipe for disaster. In fact, you may want to block incoming DHCP traffic on the second network interface using firewall rules, as discussed in Chapter 25, Configuring `iptables`. Better yet, move the DHCP server function to a computer that connects only to the first network.

ASSIGNING FIXED ADDRESSES

Client computers can often operate quite well with dynamic IP addresses. Internet protocols work by having the client initiate a connection with the server. The client must therefore be able to locate the server's IP address. The client can pass its own address to the server when making the connection. Thus, it doesn't matter if the client's IP address changes periodically, and especially not if the address changes when the client reboots. (A change in IP address mid-session would cause problems because it would break existing connections.)

There are cases when you might want to configure DHCP clients with a fixed IP address, though. The main reason for doing this is if the DHCP client is actually a server for another protocol. You might also want to do this to aid in network diagnostics—for instance, to be able to use ping to test basic connectivity with a computer by a fixed hostname rather than via an IP address. (The section "Communicating with a DNS Server" describes another way to link a dynamic IP address to a fixed hostname, though.) Fortunately, dhcpd provides the means to deliver fixed IP addresses to specific computers, although doing so requires additional work compared to a dynamic IP address configuration. The most common way of doing this is by locating the target computer's MAC address and configuring dhcpd with a fixed association between this address and an IP address of your choice.

LOCATING CLIENT MAC ADDRESSES

The MAC address lies at the heart of networking via several types of network hardware. In the case of Ethernet, the MAC address is a six-byte number, which is generally expressed in hexadecimal (base 16), using colons or some other punctuation between bytes, as in 00:80:C8:FA:3B:0A. Every packet that an Ethernet device sends onto the Ethernet cable is identified by its MAC address, so dhcpd can use this fact to identify the network card, and hence the computer to which it's attached. (Most OSs provide the means to override the MAC address, though, so it's not a truly reliable and secure way to identify a specific piece of hardware. This method is good enough for most purposes, however.) Other types of network hardware also support MAC addresses that are similar in principle to the Ethernet MAC address.

NOTE   The first three bytes of the Ethernet MAC address identify the manufacturer of the network card, and the manufacturer assigns the remaining three bytes itself. You can look up manufacturers for specific MAC addresses at sites such as http://www.coffer.com/mac_find/ or http://www.cavebear.com/CaveBear/Ethernet/vendor.html. This information isn't required to configure DHCP, but you might find it helpful in locating particular computers based on their DHCP client broadcasts. Note that the manufacturer is the manufacturer of the *Ethernet card*, which may not be the same as the computer's manufacturer. Indeed, some smaller brands, such as cards sold under computer superstores' names, are actually built by other companies, and their MAC addresses probably reflect this fact.

To let dhcpd use the MAC address to assign a specific IP address to a specific client, you'll need to locate your client's MAC address. There are several ways to do this, depending upon the hardware and the client's OS. If you're lucky, the hardware manufacturer will have printed the MAC address on the network card, usually on a sticker glued to the card. If this is the case, you can copy the MAC address from the hardware itself. This isn't a universal practice, however, and even if your manufacturer has done this, it may not be convenient to open the computer to read the MAC address from the Ethernet card. For this reason, there are software methods of obtaining the IP address.

NOTE If you configure a computer to obtain a temporary dynamic IP address from your DHCP server in order to bring its interface up so you can determine the MAC address, the client may request the same IP address when it's next rebooted. You may need to shut it down until this lease has expired in order to obtain the new fixed IP address.

Locating the MAC Address from the Client

In Linux and other UNIX-like clients, you can obtain the MAC address by using the ifconfig command. Type **ifconfig eth0** (or use another interface identifier, if appropriate) and the system will respond with a set of information about the interface. Included in this output will be a line resembling the following:

```
eth0      Link encap:Ethernet   HWaddr 00:80:C6:F9:3B:BA
```

The value identified as HWaddr (short for *hardware address*) is the MAC address—00:80:C6:F9:3B:BA in this case. This command will only work once you've loaded the Ethernet driver and brought up the interface at least minimally. The interface need not be bound to the TCP/IP stack, though.

In Windows 2000, you can obtain the MAC address through the IPCONFIG program, which is similar to Linux's ifconfig in many ways. Type **IPCONFIG /ALL** in a DOS prompt window to obtain a complete listing of information on the system's network interfaces. This listing will include a line similar to the following:

```
        Physical Address. . . . . . . . . : 00-50-BF-19-7E-99
```

In Windows Me, the equivalent to IPCONFIG is called WINIPCFG. This program is a GUI tool, though. Once launched, it resembles Figure 5.1, which shows the MAC address in the field labeled Adapter Address.

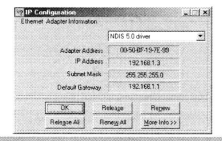

Figure 5.1   WINIPCFG presents information on network interfaces, and allows you to control a Windows 9*x*/Me DHCP client.

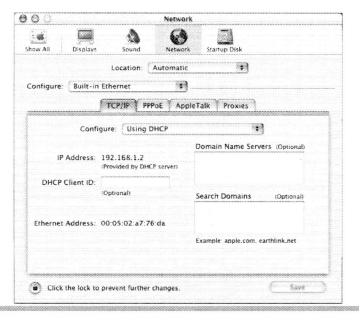

Figure 5.2   MacOS X displays the MAC address in the Network portion of System Preferences.

If your clients are Macintoshes running MacOS Classic, you can find the MAC address from the TCP/IP Control Panel. Click the Info button to get the TCP/IP Info dialog box, which displays the MAC address (called Hardware Address in the dialog box). In MacOS X, this information is available in the Network item in the System Preferences tool, as shown in Figure 5.2. It's called Ethernet Address near the lower left portion of the window.

Other OSs should provide similar methods of obtaining the MAC address. As illustrated by the preceding examples, the methods used by different

OSs are quite varied, so you may need to hunt in the OS's GUI controls or consult its documentation for the appropriate command. If you can't find a way to locate the MAC address, you may need to do it from the server, as described next.

Locating the MAC Address from the Server

Another approach to locating the MAC address is to do so from the DHCP server. This method relies upon the proper functioning of the client's network stack. One easy way to ensure at least minimal functionality is to configure the client to use DHCP and boot it, allowing your DHCP server to assign it a dynamic IP address from its dynamic address pool, as described in the earlier section, "Assigning Dynamic Addresses." You can then examine the DHCP leases file on the server (typically /var/lib/dhcp/dhcpd.leases) for information on the client's lease. This file should contain an entry like the following:

```
lease 192.168.1.50 {
  starts 4 2002/07/19 21:37:20;
  ends 4 2002/07/19 23:17:20;
  binding state active;
  next binding state free;
  hardware ethernet 00:50:56:82:01:03;
}
```

This shows the IP address assigned, the lease start and end time, and assorted other information, including the MAC (hardware ethernet) address—00:50:56:82:01:03 in this example. Of course, to use this method, you'll need to have some way of determining what IP address is associated with the new client. You may be able to spot this information on the client itself, or you may be able to deduce it from the lease times.

The Linux log file (usually /var/log/messages) may also contain the MAC address. Try the following command to search it for the most recent log entry from dhcpd:

```
# grep dhcpd /var/log/messages | tail -n 1
Jul 19 18:27:38 speaker dhcpd: DHCPACK on 192.168.1.50 to
00:50:56:82:01:03 via eth0
```

You'll need to issue this command as soon as the server has delivered an address to the client. If you're unsure of the IP address the client has received, you run the risk of getting the wrong address, particularly if some other client has obtained or renewed a lease just after your target system. If you know the client's IP address, you can double-check that you've obtained the correct MAC address by checking the IP address, as well. If they don't match, use a value higher than 1 for the -n parameter to tail in order to review earlier messages from dhcpd to find the correct entry.

Finally, whether you configure the client to use DHCP or give it a static IP address, you can use the arp command to determine its MAC address. Type this command, followed by the client's current IP address, on any Linux computer on your network:

```
# arp 192.168.1.50
Address          HWtype  HWaddress          Flags Mask   Iface
192.168.1.50     ether   00:50:56:82:01:03  C             eth0
```

You may need to initiate a data transfer to the client before you'll get a reading with arp, though. Using ping to send a single packet should do the job, as in **ping -c 1 192.168.1.50**.

DEFINING HOSTS VIA MAC ADDRESSES

To configure dhcpd to deliver a fixed IP address to a computer with a specific MAC address, you should first configure the server much as for a dynamic IP address setup. You can begin with Listing 5.1 as a template, and make the same sorts of changes you'd make for your network in any event, such as altering the DNS server and gateway addresses, or adding any global parameters you might need. You must then add one host declaration for each client that will receive a fixed address. These declarations may go within the subnet declaration or after it, and they look like this:

```
host teela {
    hardware ethernet 00:05:02:a7:76:da;
    fixed-address 192.168.1.2;
}
```

This declaration begins with the keyword host, then provides a hostname (without the domain name), although this hostname might or might not be passed on to the client, depending upon other parameters such as use-host-decl-names. Within the curly braces are two parameters. The first (hardware) lists the hardware type and MAC address to which this declaration applies. This example shows an Ethernet configuration, but you can specify token-ring if you have a Token Ring network. The second parameter (fixed-address) provides the IP address to be delivered to this client. Be sure this address is *outside* the range set by the range parameter in the subnet declaration as a whole, but *within* the specified network block. For instance, the preceding example (with an address of 192.168.1.2) is outside the range of 192.168.1.50–192.168.1.150 provided as the range for dynamic IP addresses in Listing 5.1, but within the 192.168.1.0/24 network block covered by the subnet declaration.

You can define as many specific clients as you like in this way, and you can mix clients using fixed IP addresses with clients using dynamic IP addresses. If you have both a range statement and one or more host declarations, any computer whose MAC address isn't explicitly listed in a host declaration will receive an IP address from the dynamic IP address range.

CUSTOMIZING CLIENT-SPECIFIC PARAMETERS

As noted earlier, multi-line declarations may contain parameters that apply only within the declaration. In fact, the hardware and fixed-address statements in the host declaration are both parameters. There are many other parameters you can specify for particular hosts. You can use the options described earlier, in the section "Setting Global Options." The option you're most likely to want to set on a per-computer basis is option host-name "*name*". This parameter sets the hostname provided to the client by the DHCP server. You might use this instead of get-lease-hostnames or use-host-decl-names if you want to override these options in certain specific cases, or if you only want to provide hostnames to some clients.

You can also apply options to specific groups of clients. One way to do this is to define separate subnets for each group, but this approach works best when the clients are isolated on separate physical or logical subnets. More generally, you can use the group declaration to create a group of identified hosts with some shared parameters. For instance, you might use something like the following:

```
group {
   get-lease-hostnames true;
   host teela {
      hardware ethernet 00:05:02:a7:76:da;
      fixed-address 192.168.1.2;
   }
   host nessus {
      hardware ethernet 00:50:BF:19:7E:99;
      fixed-address 192.168.1.3;
   }
}
group {
```

```
        use-host-decl-names true;
        host hindmost {
            hardware ethernet 00:50:56:81:01:03;
            fixed-address 192.168.1.4;
        }
        host louiswu {
            hardware ethernet 00:e0:98:71:60:c1;
            fixed-address 192.168.1.5;
        }
}
```

This example provides hostnames via DNS lookup for the first two clients (teela and nessus), and via the name used in the host declaration for the next two clients (hindmost and louiswu). You might use this feature in other ways as well, such as providing different boot files for different computers (using the filename and next-server parameters) or configuring certain computers with specific TCP/IP settings that optimize those systems' performance but that might degrade other computers' performance.

INTEGRATING WITH OTHER PROTOCOLS

Some types of DHCP options require that some other package exchange data with the DHCP server. Frequently, this is a matter of the DHCP client accepting and using additional information from the DHCP server. Other times, some other server must consult the DHCP server to help with its configuration. The preceding discussion has included an example in which the DHCP server uses another server to obtain information: The get-lease-hostnames parameter allows the DHCP server to set clients' hostnames based on a DNS server lookup of the IP address being assigned.

INCLUDING NETBIOS INFORMATION

NetBIOS, which serves as the underpinning for the Server Message Block (SMB)/Common Internet Filesystem (CIFS) file- and printer-sharing protocols described in Chapter 7, uses a series of structures and tools atop TCP/IP to do its job. You can configure a DHCP server to deliver information on some of these structures to Windows clients to help these systems operate most efficiently. Specifically, you can set the following dhcpd.conf parameters:

- **option netbios-name-servers *server-addresses***—Traditionally, NetBIOS has relied upon name resolution systems that are independent of those used by most TCP/IP clients. NetBIOS computers can use a broadcast model, in which computers send broadcasts on the local network to locate clients, or they can use name servers independent of the DNS name servers used by TCP/IP. These independent name servers are known as NetBIOS Name Service (NBNS) servers or Windows Internet Name Service (WINS) servers. You can give Windows clients the names of these servers with the `option netbios-name-servers` parameter. You'll usually list just one server here, although DHCP can deliver multiple WINS server addresses.

- **option netbios-node-type** *type-code*—This option is used in conjunction with the preceding one to tell clients whether to use broadcast name resolution or a WINS server. The *type-code* is a value that ranges from 1 to 8. Values of 1 and 2 mean to use broadcasts or a WINS server, respectively. Values of 4 and 8 mean to use both, with 4 causing the client to try broadcasts first and fall back on the WINS server, and 8 to use WINS first and fall back on broadcasts. Most networks that have WINS servers should use a *type-code* of 8, because this will reduce network broadcasts but provide the most reliable operation if the WINS server goes down or lacks data on a particular computer.

- **option netbios-dd-server** *server-address*—This option sets one of the more obscure aspects of NetBIOS networking: the address of the NetBIOS Datagram Distribution (NBDD) server. This server relays broadcasts to clients that might not otherwise receive them. Chances are you won't need to set this option.

- **option netbios-scope** *string*—NetBIOS *scope* refers to a group of computers across which a given NetBIOS name is known. Most NetBIOS systems leave their scopes unchanged, so any NetBIOS computer on a network can resolve the name of any other. If your network uses NetBIOS scopes, though, you may need to set this option (possibly in a `group` declaration).

It's often beneficial to set the first two of these options globally on a DHCP server that delivers IP addresses to Windows clients. (Linux's Samba package doesn't use the values delivered by DHCP, but its Windows clients may.) For instance, you might include the following two lines near the top of the `dhcpd.conf` file:

```
option netbios-name-servers 192.168.1.1;
option netbios-node-type 8;
```

To be sure that the Windows computers *use* this information, you should check the Use DHCP for WINS Resolution option in the TCP/IP Properties

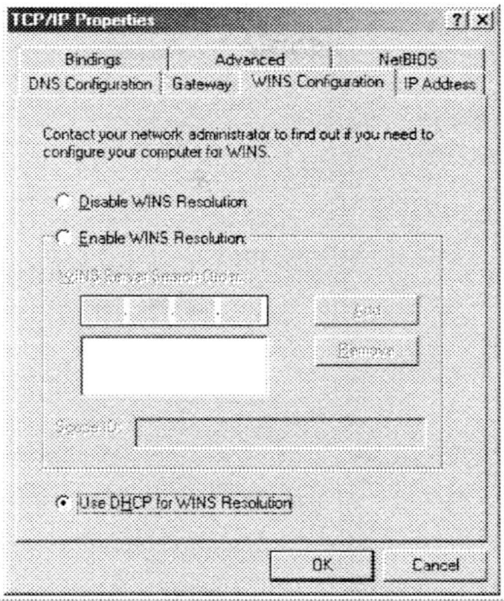

Figure 5.3 You must explicitly configure Windows clients to use NetBIOS-specific options provided by a DHCP server.

dialog box in Windows, as shown in Figure 5.3. If you select Disable WINS Resolution, the system won't use WINS at all, and if you select Enable WINS Resolution, you must manually enter the IP address of your WINS server.

COMMUNICATING WITH A DNS SERVER

If you want to be able to directly address a DHCP client from random systems, you have two choices: You can configure the DHCP server to give the client a fixed IP address, as described earlier in this chapter; or you can configure the DHCP server and the DNS server to communicate with one another, in order to update the DNS server's records to reflect the DHCP client's current address. This latter approach works best when the DHCP clients' addresses don't change very often, and when you're interested primarily in accessing the DHCP client from other systems on your local network. When Internet access is needed, a changing IP address may take some time to propagate through the Internet's DNS server collection, so there may be attempts to reach the computer at its old address for some time after that address has changed.

Prior to version 3.0, dhcpd included no explicit support for DNS updates. Version 3, though, implements two preliminary methods of DNS updates. Another is on track to become an Internet standard, and will be implemented in a future version of dhcpd, once the standard is finalized.

The two methods that are currently implemented are the *ad-hoc method* and the *interim method*.

Other update methods also exist, which are usually implemented by third-party packages. These tools monitor DHCP log files and then change the DNS server's configuration when the DHCP log files indicate important actions.

Dynamic DNS updates are enabled through the `ddns-update-style` parameter, which takes one of three values: `ad-hoc`, `interim`, or `none` (the last of these is the default). To use dynamic DNS, enable one of the first two values in the global section of the `dhcpd.conf` file—it won't work if you try to enable it for just some clients.

WARNING Both these methods of DNS updates rely upon the DNS server accepting the updates. This topic is covered in Chapter 18, Administering a Domain via DNS.

Using the Ad-Hoc Update Method

The ad-hoc method obtains a hostname for a client in one of four ways, in the following priority:

1. If a `host` declaration contains a `ddns-hostname` option, the value of that option is used.
2. If the client passes a fully-qualified domain name (FQDN—that is, a hostname complete with domain name portion), the DHCP server uses the hostname portion of the FQDN.
3. If the client passes a hostname without a domain name, the DHCP server uses it.
4. The name of the `host` declaration for the client may be used.

In all these cases, only the local hostname portion is used. If none of these methods yields a hostname, the DHCP server does *not* attempt to perform a DNS update for the client. If the DHCP server can find a hostname, the server combines the hostname with the value of the `ddns-domainname` option, if it's present, or with the `domain-name` option if there's no `ddns-domainname` option.

The DHCP server uses the FQDN it's derived to update the DNS server. It first updates the A record—the record that controls *forward lookups*, in which a user enters a hostname and obtains an IP address from that. If the A record change was successful, the DHCP server then updates the PTR record, which is used for *reverse lookups*, in which a user enters an IP address to obtain a hostname.

Using the Interim Update Method

The interim update method works much like the ad-hoc method in many ways, but it provides support for allowing the client to update the DNS server's A record, if the client makes this request. You may include the `allow client-updates` or `ignore client-updates` statements in the `dhcpd.conf` file to tell DHCP to allow clients to do this job themselves, or to ignore such requests, respectively. The default is to honor client requests on this matter.

If the DHCP server is configured to honor client DNS updates, then the DHCP server uses the FQDN provided by the client to perform PTR updates. If the DHCP server disallows this option, then the DHCP server constructs an FQDN from the client's hostname and the domain name set in `dhcpd.conf`, and uses this name to update both the A and PTR records.

When configured to disallow client-initiated DNS changes, the interim method creates results that are similar to those of the ad-hoc method. When the interim method permits client-initiated DNS changes, though, there's a difference: The client might specify a domain name that's something other than what the DHCP server is configured to use. For instance, suppose the DHCP server hands out hostnames in the `threeroomco.com` domain. Using the ad-hoc method, all clients that receive DNS updates will receive them in this domain, even if the client presents an FQDN in another domain. With the interim method configured to permit client updates, the client could claim a hostname of, say, `dino.pangaea.edu`. Assuming that this domain's DNS servers accept the update, the client could then be reached by this name. If your own DHCP and DNS servers interoperate fully, the PTR record for reverse lookups would also then return the name `dino.pangaea.edu` when asked about the name associated with the dynamically granted IP address for the client. Such a configuration isn't possible with the ad-hoc method. Whether or not it's a *desirable* configuration is something you'll have to decide for yourself. If your network connections are tightly controlled and your users are likely to need hostnames in foreign domains, such a configuration might be desirable. You might prefer to prevent such configurations if your network is relatively easy to access physically, though, because a reverse lookup of one of

Dynamic DNS Services

Some users of broadband Internet access, such as Digital Subscriber Line (DSL) and cable modems, receive dynamic IP addresses from their ISPs using DHCP or other protocols. If you're in this situation and want a fixed hostname for your computer, you probably won't be able to use the dynamic DNS features of DHCP and DNS on Linux, since what you really need to do is to interoperate with an Internet-accessible DNS server. The solution is to use one of many dynamic DNS *services* that are available for free or at low cost.

A dynamic DNS service operates its own DNS servers, which provide lookups on names on the Internet at large. Once you contract with such a service, you can use a client package on your computer to contact the provider's DNS server whenever your IP address changes. You can then have a fixed hostname (either within a domain owned by the dynamic DNS provider or within your own domain) that points to your dynamic IP address. Many dynamic DNS providers offer update software written in Perl or other common scripting languages, so most of them are Linux-compatible. You should check on this detail to be sure, though.

There are many dynamic DNS providers today. Indeed, there are a large number of *lists* of dynamic DNS providers. These include `http://www.technopagan.org/dynamic/`, `http://www.geocities.com/kiore_nz/`, and `http://dns.highsynth.com`. One of these lists should be able to point you to a dynamic DNS provider that suits your needs, if you don't operate your own externally accessible DNS server.

your IP addresses linked to a foreign domain might cause confusion or help a cracker mask illegal activities.

SUMMARY

DHCP can be a very important protocol for use on both small and large networks. By concentrating configuration details into a single server, you can greatly simplify the network configuration of client computers running just about any OS. The main cost is that the DHCP server itself requires configuration and maintenance—if it goes down or is misconfigured, clients on the network may not be able to operate correctly. You can configure a DHCP server to issue IP addresses from a pool, without regard to what computer receives a particular address, or on a fixed basis, in which a particular computer receives the same IP address time after time. The latter is probably the best configuration if you need to contact DHCP clients by name, but even dynamic IP addresses can be linked to hostnames by having the DHCP server and the domain's DNS server communicate with each other using features in version 3 of the Linux DHCP server.

Authenticating Users via Kerberos

Linux systems normally use localized authentication—that is, when a user types a username and password, the computer uses its own authentication database to decide whether to grant the user access. A further consequence of this system is that servers that require passwords for access, such as POP mail servers and FTP servers, require users to enter their passwords and send them over the network. This approach is sensible for isolated computers and for computers whose users don't have accounts on other systems on a network. When a group of users has accounts on many computers, though, maintaining those accounts can be tedious. Furthermore, with passwords flying across the network wires, often in an unencrypted form, the chance for a malicious individual to do damage by stealing passwords is substantial. These are the problems that Kerberos is intended to solve. This tool allows you to maintain a centralized user database. Individual computers defer to this centralized database when authenticating users, and use sophisticated encryption techniques to ensure that data transfers aren't subject to hijacking.

NOTE The name *Kerberos* is derived from Greek mythology; Kerberos was the three-headed dog who guarded the underworld. The Romans spelled the name *Cerberus*, but the Kerberos developers used the Greek spelling. Many Kerberos Web pages sport graphics of the three-headed dog of mythology.

To run a Kerberos server, it's important that you understand the basic principles upon which it's built, including the different versions of Kerberos and its needs. As with other network protocols, Kerberos uses both a client and a server. To do any good, you must be able to configure both, so this chapter covers both options.

Kerberos is an extremely complex protocol, and to use it fully you must configure not only a single Kerberos server, but many of your network's servers and clients. For this reason, this chapter only scratches the surface of Kerberos configuration. To do more than set up a fairly basic Kerberos system, you'll need to consult additional documentation, much of which is available from the main Kerberos Web site, `http://web.mit.edu/ kerberos/www/`. This page includes many links to official and unofficial Kerberos documentation and implementations of the protocol.

WHEN TO RUN A KERBEROS SERVER

Tools like firewalls (discussed in Chapter 25, Configuring `iptables`) are designed to protect a computer or network from the outside world, or to protect the outside world from miscreants inside a local network. Kerberos, on the other hand, is an *internal* security tool—it helps both servers and clients be sure that they're communicating with the proper systems and users, and to protect passwords so that they can't be stolen and abused by other local network users. (Kerberos can also improve external security by providing encryption to external users who need access to internal servers.) Simultaneously, Kerberos provides convenience—by centralizing the password database, Kerberos allows a user to log in to any workstation on a network and enter a login password only once, obviating the need to enter passwords for POP mail servers, FTP servers, and other local servers that would otherwise require passwords.

These features make Kerberos a very useful tool on mid-sized and large local networks, such as those operated by many colleges, universities, and corporations. Such networks frequently host mail servers, print servers, and the like internally, and allow users to log in to workstations at many locations. Rather than maintain a centralized computer system with terminals, users at these organizations use more powerful workstations. On such a network, maintaining individualized password databases is tedious at best, so Kerberos is a useful tool.

Kerberos is a cross-platform tool; Kerberos clients and servers can exist on Linux, other UNIX-like OSs, Windows, MacOS, or many other OSs. (Microsoft's own Kerberos implementation, though, is subtly incompatible

Centralized versus Distributed Computing

In the late 1960s through much of the 1980s, UNIX systems were generally intended to be used by several people simultaneously. These computers sat in machine rooms and were used via text-mode terminals or, later, X terminals that provided GUI access. As processing power became cheaper, a trend developed to place workstations on all users' desks. The modern x86 PC is a manifestation of this trend.

Today, most networks use a largely decentralized computing model, with workstations running Windows, MacOS, or occasionally Linux or some other UNIX variant. These computers may rely on network servers such as mail servers, file servers, print servers, and so on, but they do most of their processing locally. Such a network has a certain advantage in robustness, because if a server goes down, chances are the rest of the network will continue to operate. This distributed approach also means that all users can count on a certain minimum amount of processing power—whatever's available on the local workstation. In simple networks like this, users are often tied to specific computers, because they only have passwords on their own computers. This is one of the problems that Kerberos is intended to solve.

Today's x86 computers are far more powerful than the mainframes of just a couple of decades ago, and it's possible to use them in a centralized computing approach. A single powerful Linux system can run many users' programs. These users can sit at much less powerful systems that function only as terminals, using terminal software like that discussed in Chapters 13 (Maintaining Remote Login Servers) and 14 (Handling GUI Access with X and VNC Servers). Such an approach is vulnerable to problems with the central system, though; if it goes down, the rest of the network becomes useless. The centralized approach can be easier to administer, though, and it may obviate the need for user management software like Kerberos.

with the standard version. The MIT Kerberos page includes links to another implementation of Kerberos for Windows that is more compatible with the standard version.) Cross-platform compatibility can be an extremely important characteristic in many environments.

In most cases, the applications you use must include explicit Kerberos support to take advantage of the tool. For instance, your POP mail client and server must both support Kerberos authentication, or they'll continue using their own authentication methods. This chapter covers Kerberos configuration on Linux. This configuration can be used in conjunction with non-Linux systems, but I don't cover configuring Kerberos clients in Windows, MacOS, or other platforms.

UNDERSTANDING KERBEROS OPERATION

Effectively using Kerberos on your network requires you to install a Kerberos password server (more commonly called a *key distribution center*, or *KDC*) and add both client and server software that uses the KDC for authentication (these are often called *Kerberized applications*). Understanding the basics of the Kerberos protocols, including the interactions between these elements, is important for effective use of Kerberos on a network. This section therefore presents the basic principles of the protocol's operation, including information on various Kerberos products and requirements for a KDC.

BASIC PRINCIPLES OF KERBEROS OPERATION

Described in a single sentence, Kerberos is a centralized user authentication protocol that uses encryption to protect against various forms of attack. This description, however, is incomplete; Kerberos's encryption system is fairly complex so that it can meet various specific design goals. The structure of a Kerberos network also involves certain features that require some discussion.

Kerberos Network Elements

As already described, a Kerberos network is built around a KDC. This KDC is responsible for authenticating machines in a Kerberos *realm*. Typically, a realm corresponds to an Internet domain or subdomain. For instance, the threeroomco.com domain might contain a single Kerberos realm, which would probably be called THREEROOMCO.COM. Kerberos realm names are case-sensitive, unlike Internet domain names. The convention is to use all-uppercase letters for Kerberos realms simply to distinguish in writing between the functions of a realm and a domain, although the two may consist of the same set of computers. It's possible for a Kerberos realm to span less than an entire domain, or to include computers in multiple domains. If you want to use two separate Kerberos realms in a single domain, the common practice is to add a separate element to the start of the Kerberos realm names, such as REALM1.THREEROOMCO.COM and REALM2.THREEROOMCO.COM.

Kerberos works by assigning *tickets* for various services. Like an airline or movie theater ticket, a Kerberos ticket grants the holder access to something. As described shortly, there are two main types of ticket.

A *Kerberos server* is, as you might expect, a computer that runs the Kerberos server software, or the server software itself—in other words, the KDC. A *Kerberos client* is a computer or program that obtains a service ticket from the Kerberos server. Normally, this system is associated with a user who initiates a request to obtain service. The name for a computer that the Kerberos client is ultimately trying to use (say, a print server) is the *application server*.

Kerberos assigns tickets to *principals*, which as a first approximation are similar to users or server programs. Principals are described as three components: a *primary*, an *instance*, and a realm. These three components are expressed as `primary/instance@realm`. The primary is a username, in the case of a user requesting a ticket. If it's a computer that requests the ticket, the primary is the word `host`. A principal can also be associated with a specific server, in which case the primary is usually the server name, such as `ftp`. The instance is optional, and is used to create separate entries for a single primary for different purposes. For instance, the user `fluffy` might have a regular principal for ordinary use, but another principal that uses the `admin` instance for administering the realm. If the realm is `THREEROOMCO.COM`, these two principals would be expressed as `fluffy@THREEROOMCO.COM` and `fluffy/admin@THREEROOMCO.COM`.

Kerberos Design Goals and Operation

In order to better understand why Kerberos does things the way it does, it's helpful to look at the Kerberos design goals. These include the following:

- **Provide network authentication**—Servers must be able to authenticate the identities of users attempting to use their services to prevent unauthorized access to servers. As important in many environments, but less obvious, the clients must be able to verify the identifies of the servers they use to prevent one system from pretending to be a server and thus intercepting print jobs, e-mail, or other potentially sensitive data. This is Kerberos's *raison d'etre*.

- **Protect passwords**—Many services, as described in various chapters of this book, use unencrypted passwords by default. This is a security liability, because these passwords can be intercepted, thus compromising the network's security. Some protocols encrypt passwords to avoid this problem, but Kerberos uses an unusual approach: Rather than send passwords in an encrypted form, it uses the password as an encryption key for transmitting data required for Kerberos's operation. Thus, the password isn't transmitted, but only a user with the correct password can use the data.

- **Allow single-login operation**—Kerberos allows users to enter passwords once, when they log in to their computers. Subsequent transfers using Kerberized applications don't require password entry. For instance, you need not reenter your password when you retrieve e-mail using a Kerberized pull mail server or log in to another computer using a Kerberized remote login server. (Of course, if you access a system outside of your local Kerberos network, this benefit won't extend to the remote systems.) The tickets you get when you enter a password are time-limited, though, so you may need to periodically reenter your password if you use the system for a long time. You won't need to reenter the password when you use new servers or reuse old ones within the lifetime of the tickets.

NOTE Many applications that use passwords to access remote servers provide the user with the option of saving the password. This is common in pull mail clients, for instance. (Chapter 11, Pull Mail Protocols: POP and IMAP, covers these protocols.) When a password is saved in this way, the user doesn't need to reenter it; however, saving the password to disk is a security risk in the event of a break-in of the workstation. Furthermore, if the user changes a password, it may have to be changed in several programs, which can be a nuisance. Kerberos eliminates both problems.

Kerberos was also designed to meet various technical requirements that are partly dependent upon design details of the system, but the preceding three are the main requirements from a user's or administrator's point of view. To achieve these goals, Kerberos relies upon its tickets. The process works something like this:

1. A user at a workstation wants to use a service, and so enters a username and password.

2. The workstation (a Kerberos client) sends the username to the KDC with a request to obtain a *ticket-granting ticket (TGT)*. This request is processed by a particular Kerberos subset known as the *ticket-granting service (TGS)*.

3. The KDC checks for the username in its database. If the username is present, the KDC responds with a TGT. This ticket includes information such as the username for which the TGT is useful, the time the TGT was issued, and the time span over which the TGT is valid. The KDC uses the password in the username database to encrypt the TGT, and sends it back to the client.

4. The client receives the TGT, and attempts to decrypt the TGT with the password the user entered. If this process is successful, the client holds onto the ticket, transparent to the user.

5. The client sends a request to obtain a ticket for a specific server to the KDC, using data extracted from the TGT. The KDC recognizes this data as valid (because it's been successfully decrypted and then reencrypted) and replies by sending a ticket for the server. This ticket is encrypted with the *target server's* password (which is known only to the server and the KDC), and includes information such as the username of the person making the request, the name of the service being requested, a time stamp, a time period for which the ticket is valid, and a *session key*, which is another password created by the KDC and shared with the server and client. This ticket's lifetime is short to reduce the risk of its being intercepted and abused.

6. The client receives the service ticket, which it holds, transparent to the user. (The client doesn't attempt to decrypt this ticket.)

7. The client sends the service ticket to the server in question, requesting a data transfer session.

8. The server decrypts the ticket with its password; this will work properly if and only if the ticket was properly encrypted by the KDC. If the request is in order (it decrypted properly, it's from a valid user, and so on), the server uses the session key to encrypt a reply to the client.

9. The client receives the server's reply. If and only if this reply is valid, the client can assume that the server is authentic, so the client completes the connection and begins its data transfer only if it receives the correct reply from the server.

From here, the data transfer proceeds more-or-less as it would without Kerberos in the picture, although some Kerberized applications support data encryption features that are unavailable to their non-Kerberized counterparts. Eventually, the TGT and server tickets will expire, but the expiration times are set to long enough values (several hours) that this seldom poses a problem for individual users. If a ticket does expire, it can be renewed.

WARNING

The preceding procedure uses time stamps in several exchanges. If computers' clocks are set to different times, these time stamps may cause a transaction to fail, or may reduce the security on the network. It's therefore extremely important that all computers on a Kerberos network be set to the same time. You can accomplish this goal by running a Network Time Protocol (NTP) server on all computers, as described in Chapter 10, Maintaining Consistent Time: Time Servers.

REQUIREMENTS FOR THE KERBEROS SERVER

This design has several consequences. Most importantly, the KDC is an *extremely* sensitive system, from a network security point of view. The KDC should run as few other network servers as possible (normally only those required to administer it—ideally none), it should have no ordinary users except for its administrators, you should pay particular care to keeping its software up to date, and it should be physically secure. Because use of many network services depends upon the KDC, you should be prepared with contingency plans in case it fails. Keep backups of the KDC's data and have backup hardware ready in case of failure. You might even want to maintain a *slave* or *backup KDC*, which pulls its configuration from the *master* KDC, so that the slave can take over KDC functions in case of a failure of the master KDC.

The hardware requirements of the KDC depend upon the size of your network, both in terms of the number of computers and the number of users. A KDC for a small network of a few dozen systems might require what is by today's standards a very low-end computer—after all, such a system would need to field only a few requests every hour. A system with a low-end Pentium CPU, 32MB of RAM, and a hard disk of a few hundred megabytes should be more than sufficient. A KDC for a network with hundreds or thousands of computers might require more computing power, particularly in terms of CPU power and network connectivity. In any event, you should ensure that the KDC is placed somewhere on your network topology that ensures maximum reliability and minimum data transit times. If your network is large enough and segmented in such a way as to make it likely that sections of it may become isolated from each other, you may want to place slave KDCs in each segment to minimize disruption in case of a break in network routing.

KERBEROS VERSIONS AND VARIANTS

The main Kerberos package is available from `http://web.mit.edu/kerberos/www/`. This site hosts Kerberos source code and binary releases for a few platforms, but not for Linux as of Kerberos V5 Release 1.2.1. You can also obtain the older Kerberos V4 from this official site and versions of the software for Windows and MacOS (both the older MacOS Classic and the newer MacOS X). All other things being equal, Kerberos V5 is superior to Kerberos V4; V5 adds a few features and fixes bugs in V4.

The Kerberos license is similar to that of X, and so various open source and commercial variants of the original MIT code have emerged. One of these is distributed by the Royal Institute of Technology in Sweden, and is available from their Web page, http://www.pdc.kth.se/kth-krb/. This variant is known as eBones, but package filenames typically begin with the string krb4. The eBones Web site officially distributes only source code, but the FTP site includes a binaries subdirectory with some contributed binary packages, including directories for Linux. These may be out of date, though. Indeed, eBones itself is based on the Kerberos V4 release, at least as of eBones version 1.1.

The Center for Parallel Computers has developed a Kerberos implementation known as Heimdal, headquartered at http://www.pdc.kth.se/heimdal/. This variant is based on MIT's Kerberos V5. You can obtain both source code and compiled Linux executables from the Web site, including RPMs for Red Hat, although the binary versions may lag behind the latest (currently 0.4e).

Some Linux distributions now ship with Kerberos support. In particular, Debian 2.2 ships with both eBones and Heimdal, Mandrake 8.1 ships with Kerberos V5, Red Hat 7.2 ships with Kerberos V5, and SuSE 7.3 ships with Heimdal. Caldera 3.1, Slackware 8.0, and TurboLinux 7.0 do not ship with Kerberos support, but you can add packages by compiling the source, or possibly by installing a package intended for another distribution.

NOTE Subsequent sections of this chapter describe MIT's Kerberos V5. Kerberos V4 differs in some important configuration details, and even V5 derivatives like Heimdal may not work precisely as described here. In writing this chapter, I used both Red Hat's Kerberos V5 packages and builds of the original MIT source code as references.

SETTING UP A KERBEROS SERVER

The core of a Kerberized network is the Kerberos server—the KDC. As with most Linux servers, it's configured through a plain-text configuration file stored in /etc. Understanding this file's format allows you to control the Kerberos server, and thus to exercise some control over other systems on the network. This chapter cannot present details of every aspect of Kerberos operation, but this section does describe the basics of configuring the server. Subsequent sections discuss configuring Kerberos clients and application servers.

NOTE Some of the configuration steps described in this section must also be performed on Kerberos clients and Kerberos application servers. For instance, you must set up realms in the same way on all systems (described shortly in "Setting Up a Realm").

The Kerberos package must be installed on the KDC, of course. If you obtain the MIT source code, you can compile and install it in the usual way, by using a script called configure included in the package, followed by the commands **make** and **make install**. This will install the Kerberos server, Kerberos application servers, and Kerberos clients. I recommend you use the --enable-shared option to configure; this compiles Kerberos libraries in a shared form, which reduces the size of individual Kerberos programs. Some third-party Kerberos packages rely on such a configuration. Binary packages may break Kerberos components up into separate package files. For instance, Red Hat's Kerberos distribution includes packages called krb5-libs, krb5-server, and krb5-workstation. You can fine-tune your installation by omitting unnecessary packages.

MODIFYING SERVER CONFIGURATION FILES

The main Kerberos server configuration file is /etc/krb5.conf. This file consists of sections, each of which is headed by a keyword in square brackets ([]). Subsequent lines, up until the next heading, define features related to that heading. Listing 6.1 shows a sample krb5.conf file for a KDC.

Listing 6.1   Sample krb5.conf File

```
[logging]
 default = FILE:/var/log/krb5libs.log
 kdc = FILE:/var/log/krb5kdc.log
 admin_server = FILE:/var/log/kadmind.log

[libdefaults]
 ticket_lifetime = 24000
 default_realm = THREEROOMCO.COM
 dns_lookup_realm = false
 dns_lookup_kdc = false

[realms]
 THREEROOMCO.COM = {
  kdc = kerberos.threeroomco.com:88
  kdc = kerberos-1.threeroomco.com:88
  kdc = kerberos-2.threeroomco.com:88
  admin_server = kerberos.threeroomco.com:749
  default_domain = threeroomco.com
 }

[domain_realm]
 .threeroomco.com = THREEROOMCO.COM
 threeroomco.com = THREEROOMCO.COM
 outsider.threeroomco.com = PANGAEA.EDU

[kdc]
   profile = /var/kerberos/krb5kdc/kdc.conf
```

Within each section, each line consists of a variable name, an equal sign (=), and the value assigned to the variable. Some sections include subsections, indicated by curly braces ({}). For instance, the [realms] section of Listing 6.1 uses curly braces to identify the lines associated with the THREEROOMCO.COM realm. This allows you to create a file that supports multiple realms.

NOTE Kerberos application servers and clients need most of the same sections in krb.conf as does the KDC, but you can omit the [logging] and [kdc] sections from these systems. Some specific programs may require their own settings. These frequently go in a section called [appdefaults].

The KDC also uses its own configuration file, kdc.conf, which is often stored in /var/kerberos/kdc5krb, /usr/local/var/kdc5krb or a similar location, specified in the [kdc] section of krb5.conf. This file contains information specific to the KDC, as opposed to the krb5.conf file, which is used by the KDC, Kerberos clients, and Kerberos application servers. The format of the kdc.conf file is similar to that of krb5.conf.

SETTING UP A REALM

The usual way to configure a realm entails making certain realm-specific entries in the krb5.conf and kdc.conf files. In the case of the former file, you make these changes on the KDC, the application servers, and the clients. You then restart the Kerberos server and application server programs to initiate the changes.

Changing krb5.conf

The krb5.conf file contains a [realms] section that specifies the KDC and its slaves. There's also a [domain_realm] section that defines the relationship between the realm and an Internet domain. Listing 6.1 shows examples of both sections.

The [realms] section in this example specifies the master KDC and two slave KDCs for the THREEROOMCO.COM realm. These servers are conventionally called kerberos and kerberos-*n*, where *n* is a number signifying the slave number, within the domain corresponding to the realm. Although in this example the domain and realm have the same name (aside from case), this need not always be true, as noted earlier. Each of the KDC specifications includes the port number on which the KDC listens for connections—

normally 88. The `admin_server` entry specifies a computer that's used to administer the realm. This is often the same as the KDC, but the administrative functions use a different port—normally 749. The `default_domain` entry specifies the domain name associated with Kerberos principals. The default is the Kerberos realm name converted to lowercase, so in this example this entry isn't strictly necessary.

It's possible to specify multiple realms with a single `krb5.conf` file. To do so, you include a single `[realms]` section, but list multiple realm names, each of which contains its specifics within its own set of curly braces (`{}`).

TIP

When configuring a DNS server to handle your domain, you may want to use a CNAME entry to specify the KDC hostnames as listed in the `krb5.conf` file and elsewhere. This way, you can quickly and easily change the computer that functions as the KDC in the event of network problems or restructuring, without modifying numerous Kerberos configuration files scattered throughout the realm. Another option is to use virtual IP addresses—one system using Network Address Translation (NAT; see Chapter 25) is listed in the DNS server as the KDC, but it forwards its requests to another computer, which actually runs the KDC software. Thus, you can easily move KDC functions from one computer to another without adjusting your DNS entries.

The `[domain_realm]` section maps computers into specific Kerberos realms based on their hostnames or domain names. The format lists a hostname or domain name (the latter indicated by a leading period, as in `.threeroomco. com`) followed by an equal sign and the Kerberos realm to which the machine or machines belong. Listing 6.1 maps all computers in the `threeroomco.com` domain (including any computer known only as `threeroomco.com`) to the `THREEROOMCO.COM` realm, with one exception: `outsider.threeroomco.com` belongs to the `PANGAEA.EDU` domain.

Changing `kdc.conf`

The `kdc.conf` file contains entries that are similar to those in `krb5.conf`. Listing 6.2 shows an example `kdc.conf` file. You'll have to make realm-specific changes in the `[realms]` section. Most importantly, you need to change the name of the realm (`EXAMPLE.COM` in many default configuration files). The `[realms]` section also contains entries that set the types of encryption keys the realm supports, but you shouldn't change these unless you fully understand the consequences. The `[kcdefaults]` section points the server to various important configuration files.

Listing 6.2   Sample kdc.conf File

```
[kdcdefaults]
  acl_file = /var/kerberos/krb5kdc/kadm5.acl
  dict_file = /usr/share/dict/words
  admin_keytab = /var/kerberos/krb5kdc/kadm5.keytab

[realms]
  THREEROOMCO.COM = {
    master_key_type = des-cbc-crc
    supported_enctypes = des-cbc-crc:normal des3-cbc-raw:normal \
des3-cbc-sha1:normal des-cbc-crc:v4 des-cbc-crc:afs3
  }
```

CREATING A MASTER KEY

Kerberos relies on a *master key* to control access to itself. This key is essentially a password, and it may be stored locally in a *stash file*, which is a file that the server reads to allow itself to start up automatically. Without the stash file, the server requires manual intervention at startup—somebody must type in the master key.

Because of its critical nature, the stash file should be stored *only* on a disk that's local to the KDC, and be readable only by root. You shouldn't back up this file unless the backup is very closely guarded. You should apply the usual rules for selection of a master key that you use for any password—it shouldn't be a dictionary word, name, or be derived from personal data that an attacker might gain from public sources. You should use a mixed-case string of letters, numbers, and punctuation that's as close to random as you can make it and still remember it. A good starting point is an acronym based on some phrase you can remember, such as *yiwttd* for *yesterday I went to the dentist*. Randomly change the case of some letters and add punctuation and numbers. The result might be *yi9Wt%Td*.

To create a master key and store it in a stash file, use the kdb5_util command:

```
# kdb5_util create -r THREEROOMCO.COM -s
Initializing database '/var/kerberos/krb5kdc/principal' for realm
'THREEROOMCO.COM',
master key name 'K/M@THREEROOMCO.COM'
You will be prompted for the database Master Password.
It is important that you NOT FORGET this password.
Enter KDC database master key:
Re-enter KDC database master key to verify:
```

147

This command creates or initializes several files in the /var/kerberos/ krb5kdc directory, or some other location a given Kerberos package uses for this purpose, such as /usr/local/var/krb5kdc. These files include:

- The stash file, which may be called .k5.*REALM.NAME*, where *REALM.NAME* is the realm name; or .k5stash.
- Two Kerberos database files, principal and principal.ok. (The principal file is called principal.db on some systems.)
- Two Kerberos administrative files, principal.kadm5 and principal. kadm5.lock.

If you don't want to use a stash file, you can omit the -s from the kdb5_util command; this will cause the program to *not* create the stash file. You'll then need to enter the Kerberos master key whenever you start the server.

ADMINISTERING A REALM

Once you've modified the Kerberos configuration files for your realm and used kdb5_util to create a master key and initialize the Kerberos databases, you can begin administering the realm. This process is essentially one of defining principals, including some that have administrative privileges to add other principals.

Defining Basic ACLs

Kerberos principal information is stored in the form of Access Control Lists (ACLs), which are stored in the file pointed to by the acl_file entry in kdc.conf. This file consists of lines with the following format:

Kerberos principal   *Permissions*   *Target principal*

Table 6.1 Permission Codes for the ACL File

Code	Meaning
a	Allows the addition of principals or policies
A	Forbids the addition of principals or policies
d	Allows the deletion of principals or policies
D	Forbids the deletion of principals or policies
m	Allows the modification of principals or policies
M	Forbids the modification of principals or policies
c	Allows changing passwords for principals
C	Forbids changing passwords for principals
i	Allows inquiries into the database
I	Forbids inquiries into the database
l	Allows the listing of principals or policies in the database
L	Forbids the listing of principals or policies in the database
x or *	Wildcard for all "allows" ACLs (admcil)

The first entry (`Kerberos principal`) is a principal name, as described earlier. You can use an asterisk (*) as a wildcard in part of the principal name to match anything. For instance, you might use */admin@THREEROOMCO.COM to match any primary with an instance of admin in the THREEROOMCO.COM domain. Such a definition is useful to grant administrators uniform access to the KDC.

The second entry (`Permissions`) is a code for the ACLs granted to the principal. Each type of permission is signified by a single-letter code, as shown in Table 6.1. You can merge multiple codes to grant multiple types of access, as in `ali` to allow a principal to add users, list principals, or make inquiries of the database.

The final entry (`Target principal`) is optional, and provides the names of principals to which the preceding permissions apply. For instance, you might want to limit a given user's ability to access or modify rights for particular principals. As with the `Kerberos principal`, the `Target principal` may use an asterisk as a wildcard.

As an example, consider the following entry:

```
*/admin@THREEROOMCO.COM     *
```

This entry gives all principals in the admin instance full access to the Kerberos database. An entry similar to this is the default. As a starting point, you may want to modify it to point to your realm and otherwise leave it alone.

Creating Principals

You use the kadmin or kadmin.local programs to administer your Kerberos user database. The former program uses encrypted Kerberos communications to administer a KDC from a remote system; the latter modifies the local database files directly, without using network tools. You must use kadmin.local to add at least one administrative user. Thereafter, you can theoretically use kadmin from other systems in much the same way, although of course you must have appropriate Kerberos administrative servers running on the KDC, which at this point in the process they are not.

Both programs accept various parameters to modify the principal name with which you attempt to modify the database, the realm you attempt to administer, and so on. The kadmin man page provides details on these. Once you've started the program, you enter commands at its prompt. For instance, to add the principal admin/admin@THREEROOMCO.COM, you would use the addprinc command, as follows:

```
# kadmin.local
Authenticating as principal root/admin@THREEROOMCO.COM with password.
kadmin.local:  addprinc admin/admin@THREEROOMCO.COM
WARNING: no policy specified for admin/admin@THREEROOMCO.COM;
defaulting to no policy
Enter password for principal "admin/admin@THREEROOMCO.COM":
Re-enter password for principal "admin/admin@THREEROOMCO.COM":
Principal "admin/admin@THREEROOMCO.COM" created.
```

NOTE As usual when entering passwords, they don't echo to the screen, but you must type them. You should not reuse the Kerberos master key as an administrative password, or for that matter use either of these as any other password.

After you've created an administrative principal, you must create a *keytab* for the administrative principal. This is a key that Kerberos uses to decrypt administrative tickets. You don't need to specify this key yourself; Kerberos can generate it. You do need to tell Kerberos to do so, though, using the ktadd command within kadmin.local:

```
kadmin.local:  ktadd -k /var/kerberos/krb5kdc/kadm5.keytab \
kadmin/admin kadmin/changepw
```

You specify the file in which the keytab is stored by preceding the filename with -k. This file should match the one specified in the kdc.conf file's admin_keytab entry. You then list the principals for which you want to add keytabs—kadmin/admin and kadmin/changepw in this case. (These two principals are a standard part of Kerberos; you don't need to explicitly create them.)

In addition to these administrative principals, you should add principals for your users, application servers, and KDCs. You do this with the addprinc command, which works much as described earlier. For instance, suppose you want to add a principal for fluffy@THREEROOMCO.COM. You might enter:

kadmin.local: **addprinc fluffy@THREEROOMCO.COM**

For servers, you may want to use the -randkey option, which tells the system to use a randomized key for this principal. If you don't use this option, you'll be prompted to enter a password. There are many other options you can use as well; the kadmin man page explains them.

Application server entries are added in the same way, but they're typically called *service*/*hostname*@*REALM.NAME*, where *service* is the service name (such as pop or ftp), *hostname* is the hostname, and *REALM.NAME* is the realm name. You also need one entry in which *service* is host. In addition, you must extract the host's keytab with the ktadd command, as described earlier. Extract each keytab into a unique file (that is, use a different parameter to -k for each host). You'll subsequently move this file to the application server itself. Alternatively, you can later use kadmin from the computer that hosts the application server to create a principal for the server, and use ktadd to extract the keytab directly on the application server computer.

You may want to add a principal for each KDC. These principals are generally of the form host/*host.name*@*REALM.NAME*, such as host/kerberos-1. threeroomco.com/THREEROOMCO.COM. Although these aren't strictly required in slave KDCs, they can be helpful if ordinary users will be logging into the KDC (which is generally not recommended) or if you need to swap in a slave KDC in place of a master KDC. The master KDC requires this principal in order to propagate its database to slave KDCs.

When you're done with kadmin, you can exit from the program by typing **quit** at its main prompt.

STARTING THE KDC

At this point, Kerberos is configured enough to start it. You can do so through the methods described in Chapter 4, Starting Servers. If your

Kerberos package was built for your distribution or a sufficiently similar one, it should come with one or more SysV startup scripts, such as krb5kdc for the KDC and kadmin for the administrative server.

If you don't have SysV startup scripts, you can start the KDC processes by running the krb5kdc and kadmin programs that came with the package. Each program should fork from the shell, so you don't need to follow their names with ampersands (&). You can run these programs from startup scripts such as /etc/rc.d/rc.local.

CONFIGURING A SLAVE KDC

Slave KDCs are configured in much the same way as master KDCs. In particular, you should set up the krb5.conf and kdc.conf files just as you do for a master KDC, use kdb5_util to create database files, set up an ACL file, and use the ktadd command in kadmin.local to extract a keytab file.

Each KDC requires a file that lists all the KDCs (or more precisely, the principals associated with those KDCs) for database propagation purposes. This file is called kpropd.acl, and it's stored in /var/kerberos/krb5kdc, /usr/local/var/krb5kdc, or a similar location. This file might resemble the following:

```
host/kerberos.threeroomco.com@THREEROOMCO.COM
host/kerberos-1.threeroomco.com@THREEROOMCO.COM
```

Once you've configured this file on all your KDCs, you must set up the slave KDCs to run a pair of servers, kpropd and klogind. You can do this by modifying your super server to run them. For instance, appropriate /etc/inetd.conf entries look like this:

```
krb5_prop stream tcp nowait root /usr/kerberos/sbin/kpropd kpropd
eklogin   stream tcp nowait root /usr/kerberos/sbin/klogind \
klogind -k -c -e
```

You may need to change the location of the executable files, and of course if you use xinetd, you'll need to create an appropriate xinetd configuration instead. (Chapter 4 covers both super servers.) If your /etc/services file doesn't include entries for krb5_prop and eklogin, you must add them. These entries look like this:

```
krb5_prop      754/tcp         # Kerberos slave propagation
eklogin        2105/tcp        # Kerberos encrypted rlogin
```

The propagation is handled on the master KDC. It involves two steps: dumping the database and sending it to slaves. A script that handles both tasks appears in Listing 6.3—but you'll have to make appropriate changes for your own network, as well as your own installation (such as the location of the dump file). If your network uses more than one slave, you'll need a separate kprop call for each slave, or you can write a script that uses a loop to propagate the dump to each slave. You can call this script from a cron job to have it run automatically at whatever interval is appropriate for your network.

Listing 6.3   Sample Script for Propagating a Kerberos Database to Slave KDCs

```
#!/bin/sh
/usr/kerberos/sbin/kdb5_util dump
/usr/kerberos/var/krb5kdc/slave_datatrans
/usr/kerberos/sbin/kprop -f
/usr/kerberos/var/krb5kdc/slave_datatrans \
    kerberos-1.mil.threeroomco.com
```

CONFIGURING A KERBEROS APPLICATION SERVER

Configuring the KDC is an important step toward using Kerberos, but a KDC by itself isn't very useful. Indeed, it isn't even half of what's needed; you must configure both Kerberos application servers and Kerberos clients to use the KDC. This section covers the first of these topics, and the next ("Configuring a Kerberos Client") covers the second.

NOTE   In some cases, a single computer may function as both a Kerberos application server and a Kerberos client. For instance, this might happen when you use Kerberos as a login authentication protocol. In such cases, you must configure the computer in both ways (as an application server and as a Kerberos client).

CONFIGURING KERBEROS

Kerberos on an application server needs some of the same configuration as on a KDC. In particular, the [realms] and [domain_realm] sections of krb5.conf need to be adjusted to reflect your realm configuration, as described earlier. In addition, you need a keytab file for the application server. This file should contain keys for the host itself (host/

hostname@REALM.NAME) and for each Kerberized server you intend to run on the system (for instance, telnet/*hostname@REALM.NAME* if you intend to run a Kerberized Telnet server). You can create a keytab file on the KDC, as described earlier, using the kadmin.local program. Specifically, you use the addprinc command to add principals for the host, then extract the keys for these principals to a keytab file. For instance, you might issue commands like the following:

```
kadmin.local:  addprinc \
host/gingko.threeroomco.com@THREEROOMCO.COM
kadmin.local:  addprinc \
telnet/gingko.threeroom.com@THREEROOMCO.COM
kadmin.local:  ktadd -k gingko.keytab host/gingko.threeroomco.com \
telnet/gingko.threeroomco.com
```

You should then move the file that results from the final command, gingko.keytab, from the KDC to the application server system, and call that file /etc/krb5.keytab. This file is extremely sensitive, so be sure to move it via a secure method, such as by floppy disk or scp. Once on its destination system, you should delete the original from the KDC and ensure that the file on the application server is readable only by root. Alternatively, you may use kadmin on the application server to create the file locally. Omit the -k gingko.keytab option to the ktadd command, and the system should generate the file in the correct location. This will only work if the KDC's remote administration facilities are correctly configured and running and the application server's basic Kerberos configuration (its realm, for instance) is set correctly.

RUNNING KERBERIZED SERVERS

Standard Kerberos packages ship with some Kerberized servers and local authentication tools, such as variants on Telnet, FTP, shell, exec, and login. You can use these servers by replacing their non-Kerberized equivalents with these more secure versions. For instance, if your system uses inetd, you would replace any entries in /etc/inetd.conf for these services with whichever of the following are appropriate:

```
klogin  stream  tcp  nowait  root  /usr/kerberos/sbin/klogind \
klogind -k -c
eklogin stream  tcp  nowait  root  /usr/kerberos/sbin/klogind \
klogind -k -c -e
kshell  stream  tcp  nowait  root  /usr/kerberos/sbin/kshd kshd -k \
-c -A
```

```
ftp     stream tcp  nowait  root  /usr/kerberos/sbin/ftpd ftpd -a
telnet  stream tcp  nowait  root  /usr/kerberos/sbin/telnetd \
telnetd -a valid
```

Other servers are available in Kerberized forms, as well; the ones included with the Kerberos distribution are just a start. You should consult the documentation for third-party servers to determine precisely what they allow you to do.

CONFIGURING A KERBEROS CLIENT

The first step to using Kerberos as a user is to create a Kerberos principal for that user. This process was described earlier, in the section "Creating Principals." User principals usually take the form *username@REALM.NAME*, and they're created using the kadmin or kadmin.local utilities. Once you've created a user principal, the user may access Kerberos servers using matched Kerberos-enabled clients. This means you must install these clients and make them accessible to users. You can install clients by installing the entire Kerberos package, or sometimes just by installing a Kerberos base or library package along with a Kerberos workstation or clients package. Users may also need to use some Kerberos housekeeping utilities to obtain and manage TGTs. If you want to use Kerberos to control user logins to individual workstations, you need to modify the usual login authentication tools on the workstations.

ACCESSING KERBEROS SERVERS

In broad strokes, users may access Kerberos application servers by running an appropriate client program. Unfortunately, the reality is a bit more complex than this simple explanation implies. For one thing, there are several user-level utilities that come into play—users must have some way to obtain a TGT, and must be able to perform routine maintenance such as changing their Kerberos passwords. Second, the Kerberized clients themselves sometimes pose unique challenges. For instance, many require options to enable critical Kerberos features; without these options, the Kerberized clients may behave like ordinary non-Kerberized clients.

Using Kerberos Network Utilities

The Kerberos package includes a number of utilities that manage Kerberos passwords and tickets, including the all-important ticket-granting ticket (TGT). The most important of these tools are the following:

- **kinit**—This program obtains a TGT. You can think of it as a program that "logs you into" a Kerberos realm; before running `kinit` (or using equivalent functionality, as described in the upcoming section, "Using Kerberos for User Logins"), you can't use any Kerberos client. When you run `kinit`, the program contacts the KDC to obtain a TGT. Thereafter, Kerberized applications use the TGT to obtain authorization to use Kerberos application servers, as described earlier in this chapter. When you run `kinit`, you'll be asked for a password. By default, `kinit` uses your username as the primary of the principal, in the default realm. You can override this behavior by appending the principal name to the command, as in **kinit minerva@PANGAEA.EDU**. The program also accepts several other options that modify its behavior. Consult the `kinit` man page for details.

- **klist**—This program lists the tickets (including the TGT) that you currently have, including some information such as their expiration dates. Before running `kinit`, `klist` will show no tickets.

- **kpasswd**—This program doesn't help manage a single Kerberos session; instead, it's used to change the password for a principal in the Kerberos database. It's the Kerberos equivalent of `passwd`, and works in much the same way. You must have a TGT to use `kpasswd`.

- **kdestroy**—This program destroys all the tickets in a given user's ticket cache. You'd normally run this program just prior to logging off the computer, or when you know you won't be using Kerberized servers in the near future. Although Kerberos tickets expire if unused for a while, it's best to destroy them after they've served their purpose, since this reduces the risk that they might be abused in the event of a security breach.

TIP

You might want to add a call to `kdestroy` to all users' `.logout` files, to the ends of their `.xinitrc` files, or to other standard files such that the program will run when the user logs out. If you use a Kerberos PAM module, as described later in this chapter, this functionality may be handled automatically.

How do these tools work, in practice? Most sessions will use just the `kinit` and `kdestroy` programs at the beginning and end of the session, respectively. You can use the `klist` utility to see what happens with tickets, though. For instance, consider the following exchange:

```
$ kinit
Password for fluffy@THREEROOMCO.COM:
```

```
$ klist
Ticket cache: FILE:/tmp/krb5cc_500
Default principal: fluffy@THREEROOMCO.COM

Valid starting     Expires            Service principal
10/09/02 14:38:57  10/10/02 00:38:57  krbtgt/THREEROOMCO.COM@\
                                      THREEROOMCO.COM


Kerberos 4 ticket cache: /tmp/tkt500
klist: You have no tickets cached
$ kpasswd
Password for fluffy@THREEROOMCO.COM:
Enter new password:
Enter it again:
Password changed.
$ kdestroy
$ klist
klist: No credentials cache file found (ticket cache
FILE:/tmp/krb5cc_500)


Kerberos 4 ticket cache: /tmp/tkt500
klist: You have no tickets cached
```

The initial kinit command retrieved the TGT, which appears as the krbtgt service in the subsequent call to klist. As you can see from the start and expiration times, this ticket is good for ten hours (a figure that can be adjusted on a system-by-system basis). If a Kerberized client were used and klist run again, another ticket would appear for that service. Changing a password with kpasswd requires entering the original password as a precaution, then entering the new password twice. As with the password entry with kinit, none of the passwords echo to the screen. After running kdestroy, all the tickets are cleared.

Using Kerberized Clients

Kerberos client programs work much like their conventional equivalents. In most cases, you type the program name followed by the name of the server to which you want to connect. Unfortunately, many require additional parameters to take full advantage of the features of Kerberos. For instance, the telnet client requires extra parameters to obviate the need to enter a username and password when you log in. Examples of Kerberized clients, and some of their quirks, include the following:

- **telnet**—The `telnet` program included with Kerberos works much like the standard `telnet` program if run without extra options. Thus, if you just type **telnet** *remote.host*, you'll have to type your username and password again. To get the benefit of Kerberos's one-login system, you must include the -a (automatic logon) and -f (forward tickets) options.

- **rlogin**—The standard `rlogin` program is often used in a relatively insecure way, as described in Chapter 13. You can use the -f option to the Kerberized version of the program to add Kerberos authentication. The result is very similar to using the Kerberized `telnet` with -a and -f.

- **ftp**—Used without any extra parameters, this program uses Kerberos authentication, although you must still verify your username (the program presents a default, to which you can probably press the Enter key).

TIP

The Kerberos `ftp` package presents somewhat more verbose information during the initial connection phase than do some Kerberos clients. If you're having problems with a Kerberos configuration, this additional information may be useful in debugging the problems.

- **rsh**—This program is used to run a text-mode program on another computer without logging into it with `telnet`, `rlogin`, or the like. As with other Kerberized tools included with Kerberos, this version includes extra options, such as -f.

- **rcp**—The standard `rcp` program is a simple file-transfer program, to which the Kerberized version adds the usual Kerberos authentication features.

- **Other programs**—The preceding list covers only those network tools that ship with a standard Kerberos V5 package. Many other tools come standard with Kerberos support, provide Kerberos support as a compile-time option, or are available in Kerberized variants. Of course, you need both Kerberized clients and servers to use such tools.

The man pages for the Kerberized client programs provide additional details, including information on more options to set the login realm, principal, and other features of use. If you use a Kerberized tool that doesn't ship with the standard Kerberos distribution, be sure to check its options. Some provide only minimal Kerberos functionality (for instance, authentication but not encryption), but others are more full featured. One feature that's particularly noteworthy and is supported by all the standard Kerberos clients is data encryption. If you add the -x option to any of these tools' command lines, they'll encrypt all data they transfer. This feature can be extremely useful, particularly if you're connecting over the Internet or are transferring data that's potentially sensitive even for internal purposes. For instance, if you intend to log on to a computer with telnet and then use su to administer it, you may want to use encryption to protect the root password. (The ksu command, described in the upcoming section "Changing Your Account After Logging In," can also help in this respect, but only if you configure the root account to accept password-less access from your regular account.)

The standard Kerberos source code package places Kerberos user programs in /usr/local/bin by default (administrative tools go in /usr/local/sbin). Some binary Kerberos packages may use other locations; for instance, Red Hat's Kerberos builds place user programs in /usr/kerberos/bin. Chances are you want to use the Kerberized tools instead of the standard tools. To do so, you should ensure that the Kerberized tools directory appears before the standard tools directory in users' paths (set in the PATH environment variable, usually in /etc/profile or users' .bashrc files, at least for Bash users).

USING KERBEROS FOR USER LOGINS

The preceding discussion of managing a Kerberos session assumes that users have already logged into the computer. Doing so, however, reduces the appeal of Kerberos, because it means users must essentially log in twice: Once to gain access to the workstation, and again (using kinit) to use Kerberized servers. The solution is to use a tool that takes over both tasks. There are various tools that accomplish this goal. Kerberos ships with two, login.krb5 and ksu, that can help with certain text-mode tasks. Another approach is to modify Linux's underlying authentication library to rely upon Kerberos. This approach is more difficult to set up, but is also much more flexible.

WARNING

Before trying to use login.krb5, I recommend that you first test the kinit program for important accounts, including your root account. If kinit doesn't work, it's very likely that login.krb5 won't either, which means you won't be able to log into the console in text mode. You should also keep a root shell open in one virtual terminal, so that you can change your configuration if you encounter a problem with login.krb5. Similar cautions apply to changing other login tools.

Performing Text-Mode Kerberos Login Authentication

The normal text-mode login procedure for a Linux system involves the use of a program that's known generically as a *getty*. There are several getty programs, ranging from the original getty to variants such as mingetty, mgetty, and vgetty. These programs are run from /etc/inittab, and they take control of a console, serial port, or the like, and pass control to another program, /bin/login. Some network login protocols, such as Telnet, also call /bin/login. As you might guess by the name, login.krb5 is intended as a replacement for /bin/login. To use the Kerberized tool, you should replace /bin/login with the new tool. I recommend first backing up the original program. For instance, you might issue the following commands:

```
# mv /bin/login /bin/login-original
# cp /usr/kerberos/sbin/login.krb5 /bin/login
```

This action ensures that you'll be able to recover the original /bin/login program if something goes wrong. After you've replaced this program, subsequent logins will use Kerberos for the initial login. This includes obtaining a TGT, so there's no need to run kinit after such a login. Indeed, once so configured, a computer will use *only* the Kerberos authentication for logins mediated by /bin/login, although the user must still have an entry in the local /etc/passwd file, a home directory, and any other required local resources to successfully use the computer. In addition, there are other methods of logging in that you may need to adjust, such as GUI logins or logins through servers that don't rely upon /bin/login, such as SSH.

Changing Your Account After Logging In

One additional authentication tool, which is not quite the usual type of logging in, is using su to acquire another user's identity. Kerberos includes an alternative package, ksu, to permit changes in the current user account. This program has certain prerequisites:

- The computer on which you run ksu must have a host key (typically stored in /etc/krb5.keytab, and described earlier in this chapter).

- The ksu binary must be installed SUID root if anybody but root is to use the program. Most Kerberos packages do *not* install ksu SUID root, so you must do this yourself (say, by typing **chmod a+s /usr/ kerberos/bin/ksu**).

- For best security, the user whose identity you wish to acquire must have a configuration file authorizing others to gain the specified access. The .k5login or .k5users file provides this authorization, as described shortly.

To provide authorization to an account, the target user may create an authorization file. Without this file, another user may still access the account, but ksu asks for a password, which may be passed in cleartext over the network if the user is logged in using an insecure protocol such as Telnet. The .k5login file grants another user full login privileges, and is simplest to use. This file consists of a series of lines, each of which is a Kerberos principal. The .k5users file grants users limited access to the account by specifying a list of programs that the user may run; each line begins with a Kerberos principal, and is followed by specific program names separated by spaces. An asterisk (*) is a wildcard for any command. For instance, the following entry grants minerva@THREEROOMCO.COM the right to run the /bin/ls and /usr/bin/zip programs:

```
minerva@THREEROOMCO.COM /bin/ls /usr/bin/zip
```

Once configured, the ksu program works much like su—you type the program name followed by the name of the user whose privileges you want to acquire. If you haven't configured a .k5login or .k5users file, you must then enter the password for that principal. If you've created an appropriate authorization file, though, you won't need to enter any password. This approach is also more secure if you're using any unencrypted connection.

If you want to directly run a single program, you may do so by specifying the -e *progname* parameter, where *progname* is the name of the program. For instance, **ksu fluffy -e /bin/ls** runs /bin/ls as fluffy.

Using PAM with Kerberos

The replacement login and su programs included with Kerberos can be very useful, but they don't go far enough for many situations. Of particular interest is the need for a way to control GUI logins for workstations that should be authenticated through Kerberos. There are numerous other local authentication tools you may want to link to Kerberos as well, such as vlock or xscreensaver (which lock text-mode and GUI sessions, respectively, until a user enters a password). There is a general-purpose way to add Kerberos support to many such programs, but the necessary tools aren't as widely available as are the tools that ship with Kerberos. This method relies on Linux's support for the *Pluggable Authentication Module (PAM)* tools.

PAM is intended as an intermediary between programs that require authentication (such as FTP servers, login, and X-based login tools) and the underlying user and password databases (which reside in /etc/passwd,

/etc/shadow, and similar files in a standard Linux installation). The idea behind PAM is that by abstracting authentication procedures into a library, the underlying authentication files can be easily changed without altering the numerous programs that rely upon them; only PAM must be modified to understand the new file formats. In this respect, implementing Kerberos support in PAM is the ideal way to provide Kerberos support for numerous applications—if you make these changes, the programs that use PAM need no changes to support Kerberos.

NOTE The Kerberos support provided through PAM is limited in certain ways. In particular, if a program is hard-coded to request a username and password, these prompts will not change if you alter PAM to use Kerberos. The program will send the username and password to PAM for authentication, and PAM will try to authenticate them against the Kerberos database. Thus, if your FTP server, for instance, uses PAM, Kerberizing PAM won't eliminate the need to enter a username and password. It might allow you to keep your FTP passwords up to date with your Kerberos realm, though. This isn't a drawback when it comes to a Kerberized login program, which *should* always request a username and password.

Unfortunately, although PAM is a common authentication tool among Linux distributions and many non-Linux systems, Kerberized versions of PAM aren't as common as is the main Kerberos distribution. A few possible sources include the following:

- **Derrik Brashier's module**—This is a module for use with Kerberos V4. It's available from ftp://ftp.dementia.org/pub/pam/ under various filenames beginning pam_krb4; choose the one with the most recent date (all were in 1998 when I wrote this). This package ships in source code form, so you'll have to compile it to use it.

- **Frank Cusack's module**—One PAM module that supports MIT Kerberos V5 and Heimdal is available from http://www.nectar.com/zope/krb/. (The version on this page is currently being maintained by Jacques Vidrine and others.) This package is available in source code only and was originally written for Solaris, but it does compile and work under Linux.

- **Curtis King's module**—Curtis King has made another Kerberos V5 PAM module available. It can be obtained from ftp://ftp.dementia.org/pub/pam/ under the filename pam_krb5-1.1.3.tar.gz. It also requires compilation, which may not go smoothly.

- **Red Hat's module**—Red Hat has made a Kerberos V5 PAM module available as part of its distribution, under the package name pam_krb5. This is probably the easiest to install on Red Hat and similar distributions, because it comes precompiled and is distributed in RPM format. I use this package as the basis for the following discussion, but Frank Cusack's module works in much the same way.

- **Debian modules**—The libpam-krb5 and libpam-heimdal modules are available for Debian systems, and should be easy to install if you're using Kerberos V5 or Heimdal, respectively, on Debian or related distributions. These packages are difficult to find from a package search on Debian's site, though; look for them at http://ftp.nl.debian.org/debian/pool/non-US/main/libp/libpam-krb5/ and http://ftp.nl.debian.org/debian/pool/non-US/main/libp/libpam-heimdal/.

When you install the Kerberized PAM, what you're installing is a PAM *module*, which you can configure PAM to use in certain specific cases. The PAM module consists of one or more library files that are stored in /lib/security or /usr/lib/security. In the case of the Red Hat package, the files are called pam_krb5.so and pam_krb5afs.so. To use these libraries, you must alter your PAM configuration files, which are stored in /etc/pam.d. This directory contains several files named after the servers or other programs that require authentication support. For instance, /etc/pam.d/login controls how the login program interacts with PAM. To use Kerberos with these programs, you must change or add lines to the PAM control files to tell PAM to use its new Kerberos module. In fact, Red Hat's package includes a large number of sample files in /usr/share/doc/pam_krb5-*version*/pam.d, where *version* is the package's version number. To simplify configuration, you can copy the appropriate configuration files to /etc/pam.d. Files you might want to consider copying include the following:

- **login**—This controls the login program. If you install Kerberized PAM support, you can forego the official Kerberos login.krb5 program.

- **gdm**—The GNOME Display Manager (GDM) is one of three common GUI login tools in Linux. (Consult Chapter 14 for information on how to configure these servers.)

- **xdm**—The X Display Manager is another common GUI login tool, and the KDE Display Manager uses XDM's configuration files, as well. In theory, this file should enable these tools to use Kerberos for login authentication, but I've had problems with this configuration on a Mandrake system.

- **su and sudo**—The su program, described earlier, lets users change their identity once logged in. The ksu program does the same using Kerberos, but you can achieve similar results by installing the Kerberized PAM control file for su. The sudo control file provides similar Kerberization for the sudo command.

- **passwd**—This file tells PAM to send password changes, as handled through the passwd program, to the KDC.

- **vlock**—The vlock program locks a console without logging the user out; only after entering a password can the console be used again. As you might expect, this control file causes vlock to use the KDC for authentication.

- **xlock and xscreensaver**—These programs both lock an X session, much as does vlock, but xscreensaver can do so automatically after a period of user inactivity.

Naturally, there are other programs whose PAM control files you might want to modify to add Kerberos support. The details depend on your system. Note that you don't need to modify the PAM files for services you're explicitly Kerberizing. For instance, if you install a Kerberos-enabled FTP server, you don't need to modify the /etc/pam.d/ftp file. Explicitly Kerberized applications can communicate with the KDC for authentication, bypassing PAM and the need to explicitly enter a username and password that PAM requires.

If you need to modify a PAM-using program to use Kerberos, you must add or replace certain lines in the PAM configuration file. These files specify four authentication *services*: auth (authenticating a user), account (checking that an account is valid), password (changing a password), and session (setting up and terminating sessions). A PAM configuration file consists of one or more lines for one or more of these services, describing what PAM modules are to be involved in the process. For instance, Listing 6.4 shows the gdm file from Red Hat's Kerberos PAM package.

NOTE   Different distributions often use substantially different PAM configurations, so yours may call different PAM modules than those shown in Listing 6.4. In most cases, adding the pam_krb5.so module, and possibly deleting a reference to another module, is all you need to do to use a Kerberized PAM.

In this case, the important lines are the final auth and the second session lines, which tell PAM to use Kerberos for login and logout, respectively. The

Listing 6.4 A Sample PAM Configuration File with Kerberos Support

```
#%PAM-1.0
auth       required    /lib/security/pam_nologin.so
auth       sufficient  /lib/security/pam_unix.so shadow md5 \
nullok likeauth
auth       required    /lib/security/pam_krb5.so use_first_pass

account    required    /lib/security/pam_unix.so

password   required    /lib/security/pam_cracklib.so
password   required    /lib/security/pam_unix.so shadow md5 \
nullok use_authtok

session    required    /lib/security/pam_unix.so
session    optional    /lib/security/pam_krb5.so
session    optional    /lib/security/pam_console.so
```

auth line includes the use_first_pass argument, which tells the Kerberos PAM module that it's collecting the first password for a session. This causes the module to behave like kinit, acquiring and storing a TGT. Most Kerberos PAM modules can be configured in much this way, but some may need something else. For instance, the password configuration file requires the addition of a line like the following after the existing password entries:

```
password   required    /lib/security/pam_krb5.so use_authtok
```

This is the case because the password module is used by the passwd program, which changes passwords rather than authenticate users. Some files shouldn't have a session line, because this line causes authentication tickets to be destroyed. For instance, the xscreensaver and linuxconf modules shouldn't destroy tickets because when these programs exit, you're returned to a working login configuration in which the tickets you've previously obtained should remain valid.

In some cases, you may need to remove existing entries from the /etc/pam.d configuration files. Specifically, if you add a pam_krb5.so entry for a service for which there is also a reference to the pam_pwdb.so library, you should remove the latter line. The pam_pwdb.so library directly accesses the password database, and if both references are present, the local password database and the Kerberos database must *both* authenticate the password. Although this may be desirable in some very high-security situations, it limits the flexibility of Kerberos, since users must ensure they change their passwords on the KDC and on their local workstations simultaneously. If the PAM `password` configuration file includes a matching duplication, this is easily done with the `passwd` tool for a single workstation, but coordinating such changes across an entire network will be tedious at best.

After you've made changes to your PAM configuration, those changes should be immediately available; there's no PAM daemon to restart. If a configuration affects a server or program that's already running, though, you may need to restart it before it will use the new configuration. In the case of `login`, the new configuration should take effect after you log out of the console. For a GUI login tool like GDM, you may need to restart the server.

SUMMARY

Kerberos is an extremely powerful tool for centralizing authentication in a network. The protocol uses encryption and a centralized user database to allow application servers and workstations to rely on the main Kerberos server to handle authentication tasks. If used to its fullest, the result is that users can log into any workstation and then use network services within the network without providing a password again. Even the initial password is never sent over the network, so the risk of passwords being compromised is greatly reduced. The centralized user database also greatly simplifies account maintenance.

There are several Kerberos implementations available for Linux, some of which may be easier to use with any given distribution than others. Configuring a Kerberos network requires installing at least a subset of the Kerberos software on all computers. One system must be configured as a key distribution center (KDC), which houses the user database. Servers and workstations need Kerberized versions of their server and client programs, respectively. If a single-login configuration is required, workstations require modified login software. Although configuring this software can be tedious, particularly if your distribution doesn't ship with appropriate Kerberos packages, the benefits in security and centralized user administration can be substantial in a mid-sized or large network.

File and Printer Sharing via Samba

In the mid- to late 1990s, Linux earned a reputation as a "stealth" OS. Network administrators, asked to do a great deal with few resources, turned to Linux, sometimes even when it wasn't an approved solution in their organizations. In some cases, Linux replaced Windows servers that were expensive, balky, or unreliable. One of Linux's greatest tools in accomplishing this task without raising eyebrows was Samba, a server that handles the *Server Message Block (SMB)* protocol, which now also goes by the name *Common Internet Filesystem (CIFS)*. SMB/CIFS is the file- and printer-sharing protocol used atop NetBIOS, a common set of network protocols on local networks dominated by Windows systems. In other words, Samba lets a Linux system function as a file and print server for Windows computers. Samba does this job very well, and its capabilities are improving.

This chapter begins with a look at the role of Samba in a network, then moves on to general Samba configuration. These general options include configuring Samba to take on the roles of domain controller, master browser, and NetBIOS name server—NetBIOS functions that aren't directly related to file serving but that are often found on NetBIOS networks. Samba's file- and printer-sharing features are fairly straightforward, but you may need to set some parameters to alter some default behaviors. This chapter concludes with a look at how you can use Samba's automation features to do things you might not ordinarily associate with file and print servers.

Although you can get a Samba server running to a minimal extent without making extraordinary changes to its configuration files, Samba is a very complex package with many options. The Samba man pages provide unusually detailed descriptions of its configuration file format, so type **man smb.conf** for details on specific parameters. If you need an in-depth tutorial introduction to Samba, there are several books on the topic, including my *Linux Samba Server Administration* (Sybex, 2001) and Eckstein and Collier-Brown's *Using Samba* (O'Reilly, 1999).

WHEN TO RUN A SAMBA SERVER

First and foremost, Samba is a file- and printer-sharing tool. File sharing refers to the ability to mount a remote filesystem on a client as if it were local. Ordinary applications on the client can then directly access files on the server—a text editor can load files, the user can edit them, and they can be saved directly back to the server, for instance. This type of operation is most useful in office environments to consolidate the storage of users' files and applications on a single server. Printer sharing involves giving clients access to printers controlled from the server. It's useful in saving resources by allowing many computers to use the same pool of printers. These are the general tasks to which Samba may be applied.

Because of the NetBIOS and SMB/CIFS heritage in DOS and Windows, it's not surprising that Samba is most useful on networks that include DOS and Windows systems. Samba provides features that are tailored to the needs of these computers. For instance, DOS and Windows use case-insensitive filesystems, so that FILE.TXT, file.txt, File.txt, and other filenames that differ only in case are equivalent. Linux, by contrast, uses a case-sensitive filesystem, so these filenames are all different. Samba includes features to help bridge this gap, allowing Samba to serve files in a case-insensitive manner. Also, SMB/CIFS provides support for features of DOS and Windows filesystems like *hidden* and *archive* bits. These are flags to indicate that a file should be hidden from users under most circumstances, or that the file has been backed up. Linux filesystems don't include these features, so Samba provides a way to provide these bits. Samba's extensive support for these and other SMB/CIFS features makes Samba the ideal way to share files with DOS and Windows systems. A few other OSs, such as IBM's OS/2, have similar requirements and also support SMB/CIFS, so Samba is an excellent file-sharing tool for these OSs, as well.

Samba can be a useful tool even on networks that don't use DOS, Windows, OS/2, or other OSs for which SMB/CIFS is the preferred file-sharing protocol. UNIX and Linux systems, Macintoshes, BeOS systems, and others all support SMB/CIFS, either through native tools or through third-party packages. Linux often supports protocols that are more appropriate for these platforms (such as NFS for Unix and Linux systems, discussed in Chapter 8, File Sharing via NFS), but sometimes using Samba can be beneficial even in these cases. For instance, you might prefer to run as few servers as possible, and make do with SMB/CIFS for file sharing with non-Windows platforms. NFS and SMB/CIFS also use very different security models, and in some situations the SMB/CIFS security system (which uses usernames and passwords for authentication) may be preferable to the NFS model (which uses IP addresses and the client's own security).

GENERAL SAMBA CONFIGURATION

There are two aspects to Samba configuration: general configuration options and configurations for specific Samba *shares* (directories or printers that Samba serves to clients). Configuring the global options correctly is particularly important, because problems in these settings can cause the server to be completely inaccessible. The global settings also affect Samba features that aren't directly related to file and printer sharing, such as how Samba locates other systems on a NetBIOS network.

THE SAMBA CONFIGURATION FILE

Samba uses a file called `smb.conf` for its configuration. Most Linux distributions place this file in `/etc`, `/etc/samba`, or `/etc/samba.d`. Like many Linux configuration files, this file uses a pound sign (#) as a comment character. Uncommented lines are broken into separate share definitions, which are identified by a name in square brackets:

`[share-name]`

Lines following the share name control that share's settings—the directory Samba associates with the share, how filenames are handled, and so on. Global configuration options appear in a section that looks like a share definition, but it's not. This is the `[global]` section of the `smb.conf` file. Settings in this section may be defaults that carry over to other shares if they're not overridden, or they may be settings that are meaningful only in the `[global]` section itself.

Individual settings are controlled through *parameters*, which in Samba are lines that take the following form:

`parameter = Value`

Samba is very flexible in whether parameters and values are in upper- or lowercase, but by convention I list most parameters in all lowercase and most values with initial capitalization. A few values (such as those that refer to Linux filenames) are case-sensitive. Some values set binary features; for these, Yes, True, and 1 are synonymous, as are No, False, and 0.

SETTING SERVER IDENTIFICATION

NetBIOS networks use names for computers and groups of computers that are independent of the computers' TCP/IP hostnames. For instance, harding.threeroomco.com could also be known by the NetBIOS name BILLY in the USPRES domain. To avoid confusion, I use all-uppercase Net-BIOS names to distinguish these from TCP/IP names. The NetBIOS name space has just two levels: computer names and *workgroup* or *domain* names. (NetBIOS domains are unrelated to TCP/IP domains.) For this reason, Samba needs some way to specify both a NetBIOS name and a NetBIOS workgroup or domain name.

NOTE NetBIOS workgroups and domains are very similar. A workgroup is a collection of computers with a common workgroup name. A domain is a workgroup that features a computer (the *domain controller*) that provides centralized authentication and other services. Domains can also be spread across multiple network segments, which is more difficult to accomplish with workgroups. Samba can take on the role of a domain controller, as described shortly in "Becoming a Domain Controller."

You specify the workgroup or domain name with the workgroup parameter, thus:

```
workgroup = USPRES
```

This tells the computer that it's a member of the USPRES workgroup. The system can still communicate with members of other workgroups, but some functions, such as browsing a network in Windows, rely upon the workgroup name. Therefore, if you set the workgroup name incorrectly, your Samba server won't show up in Windows' Network Neighborhood or My Network Places browsers. This is a common problem with initial Samba configuration.

By default, Samba uses the first component of the computer's TCP/IP hostname as its NetBIOS name. For instance, on harding.threeroomco.com,

Samba uses the NetBIOS name HARDING. You can override this setting with the netbios name parameter. You can also use the netbios aliases parameter to set the computer to respond to multiple NetBIOS names. For instance, the following parameters tell the computer to respond to both BILLY and WILLIAM:

```
netbios name = BILLY
netbios aliases = WILLIAM
```

TIP It's usually best to use the same TCP/IP and NetBIOS names for a computer. This will avoid confusion over what the computer is called. If your computer's TCP/IP hostname is set strangely or incorrectly, though, the NetBIOS name will inherit this peculiarity. Therefore, it's a good idea to use netbios name to set the name explicitly to whatever the TCP/IP hostname should be.

SETTING SECURITY OPTIONS

Early SMB/CIFS implementations sent passwords in *cleartext*, meaning that they weren't encrypted. This made the passwords vulnerable to detection by other computers on some types of local networks, or if SMB/CIFS sessions were passed through routers. Subsequent versions of SMB/CIFS therefore added password encryption technologies. The problem is that the encryption methods used by SMB/CIFS are incompatible with those generally used on Linux systems for managing local users' passwords. It's impossible to take an encrypted SMB/CIFS password and verify the user against the normal Linux user database. Therefore, Samba must implement its own password database to handle encrypted passwords. This database is called smbpasswd, and it's controlled through a utility of the same name.

Versions of Windows since Windows 95 OSR2 and Windows NT 4.0 SP3 use encrypted passwords by default. These systems cannot connect to a Samba server that's configured using its default cleartext passwords; one or the other must be reconfigured. In the long term, it's generally easier and safer to reconfigure Samba to accept encrypted passwords than it is to reconfigure the Windows clients to send cleartext passwords.

To enable Samba to use encrypted passwords, you use the encrypt passwords parameter, which is a binary parameter that tells the system to accept encrypted passwords. Set this parameter to Yes and Samba will begin checking for encrypted passwords in its smbpasswd file. This file must contain encrypted passwords to do any good, though. To add an encrypted password for a user, issue the following command:

```
# smbpasswd -a username
```

This adds the user *username* to the smbpasswd file. The utility will ask for the password (twice, to be sure you don't mistype it). The computer must already have a valid user called *username*, or smbpasswd won't add the name. The first time you run the command, it will complain that the smbpasswd file doesn't exist; but it will create the file automatically, so you can ignore this complaint.

Another important security feature is provided by the hosts allow and hosts deny parameters. These work much like the /etc/hosts.allow and /etc/hosts.deny files of TCP Wrappers (discussed in Chapter 4): They provide lists of hosts that are explicitly allowed to connect to the server, or that are explicitly not allowed to connect, respectively. For instance, the following parameter allows computers in the 192.168.7.0/24 network to connect, as well as the system algernon.pangaea.edu, but no others:

```
hosts allow = 192.168.7. algernon.pangaea.edu
```

NOTE   For most configurations, you can skip ahead to the section entitled "Serving Files with Samba." The intervening sections are of interest only if you want your Samba server to function as a NetBIOS name server, a master browser, or a domain controller. The default settings work fine on most existing networks.

BECOMING A NETBIOS NAME SERVER

NetBIOS networks require some means of name resolution. Traditionally, NetBIOS name resolution has used methods separate from TCP/IP name resolution, but today one option is to use TCP/IP name resolution. In total, four methods are available:

- **TCP/IP names**—It's possible to use TCP/IP names for name resolution, and in fact Windows 2000, Windows XP, and Samba all default to this method, despite the fact that it's not strictly a NetBIOS solution.
- **An lmhosts file**—Systems can record mappings of names to IP addresses in a file, typically called lmhosts, which works much like the Linux /etc/hosts file.

- **Broadcasts**—Whenever a computer needs the address of another, the first system can send out a broadcast asking for the second computer's address. This approach is easy to configure and works well on small networks, but produces a lot of extraneous chatter on larger networks. Broadcasts also don't work if your network is split up into multiple segments separated by routers, unless the routers are configured to echo broadcast traffic.
- **A WINS server**—A NetBIOS Name Service (NBNS) server, also called a Windows Internet Name Service (WINS) server, works much like a TCP/IP Domain Name System (DNS) server in that it translates between machine names and IP addresses for other systems.

To configure a Samba system to function as a WINS server, you must set one parameter in the [global] section of smb.conf:

```
wins support = Yes
```

WINS servers require no extra configuration—at least not on the server side. When NetBIOS clients and servers come online, they register themselves with the WINS server, which maintains information on the systems. You need to tell all your systems to use the designated WINS server. In Windows, you do this from the TCP/IP Properties dialog box, as shown in Figure 7.1. If you click Use DHCP for WINS Resolution, you can have Windows obtain

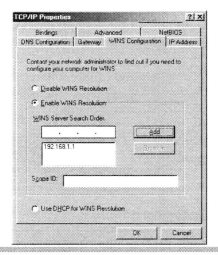

Figure 7.1 Windows' TCP/IP Properties dialog box lets you specify a WINS server address.

this information from a DHCP server. (Chapter 5 includes a discussion of how to include this information in a Linux DHCP server's configuration.)

To configure a Samba server to use a WINS server for NetBIOS name resolution, you need to set two smb.conf parameters: wins server and name resolve order. Give the IP address of a WINS server as the first parameter's value and one to four names for the four types of name resolution as the second parameter's value. Samba will attempt to use each of the name resolution methods specified in the order you list them. (The options host and bcast stand for normal TCP/IP resolution methods and NetBIOS broadcasts, respectively.) For instance, you might include the following parameters:

```
wins server = 192.168.1.1
name resolve order = wins lmhosts host bcast
```

It's important that only one system be configured as a WINS server. If you have multiple WINS servers, it's possible that name resolution will become unreliable because some systems will register with one server and others with the other server. (NetBIOS does provide for a secondary name server to improve reliability without running into this problem, but Samba doesn't support working as a secondary name server.)

BECOMING A MASTER BROWSER

Earlier, I alluded to the Windows Network Neighborhood or My Network Places browsers. These are not the same as Web browsers, although Microsoft has blurred the lines in its user interfaces. Rather, these browsers allow you to browse to SMB/CIFS servers on a NetBIOS network, as shown in Figure 7.2. You can double-click on a computer name to see the SMB/CIFS shares it's defined. File shares show up as folders and printer shares as printer icons. You can double-click a file share to access its files much as you do files on the local hard disk.

This is all well and good from a user's point of view, but it doesn't happen without effort from the software side. Think of the situation from the point of view of the Windows network browser: How does it know what computers on the local network have shares available? NetBIOS answers this question by designating one computer on a network segment as a *local master browser*. This computer maintains a list of the SMB/CIFS servers on its network segment, and delivers this information, upon request, to SMB/CIFS clients. The result is that the clients need only locate the master browser, which they do by sending a broadcast message when they boot, asking for

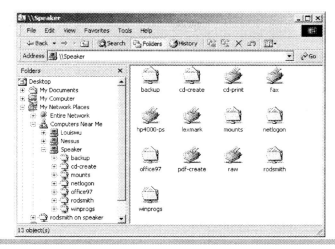

Figure 7.2 Windows lets you browse computers within your domain or workgroup, or on other domains or workgroups with a presence on your local network segment.

the master browser's address. When a server does this, it also registers itself with the master browser, thus keeping the master browser's list up to date.

NetBIOS domains include a second type of master browser, known as the *domain master browser*. This master browser communicates with local master browsers on other subnets that are part of the same domain. The master browsers exchange browse lists, thus keeping the systems coordinated, albeit with a bit of a time delay.

Domain master browsers are normally associated with domain controllers (discussed shortly). A computer must be explicitly configured to take on this role. Local master browsers, though, are designated through an *election* process, in which all the computers on a network segment present their credentials and the one with the highest score wins the election and becomes the local master browser. It's important that all master browsers be reliable systems; if the computers frequently crash or reboot, there'll be frequent periods during which browsing won't work on the network. It's also important that a Samba system not be too insistent about winning browser elections; certain parameters can cause Samba to repeatedly call for elections, which can cause browsing blackouts.

To configure a Samba system to become the local master browser, you must set it to participate in and win elections. To do this, you should create [global] parameters similar to the following:

```
browse list = Yes
local master = Yes
preferred master = Yes
os level = 65
```

The browse list parameter causes Samba to compile a browse list, which it may then share with other systems. This parameter's default is Yes, so it can usually be omitted. The local master = Yes parameter is also the default. It causes Samba to participate in elections, but doesn't guarantee victory. The preferred master parameter defaults to No. When set to Yes, it causes the system to call an election when it starts up, and periodically thereafter if it doesn't win an election. If you have multiple Samba servers, you should set this parameter to Yes on *at most* one of the servers, otherwise your network will be disrupted by frequent master browser elections. Finally, the os level parameter sets the primary criterion used in master browser elections. The higher the value, the more likely the system is to win. Setting os level = 65 should win against all Windows systems through at least Windows Me and Windows 2000, but could lose against a Samba system configured with a higher value. If you don't want a Samba system to ever win the master browser election, set this parameter's value to 0.

Domain master browser configuration requires you to set the local master browser options to win and to set the domain master = Yes parameter. You should also configure the system as the primary domain controller, as described shortly in "Becoming a Domain Controller." As with local master browser configuration, you shouldn't configure more than one system (Samba or Windows) to become the domain master browser. If your network uses a workgroup configuration rather than a domain configuration, there's no need to set this option.

BECOMING A DOMAIN CONTROLLER

NetBIOS computers are organized into either workgroups or domains. These structures are very similar to each other, but a domain is more centralized; it uses a computer known as a *domain controller* to authenticate users. Rather than have every server decide whether or not to allow users access to shares, the domain controller does this job. This can greatly simplify administration of a network with several servers, particularly if users are constantly coming and going. It does, however, require additional effort to set up initially. Domains also offer additional features, such as the ability to provide network logon scripts to clients whenever users log on, and the ability to store Windows *profiles*, which are individualized desktop customization settings, so that these settings can move with users from one client to another. In fact, domain configuration is complex enough that I can only touch upon its broad outlines in this section.

There are two types of NetBIOS domain controllers: *primary domain controllers (PDCs)* and *backup domain controllers (BDCs)*. The BDC takes over PDC functions if the PDC system crashes or becomes inaccessible. Samba handles PDC operations well, but Samba can't be used as a BDC.

To configure Samba to work as a PDC, you should add the following parameters to the [global] section of your smb.conf file:

```
security = User
encrypt passwords = Yes
domain logons = Yes
```

The security parameter sets Samba to process its own share-access requests by using Linux's usernames and passwords. (This is the default for Samba 2.0.0 and later.) The encrypt passwords parameter controls Samba's use of encrypted passwords, as described earlier. Domains must use encrypted passwords. The domain logons parameter is key to PDC operation; it tells Samba to accept domain logon requests and process them according to the contents of the smbpasswd file. Windows PDCs also function as domain master browsers and WINS servers, so it's best if you configure your Samba server to do the same (this was described earlier).

NOTE   You set the domain name through the workgroup parameter in smb.conf.

If your network includes Windows NT, 2000, or XP systems, you must take some additional configuration steps. First, Samba versions prior to 2.0.5 don't support Windows NT domain clients, versions prior to 2.2.0 don't support Windows 2000 domain clients, and versions prior to 2.2.1a don't support Windows XP or Windows 2000 Service Pack 2 (SP2) clients, so you must upgrade if you have an earlier version of Samba. Versions 2.2.0 and later add many new features to NT/2000 domain client support, even for Windows NT 4.0 users. Next, you need to create what's known as a *trust account* on Linux for each NT/2000/XP client. You can do this by issuing the following commands:

```
# groupadd -r trust
# useradd -r -g trust -d /dev/null -s /dev/null client$
# smbpasswd -a -m client
```

You only need to issue the groupadd command once; it creates a special group for the trust accounts. (In fact, you *could* use an existing group, but it's best to create a special group for this purpose.) The useradd command creates a special account for the NetBIOS computer *CLIENT*. The dollar sign ($) at the end of the username is required. Finally, the smbpasswd command adds *client* to the smbpasswd file. You should *not* include the dollar sign for the username in this command. When your Windows NT/2000/XP client next tries to access the domain, it will log on using its trust account and use Samba's password database for authenticating its own users.

Domain configuration also requires changes to the way the clients are configured. This can be handled in the TCP/IP Control Panel in Windows 9*x*/Me. Select the Client for Microsoft Networks item and click Properties. Windows displays the Client for Microsoft Networks Properties dialog box shown in Figure 7.3. Check the Log On to Windows NT Domain item and enter the domain name. In Windows 2000, open the System Properties dialog box by right-clicking My Computer on the desktop and choosing Properties from the resulting pop-up menu. Click the Network Identification tab, then the Properties button. When you activate the domain configuration, you'll be asked for an administrative username and password. Enter an ordinary username and password.

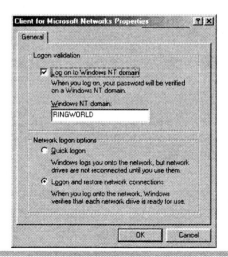

Figure 7.3   Changing to a domain configuration involves checking a box and entering the domain name on the Windows client.

SERVING FILES WITH SAMBA

Configuring Samba as a domain controller, WINS server, and so on is often desirable, but many Samba servers don't need to be configured as such. The most common use for Samba is as a file server. Configuring Samba in this way entails creating file shares, which follow the [global] section of smb.conf. You can define a basic file share in just a handful of lines. There are various additional options that can be quite powerful, which you may want to add to these lines.

CREATING A FILE SHARE

A basic Samba file share looks like this:

```
[sample]
    path = /home/samba/shared-dir
    browseable = Yes
    read only = No
```

This definition creates a share called [sample]—it appears by the name SAMPLE in Windows browse lists such as that shown in Figure 7.2. The share corresponds to the /home/samba/shared-dir directory on the computer; users who browse to the [sample] share will access files in that directory. The browseable = Yes line isn't strictly necessary, since it restates the default setting. It causes the share to appear in browse lists. (You can remove a share from browse lists by setting browseable = No, but those who know of its existence can access it by entering its name directly in the Address line of a Windows file browser.) By default, Samba creates read-only shares—clients can read files in the shares but not write to them. To make a share read/write, you should include the read only = No parameter, or one of its synonyms, writeable = Yes or write ok = Yes. Linux's ownership and permissions rules still apply to files in the share, although you can use Samba features to alter matters, as described shortly in "Configuring Ownership and Permissions."

Many networks use a Samba server to provide file storage space for users' documents. Used in this way, a special shortcut share is particularly helpful. This is the [homes] share. When you include a share definition using the heading of [homes], Samba treats things a bit differently:

- You don't need to include a path parameter. Instead, Samba uses the home directory of the user who logs into the share.

179

- The share appears in browse lists under the user's own name (such as rodsmith in Figure 7.2). If you set the browseable = No parameter, this suppresses the appearance of a share called HOMES in browse lists, but it doesn't suppress the username-based share name.

Most Linux distributions include a [homes] share definition in their default smb.conf files. Therefore, even if you don't define any shares yourself, you'll have a Samba server configuration suitable for many common uses. (You'll still need to set your workgroup name and, in all probability, adjust your password encryption policies, as described earlier.)

You can define as many file shares as you like, including a mix of ordinary shares and a [homes] share. There's no point in defining multiple [homes] shares, though. If you find yourself including some parameter in all your shares, you might consider moving that parameter to the [global] section. Doing this will make that option the default for all your shares.

SETTING WINDOWS FILENAME OPTIONS

Linux and Windows have different filename requirements. If your network still has DOS clients, DOS has still another set of filename conventions. These facts make Samba's job a difficult one, because it has to provide a way to make a Linux filesystem look like a DOS or Windows filesystem.

Perhaps the most important of the differences between Linux and Windows filename handling lies in case sensitivity. Linux treats its filenames in a *case-sensitive* manner—FILE.TXT, file.txt, and File.txt are all treated differently, so all three can exist in a single directory without conflict. Linux's case-sensitivity also means that a user must enter precisely the correct case when accessing a file. Windows, by contrast, is *case-retentive*, which means that it retains case in filenames, but it doesn't use case when matching filenames. Therefore, two filenames that differ only in case cannot exist in a single directory. DOS uses a completely *case-insensitive* system; all filenames are converted to uppercase, even if the user enters a mixed-case or lowercase filename.

The case sensitive Samba parameter controls whether it treats filenames in a case-sensitive manner or not. This parameter defaults to No, which works well with both Windows and DOS clients. When a client requests a file of a particular name, Samba checks for a name that differs from the original only in case if the original doesn't match, thus emulating Windows' behavior. The drawback is that this causes a slight performance hit. If you must have the very best performance possible, you can try setting case sensitive = Yes, but there's a good chance that at least some Windows programs will misbehave when Samba is so configured. You might also want to use this setting if you intend to use Samba with clients that are case sensitive, such as Linux.

The preserve case and short preserve case parameters define whether Samba retains case on filenames. When set to Yes (the default), Samba creates files using precisely the case specified by the client. When set to No, Samba converts filenames' case to uppercase or lowercase, depending on the value of default case, which defaults to Lower but can be set to Upper. The preserve case parameter affects the case of all files, but this setting is overridden by short preserve case for short filenames—those that conform to the length limits of DOS (eight characters plus a 3-character extension, often called *8.3 filenames*). You might want to set short preserve case = No if your network hosts a large number of DOS clients. Doing this will result in lowercase filenames stored on the Linux server, although the DOS clients will see them as being uppercase.

One SMB/CIFS feature is that it supports the delivery of 8.3 filenames even for files with long names. This allows DOS and 16-bit Windows programs (which can handle only 8.3 filenames) to access files with long filenames. Windows servers store 8.3 filenames with their files, so they can deliver these filenames without trouble. Linux, however, doesn't store 8.3 filenames, so Samba must create them dynamically. Using the default mangled names = Yes setting enables this behavior; setting mangled names = No disables the creation of 8.3 filenames.

Configuring Ownership and Permissions

Linux security is built around ownership and UNIX-style permissions. SMB/CIFS, though, doesn't use these features in the same way that Linux does. SMB/CIFS permits logins to a server using a username and password, so by default Samba uses Linux user accounts for this purpose. With cleartext passwords, Samba uses the standard Linux authentication mechanisms, but with encrypted passwords, Samba authenticates users itself. Either way, Samba provides features that allow you to alter the username associated with a login. Specifically, the force user and force group parameters allow you to treat all accesses to a share as if they came from some other user or group, respectively. For instance, consider the following share definition:

```
[jekyl]
    path = /home/samba/jekyl
    read only = No
    force user = hyde
```

Any user who accesses this share will do so as the Linux user hyde. For instance, if muriel logs in and creates a file, that file will be owned by hyde. If henry logs in and creates a file, that file will also be owned by hyde. Either user can read the others' files via Samba in this directory, even if neither can read the other's files directly from a regular login to Linux, and even if neither can read the /home/samba/jekyl directory from a regular Linux login. Anybody who uses this share can read any files within it that are readable by hyde. The force group parameter works in a similar way, but it affects the group associations of files rather than the ownership.

NOTE Users still enter their own passwords in shares in which force user is used— Muriel uses her password, and Henry uses his.

The force user and force group parameters can greatly simplify certain types of Samba configurations. For instance, if you want to create a Samba share in which individuals may freely exchange documents, you can use force user to ensure that all the files created in that directory have a single Linux owner, and that anybody using the share can read the files. You can create an account specifically for this purpose, and use Linux permissions that are as lax or restrictive as you deem necessary on the Linux side. If you need to restrict the users who may access the share from Samba, you can do so with additional parameters, discussed shortly in the section "Limiting Access to Shares."

Whereas Linux and SMB/CIFS both support usernames, Linux permissions don't map quite directly onto any SMB/CIFS concepts. When Samba supports DOS or Windows 9x/Me clients, the client doesn't understand these concepts at all. Therefore, you're free to specify the permissions of files created by clients, using the create mask and directory mask parameters, which affect the permissions on files and directories, respectively. Both parameters take 3- or 4-digit octal values that represent the permission bits that *may* be set in a file that Samba creates. The default value for create mask is 0744, and for directory mask is 0755. Both values allow read/write access to the owner and read-only access to the file's group and the world. You can adjust these values as you see fit, but be aware that they interact with the storage of DOS-style archive, system, and hidden bits.

DOS and Windows filesystems support three attribute bits that Linux filesystems don't support. Therefore, Samba can map these bits onto execute bits. You can control whether or not this mapping occurs by using appropriate Samba parameters. Specifically:

- **map archive**—If set to Yes (the default), this parameter maps the DOS archive bit onto the Linux user execute bit. DOS and Windows clients set this bit on new files, and clear it when the file has been backed up through appropriate backup software. For this reason, with the default create mask, new files created by Samba clients appear to be executable by their owners if viewed in Linux.

- **map system**—If set to Yes, this parameter causes the DOS system bit to be mapped to the Linux group execute bit. The default value is No, so this mapping doesn't occur. DOS and Windows mark a few critical system files with this bit, but such files are unlikely to be stored on Samba servers.

- **map hidden**—If set to Yes, this parameter maps the DOS hidden bit to the Linux world execute bit. The default value is No. Many DOS and Windows programs hide files that have their hidden bits set from users; the files are still accessible, but they don't show up in directory listings or file selection dialog boxes.

NOTE

By default, Samba sets the hidden bit on Linux *dot files*—files that begin with a dot (.). Linux shells treat dot files much like DOS and Windows shells treat hidden files. You can override this behavior and make dot files unhidden by using the hide dot files = No parameter.

The default create mask value mirrors the settings of the mapping parameters. If you want to change the map system or map hidden parameter defaults, you must also change the create mask value by adding 1 to the next-to-last or last digit, respectively.

Windows NT/2000/XP uses a more sophisticated internal security model than does Windows 9x/Me. Specifically, Windows NT/2000/XP supports *Access Control Lists (ACLs)*, which allow you to specify the level of access particular users may have to a file. Samba allows you to map the Linux user, group, and world permissions onto Windows ACLs, so that you can adjust read and write permissions from Windows NT/2000/XP systems. This feature is controlled through the nt acl support parameter, which defaults to Yes. You'd change this parameter to No if you want to disable an NT/2000/XP system's ability to modify Linux permissions on a fine-grained basis.

NOTE   Even a DOS or Windows 9x/Me system can adjust write access by setting or clearing the DOS read-only bit. This action affects user, group, and world permissions, though, subject to the create mask or directory mask parameter, as appropriate. ACL mapping gives finer-grained control over write access, and also gives control over read access.

LIMITING ACCESS TO SHARES

Samba provides many means to control access to itself. For instance, the hosts allow and hosts deny options were mentioned earlier, in the section "Setting Security Options," and of course Samba uses an authentication model in which users provide a username and password. (It's possible to configure Samba to perform by-share authentication rather than by-user authentication, by setting the security = Share parameter. This setting tends to be tricky to configure properly, though, because it maps poorly onto Linux's underlying security scheme.) Samba also provides several mechanisms for controlling access to individual shares. Of particular interest are the valid users and invalid users parameters, which provide lists of users who may or may not use the share, respectively. If you use valid users, you must present a space-separated list of users who are allowed to access the share; all others are denied access. You can use invalid users to blacklist certain users to keep them out of a share, even if they have access to other shares.

Another pair of access-control parameters are write list and read list. These parameters allow you to override a share's read-only or read/write settings for individual users. For instance, you might want to create a share that contains program files to which most users should not be able to write, so you'd create the share read-only. You might want to give one or two users full read/write access to the share to allow them to upgrade software, though. You'd use write list to specify these users.

As an example of these parameters, consider the following share:

```
[control]
    path = /home/samba/control
    read only = Yes
    invalid users = thomas susan
    write list = gertrude henry
```

This share is read-only for most users, but two users (thomas and susan) are denied access entirely, and two others (gertrude and henry) are given read/write access to the share.

SERVING PRINTERS WITH SAMBA

SMB/CIFS treats printer shares much like file shares. To print, a client sends a file to a share. The server then processes that file through its own printing system. Given this model, it should come as no surprise that Samba printer shares closely resemble Samba file shares. In fact, the parameters just discussed in reference to file shares, such as access control features, apply equally well to printer shares. Of course, some of these features, like filename case handling, aren't terribly important in printer shares.

Much of the challenge of handling Samba printer shares comes in passing Windows print jobs through the Linux queue in a way that modifies or does not modify them correctly given the type of queue you've configured. You may need to create very different configurations for PostScript as opposed to non-PostScript printers.

NOTE This section assumes that your printer already works in Linux, or at least that you can send data to the printer from Linux. (Some printers lack Linux Ghostscript drivers, but can still be shared via Samba.)

CREATING A PRINTER SHARE

The main difference between file and printer shares is the presence of the `printable = Yes` or `print ok = Yes` parameter (the two are synonymous). The directory you specify is a temporary spool directory (but it's *not* the Linux print spool directory, typically located in `/var/spool/lpd`). The default value is `/tmp`, which generally works acceptably, although many Linux distributions create and use a directory called `/var/spool/samba` or the like. In either case, this directory should generally have its "sticky bit" set, which prevents users from deleting files in the directory they didn't create. You can configure a directory in this way by typing **chmod 1777** **/path/to/dir** or **chmod o+t** **/path/to/dir**, where */path/to/dir* is the directory in question. (The former option also makes the directory writeable to all users, which is often desirable for a printer queue directory.) Multiple Samba printer queues can share a single spool directory. An example of a functional printer share definition is as follows:

```
[laser]
    comment = Laser printer in Room 7
    path = /var/spool/samba
    printable = Yes
```

185

The comment parameter simply provides a comment that's associated with the share name (LASER) on clients. (This parameter may also be used with file shares.) This share will work *if* your system has a *local* printer queue called laser. If your local printer queue name is something other than the share name, you should use the printer name parameter to specify it, as in printer name = lp, which tells the system to use the local queue called lp.

Linux distributions use a variety of printing systems. Currently, the original BSD lpr is quite common, but the more up-to-date LPRng is gaining ground, and the Common Unix Printing System (CUPS) is also becoming popular. Syntax details for these systems vary, and Samba must be able to adjust itself appropriately. Therefore, Samba provides an option called printing that lets you specify the printing system your computer uses. Set this to BSD, LPRng, or CUPS, as appropriate. (Several other options are available, but are quite uncommon on Linux systems.) If you use a Samba package that came with your distribution, it was probably compiled to use the appropriate package by default. If your system uses a truly oddball printing system, you may be able to rescue matters with the print command parameter, which lets you adjust the print command used by Samba to anything you specify. When you specify a command, %s is a variable that stands for the print job's filename. You may need to explicitly delete this file after you've passed it to the printing system. This parameter is actually extremely flexible, and can be a key to using Samba in some extremely unusual ways, as described in the upcoming section, "Using Pseudo-Printers."

Just as Samba's file-sharing features allow you to specify a single share that allows all users of the system to access their files, Samba's printer sharing allows you to create a single printer share that provides access to all the system's printers. This share name is [printers]. When this share is present, Samba scans the computer's /etc/printcap file for printer names and creates one share for each of the names it finds. As with the [homes] share, the [printers] share normally includes a browseable = No parameter to keep a share called PRINTERS from showing up on Windows clients. Even with this parameter set, the individual printer names appear in Windows browse lists.

SHARING A POSTSCRIPT PRINTER

The preceding description has largely bypassed one of the most important issues (and potential sources of problems) in sharing printers via Samba: printer drivers. Windows systems use printer drivers that interact with application programs to generate output that a specific model of printer can understand. Therefore, the file that a Samba printer share receives for printing will be preformatted by whatever printer driver was installed on the client. Linux, by contrast, generally uses printer queues that are configured to accept PostScript output. Depending on the type of printer that's attached to the computer, the queue may output the original file in unchanged form, or it may pass the file through *print filters*, which convert PostScript into a form that can be understood by a non-PostScript printer. The result of these two differing print models is that a clash sometimes develops. If the Windows clients feed Samba non-PostScript files, they may get garbled. Just as bad, some Windows PostScript drivers create output that can confuse Linux print filters into thinking the output is *not* PostScript, which can also produce garbled output. Fortunately, there are a handful of rules and Samba parameters that can help immensely in fixing these problems, but you may need to do some experimentation to learn what works best.

The simplest case is usually if the printer you're sharing is a PostScript model—that is, if it understands and processes PostScript output itself. This feature is common on high-end laser printers, and is available on some mid-range laser printers. It's rare on low-end laser printers and inkjets, although there are a handful of inkjet printers that understand PostScript. Consult your printer's documentation if you're unsure if it supports PostScript.

WARNING

Some printers claim to support PostScript, but that support is provided by a PostScript interpreter that resides in Windows. Such printers are *not* PostScript printers for the purposes of this discussion. They may be perfectly good printers, and your Windows clients may be able to use the Windows PostScript interpreter via Samba, but they are not configured as PostScript printers.

NOTE

PostScript was originally created by Adobe (http://www.adobe.com), which has traditionally licensed PostScript for inclusion in printers. Other companies have also produced PostScript interpreters, and these are currently common on many printers, including some models from such major manufacturers as Hewlett Packard and Lexmark. Although some early PostScript clones were far from perfect, more recent PostScript clones generally do a good job. For purposes of Samba configuration, whether your printer uses a genuine Adobe PostScript or a clone is unimportant.

If your printer supports PostScript directly, you should be able to install a Windows PostScript driver, either from the Windows CD-ROM or from the printer manufacturer. (Adobe also has PostScript drivers available, although they're licensed only for use with printers that have Adobe-created PostScript interpreters.) This driver will generate PostScript output, which Samba will pass to the Linux printer queue, which should then send the file to the printer. If all goes well, the file will print without problems.

The most common source of problems in such a configuration arises because many Windows PostScript drivers precede their output with a Ctrl+D character. Most PostScript printers ignore this character, but it confuses the Linux print queue. Specifically, Linux print filters look for certain strings at the start of a print job to identify PostScript jobs. The Ctrl+D interferes with this identification, so the print filter assumes the file is plain ASCII text. Some PostScript printers can't cope with plain ASCII text, so the print filter converts the PostScript (that the filter believes to be plain text) into a PostScript file that prints the PostScript code. The result is a printout of PostScript code, rather than the page you'd expected. There are two possible solutions to this problem.

First, you can locate the option in the Windows print driver that generated the Ctrl+D. This option can usually be found in the Properties dialog box for the printer, or in a dialog box obtained by clicking an Advanced button in that dialog box. Figure 7.4 shows an example. The Send CTRL+D Before Job option should be unchecked. (The Send CTRL+D After Job option is less likely to cause problems.) Disabling the Ctrl+D at the source is a good plan if you want to use the queue with both PostScript and non-PostScript driv-

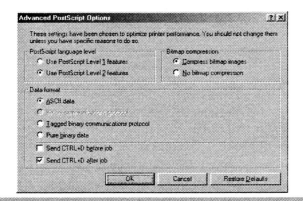

Figure 7.4   You can usually disable the Ctrl+D character that causes problems for many Linux printer queues.

ers (say, if the printer understands PostScript and some other printer language), but it can be tedious if you have many clients that need correcting.

The second solution to the Ctrl+D problem is to use the Samba parameter `postscript = Yes`. This parameter causes Samba to add the PostScript identification code to the start of the print job, before the Ctrl+D character. The end result is that the job prints fine, since the printer will then ignore both the Ctrl+D and the second PostScript identification code. This solution is easier if you have many clients that would need reconfiguring, but if you also want to be able to print using another type of driver, you'll need to create a second queue for that purpose, which may clutter your network share list.

SHARING A NON-POSTSCRIPT PRINTER

You have two options for configuring a non-PostScript printer for sharing via Samba. The first is to use a PostScript driver on the clients and configure the Linux printer queue to convert PostScript to the printer's native language, as you'd do if using the printer locally. The second option is to use the printer's native drivers on the client and share the printer with a *raw* queue, which passes data to the printer unchanged. Each option has its advantages and disadvantages, and each requires its own configuration.

Using Ghostscript

If you can print to a non-PostScript printer from Linux applications that generate PostScript output, such as Netscape, then your system is configured to pass printed output through Ghostscript (`http://www.cs.wisc.edu/~ghost/`), which is a PostScript interpreter that runs on the computer rather than the printer. The GNU version of Ghostscript ships with all major Linux distributions and supports most printers. In a few cases, you may need to locate special drivers or the Aladdin version of Ghostscript, which is more up-to-date. For information on printer compatibility with Ghostscript, check the Linux Printing database at `http://www.linuxprinting.org/printer_list.cgi`.

A Linux printer queue that's configured to use Ghostscript uses a print filter to detect the type of the file, just as does a queue that feeds a PostScript printer. This filter, however, passes the input through Ghostscript. Configuring this setup usually entails using distribution-specific printer configuration tools or following the instructions that came with the filter package. Once it's set up, the queue works almost identically to a queue for a PostScript printer. You should therefore read the preceding section, "Sharing a

PostScript Printer," to learn how to set this up in Samba and its clients. You'll need to choose a generic PostScript driver on Windows (Apple LaserWriter drivers usually work well for laser printers driven in this way, and the QMS magicolor driver usually works well for color inkjets). The Ctrl+D issue mentioned in the earlier section can occur with these queues, and the solutions are the same as for PostScript printers.

Some Windows PostScript drivers produce PostScript files that include embedded commands to display progress information on certain printers' built-in displays. This information usually produces an extra page of output with messages like %%[LastPage]%%. If you have this problem, one solution is to use a different Windows printer driver. Another option is to locate the file that calls Ghostscript and add >/dev/null to the end of the gs command line. This action redirects the error messages from Ghostscript's usual output device of the printer to /dev/null. In Caldera, this file is /var/spool/lpd/*queuename*/printfilter (where *queuename* is the name of the printer queue). In Red Hat, Mandrake, and TurboLinux, this file is /usr/lib/rhs/rhs-printfilters/ps-to-printer.fpi.

Creating a Non-PostScript Queue

If you want to use a non-PostScript driver on the client, you may do so, but you'll need to create a Linux printer queue that doesn't attempt to interpret or modify the data being sent to the printer. Some Linux print filters can recognize certain printer languages and send the results through untouched, so it's possible you'll be able to use a regular queue for this. If you try it and your print jobs disappear or come out in some garbled or unintelligible form, though, you'll need to create a raw queue.

You can create a raw queue by creating a printer queue as you normally would and then editing the /etc/printcap file (assuming your system uses the BSD or LPRng printing system). Specifically, you should remove the if= line from that queue's definition, or set it to point to nothing. This line specifies the Linux print filter, and removing it ensures that the print job will pass from the input queue to the printer without being altered. Such a queue might resemble the following:

```
lp|hp4000|raw:\
        :lp=/dev/lp0:\
        :sd=/var/spool/lpd/lp:\
        :mx#0:\
        :sh:\
        :if=:
```

This queue definition creates a printer that goes by three names: lp, hp4000, and raw. It prints to the printer located at /dev/lp0 and uses /var/spool/lpd/lp as its spool directory. (Note that this directory is *not* the same as Samba's spool directory; the file resides first in Samba's spool directory, and then moves to /var/spool/lpd/lp.) The mx#0 option disables any limit on print file size and sh disables any header page. Because the if= line doesn't point to a print filter file, the filter is empty, so the queue always passes data through unchanged.

In defining the Samba printer share for a raw queue, you should be sure that the postscript option is *not* included, or that it's set to postscript = No. Preceding a non-PostScript print job with a PostScript identification is likely to confuse most printers, resulting in a garbled printout.

Choosing an Approach

If you have a non-PostScript printer, you must decide whether to use a PostScript driver or a native driver on the client systems. These are *not*, however, mutually exclusive options. You can create two Linux and Samba print queues, or possibly even use a single queue if your Linux print filter recognizes native print jobs for what they are. (If you create two Linux printer queues, a single Samba [printers] share will detect and share both of them.) You can then install two printer drivers on the clients and choose between them.

One of the important distinctions between these two approaches is where the text or image data is converted into a bitmap. When using Ghostscript and a PostScript driver on the client, the client generates what is essentially a text file describing the text in the document (if it's primarily a text document). This file is small and is usually easy for the client to produce. It therefore imposes little CPU load on the client and generates little network traffic, but it requires CPU power on the print server to convert to a bitmap form. If you use a native driver on the client, by contrast, the client's CPU load will probably be higher, and the file it transmits to Samba will usually be larger; but the Samba server won't need to exert much CPU power to process the file. Thus, the Ghostscript approach is good for minimizing client CPU and network loads, whereas the native driver approach is good for minimizing server CPU loads. These differences are much less important when printing graphics than when printing text, though, because graphics files are large whether they're in PostScript or native printer formats.

Another difference between these approaches relates to the quality of the output. When you use Ghostscript, you rely upon Ghostscript to generate the final output image. In some cases, Ghostscript does a very good job of this, but in other cases, Ghostscript's drivers aren't as good as native Windows drivers. This is particularly true for some of the more obscure and recent color inkjets. Indeed, some of these printers don't have Ghostscript drivers at all, which means you *can't* use the Ghostscript approach, although you may be able to share the printer using a raw queue and native Windows drivers. In a few cases, Ghostscript's output can be superior to that of native client drivers. This is particularly likely if you have applications that work best with PostScript printers, such as some desktop publishing packages or if you need to print Encapsulated PostScript (EPS) files. In fact, Ghostscript can be a great way to get PostScript compatibility at low cost. Furthermore, by standardizing on one PostScript driver for many printers, you can minimize changes in formatting you might otherwise get when switching between printers—a serious problem with some programs.

Related to the print quality issues are issues of driver flexibility. When using Ghostscript, you set the printer's resolution and other print quality features via Ghostscript settings. In Linux, these are generally set in the printer setup utility when you define a print queue. To change resolutions, you must create multiple queues and switch between them. If you use native client drivers, though, those drivers typically include resolution-setting options and options to control other printout features. It's therefore usually easier to control an inkjet printer's resolution by using native drivers.

You'll have to balance all these factors based on your own network's capabilities and needs; there is no single best answer to the question of whether to use Ghostscript or native client drivers. You may want to experiment with both approaches to learn which works best on your network and with your printers. Indeed, you might find that one approach works best for some printers, while the other works better for other printers.

SAMBA SCRIPTING FEATURES

One of Samba's most exciting features is the ability to run scripts. You can feed commands to Samba in various ways, and Samba will execute those commands in specified circumstances. You can use this ability to have Samba perform tasks you might not ordinarily associate with a file and print server. This section is devoted to this capability. It starts with a description of two scripting features (preexec/postexec scripts and pseudo-printers) and concludes with several examples of how to use these features.

USING preexec AND postexec SCRIPTS

Samba provides parameters that allow it to run commands that you specify whenever a user logs into or logs out of a share. These parameters are preexec and postexec for login and logout commands, respectively. You specify the commands you want executed as the value of the parameter. For instance, if you want Samba to send e-mail to billy@harding. threeroomco.com whenever a share is accessed, you might include the following parameter in the share's definition:

```
preexec = mail -s "Share being used" billy@harding.threeroomco.com
```

Whenever somebody logs into the share, Samba sends a message in that user's name to billy@harding.threeroomco.com. The mail command's syntax gives the message the subject Share being used, and because the message is sent in the name of the user who made the connection, the message recipient knows who logged in.

The postexec command works in the same way, but it sends a message whenever the connection to the share is terminated. Because of the way Windows clients handle SMB/CIFS shares, this won't happen immediately after a user closes a window that was opened through Network Neighborhood or My Network Places, but it will happen eventually.

Two variants on these parameters are root preexec and root postexec. These parameters work just like their non-root namesakes, except that they execute the commands you specify as root. This can be useful if you need to execute some privileged commands, but you should be cautious in using these parameters. If you make a mistake in your command specification, you can cause problems or give a miscreant root access to your computer.

Samba supports many variables, summarized in Table 7.1, which can be used as part of a command specification. By including these variables, you can customize the operation of a preexec or postexec script for individual users, clients, client OSs, and so on. (Some of the variables in Table 7.1 are intended for use in printer shares.)

The preexec and postexec parameters are intended to let you execute commands that might be useful in preparing a share to be used, like a command to back up Linux configuration files that a Windows user might mistakenly delete from a home account. The limits of what you can accomplish with these commands are determined by your imagination, however. Some possibilities include the following:

Table 7.1 Variables Available in Samba

Variable	Meaning
%a	Client's operating system. Possibilities include OS2 (OS/2), Samba, UNKNOWN, WfWg (DOS or Windows for Workgroups), Win2K, Win95 (Windows 95 or 98), or WinNT.
%d	Server's process ID
%g	Primary group of %u
%G	Primary group of %U
%h	Server's TCP/IP hostname
%H	Home directory of %u
%I	Client's IP address
%j	Print job number
%L	Server's NetBIOS name
%m	Client's NetBIOS name
%M	Client's TCP/IP hostname
%N	NIS home directory server
%p	Path to the share's root directory, if automounted
%P	Path to the share's root directory
%R	Negotiated SMB/CIFS protocol level; can be CORE, COREPLUS, LANMAN1, LANMAN2, or NT1
%s	The filename passed to a printer share
%S	The share name
%T	The current date and time
%u	Effective Linux username
%U	Requested Linux username (may not match %u)
%v	Samba version number

- These scripts can create and destroy symbolic links between a shared common directory and a user's home directory. (Samba follows symbolic links by default, but this behavior can be disabled by setting follow symlinks = No.)

- A preexec parameter could mount a removable-media device for a user, and a postexec script could unmount it. This could be very useful in giving access to floppies, CD-ROMs, and the like.

- You can log information that Samba doesn't ordinarily record, or in ways Samba doesn't ordinarily do it.

- Samba can manipulate graphics files deposited in a directory. You might create a share that includes commands to convert graphics files to a particular format, for instance, and copy the converted files into another share for pickup.

- A share with restricted access could be used to help administer the server itself. For instance, a share could contain copies of critical files in the /etc directory; a postexec script could look for changes to these files and, if present, copy the changed versions to /etc and restart servers.

- Files could be copied from a share to a backup device, like a tape drive. This feature could be used for client-initiated backups—you could create a Windows batch file script to open a Samba share, copy all a computer's files to that share, and close it. Users could then insert a tape in the Samba server's drive, double-click the batch file on the client, and wait for the backup to complete. Chapter 17, Performing Network Backups, presents an example of such a configuration.

Some of these possibilities are more likely to be useful than others. Some (particularly the administrative help share) are potentially risky from a security point of view, but could conceivably be useful in some limited situations. The point of these descriptions isn't so much to suggest what you *should* do with preexec and postexec scripts, but to illustrate the range of things that are *possible* with them.

TIP

> Although you can give a fairly sophisticated set of commands directly on a preexec or postexec parameter line, past a certain point you should consider writing a shell script and calling it. This allows you to run an arbitrarily complex set of commands.

For some uses, you may want to limit the number of people who can use a share at once. You can do this with the max connections parameter, which tells Samba how many simultaneous connections it will accept to a share. To keep users from trampling each others' efforts, set max connections = 1. This may have the undesirable side effect of preventing access if a user reaches a share through Network Neighborhood or My Network Places, however, because as noted earlier, Windows tends not to close such connections in a timely fashion.

USING PSEUDO-PRINTERS

Another opportunity for scripting derives from the print command parameter used in printer shares. Although intended for specifying commands to send a print job to a printer, you can put anything in this parameter that you like, just as you can specify any command in a preexec or postexec parameter. You can use this facility to operate on PostScript files to generate effects that aren't what you'd normally call printed output. By bypassing the Windows printer drivers, you can also use it to process any single-file data you care to generate on a Windows system. Possibilities for use of this parameter include:

- Sending faxes with Linux fax software and Windows PostScript drivers. There are even Windows packages like Respond (http://www. boerde.de/~horstf/) that help provide an interactive interface for such a use, so you can enter fax numbers on the Windows system.

- Converting PostScript files into other formats, such as PDF files or graphics file formats. The upcoming section, "Example: Creating PDF Files" gives an example of this use.

- Directly printing non-PostScript data. Some such data can be correctly parsed by Linux print filters, and so needs no special configuration; however, you could create a print command to process word processor files, extract and print specific fields from database files, and so on.

- By packaging data files in a carrier like a zip file, you can pass any collection of data to Linux you like and perform actions similar to those you could perform with a preexec or postexec script. You can therefore back up a computer, convert one file format to another, and so on. The upcoming section "Burning a CD via a Pseudo-Printer" gives an example of such use.

As with preexec and postexec scripts, you can easily do dangerous things with print command. Be cautious with it, particularly if you find the need to use the force user parameter to set root privileges.

You can use the variables described in Table 7.1 with print command (in fact, some of them, like %s, don't make sense with preexec or postexec). The %H variable is particularly helpful in delivering output back to the user who initiated the job—you can use this to specify a path in which files are to be placed upon completion.

One advantage of print command over preexec and postexec scripts is that there's no problem with connections staying open, and thus the postexec command not executing for a while. Once the client submits the print job, the print command springs into action. Two consecutively submitted jobs could conceivably damage each others' files, though, depending on the nature of the operations involved.

EXAMPLE: CD BURNING

One example of scripting in action is using a Samba server as a CD creation platform. Suppose you've got a small office with a dozen clients and just one CD-R or CD-RW drive. Any of the clients may have a legitimate need to create a CD. You could put the CD-R drive on the Samba server and allow users to copy files to this server and then use a Linux CD-R creation tool to create CDs. This process requires training all the users how to use the CD-R creation software, though, and it opens the possibility for problems because users may leave files lying about, thus chewing up space on the hard disk. You can use Samba's scripting features to automate the process, eliminating many of these problems.

Burning a CD via preexec and postexec Scripts

Let's assume that you've set aside a Samba share for CD creation. This share will be used for *nothing* but CD creation. To burn a CD via preexec and postexec scripts, you need to have Samba perform several tasks:

1. Clear the share of all files.
2. Accept files for burning to CD.
3. Create a CD image file with mkisofs or a similar utility.
4. Burn the CD image file to a CD-R using cdrecord or a similar utility.
5. Delete the image file and the files from which it was created.

The following share accomplishes these tasks, albeit with a bit of help:

```
[cd-create]
    path = /home/samba/cd-create
    create mask = 0666
    directory mask = 0777
    read only = No
    max connections = 1
    preexec = /bin/rm -r %P/*
    postexec = /usr/local/bin/create-cd %H %P %U
```

The preexec parameter takes care of task 1. Task 2 is accomplished by normal Samba operations. Tasks 3–5 are handled by the postexec parameter—or more precisely, by the /usr/local/bin/create-cd script, which appears in Listing 7.1.

Listing 7.1   Script to Create a CD-R Using preexec and postexec

```
#!/bin/sh
# $1 = Home directory of job submitter
# $2 = Directory of original files
# $3 = Username of job submitter
mkisofs -J -r -o $1/image.iso $2
cdrecord speed=2 dev=4,0 $1/image.iso
mail -s "CD-R creation finished" $3
rm $1/image.iso
rm -r $2/*
```

To prepare this share, you must take the following steps:

- Type the create-cd script into your system and store it in /usr/local/bin. The script should have execute permissions set (type **chmod a+x /usr/local/bin/create-cd** to accomplish this task). You should adjust the mkisofs command for any additional CD-creation options you want to use, and you should set cdrecord for your own CD-R drive (the dev and speed parameters).

- Create a Samba share like the [cd-create] share. Use a different directory if you like, but be sure it's given full read/write permissions for all the users who may use it.

- Set the SUID bit on the cdrecord executable. You can do this by typing **chmod a+s /usr/bin/cdrecord** on most systems. Some distributions use a special group to control access to cdrecord. If yours does, you can add your CD-creating users to that group, or use the force group Samba parameter to set users to be members of this group. Alternatively, use root postexec rather than postexec in the [cd-create] share. The key here is that the create-cd script's commands be executed with sufficient privilege that the cdrecord command succeeds.

When you've taken these steps, you can use the share. In Windows, you can mount the share by locating it in Network Neighborhood or My Network Places, right-clicking the share name, and choosing Map Network Drive from the pop-up menu. You'll then assign a drive letter to the share. Once you've mounted the share, copy files that you want burned on a CD to the share. You can move files around in the share, delete unwanted files, and so on. When you're ready to burn the CD, insert a blank CD-R in the CD-R drive and unmount the share by right-clicking its icon in the My Computer window and selecting Disconnect from the menu that appears.

Unfortunately, Windows sometimes doesn't disconnect the share even at this point, forcing you to log out or (in the case of Windows 9*x*/Me) reboot the system. After some time (a few seconds or minutes), the server's CD-R drive should activate and eventually finish its operations, whereupon the `create-cd` script will e-mail the user that the job is done. It's then safe to remove the CD-R from the drive and test it.

The share definition and CD-creation script presented here are a bit rough around the edges. For instance, these scripts provide only very limited protections against two users trampling each others' work; if one tries to create a CD-R before another has removed a new disc from the CD-R drive, there'll be problems. These scripts don't report errors to the user. For instance, if the created image is too large to fit on a blank CD-R, the first indication of it may be when the disc gives problems when read. A more complex `create-cd` script might check for such potential problems and alert users to them or avoid the problems entirely. Finally, different versions of Samba treat the %P variable in different ways, so you may need to adjust the share accordingly.

Burning a CD via a Pseudo-Printer

Pseudo-printers provide a method of CD creation that's more convenient for Windows 9*x*/Me clients, but that's somewhat less obvious than a regular file share. The idea for this share is to have the Windows client pass a zip file with the CD's intended contents. The share then calls a script that's a variant on the `create-cd` script to unpack the zip file and burn a CD-R from the resulting files. The basic Samba share definition looks like this:

```
[cd-print]
    path = /var/spool/samba
    printable = Yes
    print command = /usr/local/bin/print-cd %H %s %U %P; rm %s
```

As with the earlier share, you may need to adjust the use of %P. Specifically, you may need to replace it with `/var/spool/samba`. Most of the work is done by the `print-cd` script, shown in Listing 7.2.

You must configure this share and script in a similar manner to those used with the `[cd-create]` share and `create-cd` script. Specifically, the script needs to be executable, you should adjust the `mkisofs` and `cdrecord` commands for your system, and the `cdrecord` executable should be set SUID root. Once this is done, you can create a CD by sending a zip file to the share with the DOS/Windows COPY command, thus:

```
C:\> COPY FILE.ZIP \\SERVER\CD-PRINT
```

Listing 7.2 Script to Create a CD-R Using `print` command

```
#!/bin/sh
# $1 = Home directory of job submitter
# $2 = Filename of zip file
# $3 = Username of job submitter
# $4 = Path to zip file
mkdir -p $1/cdr/samba
cd $1/cdr/samba
unzip $4/$2
mkisofs -J -r -o $1/image.iso ./
cdrecord speed=2 dev=4,0 $1/image.iso
mail -s "CD-R creation finished" $3
rm $1/image.iso
rm -r $1/cdr/samba
```

This command creates a CD-R with the contents of *FILE.ZIP*, assuming that *SERVER* is the name of the Samba server. You can place this command in a batch file (a text file whose name ends in .BAT), using a variable for the zip filename:

```
COPY %1 \\SERVER\CD-PRINT
```

You can then call that batch file followed by the name of a zip file, as in **MAKECD *FILE.ZIP*,** if the batch file is called MAKECD.BAT. If you create a desktop icon that's a shortcut to this batch file, you can create a CD by dragging a zip file to it. Alternatively, you could create a batch file that zips a directory using a text-mode zip utility and passes that zip file to the CD-creation printer share. Windows users could then place files they want on the CD in a local directory and drag that directory to a desktop icon for the batch file to create a CD.

Like the CD-creation file share, the CD-creation printer share presented here is rough around the edges. There's no checking to be sure the image file size is reasonable, and if two users submit jobs in quick succession, there'll be problems. Using a more sophisticated `print-cd` script could work around these problems.

EXAMPLE: CREATING PDF FILES

An example of using a printer queue in a more printing-oriented way is to create Adobe Portable Document Format (PDF) files from PostScript input. For this configuration, you use a Windows printer queue that's identical to what you might use when printing to a PostScript or Ghostscript-driven printer, complete with a PostScript driver. The Samba printer share looks like this:

```
[pdf-create]
    comment = Create a PDF file
    path = /var/spool/samba
    printable = Yes
    print command = gs -dNOPAUSE -q -dBATCH -sDEVICE=pdfwrite \
                    -sOutputFile=%H/%s.pdf %s; rm %s
```

NOTE The trailing backslash (\) on the next-to-last line is a line continuation character; it tells Samba that the next line is a continuation of the previous one. Such characters make for more readable configuration files when commands are long because they can produce shorter lines.

This print command parameter calls gs, the Ghostscript executable. The -dNOPAUSE, -q, and -dBATCH options produce quiet and continuous output without requiring human intervention. The -sDEVICE=pdfwrite specification indicates that the output is to be a PDF file, and the -sOutputFile=%H/%s.pdf option specifies the output filename to be the same as the print job name but with .pdf appended and stored in the user's home directory. You could modify this share definition to e-mail the file back to the user or store it in some other location or under some other filename.

SUMMARY

Samba is an unusually complex and flexible file-sharing server. Most Linux distributions ship with default Samba configurations that require only a couple of adjustments to work on a typical network. Making further adjustments (particularly if you want a Samba server to function as a domain controller) and adding shares for your particular purposes may take more effort, but most of the individual adjustments are not too onerous. One area in which Samba shows its flexibility particularly well is in its ability to run commands on demand. You can use this feature to have a Samba server provide functionality you probably wouldn't normally associate with a file server, such as the ability to create CDs.

File Sharing via NFS

The Server Message Block (SMB)/Common Internet Filesystem (CIFS) protocols described in Chapter 7 are extremely useful for sharing files and printers with DOS, Windows, OS/2, and various other OSs. These protocols, however, lack support for features that are required on UNIX or Linux filesystems, such as full support for UNIX-style ownership and permissions. For this reason, when you want to share files with another UNIX or Linux system, you generally use another protocol: the Network Filesystem (NFS). (Chapter 9 discusses Linux's native printer-sharing protocol; NFS doesn't support printing, unlike SMB/CIFS.)

WHEN TO RUN AN NFS SERVER

The usual reason for running an NFS server is that you want to share files with other UNIX or Linux systems. You might do this to share static files, such as program binary files—for instance, you might store large programs on a server and allow computers with smaller hard disks to run those large programs via NFS. Another common use of NFS is to provide a centralized server for user changeable files—rather than place users' home directories on their own workstations, you can place them on a centralized server. Particularly when used with a centralized login system such as Kerberos (discussed in Chapter 6, Authenticating Users via Kerberos), this approach provides a great deal of flexibility, because users can log in to any workstation on your network that is appropriately configured and use it as if it were any other computer. This effectively unbinds users from specific workstations. Of course, you don't need to use NFS in either of these precise ways. For instance, you could set up local home directories but provide an NFS server for files shared between users, or provide read-only access to a static database.

Although NFS was designed for UNIX systems and therefore works well with Linux, NFS clients and servers are available for other OSs, such as Windows, OS/2, and MacOS. In most cases, it's better to configure Linux to use the file-sharing protocol that's native to the other OS than to use NFS with one of these OSs. This is particularly true when that protocol is SMB/CIFS and Linux functions as the server, because Samba does an excellent job as an SMB/CIFS server, and it's usually easier to configure one Linux system with Samba server software than to add NFS client software to many clients that don't normally support it. You might want to use NFS to interact with non-UNIX or non-Linux systems on some occasions, though, such as if your network is dominated by UNIX or Linux systems and you need to add just one or two Windows or MacOS computers. (MacOS X is based on UNIX, and so supports NFS quite well, although its configuration isn't obvious from the standard MacOS X GUI interfaces.)

WARNING

As described in the upcoming section "Access Control Mechanisms," NFS doesn't rely on passwords or other typical methods of restricting access to the server. Instead, it uses a *trusted hosts* model, in which the server relies on the host to authenticate users, and the NFS server in turn trusts that these clients do their user authentication jobs. You specify clients by hostname or IP address. It's possible to spoof (that is, fake) IP addresses, though, or reconfigure local computers to circumvent this security method. You should therefore pay careful attention to security on an NFS system. Ideally, you should not serve sensitive data via NFS. You might prefer to use Samba or some other file transfer mechanism, such as the scp program that's part of the *Secure Shell (SSH)* package, for more secure transfer of sensitive data.

NFS SERVERS AVAILABLE FOR LINUX

There have been several important changes in Linux's NFS support between 1998 and 2002. This section summarizes two of these changes, in case you have older documentation or are using an older distribution. You can often use whatever NFS server ships with your distribution, but sometimes you may have to upgrade (or occasionally downgrade) your server to achieve compatibility with other systems. You can find information on the latest NFS developments for Linux at http://nfs.sourceforge.net.

USER-MODE AND KERNEL-MODE SERVERS

An NFS server basically directs data between a disk file and a network interface. The original Linux NFS servers operated in *user mode*, which means that they had no privileged access to or help from the kernel. This design, however, means that data must pass from the disk through the kernel to a user-mode program and back through the kernel and to the network (or in the opposite direction). The transfer of data from the kernel to the user-mode program and back again impedes performance, so the kernel and the NFS server were redesigned so that the kernel could handle more of the necessary transfers itself. This resulted in a speed increase. To take advantage of this improvement, you must activate the NFS Server Support option in the Network File Systems menu of the kernel's File Systems menu (see Figure 8.1); without this support, your kernel won't do its part of the NFS server job. You must also use an NFS server that's designed to use the kernel's NFS server support. This server is often called knfsd, as opposed to the regular nfsd, but this distinction is often not made explicit.

NOTE The Linux kernel configuration tools also provide an option called NFS File System Support. This option provides the kernel's NFS *client* tools, which work in conjunction with the normal mount command to mount a remote NFS server's exports on your local directory tree. The kernel's NFS client and server support options are independent of each other; you can include neither, just one, or both, as you see fit.

Figure 8.1 The Linux kernel includes support for both client and server NFS functions.

NFS VERSIONS 2 AND 3

Like many other protocols and programs, NFS has undergone periodic revisions. In 2002, version 3 of NFS, or *NFSv3* for short, is the latest version in common use. (In fact, NFSv4 also exists, but Linux support for NFSv4 is embryonic at best. Check http://www.nfsv4.org for more information.) Many NFS clients and servers, however, don't yet support NFSv3; they support *NFSv2*. Most of the Linux 2.2.*x* kernels, for instance, support NFSv2 but not NFSv3. Only with kernel 2.2.18 and later does NFSv3 support appear as a standard kernel option. (You can obtain NFSv3 patches for some earlier versions of the kernel.) NFSv3 introduces several improvements, including better file locking, improved performance via an asynchronous mode (Linux's NFSv2 implements an asynchronous mode, but in a non-standard way), extensions taken from BSD's *Not Quite NFS (NQNFS)*, and optional use of TCP connections (NFSv2 uses UDP exclusively—but TCP connections are not fully implemented in Linux's NFSv3, as of early 2002). As a general rule, NFSv2 is adequate for many small networks with casual users, but NFSv3 is very desirable for higher server loads—at least, when fully implemented. Early experimental versions of Linux's NFSv3 performed poorly because they didn't implement the faster asynchronous mode operation, but the 2.4.*x* kernel's NFSv3 support implements this feature for server operations. (Client operations are still slow as of kernel 2.4.17.)

If you want to use an NFSv3 server that uses the kernel's NFS acceleration, you must select the Provide NFSv3 Server Support option in the kernel configuration tools (this is a suboption of the NFS Server Support option described earlier and shown in Figure 8.1). Similarly, the Provide NFSv3 Client Support option is required to use NFSv3 features as a client. The NFS protocols allow for fall-back operation, so if one system provides NFSv3 support but the other system only supports NFSv2, the two computers will still be able to communicate using NFSv2 protocols. Thus, chances are you'll want to select NFSv3 support.

In addition to kernel options, you need versions of NFS support utilities that support NFSv3 if you want to use it. Specifically, you need `nfs-utils` version 0.1.6 or later for NFSv3 server support and `mount` version 2.10m or later for NFSv3 client support. Most distributions include these tools in packages of these names, so you can check your installation CD-ROM or use `rpm` or `dpkg` to check for the appropriate tools. For instance, you might type the following to check for the appropriate version of `mount` on an RPM-based system:

```
$ rpm -q mount
mount-2.11b-5mdk
```

In this example, the output reveals that `mount` version 2.11b is installed, which is more than adequate for NFSv3 client support.

UNDERSTANDING THE PORTMAPPER

Most TCP/IP servers work by attaching themselves to a port, which is set by convention to a single value. For instance, Simple Mail Transfer Protocol (SMTP) servers bind themselves to port 25, and Hyptertext Transfer Protocol (HTTP, aka Web) servers use port 80. These servers usually *can* use nonstandard ports, but most servers use the conventional port numbers so that clients can connect to them without having to be configured to use a nonstandard port. NFS, though, is one of a class of protocols that works slightly differently: It uses what's known as the *portmapper*, which is a utility that binds to a fixed port (111), monitors the ports that specific servers use, and directs clients to use the correct ports. (NFS generally uses UDP port 2049, but NFSv3 may use TCP port 2049.) This whole process is closely related to the *Remote Procedure Call (RPC)* services, of which NFS is one example. The portmapper handles RPC services.

The portmapper is implemented in a program called `portmap`. This program is normally started as part of your network startup script, or in a startup script of its own. Although it doesn't normally operate via a super server like `inetd`, recent versions of the portmapper can use TCP Wrappers. You can substantially improve your NFS server's security by blocking access to the portmapper except by computers that should be allowed access to it. The following line placed in `/etc/hosts.deny` will restrict portmapper access:

```
portmap : ALL
```

You can then loosen access to the portmapper by entering the IP addresses of computers or networks that should have access to NFS and other RPC services into `/etc/hosts.allow`:

```
portmap : 192.168.1.
```

NOTE　Chapter 4 includes a discussion of TCP Wrappers configuration, including the allowable forms of client specifications. You shouldn't specify clients by hostname in the case of the portmapper, though, because hostname lookups can cause portmap activity. Thus, in looking up the hostname, portmap can be called again, which causes another hostname lookup, and so on. This sort of infinite loop will, of course, get you nowhere while consuming lots of CPU time. Instead of using hostnames, use IP addresses or IP address fragments.

Starting the portmapper isn't enough to serve files via NFS. In addition to defining the directories you want to share (as described in the next section, "Serving Files with NFS"), you must start the NFS server itself. This is normally done by a SysV startup script called nfs or something similar. Some distributions require you to start two or more SysV startup scripts (in addition to the portmapper) to get NFS working. These scripts will probably run automatically when you boot after installing the NFS server package. If you change your configuration, you may need to call the NFS SysV startup script with the restart option, as in **/etc/rc.d/init.d/nfs restart**.

SERVING FILES WITH NFS

Actually serving files requires telling the NFS server what directories you want to *export* (that is, make available to others) and which clients should have access to specific directories. You can also include options that affect access control and other important server features. To mount an NFS server's exports from a client, you use the mount command, but instead of specifying a local device file, you point the utility at an NFS server and provide the name of the directory you want to mount.

DEFINING NFS EXPORTS

Linux uses the /etc/exports file to control the NFS server. This file consists of a series of lines, each of which defines a single directory to be exported. Each line has the following format:

```
/path/to/export  client1(options) [client2(options)[...]]
```

The */path/to/export* is the name of the directory you wish to export, such as /home or /usr/X11R6. You can list any directory you like, but of course some directories aren't useful or would be security risks when exported. For instance, exporting /etc or /proc could be potentially dangerous, because remote users might be able to view or modify sensitive system-specific information. You might think that exporting /dev would give remote users access to the server's devices, but this isn't so—device files always refer to devices on the local computer, so a /dev export would just give users a duplicate means of accessing the client's devices. These files might be named strangely or point to the wrong hardware if the export were mounted on a different OS than the server uses. Such access can also be a potential security risk to the *client* system, if a user can create device files on the server with lax permissions. (The nodev mount option, described later, addresses this issue.)

You list clients singly or via wildcards. Possibilities include the following:

- **No name**—If you provide only a list of options in parentheses, any client may connect to the export. This configuration is extremely insecure, and so isn't normally used, except occasionally when restricting access to a directory, as described shortly.

- **Single computer name**—You can specify a single computer name, such as `larch` or `larch.threeroomco.com`, to allow that computer access to the share. If you don't include the domain name, the server's own local domain is assumed.

- **Wildcards**—You can use question mark (?) and asterisk (*) wildcards to represent single characters or a group of characters in a computer name, as in `*.threeroomco.com` to provide access to all computers in the `threeroomco.com` domain. Wildcards don't match dots (.) though, so in this example, computers in `threeroomco.com` subdomains, such as `mulberry.bush.threeroomco.com`, won't match.

- **NIS netgroup**—If your network uses a Network Information Service (NIS) server, you can specify an NIS netgroup by preceding the name by an at-sign (@).

- **Network by IP address**—You can specify a restricted group of computers by IP address by listing a network address and netmask, as in `172.19.0.0/255.255.0.0`. You may also specify the netmask as a single number of bits, as in `172.19.0.0/16`. You may omit the netmask if you want to specify a single computer by IP address.

As a general rule, it's safest to specify computers by IP address, because hostnames and NIS netgroup names can be altered if the DNS or NIS server is compromised. IP addresses can also be faked, particularly if an intruder has physical access to your network, but using IP addresses eliminates one possible method of attack. On the other hand, using IP addresses can be inconvenient, and may complicate matters if clients' IP addresses change frequently, as when they're assigned via DHCP, as discussed in Chapter 5.

TIP   Specifying individual clients in this way may seem redundant with blocking access to the portmapper via TCP Wrappers, as described earlier. This is partially correct, in that both methods *should* restrict access to the server. There could be bugs or a misconfiguration in one method or another, though, so this redundancy isn't a bad thing. In fact, imposing additional blocks via packet filter rules (as described in Chapter 25, Configuring `iptables`) is advisable.

NOTE Some Linux distributions now ship with firewalls enabled by default, or easily configured at installation time. Some of these, such as those in Red Hat, have been known to block access to NFS servers, and some don't make it easy to open this access. If you're having problems with NFS access, you may want to consult Chapter 25 to learn how to examine and modify your system's firewall rules.

You can specify a different set of options for each client or set of clients. These options appear in parentheses following the computer specification, and they're separated from each other by commas. Many of these options set access control features, as described shortly in the section "Access Control Mechanisms." Others relate to general performance issues or server defaults. Examples of general options include the following:

- **sync and async**—These options force synchronous or asynchronous operation, respectively. Asynchronous writes allow the server to tell the client that a write operation is complete before the disk operations have finished. This process results in faster operation, but is potentially risky because a server crash could result in data loss. NFSv2 doesn't officially support asynchronous operation, but the Linux NFS server implements this feature despite this fact. NFSv3 does support an asynchronous option, and requires the client to buffer data to reduce the risk. The default for this option is async, although beta-test versions of Linux's NFSv3 support ignored it.

- **wdelay and no_wdelay**—By default, Linux's NFS server may delay writing data to disk if it suspects that a related request is underway or imminent. This improves performance in most situations. You can disable this behavior with the no_wdelay option, or explicitly request the default with wdelay.

ACCESS CONTROL MECHANISMS

Many of the options you specify for individual clients in /etc/exports relate to access control. As noted earlier, NFS uses a trusted hosts security model, so you can't control access to specific exports or files via usernames and passwords as you can with Samba; if the client's security can be trusted, the client will apply standard UNIX-style ownership and permissions to file access. Security-related /etc/exports options include the following:

- **secure and insecure**—By default, the NFS server requires that access attempts originate from *secure* ports—that is, those numbered below 1024. On a UNIX or Linux system, such ports can normally only be used by root, whereas anybody may use ports with higher numbers. Thus, allowing access from higher ports (as can be done with the insecure option) provides greater opportunity for ordinary users on the client to abuse the server, but also allows you to run NFS test client programs as an ordinary user.

- **ro and rw**—The ro and rw options specify read-only and read-write access to the export, respectively. The knfsd kernel-enabled server defaults to ro, but older servers default to rw. I recommend explicitly specifying one option or the other to avoid confusion or errors.

- **hide and nohide**—Suppose your NFS server stores the /usr directory tree on its own partition, and /usr/local is on another partition. If you export /usr, is /usr/local also exported? The default has varied with different NFS servers in the past, and the 2.2.x kernel included an option to set the default. Recent NFS servers include the hide and nohide options to hide a mounted partition or not hide it, respectively. Some clients don't cope well with unhidden mounted partitions, so you may want to set the hide option and explicitly export the mounted partition (/usr/local in this example). The client can then explicitly mount both exports.

- **noaccess**—This option disables access to a directory, even if the directory is a subdirectory of one that's been explicitly exported. For instance, suppose you want to export the /home directory tree, *except* for /home/abrown. You could create an ordinary /etc/exports line to export /home, then create a separate /etc/exports line for /home/abrown that includes the noaccess option. The end result is an inability to access /home/abrown.

- **subtree_check and no_subtree_check**—Suppose you export a subdirectory of a partition, but not the entire partition. In this case, the NFS server must perform extra checks to ensure that all client accesses are to files in the appropriate subdirectory only. These *subtree checks* slow access slightly, but omitting them could result in security problems in some situations, as when a file is moved from the exported subtree to another area. You can disable the subtree check by specifying the no_subtree_check option, or explicitly enable it with subtree_check (the latter is the default). You might consider disabling subtree checks if the exported directory corresponds exactly to a single partition.

- **root_squash and no_root_squash**—By default, the NFS server *squashes* access attempts that originate from the client's root user. This means that the server treats the accesses as if they came from the local anonymous user (described shortly). This default improves security because it denies root privileges to other systems, which might be compromised. If you need to allow the remote administrator local root privileges to an export, you can do so by using the no_root_squash option. This might be required in some network backup situations, for example.

- **all_squash and no_all_squash**—Normally, accesses from ordinary users should not be squashed, but you might want to enable this option on some particularly sensitive exports. You can do this with the all_squash option; no_all_squash is the default.

- **anonuid and anongid**—The anonymous user, used for squashing, is normally nobody. You can override this default by specifying a user ID (UID) and group ID (GID) with the anonuid and anongid options, respectively. You might use this feature to give remote root users access with a particular user's privileges, for instance, or in conjunction with PC/NFS clients, which support just one local user. When using these options, follow them with equal signs (=) and a UID or GID number, as in anonuid=504.

As an example of a complete /etc/exports file, consider Listing 8.1. This file exports two directories, /usr/X11R6 and /home. It includes a third entry to restrict access to /home/abrown by using the noaccess option. (Because this final line *restricts* access, it's used without explicitly specifying a host—all clients are denied access to this directory.) Both /usr/X11R6 and /home are accessible to the computer called gingko and all systems on the 192.168.4.0/24 network, but with different options. Read-only access is granted to /usr/X11R6, while clients have read/write access to /home. In the case of gingko, the anonymous user ID is set to 504 for /usr/X11R6, and no subtree checks are performed for /home.

Listing 8.1   A Sample /etc/exports File

```
/usr/X11R6 gingko(ro,anonuid=504) 192.168.4.0/24(ro)
/home gingko(rw,no_subtree_check) 192.168.4.0/255.255.255.0(rw)
/home/abrown (noaccess)
```

MOUNTING NFS EXPORTS

From the client side, NFS exports work much like disk partitions. Specifically, you mount an export using the mount command, but rather than specify a partition's device filename, you provide the name of the NFS server and the directory on that server you want to mount in the form *server*:*/path/to/export*. For instance, the following command mounts the /home export from larch at /mnt/userfiles:

```
# mount larch:/home /mnt/userfiles
```

Alternatively, if you want an export to be available at all times, you can create an entry in /etc/fstab that corresponds to the mount command. As with the mount command, you substitute the server name and export path for a device filename. The filesystem type code is nfs (you can also use this with a mount command, but Linux can normally determine this automatically). For instance, the following /etc/fstab entry is equivalent to the preceding mount command:

```
larch:/home   /mnt/userfiles   nfs   defaults   0 0
```

Users may then access files from larch's /home directory within the /mnt/userfiles directory. You can perform most operations on a mounted NFS export that you can perform on a native Linux disk partition, such as reading files, deleting files, editing files, and so on. There are a handful of operations that don't work properly on NFS exports, though. For instance, you can't use a swap file via NFS. In most cases, the performance of NFS exports won't match the performance on local filesystems; the speed of most networks doesn't match modern hard disk speed. NFS might provide superior performance if you have a particularly fast network, though, such as gigabit Ethernet, or if your clients' local hard disks are particularly old and slow. The server's disk speed and number of clients being served will also influence NFS performance.

Ownership and permissions are exported along with filenames and file contents. Thus, you and your users can use ownership and permissions much as you do locally to control access to files and directories. You can even use these schemes to control access across multiple computers—say, if a single NFS server supports several clients. There is a potentially major problem, though: NFS uses UIDs and GIDs to identify users, so if these don't match up across clients and the server, the result is confusion and possible security breaches. There are several ways around this problem, as discussed in the section "Username Mapping Options."

The upcoming sections describe some options you can give to the mount command to modify the behavior of the NFS client/server interactions with respect to performance, username mapping, and so on. A few additional miscellaneous options include the following:

- **hard**—If the server crashes or becomes unresponsive, programs attempting to access the server hang; they wait indefinitely for the response. This is the default behavior.

- **soft**—If your NFS server crashes or becomes unresponsive frequently, you may want to use this option, which allows the kernel to return an error to a program after the NFS server has failed to respond for some time (set via the `timeo=time` option).

- **nodev**—This option prevents the client from attempting to interpret character or block special devices on the NFS export. This can help improve security by reducing the risk of a miscreant creating a device file with lax permissions on an NFS export and using it to wreak havoc on the client.

- **nosuid**—This option prevents the client from honoring the set user ID (SUID) bit on files on the NFS export. As with `nodev`, this can be an important security measure, because if a user could create an SUID `root` program on an NFS export, that user could potentially gain superuser access to the client.

- **noexec**—This option prevents the client from honoring the execute bit on files on the NFS export—in other words, users can't run programs from the NFS export. This option is clearly inappropriate in some cases, such as when you're deliberately sharing a binaries directory, but it may further enhance security if the export shouldn't hold executable files.

You can include any of these options in a `mount` command following the `-o` option, as in the following example:

```
# mount -o noexec,nodev larch:/home /mnt/userfiles
```

If you create an `/etc/fstab` entry, place these options in the options column (where the previous `/etc/fstab` example lists `defaults`).

OPTIMIZING PERFORMANCE

Two of the most important performance enhancements have already been described: Using the kernel's NFS support in conjunction with `knfsd`, and using asynchronous mode whenever possible. (The latter option imposes an increased risk of file loss in the event of a server crash, though.) Other performance enhancements include the following:

- **Optimizing mount transfer size options**—The `rsize` and `wsize` options to `mount` specify the size of data blocks passed between the client and server. The defaults vary from one client and server to another, but 4096 is a typical value. You may want to adjust these values, as in **mount larch:/home /mnt/userfiles -o rsize=8192**. Place these options in the options column of /etc/fstab (where defaults is in the preceding example) when you want to mount an NFS export automatically.

- **Optimizing access time option**—The noatime option to mount tells Linux not to update access time information. Ordinarily, Linux records the last time a file was accessed, as well as when it was created and changed. Omitting access-time information can improve NFS performance.

- **Number of running NFS servers**—The NFS server startup scripts in most distributions start eight instances of the server. This number is arbitrary. On a lightly used system, it may be too high, resulting in wasted memory. On a heavily used system, it may be too low, resulting in poor performance when clients connect. You can adjust the value by editing the NFS server startup script. These frequently set the number of instances via a variable near the start of the script, such as RPCNFSDCOUNT=8.

- **Non-NFS performance issues**—Many networking and non-networking features can influence NFS performance. For instance, if your network card is flaky or slow, you'll experience NFS performance problems. Similarly, a major NFS server relies upon its hard disks, so it's important that you have a fast hard disk, ideally driven by hardware that imposes low CPU overhead (such as a DMA-capable EIDE controller or a good SCSI host adapter; SCSI is often preferable because SCSI hard disks often outperform EIDE hard disks).

If your NFS server is experiencing poor performance, you should first try to ascertain whether the problem lies in the NFS server software, in the NFS client systems, in the network configuration generally, or in some more generalized area such as disk performance. You can do this by running performance tests using a variety of protocols and clients, as well as entirely local tests (such as using the -t option to hdparm to test your hard disk performance).

USERNAME MAPPING OPTIONS

On an isolated Linux computer, the /etc/passwd file controls the mapping of usernames to UIDs, and /etc/group does a similar job for groups. With NFS, there are usually at least two independent /etc/passwd files—one for the server and one for each client. Thus, a situation in which a user has one

UID on the server and another UID on the client is possible, and perhaps even likely, unless care is taken in setting up accounts. There are several possible ways to work around or avoid this potential problem.

NOTE This discussion assumes that users have accounts on both the client and the server. If the server is used *only* as a file server, it might lack user accounts. This may be a reasonable configuration for read-only servers, and even for some read/write configurations. If a read/write server has several clients, though, synchronization of UIDs among the clients is important, even if the server doesn't have accounts for all the users. It's often simplest to configure an NFS server that holds user files with user accounts, even if those users can't log onto the NFS server directly. If the server doesn't hold files that are owned by users, username mapping is probably unimportant.

SYNCHRONIZING CLIENT AND SERVER USER IDs

The solution that is conceptually simplest is to synchronize the UIDs and GIDs on the client and server. For instance, if a particular user has a UID of 504 on the server, you should ensure that this user has a UID of 504 on the client as well. GID assignments should be synchronized in a similar way. Unfortunately, manually adjusting UIDs in this way is tedious. This may be a viable option on a very small network with few client computers and few users, though. If you need to adjust existing UIDs, you can use the usermod command to alter a user's UID. For instance, to change abrown's UID from 507 to 504, you'd issue the following command:

```
# usermod -u 504 abrown
```

This command will change the entries in /etc/passwd and change the UID associated with files in the user's home directory, so the user won't notice a change after logging back in. (If the user has stored files outside of the home directory, you need to manually change the ownership of those files.) This command can take some time to complete. If you interrupt it, you may need to change the ownership of some files and directories (including the user's home directory) manually.

The groupmod command serves a similar function for altering group information, but you pass the new group ID using the -g parameter. For instance, to change a GID number for the group project3 to 127, you'd issue the following command:

```
# groupmod -g 127 project3
```

WARNING Don't try to change a UID or GID when the user or members of the group are logged on. Doing so is likely to result in an inability to save work or read files, and running programs may misbehave in program-specific ways when this happens. If you make such a change accidentally, you might try undoing it, or advise the user to log out and then back in. If the user needs to save any files, they can be saved in a common area, such as /tmp.

One point to note about this approach is that the usernames used on the client and server don't need to match. For instance, a single user might have a username of abrown on the server but alyson on the client. When this person uses the client to access files on the server, they will appear to be owned by alyson; but if the user logs into the NFS server, the files will appear to be owned by abrown. This feature could be confusing, but it might also be useful in some situations.

A variant on the idea of keeping UIDs and GIDs synchronized is to use an outside server to authenticate users on both the client and server. This practice will give users the same UIDs, and groups the same GIDs, on both the NFS client and the NFS server. You can use Kerberos, described in Chapter 6, for this function. Linux's NFS implementation includes explicit support for NIS authentication, via the map_nis option. When you include this option in a definition for a specific client in /etc/exports, the NFS server defers to the NIS server in creating a username mapping for that client and export.

USING A SERVER-SIDE USER ID MAP

Suppose you're administering a two-computer network with four users whose usernames and UIDs are outlined in Table 8.1. In this example, gingko is the server and larch is the client. Of these four users, only one (james) has the same UID on both systems. Without special configuration,

Table 8.1 Hypothetical User and Group IDs on Two Computers

User	User ID on gingko	User ID on larch
alyson	500	504
james	501	501
jennie	502	503
samuel	503	502

james would be able to access his own files correctly. From larch, though, alyson would find that her files stored on gingko would be owned by an unidentified user (UID 500, which has no counterpart on larch). The final two users, jennie and samuel, would seem to own each others' files.

One way to work around the mapping problem is to have the NFS server maintain a file that includes mapping information akin to that in Table 8.1. You tell the server to use such a file with the map_static option, and you pass the name of the mapping file along with this option. For instance, an entry in /etc/exports might look like this:

```
/home   larch(rw,map_static=/etc/nfs/larch-map)
```

This tells the system to export /home to larch, and to use the file /etc/nfs/larch-map for the mapping file. Because the map_static option is part of the option list for a client, it's possible to create separate mapping lists for different clients. The contents of larch-map, matched to Table 8.1, might resemble Listing 8.2. Lines beginning with pound signs (#) are comments and are ignored; Listing 8.2 includes a couple of comment lines to document the file and remind you of the meaning of each column of information. Each noncomment line begins with uid or gid to identify the mapping of UIDs or GIDs, respectively. The next item is the ID number or numbers (expressed as a range, as in the first entry's 0-99) on the client system. The final entry is the local UID or GID to which the remote ID is mapped. Thus, for instance, Listing 8.2 maps the client's UID 504 to the server's UID 500. If the server column consists of a single dash (-), the NFS server squashes access—converting it to that of the anonymous user, as discussed earlier.

Listing 8.2 Sample Contents of a UID Mapping File

```
# Mapping for client larch
#     remote     local
uid   0-99       -         # squash
uid   504        500
uid   501        501
uid   503        502
uid   502        503
gid   0-99       -         # squash
gid   100-102    100
```

It's important that *every* user's ID appear in the mapping file. Listing 8.2, for instance, doesn't omit UID 501, although it maps to the same number on both systems. Omitting the UID is likely to result in a spurious mapping, and therefore problems. Listing 8.2 explicitly squashes all the system UIDs (those numbered below 100). It also squashes all GIDs below 100, and maps client GIDs of 100–102 onto a local GID of 100. Although you can map a range of client IDs onto a single server ID, doing the reverse is meaningless—the server would have no idea which of the local IDs to use when it saw an attempt to create a file with a particular remote ID.

As with manual client and server ID synchronization, it's possible for the usernames on the client and server to be different with this approach. The mapping file works exclusively on user and group IDs; it doesn't care about usernames. To avoid confusion, it's probably best to keep usernames the same across clients and servers, whenever possible.

USING A CLIENT-SIDE MAPPING DAEMON

Another way around the mapping problem is to use the map_daemon option in the server, which allows a special server (called ugidd or rpc.ugidd) that runs on the client to perform username mapping. Unfortunately, this option has several problems. For one thing, the ugidd server is difficult to find. Of the distributions discussed in this book, only Debian ships with it. Another problem is that the ugidd server runs on the client, which can result in much more complex configuration, as you must install the program on all your clients. Unless you block access to ugidd (say, using /etc/hosts.allow), the server can be used by miscreants to discover all the usernames on your NFS clients, which is better made impossible. Finally, and in many ways most important, the server is very finicky and may not work at all, or it may map all users to nobody.

SUMMARY

NFS is an extremely useful tool for performing file sharing between UNIX and Linux systems. Unlike Samba, NFS provides explicit support for UNIX-style file ownership and permissions. NFS configuration tends to be simpler than Samba configuration, as well. On the other hand, NFS relies upon a trusted hosts security model, and if you don't keep your usernames synchronized across clients and servers, you'll have to resort to a username mapping scheme such as storing user IDs in a special configuration file.

Printer Sharing via LPD

Linux has inherited its printing system from the Berkeley Software Distribution (BSD) UNIX variant. This system, which is often referred to by the name of its most critical component, the *Line Printer Daemon (LPD)*, is both extremely flexible and very primitive when compared to the printing systems on modern desktop OSs such as Windows or MacOS. LPD's flexibility derives from the fact that it's a network-capable printing system. Thus, there's no need to run a separate print server or print client to perform network printing operations; the basic printing system includes both network client and network server functionality. The primitive nature of LPD relates to its handling of drivers to process output for the wide variety of printers that are on the market today. LPD doesn't explicitly support printer drivers in the way they're used on other OSs, although a common add-on package (Ghostscript, see http://www.cs.wisc.edu/~ghost/), in conjunction with a *smart filter* to identify and process different types of files, roughly fills this role.

This chapter discusses the network features of LPD, as well as a more modern protocol that's becoming increasingly popular. This chapter does *not* cover configuring a computer to drive a particular model of local printer via Ghostscript and a smart filter. For that information, consult your distribution's documentation or an introductory book on Linux. This chapter begins with an overview of the LPD landscape—when you should run an LPD server and what options exist for printing software under Linux. This chapter then proceeds to examine how to configure each of the three most common printing systems under Linux: the original BSD LPD, the LPRng replacement package, and the newer CUPS package.

When to Run an LPD Server

Conceptually, network printing is similar to file sharing. In network printing, the client sends a file to the server, much as a file-sharing client may send a file to a file-sharing server. The main difference is what happens to the file. In the case of file sharing, the server stores the file on its disk, presumably to be accessed at a later date by the same or some other user. In network printing, the server sends the file on to a printer, and usually deletes the spool file once this is done. These two tasks are so similar at a network level that some protocols—most importantly, the Server Message Block (SMB)/Common Internet Filesystem (CIFS) protocols—use a single server (Samba in the case of Linux) to handle both tasks. Native UNIX tools, though, separate these two functions into two servers: the Network Filesystem (NFS) server for file sharing, and LPD for printer sharing.

As noted earlier, Linux's standard LPD tools integrate local and network printing operations, so if your Linux system is configured to print using these standard tools, it takes very little additional effort to configure the system to either accept remote print jobs or send print jobs to a networked printer. In some sense, therefore, the question of when to run an LPD server is one of when you want to do network printing. As a general rule, network printing is useful in many small- and mid-size offices as a method of stretching available resources. Rather than buy inexpensive (say, $300) laser printers for a dozen computers (for a total cost of $3600), you can buy one much more capable $1500 laser printer. For that price difference, you could even throw in an inexpensive color inkjet or further upgrade the laser printer to one that can handle color, and still come out ahead. LPD is one of the critical components that allows you to do this.

LPD isn't the only network printing protocol, though. As noted earlier, SMB/CIFS includes printing capabilities. So do competing protocols and packages like AppleTalk (via Linux's Netatalk). On another level, then, the question becomes: When should you use LPD as opposed to some other printer-sharing tools? This question is more subtle than the earlier question. There are two major points to consider in answering it:

- What is best supported by the client? Linux supports a wide variety of network printing protocols, so a Linux computer can function as a print server for many different types of clients. Because clients usually outnumber servers on any given network, you'll save yourself considerable effort by using whatever protocol is best supported by the clients. When your clients are UNIX or Linux systems, this means LPD. When they're DOS, Windows, or OS/2 systems, this means SMB/CIFS. When they're Macintoshes, AppleTalk is a good bet, although MacOS X also works well with LPD.

- Do the competing protocols provide differing levels of support for features you need? Network printing is simpler in many ways than is file sharing—for instance, filename and permission issues are less troublesome in network printing than in file sharing. Nonetheless, each protocol supports its own set of options, such as authentication procedures. You might want to use a protocol that's not the default for your clients in order to obtain one of these features.

This second point deserves some elaboration. LPD, like NFS, uses a *trusted hosts* security model, in which the server relies on the client to control access to the shared resource. The server restricts access based primarily on the IP address of the client. This method is convenient when working with multi-user client OSs, but it's not as secure as a method that requires usernames and passwords to access the server. SMB/CIFS, in particular, works in this way, so you might want to favor it if you prefer to require a password for printer access. (If your clients are Linux or UNIX computers, though, you'll end up storing printer passwords in some globally readable configuration file unless you write new printing scripts from scratch. The result may not be an improvement over trusted hosts security.) The newer Internet Printing Protocol (IPP) favored by CUPS also supports the use of usernames and passwords, but this feature is optional in CUPS.

If your clients are Windows computers, chances are you'll want to use SMB/CIFS for printer sharing, although there are LPD clients available for these systems. You might consider foregoing SMB/CIFS, and the complications of Samba configuration, if you have just a few Windows clients on a network dominated by UNIX, Linux, MacOS, or some other system that doesn't normally use SMB/CIFS.

A related question is when to use *Linux* as a print server. You can run most Linux print servers on other UNIX-like OSs, so when you have a choice of Linux versus another UNIX-like OS for using BSD protocols, the issue is one of convenience. Linux makes an excellent unifying platform if you need to share printers with Linux, UNIX, Windows, MacOS, and other OSs because you can run so many different printer-sharing protocols simultaneously.

Another option in many situations is to use a dedicated printer-sharing box. These devices are dedicated network appliances with an Ethernet interface, server protocols built into firmware, and parallel, RS-232 serial, or USB ports for connecting one or more printers. They can be very good choices if you don't want to configure printer sharing on a regular computer—say because the computer won't be powered up at all times or because you're concerned about the security aspects of running a server on whatever computer might be convenient. Some high-end printers come with network connectors that function much like dedicated print servers.

TIP You can convert an old computer into a dedicated print server by using Linux. Install Linux, strip it of unnecessary tools and servers, and even an old 386 makes an adequate print server. With a fast enough CPU, the print server can use Ghostscript to process PostScript files, turning the combination of the dedicated computer and an inexpensive non-PostScript printer into a networked PostScript printer. Particularly if you add extra parallel ports or use USB devices, a single Linux computer can serve several printers. Of course, a more powerful computer can function as a print server *and* perform other server or nonserver tasks.

LPD SERVER OPTIONS FOR LINUX

UNIX systems generally, and Linux systems in particular, support a large number of printing packages, most of which implement the LPD protocol. In 2001, the three most popular printing packages for Linux are:

- **The original BSD LPD server**—This package has long been the standard in Linux, and many Linux programs assume that BSD LPD utilities are installed. For this reason, both LPRng and CUPS emulate the BSD LPD tools, although to differing extents. BSD LPD is very simple in its access control mechanisms, which is one of the reasons many distributions have begun shifting away from it.

- **The LPRng package**—This system, headquartered at http://www.astart.com/lprng/LPRng.html, is designed as a more-or-less direct replacement for the BSD LPD system. It deviates from the BSD LPD system in some of its configuration file formats, but retains the BSD LPD format in other configuration files. It doesn't alter the basic printing model, which requires that the application know something about the printer to which it's printing (in Linux, most applications assume the printer is a PostScript model).

- **The Common UNIX Printing System (CUPS)**—This system, whose home page is http://www.cups.org, is a more radical deviation from the BSD LPD system than is LPRng. Like LPRng, CUPS provides workalike commands for some of the common tools, but CUPS uses an entirely different set of printer configuration files. CUPS also provides information on the printers it drives to applications that are written for CUPS. (To use this feature over a network, both the client and the server must run CUPS.) In addition to the LPD protocol, CUPS supports a newer network printing protocol, IPP.

NOTE Other printing systems are common on some other UNIX-like OSs. For instance, versions of UNIX derived from SysV often use a different system. The SysV printing system can interoperate with the BSD system, but it uses different commands, such as 1p rather than 1pr to submit a print job.

Table 9.1 details the printing systems that ship with several popular Linux distributions. Of course, you can install a printing system on a distribution even if that printing system doesn't ship with the distribution, but you may need to put additional effort into configuring the software. Getting the software to start up automatically may be a particular challenge, as described in Chapter 4, Starting Servers.

NOTE The distinction between "standard" and "alternative" printing systems in Table 9.1 is sometimes very slim. For instance, Mandrake gives you the option at installation time of using LPRng or CUPS. The default choice is LPRng, but it takes only a single mouse click to change this to CUPS. Debian doesn't install any printing system by default, so listing BSD LPD as the standard is entirely arbitrary.

Table 9.1 Standard Printing Software with Several Linux Distributions

Distribution	Standard Printing System	Alternative Printing Systems
Caldera OpenLinux Server 3.1	CUPS	none
Debian GNU/Linux 2.2	BSD LPD	LPRng, CUPS
Linux Mandrake 8.1	LPRng	CUPS
Red Hat Linux 7.2	LPRng	none
Slackware Linux 8.0	BSD LPD	none
SuSE Linux 7.3	LPRng	CUPS
TurboLinux 7.0	LPRng	none

Most Linux documentation has been written with a BSD LPD system in mind. Most of this documentation applies almost as well to an LPRng system, although the details of how to restrict access to a networked print server differ between the two, as the following sections illustrate. Most of the generic Linux printing documentation applies only loosely to CUPS, because CUPS uses entirely different configuration files.

Configuring a BSD LPD Server

Two files are most important for configuring a BSD LPD server: `/etc/hosts.lpd` and `/etc/printcap`. The first of these controls which clients may connect to the server for network operation. The second defines the printers that are available to both local and remote users. Note that `/etc/printcap` defines both local and remote printers, and defines printers that are available both locally and remotely. Therefore, it's possible for a remote user to submit a print job to a queue that corresponds to a remote system. When this happens, the print job comes in over the network and is immediately sent out again. Normally, this is wasteful of bandwidth, but in some cases it might be desirable, as when the print server uses Ghostscript to convert a PostScript file into a format that the ultimate destination printer can understand.

Configuring /etc/hosts.lpd

By default, a BSD LPD system doesn't accept print jobs that don't originate on the local computer—that is, the software does *not* function as a networked print server. Changing this configuration requires editing a single file: `/etc/hosts.lpd`. This file contains a list of computers, one per line, that are allowed to access the local print queues. Computers may be specified by hostname, by IP address, or by NIS netgroup. In the final case, the netgroup name is identified by a leading at-sign (@), which in turn must be preceded by a plus sign (+). A plus sign alone makes the server accept *any* print job, which is a potentially major security hole. Preceding a name by a minus sign (-) indicates that the host is explicitly *disallowed* access. For instance, Listing 9.1 shows a completely functional `/etc/hosts.lpd` file. In the case of `gingko`, the server's own domain name is assumed. The `+@group1` line gives access to all the computers in the NIS netgroup called `group1`, but `oak.threeroomco.com` is denied access, even if it's part of the `group1` netgroup.

Although you can place comments in the `/etc/hosts.lpd` file by beginning a comment line with a pound sign (#), you should *not* place comments on

Listing 9.1 A Sample `/etc/hosts.lpd` File

```
gingko
birch.threeroomco.com
192.168.1.7
+@group1
-oak.threeroomco.com
```

lines that also contain client specifications. Instead, you should place comments on lines that precede or follow the line you want to explain.

WARNING

It's possible to use `/etc/hosts.equiv` much as you can use `/etc/hosts.lpd`. The `/etc/hosts.equiv` file, however, has an effect far beyond that of printing; it provides access to clients that use `rlogin` and other protocols. I strongly recommend against using `/etc/hosts.equiv`; you can configure the servers that it controls individually, giving you much finer-grained control over access to the computer. You might want to look for this file and, if it's present, rename it and adjust the configuration of other files as appropriate.

Specifying the Server on a BSD LPD Client

The `/etc/printcap` file controls the BSD LPD printing system's printer definitions (`printcap` stands for *printer capabilities*). This file contains entries for each print queue on the system, whether it's a local queue (that is, prints to a printer that's connected directly to the computer via a parallel, RS-232 serial, or USB port), or a network queue (printing to another LPD printer, or even a printer that uses SMB/CIFS, AppleTalk, or some other protocol). In theory, each printer definition occupies one line, and options are separated by colons (`:`). In practice, most `/etc/printcap` definitions use the backslash (\) line continuation character to allow a single entry to span multiple lines, to make it easier to read—every line but the last one ends in a backslash to indicate that it's continued on the following line.

Most details of printer configuration via `/etc/printcap` are beyond the scope of this book; as noted at the start of this chapter, you should consult your distribution's documentation or an introductory book on Linux system administration to learn how to configure printers, including smart filters, Ghostscript, and most `/etc/printcap` options. There are a few options that require comment from the point of view of configuring a network print client, however. These options are:

227

- **lp**—The lp option points the BSD LPD system to the device file to which the printer is attached. For instance, lp=/dev/lp0 tells the system to use /dev/lp0 (the first parallel port). If you're configuring an LPD-style network printer, you should omit this option, or leave it blank (as in lp=).

- **rm**—The rm option specifies the name of the LPD-style print server. For instance, if oak is the print server for a given queue, you'd include the option rm=oak in the queue's definition. Note that this isn't enough to print to a specific remote queue; it only identifies the *computer* on which the queue resides. You can specify the remote machine as a hostname (with or without the domain name) or as an IP address.

- **rp**—The rp option picks up where rm leaves off, specifying the name of the remote print queue. For instance, if the remote queue is called inkjet on the print server, you'd include rp=inkjet in the client's /etc/printcap. Note that the name of the remote queue need bear no resemblance to the name of the local queue. For instance, the server's inkjet printer might be known on the client as lp1 or canon. Particularly in a large network, though, you might want to keep the names synchronized to avoid confusion.

In sum, if you have an existing local print queue, you can convert it into a network print queue by replacing the lp option with an rm option and an rp option. Once this is done, the computer will send its print job to the computer identified by rm and the queue specified by rp, rather than to the printer attached to the device indicated by lp. On the server, the queue will probably include an lp specification, although it *could* include rm and rp specifications—but in this case, it's usually simpler to specify the ultimate destination more directly in the ultimate print client. (Exceptions include cases where you want to offload Ghostscript processing onto an intermediate system or when network topologies prevent a direct connection between the client and server, but where an intermediate system can connect to both.)

If the print server doesn't accept LPD connections, you'll need to use a more complex arrangement. For instance, the server might expect SMB/CIFS or AppleTalk print jobs. In such cases, you'll need to write a script that processes the print job using whatever tools are appropriate, and call that script with the if option, which sets up an input filter. The Samba and Netatalk documentation both include examples of doing this.

CONFIGURING AN LPRNG SERVER

As an intended replacement for BSD LPD, LPRng works much the same way from a user's perspective. Indeed, LPRng even uses an /etc/printcap file that's very similar to the file of the same name in a BSD LPD system. LPRng's access control system for operation as a print server, however, is very different. Instead of a simple list of allowed clients in /etc/hosts. equiv, LPRng supports a much more complex security system, controlled through /etc/lpd.perms.

CONFIGURING /etc/lpd.perms

The /etc/lpd.perms file controls access to the printing system as a whole. There may also be lpd.perms files stored in the spool directories for individual queues (typically /var/spool/lpd/*queuename*). If present, these files provide control over individual queues—/etc/lpd.perms sets global options.

Whatever the location, lpd.perms contains five types of lines. The first is a comment line, which begins with a pound sign (#). Unlike /etc/hosts.lpd, you may add a comment to a line after the main command. These commands take one of four forms:

```
DEFAULT ACCEPT
DEFAULT REJECT
ACCEPT [ key = value[,value]* ]*
REJECT [ key = value[,value]* ]*
```

The first two forms set the system's default policy—to accept or reject connections. Most LPRng packages that ship with Linux distributions include a DEFAULT ACCEPT line in /etc/lpd.perms, so these packages are, by default, much more promiscuous than are BSD LPD packages, which normally accept connections only from the localhost address (127.0.0.1, the computer on which the software runs). For this reason, it's important that you tighten restrictions on connections by using ACCEPT and REJECT options.

The ACCEPT and REJECT options set specific types of accesses that the server will accept or reject, respectively. You normally follow these options with one of the keys from the Key column of Table 9.2, which you set to a value defined by the Connect through lpc columns of that table. The Connect column defines a basic ability to connect. The Job Spool and Job Print columns define the ability to send a job to the spooler and cause it to print, respectively. The lpq, lprm, and lpc columns define the ability to perform tasks that are normally controlled by the printing utilities of these names. In most cases, giving access to one of these features gives access to all of them—or at least to all of them that make sense. Some features are meaningless with

Table 9.2 Keys and Associated Value Types for `lpd.perms`

Key	Connect	Job Spool	Job Print	lpq	lprm	lpc
SERVICE	X	R	P	Q	M	C for control or S for status
USER	-	Username	Username	Username	Username	Username
HOST	Remote Host	Host Name	Host Name	Host Name	Host Name	Host Name
GROUP	-	Username	Username	Username	Username	Username
IP	Remote IP Address	Host IP Address	Host IP Address	Remote IP Address	Host IP Address	Host IP Address
PORT	Port Number	Port Number	-	Port Number	Port Number	Port Number
REMOTEUSER	-	Username	Username	Username	Username	Username
REMOTEHOST	Remote Host	Remote Host	Host Host	Remote Host	Remote Host	Remote Host
REMOTEGROUP	-	Username	Username	Username	Username	Username
REMOTEIP	Remote IP Address	Remote IP Address	Host IP Address	Remote IP Address	Remote IP Address	Remote IP Address
CONTROLLINE	-	Pattern Match	Pattern Match	Pattern Match	Pattern Match	Pattern Match
PRINTER	-	Printer Name	Printer Name	Printer Name	Printer Name	Printer Name
FORWARD	-	-	-	-	-	-
SAMEHOST	-	-	-	-	-	-
SAMEUSER	-	-	-	-	-	-
SERVER	-	-	-	-	-	-

some keys, or don't take an explicit parameter, as indicated by "-" entries in Table 9.2. You can reverse the meaning of a value by preceding it with NOT. IP addresses may be followed by a slash (/) and a netmask to apply to an entire network.

The options for controlling access can seem quite complex, so it may help to examine some examples. First, consider some lines that are part of most standard /etc/lpd.perms files:

```
ACCEPT SERVICE=M SAMEHOST SAMEUSER
ACCEPT SERVICE=M SERVER REMOTEUSER=root
REJECT SERVICE=M
```

These three lines specify who may use the lprm utility to delete jobs. All three lines include the SERVICE=M option, which indicates that they apply to the lprm functions, as shown by the SERVICE line in Table 9.2. The first line includes the SAMEHOST and SAMEUSER options, which mean that the command will be accepted if it comes from the same computer that submitted the job, and from the user who owns the job. The second line includes the SERVER and REMOTEUSER=root options, which tell the system to allow root on the server system to delete jobs. The final line rejects all other requests for lprm service. (LPRng searches through its control file until it finds an option that matches the incoming command; as long as the two ACCEPT SERVICE=M lines come before the REJECT SERVICE=M line, the ACCEPT lines take precedence for commands that they match.)

As noted earlier, the default LPRng configuration on many distributions is to accept connections from just about anywhere. This is a potentially dangerous configuration, because an outsider could submit print jobs that could waste your paper, ink, and toner, as well as fill your print spool partition or possibly even compromise your system, if there's a security flaw in LPRng. For this reason, it's generally a good idea to limit access to LPRng. You can do this with a packet filter firewall rule, as discussed in Chapter 25, Configuring iptables. I recommend doing this, but I also recommend implementing redundant protections in LPRng itself. Suppose you have a print server that should accept jobs from the 172.22.0.0/16 network, and from the server computer itself, but not from other addresses. You could accomplish this goal with a pair of lines like the following:

```
ACCEPT SERVICE=X SERVER
REJECT SERVICE=X NOT REMOTEIP=172.22.0.0/16
```

These lines restrict basic connection to the server, and thus the ability to submit print jobs or do anything else. The first line explicitly allows connections from the server itself. (These come over the 127.0.0.1 interface, so using REMOTEIP=127.0.0.1 instead of SERVER will have the same effect.) Without this line, the next one would block access to the server from itself, which you probably don't want to do. The second line rejects all accesses that don't originate from the 172.22.0.0/16 network, or which weren't accepted by a preceding line. If you wanted to accept jobs from multiple subnets, you could include an ACCEPT line that accepts jobs from an additional subnet just prior to the REJECT line. It's best to place these lines that operate on service X earlier than other lines that operate on more specific services, unless those other lines are written in a restrictive way; placing the more specific lines earlier could inadvertently let through some types of connection you might prefer not to permit.

Specifying the Server on an LPRng Client

LPRng uses an /etc/printcap file that's very similar to the one use by BSD LPD. In particular, the lp, rm, and rp options, described earlier in the section "Specifying the Server on a BSD LPD Client," apply to both BSD LPD and LPRng. Most other options also apply to both printing systems, although there are a few differences. These are outside the scope of this chapter, though.

BSD LPD and LPRng use the same LPD protocol for network printing, so you can configure an LPRng client to print to a BSD LPD server or vice versa. This interoperability also extends to CUPS, although CUPS also supports extended protocols that are useful only when two CUPS systems interoperate.

Configuring a CUPS Server

CUPS is an unusually flexible printing system for UNIX and Linux computers. Rather than a re-implementation of the BSD LPD package (which is what LPRng is), CUPS is a new framework around which printing on Linux can work. *Part* of this framework is a compatibility layer, so that applications and users can use familiar printing commands, and so that CUPS clients can use LPD print servers, and vice versa. Major additional features include support for a new network printing protocol, IPP, which is based on the Hypertext Transfer Protocol (HTTP) used by Web servers and browsers; the ability to pass file type information with files to simplify the selection of print filters on the print server; the use of PostScript Printer Description (PPD) files to define printer capabilities; and "printer browsing," a feature that allows a client to search for printers on the network without having to explicitly configure the client to use a specific printer. If CUPS is widely adopted, these features will greatly simplify printer configuration, both for non-networked and networked use.

One major hurdle faced by CUPS is the fact that it doesn't use the same types of configuration files that BSD LPD or LPRng use. Therefore, if you're already familiar with these systems, you'll have to learn to configure your printers in an entirely new way. If you like to work with GUI tools, you may want to look into a GUI front-end to CUPS for general configuration, such as KUPS (http://cups.sourceforge.net/kups/) or ESP

Print Pro (http://www.easysw.com/printpro/). CUPS also comes with a Web-based tool, as described shortly; you can point your Web browser at http://localhost:631 to configure the computer on which the Web browser is running.

NOTE   As with the other printing systems, a complete description of CUPS printer configuration is beyond the scope of this book. This section assumes that you can create a minimally functional local print queue; I describe only those options related to the networking aspects of the printer definition. For more information on basic CUPS configuration, consult the CUPS documentation at http://www.cups.org/sam.html.

CONFIGURING /etc/cups/cupsd.conf

The CUPS server is controlled through the /etc/cups/cupsd.conf file. This file is modeled after the Apache configuration file (discussed in Chapter 20, Running Web Servers), as CUPS borrows many HTTP server features. CUPS also uses several other configuration files, such as /etc/cups/printers.conf and /etc/cups/classes.conf, which define specific printers and groups of printers, respectively. Both these files are normally edited via the lpadmin configuration tool or a GUI front-end, but the CUPS documentation recommends editing cupsd.conf manually.

The cupsd.conf file consists of a series of *directives* that set specific features of the server's function, such as the server's name or where logs are stored. Directives that are particularly important for network print server functions include the following:

- **Allow**—This directive is followed by the keyword from and the wildcards All or None, a hostname, a hostname with an asterisk wildcard (such as *.threeroomco.com), a partial or complete IP address, or an IP address with a netmask (in either CIDR or 8-byte formats). Any of these forms specify computers that are allowed access to the server. You can include multiple Allow directives to grant access to multiple computers or groups of computers. This directive must appear within a Location directive.

- **AuthClass**—This directive takes a value of Anonymous (the default), User, System, or Group. Anonymous results in no need to authenticate clients; this works much like a BSD LPD system. The remaining three options require clients to provide a valid username and password.

System further requires that the user belong to the sys group, as set by the SystemGroup directive. Group requires that the user belong to the group named by the AuthGroupName directive.

- **BrowseAddress**—The CUPS printer browsing features works best when a central server collects information on available printers on a network. You can set this server with the BrowseAddress directive, which takes an IP address or hostname and port number as an option, as in 192.168.23.34:631. (631 is the usual port number for this and most other CUPS connections.) The default is 255.255.255.255:631, which results in a broadcast to all computers on the local network.

- **BrowseAllow**—To use printer browsing from a client, your server must accept browse packets from the client. This directive is followed by the keyword from and the partial or complete hostname or IP address of the computers from which the server will accept browse packets. The default is to accept browse packets from all computers.

- **BrowseDeny**—This directive is the opposite of BrowseAllow; you can blacklist just certain networks or clients using this directive.

- **BrowseOrder**—When you use both BrowseAllow and BrowseDeny, this directive determines the order in which the first two directives are applied. Options are BrowseOrder Allow,Deny and BrowseOrder Deny,Allow.

- **BrowseInterval**—This directive sets the time in seconds between outgoing browse queries. A value of 0 disables outgoing browse queries. This value should always be less than the value of BrowseTimeout, or printers will periodically disappear from your local browse list.

- **BrowsePoll**—You can set the name or IP address of a print server you want to poll for printers using this directive. You can poll multiple servers by using this value more than once.

- **BrowsePort**—The default port for printer browsing is 631, but you can override this value by using this directive.

- **BrowseTimeout**—CUPS removes information on network printers and classes at an interval determined by this directive. This value should always be greater than the BrowseInterval value, or printers will periodically disappear from a CUPS client's browse list.

- **Browsing**—You can enable or disable network browsing by setting this directive to On or Off, respectively. The default value is On.

- **Deny**—This directive is the opposite of Allow; it's a specification of computers that are not allowed access to the server. It must appear within a Location directive.

- **HostNameLookups**—This directive takes values of Off, On, and Double. These cause CUPS to not look up hostnames of clients, to look up hostnames for every client that connects, and to look up the hostname and then look up the IP address from the obtained hostname, respectively. The Double option in particular provides some protection against certain types of attack, because it prevents connections from systems with misconfigured DNS entries. The default is Off, because this setting results in the least performance cost and because it's most reliable (the other options can cause problems if your network's DNS server goes down or becomes slow).

- **Listen**—You can tell CUPS to use only a subset of your computer's network interfaces by using one or more Listen directives. Follow the directive name with the IP address associated with the network interface, a colon, and a port number (normally 631). For instance, Listen 192.168.23.8:631 causes the computer to use the interface associated with the 192.168.23.8 address. You can use more than one Listen directive (and probably should, to bind to the 127.0.0.1 interface as well as whatever network interface you want active).

- **Location**—This directive is unusual in that it surrounds others, defining a location within the CUPS document tree to which the surrounded directives apply. For instance, you must include Allow and Deny directives within a Location directive, in order to restrict access to particular document types (and hence particular types of operations) for specific clients. To start a Location directive, you include that keyword in angle braces (<>) along with the name of the location. To end such a directive, you use the string </Location>. Possible locations you can restrict include /admin for administrative actions, /classes for printer classes, /jobs for print jobs, and /printers for printers.

- **MaxClients**—You can limit the number of clients that can connect to a server using this directive. The default value is 100.

- **Order**—This directive is similar to the BrowseOrder directive, but it applies to the Allow and Deny directives. Order Allow,Deny causes Allow directives to be applied before Deny directives, whereas Order Deny,Allow does the opposite.

- **Port**—CUPS normally listens on port 631 for IPP transfers, but you can change the default port with this directive. You can specify multiple ports by using this directive more than once. Note that this does *not* affect the port CUPS uses for interacting with BSD LPD clients and servers, or compatible programs.

The default /etc/cups/cupsd.conf file provided with most CUPS pack-ages leaves the server fairly open to access from outsiders. You should probably tighten access by applying CUPS configuration rules to restrict access to the server. For instance, the following directives block access to anything but the server computer itself and systems on the 172.22.0.0/16 network:

```
<Location /printers>
BrowseAllow from 127.0.0.1
BrowseAllow from 172.22.0.0/16
Allow from 127.0.0.1
Allow from 172.22.0.0/16
</Location>
```

Because it applies to the /printers location, the preceding example does not completely close off access to the server. For instance, administrative tasks (via the /admin location) and access to specific print job information (via the /jobs location) is still available to other systems. You should probably restrict access to these locations as well, and apply packet filter firewall rules (as discussed in Chapter 25). The latter will completely block access to systems you don't authorize, assuming no bugs or mis-configuration.

ACCEPTING JOBS FROM BSD LPD OR LPRNG CLIENTS

The preceding discussion of /etc/cups/cupsd.conf directives applies most directly to clients that support IPP. Neither BSD LPD nor LPRng uses IPP, though; they use the older LPD protocol. (Work is underway for adding IPP support to LPRng, though.) Therefore, if your CUPS print server must accept print jobs from clients that use the LPD protocol, CUPS needs a helper program to let it do the job. This program is called cups-lpd, and it comes with CUPS.

To use cups-lpd, you must configure it to work via a super server such as inetd or xinetd, as discussed in Chapter 4; the package doesn't work as a standalone server. It's normally located in the /usr/lib/cups/daemon direc-tory. An appropriate /etc/inetd.conf file entry is as follows:

```
printer stream tcp nowait lp /usr/lib/cups/daemon/cups-lpd cups-lpd
```

Chapter 4 covers the differences between inetd and xinetd, should you need to configure cups-lpd to work with xinetd. Some distributions ship preconfigured to work correctly with BSD LPD clients, so you may not need to make such a modification.

WARNING

CUPS provides no means to control printer access to clients using the LPD protocol. Such jobs are submitted locally using the server's own address, so the normal /etc/cups/cupsd.conf directives don't have any effect. To limit outside access to a CUPS server that supports the LPD protocol, you must use a packet filter firewall or some other outside mechanism.

SPECIFYING THE SERVER ON A CUPS CLIENT

You can add printers to CUPS by using the command-line lpadmin utility, by using a GUI front-end to lpadmin, or by entering http://localhost:631 in a Web browser running on the computer (or the hostname and :631 on another computer that's allowed administrative access). Each of these methods of administration allows you to add or delete printers accessible from the computer in question, or to perform various other administrative tasks.

To add a network printer, you could use lpadmin to enter a command like the following:

```
# lpadmin -p PrinterName -E -v lpd://server.name/queuname -m \
ppdfile.ppd
```

In this example, *PrinterName* is the name of the printer queue to be used locally, *server.name* is the hostname of the print server, and *queuename* is the name of the print queue on that server. This example shows access to a print queue that uses the BSD LPD protocol, as indicated by the lpd that precedes the server and queue names. To use another CUPS server, you might prefer using ipp in place of lpd. This tells CUPS to use IPP rather than the BSD LPD protocol. (You can create a local queue in much the same way, but the parameter to -v would be parallel:/dev/lp0 or some other local device identifier.) Finally, the -m parameter identifies the PPD file for the printer, so that CUPS can pass information on the printer's capabilities back to CUPS-aware applications. On most installations, you can find a collection of PPD files in the /usr/share/cups/model directory tree. Many PostScript printers also ship with their own PPD files, which you can use. You can also attempt to use the driver listings at the Linux Printing Web site, http://www.linuxprinting.org/driver_list.cgi. Click on a Ghostscript driver name, then select your printer model in the

CUPS-O-Matic area and click Generate CUPS PPD. After a brief delay, the result should be a PPD file that describes your printer's capabilities. As the comments in the generated file note, though, this machine-generated PPD file might have quirks, or it might not even work at all. For this reason, you're better off using a PPD file that's provided by your printer's manufacturer, if possible.

TIP

If you've configured both the client and the server to perform CUPS browsing, as described earlier, you shouldn't need to explicitly add CUPS IPP printers; the client should retrieve the list of available printers and make them available automatically. Adding a printer manually is most useful for LPD print queues.

If you want to modify an existing print queue, you may do so with the lpadmin tool just as if you were adding a new queue. Specify the original name and any other options you include override the originals. For instance, you can change a local queue to a network queue by using the -v option and specifying the new location.

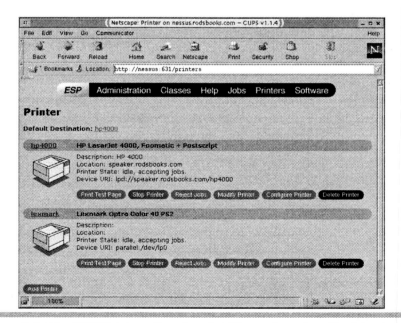

Figure 9.1 The CUPS Web-based interface simplifies configuration of both local and network printers.

If you prefer to use a GUI tool, the Web interface (shown in Figure 9.1) is supported by default on a standard installation. After you enter the URL to your computer (including the port 631 specification), CUPS prompts you for an administrative username and password. You can then select from several options, such as Do Administration Tasks and Manage Printers. Figure 9.1 shows the latter, in which you can create, delete, and administer printers. Figure 9.1 shows two defined printers. The first, hp4000, is the default and is an LPD printer. The second, lexmark, is connected to the parallel port. You can click Modify Printer to modify the basic settings, such as the server name, or you can adjust printer-specific settings such as page size and printer memory by clicking Configure Printer.

SUMMARY

Historically, Linux systems have used the BSD LPD printing system, but this system is showing its age. Various alternatives exist to this system, and Linux distributions are increasingly using them—usually LPRng or CUPS. These alternatives offer improved access control mechanisms and other features. CUPS, in particular, offers an improved ability to interact with printing applications in order to convey printer-specific features to the applications, and a Web-based configuration tool for print client configuration.

Security should be a concern on any computer that functions as a print server. Ideally, you should use packet filter firewall rules to block access to ports 515 and 631 (the LPD and IPP printing ports, respectively) to any but authorized hosts, and use access control features specific to each printing tool as a redundant measure. LPRng offers the best control over LPD printing mechanisms, while CUPS offers good control over IPP tools.

Maintaining Consistent Time: Time Servers

Every time you set up a computer, you must set its clock. What's worse, computer clocks are imperfect, so they drift from the true time—and they drift at different rates. The result is that, on a network of any size, a few weeks (or possibly just a few hours) after you've set all the computers' clocks to the same time, they'll show annoying differences. Daylight Savings Time can also cause problems, because you'll have to set the computers' clocks again or allow the computers to adjust their own times—a process that can itself cause problems if a computer has more than one OS installed on it. All told, keeping all your systems' clocks synchronized can be an administrative headache. Fortunately, a class of programs exists to help work around this problem: *time servers*. These programs deliver accurate time measurements to their clients, so setting up a central time server and configuring clients to use it can keep all your computers set to the same time. You can even have your central time server synchronize itself to an outside time server that sets its time using an atomic clock, thus allowing for very accurate time settings across your entire network.

WHEN TO RUN A TIME SERVER

One of the primary reasons for running a time server is to deliver accurate time settings to clients on your network. By having clients set their clocks to a time maintained by one of your systems, you can keep your computers' clocks set to reasonably consistent values. (Depending on the protocol in use, "reasonably consistent" can mean variations of just a few milliseconds.) This can avoid problems caused by time mismatches. For instance, with mismatched clocks, a client might save a file to a server, but become confused when reading the file back one minute later because the save date might appear to be two minutes in the future. Mismatched times can also be a real headache when tracking down information in log files. It can also be annoying to see different times on different computers' displays. Some tools, such as Kerberos, rely on clients and servers having consistent times, so running a time server with such tools is a practical necessity.

The time server program that's discussed at greatest length in this chapter is a bit unusual in that it functions as *both* a server *and* a client. Therefore, another reason to run this particular time server is to set the clock of the computer on which the server runs. In a network that contains several Linux or UNIX computers, you'll set one machine to obtain its time from an outside server, then configure the rest of the systems in exactly the same way, except that you'll point these systems to the first one to obtain their time locally. This multi-tiered configuration reduces the load on the ultimate sources of time signals, such as computers that are linked to atomic clocks or radios that can receive broadcast time signals from official time sources. If you don't want to run the complete server package on clients, you may be able to make do with a simpler program that functions only as a client, but you'll need to call it explicitly every now and then to keep the system's time set correctly.

SETTING UP AN NTP SERVER

One of the more popular time server protocols is known as the *Network Time Protocol (NTP)*, which is described by RFC 1305 (http://www.ietf.org/rfc/rfc1305.txt). Previous versions were described in RFCs 958, 1059, and 1119. The current version number is 4, although version 3 NTP servers are still common in 2002. The main NTP Web site is http://www.eecis.udel.edu/~ntp/. NTP allows for a hierarchical structure of time servers, so those closest to accurate clocks can serve others, which in turn serve the ultimate clients. NTP clients and servers are readily available for Linux and other OSs. Configuring NTP for Linux requires editing a single configuration file. You can monitor the server's operation using dedicated tools. Limited-functionality clients are also available for easy use if a system is to be a terminus in the time server hierarchy.

NOTE   There's a simplified variant of NTP that's known as Simple NTP (SNTP). SNTP clients can synchronize to NTP servers.

UNDERSTANDING HOW A TIME SERVER FUNCTIONS

Time server functionality begins with a veridical time source, such as an atomic clock or a radio or modem receiver that can synchronize with an official time source. Global Positioning System (GPS) receivers work in part by using time signals from satellites, so these may be used as a way to acquire such an accurate time source. (The NTP Web page includes a discussion of such hardware devices at http://www.eecis.udel.edu/~ntp/hardware.html.)

The atomic clock, radio hardware, or similar device is known as a *reference* or a *stratum 0* time server. Unless you own such a device, you won't connect directly to it, since they don't have network connections (they usually interface through an RS-232 serial port and require special drivers). The computer that synchronizes its clock to the reference is known as a *stratum 1* server. In theory, these computers have the most accurate times available on the Internet, although in practice, surveys suggest that roughly a third of them have times that are incorrect by a second or more. Systems that synchronize to stratum 1 servers are known as *stratum 2* servers, and so on.

Synchronization involves transferring several packets (typically at least five over roughly a five-minute period) between the client and the server. The client sends a packet with the client's current time to the server. The server responds with a similar packet. By comparing the send and receive times using its local clock, the client can estimate the round-trip network delays between it and the server, and thus compensate for these delays in adjusting its own time. The client may also be configured to use several servers, and thus to compare the times, network delays, and other salient factors between these servers in order to select the best time from among these servers.

Locally, a full NTP server runs continuously, checking back with its parent servers every once in a while (initially every 64 seconds, but this interval usually increases to 1024 seconds, or possibly higher with some configurations). The NTP server program can adjust the clock on the computer on which it runs in several ways. NTP typically ignores large differences (those over a second or so) for a while, on the grounds that the large difference might be a protocol error; but after the difference has persisted for a while, NTP compensates either by resetting the time at once or by running the system clock faster or slower (that is, *slewing* the clock) until the system and external time are synchronized. Small errors are compensated by slewing the system clock until the measurements are synchronized. The NTP server also maintains a file, typically /etc/ntp/drift, /var/state/ntp.drift, or something similar, in which a number is stored that allows the server to compensate for the bulk of a computer's clock drift even if contact with lower-stratum time servers is lost or if the computer is powered off for a while.

TIP

Errors of more than 1000 seconds usually cause NTP to exit, on the assumption that something is seriously amiss and requires human intervention. Thus, you may need to manually set your system clock to a value that's at least *approximately* correct before running an NTP server. Alternatively, you can use the ntpdate program, described in the upcoming section "Using an NTP Client Package," to set the time before running the NTP server. Some distributions call ntpdate in the NTP server startup script.

Normally, an NTP server on a small network synchronizes its clock to about three external time servers. (Three is a somewhat arbitrary number; you may increase it or decrease it as you see fit, but three usually provides enough redundancy and cross-checking to work well.) The external time servers for a small network should normally be stratum 2 servers; there's very little accuracy to be gained by using stratum 1 servers, and because there are so few of them, stratum 1 servers are best reserved for use by servers with over a hundred clients. Clients on the small network may then run NTP servers for near-continuous updates from the network's stratum 3 NTP server, or they may use NTP clients or other time protocol clients to update their clocks less frequently. If your network has more than a couple dozen computers and continuous service is important, you might consider running two stratum 3 time servers to reduce the chance of problems should your main time server computer go down or become unreliable. If extremely precise time is important, you might obtain a GPS-based clock and run your own stratum 1 time server. Such clocks sell for a few hundred dollars. Devices based on AM radio time broadcasts are less costly, but are also much less accurate (they're usually accurate to less than a second, but if the goal is high accuracy, that may not be enough).

NTP uses Coordinated Universal Time (UTC) as the basis for all operations. UTC is similar to Greenwich Mean Time (GMT)—the time in Greenwich, England, unadjusted for Daylight Savings Time. UTC differs from GMT in several technical details, but the main point of interest is that it's defined more precisely and in terms of highly reliable atomic reactions, rather than the rotation of the Earth, which varies by small but measurable amounts. When necessary, UTC is adjusted for variation in Earth's rotation by the addition or subtraction of a second from a day (a *leap second*). Local time is related to UTC by adding or subtracting your time zone, with Daylight Savings Time adjustments, if necessary. Linux systems use UTC internally, so UTC is a good choice for a time protocol from a Linux point of view.

Most *x*86 OSs require that the motherboard's hardware clock be set to local time, not UTC. For this reason, Linux supports motherboard clocks that are set to either local time or UTC, and maintains a separate software clock set to UTC. On a Linux-only system, UTC is the better option because Daylight Savings Time requires no adjustments to the hardware clock. On a system that dual boots Linux and Windows (or some other OS that requires a clock set to local time), you may be forced to use local time, and both OSs may attempt to make Daylight Savings Time adjustments. Using a time protocol at system boot time can help alleviate this problem, but Linux doesn't automatically adjust the hardware clock when the system clock is set, so the benefit of NTP running under Linux may not manifest itself in the other OS. You can type `hwclock --systohc --localtime` to set the hardware clock from the system clock on a system that sets the hardware clock to local time. Substitute `--utc` for `--localtime` if the computer stores time in UTC.

TIME SERVER PROGRAMS FOR LINUX

The main NTP server package for Linux is known as `ntp`, or some variant of that, such as `xntp`, `xntp3`, or `xntpd`. The x in the name stands for *experimental*, although that's something of a misnomer, since the software has been in common use for several years. NTP version 4 packages usually omit the x. Most Linux distributions ship with one of these packages—usually version 4, although in 2002 some distributions still ship with version 3.

The NTP package included with most distributions includes the main NTP server and several support programs, including the following:

- **ntpd**—This is the main NTP server program. (It's sometimes called `xntpd`, particularly with version 3 servers.) As noted earlier, although this program is referred to as a server, it functions both as a server for higher-numbered strata and as a client to one or more lower-strata NTP servers. Thus, you might run this program even if you want your system to function only as a client to other time servers.

- **ntpdate**—This program is a much simpler client-only package. You can call it periodically on systems for which a constant accurate time is less important, as described in the upcoming section "Using an NTP Client Package."

- **ntptrace**—Occasionally, you might want to know the source of a time setting. This program traces backwards, from the local computer to the NTP server to which it's currently synchronized, and so on. This can sometimes be useful diagnostic information.

- **ntpq**—This is the NTP monitoring program, described shortly, in the section "Monitoring NTP's Operations."

- **xntpdc**—This is another NTP monitoring and control program. It's used for more advanced operations than is ntpq.

In addition to the main NTP package, there are other time-setting programs available for Linux. The most common of these is rdate, which is similar to ntpdate in general principles—you use rdate to set the clock on a one-time basis. Most distributions don't install rdate by default, but many do ship with it. One advantage of ntpdate over rdate is that ntpdate provides much greater precision—to within a few milliseconds, depending upon network connections and the precision of the parent server. By contrast, rdate provides a precision of only about a second.

CONFIGURING ntp.conf

NTP is configured through a file called ntp.conf, which is usually located in the /etc directory. This file contains comment lines, which begin with a pound sign (#), and option lines that set various NTP options. Important options include the following:

- **server *address* [key *key*] [version *number*] [prefer]**—This option sets the name of a server to which NTP should synchronize itself. The *address* may be a hostname or an IP address. You may include several server options, one per line; your NTP server tries to contact each one and picks the best one for synchronization. (I discuss locating an NTP server shortly.) You may also include some additional information on this line. Specifically, key *key* provides an authentication key if you want to implement security to restrict access to the server, version *number* tells the server to use the *number* version of the protocol, and `prefer` tells the system to give this server preference over others.

- **fudge** *address* **stratum** *number*—This option is used mainly in reference to the 127.127.1.0 server (which corresponds to the local system clock) to make NTP treat it as a stratum 7 server—that is, well below most NTP servers in priority. This allows NTP to operate even if it can't reach any other servers.

- **driftfile** *filename*—The drift file contains a number that NTP uses when it starts up after having been shut down for a while, or when it can't reach a server. This number allows NTP to compensate for the computer's average clock drift, thus reducing the clock's inaccuracy when isolated.

- **broadcast** *address* **[key** *key***] [version** *number***] [ttl** *number***]**—If you include this option, the server will periodically broadcast its current time to all clients on the network specified by *address*, which should be the computer's address on that network or a multicast address of 224.0.1.1. Using broadcasts may reduce network traffic on a large local network with many NTP servers that function mainly as clients.

- **broadcastclient [yes | no]**—You can tell an NTP server to listen for broadcasts from other local NTP servers with this option.

There are many other `ntp.conf` options available for performing more exotic functions. Consult the documentation, which ships in HTML format and usually appears in /usr/share/doc/xntp-*version* or a similar directory.

The default `ntp.conf` file on most distributions is nearly functional; you need only edit or add one or more `server` lines to point the computer to appropriate NTP server systems. Your choice of servers is important, because a server that's very distant from you in a network topology sense, that has unreliable network connections, or that has synchronized to an unreliable source, can cause your own time to be incorrect or of highly variable accuracy. As noted earlier, unless you're setting up a time server that will serve hundreds or more clients, or unless you have some compelling reason to have the most precise time possible, you should synchronize to a stratum 2 or higher server. You can find an extended discussion of these issues at http://www.eecis.udel.edu/~mills/ntp/servers.htm. The bottom of this document includes links to lists of public stratum 1 and stratum 2 time servers, so you can search the stratum 2 list for suitable time server candidates. Try to find a server that's close to you in a network topology sense. Network topology corresponds only very loosely with geography—if you're in Philadelphia, a server in Canberra, Australia, is likely to be farther than one in Boston, but the Boston server might be closer than one in New York City, depending on how your network links work.

TIP You can use ping to get a rough idea of the network delays involved in reaching two different NTP servers. As a very rough rule of thumb, NTP servers with shorter ping times are preferable to those with longer ping times.

If the time server list indicates that a server's operators want to be notified before you use the server, be sure to do so. You might also want to investigate time server options that might be less public, but closer to you. Many large organizations, including many Internet service providers (ISPs), operate time servers. You might therefore find a time server that's very close to you on the Internet. Consult your ISP, or your network manager if you want to set up a time server for a department in a larger organization.

If you buy a GPS time receiver or other external clock hardware, you can synchronize your system to it to become a stratum 1 time server. You'll need to install special drivers for the external clock hardware. These drivers make the hardware appear to be a device on the 127.127.0.0/16 network, so you can use an ordinary server option line, but point it to the appropriate IP address. You must consult the documentation for your device's Linux drivers for details. The NTP Web site includes a list of hardware product manufacturers at http://www.eecis.udel.edu/~ntp/hardware.html.

When you're done reconfiguring ntp.conf, you should restart the NTP server. This is usually done through a SysV startup script, as discussed in Chapter 4, Starting Servers. Unless your startup script calls ntpdate prior to starting ntpd, you won't see your system time change dramatically, even if it's off by a few minutes. Instead, NTP will wait a while as it receives multiple time checks, then either change the time quickly or adjust it more slowly to synchronize it with its own parent server's time. You can monitor its operations using ntpq, as discussed in the next section.

MONITORING NTP'S OPERATIONS

Aside from watching the time with a program like xclock, the usual way to monitor NTP's operation is to use the ntpq program. You launch this program and then enter any of a large number of text-based commands at its prompt. The program then displays information in response to these commands. Some of the more important `ntpq` commands include the following:

- **host** *hostname*—By default, `ntpq` queries the server running on the localhost computer. You can change this behavior by issuing the `host` command, so you can easily monitor the functioning of NTP servers throughout your network. You can achieve the same effect by providing the target hostname when you launch `ntpq`, as in **ntpq remote. threeroomco.com**.

- **hostnames [yes | no]**—If you provide the `yes` option, `ntpq` displays hostnames rather than IP addresses when reporting on remote computers (this is the default behavior). The `no` option causes `ntpq` to display IP addresses. Using `-n` when launching `ntpq` has the same effect as typing **hostnames no** after launching the program.

- **ntpversion** *versionno*—You can specify the NTP version number (*versionno*) to use in queries of the NTP server with this option.

- **quit**—When you're done, issue this command to quit from the program.

- **peers**—This command is one of the more useful initial diagnostic tools. It displays a list of the servers with which yours is communicating. Unless you use the `host` command, this list should include the localhost and all the servers you listed in `ntp.conf`. Additional information includes the server to which each of the listed servers is synchronized; the stratum of each server; when each server was last contacted and the interval between contacts; a numeric code indicating how reliable the connection between the systems is; and delay, offset, and jitter information, which are measures of how accurate and variable the time data are. To the left of each entry is a one-character code indicating how your server is using data from each server. A plus sign (+) means that the server was considered for synchronization, but was beaten out by a better server; an asterisk (*) indicates that the server is your own server's parent; an x indicates a *false ticker*—a server whose time is just plain wrong; and various other characters indicate servers that have been rejected for assorted other reasons. Variants on `peers` are `lpeers` (which may list more servers) and `opeers` (which doesn't display the names of servers to which yours is connected).

- **associations**—This command produces a list of association statistics for each server. Servers aren't identified by hostname or IP address, but by an association ID that's used in some other commands. Variants on this command are lassociations, passociations, and lpassociations.

- **readvar** *assocID* *varname*—You can read a raw variable using the readvar command, which takes an association ID and variable name as arguments. This command is most likely to be useful in advanced debugging sessions. Variants are mreadvar and rv (the latter is actually an exact synonym).

- **readlist** *assocID*—This command is like readvar, but it produces a list of all the standard variables. A synonym is rl, and a variant is mreadlist.

- **pstatus** *assocID*—This command requests that the system indicated by *assocID* return status information. In practice, the effect is very similar to the readlist command.

- **writevar** *assocID* *varname=value*—You can alter the value of a variable with the writevar command. You won't normally have to do this.

The first time you configure NTP, whenever you reconfigure it, and possibly periodically thereafter, you may want to use ntpq to check that it's doing what you expect. Figure 10.1 shows ntpq in action on a server that's been running for some time. When you first run ntpq after starting ntpd, many of the fields will be blank or will hold dummy values (typically 0). Over the course of a minute or so, most of those fields should fill with values similar to those shown in Figure 10.1, but the plus signs and asterisks to the left of most of the entries in Figure 10.1 won't appear for several minutes because the server will take a while to determine which of the would-be peers is most reliable. Some other values will change over the course of several minutes, as well, and then stabilize. If you see an x to the left of a server name, you may want to consider removing it from your configuration, because chances are that server is seriously misconfigured.

If you notice your system time drifting or changing in some odd way, you may want to use ntpq to check your NTP server's configuration. It may

```
ntpq> peers
     remote           refid        st t when poll reach   delay   offset  jitter
==============================================================================
 LOCAL(0)        LOCAL(0)          7 l   47   64  377    0.000    0.000   0.000
+cs.columbia.edu clepsydra.dec.c   2 u  638 1024  377   52.667  -22.793   3.686
*caesar.cs.wisc. ben.cs.wisc.edu   2 u  578 1024  377   54.510  -24.900   4.793
+ns2.bos.pnap.ne navobs1.wustl.e   2 u  582 1024  377   60.646  -17.340   4.289
ntpq>
```

Figure 10.1 The ntpq program lets you monitor NTP server activities.

SETTING UP AN NTP SERVER

How to Keep Precision Time

Most computers use internal clocks that are based on *oscillators*—electronic devices that produce a signal that changes in a regular manner. If the oscillator produces, say, a 100Hz signal, this means that it changes state 100 times per second. By counting the oscillations, the computer keeps time. As noted earlier, however, computer clocks are imperfect. There are several causes of such imperfections. For one thing, the oscillators may not operate at *precisely* the values they're supposed to. If a 100Hz oscillator actually operates at 100.1Hz, time measurements will be off. In fact, an error of this magnitude would cause a clock to gain over a minute a day. What's more, the oscillation rate may vary over time, as the circuit's temperature changes as a computer heats up after being turned on or as room temperature varies. The oscillation rate may also vary as the circuit ages or for assorted other reasons.

Factors outside of the oscillator can also influence the precision of the time measurement. Normally, the oscillator signals the computer that its time period has come by using an interrupt (interrupt 0 on *x*86 computers). If the computer is busy processing other important events, though, it may not be able to process this interrupt in a prompt fashion, and so the computer may miss a "tick" of the clock.

These sources of error contribute to general clock drift, and for most users, they're a modest annoyance. In some cases, though, precision time measurement is important. For instance, computers used in extremely time-sensitive scientific experiments may need extreme precision. (Linux isn't really well-suited to such functions, although the *Real-Time Linux* variant, `http://fsmlabs.com/community/`, does much better in this respect.) The Enhanced Real Time Clock kernel option (in the Character Devices menu) enables user access to a high-precision clock, should you need it.

Inserting kernel modules is one task that's particularly likely to result in missed oscillator beats, so if high timing precision is important, you should compile a kernel with as many drivers built in as possible, rather than leaving lots of options as modules. Leaving the computer powered on at all times and keeping it in a temperature-controlled room can both help minimize changes in clock drift due to temperature factors. The NTP server tracks clock drift and attempts to compensate, and periodically checks back with its parent server, so running an NTP server can help keep an accurate time—but if there's a chance that NTP will step the time at some critical point, you might want to temporarily disable it during particularly time-sensitive operations.

have lost synchronization with a server because of a change in IP address or some permanent network connectivity problem. (A temporary network outage shouldn't create noticeable problems; the server will just switch to the local clock until the network comes back online.) If your system doesn't synchronize with any time server for several minutes after starting `ntpd`, you should investigate general network connectivity. Can you ping the remote server? Do you have a firewall in place that might block NTP queries? (You may need to reconfigure the firewall to pass through UDP port 123 packets, at least to and from the servers in question—both yours and the remote servers.) Do you have authorization to use a remote server? (That server might use a firewall or an authentication key to keep out unwanted clients.)

USING AN NTP CLIENT PACKAGE

If you've configured an NTP server on one computer on your network to acquire its time from a remote system, you can install and configure NTP servers on all other systems on your network in much the same way, but point these computers to your first NTP server instead of to external servers. The result is that your entire network will generate relatively little in the way of Internet traffic related to NTP, although the entire network will be set to the correct time via local NTP queries. You'll get the full benefits of `ntpd` on each of the clients, even though most or all of them won't be used as servers. On a complex network, you might implement several strata of time servers yourself. For instance, you might run an NTP server on each subnet for the benefit of clients on that subnet, and have each of these subnet servers connect to a system on the subnet that's one closer to the Internet at large to obtain its own time. This design will minimize NTP-related network traffic within your own network.

For many systems, running `ntpd` is overkill. This program is designed to keep the time on an entire network synchronized to within a few milliseconds, and to keep the entire network's time set to well under a second of UTC. Furthermore, `ntpd` is designed to keep this time accurate constantly, with little drift from accuracy during the course of a day. Your needs might be more modest; for instance, you might not be concerned if the time on any given system drifts a few seconds each day. Furthermore, `ntpd` is a server, and as such poses a potential risk; a security-related bug could conceivably be found and exploited in `ntpd`, resulting in a potential vulnerability for all your systems, or at least all those that are exposed to the Internet at large. (In fact, such vulnerabilities have been found in `ntpd` in the past.) For these reasons, the `ntpdate` program may be useful in many situations. As noted earlier, the `rdate` program can be used in a similar manner, but it uses its own protocol and is less precise than is `ntpdate`.

NOTE
The designers of NTP are working to phase out ntpdate, with the goal of allowing ntpd to be used for one-time clock settings, much as ntpdate can be used today. Future versions of the NTP package may omit ntpdate and provide some way to use ntpd in a more limited manner in its place. In fact, some NTP version 4 packages lack ntpdate.

To run ntpdate, you type its name followed by the name or IP address of the time server against which you want to synchronize your system's time. You can specify multiple time servers if you want the program to automatically select the best one. You can also include several optional parameters before the program name and the time server addresses:

- **-B**—Normally, ntpdate slews the system clock speed if the time difference is less than half a second, and resets the clock if the difference is greater than half a second. This option forces the program to always slew the clock speed, even with large errors.

- **-b**—This option forces ntpdate to set the clock to the value sent by the server, even if the error is small.

- **-o** *version*—You can tell the program to use a specific version of NTP with this option.

- **-p** *samples*—Normally, ntpdate sets the clock by using four time samples from the server. You can adjust this value up or down (within the range 1 to 8) using this option.

- **-q**—You can query the server without setting the clock by including this option. This will *not* return a human-readable time, though; it returns information on the delays and offsets to the servers.

- **-s**—You can force ntpdate to send its output through the system logger with this option. You might do this if you call the program as a cron job.

- **-u**—Normally, ntpdate uses the standard NTP port of 123 for its outgoing packets. You can have it use an unprivileged port (numbered above 1024) by using this option. This might be necessary to work around some firewalls.

When you run ntpdate to synchronize your clock with a server, the program reports various statistics, such as the stratum, offset, and delay associated with the server you contact. Unless you specify -q or there's an error, the program then either slews your clock's speed or sets the absolute time on your computer.

One common method of using ntpdate is to run it as a cron job. You might run it once an hour or once a day, for instance. This may be often enough for many purposes, and it can reduce network loads to run ntpdate on a periodic basis, as opposed to running ntpd constantly.

WARNING *Do not* call ntpdate on a regular basis at midnight to synchronize with a public time server. Such servers are often bombarded by requests at midnight, generated by people who think that's a reasonable time to synchronize their clocks. Instead, pick some unusual time that's otherwise convenient, like 1:23 PM or 3:48 AM. This will reduce unnecessary congestion on public time servers, and may result in more accurate and reliable clock setting for your system, because you won't experience delays or dropped packets from midnight congestion.

USING SAMBA TO SERVE TIME

NTP is an extremely useful protocol, and as noted earlier, it's one of the most precise methods of setting the time on a Linux computer. Other time protocols do exist, however. One of these that deserves mention is the time server functionality that's included in the Server Message Block (SMB)/Common Internet Filesystem (CIFS) file- and printer-sharing protocols used on Microsoft networks and implemented in Linux by Samba (described in Chapter 7, File and Printer Sharing via Samba). If you run NTP on a Samba server, it may be simpler to configure Samba to serve the time rather than install NTP clients on all your Windows computers. (Samba can't set your system's time from a Windows SMB/CIFS time server, though.)

SAMBA'S TIME SERVING OPTIONS

Samba's configuration file, smb.conf, is broken into several sections, most of which define particular directories you want to share with SMB/CIFS clients. The first section, though, is known as [global], and it defines global defaults and other options that don't make sense in individual shares. One of these is the time server option, which you can activate by setting the following parameter:

```
time server = Yes
```

This tells Samba to respond to time queries from SMB/CIFS clients, using the SMB/CIFS time server features. You can set this option whether or not your computer uses NTP, rdate, or some other time-setting protocol to set its own time, but it's most useful if the Samba server's time is set correctly through such a mechanism.

NOTE The SMB/CIFS time protocols aren't as precise as are those of NTP. Windows systems may vary by a second or so after being set in this way, even before their clocks begin to drift.

CONFIGURING A WINDOWS CLIENT TO SET ITS CLOCK

To set the time on a Windows client, you can use the following command in a DOS prompt window:

```
C:\> NET TIME \\SERVER /SET /YES
```

In this command, SERVER is the NetBIOS name of the Samba server. You can manually type such a command to set the time much as you can use ntpdate to set the time on a Linux computer. You might want to create a Windows batch file to execute this command whenever a user logs in, though. You can do this by typing the command (without the DOS C:\> prompt) into a file (you might call it SETTIME.BAT) and copying that file to the Windows StartUp folder. This way, whenever the user boots the computer or logs in, the command will execute. Alternatively, if your network uses a domain configuration, you can include the command in your default network login script. (Because networking hasn't started when Windows executes AUTOEXEC.BAT, though, you should *not* include this command in that script.)

NOTE Windows 2000 and XP support NTP more directly. Specifically, the command NET TIME /SETSNTP: *ntpserver* should synchronize the time with the *ntpserver* system. There's even a full NTP server that ships with these systems, but its configuration is outside the scope of this book.

SUMMARY

A time server allows you to keep your computers' clocks synchronized with each other, and with an external time server that is ultimately tied to a veridical time source. Using time servers can be useful when referring to time stamps on files and in system logs. One of the more popular and powerful time server protocols is NTP, which allows for a time server (generally called ntpd or xntpd) to run constantly, periodically checking its notion of time against that of another NTP server. On a small network, you'll probably configure one server to synchronize itself to a stratum 2 server (that is, one that's two links away from a veridical time source), then synchronize all your other computers to your stratum 3 time server using ntpd or a client-only NTP program like ntpdate. A larger network might use multiple stratum 3 time servers or a veridical time source like a GPS clock.

Other options for handling time setting include the Linux rdate command (a time client) and the time server functionality in SMB/CIFS, including the Samba server and Windows NET command. You can use the latter to easily synchronize the time on Windows clients, without installing NTP software on them.

Pull Mail
Protocols:
POP and IMAP

E-mail is one of the most important network functions in use today. Whether it's used to send a memo to a co-worker across the hall or a correspondent across the globe, e-mail has come to be something we rely upon on a daily basis. Linux includes extensive support for several different e-mail protocols. This chapter covers one class of e-mail protocols that are known as *pull protocols*, because the mail recipient initiates the transfers. These protocols contrast with *push protocols*, in which the sender initiates the transfer. (Chapter 19, Push Mail Protocol: SMTP, covers the most common push mail protocol.) Because e-mail originates with a sender, push protocols are always involved in e-mail delivery. E-mail transfers, though, typically involve several weigh stations. Pull protocols come into the picture in the last stage of a transfer, or occasionally at an intermediate stage.

NOTE Although this chapter comes before Chapter 19 in this book, you must have a working push mail server before a pull mail server will be useful. Most Linux distributions install a working push mail server by default, so you should have at least minimal functionality from the start. If you're having problems with your push mail system, or if you need to configure it in something other than the default way, you may need to skip ahead to Chapter 19 and then come back to this chapter.

This chapter begins with a discussion of pull mail protocols, including when you should use one, and an overview of the two pull protocols discussed in this chapter. The chapter then proceeds to a discussion of how to configure Linux to serve both of these two protocols. This chapter concludes with a look at Fetchmail, which functions as a pull mail client that can then forward mail to other destinations using push mail protocols.

WHEN TO RUN A PULL MAIL SERVER

Suppose you want to provide e-mail services to a small office, clients of an ISP, or some other group of users. The push mail servers that come with all Linux systems, and that are described in Chapter 19, allow you to set up a server to receive incoming e-mail addressed to your users. The question then becomes: How do you provide access to the mail that the mail server computer is collecting? There are two main approaches to this problem:

- You can provide users with login accounts on the mail server computer and allow users to read mail locally, using Linux e-mail programs like pine, mutt, or KMail (known technically as *mail user agents*, or *MUAs*). These programs can read the incoming mail spools directly, so they don't need any special support software. This approach requires users to either sit at the mail server computer proper or log into it remotely, using protocols like Telnet, Secure Shell (SSH), or some form of X-based remote login. (Chapters 13, Maintaining Remote Login Servers, and 14, Handling GUI Access with X and VNC Servers, discuss such servers in more detail.)
- You can run a pull mail server, which allows users to run mail readers on their own computers in order to read the mail that's been collected on the mail server. The mail readers function as pull mail clients to the mail server computer's pull mail server program. The pull mail server program effectively takes the role of the *local* mail reader, filling in for the remote mail reader used by the user.

The first option was common when UNIX systems served as the only real computers in organizations, and users accessed the UNIX computers through dumb terminal hardware. Today, though, users prefer to use GUI programs, often running in Windows or MacOS, to read their mail. Although there are local GUI mail readers that run on Linux, they require that the user run an X server, which is uncommon on Windows and MacOS systems. For this and other reasons, the second approach is usually more convenient for users who sit at Windows or MacOS computers.

From the user's point of view, the mail reader needs to be configured with the hostname or IP address of the pull mail server, and mail can be checked by launching the mail reader and clicking a button. Many mail readers can periodically check for new e-mail, so the button click may not even be necessary.

Thus, running a pull mail server makes sense when you want to provide access to your e-mail server for users who want to run mail readers on their own computers, without logging in to the mail server using tools like Telnet or SSH. Pull mail servers are commonly used on local corporate and educational networks, as well as by ISPs, who use it to provide e-mail to subscribers. These servers can support just a handful of users or many thousands of them when given adequate hard disks, network connections, and other hardware resources.

UNDERSTANDING POP AND IMAP

The preceding discussion has outlined some key points of mail delivery. To fully understand pull mail protocols, though, it's useful to study this issue a bit more to better comprehend how pull mail protocols can be used and how they interact with other e-mail delivery systems. The two pull mail protocols described in this chapter are the *Post Office Protocol (POP)* and the *Internet Message Access Protocol (IMAP)*. The discussion to this point has applied to both protocols, but there are important differences between them, as described next. You might not want or need to use both POP and IMAP, or you might have some active reason to *not* use one or the other protocol. Understanding the tasks for which each protocol is most useful is very important when planning your pull mail server implementation.

PULL MAIL'S PLACE IN THE MAIL DELIVERY SYSTEM

As noted earlier, a pull mail server computer also normally functions as a push mail server—without the push mail server, the pull mail server won't have any e-mail to deliver to clients when it's queried. Where does the mail come from, though? In most cases, the mail originates on one computer, passes through one or more mail server computers using push mail protocols, and arrives at the pull mail server system, where it waits for a client to read the mail via the pull mail protocol.

Unlike some protocols, e-mail delivery (especially push, but also pull) is based on the idea of a *relay*. Instead of delivering a message directly to the ultimate recipient computer, the e-mail system is designed to allow each computer to pass the message closer to the destination. Indeed, the sender may not be able to identify the *true* and *ultimate* destination of the message. For instance, if you send a message to sammy@threeroomco.com, you may be able to tell by checking Domain Name System (DNS) entries that the message will be sent to the computer called mail.threeroomco.com. This system, though, could be configured to forward mail addressed to sammy to another computer, such as gingko.threeroomco.com. The user sammy might then use a pull mail protocol to read the mail from a different computer, such as larch.threeroomco.com. Similarly, when you send a message, you configure your mail package (let's say it's on trilobite.pangaea.edu) to relay the mail through some computer's push mail server (let's call it franklin.pangaea.edu). That computer could be configured to relay mail through another server (osgood.pangaea.edu). The result can be a fairly long chain of mail servers involved in the delivery of a message, as illustrated by Figure 11.1. Most of these transfers use the Simple Mail Transfer Protocol (SMTP) push mail protocol; they're initiated by the sender. Assuming the network and all intervening servers are functioning smoothly, mail moves quickly from trilobite.pangaea.edu to gingko.threeroomco.com. This penultimate system,

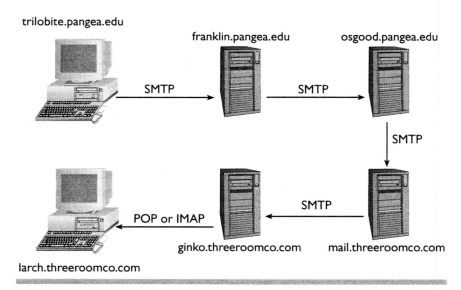

Figure 11.1 E-mail delivery can involve several push mail relay systems, often concluding with a pull mail transfer to the ultimate recipient.

though, may sit on the message for quite some time, waiting for a pull mail client system such as larch.threeroomco.com to retrieve the message. For this reason, pull mail server computers may need large hard disks to store the messages. As described shortly, this is particularly true of IMAP servers.

Figure 11.1 depicts just one possible path of mail delivery. Mail may involve as few as one computer (for mail from a user of a computer to another user of the same system), or many more than are depicted in Figure 11.1. There might be more systems within the sender's domain or more within the recipient's domain. Other domains may be involved in the transfer, especially if mail for specific users is forwarded from one system to another, say because users have graduated from college or moved on from one job to another. As described in the upcoming section, "Using Fetchmail," it's even possible for a pull mail transfer to occur in something other than the last leg of the mail's journey. In such a configuration, one system pulls mail using Fetchmail or a similar program, then passes it on again, perhaps to a local mail queue maintained by a push mail server on the same system, or possibly to another computer altogether.

One important point to remember is that pull mail servers are used for *retrieving* mail, not *sending* it. Sending mail is accomplished with a push mail protocol like SMTP. A single mail server *computer* may operate as both a push and pull server, so an end user may both retrieve incoming mail from and send outgoing mail through a single computer, but the protocols involved are different. Some organizations separate these two functions. For instance, you might specify franklin.pangaea.edu as your outgoing (SMTP) mail server, but use ponyexpress.pangaea.edu as your incoming (POP or IMAP) mail server. The latter computer would also run an SMTP server, but it might not be accessible to end users; it might be used only for accepting mail from the organization's externally-accessible push mail server.

STORING MAIL: ON THE CLIENT OR THE SERVER

As described earlier, one role of a pull mail server is to store mail until the recipient can retrieve it. At that time, the recipient's mail reader contacts the mail server and downloads the messages. You might infer from this description that the mail is then deleted from the mail server. This inference is often correct, but it need not be. There are circumstances in which the mail server might retain a copy of the mail:

- With either POP or IMAP, you can configure a mail reader to download messages but leave the originals on the server. You might do this if you regularly use two different mail readers or computers. With POP, however, this procedure can quickly become awkward, because POP has only very primitive provisions for identifying and manipulating individual messages. Therefore, as the number of messages on the server grows, this method can become extremely awkward.

- With IMAP, you can organize messages into message "folders" *on the server*. Thus, if you regularly use several different computers, you can organize your messages on the IMAP server and not wade through duplicate messages when you switch computers. IMAP also includes the ability to retrieve only message *headers* (information such as the subject and sender address) without the message *bodies* (the bulk of the text and attachments), so you need not waste undue bandwidth to check your mail.

These distinctions between POP and IMAP are unimportant in some situations, but crucial in others. If you use just one computer and want to store and organize your messages locally, POP and IMAP both do the job. If you switch computers regularly or use multiple mail packages on a single computer, IMAP can be much more convenient. On the other hand, the network transfers involved mean that storing messages on the server could cause you to wait longer to read any given message, particularly if you store many messages and read old messages on a regular basis. From the point of view of administering the pull mail server, though, IMAP offers more challenges, because it increases the demand for disk storage and network bandwidth, as users may recover the same message multiple times. (To be sure, though, users who use IMAP just like POP won't impose such additional overhead for IMAP; it's only if users take advantage of IMAP's extra capabilities that you'll see increased demands on the server's hardware.)

A SAMPLE POP SESSION

POP is actually several different protocols. The most common version today is POP-3, which uses TCP port 110. (The earlier POP-2 uses port 109.) Like many Internet protocols, POP is built around text-based commands sent by the client and text-based responses sent by the server. POP-3 supports about a dozen commands, including USER (to specify a username), PASS (to specify a password), RETR (to retrieve a message), DELE (to delete a message), and QUIT (to terminate a session). Mail readers that support POP can send these and other POP commands to a POP server, capture the results, and use the results to store mail and present it to users in an intelligible fashion.

As an example of POP in use, consider Listing 11.1, which shows a simple POP session in which a single message is retrieved. This listing uses telnet to connect to the POP-3 port and issue commands manually. Most POP sessions hide these details behind the mail reader, but it's informative to see what the mail reader and POP-3 server do to exchange messages.

Listing 11.1   A sample POP-3 session

```
$ telnet nessus 110
Trying 192.168.1.3...
Connected to nessus.rodsbooks.com.
Escape character is '^]'.
+OK POP3 nessus.rodsbooks.com v7.64 server ready
USER rodsmith
+OK User name accepted, password please
PASS password
+OK Mailbox open, 1 messages
RETR 1
+OK 531 octets
>From rodsmith  Wed Aug  8 14:38:46 2001
Return-Path: <ben@pangaea.edu>
Delivered-To: rodsmith@nessus.rodsbooks.com
Received: from speaker.rodsbooks.com (speaker.rodsbooks.com
[192.168.1.1])
        by nessus.rodsbooks.com (Postfix) with SMTP id EB2A01A2BD
        for <rodsmith@nessus.rodsbooks.com>; Wed,  8 Aug 2001
14:38:26 -0400 (EDT)
Message-Id: <20010808183826.EB2A01A2BD@nessus.rodsbooks.com>
Date: Wed,  8 Aug 2001 14:38:26 -0400 (EDT)
From: ben@pangaea.edu
To: undisclosed-recipients:;
Status:

This is a test message.
.
DELE 1
+OK Message deleted
QUIT
+OK Sayonara
Connection closed by foreign host.
```

As you can see from Listing 11.1, POP refers to messages by number. In this example, the server had only one message available, as indicated by the message +OK mailbox open, 1 messages. Messages may be retrieved or deleted by number, as in the **RETR 1** and **DELE 1** commands. Messages must be retrieved in full or not at all—POP provides no mechanism for discovering a message's sender, length, or other important information prior to retrieving it. Much of this information *is* included in the message itself, though. In this example, the bulk of the message consists of its *headers*—lines that include information on the servers through which the message has passed, the sender's address, and so on. A real message is more likely to consist of more lines of the message than of headers.

NOTE

The headers shown in Listing 11.1 illustrate a feature of e-mail that's both flexible and frustrating: It can be difficult to determine the true sender of the mail. You'll note From: and Return-Path: headers that indicate the message was sent by ben@pangaea.edu. Those who are used to reading e-mail headers, though, know that these headers are easily forged. Every mail server adds a Received: header to specify who the server is and from where it received the message. I sent this sample message directly from one computer on my network to another one, and the Received: header reflects this fact, showing the message having come from speaker.rodsbooks.com and being delivered to nessus.rodsbooks.com. No computers in pangaea.edu were involved in the transfer.

A SAMPLE IMAP SESSION

In very broad outline, IMAP fills the same role as POP—both are pull mail protocols. IMAP, however, provides finer-grained control over messages. IMAP includes the ability to examine headers before retrieving the body of the message, so a user can decide whether to download a message. (From the user's point of view, a mail reader may present information on the available messages, allowing the user to choose which to read in detail at any given moment.) These additional features require additional commands: a total of about two dozen in IMAP-4, the current version of the protocol, which uses TCP port 143. Listing 11.2 shows an IMAP retrieval session that's roughly equivalent to Listing 11.1, except that it includes a command to copy the message into an IMAP folder.

Listing 11.2 A sample IMAP-4 session

```
$ telnet nessus 143
Trying 192.168.1.3...
Connected to nessus.rodsbooks.com.
Escape character is '^]'.
* OK nessus.rodsbooks.com IMAP4rev1 v12.264.phall server ready
A1 LOGIN rodsmith password
A1 OK LOGIN completed
A2 SELECT Inbox
* 1 EXISTS
* NO Trying to get mailbox lock from process 29559
* 1 RECENT
* OK [UIDVALIDITY 997295985] UID validity status
* OK [UIDNEXT 4] Predicted next UID
* FLAGS (\Answered \Flagged \Deleted \Draft \Seen)
* OK [PERMANENTFLAGS (\* \Answered \Flagged \Deleted \Draft \Seen)]
Permanent flags
* OK [UNSEEN 1] first unseen message in /var/spool/mail/rodsmith
A2 OK [READ-WRITE] SELECT completed
A3 FETCH 1 BODY[HEADER]
* 1 FETCH (BODY[HEADER] {494}
>From rodsmith  Wed Aug  8 16:02:47 2001
Return-Path: <ben@pangaea.edu>
Delivered-To: rodsmith@nessus.rodsbooks.com
Received: from speaker.rodsbooks.com (speaker.rodsbooks.com
[192.168.1.1])
        by nessus.rodsbooks.com (Postfix) with SMTP id 2C7121A2BD
        for <rodsmith@nessus.rodsbooks.com>; Wed,  8 Aug 2001
16:02:25 -0400 (EDT)
Message-Id: <20010808200225.2C7121A2BD@nessus.rodsbooks.com>
Date: Wed,  8 Aug 2001 16:02:25 -0400 (EDT)
From: ben@pangaea.edu
To: undisclosed-recipients:;

)
* 1 FETCH (FLAGS (\Recent \Seen))
A3 OK FETCH completed
A4 FETCH 1 BODY[TEXT]
* 1 FETCH (BODY[TEXT] {25}
This is a test message.
)
A4 OK FETCH completed
A5 COPY 1 demos
A5 OK COPY completed
A6 LOGOUT
* BYE nessus.rodsbooks.com IMAP4rev1 server terminating connection
A6 OK LOGOUT completed
Connection closed by foreign host.
```

Listing 11.2 illustrates some of the added features and complexity of IMAP over POP. IMAP requires the client to submit numbered commands, such as **A6 LOGOUT** rather than simply **LOGOUT**. This detail is unimportant from the user's point of view, because the mail reader handles it. IMAP allows the client to retrieve the message headers separately from the body, as illustrated by the A3 and A4 commands in Listing 11.2. The use of folders requires the client to move into a folder (the A2 command in Listing 11.2) before reading messages, and allows the client to copy messages into folders (the A5 command in Listing 11.2). Listing 11.2 illustrates a smaller fraction of what IMAP can do than does Listing 11.1 with respect to POP. There are many variants on the way these commands can be used, such as different message features that can be retrieved with FETCH. For more information on what these commands can do, consult an IMAP reference, such as the IMAP RFC (http://www.ietf.org/rfc/rfc2060.txt).

Although a quick look at the low-level commands used in IMAP can be informative, you probably don't need to be too concerned about them as an IMAP administrator. Some of these commands do have consequences, however. Specifically, the ability of IMAP to use folders means that the IMAP server must have somewhere to store those folders. The most common IMAP server is the University of Washington IMAP (UW IMAP; http://www.washington.edu/imap/). This package stores IMAP folders in the user's home directory, except for the INBOX folder, which corresponds to the standard mail spool directory (at /var/spool/mail/*username* on most systems). When a user first connects using IMAP, there will be no folders defined, aside from the default INBOX. Users can create folders using appropriate mail reader commands, and the UW IMAP server responds by creating a file in the user's home directory in which mail messages placed in that folder will reside. Other packages may store mail folders in other locations; consult their documentation for details. You should be aware of where these messages are stored so that you can allocate adequate disk space for them, particularly on large servers or those on which users will be storing large messages.

DETERMINING WHICH TO USE

The choice of POP or IMAP is partly a matter of personal preference, partly one of the capabilities of your user's mail readers, and partly one of your available resources. POP minimizes your need for disk space and network speed on the mail server, because users will be more likely to download and permanently store e-mail on their local computers rather than leave the e-mail on the server for later perusal or archival purposes. For this reason, an IMAP server is likely to require more disk space on the server, and possibly more network bandwidth to clients. This server may be preferable to at least some users, though. The vast majority of modern mail readers support POP. IMAP support is common, but not as prevalent as is POP support. Therefore, if you provide IMAP, it's usually a good idea to provide POP as well. The added load on the server should be minimal, but it will allow users who prefer mail readers that don't support IMAP to retrieve their mail. A POP client may clean out a user's inbox, but it won't disrupt folders created via IMAP. On the other hand, running POP also means leaving another port open. If the POP server turns out to have a security flaw, this could allow miscreants access to your system.

WARNING

!

By default, both POP and IMAP send all information, including passwords, in an unencrypted (cleartext) form. Therefore, if possible you should use POP or IMAP passwords *only* for e-mail retrieval, not for other purposes, such as regular logins. There are secure variants of POP and IMAP available, such as versions that encrypt the transfers using the *Secure Sockets Layer (SSL)*. These are more difficult to configure, but well worth the effort if security is a concern. This is particularly important when e-mail is likely to be accessed over the Internet, rather than restricted to a local network segment that you control. If you want to restrict access to your pull mail servers to your local network, you can apply TCP Wrappers or xinetd rules, as described in Chapter 4, Starting Servers. Another option is to create packet filter firewall rules, as described in Chapter 25, Configuring iptables.

CONFIGURING A POP SERVER

As a general rule, POP servers are simple to set up and run. Most require no configuration, aside from that needed to start the server, as described in Chapter 4. It's important, though, that you use a POP server that's suited to your SMTP server. Most importantly, there are two formats used for storing incoming mail: mbox and maildir. Most mail servers use mbox by default, but many can use maildir instead, and a few use maildir by default. Specifically, sendmail, Postfix, and Exim use mbox by default, and qmail uses the maildir format by default. Postfix, Exim, and qmail can all be configured to use either mbox or maildir. Your POP server must be able to read mail from the appropriate format, and so must understand the format used by your SMTP server.

POP SERVERS FOR LINUX

POP servers ship with every major Linux distribution. It's usually easiest to use the tool that ships with your distribution, but if you've replaced or reconfigured your SMTP server to use an unusual incoming mailbox location or format, you may need to replace the POP server to match the new format. POP servers you might use include the following:

- **UW IMAP**—The University of Washington IMAP server (http://www.washington.edu/imap/) includes a POP server that uses IMAP as a back-end. This server ships with many Linux distributions, and uses the mbox format that's the default with most Linux SMTP servers.

- **Cyrus IMAP**—Like UW IMAP, Cyrus IMAP (http://asg.web.cmu.edu/cyrus/imapd/) supports POP in addition to IMAP protocols. This system uses its own mailbox format for folders, and mbox for incoming mail.

- **nupop**—This server (http://nupop.sourceforge.net) was written with efficiency for high-volume sites in mind, so you may want to look into it if your server must handle mail for many users. It requires mail to be stored in the maildir format favored by qmail.

- **Courier**—The Courier server (http://www.courier-mta.org) is an integrated POP/IMAP/SMTP mail server. Its POP and IMAP servers are available in a separate package, Courier-IMAP (http://www.inter7.com/courierimap/). These servers rely on the maildir format.

- **QPopper**—Despite the name, this package (http://www.eudora.com/qpopper/) is unrelated to the Linux qmail SMTP server; versions 3.0 and earlier are commercial POP3 servers, but version 4.0 is open source. QPopper works with the mbox format that's most common on Linux systems. Version 4.0 includes SSL encryption, should you wish to experiment with it.

- **qmail-pop3d**—This program comes with the qmail mail server (http://www.qmail.org), and uses the maildir format favored by that server. It's a good starting point if you choose to use qmail for handling SMTP.

The preceding list is only a beginning; a search on Sourceforge (http://www.sourceforge.net) or a Web search will turn up more POP servers, some of which are part of integrated packages that support IMAP, SMTP, and even other protocols. Most Linux distributions ship with UW IMAP, and some also ship with Cyrus, QPopper, or others.

POP SERVER INSTALLATION AND CONFIGURATION

Most distributions ship with a POP server in a package called imap or some variant of that. The POP server usually runs from a super server, as described in Chapter 4. The POP server may set up a xinetd configuration file to run automatically, or you may need to modify the /etc/inetd.conf file to have the server run. You'll probably have to restart inetd or xinetd before the POP server will begin responding to queries. If you install a server that's not part of your distribution, you should consult its documentation to learn of any quirks for running it.

The default UW IMAP, and most other POP servers, rely on Linux's normal user database for authentication. Thus, you shouldn't need to do anything special to configure the server for users on your system; so long as a user has a regular account, and so long as that account can receive push mail via an SMTP server, the POP server should be able to deliver mail to the user. Users must enter their normal login passwords in their POP mail clients in order to retrieve mail. Because the jobs these servers do is so simple, they often have no configuration files, unless you count entries in inetd or xinetd configuration files.

CONFIGURING AN IMAP SERVER

IMAP server installation and configuration works much like that for POP servers. As noted earlier, UW IMAP ships with most Linux distributions, and some distributions include other servers as well. Configuration is usually a matter of installing the package, checking or making a small change to a super server configuration, and restarting the super server.

IMAP SERVERS FOR LINUX

Many of the packages described in the earlier section, "POP Servers for Linux," include IMAP functionality. Specifically, UW IMAP, Cyrus IMAP, and Courier all support IMAP as well as POP. In 2002, searches on http://www.sourceforge.net and Web search engines reveal several other IMAP server projects, but many of them are very new and have no working code available, or they fill rather esoteric niches, like a proxy server to allow Web browsing via IMAP.

UW IMAP, the most popular IMAP server for Linux, stores most mail folders as files in mbox format in the Linux user's home directory. This may be undesirable if users have regular login accounts on the computer, because users might not recognize the purpose of the files and so might delete or move them. (You can change the default location of the mbox files by editing the source code and recompiling, as described in the CONFIG file that comes with the program's documentation.) Cyrus IMAP, on the other hand, uses its own proprietary format for everything but the mbox-format incoming mail folder. Courier IMAP uses the maildir format, which qmail uses by default and that is available as an option in Postfix and Exim, among others.

IMAP Server Installation and Configuration

Most distributions ship with UW IMAP in a package called imap or something similar. You can install this package and configure the IMAP server to run using your super server, as described in Chapter 4. Once it's running, UW IMAP uses your normal login database to authenticate users, so any user with a regular account and an active password can read e-mail using IMAP. As with POP configuration, there's no separate configuration file for IMAP options; just run it from your super server, and it should work.

Using Fetchmail

Fetchmail is an unusual mail program. It is neither a mail server nor a mail reader, although it contains elements of both. Fetchmail's job is to fetch mail from a pull mail server and then to pass it on to some other program—most commonly, Fetchmail uses a push mail protocol to forward the mail it retrieves from a pull mail server. This last mail push often occurs entirely on the same computer—that is, Fetchmail acquires mail from another computer, then mails it to a local user of the computer on which it runs. There are many variant ways to configure Fetchmail, though. The program may be set up by individual users by editing its configuration file, .fetchmailconf. There's also a GUI Fetchmail configuration tool available, known as fetchmailconf, that can be used to configure the program for many common tasks.

NOTE   Earlier sections of this chapter deal with running a pull mail server. Fetchmail, though, is generally used to retrieve e-mail from a pull mail server that's run by somebody else.

Fetchmail's Place in Mail Delivery Systems

Pull mail protocols were designed to allow mail reader programs to retrieve e-mail from mail server computers. The idea is that a computer capable of running a mail server is likely to be available at all times, and so can run a push mail server to accept mail at the sender's convenience. Only the end user's connection is likely to be transient or variable in some other way, such as in having a dynamic IP address. Although this generalization is true of many traditional networks, it's not true of all of them. There are situations in which it may be desirable to transfer mail with a pull mail protocol and then continue sending it through additional mail server programs:

- **Dial-up Linux systems**—Linux computers generally run mail servers locally, even when the computers are connected to the Internet only through dial-up Point-to-Point Protocol (PPP) connections. The local mail servers on such systems can exchange mail between multiple users or can be used to notify a single user of messages generated by the computer. One way to integrate these messages with those that arrive at the user's ISP mail account is to pull the mail using POP or IMAP and then inject the pulled mail into the local mail queue. The user can then read all mail (local and remote) using a single mail program configured to read the mail locally rather than using POP or IMAP.

- **Dial-up with a LAN**—Some small businesses and even homes use local area networks (LANs) on which e-mail passes between users. Such LANs may connect to the Internet via a dial-up account with one or more associated e-mail accounts. You can retrieve the dial-up e-mail accounts' messages and route them to appropriate individuals on the LAN's e-mail system.

- **Multiple pull mail accounts**—If you have multiple mail accounts, managing them all can be a nuisance. As with the dial-up Linux system just described, it's often possible to use a pull mail protocol to collect mail from these multiple sources and send them on to a single account. (This account could be local to the computer on which Fetchmail runs, but it might also be an account on a remote server.) Alternative ways to handle this situation include using the forwarding features of many mail accounts or using a mail reader that can handle multiple accounts.

- **One mailbox, multiple users**—Sometimes multiple users may share a single e-mail account. If you have some way to filter the mail intended for different users, you can retrieve it, filter it with features built into Fetchmail or available in separate programs, and send the mail to separate mail queues that can be used by appropriate individuals.

- **Converting POP to IMAP**—Your main external mail account might use POP, but if you want to use IMAP and if you control a Linux computer with appropriate network connections, you can retrieve the mail from the POP account and send it to a local mail queue. If you then run an IMAP server on this computer, you can read your mail using IMAP.

271

Put another way, pull mail accounts are usually intended for single mail users using fairly simple local configurations. This is especially true of POP, which works best when the user reads mail from a single computer using just one mail program. When the mail setup associated with an account becomes more complex, it may be helpful to add another step to mail delivery in order to merge mail from multiple sources or to separate mail into separate streams. Fetchmail is a tool that allows you to do this.

It's important to realize that Fetchmail functions as a client to both a pull mail server and a push mail server. (Alternatively, it can deliver mail in ways that are unrelated to a push mail server, but such configurations are

Scheduling Mail Retrieval

Whether you run Fetchmail as a cron job, in daemon mode, or manually, the pull nature of the protocols used for mail retrieval means that you must schedule checks of your mail; you can't simply wait for mail to arrive, as you can when your system receives mail directly via a push protocol. How often you do this, and under what circumstances, is a matter that you'll have to decide based on your needs. If your mail is very time-sensitive, you might want to use a tight schedule for mail checks, such as every five minutes. This has the drawback of consuming more network bandwidth and resources on the server, though. It also makes it more likely that your password will be intercepted and abused, especially if you're checking a mail server on the Internet, rather than on your local network. Checks at wider intervals (say, once every six hours) place less load on the servers and may slightly reduce the risk of your password being intercepted, but your mail may be delayed in reaching you for up to the interval you've selected. If you use cron to schedule mail checks, you can adjust your check interval based on the time of day. For instance, you might check for mail every half hour during business hours, but less frequently or not at all at night.

If the network link between your Linux computer and your pull mail server is transient (such as a PPP connection), you may not want to have Fetchmail check for mail at all times. Instead, you might want to add a call to Fetchmail to your network startup scripts. For instance, you might add a call to Fetchmail in the ppp-on-dialer PPP dialing script described in Chapter 2, TCP/IP Network Configuration. If you configure Fetchmail to run in daemon mode, you might then add a line to kill the program in the ppp-off script. Alternatively, you can use the interface or monitor options, described in the upcoming section "Configuring .fetchmailrc," to have Fetchmail attempt message retrieval only when the connection is up and in use.

rarer.) Because Fetchmail fills a dual-client role, it's in charge of the scheduling of e-mail acquisition and delivery, assuming both servers to which it connects are available. Fetchmail can run in both a batch mode, in which it runs, checks one or more pull mail accounts, forwards any mail it retrieves, and exits; or in a daemon mode, in which it runs constantly and performs a check for new mail at some interval you specify. The latter mode sounds convenient, but Fetchmail occasionally crashes or runs into problems when run in daemon mode for long periods, which can result in a failure to retrieve mail. I therefore favor running Fetchmail in batch mode except for configurations in which daemon mode is used for limited periods of time. If you want to schedule regular checks of the pull mail account, you can use cron to schedule Fetchmail runs on a regular basis. You can also run Fetchmail manually, checking for mail only when you decide to do so.

NOTE   Fetchmail can handle challenge/response password authentication, as used by Microsoft's Exchange mail server. Thus, if your upstream provider uses this feature, Fetchmail can take advantage of it.

USING fetchmailconf

Fetchmail configuration involves editing a text file that's traditionally stored in the home directory of the user who runs the program. Thus, several users can run Fetchmail on a single computer, if desired. If you prefer GUI configuration tools, though, Fetchmail supports one, known as fetchmailconf. I describe this tool in this section; the next section, "Configuring .fetchmailrc," describes the Fetchmail configuration file that fetchmailconf modifies.

Most distributions include fetchmailconf in a separate package from Fetchmail proper, so you may need to install two packages to get both programs. As an X program that's based on Tcl/Tk, fetchmailconf also requires that you have additional libraries installed. Once you've installed it, you can configure Fetchmail to retrieve e-mail from a pull mail account as follows:

1. As an ordinary user, type **fetchmailconf** in an xterm window. This action opens the Fetchmail Launcher window, which allows you to click one of four buttons to configure Fetchmail, test Fetchmail, run Fetchmail, or quit.

NOTE You *can* configure and run Fetchmail as root, but doing so offers no advantages over running the program as an ordinary user. Thus, to avoid the risk of damage should a security problem be found in Fetchmail, it's best to configure and run Fetchmail as an ordinary user. One ordinary user can retrieve mail intended for several different users, although in this case, the mail-retrieving user must have access to the passwords for all the pull mail accounts. This may be acceptable in some situations, but in others you may prefer to allow all users to create Fetchmail configurations for their own mail accounts.

2. Click the Configure Fetchmail button in the Fetchmail Launcher window. This action produces a Fetchmail Configurator dialog box that allows you to choose from novice or expert configuration modes. The former produces dialog boxes that contain a subset of the options in the latter. Although I don't emphasize the expert-only options in this procedure, I do describe this path so that you can see what some of these options are.

3. Click the Expert Configuration button in the Fetchmail Configurator dialog box. The result is the Fetchmail Expert Configurator dialog box shown in Figure 11.2. If you want to run Fetchmail in daemon mode, enter the number of seconds between mail checks in the Poll Interval field (for instance, 1200 for a check every 20 minutes). Leave this field at 0 if you intend to run Fetchmail in batch mode. The Postmaster field is the name of the local mail account that's to receive reports of problems with Fetchmail's activities. It defaults to the user who runs the pro-

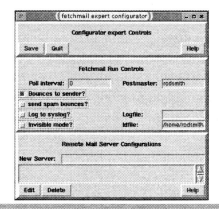

Figure 11.2 The Fetchmail Expert Configurator dialog box lets you enter global options and name specific mail servers from which Fetchmail will retrieve mail.

gram. You can leave most of the other options in the middle section of the window at their defaults, or click the upper Help button to learn more about them.

4. The most important item in the Fetchmail Expert Configurator dialog box is the bottom panel, in which you enter the name of the mail server from which you want to retrieve mail. Type in the hostname and press the Enter key, and a new dialog box will appear called Fetchmail Host *Hostname*, as shown in Figure 11.3. The hostname should also appear in the scrollable list below the New Server data entry field in the Fetchmail Expert Configurator dialog box. If you want to retrieve mail from multiple servers, you may enter multiple server hostnames, although you may want to do so after configuring the first server.

5. The most important sections of the Fetchmail Host *Hostname* dialog box are the Protocol, User Entries for *Hostname*, and Security sections. The Run Controls section sets options related to the timing of retrieval and the server name if it's different from what you specified earlier. The Multidrop Options area allows you to enter rules with which to duplicate or redirect mail based on mail headers that you specify. You can use this to let multiple users share a single pull mail account, although this use can result in problems with certain types of mail (such as mailing lists), and so is discouraged.

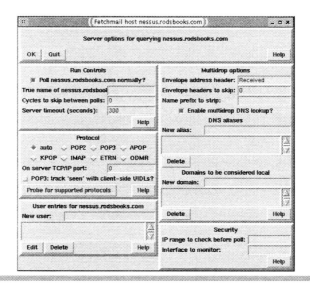

Figure 11.3   You enter most information about specific pull mail servers in the Fetchmail Host *Hostname* dialog box.

6. In the Protocol section of Fetchmail Host *Hostname*, you specify the pull mail protocol you want to use. Auto is the default, and works with some servers, but you may want to specify the protocol if you know what's supported on your server. You can click Probe for Supported Protocols to check the server for the protocols that Fetchmail supports, but this option doesn't always work correctly. If necessary, you can ask your ISP or try using `telnet` manually, as illustrated in Listings 11.1 and 11.2.

7. The Security section is particularly helpful if you use a dial-up network interface that's not always active. Enter an interface name, such as `ppp0`, in the Interface to Monitor field to have Fetchmail poll a server only when that interface has been used by another program since the last poll. (This behavior prevents Fetchmail from keeping a link up unnecessarily if it would otherwise be brought down automatically.) The IP Range to Check Before Poll field can be used to check for the presence of an IP address on a given interface. Enter an interface name, IP address, and netmask, separated by slashes (/), and Fetchmail will run only if an IP address within the specified range and on the specified device exists. For instance, `ppp0/172.20.0.0/255.255.0.0` requires that the computer have an address in the 172.20.0.0/16 network on `ppp0` before Fetchmail will poll the host.

8. In the User Entries for *Hostname* section, enter your username on the mail server in the New User field and press the Enter key. This produces the Fetchmail User *Username* Querying *Hostname* dialog box shown in Figure 11.4. As when you enter a pull mail server name, you may finish with this dialog box and enter additional accounts to query on the same server.

9. The most important item to specify in the Fetchmail User *Username* Querying *Hostname* dialog box is the Password field in the Authentication section. This information is required for retrieving mail from most servers. You should also be sure that the Local Names field lists all the local users who are to receive the mail retrieved from this account. The default is to use the same username locally as is used on the pull mail server, but you may need to change this. The Forwarding Options field lets you change the host that's to receive the mail—the default is to use the local mail system, but you can use Fetchmail to retrieve mail from one system and forward it to another. The Forwarding Options, Processing Options, and Resource Limits sections all let you set assorted options, most of which are self-explanatory, the rest of which are required only in some circumstances. When you first set up Fetchmail, you may want to select the Suppress Deletion of Messages After Reading option in Processing Options, so you can test Fetchmail without fear of losing mail. You'll want to remove this option once you're convinced

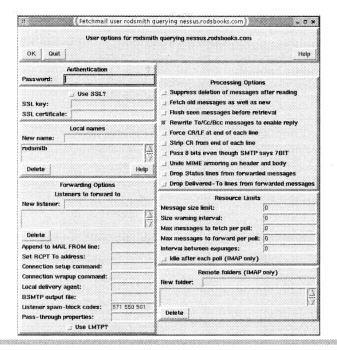

Figure 11.4 Many Fetchmail options apply to specific pull mail server accounts.

Fetchmail is working, though. Remote Folders lets you set the names of IMAP folders that Fetchmail is to check in addition to the default INBOX.

WARNING

Fetchmail stores the mail retrieval password in cleartext in its configuration file, .fetchmailrc. Fetchmail refuses to run if the permissions are set more loosely than 0600 (rw-------), but this is still a potential security risk should there be a local security breach. At the very least, you should ensure that the passwords used for remote e-mail retrieval aren't used for any other purpose, including access to the same account on the local computer or on any other computer.

10. Click OK in the Fetchmail User *Username* Querying *Hostname* dialog box, then in Fetchmail Host *Hostname*. You can then click Save in the Fetchmail Expert Configurator dialog box to save your changes to .fetchmailrc.

11. To test your setup, click Test Fetchmail in the Fetchmail Launcher window. This runs Fetchmail with debugging options, so you can see the commands that Fetchmail sends to the pull and push mail servers, and the replies that Fetchmail receives in return. This information can be

invaluable in tracking down problems. When your configuration works, exit from Fetchmail by clicking Quit.

WARNING

The Test Fetchmail button, although useful for debugging, *does not* preserve mail on your pull mail server. Thus, if there's a local configuration problem that causes Fetchmail to discard messages (for instance, if your local mail server isn't running or refuses delivery of the messages), you'll lose mail. This is why you may want to configure Fetchmail to *not* delete mail from the pull mail server in Step 9 for your initial tests.

For many people, Fetchmail configuration via `fetchmailconf` is quite adequate. Particularly in Expert mode, `fetchmailconf` can set the options you're most likely to need for retrieving mail from one or more mail accounts, and even for delivering mail from multiple pull mail accounts to multiple local users. Some people, though, prefer editing text files to using GUI configuration tools; or you might want to edit a text file to make a quick change or to create a particularly complex configuration. For whatever reason you want to do it, manual editing of `.fetchmailrc` is certainly possible.

CONFIGURING `.fetchmailrc`

When you run `fetchmailconf`, as just described, the program converts your selections into entries in the `.fetchmailrc` file in your home directory. The structure of and options in this file therefore mirror those in `fetchmailconf`. Listing 11.3 shows a sample `.fetchmailrc` file.

Listing 11.3 A sample `.fetchmailrc` file

```
# Fetchmail file for retrieving mail from mail.abigisp.net
# and imap.asmallisp.com
set postmaster rodsmith
set bouncemail
set daemon 1800
set syslog
poll mail.abigisp.net with proto POP3
    user rodericksmith there with password abc123
    is rodsmith here fetchall forcecr
    smtphost speaker.rodsbooks.com
poll imap.asmallisp.com with proto IMAP
    user rodsmith there with password A1B2C3
    is rodsmith here
```

As with many configuration files, a pound sign (#) denotes a comment, so Fetchmail ignores the first two lines. The remainder of Listing 11.3 is broken into two parts. First, a series of `set` statements set global options, most of which relate to features you can set in the Fetchmail Expert Configurator dialog box's Fetchmail Run Controls section (Figure 11.2) of `fetchmailconf`. Many of these options can be set or overridden using command-line arguments, as well. Second, Listing 11.3 includes two `poll` statements, each of which defines a remote e-mail account to be accessed, including how the mail retrieved from that account should be delivered. (This information appears in the Fetchmail Host *Hostname* and Fetchmail User *Username* Querying *Hostname* dialog boxes in `fetchmailconf`, as shown in Figures 11.3 and 11.4.) These `poll` statements may exceed one line in length, *without* using special characters to indicate a line continuation, as some other file formats require. Line breaks in Listing 11.3 are arbitrary.

Fetchmail supports a huge number of options, so I can't describe all of them here. For more information, consult the Fetchmail man page or other Fetchmail documentation. Some options take a string, such as a username, as an argument. If this string contains spaces, you should enclose it in quotes ("). Some of the more important global options include the following:

- **set postmaster** *username*—This option sets the username used for mail delivery if other options fail to specify one. This user also receives certain types of error messages. It's normally an ordinary user, but you can use `postmaster` or `root` for *username*, if you like. (All SMTP mail servers are supposed to support a user called `postmaster` to handle queries concerning the computer's mail system. The Fetchmail `postmaster` may or may not be the same as the SMTP server's `postmaster`.) The `--postmaster` *username* command-line option overrides this configuration option.

- **set bouncemail**—This option tells Fetchmail to send error messages to the mail's sender. You can alter this option by using `set no bouncemail` instead; in this case, the Fetchmail `postmaster` receives the error messages.

- **set daemon** *interval*—This option tells Fetchmail to run in daemon mode, and to query mail servers every *interval* seconds. If you want to run Fetchmail in batch mode, omit this option. You can override this value with the `--daemon` *interval* command-line argument. Using the `--daemon 0` command-line argument causes Fetchmail to do one fetch operation, even if it's configured to use daemon mode in `.fetchmailrc`.

- **set logfile** *filename*—You can tell Fetchmail to log its activities to a particular file with this option.

- **set syslog**—If you want Fetchmail to log its activities through the system logger, you can do so with this option.

The poll statements can be fairly simple or quite complex. The format of a poll statement is as follows:

poll *server.name server-options user-descriptions*

The keyword server is synonymous with poll. You can replace either of these with skip to tell Fetchmail to skip this entry. You can use this feature to easily disable an entry without deleting it from the .fetchmailrc file. The server options define how Fetchmail is to interact with the server, and the user descriptions define accounts on the server and locally. You can intermix options within each of these two categories, but not between them. (A common source of problems in manually configuring Fetchmail is to intermix these two option classes.) The words and, with, has, wants, and options are all ignored, as are the punctuation symbols colon (:), semicolon (;), and comma (,). You can place these anywhere within the server options or user descriptions to make the poll entry easier to understand.

Some of the more common or important server options include the following:

- **proto** *name* **or protocol** *name*—These synonymous options specify the pull mail protocol to be used. The *name* will most commonly be POP3 or IMAP, but Fetchmail supports several others, including some fairly obscure pull mail protocols. You can override this value with the -p command-line argument.

- **interface** *interface/IP.address/net.mask*—You can specify a network interface that must be up before Fetchmail will poll a given server with this option. You specify the interface with a device name (*interface*), such as eth1 or ppp0; an IP address, such as 192.168.1.0; and a netmask that determines the range of acceptable IP addresses. For instance, interface eth1/192.168.1.0/255.255.255.0 specifies that the computer must have an address between 192.168.1.1 and 192.168.1.254 on eth1 before Fetchmail will try to contact the server. You can also provide this information with the -I command-line option.

- **monitor** *interface*—This option causes Fetchmail in daemon mode to watch a network interface for activity. If Fetchmail detects no activity between the previous poll and a scheduled one, Fetchmail skips the poll. This behavior can keep Fetchmail from keeping an auto-dial device up with its own polling. You can use the -M command-line argument to provide this information, as well.

Some of the more common user options include the following:

- **user** *name* or **username** *name*—These options usually mark the start of the user description portion of the poll option, and they specify a username. This is normally the remote username, but if the sequence is followed by here, the username is local. The keyword there forces interpretation of the user as a remote account. The -u command-line argument overrides this option.

- **pass** *pw* or **password** *pw*—These options specify the password (*pw*) to be used on the pull mail account. You provide the password in cleartext (unencrypted), and it's stored that way in the configuration file.

- **is** *name* or **to** *name*—These options link a pull account to a local user. One of these options normally appears after the description of the pull mail account (using a sequence such as user *name* with pass *pw*). When the remote account description precedes the local account description, here follows these options to identify the account as being local. The keyword there identifies a remote account.

- **smtphost** *host.name*—Normally, Fetchmail attempts to use the address localhost, which corresponds to the computer on which it runs, to send mail. You can have the program use another computer's mail server for sending mail on its way, though, by using this option. You can also use this option and specify your computer's regular hostname, in which case the addresses in your mail headers corresponding to Fetchmail transfers will include that hostname rather than localhost. The -S command-line argument overrides this setting.

- **keep**—By default, Fetchmail deletes messages from the server once it's retrieved them. This option causes Fetchmail to leave messages. You might use this when testing a new configuration. The -k command-line argument is another way to specify this option.

- **fetchall**—Normally, Fetchmail doesn't retrieve messages that it has already retrieved. You can force the program to retrieve all messages with this option, which has a command-line equivalent of -a.

- **forcecr**—Technically, mail messages should have lines that end with a carriage return/line feed pair of characters. Most mail programs tolerate messages that lack the carriage return, and a few systems send such messages. The qmail push mail server can't tolerate such messages, though, so the forcecr option corrects matters for users of qmail.

When you specify more than one local name, Fetchmail examines the mail headers to try to determine who should receive the mail. For instance, if you specify local accounts of jack and jill, and if incoming mail is addressed to jill, Fetchmail delivers the mail to jill. This is *multidrop mode*, in which mail from a single account may be processed in different ways according to the headers in the mail.

TIP For many additional options relating to local delivery of mail after Fetchmail has done its job, look into Procmail. This package is described in Chapter 19. You can use Procmail to help identify and delete unwanted messages, move incoming mail into mail folders according to type, and more.

SUMMARY

Pull mail servers are frequently installed on an organization's main SMTP server in order to allow users to read their mail from client computers located within the organization, or potentially anywhere else on the Internet. Using a pull mail protocol obviates the need for users to log in using Telnet, SSH, or some other remote-access protocol, and allows users to use mail readers in their OS of choice. Two pull mail protocols are in common use today: POP-3 and IMAP-4. Of the two, IMAP is more powerful, as it allows retention and organization of mail on the server; but this very fact may increase demands for disk space and network bandwidth on the server, so you may prefer to use POP.

The Fetchmail program can be used as a bridge between a mail server to which you have access through a pull mail protocol and other mail systems, such as a mail server on a LAN. You can use Fetchmail to retrieve external mail and inject it into a local mail queue, simplifying users' mail experiences.

Running a News Server

Chapter 11 discussed the use of pull mail servers, which allow users to read messages directed to them personally. This chapter covers a different type of messaging system: *news servers*. Where e-mail is a one-to-one correspondence, news (or Usenet news or Netnews, as it's often called) is a one-to-many transmission medium. A user may *post* a message to a news server, and any user of that news server may then read that message. What's more, news servers often communicate amongst themselves, resulting in propagation of messages across the world. Whether you run a news server that's only used locally or one that's connected to others, news servers can provide a useful group communication system for your users.

Traditional news servers talk to each other as equals, exchanging all messages in newsgroups. These servers support multiple clients on the same or other computers, which read a small subset of all messages. One variant on a regular news server is a program that connects to a conventional news server as a client in order to download only a subset of the messages that the local users want to read. Such miniature news servers are often run on personal computers to permit *offline* news reading—rather than connect to the Internet and stay connected while reading news, the system can connect, download messages, and allow the user to read them while disconnected. This approach can minimize network connection times, which can be important if you're billed by the minute.

NOTE Although the preceding discussion refers to news as a one-to-many communications tool and e-mail as a one-to-one tool, e-mail is somewhat more flexible than this. You can specify multiple recipients for your e-mail, for one thing. There's also a tool, known as a *mailing list*, that allows for the creation of a group discussion similar to news. Mailing lists are typically set up to support special interest groups, and their subscription methods aren't quite as standardized as news group subscriptions.

WHEN TO RUN A NEWS SERVER

News servers tend to be used in three ways:

- **Usenet news**—The global network of news servers is known as *Usenet*. When a server participates in Usenet news, it exchanges one or more *newsgroups* (named discussion forums) with other news servers, resulting in the worldwide message system described earlier. Most Internet Service Providers (ISPs) and universities run Usenet news servers, as do some companies.

- **Internal communications**—An organization may set up a news server to facilitate communications among members of the organization, or associated individuals. For instance, employees working on a single project or students in a class might use a news server to communicate amongst themselves. Similarly, some companies run news servers that host discussions of the companies' products for the benefit of customers.

- **Offline news reading**—As noted earlier, offline news reading allows an individual or small group to read news without tying up a network connection while doing so. This is often desirable in homes with just one phone line or when telephone connection costs are billed by the minute. Such a use involves the transfer of only a few Usenet news groups.

Both full Usenet news and internal news use the same software. The main theoretical difference between the connected and isolated systems is one of the external connection or lack thereof. In practice, there's another major difference: A full Usenet news server (one that hosts more than a trivial fraction of the thousands of available newsgroups) consumes a great deal of disk space and network bandwidth in exchanging the news messages. A system that hosts a full Usenet news server is likely to require so much disk space and bandwidth that it won't be useful for much of anything else. Such a system will need a hard disk that's tens or even hundreds of gigabytes in size just for the news articles. Of course, a system with much more limited newsgroup availability, such as a personal system intended for offline news reading, won't have such huge resource requirements.

WARNING

News servers typically place their news articles in the /var/spool/news direc-tory tree. If you didn't install Linux with a news server in mind, this directory may reside on the root partition, or possibly on a smallish /var partition. A dedicated news server generally uses a huge /var or /var/spool/news parti-tion to hold the news posts. You should be sure the computer you intend to use for this purpose has adequate disk space in /var/spool/news, or possibly change the spool directory to some other partition where you do have ade-quate space.

TIP

Using a journaling filesystem, such as ReiserFS or XFS, can greatly reduce startup times after a system crash or power outage, particularly for a system like a news server that has a large hard disk. Keeping the news spool directory on its own dedicated partition can enhance system stability, because a filesys-tem error involving the spool directory (which is transient in nature) need not affect system stability.

Because of the need for dedicating an entire computer and bandwidth that's measured in megabits per second to a full Usenet news server, it's unlikely that a small office or home will need such a server. Instead, such users are better served by using their ISPs' news server or a third-party news server. (Some popular commercial news providers include Giganews, http://www.giganews.com; Supernews, http://www.supernews.com; and NewsGuy, http://www.newsguy.com. You can find a list of free third-party news servers at http://www.newsservers.net. The http://groups. google.com archive site holds archives of many popular newsgroups, accessible through a Web-based interface.) The discussion of regular news servers in this chapter (in the section "Running INN") focuses on the internal communications use of a news server, although it doesn't com-pletely ignore the data transfer configuration required of a regular Usenet news server.

Offline news reading is often done through a feature of news readers (news client programs), but it can be done through a special limited-func-tion news server, such as the Leafnode program described in the "Using

Leafnode" section of this chapter. Such programs have different configuration requirements than do conventional news servers, but they work much the same from the client's point of view. If you have a full-time connection to the Internet (via a corporate LAN or home broadband account), chances are you'll find it easier to use your ISP's news server directly rather than use an intermediate news server. You might use such an option when your Internet connection is limited or costly, or if your ISP's news server is overloaded when you want to use it—you can configure Leafnode to transfer messages during off hours, thus making your news reading quicker. You might also want to use Leafnode if your system serves one or two dozen people who read largely the same newsgroups, because in such a scenario, running your own server can reduce your external news-related data traffic.

UNDERSTANDING NNTP

Modern news servers use a protocol known as the Network News Transfer Protocol (NNTP) both among themselves and with news clients (often called *news readers*). An NNTP server normally runs on TCP port 119. NNTP was designed for the transfer of news on TCP/IP networks, but Usenet isn't restricted to such networks. Indeed, the earliest news servers used other network protocols. NNTP is therefore not the only news transfer protocol in existence, but it is the one that's most common on TCP/IP networks today.

The basic currency of NNTP is the *message* (aka the *post* or *article*), which is a single document that normally originates from one person at one site. (Multiple people may collaborate on a single message, but this is rare.) Messages are collected into newsgroups, as described earlier, but a single message may be posted to multiple newsgroups. Such *cross-posting* is discouraged, especially when it's taken to extremes with dozens of newsgroups. Newsgroups are arranged hierarchically, with multiple names similar to directory names that combine to form a complete newsgroup name. These names are delineated by periods (.), with the least specific name to the left. For instance, comp.os.linux.misc and comp.os.linux.hardware are both newsgroups in the comp.os.linux hierarchy, and so are closely related, as you might expect. A newsgroup that's somewhat more distant from these is comp.dcom.modems, and a still more distant one is rec.arts.sf.dune.

When a user posts a message, the news server attaches an identifying code to the message, using a message header line of Message-Id. This code includes a serial number of some sort generated by the server followed by the server's name. Because the ID includes the server's name, this code should be unique, assuming the server can keep track of the serial numbers that it generates for messages. News servers use the message IDs to keep track of which messages they've seen, and therefore which messages are worth transferring.

When two news servers connect to each other, they can transfer messages using either of two types of protocols. As with mail, these are known as *push* and *pull* protocols. For purposes of this transfer, one server assumes the role of the server, and the other takes on the role of a client. In a push protocol, the client tells the server about each message it has available in turn, using the message ID numbers. The server can then check its database and decide whether it needs a specific message. The process repeats for the next message, and so on. This procedure requires that the server do a lot of work, because it must check its database of message IDs with every exchange. The alternative is a pull protocol, in which the receiving system takes on the role of the client. This system requests a complete list of articles that arrived on the server after a given date. The client can then request specific messages. This process can be more efficient, but it requires careful checking so that the server doesn't accidentally deliver messages from newsgroups that should be private.

Because people are constantly generating news messages, news servers need some way to purge old messages; if this weren't done, news messages would soon fill the server's hard disk (a danger that's very real on full Usenet servers even with careful pruning of old messages). Typically, a news server will automatically *expire* old messages, meaning that they're deleted after they've been made available for a certain period of time. How often a server expires messages depends on many factors, including the available disk space, the number of newsgroups carried, the traffic on these newsgroups, and the popularity of various groups. It's possible to set different retention intervals for different newsgroups.

Whichever transfer method is used and however often messages are expired, transfers can involve far more than two computers. News servers can link to each other in an extremely complex web of connections. Each of these connections is known as a *news feed*. Typically, a smaller or less-well-connected site requests a news feed from a larger or better-connected site. For instance, the news administrator at Tiny College might request a news feed from the much larger Pangaea University. This means that most of the news articles to be made available on news.tiny.edu would come from news.pangaea.edu. The bulk of the transfers would flow in this direction, but of course Tiny College users might post news, so news.pangaea.edu would also accept some messages from news.tiny.edu. Pangaea University, in turn, has a news feed from some other source, which leads to others, and so on.

This relationship need not be entirely linear, though. For instance, it's possible that news.pangaea.edu doesn't carry some newsgroups that the Tiny College news administrators want. In this case, those administrators might seek out a secondary news feed for those newsgroups, and perhaps more news feeds for others. Pangaea University might do the same to obtain the groups it needs. In all these cases, not all newsgroups need be transferred. A site might drop a newsgroup or even an entire hierarchy from its feed to conserve disk space, because the group isn't of interest at the destination site, or for any other reason.

The end result is a system of interconnected news servers that includes a few very large servers that feed other large servers and smaller servers. These in turn feed others, and so on. Any of these servers may also function as a server to news client programs. These news readers also use NNTP, and they can both retrieve and post messages, but they don't feed other sites. Also, a news server adds and modifies some news headers to indicate that the post originated with it, and often to identify the client that originated the message.

It's important to remember that the flow of news articles goes both ways. Indeed, if it weren't for posts at the extreme branches of the news-feeding "tree," the large sites that constitute the "trunk" wouldn't have any news to feed to smaller sites. The large sites simply serve as aggregation points for the massive amounts of news generated by individuals who read and post to newsgroups. Individual news servers, though, receive far more news from their feeds than they generate locally.

RUNNING INN

The most popular conventional news server on Linux today is InterNet-News (INN; http://www.isc.org/products/INN/). This package actually consists of several programs that work together as a unified system. The core program is innd, which processes news articles and handles incoming connections. The nnrpd program takes over connections from news readers (as opposed to other news servers). INN initiates connections with other news servers using the innxmit program, which in turn uses nntpsend to do much of the work. Each of these programs has an associated configuration file; indeed, some use multiple files. The most basic configuration files usually reside in /etc/news, but some files are stored in /var/lib/news or elsewhere.

INN is usually shipped with Linux distributions in a package called inn or some variant of that. This chapter describes INN version 2.2.2, but configuration for other INN 2.x-series packages should be virtually identical. Some distributions make INN dependent upon Cleanfeed, which is an add-on package that can automatically remove some types of spam from the news server. (Newsgroup spam is a major problem that most end users don't notice because of the automated spam cleaning that's so common today.)

Obtaining a News Feed

If you want to run a news server that carries even part of Usenet, you need to obtain a news feed for the server, and configure your system to use that feed. The latter task is covered in the upcoming section, "Controlling Access," but the former deserves a few words, as well. NNTP is designed such that you can use just about any existing news server as a feed. The trouble is that you can't simply enter some random news server in a configuration file and expect the feed to work; most news servers accept feeds only from selected sites. You must therefore locate a site that will agree to serve as your news feed. Indeed, you might need to locate multiple feeds if you can't find a single site that can provide all the newsgroups you want to carry.

One place to start looking for a news feed is with whoever provides your network connectivity—your ISP. Assuming you have a connection fast enough to support a full news feed, your ISP might be willing to feed your news server, or at least give you a pointer to some potential providers. Many ISPs, though, don't provide news feeds to their customers. This is particularly common for ISPs that sell primarily to residential and small business customers, and such customers seldom have enough bandwidth to handle the news feed in any event. Another potential source of news feeds is third-party news providers like those mentioned earlier. For instance, NewsGuy (http://www.newsguy.com) offers news feeds as well as access via news readers.

A full news feed is likely to be costly, both in terms of a cash outlay for the service and in terms of the hardware and bandwidth required to support it. For instance, the NewsGuy feed costs $1200 a month in 2002, and the recommended hardware is a 400MHz Pentium with 500MB of RAM and 64GB of disk space, connected to a link with at least 3Mbps of bandwidth. You'll also need bandwidth for the news readers that will connect to your server. Of course, the exact requirements may be higher or lower than this,

Serving News on Limited Resources

If you want to run a regular news server on limited hardware and network connectivity, drop the *binary* newsgroups. These newsgroups carry binary files, encoded to be transmissible as Usenet posts, which were originally intended for text. Binary newsgroups carry sound clips, digitized photos, program files, and more. Some carry material that's copyrighted and should not be distributed in this way. Most see a huge amount of traffic, in terms of the size of posts, because the binary files are much larger than a typical post in a text newsgroup. Most binary newsgroups have binary or binaries in the newsgroup names. Many are in the alt hierarchy, but some are in comp or elsewhere.

If you want to provide a full news feed but lack the resources to host it, an outsourcing arrangement is often a reasonable compromise. You contract with a news provider and create a DNS entry for your domain to point to your news provider's IP address. From the point of view of your users, it appears that you're running a news server, when in fact somebody else is doing the bulk of the work. Many small ISPs use outsourced news servers. One potential drawback is that a news provider might or might not be willing to create special news groups for your local use.

depending upon the exact mix of newsgroups you want to carry, how long you want to retain posts, and so on. As a general rule, the requirements have gone up every year, so the values cited here are likely to be very inadequate in the not-too-distant future.

CONFIGURING INN

Configuring INN involves setting many options in many different files. A default installation will probably set many of the options to reasonable values, but you'll have to adjust some settings to fit your own system. For instance, you must define your newsgroups and set up access control features. (If you want to run a full Usenet server, your news feed may be able to provide you with help on control files relating to newsgroups and access to their own server.) You must also set up message expiration policies and tell INN how to handle any special control messages it may receive (these may tell the server to cancel a message, add a new group, and so on).

General Configuration

The main INN configuration file is /etc/news/inn.conf. This file sets options using the following syntax:

optionname: *value*

Many other INN configuration files use a similar syntax. Most of the options in inn.conf may be left at their default values. The most important options to change are the first few. These include:

- **organization**—This option sets the name of your organization. This string will be included in the headers of all the posts made through your news server.

- **server**—This is the name of the computer on which INN is running. It's critical because some of the programs that make up the INN package establish a network connection with this computer in order to deliver articles. The default value of localhost may work, but it's best to change this to your true hostname.

- **pathhost**—Whenever INN accepts a post, the server adds its name to a header line called Path. This header helps identify where a message has been, and thus helps prevent loops in which a message is passed back and forth between various servers. You should place your news server's fully-qualified domain name here, such as news.threeroomco.com.

- **moderatormailer**—Some newsgroups are *moderated*, which means that an individual (the *moderator*) must approve posts to the group before they appear. You can either keep track of moderator mailing addresses yourself, or send posts to moderated newsgroups to a centralized address, which will forward them to the moderator. Entering %s@uunet.uu.net will do the latter.

- **domain**—This is the name of your domain, such as threeroomco.com. It's used internally for DNS-related functions by INN component programs.

- **fromhost**—When a local user posts a message, INN creates a From header to identify the poster. The program uses the value of this line as the machine name, so you should use something appropriate here—probably your domain name, but possibly a mail machine within the domain.

- **complaints**—Unfortunately, some users abuse news. They may spam, post offensive material, post binaries to text newsgroups, or do other obnoxious things. The complaints option lets you specify an e-mail address that will be visible in the headers of messages that originate from your site, so that others can contact you in the event some abuse occurs.

There are many additional options in the `inn.conf` file, but these should have reasonable default values. Consult the `inn.conf` man page for further information about the meanings of these options.

Setting Up Newsgroups

The `inn.conf` file doesn't include any newsgroup definitions or descriptions. That task is left to two other configuration files: `active` and `newsgroups`, both of which are stored in the directory set by the `pathdb` option in `inn.conf` (normally `/var/lib/news`).

The `active` file contains a list of newsgroups that are supported on the system. Newsgroups appear one to a line in this file, and order doesn't matter. Each line contains four fields, separated by whitespace:

```
newsgroup.name himark lowmark flag
```

As you might expect, *newsgroup.name* is the name of the newsgroup, such as `comp.os.linux.misc`. The *himark* and *lowmark* fields specify the highest- and lowest-numbered posts in the group, respectively. These values begin at `0000000000` and `0000000001`, respectively, for a new group. (INN stores posts as individual files with filenames being sequential numbers corresponding to a local post number. This local post number is unrelated to the message ID, and is likely to be different from one news server to another.) The *flag* field contains a flag that denotes how the newsgroup is to be treated:

- **y**—This is the most common flag; it indicates a newsgroup to which users can post.
- **n**—Newsgroups with this flag accept new messages from news feeds, but not posts from local users or news clients.
- **m**—This flag indicates a moderated newsgroup; local posts are mailed to the group moderator for approval.
- **j**—Newsgroups with this flag accept posts, but don't keep them; INN only passes on new posts to its feeds.
- **x**—This newsgroup is static; new posts aren't accepted, either locally or from news feeds.
- **=*news.group***—Posts to this group are moved into the group specified by *news.group*. You might use this flag to redirect posts made to a defunct newsgroup.

A news server that only supports local operations is likely to have just a few news groups. You can call these whatever you like, but following the tiered naming convention of Usenet makes sense. For instance, you might create all your local groups in a hierarchy that's named after your organization, like threeroomco.support, threeroomco.support.bigproduct, and threeroomco.accounting for three discussion groups at threeroomco.com. If you acquire a news feed from an outside source, that source should be able to provide you with a list of newsgroups, or even a complete active file, that you can use.

As your news server operates, INN will modify the *himark* and *lowmark* fields of the active file. As articles are added, the *himark* value will increase. As older articles are expired, the *lowmark* value will increase, although it may not change with *every* expiration or cancellation—as described later, articles may not expire in exactly the order in which they're created.

The newsgroups file is less critical to day-to-day operation of the news server than is the active file. Like the active file, the first field of each line of newsgroups is the name of the newsgroup. After this group name comes one or more tabs and a description of the newsgroup. Clients can retrieve this file to help users locate groups, or differentiate between two groups whose names are similar.

Controlling Access

Most sites restrict access to their news servers to prevent abuse and conserve their network resources. There are three aspects to this configuration: feeding news to other sites, restricting access for news feeds, and restricting access for news clients. The first two options are important mainly when your news server exchanges messages with others, but even if you operate a standalone news server, you should check that it's not configured to accept exchanges with other news servers, to avoid abuse. Configuration for news clients is important for all news servers

Feeding News to Other Sites

If you want messages posted by your users to reach other sites, or if you've arranged to feed entire newsgroups to some other site, you need to configure your system to contact other news servers to send messages on their way. This is controlled through the /etc/news/newsfeeds file, which contains lines of the following format:

sitename:*pattern*[,*pattern*...]:*flag*[,*flag*...]:*param*

These lines can become quite long, so you can split lines by using the backslash (\) line continuation character—any line that ends in a backslash is continued on the following line, so you can break a very long line across multiple lines for ease of reading and editing. Each of the colon-delimited fields has a specific meaning, as follows:

- *sitename*—This is a code for the site. This code need not be a conventional hostname; it's matched to a hostname in another configuration file, described shortly.

- *pattern*—A *pattern* is a code for one or more newsgroups. You may specify newsgroups individually if you want to pass on posts in just a few, or you may use the asterisk (*) wildcard to match any string; for instance, comp.os.* matches all newsgroups in the comp.os hierarchy. If you precede a pattern by an exclamation mark (!), posts in that group will *not* be passed on unless they're cross-posted to another group. The at-sign (@) has a similar meaning, but cross-posted messages are blocked, as well. For instance, if you specify !comp.os.linux, a message cross-posted to comp.os.linux and comp.os.linux.hardware will be passed on as part of the latter group; but @comp.os.linux will cause the message to not be passed on at all. INN applies patterns in sequence, so if you specify comp.os.*,!comp.os.linux, INN will pass on messages in the comp.os hierarchy *except* for those in comp.os.linux. Reversing the order would pass on all groups, because the less-specific comp.os.* would override the more specific !comp.os.linux.

- *flag*—You can include one or more flags that limit what types of messages are passed on to the remote site. For instance, <*size* restricts messages to those less than *size* bytes, and G*count* passes a post only if it's posted to fewer than *count* newsgroups. The newsfeeds man page includes a description of additional flags.

- *param*—This final field's meaning depends upon the type of news feed. It's usually the name of a file in which the outgoing feed is stored. In other cases it may be blank. The default newsfeeds file includes many examples that are commented out.

The newsfeeds file controls the creation of a file that will ultimately be transmitted to another site. The /etc/news/nntpsend.ctl file controls how INN contacts that site. Like newsfeeds, nntpsend.ctl consists of four colon-delimited fields:

```
sitename:site.host.name:max_size:[args]
```

The *sitename* is the name of the site from the newsfeeds file, and the *site.host.name* is the site's conventional hostname. You can restrict the amount of data you'll pass in a single transfer with the *max_size* argument;

for instance, 2m limits transfers to 2MB or less. Finally, you can include optional arguments that are passed to the innxmit program, which does the actual transmission. Consult the innxmit man page for information on the arguments it accepts.

You'll only need to deal with these configurations if you're feeding news to other sites, or if you want to set up a feed from another site. To be truly effective, a news feed from another site must accept posts that originate with your users. Without this reciprocal connection, posts from your users won't be available to readers on the Internet at large, just locally. Thus, although you may think of yourself as accepting an external news feed, you must configure your system to provide a feed *to* your feeder, as well as accepting its input.

Setting News Feed Access

INN can control access to itself. The main daemon, innd, accepts connections from your feeder news sites and from various other programs in the INN package. Although innd handles the initial connection from news clients, it passes those connections to another program as quickly as possible. Therefore, the main innd connections control file, /etc/news/incoming.conf, should list only the local computer and news feeder sites.

The basic unit in the incoming.conf file is a *key/value pair*, which is how you specify attributes and their values. These take the form *key* : *value*. These pairs may be collected into *peers*, which are specifications of individual computers. (Some key/value pairs are global in scope, though; they don't appear in peers.) Peers may also be collected into *groups*. Both peers and groups use curly braces ({}) to delimit their extent. Listing 12.1 shows a typical incoming.conf file for a site that uses one news feed.

Listing 12.1   A sample incoming.conf file

```
# Global settings
streaming: true
max-connections: 50
# Allow NNTP posting from localhost
peer ME {
    hostname: "localhost, 127.0.0.1"
}
# Allow fiveroomco.com to send us most groups
peer fiveroom {
    hostname: news.fiveroomco.com
    patterns: *,!threeroomco.*
}
```

The most important key is hostname, which specifies the hostname of the computer that's to be allowed a connection. You can list specific newsgroups that may be transferred using the patterns key, using the newsgroup-naming conventions of the newsfeeds file. The default is to accept all newsgroups fed by the remote system. Various other keys are described in the incoming.conf man page.

Setting News Reader Access

Chances are you want authorized users to be able to access your news server. Because innd delegates this task to another program, you don't configure news reader access in the incoming.conf file; instead, you use the /etc/news/nnrp.access file for this purpose. Each line in this file consists of five colon-delimited entries, thus:

hostname:permissions:username:password:newsgroups

The meanings of specific entries are as follows:

- **hostname**—This is the name or IP address of an individual host, or a pattern using an asterisk wildcard to match a range of hosts, such as *.threeroomco.com to match any client in the threeroomco.com domain. When using IP addresses, you may use an IP address/netmask pair, as in 172.20.0.0/16.
- **permissions**—This field contains one or more of R (message reading is allowed), P (posting is allowed), N (the client may use the NEWNEWS command), or L (the client may post even to groups to which local posting is prohibited). These last two options override global settings for specific clients.
- **username**—If you want to restrict access to the server based on a username and password, you should specify the username here; when this is done, the user must authenticate before being allowed to post. A plus sign (+) causes the server to try to use the Linux password database for authentication, but this often doesn't work, particularly when the system is configured to use shadow passwords. If you leave this and the next field blank, no authentication will be required to read or post news.
- **password**—This field contains the password that's required to access the news server. Leaving this field and the *username* field blank causes the system to not require authentication.
- **newsgroups**—You can specify newsgroups using patterns like those used in the newsgroups file if you want to restrict the newsgroups to

which certain hosts have access. Leaving this field blank causes the server to make *no* newsgroups available to the client, so to make all newsgroups available, the entry must end in an asterisk (*).

If you include multiple lines in the nnrp.access file, later lines take precedence over earlier ones. Thus, if you want to make global settings but provide exceptions for specific hosts, you should place the lines for the global settings earlier in the file.

Setting Message Expiration Options

The /etc/news/expire.ctl file controls the automatic expiration (deletion) of messages. Most of the lines in this file follow a pattern similar to that in other configuration files, with five colon-delimited fields:

pattern:modflag:keep:default:purge

The meanings of these fields are as follows:

- *pattern*—This is a newsgroup specification. As with others, an asterisk (*) is a wildcard, so * alone matches all newsgroups, comp.os.* matches the entire comp.os hierarchy, and so on.
- *modflag*—This flag is a single character that indicates the rule applies to moderated groups only (M), unmoderated groups only (U), or all newsgroups (A).
- *keep*—Articles may include a header called Expires that specifies a unique expiration time for a specific article. You may set an overriding minimum value (in days) in this field. For instance, if *keep* is set to 6, 7.5, or some higher value, an article that's set to expire in only five days won't expire until the later date you specify. The value of *keep* may be a floating-point number, and never indicates that the article will never expire. (Use never very cautiously, though, since it can cause your hard disk to fill quite quickly.)
- *default*—This is the most important value, since it sets the expiration time for articles without an Expires header, which most news postings lack. As with *keep*, you specify the value in days, which may be expressed as a floating-point value. The value never means that articles are never expired.
- *purge*—The *keep* field lets you override an Expires header when it's lower than you might like. The *purge* field lets you override an Expires header that's longer than you might like. For instance, if you set *purge*

to 10 and receive an article with an Expires header that specifies it's to be kept for 100 days, your system will expire the article after only ten days. As with *keep* and *default*, the value of *purge* may be floating-point or *never*.

ONGOING NEWS SERVER MAINTENANCE

INN normally runs directly as a daemon, started by SysV startup scripts as described in Chapter 4, Starting Servers. If you installed INN from a package included with your distribution, you should be able to start it by running such a startup script.

Some of the tasks described earlier, such as sending messages to other servers and expiring articles, aren't handled automatically by innd as it runs in normal operation. Instead, these tasks are controlled by scripts or utility programs that are called by cron. If you installed INN from a package that came with your distribution, chances are that it created appropriate configuration files to have these tasks occur automatically by placing crontab files in /etc/cron.d, /etc/cron.*interval*, or some other location. If you want to change the frequency with which these tasks occur, you should check these locations or use your package manager to find out what cron files were placed where. You can then modify, move, or delete the files, and if necessary create new ones to take over these tasks.

Other server maintenance tasks involve modifying your configuration. For instance, you may need to add a new newsgroup, delete an existing newsgroup, or temporarily disable access to the server. These tasks can be accomplished with the ctlindd utility, which accepts a large number of options. Type **ctlindd -h** to view a list of its options.

USING LEAFNODE

INN is a tool that's used mainly by large ISPs or other organizations that want to provide full news feeds, or by organizations that want to provide limited local newsgroups in support of their own activities, but not full news feeds. As described earlier, though, in the section "When to Run a News Server," some people want to run local news servers in order to facilitate their own local news reading. Such a server should retrieve messages from just a few newsgroups, make them available whether or not the main Internet connection is active, and upload the user's postings during the next round of message downloads. These scheduled message exchanges could take place just once or twice a day, at times when the news server is not heavily loaded or when a Point-to-Point Protocol (PPP) dialup connection is inexpensive or easy to obtain. In principle, INN could serve this function, but considered as a server for just a few local users reading a handful of newsgroups, INN is overkill. The program is also designed to work as a peer on the Usenet network, so chances are you'd have trouble finding an ISP that would agree to feed a limited number of newsgroups to you on your own schedule. For these reasons, other tools exist to help users perform offline news reading. One of the more popular of these is Leafnode (`http://www.leafnode.org`).

NOTE Leafnode isn't alone in the class of NNTP servers for small or offline sites. Others that fill similar roles include NNTPCache (`http://www.nntpcache.org`), Noffle (`http://noffle.sourceforge.net`), sn (`http://infa.abo.fi/~patrik/sn/`) and NewsCache (`http://www.infosys.tuwien.ac.at/NewsCache/`).

UNDERSTANDING LEAFNODE'S CAPABILITIES

Like INN, Leafnode is actually composed of several programs. The most important of these are:

- **leafnode**—This is the NNTP server program. It's launched from a super server, as described in Chapter 4, and communicates with your news reader program on the same or a different computer.

- **fetchnews**—This program, as its name implies, is responsible for retrieving news from your upstream news server. It also delivers your posts to the upstream news server. You can run it as a cron job to retrieve news on a regular basis, run it in a PPP dialup script, or run it manually.

- **texpire**—Just like a normal news server, Leafnode retains news messages in subdirectories of `/var/spool/news`. Because of this, it's necessary for Leafnode to delete old messages, lest your hard disk fill up. Doing this is `texpire`'s job. It's normally run as a cron job on a daily basis.

- **newsq**—This is a local information display program; it reports a summary of news articles that have been posted locally but not yet uploaded to your upstream news server.

Leafnode is designed for dynamic newsgroup configuration. If a user tries to start reading a newsgroup, Leafnode will begin fetching that newsgroup with the next run of `fetchnews`. If Leafnode detects no attempt to access a newsgroup for some period (a week, by default), then it stops retrieving the group. This means that you can provide the illusion that you're carrying all the newsgroups available on your upstream news provider without actually doing so. Your local users will, however, experience a delay of one fetch cycle between attempting to access a new group and seeing the posts that are available in it.

One of the more unusual characteristics of Leafnode is that it doesn't require a full news feed arrangement with the upstream provider; Leafnode (or fetchnews, to be precise) presents itself as an ordinary news reader to the feed site. This means that you can use Leafnode in conjunction with your ISP's ordinary news server.

NOTE Leafnode uses both greater and fewer resources than an ordinary news reader. Fetching all the posts in a typical text newsgroup will probably consume far less time than would a news-reading session in which you're constantly connected to the remote server. This can reduce consumption of connections on the server (which are sometimes limited), as well as your online connect time. On the other hand, this process consumes far more bandwidth, in terms of bytes transferred, than would a typical online reading session, since Leafnode downloads *all* the articles—even those you ordinarily wouldn't read. If Leafnode serves several users who normally read much the same set of newsgroups, though, the total amount of data transferred might not be more with Leafnode than with individual direct connections.

In early 2002, the current version of Leafnode is 1.9.19. Work is underway on a 2.0 release, which will add support for local newsgroups, making Leafnode suitable for running a small news server for local newsgroups. The 1.9.*x* versions don't support this feature, though.

It's important to remember that Leafnode was designed as a news reader for *small* sites. It doesn't scale well, meaning that as you add users and large numbers of newsgroups, Leafnode's performance suffers. Leafnode works well for up to a few dozen clients, but it's not very useable beyond that point. If you're experiencing performance problems that are caused by a heavy server load, you should seriously consider switching to INN or some other conventional news server and obtaining a full news feed.

Another problem with Leafnode is that it may drop messages if it encounters a problem. This may result in posts that aren't posted to Usenet, or in existing Usenet posts that aren't readable. Some fetchnews options attempt to work around some of these problems, as described shortly, but you may lose posts if your connection to your upstream news server is unreliable.

Configuring Leafnode

Configuring Leafnode requires setting up three programs: The `leafnode` server itself, the `fetchnews` program, and `texpire` to expire old news. Functions relating to all three programs are contained in a general configuration file, but you'll need to set up each program to run in its own way. If you use a Leafnode package from your Linux distribution, you shouldn't need to edit many files to get it all running.

General Configuration Settings

The main Leafnode configuration file is called `config`, and it's usually stored in `/etc/leafnode`. Aside from comments, which begin with a pound sign (#), this file consists of lines of the following form:

```
parameter = value
```

A minimal Leafnode configuration needs to set just a couple of parameters: `server` and `expire`. Other parameters are optional; they take on reasonable default values if you don't set them. The more important parameters are as follows:

- **server**—This parameter sets the name of your upstream news server, as in `server = news.abigisp.net`. You can configure Leafnode to fetch news from multiple news servers by including more than one `server` line.
- **expire**—This parameter sets the number of days Leafnode retains messages before deleting them.
- **username**—If your upstream news server requires you to enter a username, specify it with this parameter.
- **password**—If you need a password to access your upstream news server, enter it with this parameter.

WARNING

!

Your password is stored in a plain text file, and so could potentially be stolen. The default permissions on the `config` file in most distributions make it accessible only to `root`, so the risk is minimized. It is also sent unencrypted to the news server. If possible, you shouldn't use the password for anything except access to your news server.

- **port**—Most news servers operate on port 119 (the default), but you can specify another port with this parameter.

- **nodesc**—Most news servers provide a newsgroup descriptions file when asked for it. A few don't, though. Leafnode works best with these when you use the nodesc = 1 parameter.

- **timeout**—When connecting to a news server, fetchnews normally waits ten seconds, then stops trying. You can set another timeout interval with this parameter.

- **groupexpire** *group.name*—If you want to set different article retention intervals for different newsgroups, you can adjust the value set via expire for specific groups or collections of groups with this parameter. The *group.name* may contain wildcards, such as comp.os.linux.* for the entire comp.os.linux hierarchy.

- **maxfetch**—Leafnode limits the number of new articles it will fetch from any one group with this option. Setting this value too low can cause problems, because it might regularly fail to fetch all the new articles, and thus fall behind the current postings.

- **initialfetch**—You can set a lower number of articles to fetch for a newly-subscribed group with this parameter, the idea being that you might not want to fetch all the posts in a new group from a server with retention of several days because this might take a long time.

- **delaybody**—Leafnode normally fetches all new message headers and message bodies with each run, within constraints such as those set by maxfetch and other options. You can have Leafnode fetch only headers, however, and then fetch message bodies only after a user has clicked on a message in a news reader, indicating a desire to read the message. When an unfetched message is read, the message body indicates that Leafnode has marked it for download. After the next fetch, the message title appears again as an unread message, which then contains the true message. Setting this parameter to 1 will delay your ability to read new messages, but this option can greatly reduce the amount of data that must be transferred.

- **maxcrosspost**—Leafnode offers this option as an anti-spam measure. It kills messages that have been cross-posted to more than the specified number of groups. The default is to accept unlimited cross-posting.

- **maxage**—Occasionally, misconfigured news servers repeatedly bounce the same messages onto Usenet, resulting in massive numbers of repeat postings. Using this parameter causes Leafnode to ignore messages that are more than a specified number of days old. This might limit the severity of such problems. The default is to not use this criterion.

- **maxlines**—You can have Leafnode reject messages that have more than the specified number of lines. By default, this limit isn't used.

- **minlines**—You can have Leafnode reject messages that have fewer than the specified number of lines. By default, this limit isn't used.

- **maxbytes**—You can have Leafnode reject messages that have more than the specified number of bytes. By default, this limit isn't used.

- **timeout_short**—By default, Leafnode retrieves posts for two days after a newsgroup has been opened accidentally. You can change this value with this parameter.

- **timeout_long**—By default, Leafnode retrieves posts for seven days after a newsgroup is no longer being read. You can change this value with this parameter.

- **timeout_active**—Leafnode periodically refreshes its list of available newsgroups from the upstream server. This parameter sets how frequently this occurs, in days. The default is 90 days.

- **filterfile**—This parameter sets the path to the filter file, described in the upcoming section, "Filtering Articles." The default is not to use a filter file.

- **hostname**—Most news readers create message IDs for their messages, but if they don't, Leafnode does it for them, using the hostname of the computer on which it runs. If this hostname is inappropriate, you can change the value with this parameter.

These parameters set options that relate to all three of the major Leafnode component programs (leafnode, fetchnews, and texpire). These programs don't have separate configuration files, but they must be run in different ways.

Setting Up the Server

As mentioned earlier, the leafnode server program is designed to be run from a super server, such as inetd or xinetd. This topic is covered in Chapter 4. A typical inetd.conf entry for Leafnode resembles the following:

```
nntp stream tcp nowait news /usr/sbin/tcpd /usr/sbin/leafnode
```

Distributions that use xinetd usually include an appropriate startup file in their Leafnode packages that go in /etc/xinetd.d, so you shouldn't need to create such a file. You might need to enable it, though. Whether you use inetd or xinetd, chances are you'll need to restart the super server before your Leafnode server will become available to your clients. Once you've done this, the Leafnode server computer will respond to requests from news readers as if it were running INN or some other full news server package.

WARNING

Leafnode's main configuration file doesn't include access-control features. You should add such controls to your xinetd or TCP Wrappers configuration to prevent unwanted access to your Leafnode system.

Fetching News

A single run of the fetchnews program will retrieve news from your upstream news server, assuming you've configured the appropriate news server hostname in /etc/leafnode/config. The same process uploads any pending messages to your upstream news server. (You can use the newsq command to see how many outgoing messages you have waiting, as well as their titles, newsgroups, and senders.) The first time you run fetchnews, chances are the operation will take some time, as the program will fetch the active newsgroups list from the upstream server.

The fetchnews program accepts several arguments, which are as follows:

- -v—This option increases the verbosity of the program's output. You can increase the number of vs, up to four (as in -vvvv) to further increase the verbosity of output. This can be a useful diagnostic tool when fetchnews isn't working as you expect.

- -x *number*—If you ran into a problem on the previous fetch operation, this option will attempt to re-fetch articles up to *number* back.

- -1—As noted earlier, Leafnode supports fetching from multiple servers. Using this option forces it to fetch news from just the first one.

- -n—This option causes Leafnode to not automatically unsubscribe from newsgroups that aren't being read.

- -f—If your newsgroup list seems stale, you can force fetchnews to update the list using this option. (The program does so automatically every 90 days, by default.) This operation can take some time, though.

- -P—This option causes fetchnews to post articles it's accumulated in its outgoing queue without retrieving new ones.

The real trick to `fetchnews` operation is in determining when and how to run it. Two common options are to run it as a cron job and to run it in a PPP dialup script, such as `ppp-on-dialer` (described in Chapter 2, TCP/IP Network Configuration). Running `fetchnews` as a cron job makes sense when you have a connection that's constantly active, or if you want to have your computer automatically dial out and retrieve news when unattended, such as early in the morning. How often you should do so is a matter of personal preference and practical matters specific to your configuration and your upstream provider's availability. Running `fetchnews` as part of a PPP connect script ensures that you'll be able to read the latest news soon after you connect to the Internet.

Expiring Old News

The `texpire` program peruses the news messages stored in the news spool directory and deletes old messages according to default values or those set in `/etc/leafnode/config`. This task should be performed on a regular basis to ensure that your hard disk doesn't overflow with old news postings. The usual way to accomplish this task is to run `texpire` from a cron job on a daily basis. Some distributions' Leafnode packages include an appropriate script that's dropped in `/etc/cron.daily` or some other location, but you shouldn't assume that your distribution maintainer has seen to this detail; you should check for such a script and, if necessary, create one or use the `crontab` utility to do the job.

When `texpire` runs, it expires articles based on *threads*. (A thread is an original posting and associated replies.) Specifically, `texpire` deletes a message only if the thread hasn't been read by local users in more than the expire time. Thus, articles may be kept around for longer than you might expect, if the thread in which they reside has been recently read by Leafnode clients.

Like `fetchnews`, `texpire` accepts one to four `-v` options to increase its verbosity. Another potentially important `texpire` option is `-f`. Ordinarily, `texpire` relies upon the last-access dates that Linux stores with files to determine when a thread has gone unread. Adding `-f` causes `texpire` to ignore this information. You might do this if you regularly back up your news spool directory with a program like tar, which modifies the last-access date as part of its operation, causing texpire to erroneously believe that messages are being read when they aren't.

FILTERING ARTICLES

Leafnode includes the capability to delete messages that match arbitrary criteria based on the contents of the messages' headers. For instance, suppose you read a newsgroup that's regularly disrupted by a person who posts from the account obnoxious@annoying.edu. This username will appear in the From header, so Leafnode can filter messages based on this information. To tell it to do so, you must edit a filter file, such as /etc/leafnode/filters, which contains filtering information in regular expression form. For instance, to remove posts from obnoxious@annoying.edu, you might include a line like the following:

```
^From:.*obnoxious@annoying\.edu
```

Each expression in this file begins with a carat (^), then the name of the header line that's to be filtered (From:, in this case). The period and asterisk characters (.*) indicate that an arbitrary number of characters may intervene. The string obnoxious@annoying can be represented directly, and so is; but the period has special meaning, so the period in .edu must be escaped with a backslash (\) character.

NOTE This description barely scratches the surface of what regular expressions can do. The "Using a Procmail Filter" section of Chapter 19, Push Mail Protocol: SMTP, provides more information on regular expressions.

You must tell Leafnode where to find the filter file you use. You do this with the filterfile parameter in /etc/leafnode/config, as described earlier. Although the filter file often goes in /etc/leafnode/filters, you can select any other filename you like.

SUMMARY

News servers can be very resource-intensive; the global Usenet news involves transfers of huge amounts of data every day, and storage of that data for a period of days on news servers around the world. Running a news server may therefore require dedicating a machine with tens or hundreds of gigabytes of disk space to the task. If your needs are more modest, though, you can run a news server without connecting it to Usenet. Such a server can host private local discussion groups, or even public discussion groups (say, for customer support purposes). In either case, the INN server is the usual choice for running a news server on Linux. This server consists of several subprograms that interact and that are configured through several files. You must set overall configuration parameters, define newsgroups you wish to carry, and set policies for who may connect to the news server as both a news feed and as a client.

Still more modest servers may run using alternative news server software. The Leafnode package, for instance, is intended for news servers with limited connectivity and few users. It fetches only those newsgroups that its users read from its upstream provider, and it transfers messages using the subset of NNTP intended for news readers. It's therefore well-suited to small sites such as very small businesses or homes, where just a few users will read news. Its main advantage over configuring local news readers to read messages directly from the ISP's news server is that it permits quick scheduled transfers of all news postings in a few groups, allowing users to read news at their leisure without keeping the network connection active.

Maintaining Remote Login Servers

Many servers provide users with access to very limited and specialized parts of the server computer. For instance, a time server (see Chapter 10, Maintaining Consistent Time: Time Servers) allows clients to read the server's clock, and a font server (see Chapter 15, Providing Consistent Fonts with Font Servers) delivers font bitmaps to clients. There is a class of server, though, that provides more-or-less complete access to the server computer: *remote login servers*. These allow an individual to log in to the computer and run arbitrary programs on the system, much as can be done by sitting at the console. Remote login servers also allow many people to use a single computer simultaneously.

There are several different types of remote login server that can be useful in different situations. This chapter covers a broad class of remote login server that provides text-mode access to the system. Using these programs, you can run text-based tools like the pine or mutt mail clients, development tools like gcc, and text-based editors like Vi or Emacs. By themselves, these tools don't allow you to run X-based programs like KMail or Nedit, though; that's the job of GUI access tools like those discussed in Chapter 14, Handling GUI Access with X and VNC Servers. (Sometimes you'll use a text-based login tool as part of the process of establishing GUI access, though.)

This chapter covers three specific text-based remote login tools: rlogind, Telnet, and SSH. Each of these has its unique characteristics, and is therefore best suited for particular types of uses. These differences relate to security and number of extra features, with rlogind providing the least security and features and SSH the most. If you run Kerberized versions of rlogind or Telnet, though, these servers can provide security on a par with that available in SSH. Chapter 6, Authenticating Users via Kerberos, covers this matter.

When to Run a Remote Login Server

The principal reason for running a remote login server is to let users run arbitrary text-based programs from other computers. You might want to make the computer accessible from distant locations (potentially even somewhere on the other side of the planet), or to allow several people to log in and use the system simultaneously. A single Linux computer can support anywhere from one to thousands of simultaneous users, depending upon the programs they run and the hardware used in the computer. As a general rule of thumb, a user load in the dozens on reasonably modern hardware is probably not excessive, so long as users don't need to use extremely resource-intensive programs.

WARNING Remote login servers are unusually sensitive from a security point of view. If a miscreant somehow obtains a username and password for a computer that runs only, say, a Post Office Protocol (POP) server, and if the POP server has no security flaws, the miscreant won't be able to do serious harm to the computer. Of course, the e-mail the miscreant might read could be sensitive, but in terms of harm to the computer, the impact is minimal. With remote login access, though, the miscreant has the opportunity to exploit any bugs or flaws that might exist in dozens or hundreds of other programs, and thus do serious damage. For this reason, it's particularly important that you configure your remote login servers carefully, and diligently guard the passwords for computers that run such servers. If you aren't using a remote login server on a computer, you should disable it, even if you're using *other* remote login servers.

Configuring rlogind

The rlogin program is one of several *r-commands*. These commands were developed to provide various types of remote access to a UNIX system (hence the name; rlogin is short for *remote login*). When you run the rlogin client, it attempts to connect to a server that's called rlogind or in.rlogind. One of the merits of rlogind is that it's easy to configure; it has few options, so you don't need to deal with complex configuration files. Unfortunately, the protocol is also very primitive by today's security standards. Although it's easy to use, controlling access to a system that uses rlogind can be tricky.

SETTING rlogind STARTUP OPTIONS

The rlogind server is usually launched from a super server, as described in Chapter 4, Starting Servers. Most distributions that use inetd include an entry for rlogind in their /etc/inetd.conf files, although that entry is often commented out by default. To run the server, you need only uncomment the line and restart the super server. Distributions that use xinetd generally provide a startup file in /etc/xinetd.d to start the server. This file is often configured to disable the server by default, so you may need to edit it to enable the server, as described in Chapter 4.

The rlogind server accepts a handful of parameters that influence its behavior. These are:

- **-n**—Normally, rlogind checks back with the client periodically to be sure it's still working, even if no data have been transferred recently. This option disables these "keepalive" messages.

- **-a**—This option is supposed to enable an increased level of password authentication, but it's broken on many distributions, and has little effect.

- **-h**—Normally, rlogind doesn't honor the superuser's .rhosts file, if present, as described shortly. This option causes rlogind to honor this file.

- **-l**—This option disables .rhosts authentication for all users. The superuser is an exception, if -h is also used.

- **-L**—This option disables authentication based on .rhosts or hosts.equiv files.

WARNING

!

Although the -h, -l, and -L options are all officially part of rlogind's repertoire, they're ineffective on most modern Linux distributions as delivered. This is because these options do not work on systems that use the *Pluggable Authentication Module (PAM)* security system, which is used on most modern Linux distributions.

UNDERSTANDING rlogind SECURITY

All of the r-commands use a security model that's generally considered by today's standards to be quaint at best, and hopelessly insecure at worst. In part, this is because the protocol is built on a *trusted hosts* security model, in which the server trusts the client with much of the authentication task. There are ways to tighten rlogind's security to a limited extent, though, and using a Kerberos-enabled version of the program can help even more. When a user attempts to connect to an rlogind server, the system takes the following steps to authenticate the user:

1. The server checks the originating port of the client's connection request. A normal rlogin client uses a port in the range 512–1023, so rlogind drops the connection if the origin port isn't in that range. This step is designed to prevent an ordinary user of another system from writing a modified rlogin client to get around the trusted hosts security features, because only root may open ports numbered below 1024. Today it's easy for an individual to set up a Linux computer and so have root privileges, or initiate connections from OSs that allow anybody to open ports numbered below 1024, so this test isn't as effective as it might be.

2. The server performs a DNS lookup on the connecting IP address to find the client's hostname.

3. If the DNS lookup produced a hostname in the same domain as the server or if the -a option is used, rlogind looks up the IP address based on the hostname. If the two IP addresses match, and if the -L or -l option is not used, rlogind checks the ~/.rhosts and /etc/hosts.equiv files to see if the client is trusted. If it is, and if the remote user has an account on the server, rlogind permits a login without further verification.

4. If the DNS lookups yielded a mismatch on the IP address, if -L or -l was in use, or if the client can't be found in any of the trusted hosts authentication files, rlogind prompts the user for a password. If the user enters the correct password, rlogind allows entry to the system. If not, the server prompts again, then prompts for a username and password. If the user can't produce a correct combination after several tries, rlogind drops the connection.

Several of the preceding steps rely upon rlogind knowing the connecting user's username. This information is passed quietly from one system to another, or you can specify the username with the rlogin client's -l parameter, as in **rlogin -l sjones**.

Because rlogind uses a trusted hosts security model, and because the hosts it trusts can be configured by individual users via their .rhosts files, the server's security may be circumvented in several different ways. These include compromising the security of the client, spoofing a trusted client's IP address, removing a trusted client from the network and replacing it with one that the attacker controls, and replacing or adding to the .rhosts file in the target user's account. Many of these modes of attack aren't trivially easy, particularly on a network with otherwise strong security, but the combination makes rlogind a poor choice of remote login protocol in most situations. It does have one advantage, though: Under many circumstances, rlogind doesn't require the user to enter either a username or a password, so access to the server system is quick and easy:

```
[rodsmith@nessus rodsmith]$ rlogin speaker
Last login: Mon Aug 12 14:48:58 2002 from nessus on 4
[rodsmith@speaker rodsmith]$
```

Another characteristic of rlogind is that it uses unencrypted data transfers. These are discussed in more detail in the upcoming section, "Understanding Telnet Security." The bottom line is that your data may be intercepted, so you should use rlogind only on small private networks that you're confident have not been compromised.

In sum, if a scripted login or otherwise quick access is required, rlogind may be worth considering, but its weak security model means you should be wary of it in most circumstances. The Telnet protocol requires use of passwords in most situations, and SSH is even more secure.

CONTROLLING rlogind ACCESS

If you do choose to use rlogind, the server prompts for a password when a login is attempted from an untrusted host. Chances are, though, that you want to use rlogind because it doesn't require the use of a username or password, so you want to configure it to trust certain hosts. This may be done in two ways:

- **/etc/hosts.equiv**—This is a system-wide configuration file to set r-command access. If a system is listed in this file, any user of that system may access r-command services on the server, provided the same username exists on the server or the username is remapped as described shortly. In the event of a name mismatch (for instance, if the user julia tries to use rlogin to access the account fred), the user must provide a password.

- **~/.rhosts**—This file, which is stored in a user's home directory, specifies clients that are to be trusted *for an individual user.* A remote user
with the same username as the user on the server can access the
server's resources as that user. (It's possible to remap this username, as
described shortly.) Users are responsible for maintaining this file in
their own accounts, if it's to be used at all.

WARNING

The availability of ~/.rhosts files means that you as a system administrator
delegate some of the authority for security on your system *to your users* when
r-command servers such as rlogind are installed. This thought makes some
administrators quite nervous, and it's one of the reasons you are well advised
to not use rlogind, or to carefully restrict its use via TCP Wrappers or other
means, as described shortly.

Both these files control access to all r-command servers—principally
rlogin, rcp, and rsh. When the computer uses the BSD LPD printing system
(described in Chapter 9, Printer Sharing via LPD), these files also control
access to that system. (As described in Chapter 9, a printer-specific configuration file may be used instead of these general-purpose r-command control files.)

Both these files have the same format, although the interpretation of some
elements differs slightly from one file to the other. The file consists of a
series of lines that describe individual hosts or groups of hosts. Each line's
format is specified as follows:

```
[+|-][hostname] [username]
```

The leading plus (+) or minus (-) sign explicitly allows or denies access
from the specified client. The default is to allow the host, so the plus sign
may be omitted in most cases. The minus sign, by contrast, may be used to
explicitly deny a client access when it would otherwise be allowed by a
preceding line that specifies several hosts, as described shortly.

WARNING

Be *very* careful if you use a plus sign. A line that consists only of a plus sign
(without a hostname) means to grant access indiscriminately to *all* clients.
This makes for an extremely poor security policy. If you mistakenly include a
space between a plus sign and a hostname, the system will interpret the
hostname as a username, giving full access to anybody who cares to try to
access your system.

You may specify the hostname as either an IP address (such as 192.168.34.56) or as a hostname (such as gingko.threeroomco.com). In the latter case, the hostname may be either a fully qualified domain name (FQDN), such as the full gingko.threeroomco.com, or a machine name alone if the two computers are in the same domain, such as gingko if the server is in the same domain as gingko. If you precede a name with an at-sign (@), it refers to an NIS domain (your system must be configured to use NIS for this form to work). The safest form in which to specify hosts is as IP addresses, followed by FQDNs, followed by machine names only.

If you include a username in the list, this gives the listed user full access to the system. In the case of the .rhosts file, this means that the listed user is equivalent to the user in whose directory the .rhosts file resides. For instance, suppose julia includes the following line in her .rhosts file:

```
172.21.13.14 jbrown
```

This configuration grants the user jbrown on 172.21.13.14 access to julia's account on the server using rlogin, and similar privileges using rsh and rcp. (From the jbrown account on the client, the user will have to use the -l julia option to rlogin to log in to julia's account on the server.)

The phrase "full access to the system" has a stronger meaning in the case of /etc/hosts.equiv. When a username appears in this file, the effect is that the named user of the remote system has unfettered access to *all* accounts on the server, with the exception of root. Thus, if the preceding example line was added to /etc/hosts.equiv, jbrown on 172.21.13.14 could use rlogin to gain access not just to the julia account, but to any other ordinary user's account. In this context, "ordinary user" includes system accounts like daemon, which can often be abused to acquire root privileges. Thus, specifying a username isn't safe in /etc/hosts.equiv, except possibly in explicit denial situations (when the line begins with a minus sign).

In addition to the access controls provided by ~/.rhosts, /etc/hosts.equiv, and passwords in case these files don't give automatic access to a client, you can use other control mechanisms to restrict access to an rlogind server. Because this server is usually run from inetd or xinetd, you can use TCP Wrappers or xinetd's access control features to limit access to specific IP addresses or by other means. I strongly recommend you do so. A packet filter firewall rule can also block access to the rlogin port (TCP port 513), as described in Chapter 25, Configuring iptables.

CONFIGURING TELNET

Telnet may be the most common login protocol on the Internet. Most OSs, including Linux, ship with Telnet client programs (usually called `telnet`). There are Telnet clients available for those few OSs that don't ship with them. Telnet servers are also quite common, although they're most common on OSs that support multiple simultaneous users, such as Linux, UNIX, and VMS. In many ways, Telnet is a more complex protocol than is that used by `rlogind`, but it's still fairly simple as TCP/IP protocols go. Configuring Telnet on Linux usually involves installing a package and ensuring that the protocol is enabled in your super server, although in some cases you'll want to investigate startup options. You can also configure a few other elements of Telnet's operation, such as the login message it returns to clients.

Telnet's security is weak by modern standards, but it's not quite as bad as is `rlogind`'s. Understanding precisely how Telnet's security is weak can help you know where it is and is not appropriate to use this protocol, and how to minimize risks if you must use it in situations where it's less than ideal to do so. As with `rlogind`, you can improve Telnet's security by using a Kerberized version of the client and server, if your network supports Kerberos.

SETTING TELNET STARTUP OPTIONS

The Telnet server may or may not be installed in your Linux distribution by default. There's little standardization in terms of the package names under which this server is distributed. For instance, it's included in Caldera's `netkit-telnet`, Debian's `telnetd`, Mandrake's `telnet-server`, Red Hat's `telnet-server`, Slackware's `tcpip1`, SuSE's `nkitserv`, and TurboLinux's `telnet`. Some of these, like Debian's `telnetd`, contain the Telnet server only; others, like TurboLinux's `telnet`, include the client and server together in one package. Most distributions install the relevant packages by default with most installation options, but the server may or may not be configured to run by default. Consult Chapter 4 for information on how to launch the Telnet server (which is usually called `telnetd` or `in.telnetd`) via your distribution's super server.

The Telnet server accepts a number of arguments that can modify the way it operates. Some of these, however, relate to optional security features that aren't available on most standard Telnet servers. The more useful options include the following:

- **-D** *debugmode*—This option is intended for debugging Telnet or its connections. To use it, you launch `telnetd` from the console, rather than via a super server. Depending on what you enter as *debugmode*, the server displays information on the connection or the data it receives. Possible *debugmode* values include `options` and `report` (both of which show information about the negotiation of connections), and `netdata` and `ptydata` (which display the incoming and outgoing data streams, respectively).

- **-h**—Normally, `telnetd` sends a login *banner* to clients, identifying the computer for the user's benefit. This banner sometimes contains information you'd prefer that random outsiders not have, such as the version of the OS you're running. Using -h suppresses the display of this banner, thus giving a would-be intruder less information on your system.

- **-L** *loginprog*—By default, `telnetd` uses `/bin/login` to handle login interactions. You can specify some other program if you like, though.

- **-n**—Like `rlogind`, `telnetd` uses keepalive messages to check that a client is still active, and to close a link if a client becomes inaccessible. This option disables the use of keepalive messages.

The server supports several additional options, mostly related to data encryption and security, but most of these options aren't useful except on comparatively rare Telnet servers that include these features. Although encrypted versions of Telnet exist, and in theory can be a good solution for secure text-mode logins, these Telnet variants haven't become very popular; that role has been filled largely by SSH. If your network uses Kerberos, though, the Kerberized version of Telnet that ships with Kerberos is well worth investigating, as described in Chapter 6.

ADJUSTING THE TELNET LOGIN DISPLAY

The `telnetd` server reads the contents of the `/etc/issue.net` file and displays it to clients when they first connect. This file is displayed *before* the user has a chance to log into the system, and it's what is suppressed by inclusion of the -h startup option to `telnetd`. The intent is that this message announce something about the computer to let users know that they've connected to the correct system. The default message, though, usually announces the Linux distribution name, and often additional information such as the kernel version. Most users don't need or want this information, but it can be very helpful to those who would break into your computer because it may give them clues about what other software may be running on your system, some of which may have security-related bugs.

NOTE A similar file, /etc/issue, displays a login message for *console* logins—those done at the keyboard and display connected directly to the computer. (X-based logins don't use either file, though; they're handled through a display manager program such as those discussed in Chapter 14.)

On many systems, you can edit /etc/issue.net directly. Change the text to whatever you'd like. You can include several variables in your text, which telnetd replaces with system-specific information. These are summarized in Table 13.1. For instance, you might change **/etc/issue.net** to read as follows:

```
Welcome to %h.
Current time is %d.
Notice: For authorized users only!
```

If your computer were called maple.threeroomco.com, this might result the following login banner:

```
$ telnet maple.threeroomco.com
Trying 172.21.32.43...
Connected to maple.threeroomco.com.
Escape character is '^]'.
Welcome to maple.threeroomco.com.
Current time is 10:57 on Monday, 12 August 2002.
Notice: For authorized users only!
```

Table 13.1 Variables Usable in /etc/issue.net

Variable	Meaning
%t	The current tty (a number corresponding to a text input/output device)
%h	The computer's FQDN
%D	The name of the NIS domain, if the computer uses NIS
%d	The current date and time
%s	The name of the operating system (Linux)
%m	The hardware (CPU) type
%r	The kernel version number
%v	The OS version (generally not a useful value)
%%	Displays a single percent symbol (%)

Unfortunately, there's a potentially major wrinkle in this picture. Some distributions (notably Caldera, Mandrake, and some versions of Red Hat) recreate /etc/issue and /etc/issue.net on every boot. They do this via the /etc/rc.d/rc.local script, which includes lines resembling the following (in Mandrake 8.1):

```
# This will overwrite /etc/issue at every boot.  So, make any \
changes you
# want to make to /etc/issue here or you will lose them when you \
reboot.

if [ -x /usr/bin/linux_logo ];then
    /usr/bin/linux_logo -c -n -f > /etc/issue
    echo "" >> /etc/issue
else
    > /etc/issue
fi
echo "$R" >> /etc/issue
echo "Kernel $(uname -r) on $a $SMP$(uname -m) / \1" >> /etc/issue

if [ "$SECURITY" -le 3 ];then
    echo "Welcome to %h" > /etc/issue.net
    echo "$R" >> /etc/issue.net
    echo "Kernel $(uname -r) on $a $SMP$(uname -m)" >>
/etc/issue.net
else
    echo "Welcome to Mandrake Linux" > /etc/issue.net
    echo "------------------------" >> /etc/issue.net
fi
```

NOTE Red Hat has shifted to static issue and issue.net files with version 7.2, but Caldera 3.1 and Mandrake 8.1 continue to create these files from the /etc/rc.d/rc.local files.

Some of these lines reference variables that are defined earlier in the script. This procedure allows the system to create a login banner that's slightly more dynamic than might otherwise be possible, such as specifying the number of CPUs in the computer. On the other hand, it means that if you want to change your login banner, you must modify the /etc/rc.d/rc.local script. You can either comment out or delete the lines that modify /etc/issue and /etc/issue.net and adjust those files directly, as just described, or you can modify the lines in /etc/rc.d/rc.local to better reflect your intended message.

UNDERSTANDING TELNET SECURITY

After telnetd sends the contents of /etc/issue.net (with any applicable variable substitutions) back to the client, it passes control of the connection to /bin/login, or whatever program was specified by the -L *loginprog* parameter to telnetd. The /bin/login program is used for local text-mode logins, as well as remote logins. It presents two prompts, login: and Password:, at which users should enter their usernames and passwords, respectively. Assuming these are entered correctly, /bin/login notes when the last login occurred and passes control to the user's default shell.

One very important consequence of this sequence, in conjunction with the fact that most Telnet servers are not configured to encrypt data transfers, is that both the username and the password are sent unencrypted over the network. This is true even though the user won't see the password echo to the screen. Unless you use -L *loginprog* to change the login program that telnetd uses, this unencrypted username/password pair is the only authentication method used by telnetd; it does *not* use a trusted hosts model like rlogind, and it doesn't even rely upon the client to automatically transmit the username (although this information does ultimately come from the client computer, and some Telnet client programs can be configured to send the username and even the password automatically).

The unencrypted nature of Telnet logins is a potential threat because the data stream might be intercepted between the client and the server. In most Internet transfers, packets pass between a dozen or more routers. If any of these routers has been compromised, the cracker who's done so might note the password that's passed over the Telnet session and use it to gain access to your computer. A threat that's at least as great is the potential for *packet sniffing* on the network that's local to either the client or the server. In this approach, a computer (which may not be directly involved in the data transfer) "sniffs" the network wires for data such as passwords. Again, the result is a compromised password.

In addition to risking login passwords, Telnet's unencrypted nature means that all the data passing over the connection after it's established may be compromised. This includes private e-mail that's read, confidential files that are edited, and any additional passwords that might be typed (for instance, if the user connects to another computer or uses su to acquire superuser privileges). The same comments apply to rlogind and other unencrypted protocols (which includes most protocols in common use today). The unencrypted nature of Telnet and rlogind is potentially more serious than, say, unencrypted e-mail transmission because Telnet and rlogind are general-purpose protocols—in one connection, you can give away your login password, the contents of private e-mail, the contents of sensitive files, and more.

Short of switching to an encrypted protocol, what can you do to minimize your risks with Telnet? The basic rule of thumb is to transfer as little sensitive data as possible. Don't read confidential or otherwise sensitive files or e-mail using Telnet. Don't log directly into another computer, even if you use Telnet to reach the first computer but then use SSH or some other secure channel. Don't use su to acquire root privileges. Don't use the password for any computer you access via Telnet on any other computer. Telnet is best used on small private networks that you're confident haven't been compromised, like a private LAN with no Internet connectivity. If you must use Telnet, change your password frequently (preferably *not* over a Telnet link) to give any would-be attackers a limited window of opportunity for doing more damage should they abscond with your password.

CONFIGURING SSH

In the Linux world, the most popular secure login protocol is the Secure Shell (SSH). This protocol uses encryption technology to digitally "scramble" transmissions so that any data that might be intercepted on compromised routers or via packets sniffers can't be descrambled and used, at least not with any technology that's readily available in 2002. (In theory, a fast enough computer could break SSH's encryption, but computers capable of doing this either do not exist or are *very* rare.)

In 2002, SSH servers are becoming more common, although they're not yet universal. Like other login servers, basic SSH configuration is fairly painless, but there are both startup options and configuration files you may need to adjust to get the system working in precisely the way you want. Understanding something of how SSH operates may help you plan your SSH setup to best effect.

NOTE There has been some discussion in 2001 concerning the trademark status of the name *SSH*. It is possible that the protocol will acquire a new name in the not-too-distant future, that one major implementation (SSH) will retain its name, and that the other major implementation (OpenSSH) will change its name. This matter appears to be unresolved as I write these words, so I use the names that are on the products' Web sites. Proposals I have seen for changes do not involve changing the names of the programs distributed in packages, just the package names and names used in documentation.

AVAILABLE SSH SOFTWARE

There are two major SSH packages for Linux: the original commercial SSH (http://www.ssh.com/products/ssh/), which is produced by a company called SSH, and an open source reimplementation (http://www.openssh. org). Many Linux distributions now ship with the latter, but you can use the former if you prefer. (If you use the original SSH, some uses may require you to purchase a license, but others allow you to use the software for free. Consult the SSH license for details.) Distributions that ship with OpenSSH include Caldera 3.1, Debian 2.2 (in the non-US package set), Mandrake 8.1, Red Hat 7.2, Slackware 7.0, and SuSE 7.3. You can obtain OpenSSH for other distributions, or the latest version if yours is older, from the OpenSSH Web site. For simplicity's sake, I use *SSH* to refer to any implementation of the SSH protocol, and differentiate this as necessary when referring to specific packages.

NOTE The OpenSSH project is closely associated with the OpenBSD OS. OpenSSH binaries for other OSs are therefore separated slightly from the main Web page. Specifically, the page http://www.openssh.org/portable.html contains information on OpenSSH for OSs other than OpenBSD, including the Linux versions. You can download portable source code or precompiled binaries for Linux.

In December of 2001, version 3.1 of the original SSH was released. In the same month, OpenSSH 3.0.2 was released. These version numbers are designed to be comparable; the original SSH and OpenSSH products support roughly the same features and cryptographic technologies in their version 3.0.*x* products, for instance. Version 3 of the SSH protocol adds Public Key Infrastructure (PKI) support, in which digital certificates "signed" by certificate authorities verify the identity of one or both parties in a transaction; smart card support, a hardware-based system of identity checking; and various other enhancements. Because the SSH company developed the protocol, they're likely to lead the OpenSSH project slightly in features.

The original SSH and OpenSSH implementations interoperate, so you shouldn't have to be concerned with who created the clients that your server will serve, or who created a server to which you want to connect. There are occasional incompatibilities between specific versions of the packages, though, even within a single line. The protocol is designed to negotiate the maximum common level of the protocol, so an SSH version 2 client can connect to a version 3 server, for example. Of course, such a connection uses the lowest common denominator level of the protocol.

Most OpenSSH packages come as several separate files. Most important are the base openssh package and the openssh-client and openssh-server packages that contain clients and servers, respectively. To use any SSH program, you must install the base package and at least one of openssh-client and openssh-server.

SSH is not yet as widespread a protocol as is Telnet, so you may need to distribute SSH client software for your users. These packages are available for many OSs. You can find links to free implementations of SSH for many OSs at http://www.freessh.org. Many commercial terminal programs for OSs like Windows and MacOS include SSH support, as well. The main problem in using SSH is not in locating the SSH clients, but in distributing them and convincing your users to use them.

UNDERSTANDING SSH CAPABILITIES

SSH does more than most other remote login protocols, and in more ways than simply providing encryption. Two extra features of SSH deserve special attention. First, it can *forward* or *tunnel* network ports between the client and server. This means that the forwarded protocol benefits from SSH's encryption. Depending on your configuration, this may be done automatically for X, so that when you log into an SSH server from a system on which X is running, you can launch X programs without worrying about setting further options. (Chapter 14 covers these matters in more detail.) With some extra work, you can tunnel just about any other protocol you like, providing an encrypted version of that protocol. In fact, it's even possible to use the Point-to-Point Protocol (PPP) to set up a network interface that's tunneled through SSH. The result is a Virtual Private Network (VPN) that's implemented via SSH. The VPN HOWTO document (http://www.linuxdoc.org/HOWTO/VPN-HOWTO.html) covers such configurations in detail.

The second SSH feature that deserves mention is the direct implementation of non-login tools. Specifically, the SSH package comes with a program called scp, which is used for copying files from one computer to another, as follows:

```
scp [[user1@]host1:]filename1 [[user2@]host2:][filename2]
```

This syntax is very similar to that of the rcp program, which is an r-command program that scp is intended to replace. Unlike rcp or many other file-transfer tools, such as FTP, scp transfers the files in an encrypted form and encrypts the username and password. Thus, it's a good choice for transferring files between computers over an untrusted network.

For more interactive file transfers, clients can use the sftp program, which works much like the more conventional text-mode ftp program, but uses SSH encryption to protect passwords and the contents of data being transferred. Some GUI FTP clients, such as gFTP (http://gftp.seul.org), also include support for SSH-based transfers, so it's becoming possible for SSH to replace both a Telnet and an FTP server from a functional point of view.

The standard SSH server program (sshd) handles both the SSH text-mode login client (ssh on Linux) and transfers initiated through scp or sftp. This server also handles port forwarding as implemented via ssh. All this traffic passes through the standard SSH port, 22.

SETTING SSH STARTUP OPTIONS

Whatever implementation of the protocol you use, the SSH server is traditionally started from a SysV startup script, as described in Chapter 4. Although the server can be run from a super server, older versions of the program imposed a delay when so started because they had to perform some CPU-intensive operations. Modern versions of sshd, run on modern hardware, typically impose very short delays when run from a super server, so if you prefer, you can reconfigure your sshd to run in this way—but be aware you must add the -i argument to the sshd launch command, as described shortly.

The SSH server program, sshd, accepts a number of arguments that can modify its behavior. In OpenSSH 3.0.2, these arguments include:

- **-d**—The server normally runs as a daemon, but this option causes it to run in debug mode, in which it remains in the foreground, processes a maximum of one connection, and logs additional debugging information. You can increase the debugging verbosity by including up to three -d arguments.
- **-D**—This option causes sshd to not detach as a daemon, but unlike -d, it doesn't cause the server to enter full debug mode.
- **-e**—This option causes sshd to send error output to standard error rather than to the system log.
- **-f** *config-file*—The server normally uses /etc/ssh/sshd_config as its configuration file, but you may specify another file using this option.

- -i—This option tells sshd that it's being run from a super server (such as inetd or xinetd). This option is *required* if you run sshd in this way.
- -p *port*—This option sets the port that the server uses, which is normally 22.
- -q—This option disables routine logging, which normally includes connection initiations, authentications, and connection terminations.
- -4—Normally, sshd accepts connections using either IPv4 or IPv6 addresses. This option causes it to accept only IPv4 addresses.
- -6—This option causes sshd to accept connections only from systems with IPv6 addresses.

There are additional options for sshd, most of which relate to setting details of how encryption is to be handled. Consult the sshd man page if you need information on these options.

Before you run sshd for the first time, you need to generate some encryption key files. These files contain the keys used by SSH's algorithms to identify itself and encrypt data. Most SSH distributions include code to check for and, if necessary, generate these keys in their SysV startup scripts for the server. If your system doesn't do this, try using the following commands:

```
# ssh-keygen -q -t rsa1 -f /etc/ssh/ssh_host_key -C '' -N ''
# ssh-keygen -q -t rsa -f /etc/ssh/ssh_host_rsa_key -C '' -N ''
# ssh-keygen -q -t dsa -f /etc/ssh/ssh_host_dsa_key -C '' -N ''
```

Each of these commands generates two keys: a *private key* used only on the server, and a *public key* that's given to clients so that they may send encrypted data to the server. The latter is placed in a file whose name is based on the name of the former, but with .pub appended. You can check for the existence of these six files (ssh_host_key, ssh_host_key.pub, ssh_host_rsa_key, ssh_host_rsa_key.pub, ssh_host_dsa_key, and ssh_host_dsa_key.pub, all normally in /etc/ssh) to see if they exist before running these commands. If you overwrite existing keys, it's possible that clients that have already been configured to trust the server with the old keys will need to be reconfigured, so don't replace these keys unnecessarily.

ADJUSTING THE sshd_config FILE

The sshd server is controlled through a file called sshd_config, which normally resides in /etc/ssh. (The ssh client program uses a configuration file called ssh_config in the same location; don't confuse the two.) This file consists of options and values, each pair on a line by itself, thus:

Option value

As with many configuration files, comment lines begin with pound signs (#). Some of the options mirror options you can set at startup time via command-line arguments. Others are unique to the configuration file. A default configuration works well enough for many systems, but you may want to review your configuration file, especially for certain security-related options like PermitRootLogin. The most important sshd_config options include the following:

- **Port**—You set the port to which sshd listens using this option. The default value is 22.

- **HostKey**—This option tells the server where to look for host keys. These are the private files generated prior to the program's first launch, such as /etc/ssh/ssh_host_key. You can specify several key files.

- **KeyRegenerationInterval**—SSH negotiates an encryption key when it makes a connection, then negotiates a new key from time to time thereafter to reduce the damage should a single key be somehow intercepted or decoded. (These keys are generated *in addition to* the keys sshd needs before you run it for the first time, and they're never stored on disk.) This option sets the length of time, in seconds, between new key generation.

- **PermitRootLogin**—This option defaults to yes on most installations. This default allows sshd to accept logins from root. It's safer to set this value to no, because doing so requires that a would-be intruder have two passwords (one for a normal user, as well as the root password) to gain root access to a system via SSH, assuming there are no other security flaws on the system. If this option is set to no, you can still use SSH to administer a system remotely, but you must log in as a normal user and then use su or a similar program to acquire root privileges.

- **IgnoreRhosts**—This option is normally set to yes, which causes sshd to ignore the ~/.rhosts file. If this option is set to no, and if RhostsAuthentication is yes, sshd permits authentication based on a trusted hosts model similar to that used by rlogind. Setting this option to no is generally unwise.

- **RhostsAuthentication**—SSH uses *two* options to enable rlogind-style trusted hosts authentication: IgnoreRhosts is one, and

`RhostsAuthentication` is the other. The latter enables trusted hosts authentication generally. It's usually best to set this option to no.

- **RSAAuthentication**—When using version 1 of the SSH protocol, the computer can use a public key authentication method that permits a login without sending a password by using a public key file. Alternatively, you can use the public key in conjunction with a pass phrase to improve security. You can enable this feature by setting this option to yes, which is the default.

- **PubkeyAuthentication**—This option works much like `RSAAuthentication`, but applies to SSH protocol version 2.

- **PasswordAuthentication**—If set to yes, this option permits users to authenticate by sending their passwords at a prompt. This is a common method of SSH authentication, so you should probably leave it enabled.

- **X11Forwarding**—As mentioned earlier, SSH can be used to tunnel X connections. Both the client and the server must be configured to do this, though. This option determines whether the server forwards X connections; set it to yes to enable this feature. The SSH client must have a similar option set. It's called `ForwardX11` in the `/etc/ssh/ssh_config` file.

There are many additional SSH configuration options you can set. Some of these relate to alternative authentication methods, others fine-tune options described here, and still others set miscellaneous features. Many default `sshd_config` files include these options, so you can peruse your file to see how your system is configured. You can also consult the `sshd` man page for information on these options.

SSH AUTHENTICATION OPTIONS

When an SSH client and server communicate, they encrypt all communications using a variety of encryption methods. In brief, the two servers agree on a temporary encryption method that they use to exchange *public keys*, which are long numbers that can be used in encryption algorithms to encrypt transmissions intended for each other. Each side also retains for its own use a *private key*, which it uses to decrypt data received from the other computer. The systems use this technique to encrypt the exchange of another type of key, known as a *secret key*, that's used for another encryption method. This secret key encryption method, which uses a single key, is faster than the public/private key method used to exchange the secret key. The public/private key method exists to protect the secret key from discovery. SSH also uses a public/private key pair as one of several possible methods of authentication—confirming that users are who they claim to be, and not malicious interlopers.

Understanding SSH Authentication

From a user's point of view, there are several different methods that SSH may use to authenticate users. The exact details of these methods differ from SSH version 1 to SSH version 2, but the systems attempt to use each of several authentication methods in turn. Specifically:

1. The client attempts to use trusted-hosts authentication. This attempt is usually blocked by settings on the server's `RhostsAuthentication` or `IgnoreRhosts` configuration options. If this attempt is successful, though, the user gains access to the server without having to enter a password.

2. The client attempts to use a hybrid of trusted-hosts with Rivest/ Shamir/Adleman (RSA) authentication. Again, this attempt usually fails.

3. The client attempts to use an RSA authentication method in which the server sends a special server identity file. If this file is stored on the server, and if subsequent steps in this method work, the user gains access to the system. Depending on the encoding of the RSA files, the user might have to enter a pass phrase, or might gain entry without having to type a pass phrase or password. This method requires per-client and per-user configuration on the server.

4. If all other authentication methods fail, SSH asks the user for a password. This password is sent to the server in an encrypted form, decrypted, and used to verify the user's identity using the server's normal password authentication methods.

The server stores its keys in /etc/ssh; they're used for *all* users. SSH clients receive public keys from specific servers, so that the client may verify the server's identity at a later date. These keys are stored in a user's ~/.ssh directory, so they're maintained individually for each user. The first time you connect to a server using ssh, the program notifies you that it's adding a new key to the file. (With some configurations, you may be asked to authorize this action.) If the key for the server changes, ssh displays a very noticeable warning message, like this:

```
@@@@@@@@@@@@@@@@@@@@@@@@@@@@@@@@@@@@@@@@@@@@@@@@@@@@@@@@@@@@@@@
@    WARNING: REMOTE HOST IDENTIFICATION HAS CHANGED!    @
@@@@@@@@@@@@@@@@@@@@@@@@@@@@@@@@@@@@@@@@@@@@@@@@@@@@@@@@@@@@@@@
IT IS POSSIBLE THAT SOMEONE IS DOING SOMETHING NASTY!
```

The message goes on to provide further details, and will not connect to the server. If the change was legitimate, you can force a connection by removing the server's entry from your ~/.ssh/known_hosts or ~/.ssh/ known_hosts2 file, depending upon whether you're using SSH protocol version 1 or version 2.

Unlike telnetd, sshd doesn't normally use the /bin/login program to handle logins. Instead, sshd performs this task itself. (The UseLogin option in sshd_config causes sshd to use login, though.) In some sense, therefore, sshd alone is like the combination of telnetd and login. It's this combination that allows sshd to perform public key authentication; only by bypassing login will such alternative authentication methods work.

Generating Keys to Automate Logins or Improve Security

Individual users may also generate keys to uniquely identify themselves. These are stored in the ~/.ssh directory on the client. You can transfer the public key stored here to your ~/.ssh directory on the server to bypass the need to enter a password, which is the normal method of authentication with a default configuration of SSH. Alternatively, this method may be used to increase security by requiring a pass phrase, which in conjunction with the public key itself may make it more difficult for an outsider to break into your account. To use this public key authentication for either purpose, follow these steps:

1. Log into the SSH client system.
2. Type the following command, which may take a few seconds to complete, to generate an SSH version 2 key:

   ```
   $ ssh-keygen -q -t rsa -f ~/.ssh/id_rsa -C '' -N ''
   ```

NOTE If you omit the -N '' option, ssh-keygen will prompt you for a pass phrase. If you enter anything other than a single carriage return, you'll have to enter this pass phrase whenever you make a connection to the server. If you do this, you'll trade the need to enter a password for the need to enter a pass phrase.

3. Transfer the ~/id_rsa.pub file to your account on the server. (Note that this file is the public key, and was automatically generated along with the private key whose filename you entered with the preceding command.) You may use the scp command to do this, thus:

```
$ scp ~/.ssh/id_rsa.pub server:.ssh/id_rsa.client
```

4. Log into the server. You may use ssh to do this, but you'll need to enter a password.

5. Change to the ~/.ssh directory. If you list the files in this directory, you should see one called id_rsa.client.

6. Add the client's public key to the authorized_keys2 file. You can do this with the following command:

```
$ cat id_rsa.client >> authorized_keys2
```

From this point on, you should be able to connect from the client to the server using version 2 of the SSH protocols. If you didn't use a pass phrase, you'll be able to log in without using a password or a pass phrase, but if you entered a pass phrase when creating your keys, you'll need to enter it when logging in. You can force the SSH client to use version 2 with the -2 option, thus:

```
$ ssh -2 server
```

WARNING

If you use public key authentication, your private key becomes extremely sensitive. If somebody acquires your client's private key file, that person may be able to masquerade as you. SSH links the private key to a particular computer, so the interloper can't log in from any IP address, but crackers have ways around such restrictions, which is part of why rlogind is not very secure. The pass phrase that was explicitly omitted in Step 2 of the preceding method is designed to protect the private key; without the pass phrase, the private key file isn't very useful to a miscreant. Of course, using a pass phrase defeats the convenience function of this method. On the other hand, using this method *with* a pass phrase improves security, because an intruder would require both your pass phrase and your private key to break in, assuming no other security problems exist on the server.

You can follow a similar procedure to enable SSH protocol version 1's RSA authentication. You'll need to implement the following changes to the procedure:

- In Step 2, change `-t rsa -f ~/.ssh/id_rsa` to `-t rsa1 -f ~/.ssh/identity`. This generates a version 1 RSA public/private key pair rather than a version 2 key pair. You'll need to make appropriate changes to the filenames throughout the rest of the procedure.
- In Step 6, you must copy the public key from `identity.pub` into `authorized_keys`, not into `authorized_keys2`.
- When making the connection, you should omit the `-2` option to `ssh`, which forces use of version 2 of the protocol.

Both of these procedures assume that the server is configured to accept public key (aka RSA) authentication. As described earlier, these options are enabled via the `RSAAuthentication` (version 1) and `PubkeyAuthentication` (version 2) configuration options in `/etc/ssh/sshd_config`.

It should be emphasized that you don't need to enable public key authentication. With a default configuration, using SSH without this option works just fine. Using public key authentication either obviates the need for entering a password, relying upon the integrity of a key file instead, or improves security by requiring both a key file and a pass phrase to gain entry to the system.

Using `ssh-agent`

Another option for SSH authentication is to use a tool called `ssh-agent` along with associated utilities. This program manages SSH keys so that you only need to enter an SSH pass phrase once per local session. To use it, follow these steps:

1. Follow the procedure outlined in the section entitled "Generating Keys to Automate Logins or Improve Security" to create a public/private key pair on your SSH client system and transfer the public key to your account on the SSH server system. You should be sure to omit the `-N ''` option to `ssh-keygen`, so that you protect your private key with a pass phrase.
2. On the SSH client system, type **ssh-agent /bin/bash**. This launches the program and a new Bash shell. The `ssh-agent` program monitors all the programs you launch from your new shell. (You can use another shell if you prefer.)
3. Type **ssh-add ~/.ssh/id_rsa** to add the SSH RSA key to the `ssh-agent` program's cache of keys. (You can omit the `~/.ssh/id_rsa` option if you use version 1 keys.) Assuming your key is protected by a pass phrase, `ssh-add` asks for it at this time.

At this point, you should be able to reach your SSH server system by using the SSH client as usual, but you won't be asked to enter a password or pass phrase. The `ssh-agent` tool works by holding keys in memory and setting environment variables that allow the SSH client to locate `ssh-agent` to retrieve those keys. Only programs run as children of `ssh-agent` gain access to its keys, though, which is why this procedure has `ssh-agent` start a new Bash shell; the shell and all its children, including `ssh` when it's launched from Bash, can manipulate or retrieve these keys.

For a single connection, this approach can actually complicate matters, because you need to run `ssh-agent` and use `ssh-add` to add keys before you can launch `ssh`, and you'll still have to enter your pass phrase once. If you routinely use SSH to log into several computers using the same key, or if you routinely log in and out of the same system, however, this procedure can save time, because you'll only have to enter your pass phrase once. Furthermore, there are some ways you can streamline the procedure:

- You can edit the /etc/passwd file to call your shell via `ssh-agent`. For instance, if your shell is normally /bin/bash, you can replace that with /usr/bin/ssh-agent /bin/bash. (You may need to alter the path to /usr/bin/ssh-agent, and of course you can use other shells if you like.) Thereafter, you won't need to manually type **ssh-agent /bin/bash**; you can log in, type **ssh-add ~/.ssh/id_rsa**, and use `ssh` to log into the remote system. This method is likely to be useful only if you use text-mode logins only; in a GUI environment, it creates a new `ssh-agent` environment for each xterm window you have open, which is likely to be counter-productive.

- If you log in via text mode and start X by typing **startx**, you can change this command to **ssh-agent startx**. This puts `ssh-agent` at the root of all your X programs, so it's available to all of them.

- If you use a GUI login, you can copy your .xsession file (or equivalent) to another name, such as .xsession-nosshagent, then create a new .xsession file that includes only the command ssh-agent ~/.xsession-nosshagent. This causes `ssh-agent` to run as the parent of all your other X processes, so that your SSH keys, once added using ssh-add, won't need to be re-entered, even if you launch SSH from several different windows or desktop tools.

Once you've set up `ssh-agent` and entered a key, you can view the keys you've entered by typing **ssh-add -l**, or you can delete the keys by typing **ssh-add -d**. The latter command configures the system so that you must re-enter the keys (or enter a password or key in the normal way for SSH) if you try to use SSH again.

One of the advantages of ssh-agent is that you need not type the key multiple times if you connect to multiple SSH servers. You must copy the public key to each server, as described in Steps 3 through 6 in "Generating Keys to Automate Logins or Improve Security," whereupon you can use the same private key loaded in ssh-agent to connect to each system. If you prefer to use different keys for different systems, you can do so, but you'll need to store them in separate files and type their associated pass phrases when you load each one. If you try to connect to a system on which you've not stored your public key, you'll need to enter a password, just as if you weren't using ssh-agent.

SUMMARY

Remote login servers allow your users to run programs and perform other ordinary command shell tasks from just about any computer that can reach your system via a network connection. This is an extremely useful feature, but also one that presents many security challenges.

Common login servers for Linux include rlogind, Telnet, and SSH. Of the three, SSH is the most sophisticated and secure, and is the best choice for a login server to be used over the Internet. (Secure Telnet variants may be an exception in some cases, but these are very rare.) Telnet and rlogind are acceptable for use on trusted private networks, but you should take great care if you must use one of them on the Internet because their security models are inadequate to the task of protecting a system in today's hostile Internet environment. All three servers are fairly simple to configure for basic operation, but you can add options to modify their configurations in various ways. This is particularly true of SSH, which supports several security and other options.

Handling GUI Access with X and VNC Servers

Chapter 13 covered remote text-based login servers (rlogind, Telnet, and SSH). These servers, in conjunction with appropriate client programs on other computers, allow users to log in and run text-based programs on a Linux computer. Because Linux (and UNIX more generally) supports a wide range of text-based tools, such text-based remote access servers allow users to perform most types of tasks with Linux. Many users, though, are most comfortable with a graphical user interface (GUI) for running programs. By themselves, text-based login servers don't support full GUIs, so users can't run popular GUI programs like The GIMP, Netscape Navigator, or StarOffice. (A few programs, like Emacs, support both GUI and text-based operation.) In order to provide access to GUI tools, you need to run special GUI servers. The most common of these in Linux is the X Window System (or X for short), which is Linux's native GUI environment. X is inherently network-capable, so you only need appropriate X software on the remote system. In some cases, you can use text-based login tools as part of the process, but in other cases you may want to run a special X-based login tool. Another option is to use a package called *Virtual Network Computing (VNC)*, which provides network GUI access similar to that of X, but using different protocols. This chapter covers all of these options.

WHEN TO RUN A GUI ACCESS SERVER

GUI access servers are most useful when a computer's primary function is to provide workstation-like functions to multiple or remote users. For instance, a company with a dozen employees might purchase one high-powered central system and a dozen much less powerful computers that function as GUI terminals for the central computer. This central system could host applications like StarOffice, The GIMP, KMail, and so on. Individuals would sit at the less-powerful systems, log into the central system, and run their applications remotely. Compared to an environment in which individuals sit at workstations that run their programs, this configuration offers several advantages, including:

- **Central software administration**—To add, delete, or upgrade an application, you need only modify the configuration on a single computer. (For many applications, an alternative is to use NFS to store applications on a file server, but run those programs on individual users' workstations.)

- **Simpler workstation configuration**—The workstations or other dedicated systems at which users sit can be very simple, both in terms of hardware and software. These systems will therefore require little in the way of routine maintenance and software updates. In some cases, you can handle these in a centralized manner, as well, if you use some variety of network boot protocol for the workstations. In fact, you can use a device known as an *X terminal*, which is a very simple computer that supports X and has little computing power of its own.

- **Central hardware upgrades**—If new or updated applications need hardware upgrades, a central server strategy allows you to perform upgrades on a single system, which can be simpler than upgrading a dozen or more computers. On the other hand, this also makes your workplace quite vulnerable to failure of the central system's hardware. This system must also have much more capable hardware than would any single workstation.

- **Central storage**—It's usually easier to back up a single system than an entire network of computers, so this approach can simplify data backups. Depending upon the client systems you use, they may require no backups, or they could use simple backups of a default configuration that would probably fit on a single CD-R.

- **Central user accounts**—Using a single system permits centralized maintenance of user accounts. Users may need accounts on only one computer, which can greatly simplify network configuration.

(Depending upon the access terminals' types and configuration, though, users may need accounts on them, as well.) Users can sit at any computer, log in, and be greeted by their own desktops and user preferences. This feature also means that you can easily replace any individual's computer, since it contains little or nothing in the way of customizations. Another way to attain this goal is to use a centralized login server protocol such as Kerberos (described in Chapter 6, Authenticating Users via Kerberos).

Of course, a network configured in this way has its drawbacks, as well. Most importantly, the reliance upon a single computer means that if that system goes down, all the other computers become effectively useless. If you decide to configure a network in this way, you should be particularly diligent about backing up the central system, and have spare parts on hand in case of a failure. You might even want to configure a computer as a backup, ready to take over the primary system's duties on a moment's notice.

Even if you aren't configuring a large network for which you want to use a central system to handle all normal user logins, you might want to use a GUI login tool to allow smaller-scale or peer-to-peer logins. All your users might have their own workstations, for instance, but if they occasionally need to do work from remote locations, those workstations can be configured to accept remote accesses, allowing a user to work from another user's workstation, from home, or from some other location.

Remote GUI access tools are most often used on a local network. Because GUI displays transfer a great deal of data, the use of these protocols across the Internet at large often results in a sluggish display. Indeed, even on a local network with 100 Mbps hardware, GUI protocols are noticeably slower than local GUI displays, although the speed on a local network is usually acceptable. As with text-based remote access tools, GUI tools provide users with full login privileges, and a password must be exchanged, so there are security risks to running such protocols. (The VNC tools encrypt passwords but not regular data, reducing risks slightly. Using SSH for the initial login allows you to encrypt the password and *all* session data.)

CONFIGURING BASIC X ACCESS

X is the GUI environment that's most often used with Linux. As noted earlier, X is a network-enabled GUI environment. This means that X programs use network protocols to display their windows, menus, dialog boxes, and so on, even when they're run on a single computer. Understanding how these protocols work is vital to understanding how to configure two computers to allow remote GUI access. You must set options on both the client and the server.

UNDERSTANDING THE X CLIENT/SERVER RELATIONSHIP

Most people who aren't intimately familiar with network protocols tend to think of a server computer as being a big, powerful box that sits in a room somewhere, whereas a client computer is a much smaller and less powerful computer at which the user sits in order to interact with the server. Although this conception is technically inaccurate, it's usually not misleading—as a practical matter (not a matter of definitions), servers usually are powerful systems that handle data requests from less powerful systems at which users sit. This conception leads to confusion, however, in the case of X servers, because the arrangement is exactly the opposite of what most people expect: The user sits at the computer that runs the X server, and this computer can be quite limited in capabilities. The X client programs run on a computer that's often much more powerful than the X server computer.

To understand this peculiar twist, it's useful to think of the situation from the point of view of the *client program*. When a network client program engages in network interactions, it initiates a connection with a server program in order to transfer data. The server program exists to *serve*. Consider for comparison a word processor like WordPerfect and its interactions with an NFS server. (Technically, a Linux kernel module functions as the NFS client, but WordPerfect is the program that causes the kernel module to initiate transfers.) You as a WordPerfect user select the options to open a file on an NFS export, so WordPerfect initiates the network transfers, telling the NFS server to deliver a file. The NFS server responds to these requests, delivering a network service to the client. Now, suppose you're running WordPerfect remotely, from a computer in another room, via an X server. WordPerfect functions as a client for the X protocols. When WordPerfect opens a file selector dialog box, it does so by requesting that the X server display a dialog box, text, and so on. To WordPerfect, the X server is just another input/output resource, like an NFS server. The fact that the ultimate destination of the data is a human being is irrelevant to the program. This relationship is illustrated in Figure 14.1.

An X server provides a GUI display device and one or more input devices (typically, a keyboard and mouse). The X server may itself be a client for

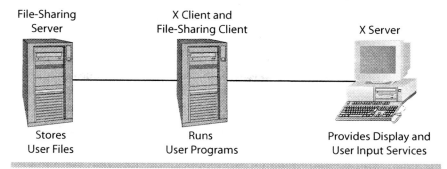

File-Sharing Server	X Client and File-Sharing Client	X Server
Stores User Files	Runs User Programs	Provides Display and User Input Services

Figure 14.1   An X server provides an interface between the user and a program that may run on another computer.

other servers, such as font servers (described in Chapter 15, Providing Consistent Fonts with Font Servers). A font server delivers fonts to the X server upon request, allowing many X servers to provide a consistent set of typefaces for users.

> **NOTE** The overall VNC client/server relationship is opposite to that of X, but VNC includes its own special X server. The upcoming section, "Understanding the VNC Client/Server Relationship," covers the details. The fact that these relationships are reversed means that one protocol may work when another fails when a firewall sits between the client and the server. Specifically, the firewall must allow through packets targeted at the server. Thus, a firewall designed to protect computers that are generally considered client *computers* may need special configuration if these computers run X servers. With VNC, no such special configuration is required. SSH can also be used to twist the X client/server relationship, but in a more subtle way, as described in the upcoming section, "Tunneling X Connections Through SSH."

When you install Linux on a computer, most distributions allow you to configure an X server. This server can be used to provide local computers with access to the display. Referring to Figure 14.1, such a configuration makes the X client and X server computers one and the same. For instance, Figure 14.1's X server system might have its own X programs that it runs. The X server on a Linux system can also be used to interface with X clients running on other systems, though. Doing so requires issuing a few commands, as described shortly. If both X and other network protocols function normally on a system, it already has all the software it needs to function as an X server, so you need not install any special packages.

X client computers (those that host the programs you want to run remotely) need no special software; the X programs you want to run *are* the clients. To be sure, these clients almost invariably require various GUI libraries, like Qt or GTK+. With systems based on RPM or Debian packages, though, you'll be told if you need to install such libraries when you install the client program itself. In theory, you don't need to install an X server on this system, although in practice it's often simplest to do so, because dependencies between packages end up requiring you to install most of X. Technically, the X server itself is a single program that interfaces to the screen, mouse, keyboard, and so on. You may be able to omit this server, but it's often convenient to have it installed to test X-based pro-

X Servers for Various OSs

X server packages are available for OSs other than Linux and UNIX. If you want to use a Windows, OS/2, MacOS, or some other system as a GUI access terminal, you can do so by installing an appropriate X server on the OS in question. Options include XFree86 (http://xfree86.cygwin.com for Windows, http://ais.gmd.de/~veit/os2/xf86os2. html for OS/2, or http://mrcla.com/XonX/ for MacOS X), MI/X for Windows and MacOS Classic (http://www.microimages.com/freestuf/mix/), Exceed for Windows (http://www.hcl.com/products/nc/exceed/), Xmanager for Windows (http://www.netsarang.com/products/xmanager.html), and Xtools for MacOS X (http://www.tenon.com/products/xtools/). This list is far from complete, though, particularly for Windows; there are many X servers available that can be used to access a Linux system. MicroImages maintains a comparison chart at http://www.microimages.com/mix/prices.htm.

As noted earlier, there are also dedicated hardware devices, known as X terminals, that support X, TCP/IP networking, and very little else. These devices function as dedicated X servers. Companies such as Network Computing Devices (NCD; http://www.ncd.com) and Hewlett Packard (http://www.hp.com) sell X terminals. These devices often require that a computer on your network run a Trivial File Transfer Protocol (TFTP) server so that they can obtain critical boot files. (The TFTP server computer need not be the same as the computers you intend to use from the X terminal, though.) X terminals usually require that the system you intend to run use a GUI login server, as described in the upcoming section, "Configuring a Login Server to Accept Connections." You can configure even an old computer to function as a dedicated X terminal by installing a minimal Linux system and altering the configuration files so that the system uses a GUI login server to log into another system.

grams locally. To make use of the X server program, you must have X client programs, either locally or on another computer.

CONFIGURING AN X SERVER TO ACCEPT X CLIENT ACCESS

An X server, like other types of server, must respond to connections initiated by clients. Most Linux distributions, however, are designed with the premise that the system will be used as a workstation or a server for other protocols, not as an X terminal. Therefore, to use a Linux system as an X server for anything but programs run locally, you must reconfigure the system to accept X connections from other systems. There are two main ways to do this: You can use xhost on the X server, or xauth on both the X server and the X client.

Using xhost

One way to grant access to an X server is to use the xhost program to allow specific remote computers to access your X display. In an xterm or similar command-prompt window, you can type a command resembling the following:

```
$ xhost +biggie.threeroomco.com
```

This command instructs the X server to accept connections from biggie.threeroomco.com for your display. Consequently, any user on that computer can connect to your X server to display windows, accept keyboard and mouse input, and so on. If you omit the hostname (typing just **xhost** +), your X server will accept connections from *any* source.

NOTE   Most X servers for Windows, MacOS, and other non-UNIX systems are configured by default to accept X connections from anywhere, much like xhost + does in Linux.

Using xhost to open your X server to connections from other systems is simple and convenient, and may be acceptable in a low-security environment. It has its problems, though. Most importantly, it doesn't provide you with any way to restrict access to specific users of a remote system. If you want to run programs that are stored on a system that has many users, a shady character on that remote system might be able to display windows and pull other pranks, or even read your keystrokes, if you use xhost in this way to open your system. For this reason, another method exists: xauth.

Using xauth

The idea behind xauth is to provide a more-or-less transparent authentication system for X connections. This utility is used transparently by the X login protocols described shortly in "Using a Remote X Login Server," but you can use it manually when connecting in some other way, as well. Although it's a bit more tedious to set up xauth than to use xhost, it's far better from a security point of view, because your X server is much more selective about the clients from which it accepts connections.

The xauth system relies on a file called .Xauthority in each user's home directory. This file must be present on both the X server and the client system, although if it's not present on one system or another, the xauth tool will create it. Unlike most Linux configuration files, .Xauthority isn't a text-mode file; you manipulate it with the xauth tool. Using xauth, you can add, delete, or otherwise manipulate X connection keys. Certain methods of starting X, such as the GUI login servers described later, check .Xauthority and, if necessary, generate a new key for the server in this file. The X server then accepts connections from any client that possesses this key. (Because .Xauthority is stored in an *individual user's* home directory, this key generation occurs when a user logs in or the user starts X, whichever occurs later. Different users can have different .Xauthority files.) To allow an X client to use an X server, you must copy the key from the user's .Xauthority file on the server to the user's .Xauthority file on the client. Client applications automatically try to use the key when they try to use the X server. There are several different ways to transfer an authorization key. One such procedure is as follows (a quicker one appears after this):

1. On the X server computer, type **xauth** to start the utility as the user who will be using the system for remote access. Note that although xauth is, in some sense, an X utility, it doesn't rely on X to operate; it runs in text mode.

2. Type **list**. This displays a series of keys in the .Xauthority file. Each key begins with a display name, which is a computer hostname followed by a display number, such as term.threeroomco.com:0. Some machine names may be followed by /unix, and you may see entries for localhost, both of which you can ignore. If some entries end in numbers higher than 0, those refer to second, third, or subsequent X server sessions run simultaneously with the first. You want to locate the display name for your main display, which will probably be your computer's hostname followed by :0. After this name on the line will be an

encoding type (probably MIT-MAGIC-COOKIE-1) and a 32-byte hexadecimal number. You can ignore these items, although ultimately they're what you'll be transferring.

3. Type **extract** *xfer-auth displayname*, where *xfer-auth* is any convenient filename and *displayname* is your X display name, as identified in Step 2. For instance, you might type **extract xfer-auth term. threeroomco.com:0**. This step copies the .Xauthority entry for your display to a file that you can transfer to the X client system.

4. Type **exit** to quit from xauth.

5. Copy the *xfer-auth* file generated in Step 3 to the X client system (the computer that hosts the programs you want to run from a distance). You can use any method you like to do this, such as FTP, scp, an NFS mount, a floppy disk, or so on.

6. Log onto the X client system.

7. Type **xauth** to start this utility on the client system.

8. Type **merge** *xfer-auth*, where *xfer-auth* is the name of the file you generated in Step 3 and transferred to this computer. (Include the path to this file, if necessary.)

9. Type **list**. This action should generate a list of the authorizations on this system, including the one you've just merged. If you don't see the X server you want to add, something went wrong in the process, so review the preceding steps.

10. Type **exit** to exit from the program and save the changes. (Note that xauth also supports a command called quit, but this abandons the changes, so don't use it unless you've made a mistake.)

If your systems both have SSH installed, you can use the following command, typed on the X server system, in place of this ten-step procedure:

```
# xauth list xserver :0 | sed -e 's/^/add /' | ssh xclient -x xauth
```

This procedure compresses the preceding ten steps into a single long command, using xauth in command line mode, sed to add the command add to the start of the output, and SSH's ability to run programs remotely to execute xauth on the X client system. You should note the following features of this command:

- Type the name of the computer at which you're sitting as *xserver*, and the client whose programs you want to run as *xclient*.

343

- Be sure there's a space after add and before the following slash (/). This is a command that's passed to xauth on the X client system, and a space must separate the add command from the display name that the first xauth call extracts.

- You'll be prompted for a password or pass phrase, unless your SSH configuration circumvents this requirement, as described in Chapter 13, Maintaining Remote Login Servers.

At this point, your X server should accept connections from the X client system, although you may still need to set an option on the client system to connect to the X server, as described in the next section, "Setting Client Options to Use an X Server." When the X client program makes the connection, it will check its local .Xauthority file for the key associated with the X server.

Because the xauth system relies on keys that are, ideally, known only to the X server and its authorized clients, it's more secure than is the xhost system, at least in some respects. If you use xauth, for instance, the server will only accept connections from specific users on a client that are authorized to use the display. The X server using this system is also less susceptible to IP spoofing attacks. On the downside, the keys used by xauth are sent in an unencrypted form, so if your local network isn't secure, or if you use this method over the Internet, these keys are vulnerable to interception, thus allowing anybody with access to the key to connect to your X server. Ultimately, if highly secure X connections are desirable, SSH is a superior connection method, as described in the upcoming section, "Tunneling X Connections Through SSH."

NOTE　Not all X servers are configured to use xauth. This feature normally is active for X servers started through XDM, GDM, or KDM, as described in the upcoming section, "Using a Remote X Login Server." If you start your X server through startx, though, it may or may not be present, depending upon your X version and distribution. In some cases, you may need to edit the startx script (usually in /usr/X11R6/bin) so that it calls xinit with the -auth authority-file option, where authority-file is the authority file (normally .Xauthority in your home directory). This step usually isn't necessary, though.

SETTING CLIENT OPTIONS TO USE AN X SERVER

Whether you use xhost or xauth to control access to the X server, you must configure the client to use the correct server. If you sit down at term.threeroomco.com and log in to biggie.threeroomco.com, and if that system tries to use wrongone.threeroomco.com as an X display, you won't be able to use the display. In fact, many Linux systems default to using their own X servers, even when you log in remotely.

When an X program starts, it checks the value of the DISPLAY environment variable to determine what X server to use. You can check the value of this variable yourself with the following command, which you type on the X *client* system:

```
$ echo $DISPLAY
biggie.threeroomco.com:0.0
```

If the output (biggie.threeroomco.com:0.0 in this example) is your X server, then you need do nothing. (The first display is usually numbered 0 or 0.0, and these two values are equivalent.) If the output shows your X client or some other system, or if there is no output (indicating the DISPLAY environment variable isn't set), then you must set it, thus:

```
$ export DISPLAY=term.threeroomco.com:0
```

You should use your own X server's hostname, of course. Subsequent attempts to run X programs will use the server you specify. In order for these attempts to succeed, though, you need to have configured the X server to accept connections from your X client by running xhost on the server or transferring an xauth record to the client, as described earlier.

Tunneling X Connections Through SSH

The preceding discussion relates to initiating an X connection using two distinct and independent protocols. First, you connect from the X server computer using a text-mode remote login client, such as a Telnet client. Second, you use this text-mode connection to initiate a link in the opposite direction for X clients. After performing basic setup tasks, you might type **xclock** in your Telnet program to start the xclock program, for instance. This configuration is adequate for many purposes, but it's not without its problems. For one thing, all the data transferred over the X connection is unencrypted, and so is vulnerable to interception by third parties. The fact that each side must run a server is also a drawback in some situations, because firewalls or Network Address Translation (NAT)/IP masquerading routers may require special configuration to allow this procedure to work. One possible solution to both of these problems is to use the Secure

Shell (SSH) protocol, as described in Chapter 13, to both make the initial connection from the X server system to the X client system and to tunnel X data back from the X client to the X server.

Chapter 13 describes the basics of SSH configuration and use. There are specific configuration options you need to set for SSH tunneling of X protocols to work, though:

- In /etc/ssh/ssh_config on the SSH client system (the X server system), set ForwardX11 to yes. This option enables the SSH client to accept the X data from the SSH server. Alternatively, you can launch ssh with the -X option. (Note that this is an uppercase -X; a lowercase -x disables X11 forwarding.)
- In /etc/ssh/sshd_config on the SSH server system (the X client system), set X11Forwarding to yes. This option tells the SSH server to intercept local X calls and forward them on to the SSH client.

X forwarding by SSH works by having the SSH server run what is essentially a stand-in for a local X server. When properly configured, SSH sets the DISPLAY environment variable so that X programs send data to a particular *local* X server port (X server 10 by default, or TCP port 6010). The SSH server then connects to this port. Rather than display data locally, SSH encrypts the data and passes it to the SSH client. This client then makes requests of its own local X server (as determined by the SSH client machine's DISPLAY environment variable), and passes any results back to the SSH server, which delivers these results to the ultimate X client program. Essentially, the SSH server pretends to be an X server, and the SSH client pretends to be the originating X client program.

This procedure has certain advantages. For one thing, the fact that there need be only one network connection between the two computers simplifies network configuration. If you want to use an X server behind a firewall or NAT router, you may find it easier to do so if you use SSH than if you use Telnet or some other remote login protocol. Second, because SSH supports encryption, passing X data through SSH can greatly enhance security. Passwords and other sensitive data are not likely to be useable even if data packets are intercepted. The drawback derives from this encryption: Encryption requires computation, so using SSH to tunnel X connections consumes CPU time on both computers, thus slowing X displays. On CPUs of more than about 200MHz, these effects may be noticeable, but probably won't be objectionable when security is important. In some cases, the -C option to ssh, which enables compression, can improve matters by reducing bandwidth requirements. On the other hand, the compression adds further to the CPU load, which can make matters worse. You'll have to try it both ways and decide which is better on your hardware and network.

These instructions assume that you're using Linux or UNIX systems on both sides of the connection. If you're using Windows, MacOS, OS/2, or some other system as the X server, it's possible that the SSH client software won't support tunneling X connections. Even if it does support this option, you may need to determine how to activate this feature in a configuration dialog box. Consult your SSH client's documentation for more details.

A SUMMARY OF REMOTE-LOGIN X ACCESS

The preceding discussion illustrates several steps and options available to you in establishing an X connection by working off a text-mode login. There are so many possibilities, though, that it's easy to get lost. To summarize, then, a prototypical connection involves steps like the following:

1. **Start the X server**—Your X server might run automatically if you use a Linux system and it's configured to boot into an X login screen; or you might need to run it by typing **startx**. On a Windows, MacOS, or other system running an X server, you'll need to run the X server program manually or configure the system to start it automatically.

2. **Configure the X server to accept connections**—You must tell the X server to accept remote connections. This may be done by using xhost on the X server or by transferring its xauth key to the client system. This step isn't necessary if you use SSH to tunnel connections, although in that case, you must configure both the SSH client and server to perform the tunneling.

3. **Connect to the X client computer**—You can use any text-mode remote-access protocol, such Telnet or SSH, to connect to the computer on which you want to run programs. Note that the remote computer runs a text-mode remote-access *server*, but it functions as an X *client*.

4. **Configure the X client to use the correct X server**—X client programs use the DISPLAY environment variable to determine what computer to use for X displays. Some systems set this environment variable correctly automatically, but on others you must adjust it with a command like **export DISPLAY=*term.threeroomco.com*:0**.

5. **Run X programs**—You can run X programs by typing their names in your original remote-login program window. If you launch an xterm or similar program, you can use it to launch further programs.

Some of these steps, such as 2 and 4, may not be necessary depending upon the methods you use to connect and authenticate. Also, some X servers for Windows and MacOS automate some of these steps. For instance, some X servers include minimal automated Telnet or other remote-access tools that can log in using the appropriate protocol, and that then launch an xterm. Thus, once configured with your username and password, these X servers can start a connection at the click of a button, with the result being an xterm window. Consult your X server's documentation for details.

The procedures described here result in the remote system's programs being displayed on the X server computer's desktop, or sometimes in a separate window that the X server opens to host the client's desktop. (This option is particularly common on MacOS and Windows X servers.) Typically, the local system runs a window manager, although that's not always true, particularly of MacOS and Windows X servers. (X supports running the window manager from either computer.) Likewise, the desktop environment is normally run locally. If you want to maintain a minimal system locally and run the window manager and desktop environment on the remote system, you can adjust the local and remote X startup scripts to disable these features on the X server computer and enable them on the remote system. Another approach is to use a remote X login server, which typically shifts more of the burden for maintaining window managers and desktop environments to the remote system.

USING AN XDMCP SERVER

Assuming there are no obstructing firewalls or other obstacles, any system running an X server may be used as a display for any computer that can run X applications. Sometimes this isn't quite enough, though; sometimes you want your X server to work just like a local X server would, displaying a desktop environment that's controlled by the remote system. The login procedure that uses Telnet, SSH, or other remote-access protocols can also be a bit on the tedious side, particularly when you want to give complete control to the remote system. These issues are both addressed by entirely X-based login protocols, such as the X Display Manager Control Protocol (XDMCP). Most Linux systems come with the software that's necessary to use XDMCP as a server (on the X client side), but most configurations restrict access to the XDMCP server to the local system. Reconfiguring the server allows it to serve many XDMCP clients (X servers). It's possible to use a Linux system as an XDMCP client, but this requires modifying the X configuration to use XDMCP to present a login display that's generated remotely rather than locally.

UNDERSTANDING XDMCP OPERATION

Preceding sections of this chapter have presented a model of remote X use that involves using a remote login protocol such as Telnet, running the Telnet server on the X client in order to establish the initial connection and allowing the user to establish a reciprocal X connection. XDMCP effectively replaces Telnet, SSH, or some other text-based remote access protocol. When a user connects to a remote system with Telnet, the Telnet server launches a login process and, ultimately, a text-based shell. The textual data from these processes pass back over the Telnet session to the client system. XDMCP is similar in some ways, but instead of launching a text-based shell, the XDMCP server initiates an X-based login process, including a GUI login prompt and the launching of the user's normal window manager, desktop environment, and so on. These programs run through a reciprocal X connection; XDMCP automatically configures both the client and the server via xauth, and sets the DISPLAY environment variable appropriately. In short, XDMCP automates many of the login steps described earlier.

In fact, the XDMCP server isn't used only for remote X connections; it's used by Linux computers that are configured to boot directly into X. When so configured, the XDMCP server runs and connects directly to the X server, creating a GUI login prompt such as the one shown in Figure 14.2. Because the XDMCP server creates this prompt, it differs from one server to another; in fact, it can be customized, and so varies from one distribution to another.

Figure 14.2   An XDMCP server's login prompt lets you enter your username, password, and sometimes additional information, such as the desktop environment or window manager you want to use.

CONFIGURING A LOGIN SERVER TO ACCEPT CONNECTIONS

XDMCP servers are configured through files that are typically stored in the /etc directory tree, and usually in /etc/X11. Most distributions ship in such a way that their servers are only accessible from the localhost as a security precaution. If you want to permit remote XDMCP logins, you must loosen this configuration. In addition, you must ensure that the XDMCP server is running. There are three XDMCP servers commonly used in Linux: The original X Display Manager (XDM) and the newer KDE Display Manager (KDM) and GNOME Display Manager (GDM).

XDM Configuration

XDM is the oldest and simplest of the popular XDMCP servers. Unlike GDM and KDM, XDM has no link to any Linux desktop environment. It allows users to enter their usernames and passwords, but no additional information, such as what window managers they want to use. Instead, users' login parameters are controlled through the .xsession files in their home directories. (This script is run from the global Xsession script, normally found in /etc/X11 or /etc/X11/xdm). Users' .xsession files normally end with a line that starts a window manager or desktop environment; when the script terminates (after the user logs out, thus terminating the window manager), the X session ends, and XDM terminates the remote link or (on a local display) redisplays the login prompt.

Adjusting XDM's Availability

XDM's availability to nonlocal systems is controlled through its main configuration file, /etc/X11/xdm/xdm-config. Specifically, many distributions ship with a line like the following:

```
DisplayManager.requestPort: 0
```

This line tells XDM not to listen on its usual port (UDP port 177) for external connection requests. You should comment out this line by adding a pound sign (#) to its start if you want to allow others to use XDMCP to log onto the computer.

In addition to editing xdm-config, you may need to adjust the /etc/X11/xdm/Xaccess file. This file indicates the specific computers that may access the XDM server. This file consists of a series of lines, each of which contains a host specification followed by an indication of what type of access the host is allowed. (Lines that begin with pound signs are comments, and are ignored.) If the access type is not specified, the clients are permitted direct access, which is the most important type. Other common options include CHOOSER, which causes XDM to display a list of other computers that have XDMCP servers running on the local network when the XDMCP client sends a so-called *indirect* query; and BROADCAST, which is generally used in conjunction with CHOOSER to tell the chooser to broadcast a query for other XDMCP servers when the system receives an indirect request. An asterisk (*) as the host list causes XDM to allow any host to connect. For instance, the following entries allow any computers to connect to the system directly or use it as an indirect server, to obtain a list of local XDMCP servers:

```
*
* CHOOSER BROADCAST
```

If you want to restrict access to certain hosts, you should create lines that list those hosts, and eliminate the asterisk entry. You may also use an asterisk as *part of* a name to grant access to a domain. For instance, the following system allows only the members of one domain and two outside computers to connect to the XDMCP server for remote logins, and only the outside systems for indirect queries:

```
*.threeroomco.com
bronto.pangaea.edu
stego.pangaea.edu
bronto.pangaea.edu CHOOSER BROADCAST
stego.pangaea.edu CHOOSER BROADCAST
```

NOTE   It's possible to configure a computer to not accept XDMCP connections through means other than the XDM configuration files. For instance, a computer's firewall rules (described in Chapter 25, Configuring iptables) could block access to a server.

Setting Displays XDM is to Manage

The /etc/X11/xdm/Xservers file specifies a list of displays that XDM is to manage. When XDM starts, it tries to connect directly to these displays, presenting a login screen for them. By default, this file contains a line similar to the following (the details differ from one distribution to another):

```
:0 local /usr/X11R6/bin/X
```

This line tells the system to connect to and manage the local display (:0). Thus, XDM manages the local X display, starting X in the process if necessary. (This is the reason that starting XDM in a SysV startup script or the like launches X.) If you want XDM to directly manage the displays of remote systems such as X servers without using an intervening login prompt, you can list those systems here:

```
term.threeroomco.com:0 foreign
```

The `foreign` specification tells XDM that this is a remote system, and to contact it as such. Of course, that system must be configured to allow the XDMCP server to connect to it and display the login prompt. Another reason to edit the `Xservers` file is to *remove* the default `local` specification. If you do this, the computer won't launch X locally when you start XDM. This might be useful if you want to use a powerful central system via remote X terminals or the like. Such a system might run many X programs, but have no need of an X server running locally.

NOTE   You do *not* need to tell XDM to manage a display if you can configure that server to locate XDMCP servers, as described in the upcoming section, "Configuring a Remote X Login Client." You should tell XDM to manage a display only if the X server in question should be used *only* to connect to the computer on which XDM is running. You might use this approach with an X terminal that connects to just one computer, for instance.

KDM Configuration

KDM is designed as a "drop-in" replacement for XDM, but KDM offers expanded capabilities. Of most interest to most users, KDM offers a clickable list of usernames, a Session Type list box in which users may enter a window manager or desktop environment, and a Quit or Shutdown button to exit from the local X server (when run remotely) or shut down the computer (when run locally). Figure 14.2 shows a KDM login display.

KDM uses the same configuration files as does XDM, so you should refer to the preceding section, "XDM Configuration," for instructions on setting up KDM to accept remote logins. Some of KDM's additional features require configuration above and beyond that of XDM, though. These features are controlled through the `kdmrc` file, which is stored in different locations on different distributions. Common locations include `/opt/kde2/share/config` and `/usr/share/config`. Options in this file control the size of the login window, the GUI style, and so on. One of the most important of these options is called `SessionTypes`. It determines the names of the session types displayed for users—that is, the window managers or desktop environments from which they can select. If you add session types to this list, you must also add them to the Xsession or Xsession.d file in /etc/X11 or /etc/X11/xdm. Unfortunately, deciphering this file is tedious at best, and it differs from one distribution to another. Look for lines that use the variable SESSION or something similar. Some distributions ship with a tool called chksession, which can automatically add window managers or desktop environments to both KDM and GDM configurations—*if* the window manager or desktop environment ships with appropriate configuration files. In most cases, it's simpler for users to customize their environments as they do in XDM, by editing the .xsession files in their home directories. Users must select a specific KDM session entry, usually called Default, to have the system use this file.

GDM Configuration

GDM is GNOME's entry to the display manager race. Like KDM, it offers users features such as the ability to select from among several desktop environments and the ability to terminate a remote X session or shut down the local computer. Unlike KDM, GDM uses its own configuration files, which are normally stored in /etc/X11/gdm. The most important of these files is gdm.conf.

Systems that use GDM, like those that use most other XDMCP servers, ship with the server configured to *not* accept logins from remote servers. You can change this by locating the [xdmcp] section in gdm.conf and altering one or two entries. Most importantly, you should change the line that reads Enable=0 to read Enable=1. If you want GDM to provide a list of other XDMCP-enabled computers to X terminals or the like, you should also change the HonorIndirect=0 line to read HonorIndirect=1.

If you want to run GDM for remote access without starting X locally, you can do so by commenting out the local servers in the [servers] section. Normally, this section contains an entry like the following:

```
0=/usr/bin/X11/X
```

This entry tells GDM to start X (the program /usr/bin/X11/X, to be precise) to manage the first X session, much like the default Xservers configuration for XDM or KDM. Commenting out this entry causes GDM to run without managing the local display, or starting X if it's not already running.

Like KDM, GDM gives users a choice of window managers or desktop environments. (In GDM, these choices are accessible from the Session menu.) You can add or delete sessions by creating appropriate scripts in the /etc/X11/gdm/Sessions directory. The default scripts usually call /etc/X11/xdm/Xsession, sometimes passing it a parameter to indicate what environment should be launched. You might therefore have to edit this script, or create one that does some of the same job, but add the capability to launch whatever new window manager or desktop environment you want to use. Alternatively, on most systems, users can edit their .xsession files to customize their startup environments.

Running an XDMCP Server

Running an XDMCP server is normally accomplished by setting the computer to start X and accept GUI logins automatically. Most distributions reserve runlevel 5 for this purpose, but some use other runlevels—specifically, SuSE prior to version 7.2 uses runlevel 3 for GUI logins, and Slackware uses runlevel 4. Debian and its derivatives try to start X in all multi-user runlevels.

You can set the default runlevel in /etc/inittab by editing a line that resembles the following:

```
id:5:initdefault:
```

Most distributions include comments preceding this line that describe the purpose of various runlevels. The number in the second colon-delimited field is the runlevel that the system enters when it boots. If this number is associated with the computer starting X, then the XDMCP server will also run.

You can change runlevels with the telinit command. For instance, **telinit 5** changes to runlevel 5. This change remains in effect until you issue another telinit command or reboot the computer.

TIP

If you make changes to your XDMCP server's configuration, one way to implement those changes is to use telinit to switch out of the X runlevel and into a text-mode runlevel, then switch back to the X-related runlevel. Another method is to use kill or killall to stop the XDMCP server, then run it again. You can use the SIGHUP signal to cause the XDMCP server to reread its configuration files without exiting. (When the XDMCP server exits, it normally terminates the local X display.)

Each distribution has its default XDMCP server, but you can reconfigure any distribution to use any XDMCP server. Different distributions use different methods to specify which XDMCP server is run. Methods of selecting the XDMCP server include the following:

- **prefdm**—Some distributions, such as Red Hat and Mandrake, use a script called `prefdm` (usually stored in `/etc/X11`) to launch the XDMCP server. This script in turn loads the contents of the file called `/etc/sysconfig/desktop` to determine the default desktop environment and XDMCP server. Common values of this file include `KDE`, `GNOME`, and `AnotherLevel`, which result in KDM, GDM, and XDM as the XDMCP servers, respectively.

- **SysV startup script**—Debian and its derivatives start the XDMCP server through a standard SysV startup script, such as `/etc/init.d/xdm`. You can edit or replace this file to have the system use a different XDMCP server, as described in Chapter 4, Starting Servers. SuSE Linux uses a similar method, but its `xdm` startup script starts a specific XDMCP server according to the value of the `DISPLAYMANAGER` environment variable, which is set in `/etc/rc.config`.

- **Other startup scripts**—Slackware uses the `/etc/rc.d/rc.4` script to start the XDMCP server. As described in Chapter 4, Slackware doesn't use runlevels in quite the same way as most other Linux distributions, but the `rc.4` script is conceptually similar to the `xdm` SysV startup script of Debian or SuSE. Caldera uses a similar approach, but calls its startup script `/etc/rc.d/rc.gui`. The Slackware script is hard-coded to try to use KDM, then GDM, then XDM; the Caldera script only starts KDM. You can edit the script to change this order or add other XDMCP servers, if you like.

CONFIGURING A REMOTE X LOGIN CLIENT

As with other protocols, an XDMCP server alone isn't useful; it must be matched with one or more XDMCP clients. These clients are normally built into or included with X servers or X terminals. The XDMCP client may contact an XDMCP server directly, or it may present a list of available X servers, as shown in Figure 14.3, which shows the chooser for the Xmanager (`http://www.netsarang.com`) X server for Windows. When you select a computer and click Connect (or your chooser's equivalent), you'll see an XDMCP login display such as the one shown in Figure 14.2. When you log in, the X server will either take over your entire display or open a large window in which your X desktop will appear, depending upon the X server's capabilities and configuration.

Figure 14.3 A chooser displays a list of available XDMCP servers; you select one to run X programs hosted on that computer.

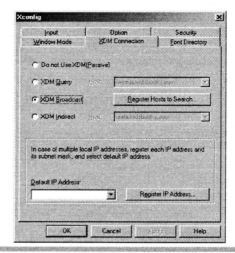

Figure 14.4 Most XDMCP clients provide several options for how to locate and interact with XDMCP servers.

Most X servers for Windows and MacOS provide a dialog box in which you can configure their XDMCP operation. Figure 14.4 shows this dialog box for Xmanager. Of particular interest are the radio buttons in the top half of the dialog box. These may be called slightly different things in different programs, but they illustrate methods the XDMCP client that's built into the X server may use to create the initial connection to the XDMCP server:

- **Do Not Use XDM (Passive)**—This method requires that you initiate a manual connection from the X server computer using Telnet or some

356

other login technique, or that you configure the XDMCP server to manage the X server's display (as for instance by creating a foreign entry in the /etc/X11/xdm/Xservers file, as described earlier). If you elect the latter option, the XDMCP server will try to create a login window on the X server computer when the XDMCP server starts. If you restart the X server, though, this login window will disappear and may not reappear until you restart the XDMCP server.

- **XDM Query**—This option causes the X server to send a login query directly to the specified host, whose name or IP address you must enter. This server presents an XDMCP login display such as that shown in Figure 14.2 if it's running an XDMCP server. You can't log directly into another computer if you use this option. This option is similar to the preceding one in many ways, but XDM Query causes the X server to query the XDMCP server whenever the X server starts up, which is usually a more sensible behavior than having the XDMCP server manage the X server.

- **XDM Broadcast**—If you're on a local network with several X servers, this option may be the best one. It causes the X server to send out a broadcast query to locate all the XDMCP servers on its local network, and to display a list of the servers, as shown in Figure 14.3. Some servers let you limit the broadcast to just some addresses (the Register Hosts to Search button in Figure 14.4 lets you do this).

- **XDM Indirect**—This option is useful if you want to allow users to log into any of several computers that are on a remote network. Enter the name or IP address of an XDMCP server on that network, and the X server connects to this system to obtain a list of servers. The XDMCP server must be configured to accept indirect queries, though, as described in the preceding sections.

Windows X servers aren't the only ones that can present a list of available XDMCP servers. You can have XFree86 on Linux do the same thing, although in this case you tell it to do so by starting X in different ways. Specifically, you use the -query *host.name*, -broadcast, and -indirect *host.name* options, as in:

```
$ /usr/X11R6/bin/X -indirect xdmcp-server.threeroomco.com
```

These options work much like those in Windows X servers, as just described, with one major exception: The XFree86 -broadcast option doesn't present a chooser list; it connects to the first XDMCP server that responds to the query, allowing you to log into that computer only.

TIP If you want to configure a Linux computer as a dedicated X terminal, you can do so. You should configure it so that X does *not* start automatically via the XDMCP server—that is, run Linux in text mode. You can then create a custom startup script or SysV startup script that runs X with an appropriate -query, -broadcast, or -indirect option. If you want to see a list of available local servers, you'll need to configure one regular XDMCP server as an indirect server and use the -indirect option when starting X. Used in this way, even an old 386 system can make an adequate X terminal.

RUNNING A VNC SERVER

Because X is the GUI environment that's most common on Linux, and because X was designed with network operations in mind, X is a common method of remote GUI access in Linux. X is not, however, the only method. Another tool, VNC, is available for providing remote GUI access to Linux. As described shortly, VNC uses a different network model than does X, and so has certain inherent advantages and drawbacks. Installing and configuring a VNC server is also a very different task than is installing and configuring an X server. Likewise, using a VNC client for remote access is different than using an X server.

UNDERSTANDING THE VNC CLIENT/SERVER RELATIONSHIP

I've taken pains in the preceding discussion to make the client and server roles of different programs explicit. This can become confusing at times, because in any connection, one computer functions as a client and the other as a server for one protocol, but this client/server relationship is reversed for another. VNC is somewhat easier to discuss because the connections between the two computers are simpler and more intuitively understandable to most people: The user sits at a VNC client and runs programs on the VNC server. This relationship is like that of a Telnet or SSH server.

If you recall the earlier discussion of the relationship between X clients and servers, though, you may wonder how this happens. After all, the X server controls the keyboard, mouse, and display, so how can the user *not* sit at the X server but still use X programs? The answer is an added layer of network complexity that's hidden from the user. The VNC server computer runs the X clients, which talk to an X server that runs on the local computer. This X server interfaces to the VNC server as if the VNC server were

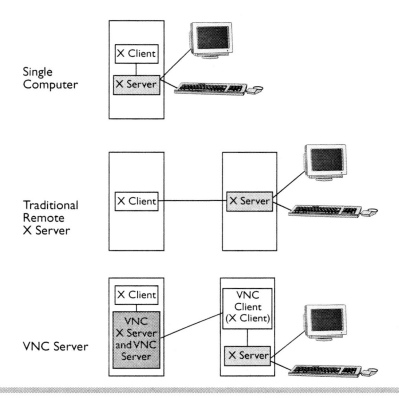

Figure 14.5   A VNC server runs its own custom X server locally, and interfaces to a simple remote network client that provides a keyboard, mouse, and monitor for the X server.

the human input and output devices. Instead of using the local keyboard, mouse, and display, though, the VNC server uses a network connection to communicate with a remote VNC client, which provides the input/output devices. This arrangement, and a comparison of it to a normal local X server and a networked X server, is shown in Figure 14.5. As you can see, it adds considerable complexity compared to a traditional remote X server configuration, but this complexity is largely hidden from the user.

The X server that's run on the VNC server system can maintain its state even if the VNC link is broken. For instance, if the VNC client system crashes, or if the user simply exits from the VNC server without logging out, the VNC server continues to run, and the next time a user makes a connection to the VNC server, all the applications that were run on the VNC server will remain open. This feature can be extremely convenient in some environments, but you shouldn't rely on it too heavily. Just as when you step away from a computer console for an extended period, the VNC server might crash, or the connection might be hijacked. (This maintenance of the local state doesn't apply when you use VNC in conjunction with XDMCP, as described in the upcoming section, "Running an XDMCP Login Server in VNC.")

In terms of security, VNC sits in-between a plain X connection via Telnet or XDMCP and an SSH-encrypted X connection. VNC encrypts its passwords, so they should be reasonably secure; but VNC doesn't encrypt other data, so anything you type or display after logging in could conceivably be viewed by others, particularly if your connection passes over the Internet at large.

X was designed with network operations in mind; it passes data in terms of lines, characters, and so on, not the bitmaps that are displayed on the screen. This results in a large number of back-and-forth transactions that transfer relatively little data. VNC, by contrast, is more bitmap-oriented; it performs relatively few transactions, each of which transfers more data. This fact means that on some networks and for some applications, VNC is more sluggish than a normal X connection, because more data must pass between the computers. For instance, if you use a text editor, the text editor can pass words to the X server, which generates the bitmaps for those words locally. VNC, however, must pass the entire bitmap, which is usually larger than a higher-level description of the display. This advantage may be small or nonexistent on a fast network or when running programs like bitmapped graphics editors, though. On the other hand, VNC's use of fewer data exchanges means that it can be faster if your connection has a very high latency, such as a satellite link; the many back-and-forth exchanges of conventional X slow it down in such situations. If you're dissatisfied with VNC's speed, you might look into an expanded version of VNC that supports more efficient encodings, such as TightVNC (http://www.tightvnc.com) or TridiaVNC (http://www.developvnc.org). These more bandwidth-efficient encodings consume more CPU time, though, so they're best used when both systems have fast CPUs. Likewise, tunneling VNC through SSH and using its compression features can improve or degrade performance, depending on available bandwidth and CPU time.

One of the big advantages of VNC over X is that you can use VNC to control a Windows or MacOS system. Although they don't use an X server internally, as shown in Figure 14.5, VNC servers for Windows and MacOS are available. These servers intercept the Windows or MacOS screen display and user input calls and echo the results to the VNC client, or take input from that client. I don't describe the operation of these Windows and MacOS VNC servers, though. They're conceptually similar to the Linux VNC server, but the Windows and MacOS servers offer fewer options and are configured through dialog boxes rather than text files. You can connect to the Windows and MacOS VNC servers exactly as you connect to a Linux VNC server. Because the Windows and MacOS VNC servers intercept screen calls, it's only practical for one person to use the computer at once.

INSTALLING A VNC SERVER

You can obtain a VNC server from the main VNC Web site, `http://www.uk.research.att.com/vnc/`. Both the VNC server and the VNC client also ship with many Linux distributions (VNC is an open source package). Some distributions ship both server and client in a single package (usually called vnc), but others break out the server and client packages (usually called vncserver and vnc, respectively). The TightVNC and TridiaVNC sites have their own packages, but their installation and use is similar to what's described here.

If your distribution ships with VNC, or if you want to install it from an RPM or Debian file obtained from another source, you should be able to accomplish the task by installing the package in the usual way. As of version 3.3.3r2, the original VNC's official distribution form is precompiled *x*86 binary code in a tarball or zip file, or source code. Assuming you obtain the code as a binary tarball, you can install it as follows:

1. Uncompress the tarball with a command such as **tar xvfz vnc-3.3.3r2_x86_linux_2.0.tgz**. This creates a directory called vnc_x86_linux_2.0.

2. Copy the files vncviewer, vncserver, vncpasswd, vncconnect, and Xvnc from the vnc_x86_linux_2.0 directory to a directory on your path, such as /usr/local/bin. Alternatively, you can move the entire vnc_x86_linux_2.0 directory to a location such as /opt and either add it to your path or create links from these program files to a location on your path.

3. Create a directory called .vnc in the home directory of the user who is to use VNC. This directory should be owned by the user in question. It will hold individualized VNC configuration files, including a VNC password file. To prevent snooping, you might want to set this directory's permissions to 700 (rwx------).

4. *As the user who will use VNC*, type **vncpasswd**. The vncpasswd program, as you might expect, sets a password. Unlike most other Linux login servers, VNC doesn't rely on the Linux username and password database to control access. Instead, it's run as a normal user, and so the server itself must provide password authentication. (If you pair VNC with an XDMCP server, as described shortly, Linux handles authentication, so you can skip this step and Step 3.)

NOTE   These instructions describe installing and using the conventional VNC server and client. VNC also supports a Java server mode, which allows you to access the VNC server from any Java-enabled Web browser. The necessary Java classes appear in the classes subdirectory of the installation directory. Read the README file for more information on installing and using these classes.

RUNNING A VNC SERVER

At this point, the VNC server is installed and configured. To run it, you must first log into the server as an ordinary user. Typically, you'll do this from the computer from which you want to use VNC, much as you'd log into a remote computer using Telnet or SSH in order to use X programs via an X server. There are other ways to do this, though; for instance, you could run VNC from the console in preparation for accessing the system from some other location. You can run the server by typing its name *as an ordinary user*:

```
$ vncserver

New 'X' desktop is vncserv.threeroomco.com:1

Starting applications specified in /home/rodsmith/.vnc/xstartup
Log file is /home/rodsmith/.vnc/vncserv.threeroomco.com:1.log
```

It's important to pay attention to the output of this command, and particularly the line that identifies the desktop number—1 in the preceding example, as indicated by the number at the end of the hostname (vncserv.threeroomco.com:1). VNC operates by starting an X server (the Xvnc program), which doubles as a VNC server. You can think of this X server as being like an X session started from a text-mode console login by typing **startx**—it has no login prompt, and starts an individual's desktop environment or window manager, as described shortly. If two or more individuals run VNC servers on a single computer, they must be differentiated from each other in some way. The method used is the X server number. The number 0 is often taken by the local console's X server, so chances are the first VNC session will use a number of 1. Subsequent VNC sessions may use higher numbers.

WARNING

If you used SSH to log into the VNC server system in order to run the VNC server, you may find that the VNC server runs, but all X programs (including window managers) fail to run in it. The result is that when you try to access the VNC server, you see a gray background with no windows, and you can't do anything with it. The cause is that SSH adjusts the `xauth` configuration for its own X forwarding features. A quick and dirty workaround is to type `export XAUTHORITY=~/.Xauthority` before running `vncserver`. This resets the X authority file to its default, so VNC won't become confused. Another workaround is to copy the authority entries from the default file into SSH's temporary authority file, which it maintains in the `/tmp` directory tree (typing `xauth` from an SSH login will use this file).

If you've finished with a VNC session, you can shut it down by using the -kill option, thus:

```
$ vncserver -kill :1
```

The number you use is the VNC session number, as reported when you started that session. Shutting down the VNC server when it's not in use isn't necessary, but reduces the memory load on the server computer and improves security—a server that isn't running can't be broken into. Be sure you've exited from any important programs before you do this, though—when you shut down a VNC server in this way, you won't be prompted if you want to save open files.

USING A VNC CLIENT TO ACCESS THE SERVER

The Linux VNC client is called **vncviewer**. To use it, you type its name, optionally followed by the name of the VNC server and its display number, thus:

```
$ vncviewer vncserv.threeroomco.com:1
VNC server supports protocol version 3.3 (viewer 3.3)
Password:
```

The password doesn't echo when you type it. The VNC client then displays additional information on the nature of the connection, such as the color depth and some other technical information. If all goes well, you'll see a window appear showing a Linux desktop on the VNC server. As noted in the next section, however, the defaults for the VNC server may not be to your liking, so you may want to adjust them.

If you don't include the display number, the VNC client tries to connect to display number 0, which won't work with most Linux systems, since that number is generally used by the local X server. Omitting the display number will usually work when connecting to a Windows or MacOS VNC server, though. If you omit the hostname, in addition to the display number, the VNC client prompts you for the hostname and password using an X-based dialog box.

Windows and MacOS VNC clients work in a way that's similar to that of the Linux VNC viewer, but the program is somewhat more GUI-centric. Specifically, you double-click the VNC viewer icon to launch the program. It then presents a dialog box in which you enter the VNC server's name and display number (such as vncserv.threeroomco.com:1). If this corresponds to a valid VNC server, the program then asks for a password and, if the password is correct, displays a window in which the VNC server's desktop appears.

ADJUSTING VNC SERVER CONFIGURATION

VNC can be a useful remote-access tool, but it's not without its problems. Some of these are inherent to VNC. For instance, many people report problems with the NEdit editor (http://www.nedit.org) and VNC. On my systems, NEdit doesn't accept keystrokes, making it essentially useless. Fortunately, such serious problems are rare. Other VNC problems aren't so severe; they can be overcome by adjusting VNC's configuration. You can change several basic features by editing the main VNC server startup script. You can set other features by customizing users' configuration files.

Adjusting Basic Server Features

The main VNC server program is Xvnc. This program includes both an X server (which communicates with local X programs) and the VNC server (which communicates with the remote VNC client). You'll note, though, that the preceding instructions don't refer to Xvnc. This is because this program is called by a script, which is used to start the server: vncserver. This script is written in Perl, and you can edit it yourself to adjust many of the

VNC server's default settings. Some that you might want to change include the following:

- **Auto-configured X defaults**—Recent versions of vncserver use the &GetXDisplayDefaults() call to retrieve various defaults for the X display, such as the display size and bit depth. Unfortunately, the system may recover a size that's inappropriate for your desired clients. You can comment out this line by preceding it with a pound sign (#) if you want to use a different display size. You'll then need to set the display size separately. The default script includes lines to do this before the &GetXDisplayDefaults() call, as described shortly.

- **Display size**—When Xvnc starts, it creates a virtual screen of a specific size. If you don't use the automatic X defaults option, you can set this display size with the $geometry variable. For instance, you might include a line like the following to set up a 900x675 display:

```
$geometry = "900x675";
```

TIP

Because VNC clients display a VNC server's desktop within a local window, it makes sense to create a display size that's slightly smaller than the client's screen size to provide for window borders. If the VNC display size is too large, users will have to scroll their local VNC windows to see the entire server desktop.

- **Color depth**—As with the display size, you can set the color depth by setting a variable, which is called $depth in the standard script. Sixteen bits is generally a good minimum for X, because color-hungry programs can rob colors from other programs. This rule doesn't apply to VNC, though; 16-bit displays tend to create corrupted color maps. This problem may be fixed in the future, though.

- **Font path**—The default vncserver script uses the default font path for the server. You can adjust it in the section that's commented Add font path and color database stuff here. The relevant line adds a font path using the -fp parameter to the $cmd string, which is ultimately used to call Xvnc. You can even configure VNC to use a font server, as described in Chapter 15.

- **Default window manager**—The default vncserver script includes a variable called $defaultXStartup, which stores the contents of the default user startup script. The vncserver script writes this file to the user's directory the first time the user runs the script. The default window manager is `twm`, which few people use today. You can adjust this default by changing the `twm` call to a call to whatever window manager or desktop environment you like, such as `startkde`, `sawmill`, or `icewm`. Adjusting the `vncserver` script will only affect the default for users who have not yet run the script, though. Consult the upcoming section, "Customizing Individual Users' Settings," for information on adjusting existing users' configurations.

Even if you're not familiar with Perl, you can peruse the script to find more advanced features you might want to adjust. Mostly the script sets options to be passed to `Xvnc` by adding them to the `$cmd` string, so if you can decipher the options added to that string, you can modify them. Typing **Xvnc -help &> Xvnc-help.txt** creates a text file called `Xvnc-help.txt` that contains information on available `Xvnc` options.

WARNING

> Be sure to back up the `vncserver` script before making any changes. If a change you make should render the script unusable, you'll be glad to have the backup.

One important caveat is that the `vncserver` scripts shipped with some distributions differ substantially from the original. Debian's script, in particular, is quite different from the original. That said, the advice presented here applies to them all, but you might need to go about making changes in slightly different ways. For instance, Debian's `vncserver` script creates a variable called `$fontpath` in which it holds the font path.

Customizing Individual Users' Settings

Global VNC server settings are controlled through the `vncserver` script. If your users want to change these settings themselves, they have three choices:

- **Create a customized startup script**—Individual users may copy the normal VNC server startup script to their home directories and modify these copies, as described earlier, then use their customized scripts to start the server.
- **Pass options to the script**—The `vncserver` script accepts several options that can be used to override the defaults. For instance, `-geometry` *widthxheight* sets the desktop size. These options are largely the same as the underlying `Xvnc` options.

- **Use individualized option files**—The standard VNC server script runs the ~/.vnc/xstartup script at the end of its running process. This is where the default script places commands to start a window manager and xterm window. Users may modify these files as they would ordinary X startup scripts. Some distributions alter the name or location of this script. For instance, Debian's configuration calls the /etc/X11/Xsession script, which in turn calls the user's ~/.xsession script.

On the whole, the last two options are usually the simplest. Each option has its role to play. For instance, users can set their desktop sizes with the -geometry option to the vncserver script, but not via an option file; and they can adjust the window manager they use by setting it in their personal startup scripts, but not by passing an option to vncserver. As a general rule, the vncserver options let users adjust how VNC's X server as a whole operates (similar to standard X server options), but their startup script options let them adjust how their desktop environments and window managers behave (as do their X session options in more conventional X servers).

Running an XDMCP Login Server in VNC

One potentially serious problem with VNC is the fact that, as just described, it requires you to log in using a standard remote-login protocol, launch the server, and remember the display number to connect to the correct display. This process can be tedious, and it requires you to run a conventional login server, assuming you want to allow convenient and truly remote access. One solution to these problems is to combine the VNC X server with an XDMCP server run on the local system.

The VNC X server supports management of its display by an XDMCP server, just as do most X servers. To enable this feature, you must launch the VNC X server with the -query *hostname* option, as described earlier, in "Configuring a Remote X Login Client." You can do this in any way you might normally launch any server, as described in Chapter 4. As an example, consider the following xinetd configuration entry:

```
service vnc
{
        disable         = no
        socket_type     = stream
        protocol        = tcp
        wait            = no
```

```
          user          = nobody
          server        = /usr/local/bin/Xvnc
          server_args   = -inetd -query vncserv -once
}
```

The server arguments are extremely important. Specifically, -inetd tells Xvnc that it's being run from a super server, -query vncserv tells it to call the computer vncserv for the XDMCP login prompt, and -once tells the server to quit after it's been called one time, which has the effect of terminating the VNC link after a user logs out. You can add more Xvnc options, such as -geometry or -fp, to customize the setup. This entry should be combined with an entry in /etc/services that defines the vnc port number:

```
vnc               5900/tcp
```

VNC uses port numbers 5900–5999 for normal connections, or 5800–5899 for Web browser (Java) access. Port 5900 corresponds to display 0, 5901 to display 1, and so on. Thus, this definition sets up VNC to respond to its first display (0), and to immediately present an XDMCP login prompt. Of course, an XDMCP server must be running on the system specified by -query for this to work. You can even set up multiple ports to respond to VNC clients, but configure them differently. For instance, you might set up display 0 to present an 800x600 desktop, display 1 to use 1024x768, and so on. You'll need multiple /etc/services entries to identify these servers, each with a unique name and port number. When run in this way, VNC doesn't prompt for a password; it leaves that detail to the XDMCP server. (Note that the username and password are transmitted unencrypted, unlike a more conventional VNC login.) One other feature of VNC when run like this is that it can accept multiple logins to the same port by different users, so users don't need to remember a potentially changing port number. As a rough approximation, then, when you run VNC with an XDMCP server, the effect is very similar to running an XDMCP server directly and using a remote X server. There are a few major differences, though:

- The VNC solution requires a single connection between the two computers. This may be helpful if the system at which the user sits is protected by a firewall, and it can help you reduce the number of servers that are available to the outside world.

- The VNC solution uses a VNC client where the user sits, rather than an X server. As open source software, a VNC client is inexpensive, but most X servers for Windows and MacOS are commercial software.

- The VNC protocols, as noted earlier, have their own unique quirks. When compared to a native X server on the user's computer, VNC may be superior or inferior in this respect, depending upon the quality of the X server and the users' specific needs.

- The VNC protocols, as noted earlier, tend to be slower than X protocols on most connections, although they may be faster on some, so using this solution has speed implications.

A COMPARISON OF ACCESS TECHNIQUES

Table 14.1 summarizes some important characteristics of the various access techniques discussed in this chapter. Note that some of these assessments depend upon the nature of the configuration or specific software products used. For instance, login security for a text-mode VNC login depends upon the text-mode tool used; if you use SSH to make the initial connection, your login security should be excellent, but if you use an unencrypted login protocol, that initial connection may be compromised, although if you use a different password for the VNC connection, its password will remain secure.

Table 14.1 Remote GUI Access Comparisons

Characteristic	Unencrypted Text-Mode X Login	SSH Text-Mode X Login	XDMCP X Login	Text-Mode VNC Login	VNC with XDMCP
Login security	Poor	Excellent	Poor	Poor to Excellent	Poor
Session security	Poor	Excellent	Poor	Poor	Poor
Potential for problems with firewalls	High	Low	High	Low	Low
Session persistence (log out, then back in to the same session)	Low	Low	Low	High	Low
Speed	High	Moderate	High	Low to Moderate	Low to Moderate
Potential for application problems	Low to Moderate	Low to Moderate	Low to Moderate	Moderate	Moderate

Which GUI access technique should you use? That's a question that has no simple answer. X is an excellent tool for connections between Linux or UNIX systems, particularly within a single subnet. Such systems almost invariably have all the necessary software installed already, so using X is fairly straightforward, and you'll get good speed. If you want to access Linux systems from Windows or MacOS, X is also a good choice, but you'll need to locate an X server for the non-Linux systems, and these can be costly. VNC is a less expensive choice for such environments, and it has the advantage of working in the opposite direction (you can control a Windows or MacOS system from Linux). VNC may also be worth considering for remote access when the system at which the user sits is protected by a firewall, because a firewall is more likely to block a return connection to the local X server than an outgoing VNC connection.

SUMMARY

Remote login servers are extremely useful tools, particularly in environments in which users have accounts on many systems or where you want to centralize access to certain programs by running them on a single powerful computer that's accessed from less powerful systems. The most common Linux GUI environment, X, is inherently network-enabled, and so can be a good way to provide remote GUI access. There are several ways to configure remote access via X, including using a text-mode access protocol to "bootstrap" X-based tools or using an XDMCP server to authenticate a remote X server's user. Another option is to use VNC, which is more complex than a direct X connection from a networking point of view, but often simpler from a user's point of view. There are several different ways to configure a VNC server to provide remote access, so the total range of options (via both direct X connections and VNC) is quite wide.

Providing Consistent Fonts with Font Servers

Every child in our culture learns the shapes of letters at an early age. Precisely what are those shapes, though? A single letter may be formed in many different ways. For instance, consider the letter *P* that begins the title of this chapter. In the chapter title font, this letter looks different than it does at the beginning of the second sentence of this paragraph. This, in turn, is different from a variant such as an italic *P*. These are examples of different *fonts* in use. A font is a design for all the characters in the alphabet, usually in both upper- and lowercase, as well as numbers and supporting characters such as punctuation symbols. A few exotic fonts aren't alphabetic at all; they contain nothing but special symbols. In any event, fonts are critical for modern computers because users today expect to be able to select from among many different fonts when using highly textual programs like word processors and Web browsers. Sometimes this ability is extremely important, as in electronic publishing tasks. In other cases, it's more of a convenience, as when you select a font for reading your e-mail.

One approach to font handling that's possible with Linux is to use a *font server*. This is a server that has access to a collection of fonts, and can deliver those fonts to clients on a network. It might at first seem that a font server is fairly pointless—after all, individual computers handle their own fonts quite well in the Windows and MacOS worlds, and even Linux systems are configured this way by default. There are situations, though, in which a font server can ease your administrative tasks or help you achieve goals that might not otherwise be achievable. To use a font server, it helps to understand something about the file formats used to store fonts, because these formats can be used in different ways and have different plusses and minuses. Most Linux font servers handle a limited set of tasks, defined as part of the X Window System. A few, though, expand on this set of tasks. Some programs, such as some word processors, rely upon these expanded font servers to help them do their jobs.

When to Run a Font Server

Part of a normal Linux computer's X configuration is the specification of the *font path* for that system. With XFree86, this is set using the FontPath entries in the XF86Config file (which is normally stored in /etc or /etc/X11). The font path consists of one or more locations where the X server can find font information. In the mid-1990s, Linux distributions tended to name local filesystem directories in the font path. These directories contained fonts and font configuration files. Such a configuration is still possible, and is even used today as part or all of the default font configuration for some distributions.

There are several problems with telling X to use fonts stored on a hard disk, though. For one thing, this relies upon X's capacity to handle the font formats in question. Prior to the release of version 4.0, XFree86 could not directly handle the popular TrueType font format, for instance. Adding support for a font format directly to XFree86 is fairly difficult, but a font server is a small and comparatively simple program, so support for True-Type appeared in font servers long before it became a standard part of XFree86. With XFree86 4.0, TrueType support isn't an issue, but this situation could arise again with new or expanded font formats, such as the Multiple Master format that's been growing slowly in popularity.

Another problem with storing fonts on disk is in administering a network of computers. If you have a collection of fonts you want to make available to all the computers on a network, installing them on all the computers on your network can be tedious. If you then want to add, delete, or change some of the fonts, you're in for more tedium. Using a font server permits you to centralize your font configuration; you need only configure all your clients to use a particular font server, then make additions and other changes to that one server. This can greatly ease your administrative burden.

372

Finally, font servers can sometimes deliver features that aren't present in X's normal font handling. This is particularly important for word processors, page layout programs, and other text-handling programs. X was designed with displays on monitors in mind, not paper printouts. Word processors and similar programs frequently need to perform textual operations that simply aren't supported by X's font handling. An expanded font server can provide these needs, thus simplifying the task of writing programs that manipulate text layouts, and especially those that provide what-you-see-is-what-you-get (WYSIWYG) printing.

Font servers may be run either locally, to serve fonts to a single computer, or as full network servers, to deliver fonts to many systems. Some Linux distributions today rely upon the first configuration to handle some or all of the computer's font needs in X. The latter configuration is something you'll have to design with your own network's needs in mind. Most aspects of font server configuration are identical for these two modes of operation; just a few details differ.

WARNING

In the United States, fonts cannot be copyrighted, but their implementation in computer-readable font *files* can be copyrighted. In many other countries, fonts can be copyrighted. In any event, you should check the licenses for your fonts before you make them available on a font server. A font's license might forbid such a use, or require that you pay a fee based on the number of computers that use the font.

UNDERSTANDING FONT FILE FORMATS

Broadly speaking, fonts come in two types: *bitmapped* and *outline* (or *scaleable*). These two types of fonts have very different characteristics and are best applied in different ways. Common Linux font servers support both types of font. It's important that you understand the differences between them, as well as know examples of specific font formats, so you know what their capabilities and limitations are.

BITMAPPED FONT FORMATS

Most computer font display devices, including the most common types of computer video cards and printers, break their display areas into a fine grid. Within this grid, each square (known as a *pixel*, a shortening of *picture element*) is assigned a color. In the case of a two-color display like a monochrome laser printer, the color may be only one of two values, such as

373

black or white. Color printers and modern monitors support multiple colors, but standard X font-handling only supports two colors. (You can set what those colors are, such as black and white or red and yellow, but there may be only two of them for any given letter.) Thus, each pixel of a font can be represented by a single bit. The point of all this is that computers must shoehorn fonts into a computer display, which can be considered a map of bits, or a *bitmap*. One obvious way to do this is to represent the fonts directly in this form. This is the bitmapped font approach.

As an example, consider Figure 15.1, which shows the representation for a single letter in a bitmapped font. This representation has many important characteristics, even aside from the details of which pixels are black and which are white. For instance, the grid used to represent the letter is of a fixed size. In a *proportionally-spaced* font, like the one used for most text in this book, some letters are wider than others. Thus, bitmapped font for-

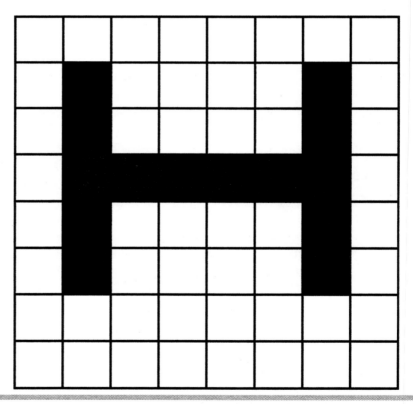

Figure 15.1   A bitmapped font precisely defines which pixels are black and which are white.

mats usually permit variable grid widths in a single font. The height is usually fixed, though. (Letters with *descenders*, which are elements that extend below the bottoms of most letters, like portions of the letters *g, j, p, q*, and *y*, simply use parts of the grid that are lower than those used by most other letters. Note that in Figure 15.1, the letter is positioned high within its grid, to permit descenders for those characters that need them.) Because the grid is fixed in size, the font appears at a fixed size on any given device, but if the resolution of the display changes, the font size will change. To support a single font on many devices, or to support variants of a font at different sizes on a single device, many different font bitmaps are required.

A display's resolution is usually measured in units called *dots per inch (dpi)*, which is the number of pixels that can be arrayed end-to-end in a single inch. Most devices have approximately the same horizontal and vertical resolutions, but sometimes these differ. Monitors usually have resolutions of between 72 and 120 dpi, while printers usually support resolutions of 144 to 1200 dpi (the lowest of these printer resolutions are used for fast or low-quality print modes, or on very old dot-matrix printers; even very old laser printers supported 300 dpi printouts). Very high-end printers and typesetting equipment support still higher resolutions. The wide variety of resolutions available, in conjunction with the need to create a new font file for every resolution and size, leads to one of the problems of bitmapped fonts: The number of font files required to support even a modest collection of font display devices is huge.

NOTE   Many printers include their own fonts, some of which may be bitmapped fonts. In the 1980s, these were commonly used instead of fonts stored on the computer. Today, some programs may use a printer's fonts, but others rely on fonts stored on the computer.

Font sizes are measured in *points*, which is a term from the printing trade. Typical sizes for body text are roughly 9–14 points, depending upon the font and the purpose of the text. Larger point sizes correspond to larger characters on the screen or page. A bitmapped font is designed to create a specific point size at a specific resolution—for instance, 12 points at 144 dpi. The same font file may be used to create a different point size at a different resolution, such as 24 points at 72 dpi, but a font designed from scratch for this new resolution might differ in subtle ways. It's possible to adjust a bitmapped font's size (for instance, displaying this 12 point, 144 dpi font at 10 points in 144 dpi), but the result is usually aesthetically unappealing,

375

because pixels will have to be added or deleted by an artistically challenged computer program.

The principal advantage of bitmapped formats is that they're simple. This simplicity translates into quick display of the fonts; the computer can move a few bits from a font it's stored in memory to the video display or printer output buffer to display text in the font. This factor was important in the 1980s and to a lesser extent in the early 1990s, when bitmap font formats resulted in noticeably snappier displays than did competing font formats. Today, CPUs are fast enough that this factor is less important.

Many different bitmap font formats exist. X supports several formats. Early versions of X used a format called Server Normal Format (SNF), but SNF fonts are rare today. Most X bitmap fonts today are in the Portable Compiled Font (PCF) format. The Bitmap Distribution Format (BDF) is another common bitmap font format for X, but it's usually not used directly by the server. Instead, you pass a BDF font through a converter program, called bdftopcf, to create a PCF file that X uses. Other OSs frequently use other font formats, and there are converters available for some of these, if you want to use a foreign bitmapped font in Linux.

NOTE XFree86 can use PCF fonts that have been compressed with gzip. Most distributions take advantage of this fact to distribute fonts in a format that consumes less disk space, so PCF font filenames typically end in .pcf.gz. You don't need to uncompress these files to make them available to X.

In addition to X, some other programs use their own bitmapped font formats. The most notable of these is the TeX layout system, which uses the Packed Font format (these fonts use the .pk filename extension). Because TeX was designed with printing in mind, not display of fonts on the screen, TeX Packed Fonts are typically created at much larger sizes, in terms of width and height in pixels, than are most other bitmap font formats.

OUTLINE FONT FORMATS

One of the major problems with bitmap font formats is that they don't scale well. If you want to support a font at different sizes on the same display device, or at the same size on a variety of devices, you need several files. Given the plethora of display devices today, and the demand of users to be able to scale their fonts in word processors and the like, this need for multiple files to create a good display is extremely unappealing. The solu-

Table 15.1   Partial Outline Description of Letter *H* from Figure 15.1

Operation	X Coordinate	Y Coordinate
Start	10,000	10,000
Line to	10,000	60,000
Line to	20,000	60,000
Line to	20,000	40,000
etc...	...	...

tion is to use an outline (aka scaleable) font format. These don't describe the fonts in terms of a bitmap; instead, they use a mathematical description of a font's curves and lines. For instance, consider Figure 15.1 again. If the 8 8 grid is replaced by one of much higher resolution (say, 80,000 80,000), the *H* described in that grid can be described in outline as a series of lines and intersections, as shown in Table 15.1.

Once the outline is complete, it's filled in with a solid color. This description offers the advantage that it can be easily scaled to just about any resolution that's desired; all that's needed is remapping the underlying coordinate grid to the actual coordinate grid. The underlying grid is of such high resolution that errors in the placement of control points are trivial. Of course, most fonts require more than simple line descriptions, as in the preceding example. Outline font formats use mathematical forms to represent various types of curves, in addition to straight lines. Many of these formats also include the capacity for *hints*, which are overrides a human designer can build into the font to improve the font's appearance at low resolutions. Without hints, outline fonts have a tendency to become illegible when displayed at small sizes on low-resolution devices like computer monitors.

NOTE   Technically, a font is a representation at a single size, and a *typeface* is a family of fonts at a variety of sizes. Thus, bitmap fonts are truly fonts, but outline fonts are more properly called typefaces. The computer industry has largely ignored this distinction, however, effectively redefining the word *font*, albeit subtly. I follow the use of the term in the computer industry in this chapter.

Because the computer has to use the outline description of a font to determine precisely which pixels will be dark and which will be light, displaying text in an outline font takes more time than does displaying the same text in a similar bitmapped font. There are various ways to minimize this problem, such as prerendering the font at a particular size and using this prerendered version. In some sense, this is part of what a font server does, because the font server, when it serves an outline font, renders it and delivers a bitmap to the client. The client doesn't know whether it's working from an outline font or a bitmap font.

Just as there are many bitmap font formats, there are many outline font formats. These include Bitstream's Speedo, Adobe's Type 1, Type 3, Type 5, and Type 42, and Apple's TrueType. (Type 42 fonts are really just TrueType fonts encoded for use on PostScript printers.) These formats differ in more fundamental ways than do bitmapped font formats, because the outline font formats can use fundamentally different types of mathematical descriptions of lines and curves. It's often possible to convert from one format to another, but such conversions frequently alter the font in subtle ways, or cause hinting information to be lost, thus degrading the font's appearance at low resolution. Whenever possible, it's best to use the font in its original format, or obtain an alternate format from the font's publisher.

Linux systems (or, more precisely, XFree86) have long supported the Speedo and Adobe Type 1 (aka *Adobe Type Manager*, or *ATM*) outline font formats. Speedo has been a fairly minor player in the font marketplace and in Linux, but Type 1 fonts are readily available on commercial font CD-ROMs and the Internet, and Linux ships with several Type 1 fonts. In the Windows and MacOS worlds, though, TrueType has outstripped Type 1's popularity, in large part because it's the standard outline font format in Windows. TrueType fonts are therefore even more available than are Type 1 fonts. TrueType fonts have a reputation for looking better at low resolutions than do Type 1 fonts, but this reputation is based largely on a handful of very well-hinted fonts. Low-cost TrueType fonts that contain little in the way of hinting often look no better on the screen than do their Type 1 counterparts.

TIP

Microsoft has made some very well-hinted TrueType fonts, intended for use with Web browsers, available from its Web site at http://www.microsoft.com/ typography/fontpack/. The easiest way to use these in Linux is to download the files intended for Windows 3.1. These are self-extracting (in Windows) zip file archives; in Linux, you can extract their contents using the unzip command. You can then install the fonts as described in the upcoming section, "Common Default Font Server Configurations." Many Web sites assume that these fonts are installed, so doing so can help your users see Web pages as they were intended to be seen.

Until version 4.0, XFree86 didn't support TrueType fonts, so the only way to use them in Linux was through a font server. Today, you can install True-Type fonts directly in X, but many distributions began using local font servers to provide support for TrueType fonts prior to the release of XFree86 4.0, and continue to use these configurations.

Just as X isn't the only tool that uses bitmapped fonts, X isn't the only user of outline fonts. There are various tools available that allow TeX to use outline fonts, for instance. Of more significance to many users, the Ghostscript program that functions as a PostScript interpreter for non-PostScript printers can use outline fonts—primarily Type 1 fonts, but also other formats, including TrueType. Some word processors require that you install fonts in them as well as in X. Most of these programs don't use font servers, although some word processors are an exception, as described in "Running an Expanded Font Server."

Running a Traditional Font Server

In this chapter, I use the term *traditional font server* to refer to a font server like the xfs program that ships with XFree86, or programs that work much like it. These programs deliver bitmapped fonts to X, based on either bitmapped or outline font files, using the standard font server protocols. These font servers are designed to support font display on monitors; they provide few or no features that help the computer coordinate on-screen fonts with those that will be printed for programs like word processors. Because XFree86 ships with xfs, chances are you already have such a font server, even if it's not currently running on your system. Configuring this server to run requires editing a few configuration files. If it's already running, you can reconfigure it to run in such a way that X servers running on other computers can access it.

Font Server Options for Linux

The most common font server in Linux is the xfs program that ships with XFree86. In some sense, this program is nothing but the font-handling code from X removed from X proper, and combined with some networking code to run as a server. This server normally resides in /usr/X11R6/bin, and is usually installed from a package called XFree86-xfs or xfs.

If you're running a version of XFree86 prior to 4.0, you may be interested in obtaining an updated font server that can handle TrueType fonts. Two such servers are available:

- **xfstt**—This package is a TrueType-only font server—that is, it doesn't serve Type 1, BDF, or any other font formats. It's a useful way to add TrueType support to older systems running pre-4.0 versions of XFree86, and it can even be used as a network font server if you only want to serve TrueType fonts. There is a major caveat, though: If your network includes machines that use different byte orders internally (such as *x*86 and PowerPC systems), you won't be able to share the server among them. This is because xfstt delivers fonts in a format that's dependent upon the CPU's internal byte order. You can download it from `ftp://ftp.metalab.unc.edu/pub/Linux/X11/fonts/`, in the `xfstt-1.1.tar.gz` file (this filename may change if the program is updated in the future).

- **xfsft**—This is a modified version of the standard XFree86 3.3.*x* xfs package. The modifications incorporate the FreeType (`http://freetype.sourceforge.net/index2.html`) TrueType renderer. The result is a font server that's capable of handling TrueType as well as Type 1, BDF, and other font formats. These modifications have been folded into the standard xfs program with XFree86 4.0, so you may be able to use the standard program even if you're running an older version of XFree86. If you prefer to use the pre-4.0 code, check the xfsft Web page at `http://www.dcs.ed.ac.uk/home/jec/programs/xfsft/`.

These two packages implement two different TrueType font renderers, which in turn are different from the ones used by Apple and Microsoft in their OSs. The result is that the same font may look quite different when displayed at the same resolution and size, depending upon the OS and (if applicable) font server you use. Both xfstt and xfsft do a good job with most fonts, but if you have problems with some fonts or if you're not satisfied with the rendering quality, you may want to investigate alternative font servers.

NOTE

Both Windows and MacOS optionally implement a feature known as *font smoothing* or *anti-aliasing*, in which some pixels are shaded grey, rather than a complete black or white. The result is that fonts appear to the human eye to have smoother outlines than they otherwise would. Some people like this effect, but others dislike it. Some X programs implement their own anti-aliasing, but most don't, and X didn't support it natively until version 4.0.2. Support for this feature is still rare, and configuring it requires taking some extra steps, which are documented at `http://sdb.suse.de/en/sdb/html/chofman_ttf_72.html` for SuSE Linux.

Although a few details differ, traditional Linux font servers are configured in largely the same way. Fonts must be placed in one or more directories, and configuration overview files listing the fonts in those directories must be created. The font server is then configured to examine those directories and make available the fonts pointed to by the directories' configuration files. The next two sections describe this process for xfs or xfsft, but xfstt's configuration isn't greatly different.

COMMON DEFAULT FONT SERVER CONFIGURATIONS

When you install Linux and XFree86, the system creates a default XFree86 configuration file called XF86Config, which resides in /etc or /etc/X11. As noted earlier, this file contains a number of FontPath entries that point to directories on your computer or font servers. For instance, you might see something like the following in the XF86Config file:

```
FontPath    "/usr/X11R6/lib/fonts/Type1/"
FontPath    "unix/:7100"
FontPath    "tcp/zapf:7100"
```

NOTE No Linux distribution ships with a font path like the preceding one by default. These three entries illustrate the three major forms that the FontPath entries may take, though.

The first of these FontPath lines illustrates the use of local fonts, without the involvement of a font server. Most Linux distributions place their fonts in several directories, so when a distribution uses fonts directly in this way, there will be several FontPath lines, each listing one directory. The system searches each directory in turn when told to look for a font of a specified name, until it's located or the path is exhausted.

The second line illustrates the use of a font server run on the local computer. The unix specifier indicates that the server is running using the UNIX domain sockets system, which permits network-like connections on the local computer. The final number (7100) is the port on which the server listens for connections. If you see such a line in your system, chances are there are few or no lines that point directly to font directories. You may adjust the configuration to add your own fonts, as described shortly in "Adjusting Font Availability."

The third line shows a network font server. The tcp in the specification indicates that this server uses standard TCP/IP networking. The name following the slash (/), zapf in this case, is the name of the font server computer. (This example lists only the machine name, not the full name. It could as easily be a full name, such as zapf.threeroomco.com.) The trailing number (7100) is the server's port number.

Font servers conventionally use port 7100, both for local servers and for full TCP/IP font servers. (A few distributions use the unusual port number of –1 for local-only connections.) This convention sometimes causes conflicts, though, because a font server other than the one you're configuring may decide to occupy port 7100. This might happen if you run a program that starts an expanded font server, such as those discussed in the upcoming section, "Running an Expanded Font Server," for its own use. In such situations, you can try another port, such as 7101 or 7102.

Font servers require configuration files. The official default location is /etc/X11/fs/conf, but many distributions use the name config rather than conf. These files specify the locations of font files and a few details of how the server operates, as discussed shortly. Font servers are normally started in SysV startup scripts, although if you add one to a system that doesn't start a font server by default, you might do so through a local startup file. The SysV files included with some distributions, such as Red Hat, carefully check the font directories to see if their font lists need to be updated. If they do, these scripts perform these updates automatically. This can make adding fonts easy, because you can simply drop the new fonts into an appropriate directory and restart the font server. On the other hand, if the utilities used to automatically generate the appropriate configuration files don't work well with a font you want to use, you may need to disable this autoconfiguration feature, at least for one font directory, so that you can create a manual configuration that works better.

ADJUSTING A FONT SERVER FOR A LAN

Most distributions that start a font server automatically take steps to ensure that it's not readily accessible from other computers. This is done as a security precaution to limit the potential for damage in case the font server has a security problem that could be exploited by outsiders. Therefore, if you want to make your font server available to other computers, you must do one of two things:

- Make a *second* font server instance available in addition to the first. If you follow this path, you can modify your font server startup script or launch a second server in some other way. You may need to use the

`-config` `/path/to/config/file` option to `xfs` to tell the second server to use a different configuration file than the first.

- Modify the configuration of the font server so that the blocks that prevent it from being accessed from outside are lifted. This may be the more efficient option in many ways, but it may not be the best choice if you want to make a different set of fonts available to clients than are available locally.

NOTE You can run a font server even on a computer that doesn't run X. Of course, you must install any packages on which the server depends, which may include much of X, but you need not actually run an X server to run a font server.

There are two main ways that distributions restrict access to a font server that runs by default. Each of these methods requires a different procedure for enabling outside access to the font server:

- **No listening for TCP connections**—Red Hat 7.2 includes an option line in its `/etc/X11/fs/config` file that prevents the server from listening for TCP connections. This line is `no-listen = tcp`. The server is otherwise configured normally, and runs on port 7100. Therefore, commenting out this line, shutting down the server, and starting it up again will make the server available to any computer that connects to it on port 7100. Red Hat uses a SysV startup script called `xfs` to start and stop the server, so you can use that to shut it down and start it up again, as described in Chapter 4, Starting Servers.

- **Port -1**—Mandrake 8.1 configures its font server to run on port −1, which is highly unusual and effectively prevents outside connections. To change this configuration, you must edit the startup script file (`/etc/rc.d/init.d/xfs`) so that the server starts on another port. Locate the line that begins `daemon xfs -port -1` and change the port number from -1 to 7100, or to some other positive port number. You must also edit your `/etc/XF86Config` file (or, depending upon your X server, the `XF86Config` or `XF86Config-4` file in `/etc/X11`) to look for the font server on its new port number. Locate the `FontPath` line that refers to `unix/:-1` and change it to point to `unix/:7100` (or whatever port number you used). You must then shut down and start up `xfs` and restart the X server (the Restart X Server button on the default Mandrake login screen can do this).

WARNING

Reconfiguring a font server for a system that is currently running X can be tricky. If the font server becomes unavailable, running programs may hang for lack of access to fonts. It's therefore best to reconfigure the font server using text-mode programs from a text-mode login. The SysV scripts for xfs used by both Red Hat and Mandrake *do not* implement your changes if you pass them the restart option, so you must explicitly send them the stop option and then start them anew with start.

After adjusting the font server to deliver fonts on your network, you should be able to point other systems' X servers at the one you've reconfigured. You can do so by adding a FontPath entry to the computers' XF86Config files. This entry should resemble the tcp example shown earlier, but of course point to your font server computer and use its port number. Depending upon what fonts are installed on each computer, you may be able to remove some FontPath entries from the client systems, but this may increase the load on the font server. To minimize the load on the font server, add its entry *after* all other FontPath entries on the clients. This will cause the clients to use their own local fonts whenever possible.

WARNING

If you configure a computer to *only* use an external font server, that system's X installation will become unusable should the font server become unavailable. It's generally best to leave a distribution's default font installation untouched, and add a font server to the existing font path. (You might want to trim fonts from some distributions, though; some come with a huge number of fonts that you may not like. You should leave the core X fonts intact, though.)

You should be concerned about the security of your font server. If you're on an isolated LAN without Internet connectivity, this may not be a major concern, but running a font server on a computer that's exposed to the Internet can be a security risk, albeit a modest one. Font servers are typically not very complex, and they don't require passwords, so you won't run into password security issues with them. Like all servers, though, font servers can potentially be buggy, and it's conceivable that some future font server bug will lead to the potential to compromise the server computer. For this reason, I recommend running font servers for other computers only on networks that are at least somewhat isolated from the Internet—for instance, on a subnet that's protected by a dedicated firewall computer. This dedicated firewall should block access to your font server's port from external computers. You should also seriously consider configuring iptables to block access to this port from anything but known local computers, as described in Chapter 25, Configuring iptables.

Adjusting Font Availability

Much of the point of running a font server is to make it comparatively easy to adjust the font configuration for an entire network of Linux or UNIX computers. (X servers for Windows, MacOS, and other OSs can also sometimes use remote font servers, so you can provide a consistent set of fonts even for X servers in these OSs, as well.) There are two steps to adjusting the fonts made available through a font server: adjusting the font server's font path (which is distinct from the X server's font path), and adding or removing fonts from the individual directories in the font path.

Changing a Font Server's Font Path

The font server's font path is set in the server's configuration file (typically /etc/X11/fs/config or /etc/X11/fs/conf). The font path isn't set using FontPath keywords, as in XF86Config; instead, this file uses the catalogue keyword, thus:

```
catalogue = /usr/X11R6/lib/X11/fonts/75dpi:unscaled,
            /usr/X11R6/lib/X11/fonts/Type1,
            /usr/X11R6/lib/X11/fonts/TrueType,
            /usr/X11R6/lib/X11/fonts/75dpi
```

This listing may span multiple lines. Commas separate directories in the font path. The last entry lacks a trailing comma; this signals the end of the list. If a directory is followed by the string :unscaled, this indicates that bitmapped fonts in this directory are to be served only if their sizes match the requested sizes *exactly*. If this string is omitted, the font server scales a bitmapped font (usually quite poorly) to match a request, if the name matches but the size doesn't. (This convention is also used in the XF86Config font path specification.) Thus, in the preceding example, the font server uses bitmap fonts from the 75dpi directory that exactly match the size of a requested font. If such a match isn't made, the system tries to find a match in the Type1 and TrueType directories, before going back to 75dpi to provide a scaled bitmap font as a last resort.

You can add or delete entire font directories by modifying this list. You might want to add a directory containing fonts you've collected from assorted sources, or a directory with fonts from a font CD-ROM. Some distributions ship with directories filled with distribution-specific fonts. If you don't want to serve these, you can eliminate them from the list. (Be sure to remove the comma from the last directory in the new list, though, if you remove the original final item.)

Adding Fonts to a Font Directory

The tricky part of X font server configuration is setting up the font directory configuration files. These files are called fonts.dir, and their format is deceptively simple looking in summary:

```
number
font-filename1 XLFD1
font-filename2 XLFD2
...
```

The first line contains a number that specifies how many fonts the file describes. Each subsequent line describes one of these fonts. Each of these lines begins with a font filename, such as goodfont.ttf or t1f32.pfb. The specified font file must exist in that directory.

NOTE   Type 1 fonts come in a multi-file format. The Printer Font Binary (PFB) file contains most of the font data, and is the filename you normally list in the fonts.dir file. Alternatively, you may list a Printer Font ASCII (PFA) file, which contains the same data but in a slightly different format. Additional filenames may end in .pfm, .afb, .afm, and others. Other utilities may use these files, but they aren't strictly necessary for the font server itself.

The rest of the line is consumed by an X Logical Font Descriptor (XLFD), which is a string that describes the font. An example looks like this:

```
-bitstream-charter-medium-r-normal--0-0-0-0-p-0-iso8859-1
```

This string consists of a series of fields, separated by dashes (-). Information in these fields is the font foundry (bitstream); the font family name (charter); the font's weight, such as light, medium, or bold (medium); the slant, such as regular or italic (r); the width (normal); an additional style name (unused here); assorted size information (the string of 0 values, which denote that the font is scaleable); spacing, namely monospaced or proportional (p); average width (again, 0 for a scaleable font); and the encoding (iso8859-1).

The XLFD can be tricky to set up manually, because it contains a lot of unlabelled information that tends to blur together in the human eye. A single typo can render the font unusable. Fortunately, there are programs that can help you create an XLFD for a font, or even a complete fonts.dir file for an entire directory.

NOTE   An X font server, like the underlying tools in many other font-handling systems, may use several font files for a complete font family. For instance, you may want to use Times in a word processing document, and apply italic, bold, or other styles to this font. In a full font installation, these variants are actually different fonts, derived from separate font files, each with its own XLFD entry in the appropriate fonts.dir file. Many word processors and other programs can derive an approximation of bold, italic, and similar attributes, but using customized files almost always produces noticeably better results, especially for italics.

The utility to create a fonts.dir file from a directory of Type 1 fonts is called type1inst. This utility ships with many Linux distributions, but it's usually not installed by default. Once you've installed the program, you can change into a directory with Type 1 fonts and run the program, thus:

```
# type1inst
```

The program will look through your font files, extract font names and other XLFD information, and create a fonts.dir file based on this information. It will also report to you on its progress and give a summary of its actions. For instance, it may tell you that it created 21 entries in fonts.dir, one of which was for a font for which it couldn't determine the foundry. You may want to edit the fonts.dir file that type1inst creates to smooth over any inconsistencies, such as fonts in the same family that list different foundries. X uses the information in fonts.dir and ignores the information that's embedded in the fonts, so changing such details will not cause problems for X. Indeed, leaving inconsistencies intact can cause problems, such as an inability to obtain a variant of a font when you select it because the foundry information doesn't match.

A similar program exists for TrueType fonts. This program is known as ttmkfdir, and is part of the FreeType library used by xfsft and XFree86 4.0. It works much like type1inst, but you must specify the output filename with the -o parameter. Also, ttmkfdir often omits fonts that are useable but that lack some characters. You can force inclusion of such fonts with the -c parameter. In sum, you can use this program by changing into a directory that contains TrueType fonts and issuing the following command:

```
# ttmkfdir -c -o fonts.dir
```

If you find that some fonts are causing problems, you can try this without the -c option. This may create a shorter list of fonts, but the fonts on the list will be more likely to work.

WARNING

!

Used as described, both typelinst and ttmkfdir overwrite any existing fonts.dir file. If you've added fonts to a directory, you may want to back up the existing file so you can restore it or use only the new entries from the new file. As already mentioned, you may need to edit the automatically created file, and if such edits have been done in the current file, you probably don't want to lose them.

Once you've changed your fonts.dir file, you must restart the font server, as described earlier. You should then either restart all the X servers that use the font server or issue the following command to have the X servers refresh their lists of available fonts:

```
# xset fp rehash
```

If you fail to do this, your X servers won't make new fonts available. If you deleted fonts and if users try to use them, the X server may appear to hang as it tries to retrieve the font, so this step is very important if you delete fonts.

RUNNING AN EXPANDED FONT SERVER

Unfortunately, X's font handling is fairly primitive by the standards of most desktop OSs at the start of the 21st century. Most users notice this in the awkward methods required for adding fonts and in poor font displays in many programs, particularly if the font path isn't set up correctly or if the system uses the default fonts, some of which aren't as good as their counterparts in other OSs. At least as important, though, is the fact that X's font system wasn't designed for integrating screen fonts with printer fonts. This fact, and other design limitations in X's font handling, make the task of creating a smooth interface between screen fonts and printed fonts difficult for applications in which this is important, such as word processors and desktop publishing packages. For this reason, there are various alternatives to traditional font servers available in Linux. Many of these are implemented internally to specific programs, but at least one is a full-fledged font server that can be used by many programs.

The most notable expanded font server for Linux is known as FontTastic (http://www.bitstream.com/categories/developer/fonttastic/). This is a commercial program that functions as an X font server *and* provides additional capabilities to applications that are written with FontTastic in mind. Specifically, FontTastic can deliver information such as an outline representation of a font, the raw font data, and kerning information. This information isn't readily obtained through a traditional font server, or from fonts handled directly by the X server. This information allows programs to do things that they might not otherwise be able to do, at least not without some other way around X's font-handling limitations. For instance, consider a word processor. If a word processor uses X's conventional font handling, a user may specify a standard X font for use in a document. When it comes time to print, though, the word processor must somehow tell the printer about the font in question. Assuming the printer is a PostScript printer, this means either telling the printer to use one of its built-in fonts or downloading the font to the printer. If the font chosen by the user is some non-standard font, though, the only way the word processor might be able to send the font is as a bitmap, because that's how it's delivered to X applications. Without knowing the printer's resolution, the word processor may have to guess what resolution to use, request characters at that resolution from the font server, and paste the results together. The result probably won't be very good.

With FontTastic, on the other hand, the word processor can request the raw font data to embed in the document, which is a superior solution because it produces a higher-quality output with less effort. (If the font is a True-Type font, the word processor might be able to convert it to a Type 42 font if it knows the PostScript printer can handle this format, or it may need to request the font in raw outline form and effectively reconstruct the font. This is more work, but will produce a cleaner result than would an attempt to print with bitmaps.) The word processor can also utilize improved information on character sizes, spacing, kerning, and so on to produce better-looking output.

Because of its commercial nature, FontTastic hasn't been widely adopted as a standard tool in the Linux community. It is used, however, by at least two major commercial programs for Linux: Corel's WordPerfect Office 2000 (which has now been discontinued) and VistaSource's ApplixWare Office (http://www.vistasource.com/products/axware/). If you run either of these programs, the package installs FontTastic and runs it automatically when its master program runs. You can create a configuration that allows other computers to use FontTastic as a conventional font server, thus simplifying your overall network font configuration requirements.

(Studying the details of FontTastic's implementation may take some effort, though.)

FontTastic isn't the only way around the problem of the disconnect between the screen and the printer. Some tools, like TeX, avoid the problem by focusing on the printer, and leaving screen fonts to fall where they may—TeX is a page description language, so TeX users edit documents using text editors that may or may not display the document in anything resembling the ultimate fonts. Other programs integrate screen and printer fonts by ignoring X's font handling. For instance, WordPerfect 8 used a very different model than its successor; version 8 of the program requires users to install fonts in WordPerfect, instead of or in addition to installing them in X. WordPerfect, not X or a font server, rasterizes fonts for display on the screen. WordPerfect can then download the fonts to a printer or create bitmaps that it downloads to the printer.

Another approach is to tell the program where the original font files are located. The program can then send those files to the printer for use in rendering files that X renders for the screen. This approach is simple, but X's lack of support for some of the finer font-handling features can still cause on-screen displays to have awkward spacing, and if the application doesn't use the appropriate information from the original font files, the printout will suffer from this problem, as well. None of these approaches is particularly network-oriented, so I don't cover them in any depth in this book; I mention them only because they're alternatives to the network-capable FontTastic, and because they may still use a network font server for on-screen font display.

SUMMARY

As network servers go, font servers are simple. They require no authentication and give users very limited access to the server computer. These servers convert font files in any of several different formats into bitmaps of specific sizes, at the request of font server client programs (typically X servers running on other computers). Running a font server for use on a single computer may allow you to add fonts of a type that's not directly supported by your X server, or you may be able to use an expanded font server to provide applications with extra font information. Network font servers allow you to quickly and easily add or change the fonts available on a large number of computers by centralizing the font configuration in one location. Adding fonts can still be a tedious undertaking, but if you use a font server, you at least need to do it only once.

Maintaining a
System Remotely

Remote access tools like those discussed in Chapters 13 and 14 allow ordinary users to use a computer from a distance. You can also use these tools to log on to the system and administer it from a distance. There are, however, more specialized tools that are designed for remote system administration. Some of these provide interfaces that are more friendly to new administrators, or they may be simpler to use than conventional administration through editing text files. All provide at least minimal help and configuration hints that can be useful even for experienced administrators. This chapter covers two general-purpose remote administration tools (Linuxconf and Webmin) and one tool that's specific to a single server (the Samba Web Administration Tool, or SWAT). This chapter concludes with a look at the unique security issues surrounding remote administration tools.

WHEN TO RUN REMOTE SYSTEM MAINTENANCE TOOLS

Specialized remote system maintenance tools are most useful when you want a dedicated and easy-to-use interface for administering a system from a distance. These tools can also be used locally—Linuxconf has both local and Web-based interfaces, but any of these tools' Web-based interfaces may be accessed from the local computer. In fact, the main aspect of these tools' utility lies in their easy-to-use interfaces rather than in their remote access features. Conventional text-based and even GUI administrative tools can be used remotely via remote login protocols like those discussed in Chapter 13, Maintaining Remote Login Servers, and Chapter 14, Handling GUI Access with X and VNC Servers.

Many new Linux administrators find traditional text-based administration intimidating, so GUI administrative tools, including those discussed in this chapter, can help them handle a Linux system. Even experienced system administrators can benefit from such tools when configuring specific systems, since few administrators fully understand every detail of every subsystem on a Linux computer. Ideally, these tools can help prevent misconfiguration by eliminating the possibility of entering typos in critical configuration files and catching certain types of improper configurations. In practice, it's still possible to misconfigure a system using a GUI or remote administration tool, so you should still exercise caution when you use such a tool. Ultimately, a good understanding of the subsystem you're configuring and its interactions with related subsystems will help you more than any GUI administrative tool.

Two of the tools discussed in this chapter, Linuxconf and Webmin, are designed as general-purpose tools to administer many different subsystems. As such, they can be good for configuring the system in broad strokes, but they lack the features needed to handle the more subtle aspects of many complex subsystems. A few of these subsystems support their own specialized administrative tools. Samba's SWAT is one such tool; there's very little you can do by editing Samba's configuration file manually that you can't do with SWAT. As a Samba-specific tool, though, SWAT isn't useful for administering non-Samba features of a Linux system.

All of the remote administration tools described in this chapter operate using HTTP (Web) protocols. Thus, you access these tools using a Web browser. By default, these tools don't work on a standard Web server port, so you can use them even if the system also runs a Web server. You must remember the port number and include it as part of the URL, as described in the following sections for each tool.

THE CHALLENGE OF A CROSS-DISTRIBUTION CONFIGURATION TOOL

All of the tools discussed in this chapter work on a wide variety of Linux distributions. One difficulty in designing such a configuration tool is that the details of what these tools must do varies substantially from one distribution to another. For instance, as discussed in Chapter 4, Starting Servers, different distributions may use different methods of starting the same servers. Some use `inetd` and others use `xinetd`, SysV startup script locations and numbers differ between distributions, configuration file locations differ between distributions, and so on. This isn't a problem for distribution-specific tools like SuSE's YaST, but tools like Linuxconf and Webmin face a challenge in working with many different distributions.

The answer to this challenge, in the case of both Linuxconf and Webmin, is to rely upon configuration *modules*. The configuration tool itself provides nothing more than a framework—code to interact with network clients, ways to allow users to select options and enter free-form strings for things like hostnames, and so on. The configuration tool relies upon modules that fill in the details, such as file locations, information on the format of server configuration files, and specific information that must be collected to configure the subsystem in question. Modules exist for general configuration, such as configuring SysV startup scripts or /etc/inittab settings, and for specific server packages, such as Apache, sendmail, and Samba. These modules can be modified for specific distributions or for specific server packages. When you install a distribution that comes with Linuxconf or Webmin, the configuration package includes modules for the servers included with the distribution, or the modules may come with the individual packages. When you install a configuration program from its home Web site, you must obtain a set of modules for your distribution. Fortunately, these module sets are readily available for most distributions, and usually ship with the configuration tool itself.

The existence of configuration modules makes tools like Linuxconf and Webmin extremely flexible, but they can also pose challenges. Specifically, if modules aren't kept up to date to reflect changes in the systems they're meant to administer, the tools can become unreliable. This may manifest in terms of an inability to configure an updated server, as errors in such a configuration, or even in unreliable operation of the configuration tool itself. These problems have been particularly troublesome for Linuxconf, and Red Hat (its main associated distribution) has ceased installing Linuxconf by default, as of Red Hat 7.1.

Server-specific configuration packages, such as SWAT, have an easier time because they don't need to deal with so much variability. For instance, SWAT needs to read just one configuration file (Samba's `smb.conf`). Although this file's location may vary from one system to another, SWAT itself is generally compiled at the same time as Samba, so it can be compiled with the same default location. (You may also specify a nonstandard location when you launch SWAT.) Thus, tools like SWAT don't usually rely upon configuration modules.

RUNNING LINUXCONF REMOTELY

Linuxconf is most strongly associated with the Red Hat and Mandrake distributions, which have traditionally shipped with Linuxconf as their default GUI configuration tool. Linuxconf wasn't developed by Red Hat or Mandrake, though, and it works with many other distributions, including Caldera, Debian, Slackware, and SuSE. The program's home page is `http://www.solucorp.qc.ca/linuxconf/`, from which you can obtain it in tarball and RPM formats.

Linuxconf includes both local (text-based and GUI) and remote (Web-based) operation modes. To use it remotely, you must enable the Linuxconf Web-based operation, which is disabled by default in most installations. Using Linuxconf in its Web-based mode is much like using it in its local text-based or GUI modes, although the displays look somewhat different.

CONFIGURING LINUXCONF TO WORK REMOTELY

A default installation of Linuxconf works in text mode, and usually in one of two GUI modes (most distributions that come with Linuxconf favor the GNOME-Linuxconf GUI, but Solucorp officially favors another called Linuxconf-GUI). There's also a Java-based GUI in the works. The default installation doesn't enable the Web-based interface, so you must do that yourself. This entails both running Linuxconf as a server and configuring it to accept logins via the network.

Running the Linuxconf Server

The most common method of running Linuxconf as a server is to run it from a super server such as `inetd` or `xinetd`. To run it in this way, you must ensure that your `/etc/services` file contains an entry that identifies the Linuxconf port, as follows:

```
linuxconf    98/tcp
```

You must also configure your super server to handle Linuxconf. To do this, have the super server run the `linuxconf` binary with the `--http` option. For instance, an `/etc/inetd.conf` entry for Linuxconf might resemble the following:

```
linuxconf  stream  tcp  wait  root  /bin/linuxconf  linuxconf --http
```

If your system uses `xinetd` and ships with Linuxconf, the Linuxconf package probably includes a startup file called `linuxconf-web` or `linuxconf` in the `/etc/xinetd.d` directory. As described in Chapter 4, you should ensure that this file does not have a line that reads `disable = yes`; if it does, change `yes` to `no` to enable Linuxconf's remote access.

Authorizing Remote Access

Once you've configured your super server to run Linuxconf, you can use any Web browser to reach the Linuxconf server; you merely type the computer's hostname, a colon, and 98 as the URL. For instance, you might type `http://remote.threeroomco.com:98` in a Web browser to administer `remote.threeroomco.com`. You can use any Web browser on any platform, so you can administer the Linux computer from a Linux system, a Windows system, or just about any other computer.

Although Linuxconf should be responsive at this point, it probably won't do much good. The default configuration allows Linuxconf to display a simple screen that summarizes what Linuxconf is, but if you click the Enter button to begin administering the system, you'll see an error message; this is a security measure. You must do more than enable basic Linuxconf operation; you must also authorize the program to accept network connections. You'll also probably want to limit the systems from which you may administer a computer via Linuxconf. The simplest way to make these changes is to use Linuxconf locally, via its text-based or GUI interface. To do so, follow these steps:

1. Start Linuxconf by typing **linuxconf** in a root shell. If you're running in text mode or if the Linuxconf GUI tools aren't installed, you'll see a text-mode menu appear. If you're in X and the Linuxconf GUI tools are installed, you'll see a new Linuxconf window appear. Figure 16.1 shows the window used by Linux Mandrake. Those used by other distributions may look slightly different, but similar options should be available.

2. Select Config ➤ Networking ➤ Misc ➤ Linuxconf Network Access Options. This should produce a set of options like those shown in Figure 16.2, but the fields will be blank. (Again, some systems display this information slightly differently, such as in a single window along with a listing of Linuxconf modules to the left.)

3. Check the Enable Network Access button. This tells Linuxconf to respond to network access attempts.

4. In the first field labeled Network or Host, enter **127.0.0.1**, and in the first field labeled Netmask (Opt), enter **255.255.255.255**. This tells Linuxconf to accept connections from the host computer itself.

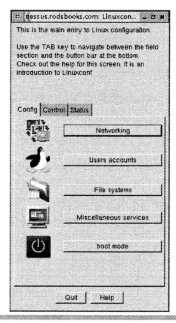

Figure 16.1 Different Linuxconf packages provide different default displays, but most provide a similar set of options.

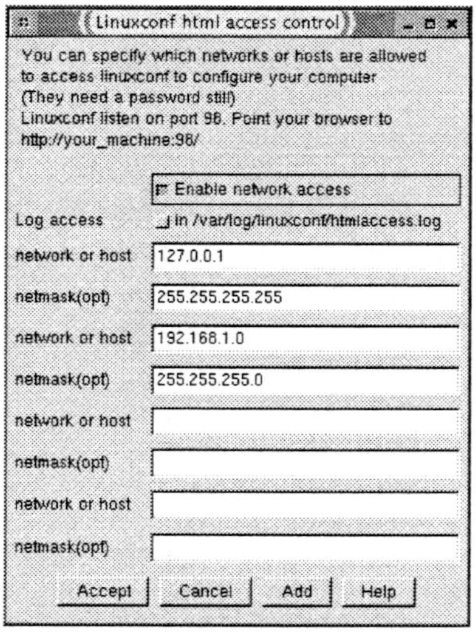

Figure 16.2 You can enable Linuxconf network access and specify what systems may access Linuxconf from one menu.

5. In the second field labeled Network or Host, enter the IP address of the computer from which you want to access Linuxconf, or an address for a network block that's to be given administrative access. Enter an appropriate netmask in the following Netmask (Opt) field. For instance, Figure 16.2 shows the system configured to accept connections from any computer on the 192.168.1.0/24 network.

6. Repeat Step 5 for any additional networks or computers you care to add, using subsequent Network or Host and Netmask (Opt) fields.

7. Click Accept, Dismiss, and Quit in the various windows or tabs to save your changes and exit from Linuxconf. The tool may inform you that the system isn't synchronized with the configuration you've created. If so, click Do It to have Linuxconf activate your changes.

At this point, Linuxconf should be configured to accept remote access from the local computer and from any other computers you specified in Step 5. Other systems will only get the basic introductory screen, as noted earlier. (If you use a firewall or some other tool to provide redundant security, would-be intruders won't even get that far.)

USING WEB-BASED LINUXCONF

To use Linuxconf's Web interface, you type `http://hostname:98` in your Web browser's URL field, where *hostname* is the hostname or IP address of the computer in question. You'll first get an introductory screen that describes what Linuxconf is. This screen will have a button called Enter. Click it to obtain a dialog box in which you enter a username and password (you must use the `root` account or some other account that's authorized to administer the system through Linuxconf). You'll then see the main Linuxconf configuration menu, as shown in Figure 16.3.

To configure the system, you click options in your Web browser just as you would select links in Web pages. The first click or two is likely to produce lists of other configuration areas, but eventually you'll reach a screen in which you can enter information in text-entry fields, toggle options, and so on. For instance, if from the display in Figure 16.3 you click Networking in the Config area, and then click Linuxconf Network Access in the Misc area, you'll see the page shown in Figure 16.4, which is equivalent to the dialog box shown in Figure 16.2 and discussed earlier. You can disable network access or change the computers that may access Linuxconf in this way.

One critical difference between Linuxconf's Web-based and GUI or text-based interfaces is that the Web-based interface typically requires less in

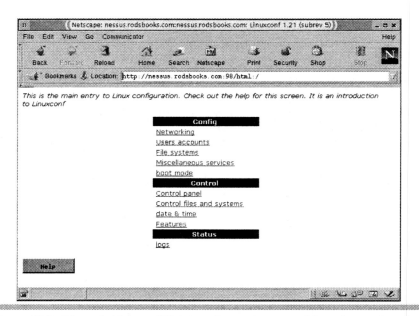

Figure 16.3 The main Linuxconf Web-based menu is comparable to the text-based or GUI menu (see Figure 16.1).

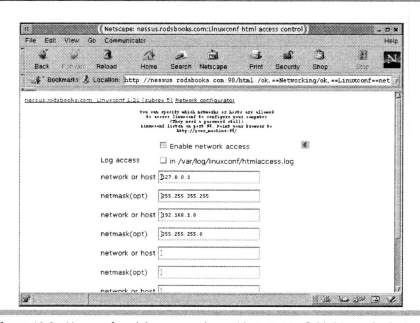

Figure 16.4 Linuxconf modules commonly provide text-entry fields, binary checkboxes, selectable lists, and other methods of setting configuration options.

the way of confirming button-presses. Although not shown in Figure 16.4, that page includes an Accept button (you'd need to scroll the Web page to see it). Click that button to accept any changes you enter, and the job is done. Using local interfaces, Linuxconf requires more in the way of button presses to exit from a module and activate the changes.

WARNING

Be sure to click the Accept button if you intend to make changes to a configuration. You can use a browser's Back button to back out of a Linuxconf module without activating its changes, so be sure to use the exit method you intend. (Some modules use a word other than Accept to activate their changes.)

As shown in Figures 16.1 and 16.3, Linuxconf uses a hierarchical structure to organize its configuration modules. The best way to learn what's available is to browse through the options—but if you don't intend to make any changes, be sure to use your browser's Back button to exit from a module, not the Accept button in the configuration page. Sometimes you might think a module should be in one location, but it will be in another. Also, you can't configure some tools through Linuxconf, either because the module doesn't exist or because it doesn't match what's installed on your system. For instance, if Linuxconf looks in /etc for the configuration file, it won't work if the file is stored in /usr/local/etc. Version mismatches can also cause problems if Linuxconf doesn't understand options that have been added to a recent version of a program, or if Linuxconf tries to use options that aren't supported if you install an older version of a program.

When you're done using Linuxconf's Web interface, it's best to exit from the Web browser. Linuxconf will eventually time out the connection, but there's no explicit exit option, and without that, anybody who has physical access to the computer you used can make changes to the configuration. You might also accidentally change some option if you leave a Web browser linked to Linuxconf.

RUNNING WEBMIN

Webmin (http://www.webmin.com/webmin/) is conceptually similar to Linuxconf in that it's a configuration system that's designed to operate on a variety of Linux distributions. Webmin explicitly supports a somewhat broader range of distributions, though, as well as non-Linux UNIX-like systems such as Solaris, FreeBSD, and MacOS X. (A complete list is available at http://www.webmin.com/webmin/support.html). Thus, configuring and using Webmin is similar to configuring and using Linuxconf. Because Webmin is designed primarily as a network configuration tool, though, initial configuration to accept remote logins is somewhat less involved than it is with Linuxconf.

CONFIGURING WEBMIN

Of the major distributions discussed in this book, only Mandrake ships with Webmin (it's planned for inclusion with the upcoming Debian 3.0, though). For other distributions, you can obtain the package from the Webmin Web site, which hosts the program in RPM and tarball formats. Installing the RPM is simplest if you're using an RPM-based distribution, because the RPM includes a script that detects your distribution type and configures the server appropriately; you do not need to do anything else to get it running. If you install the tarball, you must run a script and answer questions about your system to get the program running. The procedure for doing so is as follows:

1. As root, change to a directory that will host the Webmin subdirectory. The Webmin documentation suggests /usr/local, but other locations work as well. One other logical possibility is /opt.

2. Unpack the Webmin package with a command such as **tar xvfz /path/to/webmin-version.tar.gz**, where */path/to* is the directory in which you've stored the archive and *version* is the version number. This will create a subdirectory called webmin-*version* in which the Webmin files reside.

3. Change to the new Webmin directory by typing **cd webmin-version**.

4. Type **./install.sh** to run the installation script. This script asks you a number of questions about your system, such as the path to your Perl binary. Of particular importance is the question of which distribution you're using, followed by the version number of that distribution. You'll also have to enter an administrative username and password, which you'll subsequently use to access the Webmin server. When the script finishes, it starts Webmin so you can begin using it immediately.

NOTE Webmin is written entirely in Perl, so there's no need to compile the program; you can install the same package on any system, no matter what type of CPU it has. You do need to have a working Perl installation, though. Perl ships with all major Linux distributions, and is usually installed by default.

Webmin itself is configured through files that normally reside in /etc/ webmin (you can change this directory if you install the tarball). You probably won't need to change any of these files, but if you do, the ones that are most likely to need attention are config and miniserv.conf. Both of these files contain configuration information such as the port number to which Webmin listens by default, the system name, and the type of the host OS. In addition, the miniserv.users file contains the administrative username and password. (If you installed from RPM, the system uses root as the administrative username and copies the root password from /etc/passwd or /etc/shadow; if you installed from the tarball, you had to enter this information manually.) Subdirectories of /etc/webmin contain information relevant to specific servers and subsystems that Webmin handles.

The standard configuration for Webmin uses a SysV script to start the server. This script in turn uses the /etc/webmin/start script to actually call the Webmin Perl scripts.

Using Webmin

In broad strokes, using Webmin is similar to using Linuxconf; you enter the URL for the Webmin server (including the 10000 port number) in a Web browser, which then displays a prompt for a username and password. Figure 16.5 shows the resulting Webmin configuration screen for one system. Like Linuxconf, Webmin organizes its configuration tools into separate categories, but they don't nest as deeply in Webmin as in Linuxconf. Chances are most of what you'll do will be in the System and Servers tabs. The Webmin tab is used to configure Webmin itself, Hardware to adjust hardware (such as partitions), and Others to set a few miscellaneous items.

When you click the icon for an individual server or subsystem, you may be greeted by a final configuration screen or by a list of components of that specific server or subsystem. For instance, the DNS server configuration provides suboptions for logging, files, and so on, as well as for each zone served by the DNS server, as shown in Figure 16.6. Such nesting may continue for several levels. Eventually, you'll reach a screen in which you can alter specific settings by using text entry boxes, check boxes, lists, and so on, as shown in Figure 16.7. When you do so, click the Save button to save your changes. Many server configuration modules include a button called Apply Changes to force the server to pick up a changed configuration. Others include a Stop or Start button, depending upon whether the server is currently running; you can click the Stop button, followed by the Start button, to activate your changes.

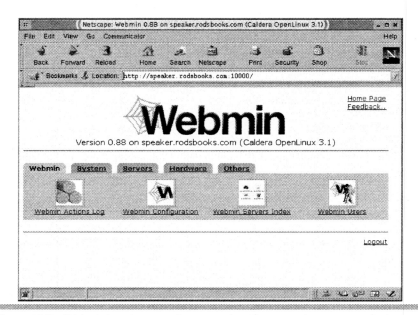

Figure 16.5 Webmin's main screen lets you select the general category and, when that's chosen, the specific subsystem you want to configure.

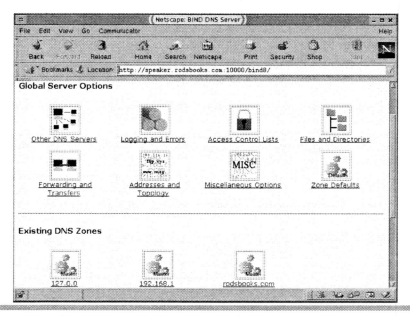

Figure 16.6 Many servers and subsystems include their own set of links to let you manage a server in reasonably sized configuration screens.

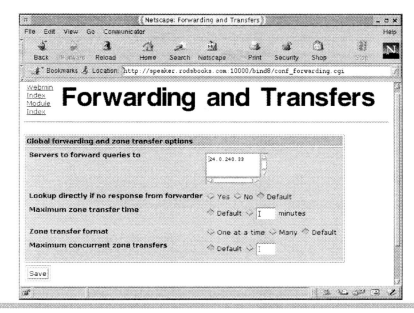

Figure 16.7 You enter information in Webmin screens much as you do in Linuxconf screens.

The main list of modules in Webmin may include servers that aren't running, or even installed, on your system. If you click such a server, you'll receive a message stating that Webmin couldn't find the configuration file, and suggesting that the module configuration may be wrong or the server may not be installed. If you've installed a server from an unusual source, you can click the Module Configuration link in this message to go to the configuration page for that Webmin module. If you know where the configuration files actually reside, you can change that information to have Webmin administer your server.

As a general rule, Webmin modules are more complete than are their Linuxconf counterparts, although there's nothing about Webmin *per se* that dictates this. On any given distribution, you might find Webmin to be better for some things but Linuxconf better for others. If you're investigating both tools, your best bet is to try both, at least on a test system.

When you're finished using Webmin, you can click the Logout link on the main page (see Figure 16.5). This action terminates your connection to Webmin, so you don't need to close down your Web browser, as is advisable when you're finished using Linuxconf.

RUNNING SWAT

The Samba Web Administration Tool (SWAT) is a much more specialized tool than are Linuxconf and Webmin. As the expanded name implies, SWAT is designed to administer just one server: Samba (which is discussed in Chapter 7, File and Printer Sharing via Samba). As such, it's not faced with so many challenges in terms of installation and configuration for multiple distributions, and it provides more complete options for Samba configuration than do Webmin or, especially, Linuxconf. SWAT is most valuable on a dedicated Samba server system, especially one that's administered by somebody who's uncomfortable with editing text files. Even for experienced Samba administrators, though, SWAT can be valuable because Samba supports many options, and SWAT's interface lets you set them without remembering their exact spelling or syntax. You can also click Help links next to options to view the smb.conf man page entries on those options. On the downside, SWAT strips comments from the smb.conf configuration file, and doesn't support the include parameter that's used to load secondary configuration files. For these reasons, experienced Samba administrators often avoid SWAT, particularly on systems with very complex Samba configurations.

CONFIGURING SWAT TO RUN

The SWAT server program is known as swat, and it can be run in any of the ways described in Chapter 4, but the most common configuration is to run it from a super server. A typical /etc/inetd.conf entry to run SWAT looks like this:

```
swat  stream  tcp  nowait.400  root  /usr/sbin/tcpd  /usr/sbin/swat
```

Distributions that use xinetd usually include a file called /etc/xinetd.d/swat in their Samba or SWAT packages, so you can check that file to be sure it doesn't include a disable = yes line. If such a line exists, remove it or change yes to no to enable SWAT. In both the inetd and xinetd cases, of course, you must restart the super server before SWAT will become available.

NOTE   Some distributions include SWAT in their main Samba packages (typically samba, samba-common, samba-server, or the like), but others place SWAT in a package of its own (typically called swat or samba-swat). Mandrake, Slackware, SuSE, and TurboLinux integrate SWAT into their main Samba packages, while Caldera, Debian, and Red Hat use a separate SWAT package.

By default, SWAT uses port 901. Both inetd and xinetd rely upon this relationship being set in /etc/services:

```
swat            901/tcp
```

This line comes standard in most /etc/services files, but it's worth checking that it exists before you try running SWAT.

USING SWAT

Once you've added SWAT to a system, you can try using it much as you use other administrative servers, except of course you need to specify port 901. For instance, you would type **http://samba.threeroomco.com:901** in a Web browser's URL entry field to access SWAT on the samba. threeroomco.com computer. As with other Web-based servers, you can use a Web browser on any platform.

NOTE Samba includes the ability to respond to NetBIOS name requests, so that SMB/CIFS clients can use their native name resolution mechanisms. SWAT doesn't include such a module, but if the client computer uses NetBIOS names in resolving Web browser URLs, the SWAT server may be accessible via the NetBIOS name, as well as its DNS hostname, assuming Samba is running. Windows clients are often configured to do this, but Linux clients aren't.

As with the other administrative servers discussed in this chapter, when you first try to access SWAT, the system asks you for a username and password. For full administrative privileges, you'll normally enter root and the root password, respectively. (You must enter the *Linux* password for the account, which may differ from the *Samba* password for the account.) If you enter an ordinary username and matching password, Samba grants access, but only to view the configuration and make changes that the user whose name you've entered can make. Normally, these are password changes. Thus, SWAT can be used as a way to allow Samba users to change their passwords. Whether you use root or an ordinary username, SWAT displays the Home page shown in Figure 16.8. You can click the icons or associated text to change to other pages—Globals, Shares, Printers, Status, View, and Password. The first three adjust the smb.conf file's global options, file share definitions, and printer share definitions, respectively. The Status page provides information such as who's using

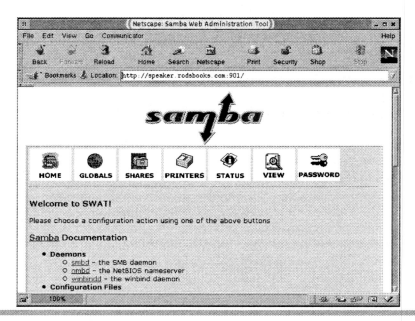

Figure 16.8 The main Samba configuration page allows you to select configuration areas or view Web-based Samba documentation.

Samba shares. The View page displays the raw `smb.conf` file, and the Password page lets you change any Samba password. The Globals, Shares, and Printers options aren't available when you enter a non-`root` username, and the Status and Password pages present a restricted set of options to ordinary users. In addition to these options, the Home page provides links to man pages and other Samba documentation.

You'll do most of your actual Samba configuration using the Globals, Shares, and Printers pages. The Globals page, shown in Figure 16.9, lets you adjust settings in the `[globals]` section of `smb.conf`—things like the computer's NetBIOS name, domain browser settings, and so on. As described in Chapter 7, you'll probably want to set the NetBIOS name, workgroup name, and password encryption options.

Both the Shares and Printers pages default to showing no information. To create or edit a share, you must take appropriate actions:

- To edit an existing share, select the share name from the selector box next to Choose Share or Choose Printer, then click the Choose Share or Choose Printer button. The information for the existing share will appear in your Web browser, and you can edit these settings.

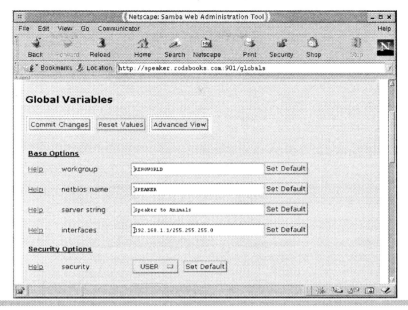

Figure 16.9 Global settings affect all Samba file and printer shares, or adjust general Samba operation.

- To delete an existing share, choose its name as just described but click Delete Share or Delete Printer.
- To create a new share, enter the name you want for the share in the text-entry field and click Create Share or Create Printer. Do not enclose the share name in square brackets ([]), as you would when editing smb.conf directly; SWAT adds the square brackets itself. After creating the share, you can edit any options you like, just as you would for an existing share.

The [homes] share has a special meaning, as described in Chapter 7, but you can create, delete, or edit it just as you would any other. Likewise, printers marked with asterisks (*) in the printer list box are default printers created by the [printers] share. You should edit the [printers] share directly rather than the asterisk-marked shares, unless you want to create a customized share for that specific printer, overriding the default [printers] share.

The Globals, Shares, and Printers pages all include buttons labeled Advanced View. (This button appears in the Shares and Printers pages only after you've selected or created a share.) The default view shows only the most commonly used Samba options. Clicking Advanced View causes SWAT to show all relevant Samba options, and changes the Advanced View button to read Basic View; clicking it returns to the original restricted range of options. Most Samba shares can be adequately configured using the basic view, but you may need to enable the advanced view for some. Setting basic view does *not* lose changes you make in advanced view, so you can use the basic view for changes even when you've made advanced changes to a share.

When you've finished entering new or changed information in the Globals page, or for an individual share in the Shares or Printers page, click Commit Changes. This writes out the changes to `smb.conf`. To have Samba acknowledge these changes, you must normally restart it. You can do so from the Status page; click Restart `smbd` and Restart `nmbd`. (Some changes might require restarting just one of those two servers, but it won't hurt to restart both.) When you're finished with SWAT entirely, it's best to exit from your Web browser to completely close the connection. As with Linuxconf, leaving a Web browser running after connecting to a SWAT server leaves the SWAT server accessible from that browser until the browser is shut down, which can be a security risk.

REMOTE ADMINISTRATION SECURITY CONCERNS

Remote system administration is a potentially huge security loophole, no matter how it's conducted—via a text-mode or GUI login or through a dedicated configuration tool like those discussed in this chapter. There are two major classes of concerns:

- **Compromised passwords**—If an unauthorized individual somehow obtains an administrative password, that person can alter your system's configuration.
- **Server bugs**—Security-related bugs have been found in many servers in the past, and it's possible that bugs will be found in remote administration tools in the future. If so, your systems may become vulnerable to attack even if your passwords are unknown by unauthorized individuals.

In both of these cases, the risks may be increased if you run a dedicated remote administrative tool in addition to a regular remote login tool, as opposed to running the remote login tool alone. As described in Chapter 13, some remote login tools send their passwords in an unencrypted form, but others (such as the Secure Shell, SSH) encrypt passwords and even subsequent data. Linuxconf and SWAT both use unencrypted passwords, so if you use only SSH locally for security reasons, Linuxconf and SWAT greatly negate SSH's advantages. Webmin may optionally use the Secure Sockets Layer (SSL; see `http://www.openssl.org`) for encryption, so Webmin can protect your passwords and other data; however, configuring Webmin to use SSL requires installing and setting up SSL. Because of the lack of encryption provided by these tools, I strongly recommend against using Linuxconf, SWAT, or non-SSL-encoded versions of Webmin on anything but a trusted local network.

The remote access tools also grant access if the user knows just one username and password. As described in Chapter 13, many remote login protocols can be configured to accept logins only from ordinary users, which means that an administrator must know *two* passwords to administer the system—an ordinary username/password pair and the `root` password (used in conjunction with `su` or a similar tool). In sum, of the remote access tools discussed in this chapter, only Webmin provides the sort of encryption features found in tools like SSH, and even at its best, Webmin is potentially slightly more vulnerable to a password that's been obtained in some way other than Ethernet sniffing.

You can reduce some of the risks of unauthorized access by limiting the systems that can connect to the administrative server. As described earlier in this chapter, Linuxconf includes tools to let you do this by specifying authorized IP addresses or network ranges. Any of these programs can be protected by TCP Wrappers or `xinetd`, as described in Chapter 4, if you start the servers from a super server, as is the default for Linuxconf and SWAT. You can also configure a firewall to limit access to the remote administration port, as described in Chapter 25, Configuring `iptables`. These measures won't limit the risks of password sniffing, though, and IP addresses can be forged or even commandeered if the intruder has physical access to a network. Thus, such procedures can't eliminate all risks, although they're important.

As a general rule, it's best to limit the number of servers a system runs, both to minimize the risk of server bugs and to restrict the number of entry points that might be abused. If a system must run a remote login server— particularly one that encrypts data, such as SSH—the safest course from a security point of view is to use that login tool to administer the system if remote administration is required; administration-specific tools like those discussed in this chapter pose an additional risk. This risk may be justified on sufficiently protected networks if administrators are more comfortable with these tools, though. Also, remote administration tools can be worthwhile if no conventional remote login servers are being run but remote administration is desirable.

You might be tempted to use limited administrative servers, such as SWAT, in place of full-access servers, such as Linuxconf and Webmin, as a security precaution. After all, if an intruder can break into SWAT, the damage that intruder can do is limited, right? This may be the case for some remote-access servers, but many provide enough leverage that an intruder could do substantial damage. For instance, somebody who breaks into SWAT can create a file share that provides full read/write access to the entire /etc directory. The intruder could use this access to alter additional key configuration files, such as activating Telnet access, adding accounts, and so on. Nonetheless, using more limited administrative tools might at least slow down an intruder.

Finally, the security precautions described here are only a start. Part IV of this book is devoted to security matters. This section highlights some of the more important issues because remote administration servers are particularly powerful tools that can be more easily abused than most other servers, if compromised.

Summary

Remote administrative tools aren't a necessity on a Linux system even if you want or need to administer the system remotely. They can be a great convenience, though, particularly when you need to administer a subsystem with which you're less than perfectly familiar. You can use these tools locally or from remote systems. Two particularly common and complete tools are Linuxconf and Webmin, both of which can theoretically handle any Linux subsystem, although in practice neither has a fully complete set of administrative modules. SWAT is another administrative tool, and is perhaps the most common specialized tool—one that administers a single server. Each of these tools can be very useful, but care must be taken in configuring and using them to minimize the security risks that they pose.

Performing Network Backups

Backing up your data is an unglamorous operation, but one that's critically important for the long-term reliability of your systems. Some networks consist of one or two large servers and a larger number of comparatively simple systems, such as X terminals, that contain little or nothing in the way of important data. In such networks, you can place backup hardware on the servers, back them up, and safely ignore the clients, except possibly for keeping a default installation backup. If a client fails, you can replace it with a new system bearing the standard configuration with minimal fuss. Other networks, though, have several servers that require backups, or client systems may house user data or other information that you can't afford to lose. Such networks require backup solutions of one sort or another. The options in this realm are quite varied, so this chapter can only scratch the surface. It begins with a broad discussion of the options available, then moves on to three specific solutions: Using tar to back up Linux or UNIX systems, using Samba to back up Windows systems, and using AMANDA to coordinate backups across a network.

Network backups can be very complex, particularly on a large network. For more information on this topic, you should read whatever documentation comes with your backup tools. There are also books on the topic, such as Preston's *Unix Backup & Recovery* (O'Reilly, 1999).

411

WHEN TO RUN NETWORK BACKUP SERVERS

In some sense, backups are most easily handled locally. If you install a tape drive or similar backup hardware in a computer, you can use software like tar, cpio, or dump to back up a Linux system without creating particularly special configurations. Attempting to perform a backup over a network adds complexity to the task, because both computers need network configurations, and the backup software must be network-aware. (You can

Backup Hardware Options

Tape drives are the most common form of backup hardware. As a general rule, the lower-cost units, such as Travan drives, use more expensive media, so by the time you buy tapes, especially for a large server or network, costs don't vary as much as the initial purchase prices might lead you to think. Small networks can often make do with a mid-range or high-end single-drive tape unit for $1,000 or so, which can typically back up 5 to 20 GB of data. Such drives generally use the *Digital Audio Tape (DAT)* or *Digital Linear Tape (DLT)* formats. Larger networks require more expensive network backup units that use DLT or various more exotic tape formats. Another option for large networks is a *tape changer*, which is a single unit that can automatically swap tapes in and out, much like a multi-disc audio CD player. Such drives present themselves to the host computer as an extra-large single-tape drive.

Tape isn't the only backup medium, though. One particularly noteworthy alternative is optical recording media, such as CD Recordable (CD-R), CD Rewriteable (CD-RW), and several recordable DVD technologies. CD-R and CD-RW drives are limited in capacity (650 MB with standard discs), and so aren't very useful for performing true network backups. These media may be useful, however, for maintaining backups of fairly static information, such as a standard installation of a client OS. Recordable DVDs have higher capacities (a few gigabytes), and so are better suited to backing up complete systems, but they're still weak as network backup media. Optical media have unusually long shelf lives (estimates for CD-R range from 10 to 100 years), so they're very well suited to archival backup duties. Using them in Linux is more complicated than is using a tape drive, because optical media need special utilities like cdrecord to be written. They can be particularly easy to restore, though, because a standard CD-ROM or DVD-ROM drive can read the media.

This chapter is written with the assumption that you'll be using a tape unit for your network backups. You may want to supplement such backups with backups of static information on optical media, though. This can make full emergency restores easier; you can restore an initial configuration using the optical media, then use that system to restore additional data from tape.

sometimes work around lack of network support in backup software by using additional tools, though.) Restoring over a network can be even more difficult, because you may need to perform the restore operation on a computer that's missing its normal package of network tools. For these reasons, it's often desirable to implement a backup policy on a small network using local backup hardware. This solution can be costly, though, particularly when the network (or at least the computers that must be backed up) grows substantially. Tape backup drives suitable for backing up workstations or small servers typically cost $100 to $1,000, and media add to those costs. Network backup drives have higher capacities and are more costly, but when considered on a per-computer basis, the cost may be much lower. Thus, one reason to perform network backups is to save money compared to individualized backups.

Network backups also offer certain convenience factors. By controlling a backup from a central location, you can eliminate backups from the tasks that individual users need to perform. The average office worker, even if given a tape backup unit, is likely to forget to perform routine backups. A centralized backup system, though, may be able to perform backups automatically and transparently to the users. (This isn't always true, though, as described shortly in the section "Types of Network Backup Solutions.")

TYPES OF NETWORK BACKUP SOLUTIONS

Broadly speaking, network backups can be performed in one of two ways: The computer that's to be backed up can initiate the backup using another system's tape drive, or the system with the tape drive can initiate the backup of another computer. I refer to the former as a *client-initiated backup* and the latter as a *server-initiated backup*. Each option has its advantages and disadvantages. This chapter discusses examples of both types of backup.

NOTE It's common to refer to the computer with the backup medium as the *backup server*, and the computer that's being backed up as the *backup client*. This terminology is in line with the usual meanings of *server* and *client* in some cases, but not in others. In the case of server-initiated backups, for instance, the backup client must normally run some type of server software that the backup server uses as a client. Although this terminology is in some sense incorrect, referring to the systems in this way greatly simplifies discussions, particularly when comparing the two types of network backups.

CLIENT-INITIATED BACKUPS

In a client-initiated backup, the backup server runs some type of server software that allows the client to access the backup hardware. The server software may be a program that's used for other purposes in addition to backup, such as rshd or Samba, or it may be a dedicated backup package. In either event, the fact that the client initiates the process has certain important consequences:

- **Scheduling issues**—If a backup should be performed regularly, you must use cron or some other scheduling tool *on the backup client* to initiate the backup. You must also have some mechanism to ensure that backups from different clients don't interfere with one another.
- **User control**—Client-initiated backups are sometimes convenient for backing up workstations, because the workstations' users can control when the backups occur and even what files to back up. A user might decide to back up just after completing a project or before going on vacation, for instance.
- **Security**—The backup clients don't need to run any server software, and so can be made quite secure. Likewise, in the case of Linux or UNIX clients, the backup process can run as root, thus providing full access to all files. The backup server, on the other hand, needs to run a server program that's accessible to all the backup clients. This is best handled by setting aside a dedicated backup server.

These characteristics make client-initiated backups a reasonable choice for operation on many small networks. Scheduling conflicts can often be resolved in a reasonable way on such networks. One important drawback is that if the backup process is placed in the hands of individual users, they may forget to do it on a regular basis. You can automate the process by using cron jobs or the like, but this requires careful planning to reduce the risk of conflicts.

SERVER-INITIATED BACKUPS

Server-initiated backups use a network client program on the backup server to open a connection to a network server program on the backup client. The backup server can then read the files from the backup client and store the files on tape. Compared to a client-initiated backup, this approach has several important characteristics:

- **Scheduling issues**—Because the backups are controlled centrally, you can more easily prevent conflicts and even schedule back-to-back backups to more effectively use otherwise idle network time, such as late at night.

- **User control**—The users of individual workstations have no control over when their backups occur. If they need a backup at a particular time, they must schedule it with the backup server or use some other means, such as backing up important files to a Zip disk.

- **Security**—All the backup clients must run some type of server program. This is most commonly a file-sharing protocol like NFS or SMB/CIFS, but in some cases a protocol like FTP might do, as well. In the case of Linux clients, the file-sharing server must provide full read access to all files to the backup server, which is a potential security risk—if a miscreant can masquerade as the backup server, the miscreant can acquire sensitive files such as /etc/shadow. The backup server, however, is less vulnerable to attack, since it needs to run only client software in order to do its duties.

The scheduling issues make server-initiated backups desirable for large networks, but the security issues may be a major concern in some cases. You can mitigate these concerns by using firewalls and other access control mechanisms to limit who may access the backup clients' filesystems. Also, dedicated backup packages like AMANDA may use techniques like setting the SUID bit on key executables to permit most of the backup processes to run as ordinary users while still allowing the package as a whole to do its job.

WARNING

Network backups pose additional security concerns for both server-initiated and client-initiated backups. If the protocol used requires a password, that password might be compromised if it's sent in an unencrypted form; likewise for data transferred in the course of the backup. Even if all data are encrypted during transfer, the security of the backup tapes can be important; if somebody steals a backup tape, or even "borrows" it for a few minutes, sensitive data such as /etc/shadow can be read from the tape, even if the file's permissions on the source computer wouldn't ordinarily allow it to be read by outsiders.

USING tar

The lowest common denominator of tape backups in the Linux and UNIX world is tar—the same program that's used to create archives for grouping multiple files into a single file for easier storage or transmission over the Internet. In fact, the name tar stands for *tape archive*. You can use tar as part of a backup procedure for a network, using either a client-initiated or a server-initiated strategy. Similar procedures apply to many other common Linux backup programs, such as cpio and dump, but the details of the commands you use with them will of course differ, so you'll need to look up the details for how to handle certain network-related options, particularly for client-initiated backups. I cover tar here both because it's the lowest common denominator and because it's used by several other tools, such as smbtar and AMANDA.

BASIC tar FEATURES

The tar utility is extremely powerful and supports a large number of options. These options come in two forms: commands and qualifiers. Commands tell tar what to do—for instance, create an archive, list the contents of an archive, or extract files from an archive. Qualifiers modify the action of commands—they're used to specify the device or file tar uses, to limit the files that might be backed up, to compress the resulting archive with gzip or bzip2, and so on. When running tar, the basic syntax is:

```
tar command [qualifiers] filenames
```

The filenames you specify are actually often directory names, possibly including the root directory (/). When you specify a directory name, tar backs up all the files and subdirectories in that directory.

Tables 17.1 and 17.2 list some of the more common tar commands and qualifiers. These are only a sample, however, particularly for qualifiers. You should consult the tar man page for information on more options.

Table 17.1 Common tar Commands

Command	Abbreviation	Purpose
--create	c	Creates an archive.
--concatenate	A	Adds a tar file to an existing archive.
--append	r	Adds ordinary files to an existing archive.
--update	u	Adds ordinary files that are newer than those in the existing archive.
--diff or --compare	d	Compares archived files to those on disk.
--list	t	Displays contents of an archive.
--extract or –get	x	Copies files out of an archive.

Table 17.2 Common `tar` Qualifiers

Command	Abbreviation	Purpose
`--absolute-paths`	P	Keeps the leading / on filenames.
`--bzip2`	I	Passes the archive through `bzip2`. (Not available on older versions of `tar`.)
`--directory` *dir*	C	Changes to the specified directory before acting.
`--exclude` *file*	(none)	Blocks *file* from being backed up.
`--exclude-from` *file*	X	Blocks all files listed in *file* from being backed up.
`--file [`*host:*`]`*file*	f	Performs backup using *file* on *host* as the archive file. (The *host* option is used in client-initiated network backups.)
`--gzip` or `--ungzip`	z	Passes the archive through `gzip` or `ungzip`.
`--listed-incremental=`*file*	g	Creates or uses an incremental backup file.
`--multi-volume`	M	Processes a multi-tape archive.
`--one-file-system`	l	Backs up or restores just one filesystem.
`--same-permissions` or `--preserve-permissions`	p	Preserves all username and permission information.
`--tape-length` *N*	L	Specifies the length of a tape in kilobytes; used in conjunction with `--multi-volume`.
`--verbose`	v	Displays filenames as they're processed.
`--verify`	W	Compares original files to archive immediately after writing it.

As an example of these options in use, suppose a computer has a SCSI tape drive, which can be accessed as /dev/st0 or /dev/nst0. You could back up the /home directory of this computer, preserving all permissions and displaying the filenames as they're backed up, with the following command:

```
# tar --create --verbose --file /dev/st0 /home
```

The abbreviations shown in Tables 17.1 and 17.2 allow for a somewhat more succinct variant of this command:

```
# tar cvf /dev/st0 /home
```

A few `tar` options deserve special discussion. These are `--one-file-system`, `--same-permissions`, `--listed-incremental`, and `--verify`. The `--one-file-system` option is particularly useful for backups because Linux systems may include virtual filesystems (such as /proc), removable media, and perhaps even regular filesystems that should not be backed up. Using

--one-file-system forces tar to back up only the directories or files you specify, so when you use this option, you should list all the partitions you want to back up. Alternatively, you could omit --one-file-system and use --exclude or --exclude-from to explicitly block directories such as /proc from being backed up.

The --same-permissions option is particularly important when backing up system files because tar sometimes loses certain permissions, particularly those that are not allowed by the current umask value. This option is important when restoring files, but not when backing them up.

The --listed-incremental option creates or uses a file that records information on the files that tar backs up. The first time the program is run with this option, the specified file is created and all files are backed up. Subsequent uses of this option cause only files that have been added or changed since the last backup to be backed up. This allows tar to create a *partial* backup, which is much smaller than the regular *full* backup. Many administrators perform full backups every week or month, and partial backups on a daily basis. This provides good protection against disaster with minimal effort. (When restoring incremental backups, though, you may find files you've intentionally deleted have been restored, because the increment procedure doesn't mark files deleted since the last backup as deleted.) In a network environment, you may want to rotate which machines receive full backups on any given day—for instance, machine1 on Monday, machine2 on Tuesday, and so on.

Finally, --verify is intended to check the accuracy of your backup. The verify pass will increase backup time substantially, but it may be worthwhile, particularly if your tape drive doesn't include its own verify feature. (Most mid-range and high-end drives do include verification in hardware, often referred to as *read-after-write*.) Any verification performed using --verify or on a second pass using the --diff command is likely to turn up some false alarms, because Linux systems are constantly active, so some files are likely to change between the backup and verify passes. Log files, files in /tmp, spool files such as mail and printer queues, and perhaps user files are particularly likely to change. If you only see a few changes in files that might reasonably have changed during the backup, there's no cause for alarm. If you see changes in other files, particularly in static files such as the contents of /usr, then it's possible that your tape, tape drive, or network connections are at fault.

Most modern tape drives support built-in compression, so there's no need to use the --bzip2 or --gzip options. Indeed, these options are potentially dangerous even on the low-end drives that lack compression features. The reason is that tar uses gzip or bzip2 to compress an entire archive, not individual files. If an error occurs when reading back a compressed archive, tar won't be able to recover, so all the data in the archive after that point will be lost. Tape drives' built-in compression algorithms are more robust against such errors; in the event of an error, you're likely to lose a file or two, but not the entire archive. Some backup programs don't use compression in this way, and so are more robust against errors. For instance, the commercial BRU (http://www.tolisgroup.com) package uses file-by-file compression when compression is enabled.

TESTING LOCAL tar AND TAPE FUNCTIONS

When setting up a backup server, you should test basic backup functions locally before introducing the network into the equation. Local backups are invariably simpler than are network backups, so if you know that local backups work, you can be reasonably confident in attributing problems with network backups to the network configuration. In addition, it's important to remember to back up the backup server itself; like any other computer, it can fail, and if it fails without a backup, the rest of your network will be at risk.

The most basic local test is to try backing up using a command like the one presented in the previous section. The trickiest part of this is in determining the correct device file to use. Four device files are common for mid-range and high-end tape devices: /dev/st0, /dev/nst0, /dev/ht0, and /dev/nht0. The first two refer to SCSI tape drives, and the second two refer to EIDE/ATAPI devices. The filenames whose names begin with n are *nonrewinding* devices—when an operation completes, the driver leaves the tape wound, so you can place multiple backups on a single tape. Device filenames without the leading n refer to *rewinding* devices, which automatically rewind the tape after every operation. Note that this is a characteristic of the *device file*, not of the hardware; every tape device has both a rewinding and a nonrewinding device file. If you have multiple tape drives, the second will have a filename that ends in 1 instead of 0, the third's filename will end in 2, and so on.

There are a few exotic hardware types that use other device filenames. For instance, some older tape drives interfaced through the floppy port and used device filenames like /dev/qft0 and /dev/nqft0. Such drives are very low in capacity and slow by today's standards, and so are unsuitable for network backups. Other drives use specialized interface hardware. Check the Linux kernel configuration for drivers for such boards.

If you have problems with a local backup, check your device hardware and check the drivers for the device. SCSI drives need both basic SCSI support and SCSI tape support enabled. Likewise, EIDE/ATAPI drives need both EIDE support and EIDE/ATAPI tape support. Be sure to check your ability to both back up and restore data; try using a small test directory, then a larger one. Use a verify function to confirm that your data are being recovered correctly.

Particularly if you want to place multiple backups on a single tape, the mt utility may be useful. This tool lets you control the tape drive, setting options such as its built-in compression and moving among various backup sets stored on the tape.

NOTE The mt man page refers to backup sets as *files*, and tar documentation often does the same. Think of the tape as a hard disk without a filesystem; your backups are really just tar files stored sequentially on the tape, hence this terminology.

You may want to experiment with tar and mt to place multiple backups on a tape using a nonrewinding tape device. The basic syntax for mt is as follows:

```
mt [-f device] operation [count] [arguments]
```

The *operation* is a command like fsf (forward space files), bsf (backward space files), rewind (rewind tape), and datcompression (set compression—send an argument of 0 to disable compression or anything else to enable it). For instance, the following string of commands creates two backups and then verifies them:

```
# tar cvplf /dev/nst0 testdir-1/
# tar cvplf /dev/nst0 testdir-2/
# mt -f /dev/nst0 rewind
# tar df /dev/nst0 testdir-1/
# mt -f /dev/nst0 fsf 1
# tar df /dev/nst0 testdir-2/
```

Most of these commands should be followed by tape activity. The first two tar commands will show the names of the files being backed up, and the last two tar commands will show the names of any files that differ between the original and the backup. The second mt command is needed when reading back the archives, but not when creating them.

PERFORMING A CLIENT-INITIATED BACKUP

A client-initiated backup using tar requires that the client have a tar program and that the backup server be running an appropriate server program to grant the client's tar program access to the tape device. There's little special that you must do on the client side, aside from changing the tar commands from those described earlier. The backup server's configuration isn't the standard one in most Linux distributions, though, so you'll have to reconfigure the backup server.

Client-Initiated Network Configurations

The --file option shown in Table 17.2 takes a filename as an option. This may be a regular disk file, a device file that corresponds to a tape device, or a path to a network resource. In this final case, the backup server must be running the rshd daemon (which is often called in.rshd). This daemon allows a remote system to execute commands on the system on which the server runs. The tar program uses this ability to pass the tar file it creates to a device file on the backup server. The rshd server comes with most Linux systems and is usually run from a super server. An /etc/inetd.conf entry to handle this server might resemble the following:

```
shell   stream  tcp  nowait  root  /usr/sbin/tcpd \
/usr/sbin/in.rshd -h
```

If your system uses xinetd, you would need to create an equivalent entry in /etc/xinetd.conf, or a dedicated startup file in /etc/xinetd.d, as described in Chapter 4, Starting Servers. A xinetd configuration probably wouldn't call TCP Wrappers (/usr/sbin/tcpd), but in either case, the security provided by TCP Wrappers or directly by xinetd is important. The rshd daemon relies almost exclusively on the caller's IP address for security. Although TCP Wrappers and xinetd provide similar access control mechanisms, the redundancy on this matter can be important in case of a security bug in rshd.

Although IP addresses are the strongest type of access control used by rshd, the server also uses usernames to control remote access in order to prevent ordinary users from running dangerous programs with undue authority on the server. Ordinarily, rshd won't accept commands from root on any remote system. The -h parameter to rshd, demonstrated in the preceding inetd.conf entry, changes this default. This is extremely important because backups of system files must ordinarily be run with root privileges in order to back up sensitive system files and all user files, depending upon your system's user file permissions. If you omit -h, ordinary users will be able to perform backups to the server, but only if the permissions for the device file on the server allow this. (Most distributions don't allow ordinary users to access tape device files in any meaningful way.)

WARNING

The -h option to rshd is broken or disabled on some systems, so this procedure won't work. You may be able to use SSH instead—run an SSH server on the backup server, and link ssh on the backup client to the rsh name so that tar calls ssh to do the network transfer. This has security advantages even for systems on which rshd works as described. This will only work if you configure SSH to accept logins without requiring a password authentication, though, as described in Chapter 13, Maintaining Remote Login Servers.

Because of the security issues surrounding rshd and its required configuration, the best configuration for a client-initiated backup server of this type is to dedicate a computer to this function. Such a computer need not be very powerful, aside from having a tape backup unit and a fast network connection. It should be protected from the Internet at large by a firewall, and ideally it shouldn't contain any vital data or run servers aside from rshd and any others needed for its configuration.

Performing the Backup

Once you've set up a backup server, you can perform backups with it. To do so, you must insert a tape into the backup server's tape drive and issue a command similar to the following on the backup client:

```
# tar cvlpf buserver:/dev/st0 /home /var /
```

This command backs up the /home, /var, and / directories on the current system to the rewinding tape device on buserver, and excludes any mounted filesystems other than those explicitly specified. If the three specified directories are the only ones on the computer, this command performs a complete network backup of the client.

You can use the same type of addressing with mt as you can with tar to specify a network backup device. For instance, **mt -f buserver:/dev/nst0 rewind** will rewind the tape in buserver's tape drive.

In sum, performing a client-initiated network backup using tar is very much like performing a local backup using tar. You must add the name of the backup server to the device specification, but otherwise the commands used are identical. The extra effort goes into configuring the backup server system.

PERFORMING A SERVER-INITIATED BACKUP

Server-initiated backups, as described earlier, have the advantage of allowing a central server to control the scheduling of backups. This type of setup places the bulk of the configuration details on the backup client, which must run an appropriate network server package. This section describes using the Network Filesystem (NFS) server, as covered in Chapter 8, File Sharing via NFS, to perform network backups. Once the client is configured, the actual backup operation is much like a local one, although you must mount the backup client's export on the backup server system in order to perform the backup.

NOTE   It's possible to use a file-sharing protocol other than NFS for network backups. In fact, the upcoming section, "Using smbmount," describes using smbmount to back up Windows file shares. For backing up a Linux system in this way, a protocol that preserves Linux file ownership and permission information is a practical necessity; hence, NFS is a good choice.

Server-Initiated Network Configurations

You should read Chapter 8 to learn how to configure a Linux computer to export specified filesystems. To perform a *complete* backup of a system, you must configure that system to allow the backup server to mount all of its important disk filesystems. You can omit /proc, removable media you don't want to back up, and so on. Ordinarily, you'll configure the backup client to export all its hard disk partitions.

For backup purposes, the backup client may export all directories with read-only access; the backup server doesn't need to write to these directories. If you need to restore data, though, you'll need to change this configuration to allow write access to the relevant directories. Alternatively, you could use some more convoluted method of restoring data, such as restoring it to a directory on the backup server, which you can then export for the backup client to read; or you could use a client-initiated restore if you configure the backup server appropriately.

One potentially dangerous requirement of a server-initiated backup configuration is that the backup server's root user must have full root access rights on the backup client—in other words, you must use the no_root_squash option when you define exports. Without this option, the backup server won't be able to read many important system files, and perhaps not many users' files, either. This requirement allows miscreants with local network access or who can spoof the backup server's address to read all the files on the backup client, and even modify those files if you export client directories using read-write mode. For this reason, you should protect the backup server and all its clients with a good firewall to minimize the risk of outside access, and carefully monitor logs for evidence of tampering or other abuse.

As an example of a configuration, consider a client with three partitions that should be backed up: /home, /var, and / (root). You can export these filesystems by creating appropriate /etc/exports entries. If the backup server is called buserver, these entries might resemble the following:

```
/home   buserver(ro,no_root_squash)
/var    buserver(ro,no_root_squash)
/       buserver(ro,no_root_squash)
```

If you need to restore files, you'll have to change the ro to rw and restart the NFS server. Another challenge, particularly at restore time, is keeping file ownership intact. If the backup specifies that a file is owned by, say, jbrown, and if this name doesn't map appropriately onto a correct UID, then the ownership of the file may be lost or mangled. As a general rule, it's simplest if the UIDs associated with specific users are the same on both the client and the server at both backup and restore time.

Performing the Backup

The backup commands are just like those described earlier, but you must first mount the backup client's exports on the backup server system. For instance, suppose the backup client is called buclient, and a mount point called /mnt/client exists for holding its backup directories. You might then mount and back up its files by issuing commands like the following:

```
# mount -t nfs -o soft buclient:/ /mnt/client
# mount -t nfs -o soft buclient:/var /mnt/client/var
# mount -t nfs -o soft buclient:/home /mnt/client/home
# cd /mnt/client
# tar cvlf /dev/st0 home var ./
```

NOTE The preceding sequence assumes that the backup client's NFS server does not export mounted subdirectories. If the NFS server does export mounted subdirectories, you only need the first mount command.

One point to note about this particular backup sequence is that it uses cd to change into the main mount point for the backup client computer. Thus, the view in this directory is of the backup client's directory tree. The tar command backs up the individual mount points in this directory tree, but omits the complete path. The result is a tape that includes no references to the /mnt/client mount point. Files on this tape may be restored by mounting the target partition at the same mount point or elsewhere and moving into the mounted directory to do the restore. It's also possible to back up with a command like the following:

```
# tar cvlf /dev/st0 /mnt/client/home /mnt/client/var /mnt/client
```

Such a command includes references to the /mnt/client directory (or, more precisely, mnt/client, missing the leading /, unless you use the --absolute-paths qualifier). Such a backup can therefore only be restored if the target system is mounted in the same way as at backup, or at least in a directory that includes a mnt/client subdirectory of its own. Restores lacking such a directory tree will create one—possibly on the backup server machine rather than the backup client.

WARNING One potentially serious drawback of this type of server-initiated backup is that the backup process may stall if the backup client goes offline during the process. The -o soft mount option used in the preceding example allows the NFS client on the backup server to return errors to tar, which may be preferable to a hung backup process.

USING SMB/CIFS

The preceding section, "Using tar," described using the tar utility in conjunction with an rshd server running on the backup server computer or an NFS server running on the backup client computer. You can use other servers to provide connectivity between the computers, though. This section describes one that's of particular interest to networks that host many Windows computers: the Server Message Block (SMB), aka the Common

425

Internet Filesystem (CIFS). As described in Chapter 7, File and Printer Sharing via Samba, SMB/CIFS support comes standard with Windows systems, and the Linux Samba package allows Linux to interact with these systems using their native file- and printer-sharing protocol. This same protocol can be used for backing up Windows systems, or possibly even Linux systems, using either server-initiated or client-initiated methods. Before proceeding, you should read or review Chapter 7 if you're not already familiar with at least the basics of Samba configuration.

BACKING UP WINDOWS CLIENTS FROM LINUX

A server-initiated backup using Samba can work very much like a server-initiated backup using NFS. Samba, SMB/CIFS generally, and Windows present certain unique opportunities and challenges, though. Of particular interest are the capabilities of the smbtar program and unique concerns of processing long filenames from a Windows system.

Sharing Files to Back Up

As with a server-initiated backup via NFS, a server-initiated backup via Samba requires that the backup client run a server to share the files that are to be backed up. In most cases, this works best with Windows backup clients. Although you can run Samba on a Linux computer to share Linux filesystems, and could back them up in this way, the resulting backup would be lacking critical information such as file ownership and permissions—or more precisely, that information would not be reliable.

Windows systems ship with the SMB/CIFS server software, but it may not be installed or configured. Details differ from one version of Windows to another, but you can use the Network or Network and Dial-Up Connections item in the Control Panel to add the necessary software component. In Windows 9x/Me, double-click Network to get the Network dialog box. In Windows NT and 2000, right-click your network icon in Network and Dial-Up Connections and click Properties. The necessary component is called File and Printer Sharing for Microsoft Networks. If this component isn't present, click Add or Install to do so. You should find it classified as a service, as shown in Figure 17.1. You may also need to set the workgroup to which the system belongs. You can do this from the Identification tab of the Network dialog box in Windows 9x/Me, or from the System object in the Control Panel in Windows 2000.

Once you've installed the SMB/CIFS server, you must share all the hard disks you want to be backed up. You can do so by following these steps:

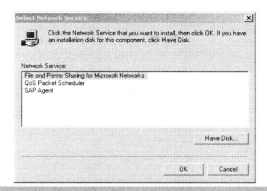

Figure 17.1   A Windows system needs the File and Printer Sharing for Microsoft Networks component to function as an SMB/CIFS server.

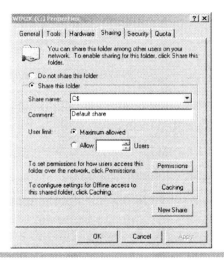

Figure 17.2   This is the Windows 2000 Sharing dialog box; the options in Windows
9x/Me are somewhat different.

1. In the My Computer window, right-click the drive you want to share
   for backups and click Sharing from the resulting pop-up menu. (If the
   Sharing item doesn't appear, chances are the SMB/CIFS server software is *not* installed.) The result is a Properties dialog box like the one
   shown in Figure 17.2.

2. Click Shared As or Share This Folder to share the drive. You must then
   enter a share name, which you'll use to mount or otherwise access the

427

share from the Linux backup server. (In Windows 2000, you enter the share name by clicking New Share.)

3. Windows 9*x*/Me systems require you to select an Access Type to specify read-only or read-write access, and to enter a password. You can specify read-only access for backup purposes, but if you ever need to restore data, you'll have to change the configuration to allow read-write access (what's called Full in the Windows 9*x*/Me dialog box). You can use the Security tab in Windows 2000 to adjust who may access the share.

4. Click OK to enable sharing on the drive.

5. Repeat Steps 1 through 4 for any additional drives you want to back up.

At this point, the drive should be accessible to remote systems. You can test this from the Network Neighborhood browser of another computer, or by using tools like smbclient from Linux. Both of the methods of server-initiated backup described next use such tools.

Using smbtar

Samba ships with a program called smbtar. As you might guess, this is a tool that combines the features of tar with an SMB/CIFS client. In fact, smbtar is really a shell script that calls the regular tar utility and the smbclient tool, combining their features into a single integrated program you can use to back up a Windows system. You can use it to back up a complete Windows share, or just some files on that share. Its basic syntax is as follows:

```
smbtar -s buclient [-x service] [-u username] [-p password] \
[-d dir] [-t device] [-r] [-v]
```

The smbtar man page provides information on a few additional options. The meanings of these options are as follows:

- **-s *buclient***—The only required option is the name of the backup client computer. You normally give the NetBIOS name for the computer, which may not be the same as the system's DNS hostname, but depending upon the name resolve order setting in smb.conf, the system might also respond to DNS hostnames.

- **-x *service***—You specify the share name, as defined in the earlier Step 2, as *service*. If you omit this value, the system defaults to a share called backup.

- **-u** *username*—If you want to connect with a username other than the one you're using to perform the backup, specify it with this option. Note that Windows 9*x*/Me doesn't use usernames on its shares unless it's part of a domain rather than a workgroup.

- **-p** *password*—If your backup share takes a password, you enter it with this parameter. This is a potentially major security hole because it means the password will show up in your shell's history if you type the smbtar command manually, and the password can also be accessed from a process listing (via the ps utility, for instance). If you run smbtar from a script, be sure the script is readable only by root to keep the password from falling into the wrong hands.

- **-d** *dir*—You can change to a directory within the share by specifying it with this option. You won't use this option to back up a complete partition.

- **-t** *device*—Use this option to specify the Linux device file associated with your tape drive, or the file to which you want to store the backup data. The default value is the value of the $TAPE environment variable, or tar.out if $TAPE isn't defined.

- **-r**—The default behavior of smbtar is to back up files. The -r option causes the program to restore files instead.

- **-v**—This option activates verbose mode, in which smbtar displays the names of the files it's backing up.

As an example, consider the following command, which backs up a share called CDRIVE on the computer WORK:

```
# smbtar -s WORK -p password -x CDRIVE -t /dev/st0 -v
```

The result of running this command is some status information, followed by a list of files, followed by a summary of the number of files and bytes backed up. The file created by smbtar is an ordinary tar file, so you can check and read back the tape using ordinary tar if you like.

Using smbmount

Instead of using smbtar, you can use Linux's ability to mount an SMB/CIFS share to back it up. You can mount such a share using either the mount or the smbmount programs. The former is the normal Linux command for mounting; you specify a filesystem type of smbfs, and you provide the Windows system's NetBIOS name, share name, and username as follows:

```
# mount -t smbfs //WORK/CDRIVE /mnt/backup -o \
username=fred,password=password
```

The equivalent command using smbmount is:

```
# smbmount //WORK/CDRIVE /mnt/backup -o \
username=fred,password=password
```

WARNING

The smbmount utility changed substantially over the course of the 2.0.x series of Samba. Earlier versions of the tool used a substantially different syntax. The command shown here should work with Samba versions 2.0.5a through 2.2.2, and probably beyond.

If you omit the password, mount and smbmount both prompt for it. This approach can make using these tools superior to smbtar if you want to perform a backup from the command line. You can also mount multiple computers' drives and back them all up with a single call to tar. This can make creating the backups easier, but it may slow restoration of a single system, because upon restoration, you may need to read through the data from other systems.

After you've backed up data from the Windows computers, you should use the umount or smbumount commands to close the connections with the backup clients. Both commands work the same way, just as umount does with local shares. For instance:

```
# umount /mnt/backup
```

Special Windows Filename Considerations

Using Linux to back up Windows systems can be a good way to back up such clients, and especially Windows 9x/Me systems. There are certain filename caveats, though. The most obvious of these is that mount and smbmount both treat filename case differently than does Windows. To understand this, it's necessary to know something of how Windows stores filenames. The File Allocation Table (FAT) filesystem used by Windows 9x/Me and optionally by Windows NT, 2000, and XP was initially designed to store filenames with only eight characters and a three-character extension, all in uppercase. This is known as an *8.3 filename*. To store longer filenames, Windows implements a separate but associated long filename using extra directory entries. These long filenames can store either filenames that are longer than the 8.3 limit, or filenames with mixed case or an otherwise forced all-lowercase or all-uppercase appearance in Windows. (Depending upon how you view the filename, the case of regular 8.3 filenames will be all uppercase or have an initial capital followed by lowercase letters, as in File.txt. You can force a filename to be all uppercase or all lowercase in file selection dialog boxes and the like by using a long filename entry.) The Linux filename problems derive from the fact that Linux has no way of knowing what the 8.3 filenames are when they differ from the long filenames; Linux uses *only* the long filenames, if they exist at all.

In contrast to Windows, Linux treats 8.3 filenames in directories mounted with mount or smbmount as being all lowercase (for instance, file.txt). When restored, these files will be restored correctly; however, if a file was created with an explicitly lowercase but 8.3 filename, the restore process will create a file that will appear as an ordinary 8.3 all-uppercase filename in Windows. This isn't normally a serious problem, because Windows treats filenames in a case-insensitive way. Users may notice small changes in filename case as a result, though, which may be confusing.

The smbtar program treats 8.3 filenames as being entirely uppercase, so it doesn't suffer from this problem, but it does suffer from a related one: Consider a file with a name that's encoded as being all uppercase using the long filename extensions, but that is still 8.3 or shorter in length. The Linux smbtar program will think that such a file is a normal 8.3 filename, and so won't restore the long filename extension that marks it as entirely uppercase. Once again, this problem isn't normally serious, but it may be disconcerting to users.

A potentially more serious filename glitch has to do with the creation of 8.3 filenames to match long filenames. Windows does this automatically, and you can see both the short and the long filenames in a Windows DOS prompt window by using the DIR command. Because Linux doesn't know what the short filename is, though, it relies upon Windows to recreate this filename when restoring files. This process normally proceeds smoothly, and the short filename isn't normally very important in any event. There are cases, though, when it is. Specifically, if a program stores the short filename in a configuration file, and if that short filename changes after restoring the file, the program won't be able to find the file. In fact, the Windows Registry stores some filenames in 8.3 form, so this problem can cause those Registry entries to be incorrect. This, in turn, can cause mysterious malfunctions and even system crashes if a critical Registry entry is affected. You can take some steps to reduce the risk of such problems, though:

- **Use short directory names**—Instead of using long directory names, use short ones. For instance, many Windows programs place themselves in the `Program Files` directory. If you instead use a directory called `APPS`, there's no chance that the short filename will be changed upon restoration. Similar changes to the names of subdirectories in which programs place themselves can go a long way towards solving this problem. Chances are data filenames don't need to be short, because Registry entries and the like aren't likely to refer to data files.

- **Use long filenames in configuration files**—If you're given the chance to enter a filename or directory name in a configuration file, use the long filename if it differs from the 8.3 name. For instance, if you want to add a directory to the `PATH` in `AUTOEXEC.BAT`, use the long filename. This action ensures that changes to the 8.3 filename won't affect functionality.

- **Create long filenames that are unique in their first six characters**— Windows creates 8.3 filenames by using the first six characters and then appending a tilde (~) and a number, which is assigned in sequence starting with 1. For instance, `longfilename.txt` might have a matched 8.3 filename of `LONGFI~1.TXT`. If all the long filenames in a directory are unique in their first six characters, they'll all have ~1 as their seventh and eighth characters, and this won't change after restoration.

In the end, the risk of filename-related problems caused by backing up a Windows system from Linux is small, particularly if you take adequate precautions. It's not nonexistent, though, so you may want to have a backup made from a Windows utility, at least for an initial installation.

 NOTE The New Technology Filesystem (NTFS) used by Windows NT, 2000, and XP also stores both 8.3 and long filenames, but it's less dependent upon its 8.3 filenames. Thus, the potential for problems caused by such changes is smaller if you use NTFS than if you use FAT.

BACKUP SHARES

Another approach to using Samba for backups is to create a *backup share*. This is a Samba share that's linked to a backup device. There are several ways you can go about creating a backup share. Depending upon the approach, you may even be able to use such a system to back up Linux computers. All of these approaches qualify as client-initiated backups.

What Is a Backup Share?

There are two common approaches for creating a backup share using Samba:

- **Direct backups**—You can create a share that's tied to the mount point for a removable media device, like a Zip or Jaz drive. When the medium is mounted, you can access it from a backup client system just as you would any other share. If you run an archiving program, or even just drag-and-drop files, you can back up those files to the removable medium.
- **Processed backups**—You can create a share that uses scripting, as described in Chapter 7's "Samba Scripting Features" section, to copy a file sent by the client to a backup medium. The script might dump the file more-or-less raw to the backup device, or process it in some way. In fact, the "Example: CD Burning" section of Chapter 7 describes precisely such a setup, using a CD-R as the backup medium.

The direct backup approach is quite limited in the size of backups it can handle because most removable-media devices are limited in this respect. Only removable hard disks could handle a backup from a client with a large disk. The processed backup approach is potentially less limiting, but if you must back up clients with large disks, your backup server will need a large disk that's mostly empty to handle the data the client sends, because the server will have to temporarily store the data on its own disk.

Creating a Backup Share

Backup shares can be created like many other types of Samba shares. In the case of a direct backup, the share definition can look much like an ordinary file share. One exception is that you might want to use Samba's scripting features to automatically mount a device when it's first accessed and unmount it when the user has finished the backup. Another feature you might want to use is max connections, which limits the number of users who may access a share at any one time. For instance, the following share definition allows remote users to back up files to Zip disks mounted at /mnt/zip:

```
[zip]
        comment = Zip Backups
        path = /mnt/zip
```

```
read only = No
max connections = 1
preexec = /bin/mount /mnt/zip
postexec = /bin/umount /mnt/zip
```

NOTE Because some SMB/CIFS clients, including Windows systems, don't explicitly unmount a share in normal operation, you may want to use the deadtime global parameter to force a disconnection after some period of inactivity. For a backup medium, deadtime = 5 might be reasonable, forcing a disconnect after five minutes of inactivity.

A backup share such as this one is best used to back up limited amounts of data or very small clients. You might use it in a small network to provide access to a removable-media drive from all systems, allowing users to back up their data files to Zip disks or the like.

You can use any filesystem supported by Linux on the removable media, but if the disks must be read by other systems, you should take that fact into consideration. For instance, if your users will take removable disks home and read them on Windows systems, you should use FAT; but if the disks will be used only on the backup server or other Linux systems, you can use FAT, ext2fs, or any other filesystem that Linux supports.

Some media, such as CD-Rs and tapes, aren't easily shared directly. To use such media for backups, you must create a share that actively copies data to the backup medium. Chapter 7's "Example: CD Burning" section presented two examples of such shares that back up data to CD-Rs. A variant on the share shown in the "Burning a CD via a Pseudo-Printer" section is as follows:

```
[backup]
    path = /var/spool/samba
    printable = Yes
    print command = /usr/local/bin/samba-backup %H %s %U \
                    /var/spool/samba; rm %s
```

This share defines a pseudo-printer, which accepts zip files from the backup client. The share uses the /usr/local/bin/samba-backup script, shown in Listing 17.1, to extract the contents of the zip file and copy it to a tape using tar. The result is a backup tape similar to what might be created with smbtar. Alternatively, you could modify the script or the print command parameter to dump the zip file directly to tape, thus preserving features such as the hidden and system bits that would be lost by extracting the files on a Linux system.

Listing 17.1 A script supporting a pseudo-printer backup share

```
#!/bin/sh
# $1 = Home directory of job submitter
# $2 = Filename of zip file
# $3 = Username of job submitter
# $4 = Path to zip file
mkdir -p $1/backup/samba
cd $1/backup/samba
unzip $4/$2
tar cvpf /dev/st0 ./ > $1/tar.out
mail -s "Backup finished" $3 < $1/tar.out
rm $1/tar.out
rm -r $1/backup/samba
```

WARNING

The approach described here requires that the backup device file be accessible to all users. There are ways around this requirement, though. For instance, you could use the root account for all connections. An intermediate approach is to use the force user parameter in the smb.conf share definition to set the effective user ID that submits the "print" command. You could set this user to root or, better yet, create a special group with full read-write access to the tape device and use the force group parameter to grant this share access to the device.

This approach can easily be adapted to process files other than zip files. For instance, if the system accepts a tar file, it could be copied directly to tape without the extraction process that occupies much of Listing 17.1. Such an approach would be faster, but might be less convenient for Windows clients because tar is less common on Windows than it is on Linux.

Using a Backup Share

As described in Chapter 7, a pseudo-printer backup system like this one requires that you create the archive file locally and send it to the backup server without using a printer driver. You can create a Windows batch file to do the entire backup by double-clicking a single desktop icon. When the job is done, the script in Listing 17.1 mails a report to the user's Linux account showing the output of tar, and hence a list of the files that were backed up.

Because this approach, at least as implemented by a pseudo-printer, requires the transmission of an archive file of some sort, you can use this method to back up Linux systems without loss of important UNIX-style filesystem data, so long as the archive format supports that filesystem data. If you set up a pseudo-printer to accept a tar file, for instance, you can use this method to back up Linux clients. This approach has the advantage of potentially better security on the backup server than is available with the rshd approach described earlier. With Samba, you can restrict access based on IP address, just as with rshd, but you can also require a password. A Samba printer share is also less powerful than is the access granted by rshd. On the downside, this method requires that the backup server have a great deal of free disk space. It may also take longer to process backup jobs, and there's the potential for conflicts if two users submit backup jobs in quick succession.

USING AMANDA

The preceding sections have described fairly basic backup options and configurations. If your network hosts just a handful of computers, you may be satisfied to perform backups manually using these methods, or to write scripts to be run from cron jobs that perform backups on an automatic basis. For larger networks, though, more sophisticated tools are in order. That's the function of the *Advanced Maryland Automatic Network Disk Archiver (AMANDA)*. This package glues together other network backup tools to help automate backups across small, mid-sized, or even large networks. The AMANDA Web page is http://www.amanda.org. You can obtain the software from there, or from the distributions that ship with it, such as Debian, Red Hat, Mandrake, and SuSE.

WARNING

❗
◆

AMANDA hard-codes some critical values in its executables, so mixing binaries acquired from different distributions may not work. If your environment includes multiple distributions, it may be best to build the package from source yourself. Be sure to specify the same user and group with the --with-user and --with-group options to configure on all your systems. You may want to create a special user and group for AMANDA operations.

THE FUNCTION OF AMANDA

AMANDA includes both backup server and backup client software. You install the server software on the backup server, and backup client software on the backup clients. These programs communicate with each other using their own protocols; NFS, rshd, and the like are not used by AMANDA. (When AMANDA backs up Windows systems, though, it uses smbclient and the standard Windows SMB/CIFS server package, as described earlier.)

In addition to functioning as a conduit for network connections, AMANDA serves as a scheduling tool. It's often helpful, or even necessary, to carefully schedule different types of backups, particularly in large networks. Specifically, you probably don't need to back up every file on every computer with every backup. Such a policy would consume an inordinate amount of network bandwidth, even if the backups were scheduled to start in off hours—the backup might not complete for days, depending on the network size. When using simple tools like tar run from cron jobs, it's common to use the --listed-incremental option, or its equivalent in other packages, to minimize the impact of backups. AMANDA can help manage network backup bandwidth by keeping track of which computers have been backed up at any given time, and whether they've received full or incremental backups. AMANDA can then schedule computers for appropriate backup types on specific days of a multiday backup rotation.

Like a Samba backup server that uses processed backups, AMANDA normally functions by first copying data from the backup clients to the backup server's hard disk, and then copying those files to tape. (You can configure AMANDA to send data directly to tape, but such a configuration is likely to be slower than the normal configuration.) Therefore, an AMANDA server works best when it has a large hard disk—large enough for at least one day's backups plus the normal system software. Having double the normal day's backup capacity allows you to dump one backup to tape while retrieving another backup set from the network. AMANDA can function with less than this amount of free disk space, but it will then have to perform a single backup in chunks. For instance, with 1GB of free space, AMANDA might grab 1GB of data from backup clients, write that data to tape, then fetch another 1GB of data, and so on.

CONFIGURING CLIENTS FOR AMANDA

AMANDA uses a server-initiated backup strategy, so the AMANDA clients need to run server software. For Linux and UNIX clients, this software ships with AMANDA, and is known as amandad. It's normally run from a super server. An appropriate /etc/inetd.conf file entry to launch this server resembles the following:

```
amanda  dgram  udp  wait  amanda  amandad  amandad
```

You may need to add an explicit path to the amandad executable for your system. If your distribution uses xinetd rather than inetd, you'll need to adjust this entry for xinetd, as discussed in Chapter 4. This entry runs the amandad server as the user amanda, which must exist on the computer; you can change this to suit your own needs.

NOTE The AMANDA documentation describes launching the package using a special username and group dedicated to backups, such as amanda, but this approach often doesn't work. You may need to launch amandad as root to get it to work.

For the super server configuration to work, your /etc/services file must contain an entry for the amanda service. A suitable entry looks like this:

```
amanda  10080/udp
```

After creating appropriate super server and /etc/services entries, you should restart your super server to make the AMANDA backup client software available to the backup server. The rest of the configuration for your client occurs on the backup server computer.

NOTE The AMANDA backup server must be backed up along with other systems on the network. For this reason, the backup server itself is usually configured as a backup client, as well as being configured as the backup server.

The backup client requires an authorization file, called .amandahosts, to be stored in the home directory of the AMANDA user's home directory. This file should contain the fully qualified domain name of the backup server and the name of the backup user on that system, separated by a space or tab. For instance, the following file allows amanda on the buserver.threeroomco. com backup server to perform backups:

```
buserver.threeroomco.com amanda
```

As noted earlier, AMANDA uses the SMB/CIFS server on Windows systems to back up those computers. You can configure Windows computers as AMANDA backup clients as described earlier in "Sharing Files to Back Up."

CONFIGURING THE AMANDA BACKUP SERVER

Because the AMANDA backup server functions as a network client for normal backup operations, it doesn't need to run actual server software for these functions. AMANDA does support client-initiated restores, though, so the AMANDA package includes two server programs that run on the backup server. These allow clients to view packages available for restoration, and to initiate a restore operation. As with the server software run on backup clients, these programs are typically run from a super server. Appropriate /etc/inetd.conf entries look like this:

```
amandaidx   stream  tcp  nowait  amanda  amindexd   amindexd
amidxtape   stream  tcp  nowait  amanda  amidxtaped  amidxtaped
```

As with the backup client software, you may need to add an explicit path to the executables, and of course if your system uses xinetd, you'll need to create appropriate configurations for that package, as discussed in Chapter 4. The matching /etc/services entries for these lines are as follows:

```
amandaidx   10082/tcp
amidxtape   10083/tcp
```

The user who runs AMANDA, which is normally the same user specified in the super server configuration file for running the AMANDA servers, should have read-write access to the nonrewinding tape device file. Without this permission, AMANDA won't be able to access the tape to perform backups.

CREATING AN AMANDA CONFIGURATION

The AMANDA package is controlled through the amanda.conf file, which may be located in a subdirectory of /etc, /usr/local/etc, or a similar location. Typically, AMANDA uses its own two-tiered subdirectory for its configuration file. This subdirectory should be readable only by the AMANDA user (amanda in this example). The first tier of AMANDA's subdirectory is called amanda, and the second tier is named after the backup configuration. For instance, there might be a /usr/local/etc/amanda/Daily for routine daily backups and a /usr/local/etc/amanda/Archive for archival backups, each with its own configuration file. If you installed AMANDA from source code, you'll find a sample configuration file in the example subdirectory of the source package.

Setting Basic Options

The `amanda.conf` file format consists of lines that contain keywords followed by one or more values. For instance, a line that tells AMANDA how long it can take to process an entire network backup might be:

```
dumpcycle 4 weeks
```

A few configuration options span multiple lines. These are surrounded by curly braces (`{}`), and define a set of related options.

You can leave many configuration options at their default values. Some that you may want to adjust include the following:

- **org**—This sets the name of your organization, as used in reports that AMANDA generates. It's largely cosmetic, but you might as well set it to something reasonable.
- **mailto**—AMANDA e-mails reports on its activities to the addresses listed in this option. You may specify multiple addresses, separated by spaces.
- **dumpuser**—This is the username that runs the backup. This defaults to the value specified with the `--with-user` option to `configure` when you built AMANDA.
- **dumpcycle**—This is the number of days in a dump cycle (a complete network backup).
- **runspercycle**—AMANDA can run every day, multiple times per day, or once every several days, as you wish, by setting this parameter. For instance, if `dumpcycle` is set to four weeks, setting `runspercycle` to 20 causes AMANDA to compute what to back up based on one run per weekday. Setting this value to 4 causes AMANDA to assume it will be run just once a week. (Note that AMANDA is actually run from cron jobs; these settings just tell AMANDA what to *expect*, and therefore how to plan its backups.)
- **tapecycle**—This sets the number of tapes used in a dump cycle. It's normally slightly larger than `runspercycle` to allow for tapes with errors.
- **tapetype**—You tell AMANDA what type of tape device you have so that the package can compute how quickly it can back up data and other information. The middle of the example `amanda.conf` file defines several tape types, and you should set the `tapetype` option to one of these. If you don't see a suitable tape type, you'll have to create one. The most reliable way to do this is to use the `tapetype` utility, which is

included with AMANDA but isn't built by default. Go to the tape-src subdirectory of the source package and type **make tapetype**. Then mount a *scratch* tape in the tape drive and type **./tapetype -f /dev/tapedevice** (where *tapedevice* is your device filename) to get a list of values for your drive. This operation will probably take several hours, and will erase all the data on the tape. If your tape drive supports hardware compression, you can probably multiply the length value by 1.5 or 2, but if you back up data that's not easily compressed, such multiplication may cause failures if the tape runs out of space.

- **tapedev**—This is the Linux device file for the *nonrewinding* interface for your tape device. In most cases, it will be /dev/nst0 or /dev/nht0.

- **netusage**—This is the maximum network bandwidth AMANDA can expect to achive.

- **labelstr**—This is a regular expression that AMANDA uses to assign names to backup tapes. You'll have to prepare tapes with names based on this value, as described shortly, in the section "Preparing Tapes."

- **tpchanger, changerfile, and changerdev**—If your tape drive is a changer model, you must define its operation by providing a changer file definition and a pointer to the changer device file. Some example files are included in the example directory of the source distribution.

- **Log files**—AMANDA sets log file locations with the infofile and logdir options. Similarly, index files containing lists of files that have been backed up are set with the indexdir option. You might or might not want to change these values, but you should definitely check them.

In addition to setting these basic values, you must also configure a holding area for data. This is achieved with the holdingdisk option, which takes a multi-line value consisting of several suboptions. These include directory (where the files are to be stored) and use (how much space you can use on the disk). If your backup server is short on disk space, you can set a negative value for chunksize. This will cause files larger than the absolute value of the chunksize to be sent directly to tape, bypassing the holding area. (Positive values of chunksize cause AMANDA to temporarily break up large files for storage in the holding area. This can be very useful if your holding disk filesystem or kernel doesn't support large files. For instance, 2.2.*x* kernels on *x*86 CPUs only support 2GB files.)

Preparing Tapes

AMANDA needs to see tapes that have been prelabeled as ones it may use. To do this, use the amlabel utility *as the user who will run backups*:

```
$ amlabel Daily DailySet123
```

The `Daily` option to `amlabel` sets the subdirectory in which the matching `amanda.conf` file resides, so that `amlabel` can read the appropriate configuration options. The `DailySet123` option is the label to give to the backup tape. This value should match the regular expression set with the `labelstr` option in `amanda.conf`, or AMANDA won't be able to use the tape. In most cases, AMANDA will back up a network to a set of tapes, so you'll need to label several tapes. You may want to develop some naming scheme for these tapes to help you differentiate among them.

Defining Dump Types

Near the end of the sample `amanda.conf` file are a number of `dumptype` definitions. These specify how a given client, or a single filesystem on the client, is to be backed up. Features you can set in these definitions include:

- **compress [client | server] [best | fast | none]**—You can specify that compression be performed on the backup client or the backup server, depending upon available CPU and network resources. You can also set compression to be more efficient but use more CPU time (best) or be faster but less efficient (fast). The none option explicitly disables compression.

- **exclude [list] "*string*"**—AMANDA passes *string* to the `--exclude` or `--exclude-from` options to `tar`, depending on whether `list` is included as well.

- **holdingdisk *boolean***—Set *boolean* to yes or no to tell AMANDA to use a holding disk area or not.

- **index *boolean***—Set *boolean* to yes or no to tell AMANDA whether to create an index of the files in the backup set. Without an index, restores are much more tedious, but an index consumes disk space you might prefer to devote to other purposes.

- **kencrypt *boolean***—You can tell AMANDA to encrypt data sent across the network with Kerberos protocols with this option. Setting *boolean* to yes requires that your network be configured to use Kerberos, as described in Chapter 6, Authenticating Users via Kerberos.

- **program "*string*"**—AMANDA may use either GNU `tar` or the OS- and filesystem-specific `dump` program to perform backups, and this is the option that sets which to use. The default is usually `dump` (set by a *string* of DUMP), but `tar` may be selected by setting *string* to GNUTAR. (When backing up via Samba, the default is to use `tar`.)

- **skip-incr** *boolean*—If *boolean* is true, filesystems that use this dump type will be skipped during incremental backups.

There are other options you can set in a dump type definition. Some of these are the same as those set in earlier sections of the file, such as dumpcycle. Others are described in the amanda man page. Most dump type definitions begin with the name of another definition. This sets a series of values based on that earlier definition. You can use this to set default values. For instance, the default amanda.conf file uses a definition called global that's included in other definitions.

Keep in mind that a single backup may use multiple dump types. For instance, you might back up critical system files without using compression, but compress data in less important directories. Similarly, you might use dump to back up ext2fs partitions, but tar to back up ReiserFS partitions.

Defining a Backup Set

The amanda.conf file includes many important backup options, but it doesn't specify the names of backup client systems or the directories to be backed up on those clients. This is the job of the disklist file, which resides in the same directory as amanda.conf. The AMANDA source ships with a sample disklist file, but of course yours will be very different from this sample.

The disklist file consists of a series of lines, each of which contains three fields: The hostname of the backup client, the area to be backed up, and the dump type to be used in backing up that area. The area to be backed up may be specified as a device filename (such as /dev/hda2 or simply hda2) or as a mount point (such as /home). This file may also include comments, which are preceded by pound signs (#). Listing 17.2 shows a simple disklist file.

Listing 17.2 A sample disklist file

```
# Back up the backup server itself
buserver.threeroomco.com  /              root-tar
buserver.threeroomco.com  /var           user-tar
buserver.threeroomco.com  /hold          holding-disk
# Back up a Linux or UNIX client
buclient.threeroomco.com  /              root-tar
buclient.threeroomco.com  /home          user-tar
# Back up a Windows client
buserver.threeroomco.com  //WINPC/DRIVEC user-tar
```

Most of these entries should be self-explanatory. You might or might not use the default dump types, but if you do they're likely to include the ones shown in Listing 17.2. The /hold partition on buserver.threeroomco.com is the AMANDA holding area. This dump type includes the holdingdisk no option to prevent an attempt to use this area to back itself up. If this partition held nothing but holding area files, you might skip it entirely. The Windows client is backed up by specifying a Linux or UNIX system on which Samba is installed and working, and listing the NetBIOS name (WINPC) and share name (DRIVEC) of the Windows client to be backed up. Listing 17.2 uses the backup server itself as the Samba system, but you can use another system if you prefer. (Using the backup server reduces unnecessary network traffic, though.) The Windows system's drive need not be mounted to be backed up; AMANDA calls on the Samba system to use smbclient to do the job. Essentially, the Samba system uses smbclient much like a regular backup client uses tar or dump. To work, you must create a file called /etc/amandapass on the Samba system. Place the Windows share name followed by the password in this file. AMANDA sends SAMBA as the username, so if you back up Windows NT, 2000, or XP systems, those systems must have such a user defined. You can change the default username by using the --with-samba-user option to configure when building AMANDA.

RUNNING AN AMANDA BACKUP

To run an AMANDA backup, you use the amdump program on the backup server computer. Type the program name, followed by the backup set name (that is, the name of the directory in which the configuration files are stored). For instance, you might type **amdump Daily**. Of course, you must first insert an appropriate backup tape that you've already prepared with amlabel, as described earlier, in the section "Preparing Tapes." AMANDA will review the areas that need to be backed up and perform an appropriate backup. This backup might not process every computer on the network, or even all of a single computer. Depending upon settings for configuration options like dumpcycle and the capacity settings in your tape type definition, AMANDA may back up just some computers, or perform partial backups rather than full backups. Assuming you haven't created a dump cycle that's too short, though, AMANDA will back up your entire network over the course of that cycle.

Of course, you probably don't want to run amdump manually. It's best to run it in a cron job, probably at some time when your network isn't being heavily used, such as late at night. You should try to ensure that the backup clients will be available at these times, though. Many users are used to shutting off their computers when they leave work, so you may need to break them of such habits.

When AMANDA finishes its backup, it sends an e-mail report of its activities to the addresses specified using the `mailto` option in `amanda.conf`. You can examine this report to spot any problems, such as computers that weren't accessible or a tape that filled up unexpectedly.

RESTORING DATA

This chapter describes the process of backing up a network. Backup is only half the story, though; in order to do any good, a backup must allow you to *restore* data. There are two types of restore that you must consider:

- **Partial restores**—In a *partial* restore, you need to restore just a few noncritical files. For instance, a user might need a file that was deleted last week, or you might need to recover an old set of log files. Such a process is usually a fairly simple reversal of the process used to create the backup. For instance, rather than use the `--create` option to `tar`, you use `--extract` and specify the filename or directory you want to restore. As noted earlier, if you use a mounted filesystem and server-initiated backup, you must ensure that the backup client's network server is configured for read-write access from the backup server, which isn't a requirement for backups alone.

- **Full restores**—The nightmare scenario for any backup procedure is a *full* restore, in which you must recover *all* the files on a disk, or at least all those required to boot the computer. Such a situation can occur because a hard disk failed or because of some software disaster, such as a computer that's been accidentally wiped out by an errant command like `rm -r /`.

WARNING   One reason for doing a full restore is to recover a system to a state prior to its invasion by a cracker. You must be very cautious when doing such restores to both wipe out all the files the invader left behind and to use a backup that predates the system's compromise. Following such a restore, you must fix whatever problems existed that allowed the computer to be cracked.

Full restores are difficult to handle because you must find some way to get the restore onto a computer that has no working software. One common approach to solving this problem is to prepare an emergency restore system on a floppy disk, bootable CD-ROM, bootable Zip disk, or the like. For network backup clients, this disk should include network configuration tools and whatever network backup clients or servers you used to create the backup in the first place.

TIP

Even if your network consists of a Linux backup server and a large number of Windows 9x/Me backup clients, you can use a Linux-based emergency restore system. Such a system can include Samba, and you can use it to run an SMB/CIFS server to which the Linux backup server can restore files. After performing a full restore, you may need to use DOS's FDISK to mark the boot partition as bootable, and use the SYS program from the version of Windows you've backed up to write a boot sector to the boot partition. If you have Windows NT, 2000, or XP backup clients, the process may be more complex, particularly if they use NTFS. In such a case, installing the systems initially with a small boot partition you can back up and restore with Linux's dd or a commercial tool like DriveImage can greatly simplify restoration.

Sometimes, you may want to use a different method for a full restore than you used for a backup. For instance, a client-initiated Samba backup using a backup share might be more easily restored by using either a client-initiated direct tar restore via rshd or a server-initiated restore using either NFS or Samba.

In some cases, and especially if you haven't adequately planned an emergency restore procedure, you may have to reinstall the base OS in order to restore normal backup client functionality. You can then use this configuration to restore the rest of the data to the system, as if it were a partial restore.

AMANDA is unusual among the tools described here in that it includes client-based restore tools. The most powerful of these is amrecover, which in turn calls other tools such as amrestore. When you type **amrecover** as root on the backup client to enter the recovery utility, the program presents you with its own prompt at which you can type commands like setdate (to set the date of a backup from which you want to recover), cd (to change into a directory in the backup), add (to add a file to a restore set), and extract (to restore files from a restore set). After you type **extract**, amrecover prompts you for the appropriate tapes to restore data.

No matter what methods you use for restoration, it's critical that you test them before they become necessary. Ideally, you should set up a test system and try backing it up and performing both partial and full restores on that test system. If your network hosts several different OSs, repeat these tests with each of the OSs. Fully document your restoration procedures, and periodically retest them, particularly if your network changes in any important way. Keep backups of your emergency restore disks—you don't want to be surprised by a bad floppy, which Murphy's Law guarantees you'd discover at exactly the wrong time.

SUMMARY

You can perform network backups in any of many different ways: client-based or server-based; using NFS, SMB/CIFS, rshd, AMANDA, or other network tools; and using tar, dump, cpio, or other backup programs. Each of these options has its place, depending on your network's details. Understanding the range of options will help point you towards a reasonable solution. For a network of just a handful of machines, a simple solution using familiar tools like tar may be adequate. For a larger network, you may need to use more sophisticated tools like AMANDA. You should not neglect the restoration aspect of the backup process. Restoring data can involve little more than reversing the backup process, or it may involve radically different techniques.

Part III

INTERNET SERVERS

Administering a Domain via DNS

In order for computers to find one another by name on a TCP/IP network, the computers need some method of *name resolution*—that is, converting a hostname like `gingko.threeroomco.com` into an IP address like 192.168. 78.109, or vice-versa. There are several ways of doing this, but one of the most common is to use a *Domain Name System (DNS)* server, also known as a *name server*. In fact, the instructions on basic configuration presented in Chapter 2, TCP/IP Network Configuration, describe configuring a computer to use a DNS server for name resolution. These instructions presuppose, however, that a DNS server exists that you can use. Furthermore, the Internet as a whole relies upon a distributed set of DNS servers. Two major reasons for running a name server yourself are closely related to these two uses of DNS. You might want to run a DNS server on your own network to translate names into IP addresses for your own computers, or you might want to run an externally visible DNS server to allow others to address your local machines by name.

In any event, DNS administration involves setting up a number of configuration files that control the DNS server, including specifications of the domains that it handles. Depending upon your needs, you may have to dig into DNS features that don't directly involve your own configuration, such as obtaining a domain name. You might also want the DNS server to coordinate its activities with other servers on your network, particularly your DHCP server, as described in Chapter 5, Configuring Other Computers via DHCP.

Linux's DNS servers fall in the middle range of server complexity; they aren't as difficult to administer as a very complex system like Kerberos, but they're harder to administer than a simple server like Telnet. This chapter can get you started, and may be all you need to administer a simple domain. For more complex configurations, you can read your DNS server's documentation, or a book on the subject such as Albitz and Liu's *DNS and BIND, 4th Edition* (O'Reilly, 2001) or Hunt's *Linux DNS Server Administration* (Sybex, 2000).

WHEN TO RUN A DNS SERVER

Administering a DNS server isn't a trivial undertaking, so it's important to understand thoroughly what you'll get out of doing so. One set of benefits accrues if you run servers on your local network that should be accessible by name to people outside of your local network. Another reason relates to purely local network access. In both cases, there are alternatives you might want to consider.

RUNNING AN EXTERNALLY ACCESSIBLE DNS SERVER

The Internet as a whole relies upon an interlinked set of DNS servers. Understanding how this system works is critical to understanding why you might want to run DNS to allow outsiders to reach your systems. Consider as an example a DNS lookup performed in response to a user's Web browsing. The user enters a uniform resource locator (URL), such as `http://www.whitehouse.gov`. This entry results in various activities on the local computer, which ultimately result in the system contacting the local DNS server to *resolve* the `www.whitehouse.gov` hostname—that is, to convert it into a numeric IP address. The local DNS server begins this process by contacting a *root server*. This is one of a handful of systems whose addresses are unlikely to change, so the DNS server encodes root server IP addresses in a configuration file. The local DNS server asks the root server for help in resolving the `www.whitehouse.gov` hostname. The root server is unlikely to know the IP address, but the root server does know the IP addresses of servers that have more information on the *top-level domains (TLDs)*, such as `.com`, `.gov`, and `.uk`. The root server therefore passes the local DNS server the addresses for the `.gov` servers, and the local DNS server redirects the request to one of these. The `.gov` DNS server is unlikely to be able to resolve the entire hostname, but it should know the

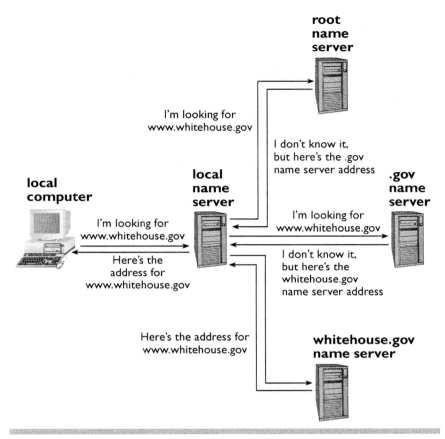

Figure 18.1   A single DNS lookup may involve requests being sent to multiple DNS servers in quick succession.

IP addresses of servers responsible for the whitehouse.gov domain, and so passes those addresses back. The local DNS server then asks one of the whitehouse.gov DNS servers for the www.whitehouse.gov address, and the whitehouse.gov server will know this address, and so will return it. The local DNS server can then return this final address to the Web browser, which uses it to request the Web page. This entire process is illustrated in Figure 18.1. Most of these details are hidden from the end user; to a program or person using this system, it appears as if the local DNS server knows the addresses associated with all the systems on the Internet.

Although this sounds like a roundabout and complicated method of resolving a hostname, the entire process typically only takes a few seconds.

453

There are also shortcuts that can help make the system even more efficient. For instance, local DNS servers may cache lookup results. Thus, if two users request the same addresses in quick succession, the DNS server won't need to go through the entire process a second time; it can simply return the original value. Also, the cache includes lookups on common domains. For instance, a local name server is almost certain to have the addresses of the .com TLD servers available, so the initial call to the root name server can be skipped. These caches aren't kept around indefinitely, though; they're occasionally flushed, which allows domain administrators to change their systems' IP addresses without causing undue problems.

If you run servers that you want to be accessible to others, it's a practical necessity to tie yourself into this DNS network. Specifically, you must run a DNS server that fills the role of the whitehouse.gov name server in Figure 18.1, but for your own domain. Some practical aspects of doing this are discussed in the upcoming section, "Obtaining a Domain Name." Once your DNS server is configured and running, and once the DNS server for the next-higher-level domain knows about yours, anybody on the Internet will be able to reach your computers by name.

NOTE The authorities who administer DNS require that every domain have at least *two* DNS servers. This isn't done because the protocols require it, but for redundancy—if one DNS server crashes, the other can still resolve hostnames. This requirement can be a problem if your network is particularly small, but you might be able to run your own primary DNS server and use an outside source for the secondary DNS server.

One alternative to running your own DNS servers is to let somebody else do it for you. Many domain registrars (discussed shortly, in the section "Obtaining a Domain Name") and Internet service providers (ISPs) offer DNS hosting services. Sometimes these are free with some other service, such as domain registration. Other times you must pay a small fee (usually a few dollars annually). At least one organization, Granite Canyon (http://www.granitecanyon.com) offers free DNS services—but remember the adage, "You get what you pay for." In any event, a third party can handle your DNS requirements for the outside world—either both servers or just one, if you want to host one yourself.

There's a specific type of DNS service that's marketed primarily to home users with digital subscriber line (DSL) or cable modem connections:

dynamic DNS. Organizations that offer dynamic DNS services operate a DNS server much like any other, but they allow you to quickly and easily update the DNS records to reflect a changing IP address. Most businesses are better off using an Internet connection that allows for static IP addresses, but dynamic DNS services may be useful for hobbyists who want to run their own servers. A few dynamic DNS providers also offer conventional static DNS services. There are too many dynamic DNS providers to list them all here, but a couple of sites that host lists of dynamic DNS providers are `http://www.technopagan.org/dynamic/` and `http://www.oth.net/dyndns.html`.

Relying on an outside source for your DNS server can make a great deal of sense if you don't want to deal with maintaining one yourself. Because DNS is so important to so many other services, it's a good idea to rely on an experienced outside source of DNS services if you're inexperienced in DNS administration or if your network connection is flaky.

Even if you rely on an outside DNS server, you may want to learn something about DNS configuration. This is because the Web-based configuration forms that are common with DNS providers typically require you to fill out much of the same information you'd enter into local DNS configuration files. Knowing what this information is will help you to configure your domain appropriately even when you don't run the DNS server yourself. The upcoming section, "Domain Administration Options," should be particularly relevant to helping you configure a domain whose name servers are being provided by a DNS hosting service.

Running a Local DNS Server

In addition to providing services to outside systems, a DNS server you run can function as your domain's DNS server—that is, the computer whose address you enter into `/etc/resolv.conf` or whose address you specify in a DHCP configuration file as the name server. This has two major advantages over relying upon an outside DNS server:

- You can configure your local systems to rely on your local DNS server for external lookups, thus potentially improving performance, particularly if your ISP's DNS server becomes unreliable or slow. Your local DNS server can maintain its own local cache, which might result in improved performance in some circumstances.

- Your local DNS server can maintain information on your local network, even for local systems that you do not want to make accessible to the outside world. For instance, you might run a local DNS server behind a firewall to allow for easy name resolution within your local network. These systems might not be visible from the outside world, and so would have no external DNS entries.

The second reason is generally more important, although on some networks the first reason may be important, as well. As a general rule, if you run a DNS server to grant outsiders access to your own network, you might as well use that server for internal access, as well. Purely local DNS servers are helpful when you run a network of more than a few computers behind a firewall.

An alternative to running a DNS server for purely local use is to configure the clients to use a name resolution method other than DNS. One common approach is to use the /etc/hosts file in Linux or other UNIX-like systems. (Non-UNIX systems also often support this mechanism, although the file may be stored in some other location, such as C:\WINDOWS\HOSTS in Windows 9x/Me.) An /etc/hosts entry consists of an IP address followed by a full hostname and a shorter "nickname." For instance, an entry might look something like this:

```
192.168.78.109  gingko.threeroomco.com  gingko
```

A typical Linux system includes at least one /etc/hosts entry to define localhost as 127.0.0.1. On a small network, it's usually not too difficult to expand this file to include definitions for all the other local computers. The effort involved on a small network is usually much less than is required to administer a full DNS package. As the number of computers grows, the effort involved in updating all the computers' /etc/hosts files grows much faster than does the effort in administering a centralized DNS server. The /etc/hosts approach is also impractical if your network uses DHCP and dynamic IP addresses (a configuration that's tricky, but not impossible, for a conventional DNS server to handle).

OBTAINING A DOMAIN NAME

Running a DNS server and obtaining a domain name are two tasks that are intimately intertwined. Without a domain name, a DNS server won't do you much good, at least not for external connectivity, because it's the domain name entries in the TLD name servers that point to your own DNS servers.

NOTE If you're running a DNS server on a private local network, you can make up your own domain name, but be sure to pick one that's not used in the real world. One good way to do this is to pick a TLD that's not in use, such as `.invalid`.

Today, there are two main types of domain names:

- **Country Code TLDs**—These TLDs (often abbreviated *ccTLDs*) are assigned to specific countries. For instance, `.us` stands for the United States and `.cc` belongs to the Cocos Islands.
- **Generic TLDs**—These TLDs (often abbreviated *gTLDs*) are not officially tied to geography, and are the most sought-after type. Examples include `.com`, `.net`, `.org`, and `.gov`. Starting in 2001, several new gTLDs are being added, such as `.biz` and `.museum`.

Registration processes differ depending upon whether you want a ccTLD or a gTLD, and even for the specific TLD within each of those categories. In most cases, you'll obtain your domain name through a *domain name registrar*. These are organizations that are authorized to submit changes to add domains to specific TLDs. Most registrars can register domains in the `.com`, `.org`, and `.net` TLDs, as well as at least some of the new TLDs. Some countries, such as the Cocos Islands, have commercialized their ccTLDs by allowing commercial registrars to register domains within those ccTLDs, even if the individuals or organizations obtaining the domains have no relationship to the host country. There are several lists of domain registrars, such as `http://www.NewRegistrars.com` and `http://www.icann.org/registrars/accredited-list.html`. Registration fees for gTLDs are in the range of $10 to $35 per year.

Some TLDs, such as the `.gov` and `.edu` gTLDs and most ccTLDs, have a more closed registration process. To use such a TLD, you must typically send e-mail or paperwork to the authority that's responsible for that TLD. (Some registrars may do this for you, but you'll probably pay more for such a service.) A list of ccTLDs, including links to some basic contact information, is available at `http://www.iana.org/cctld/cctld-whois.htm`.

NOTE The `.us` TLD's administration changed in late 2001. Before then, it was administered in a strictly geographical manner, but domains directly in `.us` are scheduled to become available in 2002. Consult `http://www.nic.us` if you want to obtain a `.us` domain.

457

Some domains, particularly in ccTLDs, are issued as subdomains. For instance, the .uk hierarchy includes subdomains for particular purposes, such as .gov.uk and .co.uk; you can't normally obtain a domain that's directly under the .uk TLD. Policies for each of the subdomains off of such ccTLDs may vary. For instance, .gov.uk domains are devoted to UK government agencies, whereas .co.uk domains are commercial (akin to domains under the .com gTLD).

When you register for a domain name, you'll have to provide some basic information, including a postal address and telephone number. You'll also have to provide the IP addresses of two DNS servers that will handle that domain's DNS lookups. If you run your own DNS servers, you can provide these addresses yourself. If you want to let somebody else handle your external DNS needs, though, you'll find yourself in a conundrum: To obtain DNS service, you need a registered domain, and to register a domain, you need DNS service. You can break out of this cycle by using the DNS service offered by your registrar. Most DNS providers also offer some sort of procedure to sign up for service before your domain is fully registered.

DNS Server Options for Linux

The first choice you must make when setting up a DNS server is *which* DNS server package to use. There are several options in Linux with varying capabilities. The most common packages include the following:

- **BIND**—The *Berkeley Internet Name Domain (BIND)* is the most popular DNS server in Linux, and it's the one upon which this chapter focuses. BIND ships with all major Linux distributions, and its Web site is http://www.isc.org/products/BIND/. The current version as I write is 9.2.0, but in early 2002, many Linux distributions still ship with the older 8.2.*x* versions. The still older 4.9.*x* versions used a different configuration file format.

- **djbdns**—D. J. Bernstein's DNS server is an alternative to BIND that's popular among some users. Originally known as tinydns, djbdns is designed to be smaller, more efficient, and more secure than BIND. It's not the standard DNS server for any distribution discussed in this book, but you can replace BIND with djbdns if you like. You can read more about djbdns at its Web page, http://cr.yp.to/djbdns.html.

- **pdnsd**—This is a proxy DNS daemon. It's designed mainly for use on a local network as a proxy for a remote DNS server. It also supports limited local domain name resolution features, but it doesn't support the full range of features implemented by BIND or djbdns. You can read more at http://home.t-online.de/home/Moestl/.

- **dnscache**—Like pdnsd, dnscache is a proxy DNS server; it's designed exclusively to speed up DNS lookups on a local network. Unlike pdnsd, dnscache provides no support for locally defined hosts, aside from localhost (127.0.0.1). The dnscache server is available from http://cr.yp.to/djbdns/dnscache.html.

Most Linux administrators who need to run DNS use BIND, because it ships with all major Linux distributions and is the most common DNS server. The security conscious sometimes pick djbdns because of its greater emphasis on security. Proxy DNS servers are often useful on small networks for local caching or even local name resolution, but they aren't good choices if you want to host your own domain and provide name resolution services to outside systems. The rest of this chapter focuses upon BIND, but some of the administrative tasks will be similar if you use djbdns.

CORE DNS CONFIGURATION

DNS configuration may be thought of as consisting of two tasks: Configuring the DNS server itself (which is called named in the case of BIND), and administering your domain. This section covers the most common options for the first task, and the next section, "Domain Administration Options," covers domain administration. (Subsequent sections cover a couple of special configurations that may be of interest to you—running a local DNS server for its cache and integrating BIND with a DHCP server.) Basic DNS configuration requires that you set basic configuration options, that you locate other DNS servers (especially the root servers), and that you tell the server about the zones you intend to administer. All but the smallest domains require a secondary name server. In theory, you could simply copy the configuration files to exactly duplicate the configuration, but it's usually better to set up the secondary server to automatically mirror the first one's files.

THE BIND CONFIGURATION FILE

Most basic BIND configuration options appear in the main BIND configuration file, named.conf. This file usually resides in /etc, but some distributions' BIND packages don't provide a default file in that location. You can usually find a sample file somewhere in the BIND documentation directory (often /usr/share/doc/bind-*version*). Listing 18.1 shows a short but complete named.conf file.

Listing 18.1   A sample named.conf file

```
options {
        directory "/var/named/";
        auth-nxdomain yes;
        forwarders {
                10.232.7.98;
                10.232.45.1;
        };
        forward first;
 };

zone "." {
        type hint;
        file "named.ca";
};

zone "threeroomco.com" {
        type master;
        file "named.threeroomco.com";
};

zone "1.168.192.in-addr.arpa"{
        type master;
        file "named.192.168.1";
};

zone "0.0.127.in-addr.arpa" {
        type master;
        file "named.local";
};
```

The named.conf file is broken up into sections. In the case of Listing 18.1, these are options and several zone sections. The options section sets global options such as the directory in which zone configuration files are stored. The zone sections define specific zones—that is, domains or other logical groupings of hostnames or IP addresses. Most lines in named.conf end in semicolons (;). This is a requirement of the file format, so you should be careful to follow it lest BIND become confused. Much of what named.conf does is to point BIND to files that provide more information about specific zones. These files reside in /var/named (or whatever location you specify with the directory option).

The following sections describe the contents of named.conf in more detail.

LOCATING OTHER NAME SERVERS

One of the first tasks you must perform when installing a DNS server is to obtain a list of root name servers. There are several ways to obtain this list. Possibilities include:

- The file may ship with your BIND package, probably under the name named.ca or db.cache under the /var/named directory. This file might be outdated, though, so you may want to check for a more up-to-date file using either of the following two methods.
- You can obtain the file via FTP from ftp://ftp.rs.internic.net/ domain/ under the filename named.ca.
- If your system has the dig program installed, you can type **dig @a. root-servers.net . ns > named.ca** to retrieve the file and call it named.ca.

The second and third options both require that your system have access to a working DNS server. If your network has no such server, you can try obtaining the file on a computer attached to another network, or temporarily set your future DNS computer to use another system for name resolution, as described in Chapter 2, TCP/IP Network Configuration.

When you've retrieved the root server list, copy it to the /var/named directory. You must also ensure that your /etc/named.conf file includes a reference to the root server list. The root server list is specified in the zone "." section, using the file option, as shown in Listing 18.1. Be sure the filename you use for the root zone file matches the one listed in named.conf. (Technically, hostnames all end in periods, so the root zone is indicated by a bare period.)

SETTING UP A FORWARDING SERVER

The default function of BIND is to perform lookups in one of three ways, in sequence:

1. If BIND is configured as the authoritative server for an address, the server responds with the address set in its configuration files.
2. If the request is for an address in the program's cache, the server returns that address. This feature improves performance, as noted earlier, and reduces network traffic.

3. If the requested address isn't in BIND's cache, the server queries a root name server, and other name servers, as described earlier. This recursive lookup usually takes just a few seconds at worst, but it is slower than a cached lookup.

BIND supports a fourth option, though: It can query a DNS server and let that server do the tedious recursive lookup. When so configured, BIND tries this option after checking its local cache but before performing a full recursive lookup. The idea is that a name server running on a small network that has access to a larger, but still somewhat local, name server may produce quicker lookups if it can rely upon the cache and faster network connections of that larger DNS server. For instance, if you operate a home or small office network that's tied to the Internet via a dial-up or satellite-based connection, you might want to configure the server to forward DNS requests to your ISP's DNS server. Connections such as dial-up and satellite broadband have high latencies, so the multiple queries of a full recursive lookup can take several seconds to perform.

Why not simply tell your local computers to use your ISP's server directly, though? Perhaps you want to run your own local DNS server to handle your local systems' names, or perhaps you want the benefit of a cache that's even closer to your systems than is your ISP's server. Also, a few ISP's DNS servers are unreliable, so having your own configured as a fallback can improve the reliability of your network connection.

In any event, a forwarding configuration like this is created with the forwarders and forward first options, as shown in Listing 18.1. The forwarders option allows you to specify the IP addresses of one or more DNS servers that yours is to query for information before trying to perform a recursive lookup. The forward option can take one of two values—only or first. If you specify forward only, BIND will rely exclusively upon the specified remote DNS server; BIND will not perform a recursive search of its own. By contrast, forward first causes BIND to attempt a lookup through the specified remote DNS servers, but if that lookup fails (say, because the remote DNS servers aren't responding), BIND proceeds with a normal recursive lookup. In both cases, BIND still relies upon its own zone configuration if it's been told it's authoritative for a zone, as described shortly.

SETTING UP ZONES

When you set up BIND, you must tell it how to handle requests for specific domains, subdomains, and IP address ranges. These different groups of names and addresses are referred to as *zones*. A zone may be either a domain or subdomain (as in the `threeroomco.com` zone in Listing 18.1) or a range of IP addresses (which are specified by zone names ending in `in-addr.arpa`). A small DNS server will set up a handful of zones:

- **The root zone**—A zone identified by a single period (.) refers to the root of the name space. This zone definition uses the `type hint` option to tell BIND to defer to the name servers listed in the file specified by the `file` option, as described earlier.

- **Your local domain**—Unless you're running a caching-only name server, you'll want to configure BIND to handle a zone that corresponds to your domain or subdomain. Listing 18.1's `threeroomco.com` zone is an example of this configuration.

- **Reverse DNS zones**—Although DNS is most commonly used to look up an IP address from a hostname, the reverse lookup is also possible. This is known as a *reverse DNS* lookup, and it's handled by zone names that end in `in-addr.arpa`. Preceding this string in the zone name is a partial IP address, in reverse order. For instance, the entry for the 192.168.1.0/24 network is called `1.168.192.in-addr.arpa`, as shown in Listing 18.1.

A basic zone configuration specifies the zone's type and lists a configuration file that provides additional information about the zone. Zone types may be any of the following:

- `master`—A *master* server is one that contains the original authoritative control file for a zone. If you're configuring a DNS server for a small network, you'll probably configure its local domain's zones as masters. Listing 18.1 illustrates this approach.

- `slave`—A *slave* server obtains information on a zone from another DNS server. The slave is still considered an authoritative source for that zone, though. The next section, "Configuring a Slave Server," covers these options in more detail. A single BIND server may function as a master for some zones and as a slave for others. It's usually simplest to set up one master and a matching slave, though.

- `stub`—This configuration is much like a slave configuration, except that the stub server copies only NS records—that is, name server specifications. You'd use this option if you want to configure a separate DNS server for a subdomain. For instance, if `threeroomco.com` has a subdomain called `sub.threeroomco.com`, and if you want to run a separate

DNS server for sub.threeroomco.com, you could include a sub.three-roomco.com zone in the threeroomco.com BIND configuration and give it a stub type that points to the sub.threeroomco.com DNS server. Alternatively, you could use one DNS server to handle the entire domain, including the sub.threeroomco.com subdomain. This would require no special zone entry for sub.threeroomco.com.

- **forward**—Like a forward option in the options section, a forward zone type tells BIND to pass on requests for information on a zone to another DNS server. Essentially, BIND issues its own DNS request to the specified servers, then responds with the results of this query. To be effective, you must include a forwarders option to tell BIND to what remote DNS servers to forward requests.

- **hint**—This zone type is unique to the root name server specification. You use it to tell the system where to find a list of root name servers. BIND should then try to update that list from one of the root name servers itself.

A simple configuration, such as that shown in Listing 18.1, can include just one hint zone and a handful of master zones. More complex configurations may include all of the preceding zone types.

CONFIGURING A SLAVE SERVER

If you're running your own DNS servers for a registered domain, you must configure two DNS servers. This is normally handled by making one server a slave of the other. The slave server stores its zone information in separate files, just like the master server. The main difference is that the slave server automatically retrieves the zone files from its master server. You tell the slave how to do this by changing the zone configuration in /etc/named.conf. For instance, suppose you want to set up a server to act as a slave to the one configured through Listing 18.1. The zone configuration for the threeroomco.com domain on the slave might resemble the following:

```
zone "threeroomco.com" {
        type slave;
        file "named.threeroomco.com";
        masters { 192.168.1.50; }
};
```

This tells the slave to obtain its configuration file for threeroomco.com from the DNS server at 192.168.1.50. If the slave is to be a slave for multiple domains, you should include several such definitions. You can include several DNS servers in the masters list, if you have more than two DNS servers for the domain; separate the IP addresses with semicolons (;). (In fact, one slave can synchronize itself from another slave.) If the server is a slave for several zones, each zone can synchronize against a different master. You might use this feature if you're administering several domains, each of which should have its own master, but for which a single shared slave is acceptable.

Remember to configure slave zones for both forward lookups (as in the threeroomco.com zone) and reverse lookups (as in the 1.168.192. in-addr.arpa zone in Listing 18.1). You should not configure a slave DNS server to use slave zones for the root name servers or for the localhost reverse lookups (0.0.127.in-addr.arpa in Listing 18.1).

When you start a server after configuring it as a slave, you should see the zone files specified in the zone options appear. If you don't, check the log files on both the master and slave systems for clues to what went wrong. One possibility is that the master might be configured to refuse zone transfers. This may be done as a security measure to keep outsiders from retrieving information on all your domain's local computers. If you want to restrict zone transfers on either your master or your slave DNS servers, you can do so with the allow-transfer option, which can go in either the options section or a specific zone section. For instance, you might use the following settings to restrict transfers to computers on the 192.168.1.0/24 network and to 172.19.98.23:

```
allow-transfer {
        192.168.1/24;
        172.19.98.23;
};
```

DOMAIN ADMINISTRATION OPTIONS

If you've created the /etc/named.conf file and set it up with global options and zones for your domain, you might be anxious to start up the server. Unless your server is a slave to another system, though, your configuration task isn't yet done. When you set up a master zone, as described earlier, you tell BIND to read a zone-specific configuration file. It's in this file that you store information on the hostnames and IP addresses for the zone. On a large name server, creating and maintaining these zone files is the bulk of the administrative work. If your domain is small and static, you may be able to set up a few zone files and then ignore them.

A SAMPLE ZONE CONFIGURATION FILE

Listing 18.2 shows a sample zone configuration file. This file begins with the name of the zone (`threeroomco.com.`) and a section that defines many defaults for the domain. These defaults are described in more detail in the next section, "Setting Master Zone Options." Following this section are a series of lines that provide information on the mapping between specific computer names and their IP addresses. Some of these actually apply to the entire domain. The upcoming section, "Specifying Addresses and Aliases," describes these lines.

WARNING Technically, DNS hostnames all end in periods (`.`). When you enter a host-name without a period in a Web browser, FTP client, e-mail client, or the like, Linux first interprets the address as being one that's missing its domain, so Linux tries adding the default and search domain names, as specified in `/etc/resolv.conf`. When this lookup fails, Linux tries again by appending a single period to the domain name. This process is transparent in normal oper-ation, but when configuring DNS, you can't afford to be sloppy. You *must* specify *all* hostnames as either fully-qualified domain names (FQDNs) *with* the trailing period or as hostnames only without the associated domain. If you provide an FQDN without the period, BIND will try to add the period, resulting in an effective doubling of the domain portion of the name, such as `gingko.threeroomco.com.threeroomco.com`.

Listing 18.2   A sample zone configuration file

```
threeroomco.com.    IN  SOA  spruce.threeroomco.com.  \
                             admin.threeroomco.com. (
                    2002043004 ; serial
                    3600       ; refresh
                    600        ; retry
                    604800     ; expire
                    86400      ; default_ttl
                    )
gingko.threeroomco.com.   IN A      192.168.1.1
birch                     IN A      192.168.1.2
spruce                    IN A      192.168.1.3
threeroomco.com.          IN A      192.168.1.4
www                       IN CNAME  gingko
kelp                      IN CNAME  jacques.pangaea.edu.
@                         IN MX     10  birch.threeroomco.com.
@                         IN MX     20  mail.pangaea.edu.
@                         IN NS     spruce.threeroomco.com.
```

The general format for lines in a zone file is as follows:

```
name   IN   record-type   record-contents
```

In such an entry, *name* is the computer's name, or a pseudo-name associated with an address in the case of a reverse DNS zone, as described in the upcoming section, "Configuring a Reverse DNS Zone." IN is a code that refers to a particular *class* of entry. It stands for *Internet*. There are other classes you can use in place of IN in some circumstances, but this chapter doesn't cover such configurations. The *record-type* is a code that stands for the type of record you're defining, such as a normal forward DNS entry, a reverse DNS entry, or an entry to specify a mail server. Finally, *record-contents* is one or more strings that go into defining the record, such as an IP address or hostname. In the case of the master options, *record-contents* is an entry that typically spans several lines. For most other records, the entire entry fits on a single line. A semicolon (;) is a comment indicator; any text after a semicolon on a line is ignored.

WARNING

!

BIND's configuration files are inconsistent in their use of semicolons. In named.conf, a semicolon indicates the end of a configuration statement. In zone files, the semicolon indicates the start of a comment. Keep this important difference in mind when editing your configuration files. If you become confused and use the semicolons incorrectly, chances are BIND won't start, or will behave strangely.

The entire zone configuration file is usually stored in /var/named and is given a name that's related to the zone name. Typically, the name is db.*zone-name* or named.*zone-name*, where *zone-name* is the name of the zone. You can call your zone files anything you like, though. The important thing is that you refer to them by their true names in /etc/named.conf.

SETTING MASTER ZONE OPTIONS

The master zone options appear in the *start of authority (SOA)* record, which has a *record-type* of SOA. The presence of this record indicates that the name server is authoritative for this domain. The *name* for this record is the zone name, as specified in /etc/named.conf—but remember to include a trailing period, as shown in Listing 18.2! The *record-contents* for this entry consists of three parts:

- **Master name server**—The first name (`spruce.threeroomco.com.` in Listing 18.2) is the name of the master name server for the zone. This name is followed by a backslash (\) in Listing 18.2. As in many configuration files, this is a line continuation character, so the second physical line in Listing 18.2 is interpreted as if it were part of the first line. Many zone files actually use a single long line instead of two lines separated by a backslash.

- **Administrative e-mail address**—The second name (`admin.threeroomco.com.` in Listing 18.2) is the e-mail address of the person responsible for maintaining this zone. The address form is somewhat unusual, though; to use it, you must replace the first period with an at-sign (@), so Listing 18.2's administrator is `admin@threeroomco.com`.

- **Timing information**—The numbers that span several lines, and that are surrounded by parentheses, provide timing information. These lines are commented in Listing 18.2 to indicate their purpose. The `serial` line is a serial number that should increase whenever you edit the zone file; slave servers use this number to determine whether or not to update their configuration files. Many administrators use the date (in *YYYYMMDD* format), followed by a number for the change number within a day, as the serial number. The `refresh` line is the time, in seconds, between checks made by the slave for updated zone files from the master. The `3600` value in Listing 18.2 translates to one hour, so the slaves will be updated within an hour of a change in the master's files. The `retry` value is the interval, in seconds, at which a slave will attempt another transfer if the first one failed; it's normally shorter than the `refresh` time. The `expire` value is the length of time, again in seconds, that a slave will wait before it discards a zone entirely because it can't reach the master. This value is normally at least a week, and it should *always* be longer than the `refresh` interval. Finally, the `default_ttl` entry sets the *time to live (TTL)* value for records. This is the length of time that remote DNS servers should keep information on individual lookups. Typical values range from a day (`86400`, as in Listing 18.2) to about a week (`604800`). If IP addresses on your network change frequently, or if you expect to implement changes soon, setting a TTL value of an hour or so (`3600`) may be worthwhile.

SPECIFYING ADDRESSES AND ALIASES

Most of the lines in a zone file provide information linking IP addresses to hostnames, either directly or indirectly. In most cases, the *name* field is the name of an individual computer or a name associated with an IP address, as described shortly. It is possible, however, to use the at-sign (@) as a stand-in for the domain name. You might use this feature in conjunction with the MX and NS records, as shown in Listing 18.2 and described in more detail shortly. Such records don't set up linkages between specific hostnames and IP addresses, but rather attach specific hostnames to take on specific duties for the domain as a whole.

The most common record types are as follows:

- **A**—An *address (A)* record uses a hostname as the *name* and provides an IP address as the *record-contents*. You can specify the hostname either as an FQDN with a trailing period, as in `gingko.threeroomco.com.` in Listing 18.2, or as a hostname without its domain or a trailing period, as in `birch` and `spruce` in Listing 18.2. It's also possible to assign a computer to use the domain name alone as its hostname, as in `threeroomco.com.` (192.168.1.4) in Listing 18.2. Such a configuration doesn't prevent you from using other names *within* the domain.

- **CNAME**—*Canonical name (CNAME)* records link one hostname to another one. As with A records, the *record-contents* may be specified as either an FQDN with a trailing period or as a hostname without a domain. In the former case, the target domain need not be in the same domain as the zone that the file defines; for instance, `kelp` in Listing 18.2 points to a machine in another domain entirely. CNAMES in general are useful if an important system's IP address isn't directly under your control. For instance, if you use a Web hosting service, you might want to link the www address to that outside computer using a CNAME entry, so that www will continue to work even if your hosting service changes the IP address of its hosting machine.

- **PTR**—Listing 18.2 contains no *pointer (PTR)* records. These records appear in the zone files for reverse DNS zones. They're discussed in the upcoming section, "Configuring a Reverse DNS Zone."

- **NS**—*Name server (NS)* records specify the name servers for a domain. Normally, at least one NS record will point to the same computer as was listed as the master name server in the SOA record. The *name* of an NS record is normally either @ or your domain name alone, and the *record-contents* field usually lists an A record that defines a name server.

- **MX**—Finally, a *mail exchanger (MX)* record provides information on a mail server for the zone. This entry uses either @ or the domain name alone as the *name*. The *record-contents* field has two components: a *priority code* and a hostname. When a mail server needs to send mail addressed to a user at the domain (such as `lorax@threeroomco.com`), the remote server asks your name server for its MX records. The remote server then tries to contact the system with the lowest priority code—birch.threeroomco.com in the case of Listing 18.2. If that system is down, the remote mail server tries the system with the next-higher priority code (such as mail.pangaea.edu. in Listing 18.2), and so on until the message is delivered or all the mail servers have failed. Of course, the mail server system must be configured to accept mail addressed to users at the domain, instead of or in addition to mail addressed to users of the specific computer. This is discussed in Chapter 19, Push Mail Protocol: SMTP.

TIP

Many record types can point to computers that reside outside of your own domain. This can be particularly helpful for CNAME records, as discussed earlier, as well as for NS and MX records if you rely upon an outside source for some or all of your DNS or mail server functions.

Listing 18.2 shows most of these record types in action. A real domain is likely to provide information on many more computers than does Listing 18.2, though.

CONFIGURING A REVERSE DNS ZONE

Listing 18.1 shows several zones, two of which are for reverse DNS entries. These zones allow the DNS server to retrieve hostnames when given IP addresses. The trick to this operation is the creation of a pseudo-domain, in-addr.arpa. Your /etc/named.conf file points BIND to zone files that are authoritative for certain subsets of this domain. Because the least significant element of a domain name is at the extreme left of the name, whereas the least significant element of an IP address is at the extreme right of the address, you enter the IP address as part of this pseudo-domain *backward*. Thus, the zone name for the 192.168.1.0/24 address is 1.168.192.in-addr.arpa.

WARNING

You can run a DNS server for your own domain after registering that domain (or even using a fake domain name, if your network is private). You should not attempt to run a reverse DNS service on an IP block unless you're in charge of that block. You're unlikely to cause problems for others if you do this accidentally, but if you set it up incorrectly, you might break reverse lookups from your own network. There are two exceptions to this rule: First, the localhost address block (127.0.0/24, or even 127/8) may be configured locally, and if you run a private network, you should set up a reverse DNS zone for the private IP address space you've used.

A reverse DNS zone is configured just like a forward DNS zone, except that PTR records dominate the reverse DNS zone. (A reverse DNS zone also includes an SOA record, and often NS records.) There's no need to define MX records, A records, or CNAME records in most reverse DNS zone files. Listing 18.3 shows a reverse DNS zone file to match the forward DNS zone file shown in Listing 18.2.

Listing 18.3   A reverse DNS zone file

```
1.168.192.in-addr.arpa.  IN SOA spruce.threeroomco.com.  \
                    admin.threeroomco.com. (
              2002043004 ; serial
              3600       ; refresh
              600        ; retry
              604800     ; expire
              86400      ; default_ttl
              )
1                        IN PTR   gingko.threeroomco.com.
2.1.168.192.in-addr.arpa.  IN PTR   birch.threeroomco.com.
3.1.168.192.in-addr.arpa.  IN PTR   spruce.threeroomco.com.
4.1.168.192.in-addr.arpa.  IN PTR   threeroomco.com.
@                        IN NS    spruce.threeroomco.com.
```

You can specify the name using either a short name—in this case, normally just the host portion of the IP address, such as 1 for 192.168.1.1—or the complete (but reverse-order) IP address followed by in-addr.arpa. Listing 18.3 illustrates both approaches. The *record-contents* field should always contain the complete hostname, including a trailing period. Because this zone is not the same as the forward zone, an attempt to abbreviate the name will result in incorrect lookups, such as birch.1.168.192. in-addr.arpa, rather than birch.threeroomco.com.

RUNNING A CACHING-ONLY NAME SERVER

One DNS configuration that's common on small networks is a caching-only system. Such a name server is configured to not be authoritative for any domains (except possibly reverse DNS on the localhost network). Instead, the server's sole purpose is to cache external DNS requests. The idea is to provide quicker DNS lookups by maintaining a cache that's local, rather than relying on a remote DNS server. This configuration is particularly likely to improve perceived network speeds in Web browsers and the like when the link to the outside world is slow, such as a satellite-based broadband connection, which must cope with high latencies—close to half a second for a two-way satellite system. Conventional telephone dial-up links also typically have latencies of around 200 ms, which is not as bad as a satellite setup, but can still produce a noticeable lag on lookups.

It's important to note that a local DNS cache won't improve lookup times if the address being looked up isn't in the local server's cache. Thus, this approach is most useful on a network with a fair number of users who tend to access many of the same sites, thus building up a cache that's likely to be exploited on a substantial fraction of DNS lookups.

A basic configuration for a caching-only name server is similar to that shown in Listing 18.1, but it would be missing most or all of the zone definitions. The only zones you might consider defining are the localhost reverse DNS zone (0.0.127.in-addr.arpa) and the root zone (.). Even these zones aren't strictly necessary.

The most important feature of a caching-only BIND configuration is the forwarders and forward entries in the options section. The forwarders entry must list your ISP's DNS servers; BIND will use those systems to do its duties, and cache the results. Rather than forward first, as shown in Listing 18.1, you may want to use forward only. This configuration will cause the server to stop trying to resolve names if the forwarder systems don't respond.

WARNING

> If you include the root zone and use forward first in the options section, BIND may attempt to look up addresses recursively if the forwarder systems fail. This is normally desirable, but it may slow down certain types of failure messages in a caching-only configuration, particularly if your Internet connection has high latencies.

As noted earlier in this chapter, slimmer packages than BIND can function as caching-only name servers, and may be superior choices for this role. Nonetheless, the caching-only BIND configuration is one of the simplest possible for BIND, and because BIND ships with all major distributions, it may be the simplest to set up. If you prefer something slimmer for this role, though, dnscache or pdnsd may be worth investigating.

When you configure a caching-only name server (or a more full-featured local name server), you should specify that system's IP address as the DNS server address for all your network's local computers. If you add a DNS server but fail to change existing local systems' DNS configurations, the local computers will continue to use whatever outside DNS servers they had been using.

COMMUNICATING WITH A **DHCP** SERVER

If your network uses DHCP to assign IP addresses to computers, you might not be able to enter a fixed IP address in your zone file because the IP address might be determined when the DHCP client boots, and could change between boots of the client. Chapter 5, Configuring Other Computers via DHCP, discusses two solutions to this problem: Configuring the DHCP server to assign a consistent address to clients or configuring the DHCP and DNS servers to communicate with one another. In the first case, you must take care to configure the DHCP and DNS servers consistently. For instance, if you want birch.threeroomco.com to be 192.168.1.2, you must set up that mapping in *both* the DHCP server's configuration files *and* in the DNS server's zone files (ideally, in both the forward and reverse lookup zone files). This is a simple solution, but it can be tedious for a large domain.

Chapter 5 discusses the DHCP configuration side of DHCP/DNS communication, so you should consult Chapter 5 in addition to this section if you want to implement the inter-server communication solution. The BIND side of the equation is implemented in the named.conf file's zone section that corresponds to the zone in question. Specifically, you must add an allow-update option. For instance, such a zone definition might resemble the following:

```
zone "threeroomco.com" {
        type master;
        file "named.threeroomco.com";
        allow-update { 192.168.1.1; }
};
```

This configuration tells BIND to accept update information sent from 192.168.1.1, which should be the DHCP server for your network. You must make a similar change to the reverse DNS zone, if your server handles that and if you've configured the DHCP server to perform both forward and reverse updates.

WARNING

!

If your DNS server is exposed to the Internet, or if your local users aren't 100 percent trustworthy, accepting DNS updates even from a single remote computer can be risky. A miscreant might manage to hijack the DHCP computer's address or masquerade as that system, then make changes to your DNS server that might compromise other systems that rely upon the veracity of the DNS server's data. You can minimize your risks by running DNS and DHCP on the same computer, and allowing updates only from the localhost (127.0.0.1) address.

STARTING AND TESTING THE SERVER

You can start the DNS server in any of the ways discussed in Chapter 4, although it's usually run from a SysV startup script or occasionally from a custom startup script. Running a DNS server from a super server produces slower name lookups, which is undesirable.

A tool that's particularly helpful for testing the operation of a name server is host. This program ships with most Linux distributions, often in a package called bind-utils or something similar. The host utility looks up a name or address using a specified name server. In its simplest form, it uses whatever the default name server is for the computer on which it runs, as specified in /etc/resolv.conf. You can use it by typing its name followed by a hostname or IP address, thus:

```
$ host www.awl.com
www.awl.com is a nickname for awl.com
awl.com has address 165.193.123.224
```

In this example, the first line of output indicates that www.awl.com is an alias (via a CNAME record) for awl.com. This system has the IP address 165.193.123.224. Such a test confirms that the name server is working for outside resolution. If you've configured your own domain, you should test its function using local hostnames and addresses as well. Be sure to test both forward and reverse lookups, if appropriate. You can also look up specific record types by specifying them with the -t option. For instance, to find the MX records for a domain, you might enter a command like the following:

```
$ host -t MX awl.com
awl.com mail is handled by 100 mailhost.uu.net.
awl.com mail is handled by 10 oldtms702.pearsontc.com.
awl.com mail is handled by 20 oldtms701.pearsontc.com.
```

This test shows that awl.com has three mail servers—oldtms702. pearsontc.com has the highest priority (10), followed by oldtms701.pear-sontc.com (priority 20), and mailhost.uu.net (priority 100). If you want to test a specific DNS server, you can append its name or IP address to the command, thus:

```
$ host www.awl.com spruce
Using domain server:
Name: spruce.threeroomco.com
Address: 192.168.1.3
```

474

```
Aliases:

www.awl.com is a nickname for awl.com
awl.com has address 165.193.123.224
```

This output is the same as that from the first command, but it adds confirmation that host used a particular DNS server to enter its query.

You can find more information on host from its man page. You may also want to investigate nslookup, which performs a similar function, but is being abandoned in favor of host.

SUMMARY

Most networks of more than a handful of computers can benefit from the presence of a local DNS server. Such a server may serve both external clients who want to find the IP addresses associated with server names within your domain, and internal clients who want to find the IP addresses of both local and remote systems. In either case, you must configure a basic set of options, including general options, a specification of root name servers, and configuration for any zones for which you want the server to be authoritative. If you want the server to deliver the names of computers within your domain, you need to set this up within zone files for the server. These files allow you to link hostnames and IP addresses, and tie specific computers to particular functions within a zone, such as mail servers for a domain.

Push Mail Protocol: SMTP

Chapter 11, Pull Mail Protocols: POP and IMAP, covered servers that dealt with part of the task of mail delivery. POP, IMAP, and other pull mail protocols allow end users to retrieve their e-mail from a central mail server system. There are two other aspects of mail delivery, though: delivering the mail to the central mail server, and sending outgoing mail. As it happens, both these tasks are handled by *push* mail protocols, so called because the sender initiates push mail transfers. The relationship between push and pull mail protocols is covered in the "Pull Mail's Place in the Mail Delivery System" section of Chapter 11.

The most common push mail protocol in 2002 is the *Simple Mail Transfer Protocol (SMTP)*. The vast majority of the mail delivered on the Internet passes through at least one SMTP transfer. Pull mail servers usually also run an SMTP push mail server so that they can accept mail for local delivery as well as accept outgoing mail from local systems, addressed to outside destinations. For this reason, SMTP servers are extremely important for any Linux system that's to handle mail. Every major Linux distribution ships with at least one SMTP server, but the default server varies from one distribution to another. This chapter covers the three most common Linux SMTP servers: sendmail, Exim, and Postfix. This chapter also covers a tool that's frequently used in conjunction with an SMTP server to process mail after it's been received by the server computer: Procmail. Before delving into the details of SMTP server configuration, though, it's important to understand when you should run such a server, which server is best to run, and how to configure your domain to handle a mail server.

Although many networks can make do with only minor changes to mail server configurations from the default, other networks require extremely complex mail server configurations. If you need more information than can be presented in a single chapter, you may want to obtain a book on your mail server of choice. Examples include Costales and Allman's *Sendmail* (O'Reilly, 1997), Hunt's *Linux Sendmail Administration* (Sybex, 2001), Hazel's *Exim: The Mail Transfer Agent* (O'Reilly, 2001), Blum's *Postfix* (Sams, 2001), Sill's *The qmail Handbook* (APress, 2001), and McCarthy's *The Procmail Companion* (Addison Wesley, 2001).

WHEN TO RUN AN SMTP SERVER

SMTP servers are often referred to as *mail transfer agents (MTAs)*. These systems potentially function as both clients and servers in a mail transfer chain. An MTA can accept mail that's sent by a user or by another MTA. It can then store that mail locally and, if necessary, send it on to another MTA. There are several possible uses for a Linux MTA:

- **Network mail recipient**—The most obvious use of an SMTP server is to function as a central mail server for a network. Such a system might support local reading of mail via local programs like pine or mutt, or remote retrieval via pull mail protocols. The SMTP server in this instance functions to receive mail (from within the local network or from outside it).

- **Network mail relay**—Users on local networks frequently need to send e-mail to others on the Internet at large. An MTA can be configured to *forward* mail—that is, to accept mail from the local network, hold it temporarily, and send it to remote systems. Such configurations are extremely important and potential sources of problems, so this chapter discusses them at some length.

- **Local mail origination**—Programs that run on the mail server computer itself may call the mail server directly in order to send mail. Such a configuration doesn't require that the MTA accept incoming mail at all. Many Linux programs assume that a local MTA is available to fill this role, although most such programs can be reconfigured to use a remote SMTP server as a relay. Some of the mail that originates locally may also be destined for local users. For instance, automatic maintenance tools frequently send e-mail to the root account on the local computer.

These functions are so important that most Linux distributions install an SMTP server by default. In particular, the local-to-local mail delivery issue makes the presence of an MTA on a Linux system very desirable. (In theory, you could track down everything that tries to send mail locally and reconfigure or rewrite it to use a remote SMTP server, but this may not always be practical.)

Most distributions' default SMTP server configurations are adequate to handle local mail delivery. The question therefore becomes one of when you should alter or at least check that configuration so that the computer can take on additional duties, such as handling mail for an entire domain. E-mail is so important in today's world that few networks can do without it. Even within a small office or a home, e-mail can be an important communications medium. Running your own e-mail server can be a way to provide e-mail, but it's not the only way. Outside e-mail providers are not uncommon, and you may already have access to an outside supplier. Such providers can be a good choice for receiving mail for a small domain, if you don't want to be bothered with creating such a configuration locally. Running your own e-mail server provides you with more control over how it operates, though. For instance, you might be able to more quickly and easily add, delete, or modify users if you run your own server. You can also configure your own server to block unwanted e-mail, adjust quotas on the size of messages the server will accept, and so on. Running your own server may be less expensive than contracting with an outsider to do the job. As a general rule, you may want to run your own mail server to handle the bulk of your mail needs if your network hosts more than a handful of users or if you have particularly exotic e-mail needs.

SMTP SERVER OPTIONS FOR LINUX

Quite a few SMTP servers are available for Linux. The four most popular are:

- **Sendmail**—The mail server with the largest installed base, and the one that ships with most Linux distributions, is sendmail. This package is large and powerful, and many programs assume that sendmail is available, so other packages usually include a binary called `sendmail` to maintain compatibility. Sendmail uses a complex configuration file format, which is one of the reasons alternatives have been growing in popularity. The main sendmail Web site is `http://www.sendmail.org`.
- **Exim**—Exim is a mail server that was designed to use a simpler configuration file format than sendmail, and to support various sophisticated filtering operations on mail. It's the favored mail server with

Debian and its derivative distributions. The main Exim Web site is http://www.exim.org.

- **Postfix**—Both sendmail and Exim are *monolithic* mail servers, meaning that they perform most tasks in a single large program. Postfix was designed in a *modular* way, meaning that tasks are broken up and handled by smaller programs. This has certain security and speed benefits. These and Postfix's simpler configuration files are its main advantages over sendmail. Linux Mandrake ships with Postfix as the default mail server. You can learn more about Postfix at http://www.postfix.org.

- **qmail**—The qmail server, like Postfix, is a modular server designed with security and performance in mind. The qmail configuration file is simpler than that of sendmail, but the program is less compatible with sendmail than either Exim or Postfix, so it's a bit more difficult to replace sendmail with qmail. Although it's turned up as the second most popular UNIX and Linux server in surveys of Internet mail servers, qmail isn't the default mail server for any Linux distribution, so I don't discuss it at length in this chapter. The main qmail Web site is http://www.qmail.org.

Although these are the most popular Linux mail servers, there are others, such as Smail (http://www.gnu.org/software/smail/smail.html), Courier (http://www.courier-mta.org), and OpenMail (http://www.openmail.com/cyc/om/00/). Most of these are open source, but some are commercial. The "big four" account for most of the discussion of mail servers in the Linux community. All four of these programs are very powerful and able to handle the mail needs for most domains—even very large ones.

Particularly if you're new to mail server administration, you're probably best off using whatever SMTP server shipped with your distribution. Many distributions now include multiple SMTP server packages. The default is probably the best choice.

If you have specific needs, and particularly if you have exotic needs, you may want to investigate the capacity of various mail servers to meet those needs. If necessary, you can replace your standard mail server with another one. Because of sendmail's popularity, this usually means replacing sendmail with another server. Exim and Postfix usually work well as "drop-in" sendmail replacements. Although the configuration files are completely different, programs that call sendmail directly usually work well with Exim and Postfix, and the mail queue format for these two programs defaults to the same format that sendmail uses—namely, the mbox format, in which all mail in a single mail "folder" is stored in a single file. Replacing sendmail with qmail is usually a bit more involved, because qmail defaults to a different mail file format (the maildir format, which uses a directory in which messages are stored as individual files), so you may need to change the standard qmail configuration or replace your mail programs (including any pull mail servers you want to run, as discussed in Chapter 11).

MAIL DOMAIN ADMINISTRATION

Many mail servers must accept mail from outside systems. There are two main ways that mail can be addressed to a mail server:

- **Direct addressing**—The mail may be addressed to a user at the mail server computer itself. For instance, if the mail server is `mail.threeroomco.com`, mail might be addressed to `jennie@mail.threeroomco.com`. This configuration is simple, because it needs only a normal address (A) record in the domain's DNS server, as described in Chapter 18, Administering a Domain via DNS. The drawback is that the address is longer than it might be.

- **Domain addressing**—To achieve shorter e-mail addresses and support for backup mail servers, DNS supports a mail exchanger (MX) record. This record tells remote mail servers to send mail to a particular computer if the mail is addressed to a user at the domain. For instance, if the `threeroomco.com` domain includes an MX record pointing to `mail.threeroomco.com`, an outside user can address mail to `jennie@threeroomco.com`, and it will be directed to `mail.threeroomco.com`. Such a configuration allows for shorter e-mail addresses and allows network administrators to set up backup mail servers (DNS supports multiple MX records). This system is slightly more complex to administer, though.

The "Specifying Addresses and Aliases" section of Chapter 18 describes configuring a DNS server's MX address. If you're setting up a mail server to handle a domain, it's usually best to do it in this way, so you should consult with your DNS system administrator, or read Chapter 18 if you're handling this yourself. In brief, an MX record looks something like this:

```
@              IN    MX    10      mail.threeroomco.com.
```

This line appears in the domain configuration file, which is normally named after the domain and stored in `/var/named`. The leading at-sign (@)

means that the line refers to the domain itself. The IN column is a standard part of Internet domain name entries. MX, naturally, identifies this as an MX entry. The 10 is the sequence number of the entry. Sending systems try the mail server with the lowest sequence number first, and work their way up if the first mail server doesn't respond. This allows you to set up multiple mail servers, using servers with higher sequence numbers as backup mail servers. Finally, the entry concludes with the complete address of the mail server, including a trailing period (.).

NOTE   Although outside users may enter a domain name only to send mail to your domain's mail server, internal users must normally specify the complete hostname when configuring an SMTP server name in mail client programs.

UNDERSTANDING SMTP TRANSPORT

Much of the material in this chapter relies upon an understanding of some key aspects of SMTP mail delivery. In particular, it's important to understand the distinction between the *envelope headers*, the *message headers*, and the *message data*. Envelope headers are From and To addresses that the sending computer provides when it makes an SMTP connection. The To envelope header, in particular, is extremely important, because that's what the receiving system uses to determine to whom the message should be delivered.

The message headers, by contrast, are provided as part of the message data, which also includes the text to be delivered to the recipient. Message headers tend to be fairly extensive on most real e-mails. They include From: and To: headers, but these are of limited value compared to the envelope From and To headers, because they're easily forged or altered. Message headers also include Received: headers, which indicate the route that the message has taken, a Subject: header that's displayed in most e-mail readers, and various others.

NOTE   Message header names are always followed by colons in the e-mail text stream, and I use that convention in this chapter. Envelope header names are usually not followed by colons, although that convention isn't universal. SMTP servers that use the maildir format don't store envelope headers under the From and To names in the message, although they're still used in SMTP transactions. Some servers can be configured to store the From and To addresses in message Received: headers, which can be a useful tool in tracking down problems.

To understand something of how SMTP works, it may help to follow an SMTP transaction. Listing 19.1 shows such an exchange, entered manually via a Telnet connection. (Most SMTP transactions, of course, don't involve a manual Telnet connection.)

Listing 19.1   A sample SMTP session

```
$ telnet louiswu.rodsbooks.com 25
Trying 192.168.1.5...
Connected to louiswu.rodsbooks.com.
Escape character is '^]'.
220 louiswu ESMTP Exim 3.12 #1 Wed, 30 Oct 2002 12:01:29 -0500
HELO nessus.rodsbooks.com
250 louiswu Hello nessus.rodsbooks.com [192.168.1.3]
MAIL FROM:<rodsmith@nessus.rodsbooks.com>
250 <rodsmith@nessus.rodsbooks.com> is syntactically correct
RCPT TO:<rodsmith@louiswu.rodsbooks.com>
250 <rodsmith@louiswu.rodsbooks.com> is syntactically correct
DATA
354 Enter message, ending with "." on a line by itself
From: <rodsmith@nessus.rodsbooks.com>
To: <rodsmith@louiswu.rodsbooks.com>
Subject: A Sample SMTP Session

This is the text of the message.
.
250 OK id=15z87H-0000CX-00
QUIT
221 louiswu closing connection
Connection closed by foreign host.
```

Most SMTP exchanges begin with the client system (which is usually a mail reader program or another MTA, or in the case of Listing 19.1 a human using telnet) identifying itself with a HELO or EHLO command. This out of the way, the client uses the MAIL FROM: and RCPT TO: commands to provide the envelope From and To headers, respectively. After each of these commands, the server MTA replies with a numeric code to indicate whether it can accept the given command. The text following those codes is generated for human consumption, should a human need to debug or oversee the process. The DATA command signals that the sender is ready to begin entering the body of the message. Thereafter, the sender enters the message headers and the text of the message. (The message headers are actually optional; they could be omitted from Listing 19.1 and the message would still be delivered.) A single blank line separates the message headers from the rest of the message body. A lone period (.) on a line signals the end of the message, at which point the recipient MTA delivers it.

There are several features of an SMTP transaction, and of the message sent during the exchange, that are important for certain configuration options. These include:

- **Sender identification**—The sending system identifies itself in several different ways. These include the HELO command, the MAIL FROM command, and the From: header. If the sender is in fact relaying mail from another site, the MAIL FROM and From: headers may legitimately differ from the sender's address. The HELO command may or may not provide accurate information in practice, although in theory it should be accurate. Another detail you should note is that the recipient system can identify the IP address of the sender. In Listing 19.1, the recipient echoes this information back to the sender—the acknowledgment of the HELO command includes the sender's IP address.

- **Envelope and message headers**—In Listing 19.1, the envelope and message headers match each other, but this need not always be the case. If you've ever received a message that doesn't appear to be addressed to you, this is how it happened—the envelope To header was to you, but the message To: header wasn't. Because the envelope To header determines delivery, the message reached you. If your mail reader lets you examine full headers, you may be able to spot the envelope To header information.

- **Options for aborting a message**—The recipient SMTP server can refuse delivery at any point along the way, from responding to the initial connection attempt to delivering the message after the sender has finished entering the data. Most message delivery and relay controls operate after the sender has issued a RCPT TO: command, but some may work before that point. Some senders re-try the delivery if a recipient aborts the transfer before the RCPT TO: command, which can cause wasted network bandwidth on the repeated attempts. Aborting after the DATA command can waste bandwidth if the sender's message is unusually long.

- **Information delivery by the server**—The exchange shown in Listing 19.1 reveals some information about the server, but not other information. For instance, the server in this example clearly identifies itself as Exim 3.12. Although it's difficult to hide the MTA package in use, some programs let you hide the version number, which can be a useful security precaution in case a security bug is found in the server—you don't want to advertise your vulnerability unnecessarily. The Exim configuration in Listing 19.1 responds to the MAIL FROM: and RCPT TO: commands with a 250 code and a fairly unrevealing is syntactically correct message. Some servers can be configured to reject mail after RCPT TO: if the specified user doesn't exist. This can provide information that could be useful to crackers—by trying many names with this or other mail server commands, crackers can locate account names. Exim in this example doesn't give out this information. On the other hand, this can cause problems because the mail server must process and then bounce messages addressed to users who don't exist.

SMTP SERVER CONFIGURATION OPTIONS

The following sections describe various features you might want to configure in your mail servers. Rather than repeat the descriptions of what these options mean in each section, I describe them once here.

ADDRESS MASQUERADING

One of the most common configuration changes required of a mail server is *address masquerading*—changing the hostname that the mail server claims to be. Ordinarily, most SMTP server installations use the hostname as set in the basic network configuration and as returned by the hostname command. The MTA uses this hostname in its HELO greeting when contacting other mail servers, as well as in the MAIL FROM command and From: message header if the mail doesn't already include that information. The server also identifies itself with this name to connecting computers, as in the 220 response in Listing 19.1.

This approach works fine in most situations, but sometimes you may need to use another name. For instance, suppose your mail server is called franklin.threeroomco.com. You might prefer that outgoing mail never be identified as coming from this computer, but instead from the threeroomco.com domain. (This might be important if you've got separate incoming and outgoing mail servers, for aesthetic reasons, or to allow you to more easily change your mail server without disrupting mail sent as replies to the default address.) You might also want to change the hostname used by a computer on a firewalled network so that return messages go to an externally accessible system. The solution is to use address masquerading to have franklin.threeroomco.com announce itself as threeroomco.com. All the mail servers discussed in this chapter can perform address masquerading, but details differ. Some include extensive options to let you fine-tune which commands, greetings, and headers use the new name, but others give fewer options. Some make it relatively easy to alter existing message headers to reflect some new address, but others discourage such actions.

NOTE Some mail administrators look down on the practice of altering mail headers, because these headers are supposed to provide a clear path back to the originating system. Other mail administrators consider the ability to rewrite mail headers absolutely vital to avoid problems that might otherwise result from mail crossing firewalls or the like. If you're unfamiliar with mail administration, you're probably best off doing as little masquerading as possible, and adding these features only if you find you have problems. If used incorrectly, masquerading can result in confusion and even bounced mail.

ACCEPTING MAIL AS LOCAL

The flip side to address masquerading is telling the mail server what addresses to treat as local. For instance, you might run a mail server that's called franklin.threeroomco.com. The default configuration in most SMTP server installations is to accept mail addressed to users at franklin. threeroomco.com. If your domain is set up with an MX record that points at this system, though, it will also see mail addressed to users at threeroomco. com. Furthermore, you might want to configure the mail server to accept mail addressed to completely different hostnames or domains. Perhaps the company has recently expanded and changed names, so you want to add fourroomco.com to the list of domains that the mail server will accept and deliver locally.

All the mail servers covered in this chapter allow you to specify what hostnames the server is to interpret as local. When you configure such a list, the server accepts mail addressed to users at these addresses and drops the messages into the users' local mailboxes (or forwards the mail, if the server is configured to forward a user's mail to another system). The details of this configuration differ from one server to another, of course.

RELAYING MAIL

One of the trickiest, and potentially most dangerous, aspects of mail configuration today is proper configuration of a mail server to handle mail *relays*. A mail relay system is one that accepts mail from one computer and delivers it to another. Most networks use at least one mail relay system, because network connections are sometimes unreliable. If a client attempted to deliver mail directly to the recipient and the connection failed, the mail client program would have to continue running to periodically attempt redelivery. An SMTP server configured as a relay, though, can accept mail from the local network with high reliability, then hold onto the mail until network conditions allow its delivery.

Unfortunately, relay configurations can be easily abused. If the MTA is too promiscuous in the systems for which it will relay, the server can be abused by third parties to send *spam* (unsolicited junk e-mail). Thus, you must find the appropriate balance to secure your server against unwelcome users while still allowing legitimate users to use the server as a relay. The correct configuration depends upon the role of the mail server program in your network, and that in turn depends in part upon your network structure.

Sometimes you may need to configure your system for third-party relaying. This is allowing an outside system to use yours as a mail relay. This is ordinarily undesirable, but there may be circumstances in which you might want to allow it. For instance, you might want to let employees who are traveling use a mail server on your own network to relay mail. Many MTA relay options that are ordinarily used to permit local relaying can be used to enable third-party relaying. You might enter the third-party IP address, domain name, or the like in the configuration options just as you would a local address or name.

 NOTE   Traveling users can be particularly troublesome, because such users frequently use dial-up ISPs with very large sets of IP addresses. You probably don't want to enable all of these IP addresses to relay, since a spammer who uses the same ISP might stumble upon your system and use it as an open relay. In such situations, it's usually better to have the traveling user use the ISP's outgoing mail server. Another option is to use an *SMTP-after-POP* configuration, in which a POP server can tell the SMTP server to accept relays from a particular IP address for some period after that IP address successfully checked or retrieved e-mail. This allows the remote user to relay mail, but only after accessing the POP server. Yet another option is to have the traveler use SSH to log on to a local system, or configure an SSH tunnel for the outgoing SMTP connection.

You may also want to configure an SMTP server to deliver all or some of its mail via another SMTP server. You might want local workstations to send mail via the departmental mail server, for instance, despite the fact that the workstations' MTAs are capable of direct delivery, in order to better track e-mail. Systems that use dial-up connections may need to use a relay in order to deliver mail at all, because some ISPs place their dial-up addresses on an anti-spam list that's used by others to block direct SMTP connections. Using the relay on such a network allows for more reliable mail delivery.

TIP

If you're configuring a system that has multiple transient Internet connections, such as a notebook that you use with different ISPs, using a mail relay may be inconvenient. Many ISPs reject relays except from systems on their own networks, so this approach will work with just one ISP. You can work around this problem by creating two SMTP server configuration files, one for each ISP, under names other than the one used by the standard configuration file. You can then add lines to your PPP dialing scripts that copy the appropriate configuration files and restart the SMTP server. For instance, if you're using sendmail, you might call the files `sendmail-isp1.cf` and `sendmail-isp2.cf`, and copy one of these to `sendmail.cf` in your PPP dialing scripts.

ANTI-SPAM CONFIGURATION

When e-mail was invented, it was considered a useful means of personal communication, and it remains that. Unfortunately, advertisers have discovered that e-mail can be an inexpensive way to communicate with potential customers. I say "unfortunately" for two reasons. First, much of the e-mail advertising today is of the lowest kind—get-rich-quick scams, ads for pornographic Web sites, and worthless products. Second, e-mail advertising is clogging mail servers around the globe, and the potential for serious harm from this form of advertising is still greater. Sending e-mail is very inexpensive, but receiving it is costlier, in terms of disk space used, recipients' time to read or even simply delete the messages, and so on. If spam becomes popular with more businesses than those of questionable repute who currently use it heavily, e-mail will quickly become completely useless, as our e-mail inboxes become clogged with thousands of worthless messages a day.

Because of concerns about spam, mail administrators frequently take steps to block it. These blocks occur at two levels: Stopping spam from getting into a mail server, and stopping it from getting out.

Blocking Incoming Spam

Your own personal concerns about spam probably revolve around the spam that's directed at your system, because this is the spam that's most obvious to you. There are several ways to control such spam. The more popular methods include the following:

- **Mail server pattern-matching blocks**—Most mail servers provide some way to block e-mail that matches certain criteria, such as mail from particular users or networks. You can use these facilities to block incoming mail from known spammers or ISPs that generate nothing but spam. Unless you review such blocks, though, you may go too far—for instance, you might block an ISP, but if the ISP cleans up its act, you'll block its legitimate users for no reason. Indeed, even an ISP that knowingly hosts spammers may also host legitimate users. Other pattern matches may be less likely to cause problems because they're more specific.

- **Blackhole lists**—Several organizations now publish lists of IP addresses that you might want to use as a basis for blocking e-mail. IP addresses on these lists may be known to have sent spam, may be open relays that are easily abused by spammers, may be associated with PPP dial-up accounts that should ordinarily relay mail through their ISPs' mail servers, or may be otherwise suspect as direct senders of e-mail. Most mail servers can be configured to use one or more such anti-spam black-hole lists. Table 19.1 summarizes some of these services, but this list is incomplete.

- **Post-MTA pattern matches**—The Procmail system, described in the upcoming section, "Using a Procmail Filter," can be used to per-form more sophisticated pattern matches than are supported by most mail servers. In fact, some sophisticated anti-spam systems, such as SpamBouncer (`http://www.spambouncer.org`), are built atop Procmail. You can use such a system or design a Procmail filter yourself.

- **Distributed pattern matching**—A fairly recent anti-spam tool is Vipul's Razor (`http://razor.sourceforge.net`). This system relies upon a catalog of spam identified by a database of spam message Secure Hash Algorithm (SHA) codes maintained by Vipul's Razor servers. You can configure your mail system to compute SHA codes on incoming mail, and if it matches the Vipul's Razor codes, you can be reasonably sure it's spam.

As a general rule, you can block a great deal of spam using just one or two methods, such as an MTA-based pattern match or a single blackhole list. One of the problems with any anti-spam measures you might take is that there is no way for a computer program using today's technology to

Table 19.1 Common Anti-Spam Blackhole Lists

List Name	URL	Server Address	Description
Dial-Up List (DUL)	`http://mail -abuse.org/dul/`	`dialups. mail-abuse.org`	This is a list of IP addresses associated with ISPs' dial-up PPP connections. The rationale is that such users shouldn't need to send mail directly, because they can use the ISP's mail relay, but spammers frequently bypass the ISP's relay.
Realtime Blackhole List (RBL)	`http://mail -abuse.org/rbl/`	`blackholes. mail-abuse.org`	This list includes systems that are known to have spammed, supported spammers in various ways, or relayed spam and not corrected the problem.
Relay Spam Stopper (RSS)	`http://mail -abuse.org/rss/`	`relays. mail-abuse.org`	This list holds systems that have been documented as having relayed spam, and which have been shown to be an open relay by a semi-automated test.
Open Relay Database (ORDB)	`http://www. ordb.org`	`relays.ordb.org`	This list is similar to the RSS, but its criteria for adding hosts are looser. Therefore, ORDB blocks more spam, but also mistakenly blocks more legitimate e-mail.
RFC Ignorant	`http://www. rfc-ignorant.org`	`Various; see Web site`	The RFC Ignorant organization maintains several blackhole lists of systems that demonstrate ignorance of one or more Request for Comments (RFC) Internet standards. Spammers often use such misconfigured systems, hence the rationale for using this as an anti-spam criterion.

determine with 100% certainty that a given message is spam. All the spam-blocking methods therefore rely upon generalizations of one sort or another, such as patterns that often appear in spam headers or the IP address from which a message comes. These generalizations often catch spam, but they may also discard legitimate e-mail, as well. Occasional *false positives* like this may be acceptable to you, or they might not be. To minimize the risk of false positives, you can use simple custom pattern-matching rules that match by very narrow criteria. Among the blackhole lists, the RBL and RSS are least likely to produce large numbers of false positives. The blackhole lists operated by the Mail Abuse Prevention System (MAPS)—the RBL, RSS, and DUL—are offered on a subscription basis, with an exception made for hobbyist sites.

How to Avoid Becoming a Spam Source

Although you're probably most concerned with blocking incoming spam, you should pay at least as much attention to preventing your system from being used to transmit spam. On a large network, you may need to be careful to police your own users to be sure they don't originate spam. This may involve creating an *acceptable use policy (AUP)* that prohibits spamming and ensuring that your users are aware of it. Some users may not realize the extent to which spam is frowned upon.

Especially on a small network or an individual workstation on which a mail server is installed, a more serious concern is that of configuring your system so that it doesn't become an *open relay*—a computer that's configured to relay mail from any system on the Internet to any other system on the Internet. (Even relaying between subsets of systems may be problematic, if those subsets are large enough.) Much of the upcoming discussion of individual SMTP servers is concerned with relay configuration. You may need your system to relay for certain systems, but it's important when you create this configuration that you don't open your system too widely.

One way to test whether a system is an open relay is to Telnet *from that system* to `relay-test.mail-abuse.org`. Doing this causes a reverse connection to your own mail server. You'll see the tests as they proceed, followed by a statement that your system is or is not an open relay. Although this test can be very useful, it's not absolutely conclusive; there are configurations that can fool the test, but it's a good place to start.

To learn more about anti-relay configurations, including tips for how to configure various mail servers, check the MAPS Transport Security Initiative (TSI) Web page at `http://mail-abuse.org/tsi/`.

BASIC SENDMAIL CONFIGURATION

In 2002, Sendmail was the most popular MTA in the world, according to surveys of MTA use. It's also the MTA that's the default with most Linux distributions, including Caldera, Red Hat, Slackware, SuSE, and TurboLinux. Debian and Mandrake, although they install other SMTP servers by default, also provide the option of using sendmail. As I write, version 8.12.2 is the latest, but some Linux distributions still ship with older versions of 8.11.*x* or earlier.

Sendmail uses a fairly obtuse configuration file format, but utilities exist to configure the software by compiling a simpler file format into the one that sendmail actually reads. Knowing how to do this is critical to configuring sendmail. In addition to the configuration files themselves, this section covers a few specific areas of sendmail configuration: address masquerading, accepting incoming mail, and relay configuration.

SENDMAIL'S CONFIGURATION FILES

Sendmail's primary configuration file is called sendmail.cf, and it's usually located in /etc. This file is difficult to edit directly, though, because there are many options, they use very non-mnemonic names, and they're formatted in a way that's difficult to read.

To work around the difficulties inherent in directly editing sendmail.cf, most distributions use the m4 macro processing utility to create the sendmail.cf file from a simpler and more easily understood file. The m4 source file usually has a filename that ends in .mc, but the exact name varies from one distribution to another. For instance, in Red Hat it's /etc/sendmail.mc, in Slackware it's /usr/src/sendmail/cf/cf/linux.smtp.mc, and in SuSE it's /etc/mail/linux.mc. No matter the name, the m4 source files are much shorter and more readable than the .cf files they create. For instance, in SuSE 7.1, the sendmail.cf file is 1669 lines long, whereas the linux.mc file that creates it is only 221 lines long—and most of those lines are comments (lines that begin with dnl). A working sendmail m4 file can be less than 50 lines long.

To create a sendmail.cf file from an m4 file, you must run the m4 command, using input redirection to feed it the m4 configuration file and using output redirection to send the output to a file. For instance, you might use the following command on SuSE Linux:

```
# m4 < /etc/mail/linux.mc > /etc/sendmail.cf
```

NOTE Some distributions require you to install a separate package of support files before you can build your m4 source files into a working sendmail.cf file. For instance, Red Hat needs the sendmail-cf package before you can rebuild a sendmail configuration file.

WARNING

> Be sure not to overwrite a working `sendmail.cf` file. It's generally best to back up this file, and your original m4 source file, to a location in another directory. This way if something goes wrong and you can't seem to get sendmail working again, you can restore the original files.

You'll have to restart sendmail after you rebuild its configuration file in order to see your changes take effect. Most distributions start sendmail through SysV scripts, so you should restart sendmail via the script's `restart` option.

Most options in an m4 configuration file take the following form:

FEATURE-NAME(` option1'[,`option2'[,...])

The *FEATURE-NAME* is a name that's at least somewhat descriptive, such as `define` or `MASQUERADE_AS`. The options (*option1, option2*, and so on) may be hostnames, sendmail-specific option names such as `always_add_domain`, and so on. Some feature definitions can omit the single quote marks, but most use them.

WARNING

> When present, the single quote marks surrounding the options are unusual because they're dissimilar. The opening quote in any given option is a backquote character (`` ` ``), which is located on the key to the left of the 1 key on most keyboards. The ending quote is a regular single quote character, which is located on the key to the right of the semicolon (;) key on most keyboards. If you use two regular single quote characters, as you would in most configuration files, either m4 won't be able to process the file or the sendmail configuration file will not work as expected.

In addition to the `sendmail.cf` file and the m4 file that creates it, sendmail relies on additional files. A couple of the more important of these include the following:

- **access.db**—This file is a binary file that's derived from the plain-text access file. This file controls what computers may access sendmail in what ways. Sendmail relay configurations, described shortly, often depend upon this file's contents. Most sendmail startup scripts run `makemap` to automatically generate `access.db` if access has changed since the last time `access.db` was built.

- **aliases.db**—This is another binary file derived from a text file with a similar name (aliases). It defines mail aliases—that is, names that are to be considered equivalent to one another. For instance, most distributions set up postmaster as an alias for root, and you may want to set up an alias for root to direct root's mail to your ordinary user account. As with access.db, many sendmail startup scripts automatically generate aliases.db from aliases.

You'll probably find these files in /etc or /etc/mail, along with other database files that control other details of sendmail's operation. These files are referenced by the m4 file, and by sendmail.cf.

SENDMAIL ADDRESS MASQUERADING

If you want your SMTP server to announce itself under a name other than its regular hostname, you must configure sendmail to perform some form of address masquerading, as described earlier. There are two lines you can set in your m4 configuration file to activate two different facets of address masquerading:

```
MASQUERADE_AS(`desired-address')
FEATURE(masquerade_envelope)
```

The MASQUERADE_AS feature enables the most basic level of masquerading, which only changes the address used in the mail header's From: field if the user's mail program doesn't specify a hostname. Because many mail programs set this field, this option is most useful as a fallback in case a user's mail program isn't completely or correctly configured. The FEATURE (masquerade_envelope) line does more, because it actively changes the From: header even if the sender's mail program set this option.

If you want your masquerading to apply only to mail from certain domains' users, you can use a couple of additional lines to limit the application of these masquerading features:

```
MASQUERADE_DOMAIN(`source-domain')
FEATURE(`limited_masquerade')
```

These options tell sendmail to limit its masquerading to addresses within the specified *source-domain*. Such a configuration is most likely to be helpful if your system functions as a mail server for two domains; you can set it to masquerade as a system within the appropriate domain for each message it sends.

CONFIGURING SENDMAIL TO ACCEPT MAIL

When a remote server sends mail to your system, the mail is addressed to a specific user on a specific computer. In order to accept delivery of local mail, sendmail must be able to recognize all the local addresses, as described earlier. Sendmail allows you to add all the names for the mail server to a local hostnames file, including the raw domain name if you've configured an MX record for it. This file has different names in different distributions, and these names are set in files loaded with the sendmail m4 package. In Red Hat, it's /etc/mail/local-host-names; in SuSE, it's /etc/sendmail.cw. If you can't find the file, try searching for a line in sendmail.cf that begins Fw. This line sets the name of the local hostnames file. Whatever its name, this file consists of a series of lines, each of which contains a hostname that the computer will consider to be local. Sendmail ignores lines that begin with a pound sign (#), though. You can omit the computer's regular hostname, although including it will do no harm.

SENDMAIL RELAY CONFIGURATION

As described earlier, relay configurations are extremely important in setting up a mail server. You must be able to configure sendmail to relay its own mail, possibly mail from the local network, and perhaps even mail from remote networks, as appropriate, without opening up the system as one that might be abused by spammers. In addition, you may want or need to configure the system to send its outgoing mail through another system as a relay. Fortunately, sendmail offers many mail relay options.

Configuring Sendmail to Relay Mail

One common mail relay configuration is to have a mail server forward mail for a local network. The idea is to use a mail server to relay mail, storing it temporarily in the event of network problems. You then point other local systems' mail programs to the mail server.

Out of the box, most sendmail installations will not work as mail relays. If you try it, the mail server refuses to relay the message. Most mail clients inform you that they've received a "relaying denied" response from the mail server. Sendmail allows you to activate several different relay options if you want it to function as a relay. You can include any of the following options in a FEATURE line:

- **relay_entire_domain**—When this option is used, sendmail accepts relay mail that originates from within its own domain, or that's addressed to any system within its local domain. Sendmail uses DNS to verify the sender's domain based upon the IP address. This can be a quick and convenient way to enable relaying.

- **relay_local_from**—This option tells sendmail to accept relays of any message that uses a From: address within sendmail's local domain. This differs from the preceding option in that this one uses only the *claimed* address in the From: header, which is easily forged. This option is therefore a poor one from an anti-spam point of view.

- **relay_based_on_MX**—This option tells sendmail to accept a relay if the domain in which the sender resides lists your sendmail system as a mail exchanger. This can be a quick and convenient way to control relaying, because you don't need to modify the sendmail configuration if you want to add domains; you need only modify the DNS records. The drawback is that spammers who control their own domains can easily adjust their MX records and hijack your mail server.

- **relay_hosts_only**—If you use this option, sendmail uses an access database, described shortly. Only individual hosts listed in this database are allowed to relay. This can be a good way to limit relays to an arbitrary set of computers.

- **access_db**—Many sendmail configurations use this option by default. Like relay_hosts_only, it causes sendmail to use an access database. This option causes the database to be interpreted a bit more loosely, though; you can list entire domains in the database by using this option.

WARNING

A final option, promiscuous_relay, should be avoided at all costs. This feature tells sendmail to accept *any* relay request. Such an open relay configuration is almost certain to be discovered and abused by spammers.

An example of a relay configuration line is the following:

```
FEATURE(`access_db')
```

This option is present in many installations' default m4 configuration files, but it doesn't actually enable practical relaying because the default access.db file permits only localhost relaying, as described shortly. If the access_db option is active, sendmail reads the access.db file when it starts.

As described earlier, this file is usually stored in /etc or /etc/mail, and it's built from a file called access. A typical access file looks like this:

```
# Allow relaying from localhost...
localhost.localdomain       RELAY
localhost                   RELAY
127.0.0.1                   RELAY
# Relay for the local network
192.168.99                  RELAY
```

The first three entries are present in most configurations; they tell sendmail to accept mail from the localhost computer (that is, the sendmail computer itself) for relaying. Some local mail programs rely on such a configuration. The final entry tells sendmail to relay any mail that comes from the 192.168.99.0/24 network. You can also provide hostnames or domain names instead of IP addresses, but IP addresses are slightly harder to forge, and so are preferable whenever possible.

All of the preceding examples end in RELAY, but there are other options you can use:

- **OK**—This option tells sendmail to accept the mail for local delivery even if other rules would cause the mail to be rejected.
- **RELAY**—As you might guess, this causes sendmail to relay mail that originates from the specified host or domain. It also causes mail addressed *to* these hosts or domains to be relayed, as well.
- **REJECT**—If you want to block mail coming from or going to a given host or domain, you can use this option, which rejects the mail and generates a bounce message.
- **DISCARD**—This option works very much like REJECT, but no bounce message is generated.
- ***nnn text***—This is another option that works like REJECT, but it generates the error code *nnn* along with *text* as a bounce message.

Once you've edited the access file, you can create a binary database file from it with the makemap command, thus:

```
# makemap hash /etc/mail/access.db < /etc/mail/access
```

Many sendmail installations include such a command in their startup scripts, so this step may not be strictly necessary. Either way, you should restart sendmail to have it reread the access file.

Configuring Sendmail to Send Through a Relay

The preceding section dealt with the question of using sendmail as a mail relay. There's one other aspect of relay configuration you may want to consider, though: Having sendmail use another system as a mail relay. You might do this if you run a small network or even a single computer, and want or need to use your ISP's mail server as a relay. Although Linux and sendmail are capable of queuing mail locally and delivering it directly, a few ISPs require you to use their own mail servers for outgoing mail. Some mail servers refuse mail that's sent directly from dial-up IP addresses that are listed on certain anti-spam lists, so dial-up users may need to use this approach to send mail reliably. Also, some Linux systems—particularly laptops—might be shut down much of the time, so you'd do well to configure them to use another system as a mail relay.

Most Linux distributions' sendmail configurations don't use an outgoing mail relay, but you can use one by adding a single line to your m4 configuration file:

```
FEATURE(`nullclient', `outgoing.mail.relay')
```

In this example, *outgoing.mail.relay* is the hostname of the computer that's to relay your mail. After you rebuild sendmail.cf and restart the server, it should relay all mail through the specified outgoing mail server. Be sure to test that mail is being delivered correctly after making this change.

SENDMAIL ANTI-SPAM CONFIGURATION

There are several ways to configure sendmail to block spam and to prevent unauthorized relay use. One simple anti-spam configuration is to use the access file and its binary equivalent, access.db, to block spam based on source hostnames or domains. If you associate a hostname, domain name, or IP address with a REJECT or DISCARD action, as described earlier, sendmail will block all mail from that address. This can be an effective tool if you regularly receive spam from certain source sites, but you should be cautious about using this approach; you can easily block a great deal of legitimate mail if spammers happen to abuse a popular ISP.

Another approach to blocking incoming spam with sendmail is to use one or more blackhole lists. You can do this with the dnsbl feature in your m4 file, thus:

```
FEATURE(dnsbl, `blackholes.mail-abuse.org', `Rejected - see \
http://www.mail-abuse.org/rbl/')
```

This line causes sendmail to use the MAPS RBL. Change the second option of FEATURE to the value listed in the Server Address column of Table 19.1 to use another blackhole list. The final argument is a string that's included in bounced mail. You should use it to point the bounce recipient to the appropriate blackhole list's Web site, so that if legitimate e-mail is mistakenly bounced, the sender can take steps to correct the problem. You can specify multiple blackhole lists if you like.

NOTE The use of blackhole lists has changed substantially with sendmail 8.10, and this discussion applies to that version and later. Prior versions had much less sophisticated blackhole provisions. Consult `http://mail-abuse.org /rbl/usage.html` for further information on this point.

Preventing unauthorized relaying with sendmail is a matter of configuring sendmail to relay in the most stringent manner possible. The simplest approach is usually to list individual IP addresses or IP address blocks in `access`, but some of the other relay options may be useful in some situations. You should *never* use the `promiscuous_relay` feature.

WARNING If you're using a version of sendmail that's older than 8.9.0, it's probably configured to allow relays by default. You should upgrade to a newer version of sendmail, or consult `http://mail-abuse.org/tsi/ar-fix.html#sendmail_8` for information on how to reconfigure sendmail to not relay promiscuously. Versions prior to 8.8.4 are not easily reconfigured to prevent unauthorized relays; they should almost certainly be upgraded.

BASIC EXIM CONFIGURATION

As the mail server that's the default for Debian GNU/Linux and its derivatives, Exim is moderately popular in the Linux world. You can also use Exim with other distributions, and in fact it ships with the PowerTools extensions for Red Hat, so it's fairly easy to install on Red Hat and related distributions. Like sendmail, Exim is a monolithic program, but the Exim configuration file format is relatively simple. Exim is capable of doing many of the same things as is sendmail, and this section describes some of these things, such as address masquerading, accepting mail addressed to multiple domains, and setting various relay options.

NOTE   Because Exim is the default MTA only for Debian among those distributions discussed in this book, this section uses Exim as shipped with Debian as a reference. Other Exim installations may be configured differently by default.

EXIM'S CONFIGURATION FILES

The main Exim configuration file is called `exim.conf`, and it's usually located in `/etc`. This file consists of lines of the form:

```
option = value
```

The file may also contain comments, which are lines that begin with a pound sign (#). In fact, a standard Debian Exim installation uses an `exim.conf` file that's mostly comments documenting what the configuration lines do. This fact can help greatly when you want to modify an Exim installation, because you can often figure out what needs to be changed by reading the comments in the configuration file.

TIP   When Debian installs Exim, the installer runs a script called `eximconfig` that generates the `exim.conf` file. You can run this script after the fact to reconfigure Exim without directly editing the `exim.conf` file. For small changes it's usually easier to edit the file yourself, because `eximconfig` requires you to respond to all its questions again. Nonetheless, `eximconfig` can be a useful tool if you're unfamiliar with Exim configuration, because it generates a configuration file with options that are appropriate for your system.

In addition to the main `exim.conf` file, Exim may use other files as sources of supplemental information. In particular, a default Debian Exim configuration uses these files:

- **/etc/aliases**— This file serves the same function in Exim as in sendmail: It associates two accounts so that mail addressed to one user is delivered to another. For instance, the line `root: amelia` causes mail addressed to `root` to be delivered to `amelia` instead. You can also specify a nonlocal account; for instance, `root: amelia@pangaea.edu` causes local mail for `root` to be sent to `amelia@pangaea.edu`. Unlike the sendmail file of this name, the Exim file doesn't need to be compiled into a binary format to be used.

- **/etc/email-addresses**—This file causes From: addresses in outgoing mail to be rewritten. For instance, `ben: bfranklin@pangaea.edu` causes mail from `ben` on the local system to appear to come from `bfranklin@pangaea.edu`.

The `eximconf` script creates an `/etc/aliases` file that directs mail addressed to `postmaster` to `root`, and in turn directs `root`'s mail to a user you specify. You can add, delete, or modify this file as you see fit. The standard Debian `/etc/email-addresses` file is empty except for some comments.

EXIM ADDRESS MASQUERADING

As described earlier, in "Address Masquerading," you may want Exim to use a particular hostname or domain name instead of the one that's returned by the `hostname` command. The most basic level of address masquerading is accomplished through the `qualify_domain` option. This sets the domain that's used for locally generated mail if the mail program does not set an address itself. For instance, suppose your `exim.conf` file includes the following line:

```
qualify_domain = threeroomco.com
```

If `ben` sends mail from a program that doesn't specify a From: domain, Exim will add the `threeroomco.com` domain to the address or replace an address that doesn't match this domain name, so that From: headers and the like will read `ben@threeroomco.com`.

Another option you might want to use is `primary_hostname`. You set this much like you do `qualify_domain`, and in fact the value of `primary_hostname` is used as the default for `qualify_domain`. The `primary_hostname` value is used in initial handshakes between Exim and the remote mail server, and the name also appears in Received: e-mail headers.

A more sophisticated address masquerading option is provided by the `/etc/email-addresses` file, described earlier. More precisely, this file is referenced by a line near the end of the `exim.conf` file. This line resembles the following:

```
*@threeroomco.com   ${lookup{$1}lsearch{/etc/email-addresses}\
                    {$value}fail} bcfrF
```

This is one of `exim.conf`'s least transparent configuration lines, and you shouldn't need to adjust it, except perhaps to alter the domain at the beginning of the line. This line matches any address that falls in the threeroomco.com domain, and causes Exim to check /etc/email-addresses for a more precise match. If the first field (before the colon) of a line in email-addresses matches that in an e-mail address, the second field (after the colon) is substituted. This tool allows you to perform address masquerading on a user-by-user basis; you need only edit the email-addresses file, as described earlier. If your mail server processes mail from multiple domains, you could duplicate the exim.conf entry for each domain, specifying a different substitution file for each domain or even using one file for all of them.

These descriptions cover only a fraction of the address masquerading features available in Exim. For more information, consult the "Address Rewriting" chapter of the Exim documentation at http://www.exim.org/exim-html-3.30/doc/html/spec_34.html.

CONFIGURING EXIM TO ACCEPT MAIL

Exim provides several exim.conf options that determine whether it should treat an address as local, and deliver it as such. These include:

- **local_domains**—You can set this option to a colon-delimited list of hostnames that Exim will treat as local. For instance, local_domains = localhost:threeroomco.com causes Exim to accept mail addressed to users at localhost or threeroomco.com as local, and deliver that mail to local users. This value defaults to the value of the qualify_recipient option, which sets the hostname on incoming mail that lacks a hostname.

- **local_domains_include_host**—If this option is set to true, Exim accepts mail addressed to the computer's current hostname. You can achieve a similar effect by adding the hostname to the local_domains list.

- **local_domains_include_host_literals**—If this option is set to true, Exim accepts mail that's addressed to the system by IP address rather than by name. For instance, if Exim is running on a computer with the 172.24.98.2 IP address, and if the user ben exists, Exim will accept mail addressed to ben@[172.24.98.2]. If you don't want to accept such mail, set this value to false.

The eximconfig script sets some of these options based upon your responses to questions about domains for which you should accept mail, so if you've run this script and answered the questions appropriately, you should find reasonable default values already set.

EXIM RELAY CONFIGURATION

Like sendmail, Exim has several relay options, relating to both relaying mail from other systems and relaying outgoing mail through another SMTP system. The `eximconfig` script asks questions about relays, and so should configure Exim properly in many situations. You can change or fine-tune this configuration by directly editing `exim.conf`.

Configuring Exim to Relay Mail

The most important `exim.conf` options relating to mail relaying are as follows:

- **host_accept_relay**—To have Exim relay mail for specific computers, you should list them using this option (separating the names by colons). Most systems use at least `host_accept_relay = localhost`, which lets Exim relay mail that originates locally. Expanding this list by specifying all the hostnames, IP addresses, or wildcards that match the desired hosts expands Exim's relaying options. For instance, `host_accept_relay = localhost:192.168.99.0/24:*.pangaea.edu` allows `localhost`, all computers in the 192.168.99.0/24 network, and all computers in the `pangaea.edu` domain to relay mail. Using this feature to specify the IP addresses of your local domain is probably the safest way to permit relaying for most installations.

- **relay_domains**—You can list one or more domains with this option (separated by colons). Exim will relay mail from any system in the specified domains. This option is most useful if your mail server should relay mail for several different domains, or even just one very large domain. You can accomplish much the same goal by using an asterisk (*) wildcard as the machine name in a hostname with the `host_accept_relay` option.

- **relay_domains_include_local_mx**—If you want to have Exim automatically adjust its relaying policy to allow new domains, you can use this option. If you set it to `yes`, it permits computers whose DNS servers have an MX record that point to your system to relay mail. This can be convenient, because it eliminates the need to adjust Exim if you routinely change domain configurations. It's potentially risky, though, because a spammer could set up a domain with an MX entry that points to your Exim server and use your system as an effectively open relay.

- **sender_address_relay**—You can provide a colon-delimited list of e-mail addresses that are allowed to relay with this option. Ordinarily, if you use this option, a mail must match *both* this and a host-based option, such as host_accept_relay. (You can change this behavior to use *either* by specifying relay_match_host_or_sender = yes, but this configuration is potentially very dangerous because e-mail addresses are trivial to forge.) You can use this feature to limit who from a given system may relay mail through Exim.

These options permit you to configure Exim to relay mail for only some systems, such as those on your local network or any remote domains for which Exim should be a relay. These options are sufficient for many purposes. For more exotic needs, Exim supports some additional options, such as host_auth_accept_relay (which requires that remote systems authenticate themselves before relaying) and tls_host_accept_relay (which requires that remote systems use an authentication and encryption system known as TLS).

Configuring Exim to Send Through a Relay

If your system must use an outgoing relay, you need to configure Exim to direct all outgoing mail through that system. Unfortunately, there is no single Exim configuration option to handle this situation. The eximconfig utility, though, can generate a series of configuration lines that have the desired effect. These lines resemble the following:

```
smarthost:
  driver = domainlist
  transport = remote_smtp
  route_list = "* franklin.threeroomco.com bydns_a"
end
```

These lines tell Exim to send all external mail via franklin.threeroomco.com. You can change this system's name if your mail relay system ever changes.

EXIM ANTI-SPAM CONFIGURATION

One of Exim's strengths is its extensive set of filtering rules. You can use these to specify hosts for which you'll refuse delivery, specify users from whom you'll refuse delivery, or perform more sophisticated checks on a per-user basis. The major filtering options are as follows:

- **host_reject**—This `exim.conf` option takes a colon-delimited list of hostnames, domain names, or IP addresses as its argument, and blocks all mail that originates from these systems. For instance, `host_reject = *.badspammer.net:10.16.8.0/24` blocks all mail from the `badspammer. net` domain, and from the 10.16.8.0/24 network block. This rejection occurs as soon as the remote system attempts to make a connection. This sometimes causes repeated attempts to connect to your server, thus consuming small amounts of network resources over an extended period of time.

- **host_reject_recipients**—This option works much like `host_reject`, except that messages are rejected after the remote system begins the transaction, and more precisely, after it's sent the `RCPT TO:` command. The result is more likely to be an immediate cessation of attempts to send the messages.

- **sender_reject**—This option rejects mail that originates from certain senders. A sender may be either an entire domain or an individual user at a domain. For instance, `sender_reject = spammer@abigisp.com: badspammer.net` blocks mail from the `badspammer.net` domain and from the user `spammer@abigisp.com`. Exim refuses to receive mail as soon as it learns the sender's identity. This quick rejection causes some sending systems to try repeatedly to send the same message.

- **sender_reject_recipients**—This option works much like `sender_reject`, but it waits to reject the mail until the sender has entered a recipient address with the `RCPT TO:` command. This approach is more effective than `sender_reject`'s approach at getting the sending MTA to stop attempting to send the messages.

- **User-specific filters**—Exim supports filters that individual users can design. These reside in the `.forward` files in users' own home directories. This facility is extremely powerful and flexible. It's similar in many ways to Procmail filters, which are described shortly in the section "Using a Procmail Filter." It's described in some detail in the `filter. txt.gz` documentation file that comes with Exim, in the `/usr/doc/exim` directory in Debian GNU/Linux (you'll need to uncompress this file with `gunzip` to read it).

If you want to create a large list of senders or sender hostnames you want to reject, you can place them in a separate file, and reference that filename with the appropriate rejection options. In addition to custom filters, Exim includes several options related to support for blackhole lists. These are controlled through several `exim.conf` options:

- **rbl_domains**—Provide a colon-delimited list of blackhole list server addresses, such as those shown in Table 19.1, to have Exim use those lists. You can append these entries with /warn or /reject to specify that Exim add a warning header (which might be used by a subsequent Procmail filter, for instance) or reject the mail outright, respectively. Two additional options are /accept (to use a blackhole-like mechanism to provide a limited "white list") and /skiprelay (which bypasses the blackhole list check if the sender's domain is listed in the host_accept_relay option).

- **rbl_hosts**—The default for this option is *, which causes Exim to check all hosts against the blackhole lists specified by rbl_domains. You might want to exempt certain senders from these checks, though, and to do so, you add their names, preceded by exclamation marks, prior to the asterisk in a colon-delimited list. For instance, rbl_hosts = !ok.pangaea.edu:* exempts ok.pangaea.edu from the blackhole list checks.

- **rbl_reject_recipients**—You can use the /warn or /reject features of the rbl_domains option to specify whether to add a warning or reject a suspected spam, as noted earlier. When you've not specified explicitly what to do, Exim defaults to rejecting the affected mail. You can change this behavior to merely add a warning header by setting rbl_reject_recipients = no.

- **recipients_reject_except**—This option lets you specify blackhole list exceptions in terms of recipients. For instance, recipients_reject_except = postmaster@*your.domain* causes Exim to accept mail addressed to postmaster@*your.domain*, even from sites included on a blackhole list.

There are a few additional blackhole list options in Exim; consult the package's documentation for details. In addition to pattern matching and blackhole lists, Exim provides a few additional options that may be used to help cut down on spam. These include the following:

- **headers_check_syntax**—Exim can check message headers for bogus syntax, such as a message addressed to user@, and reject messages that fail these checks. This is normally a sanity check on the veracity of the data, but some spam uses poorly constructed mail headers that will fail such checks. To use this option, set it to true.

- **helo_verify**—During initial connections, a calling SMTP server identifies itself with a HELO or EHLO command. Normally, Exim doesn't require this, but you can set it to be more strict by providing a list of hosts that must use this handshake. (You can set helo_verify = * to require all senders to pass this test.) In addition to requiring use of HELO or EHLO, helo_verify requires that the IP address and DNS entries on the host match one another. Spammers often use misconfigured systems for which this isn't true, but unfortunately, many legitimate mail server systems are also misconfigured in such a way that they'll fail this test.

- **message_size_limit**—This option is another that's not strictly a spam-fighting tool, but that might catch some spam. It defaults to 0, which translates into no size limit. If you set this option to a positive value, that's the maximum message size that Exim will accept. This might be useful in limiting the impact of inconsiderate or accidental delivery of overly large messages to your system.

In all, Exim's spam filtering capabilities are extremely capable, particularly if you're willing to delve into the creation of user-specific filter files.

BASIC POSTFIX CONFIGURATION

Like Exim, Postfix was designed to have a main configuration file that can be easily interpreted and edited by humans—or at least, by humans who know enough about SMTP terminology to understand the names used. Postfix was also designed to be a modular mail server, in which multiple programs work together to accomplish the tasks performed by just one program in sendmail or Exim. The general outlines of Postfix's features are similar to those of sendmail or Exim; like these other SMTP servers, Postfix allows address masquerading, acceptance of mail sent to multiple domains as local, a variety of relay options, and anti-spam features.

Postfix is the default MTA with Linux Mandrake, but it's available as an option in some others, including Debian and SuSE. The Red Hat Power-Tools collection includes Postfix, as well. The Mandrake RPM package can be installed in many other RPM-based Linux distributions, although the SysV startup script included in that package may not work. Because Mandrake is the major distribution that uses Postfix by default, this discussion focuses upon Postfix as delivered with Mandrake. Most other Postfix packages are similar in their defaults, though.

POSTFIX'S CONFIGURATION FILES

The Postfix configuration file you're most likely to modify is `main.cf`, and it's normally located in `/etc/postfix`. You specify features such as your local domains and relay configuration options here. Most items in `main.cf` take the following form:

```
option = value
```

Some of the `main.cf` options are referred to in later lines as variables. This is done by preceding the original *option* name with a dollar sign ($) and placing it in the *value* position. For instance, consider the following pair of lines, which may be separated by many other lines:

```
myhostname = franklin.threeroomco.com
myorigin = $myhostname
```

This combination sets the `myhostname` variable to the computer's hostname, `franklin.threeroomco.com`, and then sets `myorigin` to the same value. Such chains are common in Postfix, so you may find yourself tracing back through variables to determine what a given option is set to be.

The default `main.cf` file consists mostly of comments, which are lines that begin with pound signs (#). These comments do most of the work of documenting the options that they precede, so you can learn a great deal about Postfix configuration by reading its configuration file.

The `main.cf` file includes references to several other files. As with `sendmail`, some of these are binary files (with `.db` filename extensions) that are built from files of the same name, but lacking the `.db` extensions. The file of this type that you're most likely to want to edit is `aliases` (`aliases.db` in its binary form). This file sets up delivery aliases, much like the sendmail file of the same name. For instance, a line in this file that reads `root: amelia` causes all mail addressed to `root` to be delivered to `amelia`. To convert the text-format `aliases` file into the binary `aliases.db`, type **postalias aliases** from the directory in which `aliases` resides.

After you modify a text-mode file and create the matching `.db` file, Postfix will eventually discover the changes. You can speed this process up by typing **postfix reload** or by restarting Postfix through its SysV startup script.

POSTFIX ADDRESS MASQUERADING

The myorigin parameter sets the name that Postfix uses to identify itself to remote systems. A default configuration sets this parameter to the value of the $myhostname variable, which in turn defaults to the computer's regular hostname. This default configuration works well for many systems, but you may want to change it if the computer has multiple hostnames or if you want to use the domain name rather than the hostname. To do this, you should set the myorigin parameter to something appropriate, like this:

```
myorigin = threeroomco.com
```

Alternatively, you can use another variable on the *value* side of this assignment. One possible *value* is $mydomain. This variable defaults to $myhostname minus the leftmost component. For instance, if $myhostname is franklin.threeroomco.com, $mydomain defaults to threeroomco.com. You can set any of these by inserting appropriate lines in main.conf. In fact, the default main.conf includes example lines that have been commented out, so you can uncomment these and edit them to suit your needs.

Setting myorigin only performs a very basic form of address configuration. Specifically, this setting only affects initial SMTP handshaking and the default address that's used if a mail program doesn't explicitly set the domain part of a From: address. You might want to perform a somewhat more complete form of address masquerading if your mail server relays mail for other systems on your domain, which might set their own complete addresses in their headers. For instance, suppose a Postfix client wants to relay mail through Postfix, but the client specifies a From: address of ben@client.threeroomco.com. You might want to remove the client portion of that address, yielding ben@threeroomco.com. Assuming that the $mydomain variable is set to threeroomco.com, you can accomplish the goal by using the following option:

```
masquerade_domains = $mydomain
```

This option causes Postfix to strip away the nondomain portion of any hostname within $mydomain when it processes the mail message. The result is that both From: and To: headers for mail from systems within $mydomain will show $mydomain addresses, not individual systems within $mydomain.

You can implement a still more complete form of address masquerading, also known as *address rewriting*, by pointing Postfix to a rewriting database file with the sender_canonical_maps option, thus:

```
sender_canonical_maps = hash:/etc/postfix/sender_canonical
```

You can then create a set of mappings in the sender_canonical file. Each line of this file contains an address that might appear in a header followed by the address with which it should be replaced. For instance, the following two lines replace both client.threeroomco.com and localhost with threeroomco.com:

```
@client.threeroomco.com @threeroomco.com
@localhost @threeroomco.com
```

You can use a similar technique if you need to remap usernames. For instance, your e-mail system might be in transition between ones that use different username forms. You can use a canonical map file to convert all references to the obsolete addressing to the new one on a user-by-user basis (one line per user).

After creating the sender_canonical file, you must convert it to a binary form by typing **postmap sender_canonical**. You can then type **postfix reload** or restart Postfix to have it use the new mapping.

As a general rule, you should use the minimum level of address masquerading that you require. Most Postfix installations work fine with nothing more than the default settings, or perhaps an explicit adjustment to $myorigin. The masquerade_domains option is useful on mail relays that may process mail that's already passed through mail servers on Linux or UNIX workstations. Address rewriting is extremely powerful, in part because it rewrites much more of the e-mail's headers than do the other techniques, including even the contents of the Received: headers. This fact makes many administrators reluctant to use this feature, but sometimes it's very useful, particularly if you have programs that insist on using peculiar usernames or hostnames in their From: addresses.

CONFIGURING POSTFIX TO ACCEPT MAIL

Like other mail servers, Postfix accepts as local only mail addressed to specific hostnames. Postfix uses the mydestination parameter to decide what hostnames to treat as local. This parameter defaults to $myhostname plus localhost.$mydomain. For instance, if $mydomain is threeroomco.com and $myhostname is franklin.threeroomco.com, Postfix accepts mail addressed to franklin.threeroomco.com or localhost.threeroomco.com.

You can easily adjust the mydestination parameter, and in fact a mail server for a domain should have this parameter adjusted to include at least $myhostname and $mydomain. Adding localhost alone is also often a good idea. You should separate your entries with commas or spaces. In sum, a typical mail server for a single domain might include an entry like the following:

```
mydestination = localhost, localhost.$mydomain, $myhostname,
                $mydomain
```

NOTE You do *not* need to end a mydestination line with a backslash (\) if it continues to the next line, as is the case with many configuration files. Instead, the second and subsequent lines should begin with a space or tab to signal that they're continuations of the first line.

You can have a Postfix server handle multiple domains by specifying them all in a single mydestination parameter. Most of these domains would be listed explicitly, rather than through variables.

POSTFIX RELAY CONFIGURATION

Like most mail servers, Postfix supports many relay options, including both using the Postfix computer as a relay and having Postfix deliver its outgoing mail through another computer that functions as a relay. These relay options are configured through the main.cf file.

Configuring Postfix to Relay Mail

By default, Postfix relays mail that meets any of the following criteria:

- The sender is on any of the networks specified by $mynetworks. This variable defaults to the networks associated with all of the computer's network interfaces, including the localhost interface.
- The sender is in a domain specified by $relay_domains. This variable defaults to the value of $mydestination.
- The sender is attempting to relay mail to a computer in one of the $relay_domains domains, or a subdomain thereof.

The defaults mean that Postfix relays for any computer that's on any of Postfix's local network interfaces, or in the same domain as Postfix. This configuration works well for many mail servers that should function as local relays, but you may want to adjust it. To do so, you may need to alter either or both of $mynetworks and $relay_domains. For instance, suppose Postfix is to function as the MTA for a workstation called work.threeroomco.com. Such a system should never relay, so you might want to redefine these variables as follows:

```
mynetworks = 127.0.0.0/8
relay_domains = work.threeroomco.com
```

This configuration limits relaying to the localhost network and the Postfix mail server itself. On the other hand, you might want to loosen relaying to include additional domains or networks. You might do so with parameters like the following:

```
mynetworks = 192.168.99.0/24, 172.24.0.0/16, 127.0.0.0/8
relay_domains = $mydestination, pangaea.edu
```

These options cause Postfix to relay messages originating from the 192.168.99.0/24, 172.24.0.0/16, and localhost (127.0.0.0/8) networks, or from the $mydestination or pangaea.edu domains.

Underlying the mynetworks and relay_domains controls, as well as several other delivery and relaying restriction options, is the smtpd_sender_restrictions parameter. This option doesn't appear in the default main.cf file, but you can add it if you need even finer control over relaying. You can read more about it in the Postfix documentation. The permit_mx_backup value to this option is noteworthy as being similar to sendmail's relay_based_on_MX feature.

Configuring Postfix to Send Through a Relay

In a simple case, configuring Postfix to use another system as a relay requires setting just one option in main.cf: relayhost. This option specifies the hostname of a computer that can function as a mail relay for your domain, or the name of the domain if the MX record for that domain points to the appropriate mail relay system. For instance, if the mail relay for your system is franklin.threeroomco.com, you could use the following line in main.cf:

```
relayhost = franklin.threeroomco.com
```

If your system is in the same domain as the relay system and if the MX record for that domain points to the correct system, you can use $mydomain in place of franklin.threeroomco.com. Using the domain name has the advantage that Postfix will automatically adjust should your domain's mail server change.

Normally, Postfix attempts to use DNS lookups when sending mail. If your local network lacks a DNS server (for instance, if you rely exclusively upon /etc/hosts entries for local name resolution), you should include one additional line:

```
disable_dns_lookups = yes
```

This line causes Postfix to not rely upon DNS lookups for name resolution, so it can contact the relay system by means of an /etc/hosts entry or the like.

Postfix Anti-Spam Configuration

Postfix, like sendmail and Exim, provides several anti-spam measures, some of them very sophisticated. You can use a pattern matching system to block spam based on patterns in mail headers or use a blackhole list.

The main Postfix pattern-matching tool is a fairly sophisticated one that examines message headers using a regular expression system. You can specify that a message be rejected based on a match against a regular expression, similar to those used by the egrep tool. This system is frequently used in conjunction with a separate file of regular expressions, although you can specify regular expressions in the main.cf file itself. The more common configuration points Postfix to an external file by using a main.cf entry like the following:

```
header_checks = regexp:/etc/postfix/bad_headers
```

You would fill the file bad_headers with regular expressions like those shown in Listing 19.2. Postfix attempts to match the message headers sent with the message against these regular expressions, and if it matches and the file specifies that the message should be rejected, the message is bounced. The regular expressions can be either POSIX-style (indicated by a regexp: specification, as shown above), or PCRE-style (indicated by a pcre: specification).

Listing 19.2 Postfix regular expression spam filter file

```
#### Spam-sign subject headers
/^Subject: ADV:/ REJECT
/^Subject: Accept Visa/ REJECT
#### From: and Received: headers from spammers
/^(From|Received):.*badspammer\.net/ REJECT
/^From: spammer@abigisp\.net/ REJECT
```

NOTE The upcoming section, "The Recipe Conditions," describes regular expressions in more detail. For still more information, consult the egrep man page.

Postfix's header_checks option is extremely powerful, but it can be difficult to configure and maintain. A simpler approach is to use a blackhole list. You can do so by using two main.cf options, as shown here:

```
maps_rbl_domains = relays.mail-abuse.org, dialups.mail-abuse.org
smtpd_client_restrictions = reject_maps_rbl
```

The maps_rbl_domains option allows you to specify server addresses for blackhole lists, as shown in Table 19.1. You can list several domains, separated by commas or spaces. The second line tells Postfix to use those domains as a basis for rejecting mail from the sending host. The smtpd_client_restrictions option can take other values instead of or in addition to reject_maps_rbl. For instance, reject_unknown_client causes Postfix to refuse delivery if the sending system doesn't have a valid reverse DNS lookup. The Postfix documentation goes into more detail about these options.

In addition to explicit spam controls, Postfix sports a number of options that, while not strictly anti-spam measures, may have some beneficial effect on spam delivery. These include the following:

- **smtpd_helo_required**—This option defaults to no, but if you set it to yes, Postfix won't process a message unless the sender uses HELO or EHLO. This blocks some poorly written spam software, but it also blocks some misconfigured but otherwise legitimate SMTP servers.

- **smtpd_helo_restrictions**—You can further tighten Postfix's handling of HELO or EHLO transactions with this option, which takes several values. For instance, reject_unknown_hostname causes Postfix to terminate the connection if Postfix can't find an A or MX record for the specified calling hostname, and `reject_non_fqdn_hostname` requires that the sender use a fully-qualified domain name (FQDN)—one that includes both a hostname and a domain name. There are several other possible values for this option; consult the Postfix documentation for details.

- **`smtpd_sender_restrictions`**—If this option is present, it requires that the From: address meet the specified criteria. For instance, `reject_unknown_sender_domain` causes a rejection if Postfix can't find the specified From: address's domain, and `reject_non_fqdn_sender` requires that the sender use an FQDN as part of the address.

These or other Postfix options may be useful in various situations, but the defaults (which don't place too many restrictions) are a good starting point. Implementing too many restrictions too quickly can result in lost mail.

Preventing Postfix from becoming a source of relayed spam, of course, depends on appropriate anti-relay configuration. The default Postfix configuration is slightly more open than that of recent versions of sendmail because Postfix comes configured to relay mail for its local domain and network. You may want to tighten this configuration for Postfix on a workstation, as described earlier.

USING A PROCMAIL FILTER

The SMTP servers described in this chapter accept mail for delivery from remote systems. To this point in the chapter, I haven't described what happens after the mail server accepts the message. In some cases, the mail server simply appends the message to a file in which a user's incoming mail resides. Most Linux systems, though, come configured to use another tool, Procmail, for mail delivery. Procmail allows sophisticated processing of mail after it's been accepted by the MTA. You can set up a system-wide Procmail filter rule set, or individual users can design their own filters. There are also ready-made filter rule sets to accomplish specific tasks. Understanding how to use Procmail can allow you to accomplish a great deal with your mail delivery system that you could not otherwise do.

UNDERSTANDING THE ROLE OF PROCMAIL

Most MTAs are specialized to pass mail messages from one computer to another, or from one user to another on the same computer. Many mail environments, though, are complex enough that it's desirable to process or filter mail in some way once it's received. One reason for doing so has

515

already been discussed: spam filtering. You might want a spam filter to discard all spam, or at least dump it into a special folder reserved for suspected spam. Sendmail, Exim, Postfix, and other MTAs all offer at least limited abilities to do filtering like this, but these MTA features are usually limited compared to those of Procmail. Exim comes closest to matching Procmail's features; Postfix can only filter on headers, and its action abilities are limited; and sendmail is still more limited in the headers it can search. Thus, Procmail fills a gap in mail filtering abilities.

Procmail filters can do more than simply discard mail, as you might want to do with spam. You can use these filters to automatically sort mail into specific mail folders. For instance, if you subscribe to several mailing lists, you might prefer to have mail from your mailing lists sent to particular mail folders that you can read separately from your regular mail. You might check these folders once a day, rather than more frequently for your regular mail.

Procmail can even pipe mail through other programs. One use for this feature is to create a *mail-to-news gateway*, in which mailing list messages are sent to a news server (described in Chapter 12, Running a News Server). You can then read your mailing list messages using a news reader rather than a mail reader. External programs could also process the mail in various ways. For instance, you could use Procmail to pass messages that contain attachments through a virus scanner to help protect computers on your network from viruses, worms, Trojan horses, and the like. You might set up a filter to play a certain sound file when messages that contain certain words arrive, to alert you to important e-mail's arrival.

All of these features rely on Procmail's ability to scan messages. For instance, a Procmail-based spam filter might search for telltale signs that a message is spam. These might include Subject: headers that contain strings like $$$ or lines near the end of the message that reference S.1618 (a failed piece of U.S. legislation dealing with spam to which many spammers refer as if to legitimize their activities). To do this, Procmail uses regular expressions, similar to those used by Postfix in its header filters, or by the egrep program. I describe this in more detail shortly.

Procmail can be used in two ways: as a system-wide filter or as a filter for individual accounts. For instance, you might want to implement a system-wide Procmail filter to block the most egregious forms of spam or to scan e-mail attachments for viruses. Individual users might want to use Procmail to sort incoming mail into folders for mailing lists, individuals, and so on. System-wide Procmail configuration is handled through the /etc/procmailrc configuration file, while individual Procmail filters appear in the .procmailrc file in the user's home directory. The format of both files is the same.

WARNING

The /etc/procmailrc configuration file is used when Procmail is run as root on most systems. Therefore, you should be very careful about what commands you have Procmail run in such a file, and if you redirect message delivery, you may have to take steps to ensure that the files created are readable by the desired users. The user .procmailrc files don't suffer from this problem; commands run from these files run with the user's privileges.

A Procmail configuration file consists of three types of entries:

- **Comments**—A Procmail comment begins with a pound sign (#) and continues until the end of the line, as with many configuration files.

- **Environment variable assignments**—Procmail relies on certain environment variables, such as $HOME (the user's home directory) and $MAILDIR (the directory in which a user's mail folders reside) to work. You can adjust these and other environment variables much as you would in a shell script. For instance, MAILDIR = $HOME/Mail sets the $MAILDIR environment variable to the Mail directory in a user's home directory.

- **Recipes**—A Procmail filter rule is referred to as a *recipe*. The bulk of the work you put into your filter set will probably be devoted to recipes. Each recipe provides rules for what to do with a message that matches one regular expression. Thus, a complete rule set is likely to consist of many recipes. Recipes are further subdivided into two classes: *delivering* and *nondelivering*. Delivering recipes cause mail to be delivered to a mailbox file, discarded, or piped through some other program. Nondelivering recipes cause the message to be processed again by Procmail, or nest one recipe within another.

You can intersperse these three types of entries as required. Many Procmail configuration files begin by setting a handful of environment variables and then proceed with a series of recipes. In handling its configuration file, Procmail scans incoming mail and tries to match all its recipes against the mail. If none of the recipes match, Procmail delivers the mail to $DEFAULT, which is normally the default mailbox file, such as /var/spool/mail/*username*.

517

DESIGNING A RECIPE

Procmail recipes look intimidating to the uninitiated, particularly to those who aren't already familiar with regular expressions as used by egrep or similar tools. The basic format of a recipe is as follows:

```
:0 [flags] [:[lockfile]]
[conditions]
action
```

This format can be considered to consist of three parts: the recipe identification line, the conditions, and the action.

The Recipe Identification Line

Every recipe begins with the string :0. There's no special significance to the number 0, and you won't find recipes that begin with :1 or higher numbers. You can specify one or more of a variety of *flags*, which modify Procmail's behavior. You should consult the procmailrc man page for details, but the most common *flags* are:

- H—This causes the pattern match to be done on the message headers. This is the default value.
- B—This causes the pattern match to be done on the message body.
- D—By default, the pattern match doesn't distinguish between upper- and lowercase characters. This option causes case to be significant.
- c—This causes the recipe to work on a "carbon copy" of the original message; the "original" is left to match against other recipes.
- w—This causes Procmail to wait for the *action* to complete. If the action doesn't finish successfully, the message remains in the queue to be matched against other recipes.
- W—This works just like w, but suppresses program failure messages.

After any flags, you can specify a single colon (:) to have Procmail create a *lock file* when processing the mail. A lock file is a special file that signals the fact that Procmail is working with another file. If Procmail sees that a lock file is present, it delays working with the message until the existing lock file is removed. This is an extremely desirable behavior, particularly on busy queues, to keep two messages delivered in quick succession from being written to a new file in an intermingled form. The default lock file is built based on the name of the destination mail file (as specified in the *action* line). If the *action* is a pipe to another program, you may want to specify a lock file by including the name after the colon.

The Recipe Conditions

The recipe *conditions* consists of zero or more lines that normally begin with asterisks (*). These are ordinary regular expressions, which in turn are strings that Procmail tries to match against lines in the input (the message header or body). Most characters match against their equivalents in the message body. There are, however, several special characters that match groups of strings or characters that are difficult to represent in a plain text file. These include the following:

- ^—A carat signifies the start of a line. Many Procmail *conditions* lines begin with this character, after the leading asterisk.

- $—A dollar sign represents the end of a line. If you don't include this symbol, the *conditions* line matches any line that includes the specified string or other features, even if the line contains additional text.

- .—A period matches any single character except for a newline. For instance, d.g matches dog, dig, dug, or any other three-letter string that begins with d and ends with g.

- a*—This string matches any sequence of zero or more *a*s, where *a* can be any character. This is frequently used with a period as *a*, to match a string of characters of any length—for instance, if you want to match a line that contains 802 followed by some unknown characters and then 1618, you might use 802.*1618 to do the job.

- a+—This works much like a*, but it matches one or more *a* characters, rather than zero or more.

- a?—This string matches zero or one *a* characters.

- *seq1|seq2*—You can specify a match to either of two possibilities by listing them both, separated by a vertical bar (|). You can match against additional possibilities by using additional vertical bars.

- (*seq*)*—This is essentially the same as a*, but it matches the string of characters *seq* rather than a single character.

- [*chars*]—Characters enclosed in square braces are treated as a set, from which any one may match. For instance, [aeiou] matches any vowel character (a, e, i, o, or u). If one of the characters is a hyphen (-), any character between the surrounding characters matches. For instance, [m-q] matches m, n, o, p, or q.

- \—The backslash removes the special meaning from characters that possess such meanings. For instance, \. matches a single period.

For more information on these expressions, consult the Procmail man page. It's possible to build up some very complex matching patterns using a combination of regular text and these special character sequences. (I present some examples shortly.) Remember that the recipe *conditions* is *zero or more lines*. Most recipes have at least one line. If a recipe has more than one line of *conditions*, they must all match if the recipe as a whole is to match. A zero-line *conditions* matches any mail message.

It's possible to use special characters within a *conditions* line to change the interpretation of the recipe. These special characters include the following:

- !—This is an inversion operator; a *conditions* line that begins with an exclamation mark indicates that the recipe matches if the pattern provided does *not* match. For instance, you might want to create a recipe that matches all mail *except* that which is addressed to postmaster.
- <—The recipe's conditions are met if the length of the mail is less than the specified number of bytes.
- >—The recipe's conditions are met if the length of the mail is greater than the specified number of bytes.

The Recipe Action

The Procmail *action* line is exactly one line that tells Procmail what to do with the message. A simple *action* line may consist of a filename (possibly including a variable), in which case Procmail stores the message in the specified file. This works well for sendmail, Exim, Postfix, and other mail servers that use the mbox mail folder format, in which an entire mail folder fits in one file. If you're using qmail or have reconfigured another mail server to use the maildir format for storing mail, you should be sure to include a trailing slash (/) on the action line to have Procmail store the message in a qmail-style maildir. Procmail also supports a third mail-storage format, specified by an action line that ends in a slash and period (/.).

In addition to storing mail in a mail folder, Procmail supports several other actions, which you can specify by using special characters at the start of the *action* line:

- !—If the *action* line begins with an exclamation mark, Procmail interprets the line as a list of e-mail addresses to which the message should be forwarded. You might use this feature if you want to automatically make certain message types available to a group of users.

- |—A vertical bar is a pipe character in shells like Bash, and Procmail treats it in the same way. If an *action* line begins with this character, Procmail runs the specified program and pipes the message to the program. You might use this feature to scan a message in a more thorough way or to create an automated e-mail service that processes files.

- {—A left curly brace denotes the beginning of a *nesting block*. You can place additional recipes within this nesting block, and these recipes will only be used if the surrounding recipe's conditions are met. (The surrounding recipe is a nondelivering recipe, so if none of the enclosed recipes match, the message is not considered to be delivered.) You might use this feature if you have several recipes you only want to use if certain preconditions are met. For instance, you might use a nesting block that locates mail that shows certain inconclusive signs of being spam, then use recipes within the nesting block to search for other signs of the message being spam. A nesting block ends with a single right curly brace (}) on a line of its own.

Procmail supports only one action per recipe. Thus, if you want to do multiple things with a message, you may need to create a script to do them all and then call the script through a pipe. If you do this, be sure that your script reads the entire message, or Procmail will attempt to match the message against other rules. In some cases, you might use the carbon copy (c) flag on all but one recipe, but this may result in multiple deliveries of the mail, depending upon what actions are performed in each recipe.

Some Example Recipes

The preceding discussion may seem fairly abstract, but it's necessary for you to understand a Procmail filter file. Listing 19.3 shows an example of such a file, albeit a fairly simple one. This example makes more sense as an individual's .procmailrc file than as a global /etc/procmailrc file, because it delivers some messages to folders within the user's home directory.

Listing 19.3 shows several important Procmail recipe features.

- **Nested recipes**—The spam-filter recipes are nested within a filter rule that causes the spam filters to be checked only if the mail was *not* addressed to postmaster. (Note the inversion operator on the outside nesting recipe.) You could produce a similar effect by including the *! ^To:.*postmaster condition in each of the individual spam filter

---

Listing 19.3   A sample Procmail configuration file

```
MAILDIR = $HOME/Mail

# First, some spam checks, but don't ditch anything
# addressed from or to postmaster
:0
*! ^(From|To):.*postmaster
{
   :0 B
   * ^.*301.*S.*1618
   /dev/null

   :0
   * ^From:..*badspammer\.net
   /dev/null

   :0
   * ^Subject:.*\$\$\$
   /dev/null
}

# Copy anything about rugs from david to amy
:0 c
* ^From:..*david@pangaea\.edu
* ^Subject:.*rug
! amy@threeroomco.com

# Put mail to mailing list in its own folder
:0:
* ^To:..*list@mailinglist\.example\.com
$MAILDIR/mailinglist
```

---

recipes, and in this short example, this would produce a slightly shorter configuration file. In longer files, though, using a nested recipe can reduce the configuration file length. Nesting also reduces the chance for an error, because there's no need to copy the nesting condition to multiple recipes.

- **Spam conditions**—Listing 19.3 uses three spam checks. The first checks the message body (note the B flag) for a line that contains the strings 301, S, and 1618, in that order. This line is intended to catch references to the failed S.1618 bill, mentioned earlier. (These citations usually begin with a reference to section 301 of the bill.) The second spam filter blocks everything from the badspammer.net domain, and the final filter blocks everything that contains $$$ in its Subject: header. Note that both of these last two filters use the backslash (\) quoting character. All three of the spam tests "save" the mail to /dev/null, which is a quick way for Procmail to get rid of a mail message. This is an unforgiving mail filter, though; once a message is sent to /dev/null, it cannot be retrieved. There's no need to use a lock file with these spam recipes, because the messages aren't being stored; they're being destroyed.

- **Message copying**—Rather than write a message to a file, the second top-level recipe copies messages (note the c flag and the exclamation mark in the *action* line) to another user. The messages in this example must meet two criteria: They must be from david@pangaea.edu and they must contain the word rug in their Subject: headers. If either of these conditions is not met, the message isn't copied.

- **Message sorting**—The final recipe sorts mail; it directs all mail addressed to list@mailinglist.example.com to its own folder in the user's mail directory. Many mailing lists use a To: message header of the mailing list itself; they use the envelope To header to deliver the mail to the individual recipients. You may need to examine the headers of mail on mailing lists to which you subscribe in order to find a reliable way of redirecting that mail to appropriate mail folders on your system.

Listing 19.3 is a simple example that's unlikely to be useful to you directly, but you might be able to use it as a basis for something that would be suitable. Alternatively, you may want to try using or adapting a filter set you can obtain from somewhere else.

USING EXISTING FILTER SETS

Creating a good Procmail filter set for any given purpose can be a tedious undertaking. There are several ready-made filter sets designed for specific purposes, and you might be able to adapt a filter set created by a friend or colleague more easily than you could write one from scratch. Some possible sources of Procmail filter sets include the following:

- **The SpamBouncer**—This package is a set of Procmail filters designed to block spam. These filters are complex enough that they actually come as several files, and you'll probably have to edit some of these files to use the system. Consult the SpamBouncer documentation for details. You can download the package from its home page, http://www.spambouncer.org.

- **SmartList**—This is a mailing list package built atop Procmail. You can read more about it on the SmartList FAQ, `http://www.hartzler.net/smartlist/SmartList-FAQ.html`.

- **Timo's Tips and Recipes**—Timo Salmi has a Web page with Procmail tips and simple recipes at `http://www.uwasa.fi/~ts/info/proctips.html`. This isn't a complete package in the sense that SpamBouncer or SmartList is a ready-made package, but it can be a good place to go to find out how to perform specific tasks with Procmail.

- **Sample Procmail Recipes with Comments**—This Web site (`http://handsonhowto.com/pmail102.html`) presents a few Procmail recipes with comments describing their operation.

A Web search on *Procmail recipes* is likely to turn up additional hits, or you can start from the Procmail Web site (`http://www.procmail.org`) and follow links until you locate a useful example filter set.

Simple filter sets can be installed as `.procmailrc` files in users' home directories, or occasionally as system-wide `/etc/procmailrc` files. Some, such as SpamBouncer, rely on the presence of support files, so be sure to install them correctly.

WARNING

You shouldn't install a Procmail filter set blindly. Most require customization for your system, such as adjusting hostnames and even usernames. Many filter sets were designed to meet specific individuals' needs, and yours may differ. You might prefer to be more or less quick about sending suspected spam to `/dev/null`, for instance.

TIP

As a system administrator, you have the luxury of creating test user accounts. You can create such an account to test the action of a Procmail filter. You can create test messages to that account by altering the settings in a mail client program or even by using a Telnet program to reach the SMTP port (25) on the mail server program and typing envelope and message headers to simulate mail from various sources, as shown in Listing 19.2.

CALLING PROCMAIL

The preceding discussion assumes that Procmail magically runs and processes all incoming mail. This is normally true—except for the "magically" part. Most Linux mail servers come configured to use Procmail for local mail delivery. This setting can be adjusted as follows:

- **Sendmail**—There are three options that are commonly used to configure Procmail use in sendmail's m4 configuration file. The first is define(`PROCMAIL_MAILER_PATH`, `/usr/bin/procmail`). This tells sendmail where to find the Procmail binary. The second and third lines are FEATURE(local_procmail) and MAILER(procmail), which collectively tell sendmail to use Procmail for local deliveries.

- **Exim**—About two thirds of the way through the default Debian exim.conf file is a configuration section labeled procmail_pipe. This section causes Exim to use Procmail for local mail delivery. If this doesn't seem to be happening, try searching for this section and verify that it's calling the correct binary file.

- **Postfix**—The default Postfix configuration calls Procmail via the mailbox_command option in main.cf. If you omit this option, Postfix delivers mail directly, without involving Procmail.

Chances are you won't need to adjust these options, because they're included by default in most Linux mail server setups. If by chance you're using a computer on which Procmail is *not* used by default, but you want to use it for mail deliveries to specific users' accounts, you can often enable it by creating a file called .forward in the home directories of the users who need to use Procmail. This file should contain the following line:

```
"|IFS=' '&&p=/usr/bin/procmail&&test -f $p&&exec $p -Yf-||exit 75 \
#username"
```

You should be sure to include the single and double quotes exactly as reproduced here. In this example, *username* is the username for the account that's to be processed.

SUMMARY

Mail delivery is arguably one of the most important functions of the Internet today. Linux provides a plethora of options in mail servers, including the old standard, sendmail, and newer upstart servers like Exim and Postfix. No matter what SMTP server you choose to use, you can configure it to handle various common functions, including accepting mail addressed to it and relaying mail to other systems. You must attend to many details, such as the range of hosts for which a server will relay mail and any anti-spam configuration you may want to implement. After an SMTP server receives mail, it often relies upon another utility, Procmail, to further process the mail. Procmail may perform spam checks, run programs in response to mail that meets certain criteria, forward or copy mail to others, and so on. Both the system administrator and individual users may configure Procmail, so it's an extremely flexible tool.

Running Web Servers 20

To many people, the World Wide Web (WWW or Web for short) is synonymous with the Internet. In truth, there are many other protocols in use on the Internet, many of which are described in this book. The Web has grown to be arguably the most visible part of the Internet, though. For this reason, Web servers are extremely important to many organizations—without a Web site, a company or even an individual has very little visibility on the Internet.

Linux supports many different Web server options, although one program (Apache) is the most common one. This chapter therefore focuses on Apache configuration, beginning with the basic options required to get Apache up and running. This chapter then moves on to touch upon other topics, such as Linux kernel-based Web server extensions, forms, scripts, secure sites, and virtual domains. This chapter also covers issues that in some sense come before and after the Web server: generating material to serve on the Web site and analyzing your Web site's traffic.

Although it's not difficult to get a basic Web server up and running with Linux, advanced configuration options are complex enough that a single chapter isn't enough to cover them all. If you need to delve into the minutiae of Web server configuration and use, you can read your Web server's official documentation or obtain a book on the subject, such as Engelschall's *Apache Desktop Reference* (Addison Wesley, 2001) or Aulds'

Linux Apache Server Administration (Sybex, 2001). There are also books dedicated to more specific Web server subtopics, such as Meltzer and Michalski's *Writing CGI Applications with Perl* (Addison Wesley, 2001).

When to Run a Web Server

Although Web servers are extremely desirable in many situations, they aren't needed on all computers. Indeed, they aren't even needed or desirable on all networks. Understanding when to run a Web server will help you to avoid problems that can be caused by unnecessary Web servers, as well as minimize the effort and expense you put into running your network.

A Web server is a program that responds to requests that use the *Hypertext Transfer Protocol (HTTP)* to transfer files. For this reason, some people prefer the term *HTTP server* to *Web server*. Whatever the name, a Web server listens on a specified port (usually port 80) for incoming requests for data. The HTTP client (more commonly known as a *Web browser*), such as Netscape Navigator or Internet Explorer, sends a request to the Web server for a particular document. The Web server retrieves that document from the hard disk or, in the case of CGI scripts, generates a document, and sends the file to the client. Under certain circumstances, the client can send information back to the Web server for processing.

The result is that the Web server provides users with a *Web site*—a collection of documents accessible via one or more *uniform resource locators (URLs)*, which are the Web addresses you type into a Web browser's location field. URLs most frequently begin with http://, but some begin with another string, such as ftp://. Web servers handle the http:// and https:// URLs; most others indicate that another protocol, such as FTP, is to be used.

Given this information, the question of when to run a Web server seems to boil down to one of when to put up a Web site. If you run a Web server, and place appropriate files on that Web server so that users can retrieve meaningful content, you have a Web site. This is indispensable for most businesses and even many individuals today. Web sites provide a way to communicate with customers, suppliers, and others who might seek information about your organization, products, or services.

Web sites, and hence Web servers, can also be useful for *internal* communication. You might want to create a Web site that's accessible only within your local network, on which you can place important information for internal communication, such as individual employees' schedules, plans for meetings or seminars, and so on. This internal Web server might be physically distinct from one that hosts an external Web site, or you might be able to have one computer do double duty, as described in the upcoming section, "Handling Virtual Domains."

One important distinction to keep in mind is that between a Web *site* and a Web *server*. A Web site is the documents that make up your presence on the Web. These documents are associated with a particular set of URLs, which you probably want to tie to your organization's domain name. The Web server, on the other hand, is the software or hardware associated with the Web site. It's possible to have a Web site without running a Web server in your organization. You can accomplish this goal by using a *Web hosting service*. This is an ISP that runs a Web server that responds to requests directed at your URLs. This can work because, as described in "Handling Virtual Domains," a single Web server can respond differently to requests directed at different hostnames. You can configure your DNS server (described in Chapter 18, Administering a Domain via DNS) to point the hostname associated with a Web site to a hosting service's computer. For instance, if the hosting service runs its Web server at 10.102.201.1, and if you want the www address within your domain to be associated with your Web site, you can create a DNS entry like the following:

```
www            IN   A      10.102.201.1
```

The Web hosting service must then configure its system to respond appropriately to your Web address. You'll also need access to the Web hosting service's computers so you can upload your Web pages.

Using a Web hosting service has certain advantages compared to running your own Web server. For instance, you don't need to have the network bandwidth to handle the Web server. This may be important if your organization lacks a high-speed or reliable Internet connection. (Precisely what the terms *high-speed* and *reliable* mean is subjective; a 200Kbps service with five hours of downtime a month may be acceptable to a home user, but would be unworkable for a large company like IBM.) Using a Web hosting service also relieves you of the need to configure and maintain your own Web server computer. On the downside, the Web hosting service will charge money—anywhere from a few dollars a month for a small site to thousands of dollars or more for a very large and busy site. The Web hosting service may place restrictions on your site. For instance, very low-end Web hosting accounts may not support GCI scripts or SSL encryption.

A couple of other options for external use deserve mention. One is *co-location*, in which you own a computer but locate it off your own premises, usually at an ISP's office. Your Web server computer can then benefit from a high-speed and reliable connection, and you can configure it in whatever way you deem necessary. At the other end of the scale are the default Web pages offered with residential and many low-end business Internet access accounts. These typically include the ISP's name in the URL, such as http://www.abigisp.net/~yourname/. They have the advantage of being an inexpensive way for individuals or small businesses to gain a presence on the Web, because they come standard with Internet access packages. They're usually very limited in the space permitted for Web pages, though, and most businesses want their own names in the URL, not their ISP's.

You should also examine the consequences and need for internal Web servers. If you have a legitimate need for a Web site for internal communications, by all means run one. You should take active steps to configure such a site, though; don't rely on the default out-of-box Web server configuration. Depending upon how you install them, some Linux distributions install Web servers by default. Such configurations have certain downsides. The Web servers consume disk space and perhaps memory that you might prefer to devote to other tasks. These unused Web servers are also potential security holes. On the other hand, some distributions use Web servers to provide help files to local users, so they can play a legitimate role even on workstations. As a general rule, though, Web server software should not be installed on workstations, only on computers on which you want to run a Web site.

WEB SERVER OPTIONS FOR LINUX

As with most types of server, there are several Web servers available for Linux. These servers range from exotic and specialized programs to generalist tools. Some programs are small and support just a limited set of options; others are large packages and are loaded with features. Some of the more noteworthy Linux Web server options include the following:

- **Apache**—This Web server ships with all major Linux distributions, and is the package that's installed by default when you ask for a Web server during system installation. According to Netcraft (http://www.netcraft.com), 65% of the Web's active sites used Apache in March of 2002. For these reasons, this chapter focuses on Apache. This server is quite full-featured and supports the usual set of advanced options, such as CGI scripts and SSL security. The main Apache Web site is `http://httpd.apache.org`.

- **Roxen**—This is a full-featured Web server comparable to Apache in many ways. It features a Web-based configuration interface that may make it appealing to some new administrators. You can read more about it at `http://www.roxen.com/products/webserver/`.

- **thttpd**—This server is much smaller than Apache (roughly 50KB in size, compared to 300KB for Apache, both figures dependent upon compilation options). It's intended to be quick and efficient. Despite its small size, it supports CGI scripts, but not SSL security. You can read more about it at `http://www.acme.com/software/thttpd/thttpd.html`.

- **Zeus**—Most Linux Web servers are open source, but Zeus is an exception; it's a commercial product that sells for $1,700. The Zeus Web site (`http://www.zeus.co.uk/products/zws/`) claims that Zeus scales better than most Web servers to handle very high server loads.

- **Kernel-based Web servers**—An entire class of Web server has sprung up that relies upon specialized Linux kernel features to handle some of the Web serving. The idea is that the bulk of the job of serving Web pages involves taking disk files and sending them out a network port. This is a simple enough task that the kernel can do it with much greater efficiency than an external program, so various kernel-based Web servers have been developed to do the job. The upcoming section, "Configuring kHTTPd," discusses this approach in more detail.

- **Non-traditional servers**—Some products use HTTP to provide functions that are more specialized than those handled by traditional Web servers. For instance, the remote administration tools covered in Chapter 16, Maintaining a System from a Distance, are in some sense Web servers. These products typically run on ports other than the traditional Web server's port 80, but they can be accessed using Web browsers. This chapter doesn't cover such servers.

If you have some particularly exotic requirements, you may be able to find a Web server to fit the bill; people have written Web servers for various specialized or just plain strange needs. Doing a Web search may turn up some useful leads.

As a general rule, Apache is a good choice for a Web server because of its popularity and the fact that it ships with all major Linux distributions. Small sites, or those concerned with resource use, might want to look into a slimmer Web server, such as thttpd. If you simply want to run a low-traffic site that doesn't use Apache's more advanced features, such an approach might be reasonable if the slimmer server is easy to install, configure, and use. Because Apache is so common, though, it's usually the easier choice, despite being far more capable than you might need.

Extremely high-performance sites might benefit from kernel Web server enhancements, such as those provided by kHTTPd. Using such a server, you can serve more requests on a single computer, or use a computer with weaker hardware than you might otherwise require. Similarly, even userspace servers such as thttpd and Zeus might be able to squeeze more performance out of your hardware. In many cases, though, the bottleneck in Web server performance is the Internet connection, not the Web server computer or software. More efficient software won't help if your site is too popular for your Internet connection. If that's the case, you'll need to reduce the bandwidth requirements of your Web sites (say, by reducing graphics), upgrade your Internet connection, or move your site to a Web hosting or co-location service with better connectivity than you have locally.

If you opt to use a Web server other than Apache, this chapter may be useful in that some of the capabilities of your server may be similar to those of Apache, and the configuration features may be similar in a broad sense. The specifics of how you handle a configuration file will be dissimilar, however.

Basic Apache Configuration

Even if you need to use advanced features on your Web site, you should begin by getting Apache operating on a basic level. Once Apache can serve *static* Web pages (that is, those that don't use advanced features like scripting), you can begin to tweak the configuration to do the more advanced things you need it to do. Basic Apache configuration involves running the server and setting fundamental options in the server's configuration files. You should also understand something of Apache *modules*, which are extensions that handle specific types of tasks. Fortunately, most distributions ship with an Apache configuration that works with few or no changes, but you may need to tweak some of these features to customize your server for your particular needs.

Understanding Apache Configuration Files

The Apache configuration file is usually called httpd.conf. Different distributions use different locations for the file, but the format is the same.

Caldera and SuSE store the file in /etc/httpd; Debian and Slackware use /etc/apache (Slackware provides a sample file called /etc/apache/httpd. conf.default that you must rename and modify); and Mandrake, Red Hat, and TurboLinux use /etc/httpd/conf/.

Whatever the location, httpd.conf consists of comments, which begin with pound signs (#), and configuration option lines, which take the following form:

Directive Value

The *Directive* is the name of the configuration option you want to adjust, such as Timeout or StartServers. The *Value* may be a number, a filename, or some other arbitrary string. Some directives allow you to set several suboptions. These are indicated by directive names enclosed in angle brackets (<>), as follows:

```
<Directory /home/httpd/html>
    Options FollowSymLinks
    AllowOverride None
</Directory>
```

The final line uses the same directive name as the first, but without any options, and preceded by a slash (/) to indicate that this is the end of the directive block.

Some additional Apache configuration files may be important in some situations. These are normally stored in the same directory as httpd.conf, and they include the following:

- **access.conf**—This is essentially a supplemental configuration file. It's set in httpd.conf with the AccessConfig directive. The access.conf file has traditionally been used for <Directory> directives, which determine how Apache treats access to the specified directory. Many configurations today leave this file empty, or use AccessConfig to point Apache to /dev/null for this file, effectively disabling it.

- **mime.types**—HTTP relies on a file type identification system known as the *Multipurpose Internet Mail Extensions (MIME)* to allow a Web server to inform a Web browser how to treat a file. For instance, text/plain identifies a file as containing plain text, and image/jpeg identifies a Joint Photographic Experts Group (JPEG) graphics file. The mime.types file contains a mapping of MIME types to filename extensions. For instance, the .txt and .asc filename extensions are associated with `text/plain` MIME type. If these mappings aren't set appropriately, Web browsers may become confused when confronted with certain file types. The default file works well for most materials you're likely to place on a Web page, but you may need to edit or add mappings if you want to serve unusual file types.

- **magic**—This file provides another way for Apache to determine a file's MIME type. Apache can examine the file's contents to look for telltale signs of the file's type. Many file types have certain key, or *magic*, byte sequences, and the `magic` file lists these, converted to a plain-text format so that the file can be edited with a text editor. It's best to leave this file alone unless you understand its format, though, and that format is beyond the scope of this chapter.

STANDALONE VERSUS SUPER SERVER CONFIGURATION

Chapter 4, Starting Servers, describes different methods of running servers. Apache can be run in any of the ways discussed in that chapter—through a super server, a SysV initialization script, or a custom startup script. Most distributions use a SysV startup script or a custom startup script, because these methods of running Apache cause the server to run continuously, and therefore to respond quickly to incoming requests. You may elect to run Apache from a super server if you like, though, and in fact Debian gives you the option of running Apache either way when you install the package. Running Apache from a super server results in slower responses to incoming Web page requests, because the super server must launch Apache for each request. The Apache developers also recommend against this configuration.

TIP The delay caused by running a Web server from a super server can be reduced or eliminated by using a slimmer Web server, such as `thttpd`, or a kernel-based Web server. Therefore, if you want to use a super server for security reasons, you might want to more seriously consider a slimmer Web server than Apache.

Although Chapter 4 covers running servers from a super server or standalone, there is one Apache-specific option you must set: `ServerType`. This Apache configuration file option can be set to `standalone` or `inetd`. If you don't set this option correctly, Apache may behave erratically or fail to respond to requests. If you want to change your configuration, be sure to adjust the configuration file, disable the former startup method, and enable the new startup method. For instance, to convert from a SysV startup to running Apache from `inetd`, you should change the configuration file, use the SysV startup script to shut down Apache, disable the SysV startup script, edit `/etc/inetd.conf` to enable Apache, and restart `inetd`. If you forget one of these steps, you may find that Apache doesn't work correctly, or continues to work with the old configuration.

NOTE Some distributions call the Apache executable `apache`, and others call it `httpd`. If you change your startup script or want to shut down Apache directly, you may need to check both names.

SETTING COMMON CONFIGURATION OPTIONS

The default Apache configuration works on most systems. After installing the server and starting it, Apache will serve files from its default directory (usually `/home/httpd/html`; consult the upcoming section, "Setting Server Directory Options" for more details). This directory normally contains a default set of files that announce that an Apache server is present but unconfigured. You'll almost certainly want to replace these files with the files that make up your own Web site, as described in the upcoming section, "Producing Something Worth Serving."

There are a few general-purpose Apache options you might want to adjust to affect its overall behavior. These include the following:

- **ServerType**—This directive has already been mentioned, but it deserves reiteration. If you change how you run Apache, you must adjust this option to fit: either `standalone` or `inetd`.

- **User and Group**—Every Linux server runs as a particular user and group. You can tell Apache to run as a particular user and group with these directives. Most distributions set Apache to run as the user `nobody` or as a custom user with few privileges, to reduce the potential for damage should a cracker find a way to get Apache to do things you'd rather it not do. It's generally best to leave these options alone.

NOTE As a security measure, most Apache binaries are compiled so that they can't be run as `root`.

- **ServerTokens**—Apache can provide callers with varying degrees of information about the platform on which it runs by setting this directive. Most distributions set it to ProductOnly, which provides no information about the OS on which Apache is running. You can set it to Min, OS, or Full to provide increasing levels of information, but this is usually best left at ProductOnly.

- **MinSpareServers and MaxSpareServers**—When run in standalone mode, Apache starts up several instances of itself in order to provide quick responses to incoming HTTP requests. Each instance can handle a single request. These directives set the minimum and maximum number of these "spare" servers that run at any given time. If fewer than MinSpareServers are running and unused, the master Apache process starts another. If more than MaxSpareServers are running and unused, spares are killed to bring the number in line. Setting these numbers too low can result in slow responses when the load spikes on a heavily used server, while setting them too high can result in reduced performance if the server lacks sufficient memory to handle them all. Most distributions set defaults of about 5 and 10. You can experiment with lower values if your server is used very lightly, or higher values if your server is heavily used. Note that the total number of Apache processes that run at any given moment may be higher than MaxSpareServers, because some of these may be connected to clients, and so are not spares. A busy Web site, or one whose traffic spikes periodically, may need a lot of swap space to handle all the server instances. If the MaxSpareServers value is high, this may increase the need for memory, and hence swap space.

- **MaxClients**—This directive sets the total number of clients who may connect to the system at any one time. The default is usually about 150, but you can adjust it up or down to suit your hardware and traffic. Setting this value too high can cause your system's performance to degrade if your site becomes very popular, but setting it too low can keep clients from connecting to your site. As with MaxSpareServers, a high MaxClients value may require you to have a lot of swap space or memory, should your traffic level rise.

The number of connections set in MaxClients is not the same as the number of Web browsers Apache supports. Individual Web browsers can open multiple connections (up to 8), and each consumes one of the connections allocated via MaxClients.

- **Listen**—By default, Apache binds to port 80 on all active network interfaces. You can bind it to additional ports or interfaces with this directive. For instance, Listen 192.168.34.98:8080 causes Apache to listen to port 8080 on the interface associated with the 192.168.34.98 address. Listen 8000 binds Apache to port 8000 on all interfaces.

- **BindAddress**—If your system has multiple network interfaces, you can bind Apache to just one interface by using this directive. For instance, BindAddress 192.168.34.98 binds Apache to the interface associated with 192.168.34.98. BindAddress * is the default, which binds Apache to all interfaces.

TIP

✔ If you need to run Apache on a workstation for local use only, you can use BindAddress 127.0.0.1 to keep it from being accessible to other computers. You'll have to use http://127.0.0.1 or http://localhost as your URL when accessing Apache locally, though.

- **Port**—This directive tells Apache to which port it should listen. The default is 80.

- **ServerAdmin**—You should specify the e-mail address at which you can be reached with this directive. The default is usually webmaster, which you can alias to your regular user account on the server using your mail server's alias feature, as described in Chapter 19, Push Mail Protocol: SMTP. This e-mail address isn't normally apparent to users, but it's returned with some types of error messages.

- **ServerName**—You can set this directive to your computer's true DNS hostname, if that differs from the hostname configured into the computer by default.

- **DefaultType**—If Apache can't determine the MIME type of a file based on its extension or magic sequence, as described earlier in "Understanding Apache Configuration Files," it returns the MIME type specified by the DefaultType directive. This is normally text/plain, but you might want to change it if your Web site hosts many files of a particular type that might not always be properly identified.

- **HostnameLookups**—This option can be set to On or Off, and it determines whether or not Apache looks up and logs the hostnames of the clients that connect to it. Having hostname information may be convenient when you're analyzing log files, as described in the upcoming section, "Analyzing Server Log Files," but performing the lookups takes some time and network resources, so you might prefer to forgo using this feature.

- **LogLevel**—Apache logs information on its activities. You can set the amount of information it sends to its error log by setting this directive to debug, info, notice, warn, error, crit, alert, or emerg, in decreasing order of the amount of information logged. The default is usually warn. This setting does *not* affect the access logs.

- **CustomLog**—This directive takes two options: the name of a log file and the format of information sent to that log file. The log file in question holds access logs—information on what systems have requested Web pages. The format may be common, agent, referer, or combined. For still more flexibility, the LogFormat directive lets you create your own log file format. You can use multiple CustomLog directives to create multiple log files.

These are the major general-purpose configuration options in httpd.conf. Upcoming sections describe some additional options, and still more are esoteric or specialized options that are beyond the scope of this chapter. You should consult the Apache documentation or a book on Apache to learn more about such directives.

SETTING SERVER DIRECTORY OPTIONS

URLs consist of two to four components:

- **The protocol**—The http://, ftp://, or similar component of the URL specifies the protocol to be used. This chapter discusses Web servers, which deal primarily with http:// URLs. (Secure sites use https://.)

- **The hostname**—The hostname component of the URL is the same as the hostname for the computer on which the Web server runs. For instance, if the URL is http://www.threeroomco.com/thepage/index.html, the Web server's hostname is www.threeroomco.com. (A single computer can have multiple hostnames by setting up multiple DNS A address records or CNAME aliases, as described in Chapter 18.)

- **The filename**—An HTTP request is, at its core, a request for a file transfer. Following the hostname in the URL is a filename, often associated with a directory name. For instance, in `http://www.threeroomco.com/thepage/index.html`, the file, including its directory reference, is `thepage/index.html`. Note that, although there is a slash (/) separating the hostname from the filename, that slash doesn't indicate that the filename reference is relative to the root of the Linux filesystem; it's relative to the root of the *Web site's files directory*. If the filename is omitted, most Web servers return a default Web page, as specified by the `DirectoryIndex` directive, described shortly.

- **Additional information**—Some URLs include additional information specific to a URL type. For instance, HTML Web pages can include position anchors, which are specified by a pound sign and anchor name, and FTP URLs can include a username and password.

There are several Apache configuration options that let you set the directories in which you can store files for the Web server. There are also variant forms of addressing you can use in URLs to indicate which of several alternate directories Apache is to use for retrieving files. If you don't set these options correctly, some or all of your Web pages won't appear in the way you expect. The relevant `httpd.conf` options include the following:

- **ServerRoot**—This directive sets the root of the directory tree in which Apache's own binary files reside. On most Linux installations, this defaults to `"/usr"`, and you shouldn't change this setting.

- **DocumentRoot**—Apache looks in the directory specified by this directive for static Web page files. The default is usually `"/home/httpd/html"` or something similar. (The directory name is normally enclosed in quote marks in the `httpd.conf` file.)

WARNING

! Do not include a trailing slash (/) in your `DocumentRoot` directive. Although this is a valid way to refer to directories, it can cause Apache to misbehave.

- **UserDir**—If the filename specified by a Web browser begins with a tilde (~), Apache interprets the first component of the filename as a username and attempts to locate the file in a subdirectory of the user's home directory. The `UserDir` directive specifies the name of the subdirectory used for this access. For instance, if `UserDir` is set to `public_html`, and if a remote user types `http://www.threeroomco.com/`

~abrown/photos.html into a Web browser, then Apache attempts to return the public_html/photos.html file in abrown's home directory. If this directive is set to disabled, user directories are disabled. You can disable only some user directories by following disabled with a list of usernames to be disabled. This directive is often enclosed in an <IfModule> directive, which checks to see that the appropriate Apache modules for handling user directories are loaded. (The next section, "Loading Apache Modules," describes modules.)

- **DirectoryIndex**—Some URLs don't end in a filename; they end in a directory name (often followed by a single slash). When Apache receives such a URL, it first tries to locate a default *index* file, the name of which you specify with the DirectoryIndex directive. Most distributions set this to index.html by default, but you can change this if you like. For instance, with this setting, if a user enters a URL of http://www.threeroomco.com/public/, Apache returns the public/index.html file from the DocumentRoot directory. You can provide the names of several index files, and Apache will search for all of them. This is often done if Apache handles CGI forms or other non-HTML files.

Most distributions' Apache packages create reasonable defaults for directory and file handling. You may want to check your configuration files to learn where you should place your Web site's files. If you prefer to place the files elsewhere, you can of course change the default settings. You might also want to change the index filename, particularly if you're setting up an Apache server to replace another Web server that used a different index filename.

LOADING APACHE MODULES

One of Apache's strengths is that it's an *extensible* Web server. Programmers and administrators can write *modules* that extend its capabilities, without touching the Apache source code or recompiling Apache itself. These modules can add features such as access control mechanisms, parsing extended information provided by clients, and so on. In fact, a great deal of Apache's standard functionality comes in the form of modules that come with the server.

If you check your httpd.conf file, chances are you'll see references to modules. These use the LoadModule directive, and they look like this:

```
LoadModule mime_module          lib/apache/mod_mime.so
```

This directive gives the module's internal name (`mime_module` in this example) and the filename of the external module file itself (`lib/apache/mod_mime.so`). In this example, the module filename is referenced relative to the `ServerRoot`, although you can also provide an absolute path if you prefer.

It's possible to build modules directly into the main Apache binary. To find out what modules are permanently available in this way, type **httpd -l** or **apache -l**, as appropriate. In some cases, modules built into the Apache binary or loaded via `LoadModule` need to be activated in the Apache configuration file. This is done with the `AddModule` directive, thus:

```
AddModule mod_mime.c
```

You provide the module's source code filename as the value for this directive. Some distributions' Apache configuration files include both `LoadModule` and `AddModule` directives for important modules.

Frequently, you won't need to add to the standard Apache module configuration; the default configuration file loads the modules that are most commonly used. In fact, you might want to disable certain modules to eliminate features that might be abused, such as the ability to handle CGI. Unfortunately, it's not always easy to tell what modules can be safely removed from a configuration.

If Apache doesn't do something you require of it, you might want to investigate adding a module to do the trick. One Web site you might want to visit in this case is the Apache Module Register, `http://modules.apache.org`. You can search for modules others have written by typing in a key word; the site returns a list of modules, including links to the module maintainers' Web sites.

CONFIGURING KHTTPD

UNIX-like systems in general, and Linux in particular, make a clear distinction between two types of processes: *kernel space* processes and *user space* processes. The kernel handles kernel space processes. If some event that the kernel handles triggers such a process, the process can be initiated very quickly. User space processes, by contrast, impose an overhead to start, and to communicate important data back to the kernel. This fact is not a problem for many processes, because user space processes often do substantial processing *within* user space. The overhead of calling user space programs is also tolerated in the name of security and stability—kernel space

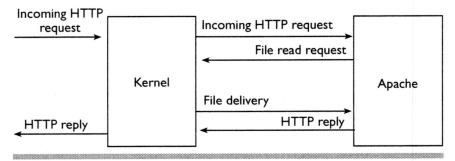

Figure 20.1   User space Web servers generate a lot of communication between the kernel and the user space server.

processes have privileged access to hardware, filesystems, and so on, so they can wreak havoc if they contain bugs or if unauthorized individuals gain control of them.

Researchers who have looked for ways to optimize the performance of Web servers have discovered that, although Web servers like Apache are user space programs, much of the work they do is performed in kernel space or in calls between the kernel and the server. Figure 20.1 illustrates the flow of requests between the kernel and a traditional user space Web server. In fact, Figure 20.1 simplifies matters considerably. For instance, the file read request by Apache results in the kernel performing fairly complex file read operations. Ultimately, in a simple transfer (the most common type on many sites), Apache does little more than receive the file from the kernel and then deliver it straight back to the kernel. This is a huge waste of CPU time, memory, and other resources.

In order to better optimize a Web server computer's performance, developers have created simple Web servers that run *within* the kernel. This eliminates the communications between the Web server and the kernel, thus streamlining the process of serving Web pages and (it is hoped) improving performance. In fact, the 2.4.*x* and later kernels include one such kernel-based Web server: kHTTPd, headquartered at http://www. fenrus.demon.nl. This server is configured by writing data to files in the /proc/sys/net/khttpd directory. To use it, follow these steps:

1. Build the kHTTPd support by including it in your Linux kernel configuration. The relevant option is on the Networking Options menu, and is called Kernel HTTPd Acceleration. You can build it as a module or directly into the kernel file.

2. Change your Apache configuration so that it listens on port 8080, or some convenient port other than the usual port 80.

3. Reboot with a kHTTPd-enabled kernel, or load the kHTTPd kernel module. It may load automatically, depending upon your configuration, or you may need to type **insmod khttpd**.

4. Tell kHTTPd to listen on port 80 for incoming requests. Do this by typing **echo 80 > /proc/sys/net/khttpd/serverport**.

5. Type **echo 8080 > /proc/sys/net/clientport** to tell kHTTPd to pass on requests it can't handle to port 8080. (If you used a port other than 8080 in Step 2, the port you specify here should match.)

6. Tell kHTTPd where to find unencrypted static files by typing **echo /home/httpd/html > /proc/sys/net/khttpd/documentroot**. You can change the directory name (*/home/httpd/html* in this example) as necessary. Be sure you specify the same directory here as you do with the DocumentRoot directive in httpd.conf.

7. If your site includes PHP3 or secure HTML documents, repeat Step 6, but echo the directory names in which these documents reside to the /proc/sys/net/khttpd/dynamic file.

8. Type **echo 1 > /proc/sys/net/khttpd/start**. This starts the kHTTPd server; it's equivalent to using an Apache SysV startup script.

You may want to create a custom SysV or local startup script to handle Steps 4 through 8 automatically when the system boots. Whether you start kHTTPd manually or through a script, the result is that it handles simple requests—those for ordinary files that exist in the specified directory, aren't CGI scripts, and so on. If a request doesn't meet kHTTPd's requirements, kHTTPd passes the request on to the user-space Web server via the port number indicated in Steps 2 and 5. This adds some overhead when dealing with these file types, so kHTTPd isn't worth using if your site handles mostly CGI scripts or other nonstatic files. Indeed, kHTTPd may not be worth using even on a site with moderate amounts of traffic; it's most worth considering if Apache is having trouble keeping up with requests to your Web site. Also, kHTTPd is officially experimental, so it might not be as reliable as Apache or some other fully debugged user-space Web server. Finally, because it runs in kernel space, the risks if a bug exists in kHTTPd are much greater than are the risks involved if a bug is present in Apache. For a truly secure Web site, you're best sticking to a well-tested user-space program such as Apache.

Although kHTTPd is the kernel-based Web server that's most readily accessible, it's not the only one available. Red Hat's TUX product is one other that's received good reviews, and researchers are working on several more. In the future, we may see a wide selection of kernel-based Web servers for Linux.

HANDLING FORMS AND SCRIPTS

Although static content is extremely common and important, it's not the only type of file that a Web server may be called on to handle. Some Web sites are much more dynamic in nature. For instance, Web search sites like Google allow you to enter information in a form, click a button, and receive back a customized Web page that the Web server built just for you. If you need to create such sites, it's vital that you understand how to configure your Web server to handle them appropriately. This topic is complex enough that this section can only provide a basic overview and a few pointers to the Apache options used in configuring such a site. For more information, you'll need to consult more specialized documentation.

UNDERSTANDING STATIC CONTENT, FORMS, AND CGI SCRIPTS

The preceding sections have focused on static content. This term refers to files that aren't unique to particular users and that don't interact with the user in any sophisticated way. Examples of static content include:

- **HTML files**—The *Hypertext Markup Language (HTML)* is the most common form for textual content on the Web in 2002. HTML files usually have extensions that end in `.htm` or `.html`, and they're basically nothing more than plain text files with a few character sequences reserved to indicate special formatting. For instance, `<P>` marks the start of a paragraph, and `</P>` marks the end. HTML also provides mechanisms for linking to other documents on the Web (or the Internet generally) by embedding URLs in the text. Users can click on links to read the linked-to files, and some (such as many graphics) can be displayed automatically, depending upon the browser's capabilities and settings. The upcoming section, "HTML and Other Web File Formats," describes HTML in more detail.

- **Text files**—Plain text files usually have `.txt` extensions. Web servers can deliver plain text files, and Web browsers can display them, albeit without the formatting and links that HTML files make possible.

- **Graphics files**—HTML files frequently include links to graphics files in various formats. These files are also static files. Note that some graphics files include animations. Although these are animated, they still qualify as static content; the word static refers to the data in the file, not to the data's appearance when displayed in a Web browser.

- **Miscellaneous document files**—Web pages sometimes include links to Adobe Portable Document Format (PDF) files, Microsoft Word files, archive files like .zip files or tarballs, and so on. Some browsers can load some of these files into appropriate applications, like a PDF viewer or word processor. Other files, if their links are clicked, can be saved to disk.

These are all examples of static content, and can be served from your DocumentRoot directory, your UserRoot directories, or subdirectories of these. When a user requests one of these files, the data flow is largely one way: The client requests a file, and the server delivers that file. To be sure, the request for a file itself contains data, but beyond the data in that request, the data flows in one direction.

Dynamic content, by contrast, is customized for individual users or allows a two-way exchange of data. You've probably encountered dynamic content on the Web before. Examples include:

- **Web search engines**—When you enter a search engine's URL, the Web server delivers a Web page that includes a form in which you can enter a search term. When you click the search button, the term you typed is returned to the Web server, which processes the data in order to create a custom Web page that's delivered to your Web browser.

- **E-commerce sites**—Clicking the "buy" button on a retailer's Web site causes your browser to request a URL that the retailer's Web server uses to register an entry into a "shopping cart." The retailer's Web server and your Web browser coordinate their actions in subsequent interactions to provide you with information on your purchase; provide the retailer with your address, credit card number, and so on; and confirm your purchase. The details vary greatly from one site to another, but at their core, the interactions are similar to those involved in a Web search engine—the Web server creates customized content, and your Web browser returns data to the Web server.

- **Personalized sites**—Some sites provide personalized "logons" that allow the Web server to deliver the content you want to see, rather than generic content. For instance, sites such as Slashdot (http://slashdot.org) allow you to register and provide preferences for the type and amount of data they're to display. These sites usually work by storing a *cookie* on your computer to uniquely identify you in the future. When you request a Web page, your browser returns the cookie, so the Web server can generate custom content. (E-commerce sites and even search engines may also use cookies.)

These are only a few examples of dynamic Web sites. The possibilities are limited mainly by the Web site designer's imagination. The key difference between dynamic and static sites from a Web server's point of view is that the dynamic sites require creating HTML (or other document formats) on the fly, based on input sent by the user in a previous interaction or in the URL. To do this, several mechanisms may be used:

- **Web forms**—A Web *form* is a Web page that provides buttons, data entry fields, lists, and other mechanisms for entering data. A search engine usually provides a small text-entry field and a button to click to begin a search. E-commerce sites usually provide a wider array of forms, including text-entry fields and selection lists (for entry of your state, for instance). Web forms are encoded in HTML, which may be generated statically or dynamically. Even fixed Web forms ultimately feed back into a dynamic system.

- **CGI scripts**—The *Common Gateway Interface (CGI)* is a common tool for interfacing programs for generating dynamic content to a Web browser. These scripts may be written in just about any language. (In fact, they can be written in compiled languages rather than scripting languages, although scripting languages like Perl are very popular for writing CGI scripts.) The Web browser calls the CGI script when the user enters an appropriate URL. The CGI script can then accept input back from the user, call other programs on the Web server, and generate an appropriate reply page.

- **SSIs**—*Server Side Includes (SSIs)* are a basic form of dynamic content. Instead of generating a complete Web page dynamically, as CGI scripts do, SSIs are used to modify a template script. This makes SSIs less flexible than CGI scripts, but they're useful for performing tasks like embedding the current date in an otherwise static Web page.

There are other forms of dynamic content available. In particular, an assortment of alternatives to CGI scripts exist, but CGI scripts remain an extremely popular way to generate dynamic content. Note that CGI scripts may create pages that contain Web forms; the two aren't so much competing forms of dynamic content as they are two aspects to one system for data exchange between client and server.

Setting Script and Form Options

In order to use CGI scripts, you must tell Apache that you want to use them. Apache must be configured to run the CGI script when its filename is provided in a URL, to process the script's output to be sent back to the Web browser, and possibly to receive return data from the Web browser for return to the CGI script for another round. Apache's role is that of a middle man, and fortunately, its configuration is not too difficult. There are two things you must do. First, you must enable CGI features. Second, you must tell Apache which types of incoming requests may be treated as CGI requests.

Adding CGI support involves loading the CGI module, thus:

```
LoadModule cgi_module          lib/apache/mod_cgi.so
```

If your CGI support is compiled into the main Apache binary (and sometimes if you load it as a module), you may need to use AddModule to activate it, thus:

```
AddModule mod_cgi.c
```

Once this is done, Apache has the basic tools it needs to handle CGI scripts. This leaves enabling CGI support for particular files or directories. There are several ways you can accomplish this task:

- **ScriptAlias**—This directive performs two tasks. First, it tells Apache to run CGI scripts within a specific directory. Second, it maps a physical directory to a directory that might be specified in a URL. For instance, ScriptAlias /scripts/ "/home/httpd/cgi-bin/" maps the /home/httpd/cgi-bin directory to the /scripts directory in a URL. For instance, with this configuration, a user who enters http://www.threeroomco.com/scripts/test.pl causes the /home/httpd/cgi-bin/test.pl CGI script to run. Many Apache installations include a default configuration along these lines; check your httpd.conf file for one. This configuration also relies upon the presence of the mod_alias module. This module is usually included by default, but you should check this detail if you have problems.

- **Options +ExecCGI**—You can provide the +ExecCGI parameter to the Options directive to enable execution of CGI scripts. You probably should *not* use this feature as a system-wide option; instead, apply it only to specific subdirectories (within a <Directory> directive).

- **.htaccess**—You can control various types of access to individual directories by placing .htaccess files in those directories. If the file contains an `Options +ExecCGI` line, Apache will run CGI scripts it finds in the directory. For this configuration to work, though, the `httpd.conf` file must include an `AllowOverride Options` line, at least for the directory in question.

WARNING

The `Options +ExecCGI` and `AllowOverride Options` methods are both potentially dangerous if applied sloppily, because users may then be able to write scripts that open the system up to security breaches. For this reason, most distributions disallow use of the `.htaccess` file, and often in other directories, as well.

Many distributions' default Apache configurations permit CGI scripts via the `ScriptAlias` option, often from a directory called `/home/httpd/cgi-bin`, using the `/cgi-bin` URL component. This configuration is convenient, because you can drop files in the CGI directory and have them be treated as CGI scripts with little additional fuss. One detail to which you must attend is permissions. In particular, the CGI scripts *are* scripts. Like other Linux scripts and programs, they must have appropriate permissions to be run. Particularly if you've written a script yourself or downloaded one from a Web or FTP site, you may need to type **chmod a+x *script-name***, where *script-name* is the script's name, to set its permissions appropriately.

WRITING CGI SCRIPTS

CGI scripts, like other scripts, are computer programs. A complete guide to writing them is well beyond the scope of this chapter. This section therefore provides just a few pointers to help get you started if you already know something about scripting. If you need more information, consult the "Dynamic Content with CGI" Web page (`http://httpd.apache.org/docs/howto/cgi.html`) for a basic introduction, or a book on CGI scripting for more detail.

CGI scripts accept standard input and generate standard output. Therefore, any text that you want your user to see can be output as if to the console, using standard output commands. The trick to creating output is to remember that the user is reading the output on a Web browser. Thus, your CGI script should generate HTML, or occasionally some other format that's friendly to Web browsers. (For instance, you might dynamically create a graphics file.)

Preceding the bulk of the HTML output, your CGI script should generate a content type header that lists the document's MIME type. This should normally resemble the following:

```
Content-type: text/html\r\n\r\n
```

This example specifies a `text/html` MIME type, which is usually what you want to create. (The `\r\n\r\n` portion of the line creates two new-lines, which is a necessary part of the specification.) Precisely how you create this output depends upon your scripting language, of course. Bringing this together with a normal script header line and a simple program might produce something like Listing 20.1, which shows a Perl script to display a line of text. If you type this program into a file in a CGI scripting directory, give it execute permissions, and specify its URL in a Web browser, you should see the text *Hello, Web* appear in the Web browser's window.

Listing 20.1   A simple Perl CGI script

```
#!/usr/bin/perl
print "Content-type: text/html\r\n\r\n";
print "Hello, Web";
```

CGI script input is a bit trickier. Your script may receive input if it has generated output that displays a form on the Web browser. The input to the CGI script from the user's entering data in the form appears as field/value pairs. Each of these pairs uses an equals sign (=) to separate the field name from its returned value, and ampersands (&) separate different field/value pairs. For instance, your CGI script might see input like this:

```
city=Oberlin&state=OH&zip=44074
```

Parsing and using such input is one of the strengths of certain scripting languages, including Perl, hence the popularity of Perl as a CGI scripting language.

SCRIPTING SECURITY MEASURES

One of the dangers of using CGI scripts is that you are giving anybody who can reach your Web server with a Web browser the right to run programs on your computer. Of course, this is true of *any* server, in the sense that outsiders can use the server itself. A CGI-enabled Web server, though, opens the door substantially wider, because every CGI script is a potential security threat. The programmers who write servers usually take great care to ensure that the server doesn't suffer from any security flaws. Even with careful attention to this detail, security problems occasionally do crop up. A Web server's CGI scripting tools are often used by administrators who are not as skilled at programming as are those who write servers, and the results can be disastrous.

Fortunately, there are certain measures you can take to help minimize the risk. Most importantly, you should double-check your User and Group settings in httpd.conf. Apache runs CGI scripts with the permissions specified by these options, so if you use an account with few privileges for this purpose, you minimize the damage that can be done if your script contains a flaw. Ideally, you should create a user and group *only* for Apache, and configure the account to not accept remote logins by any other means. This isn't a panacea, though; even with limited access, a buggy script could give a miscreant a foothold that could be used to create greater access to the server, when combined with other security problems.

You can also use existing scripting libraries. This will both ease the development task and reduce the risk that your code contains fundamental security flaws. You can find scripting libraries, such as CGI.pm and CGI::Lite, on scripting Web sites like http://www.cpan.org.

In the event that your Web server *is* compromised, you should take steps to ensure that it can do minimal damage. For instance, you should disable unnecessary servers, and restrict access *from* the Web server computer to other computers on your network. Part IV, Network Security and Router Functions, provides information on many general-purpose security measures you can take.

HANDLING SECURE SITES

One feature that's often used in conjunction with scripting is encryption. More precisely, the *Secure Sockets Layer (SSL)* is an encryption protocol that can be used to encrypt data that pass between the Web server and Web browser to protect the data from prying eyes. SSL is frequently used on e-commerce sites and others that handle sensitive data. Apache is capable of handling SSL encryption, but only with the addition of supplemental software. There are various implementations of SSL for Apache, such as the Apache-SSL project (http://www.apache-ssl.org), mod_ssl (http://www.modssl.org), and various commercial sources.

UNDERSTANDING SSL

SSL is a form of encryption technology that's similar to that used in the Secure Shell (SSH) remote login protocol. (In fact, the popular OpenSSH package relies on the OpenSSL package, which is also used by some

SSL-enabled Apache implementations.) In terms of Web transfers, SSL was designed to solve two problems:

- **Encryption**—SSL allows both sides of a connection to encrypt data in order to keep it private. This is obviously important for transmitting sensitive information such as credit card numbers or bank account numbers. Encryption alone can be handled by using *public-key cryptography*, which requires two *keys* on each side of the connection. Each party encrypts data with the other's *public* key. The encrypted data can only be decrypted with the matching *private* key, so the sender can be sure that only the recipient can decode the data.

- **Authentication**—Even with encryption, there is risk involved in sending sensitive data across the Internet. One such risk is that the other server may not be what it claims to be. For instance, if you type http://www.abigretailer.com into your Web browser, how can you be sure that you've actually reached the claimed retailer? It's conceivable that a miscreant has adjusted a DNS server to redirect requests for the legitimate retailer to a bogus site, or has modified routers to the same end. SSL provides a mechanism for authenticating parties in an exchange by relying upon a third party, known as a *certificate authority (CA)*. The CA provides *certificates*, which are digital codes used in creating public keys. If one party uses a certificate from a CA, the second party can verify the identity of the first with a high degree of confidence. (This isn't perfect, though; for instance, there was a foul-up in 2001 involving certificates that were mistakenly issued in Microsoft's name to somebody who was not affiliated with Microsoft.) Normally, secure Web servers will need certificates from a valid CA to reassure users that the site is valid.

NOTE You can serve as your own CA, but this doesn't provide good authentication except for internal uses, since outsiders can't trust that your internally generated certificates are valid. If you want to run an e-commerce site, as a practical matter you'll need to obtain certificates from a CA. One list of CAs is available at http://www.apache-ssl.org/#Digital_Certificates. Individuals browsing the Web don't usually need certificates from a CA because Web sites seldom need to be sure they're communicating with the claimed individual.

SSL encryption isn't normally done on the usual HTTP port (80). The default port for secure HTTP (or *HTTPS*) transfers is 443. You can tell a Web browser to use this port by using https:// at the start of the URL rather than http://. When you configure Apache to use SSL, you'll have to either run one server that binds to both ports and treats them differently, or run two servers, one for each port. The former is usually the simpler approach, but if for some reason you want to run two different types of servers (such as Apache for secure requests and thttpd for normal requests), you can do so.

CONFIGURING SSL

The first step in using SSL with Apache is to install and configure an SSL package. There are two SSL packages in common use in Linux:

- SSLeay (http://www2.psy.uq.edu.au/~ftp/Crypto/ssleay/)
- OpenSSL (http://www.openssl.org)

OpenSSL is rapidly becoming the standard in Linux. (OpenSSL is actually derived from SSLeay, but SSLeay remains available as a separate package.) It's included in many Linux distributions, including Debian, Mandrake, Red Hat, and SuSE. SSLeay and OpenSSL are logically equivalent; they function in the same way, although different packages sometimes place configuration files in different locations, and their main binaries are named differently (ssleay and openssl, respectively).

Once OpenSSL is installed, you need to obtain a certificate for it. For a public site, you should obtain your certificate through a CA, so that your users know you are who you claim to be. For testing purposes or to run a private site, though, you can use a certificate that you generate yourself. In fact, some Apache SSL installation scripts, like the one that ships with Debian, create such a certificate automatically. If yours doesn't, you can use a command like the following to do the job:

```
# openssl req $@ -new -x509 -nodes \
 -config /usr/share/doc/apache-ssl/examples/ssleay.cnf  \
 -out /etc/apache-ssl/apache.pem \
 -keyout /etc/apache-ssl/apache.pem
```

NOTE The preceding command assumes that the SSL-enabled Apache's configuration files will reside in /etc/apache-ssl and that an SSL example configuration file exists at /usr/share/doc/apache-ssl/examples/ssleay.cnf. You may need to change these values to suit your configuration. This command also uses backslashes (\) to indicate continuations of long lines. You can leave these in or omit them and type the entire command on one line.

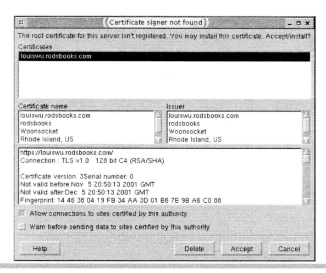

Figure 20.2 If you use a self-generated certificate, users who access your site will see a warning that the certificate has expired or is not recognized.

When you type this command, openssl prompts for some information, such as your location and computer name. This information will be encoded in the certificate, which will reside in the /etc/apache-ssl/ apache.pem file.

If you obtain a certificate from a CA, you should replace your self-generated certificate file with whatever file your CA gives you. This should eliminate the warning message that users will see if they try to access a site that uses a self-generated certificate. Figure 20.2 shows one such warning message, as displayed by Opera in Linux; other browsers may format the information differently or present it across multiple dialog boxes.

ENABLING SSL IN APACHE

In principle, Apache can be configured to use SSL through an add-on module. In practice, though, the SSL module requires a few changes to the Apache server, so some SSL-enabled Apache packages provide a rebuilt Apache server along with the SSL extensions. Other distributions release an Apache package that was built with the SSL hooks, and provide an SSL extension package that works with the standard Apache package. If you try to mix and match regular Apache and SSL-enabled Apache packages, the combination might or might not work.

Many SSL packages use a separate configuration file for the SSL-enabled server than for the standard server. For instance, Debian's SSL-enabled Apache configuration files reside in /etc/apache-ssl, whereas the standard Debian Apache files are in /etc/apache. The configuration files are largely the same as those for Apache without SSL support, so you should set details like the Web site directories in the same way. Some specific options you might need to change compared to a regular installation include the following:

- **ServerType**—SSL-enabled versions of Apache must be run standalone, not from a super server. Therefore, ServerType must be standalone.

- **Port**—The standard SSL HTTP port is 443, so you should set this value appropriately. Listen may also bind the server to a specific port number, and so should be adjusted, if used.

- **Modules**—The LoadModule and AddModule directives may reference one or more modules related to SSL. These should be set correctly in the default or example configuration file for any SSL-enabled version of Apache.

- **SSLRequireSSL**—You might use this option within a <Directory> directive to block access to a directory if the client isn't using SSL. You use this directive alone (it takes no options). This can be a convenient way to ensure that sensitive data aren't transferred without encryption, but of course you'll also need some other form of access control to ensure that only authorized users can reach the directory.

- **SSLEnable**—This directive enables SSL. Like SSLRequiresSSL, it takes no options; just list it on a line of its own.

- **SSLCACertificatePath**—This directive points Apache to the directory in which the certificate is stored, such as /etc/apache-ssl.

- **SSLCertificateFile**—This directive points Apache to the SSL certificate file, such as /etc/apache-ssl/apache.pem.

There are several other SSL-related directives you can set. Consult the comments in the configuration file, your SSL-enabled Apache's documentation, or a book that covers SSL Apache configuration for details.

Once you've configured SSL and Apache, you can start the SSL-enabled Apache server. You should then be able to reach the server by typing https:// rather than http:// in a URL for the server. If you've generated your own certificate, you'll probably see a warning like the one in Figure 20.2. You can accept the certificate (some browsers give you several options for the conditions in which they'll accept this certificate in the future) to continue testing the Web site.

WARNING

As a general rule, you shouldn't accept unverified certificates from random Web servers. Most Web sites that use SSL register with a CA, and you should not see such warnings for these sites. If you do, it may mean that the Web site operator has allowed the certificate to lapse (they are time-limited) or that the operator hasn't registered with a CA. It could also mean that somebody is attempting to masquerade as the Web site, and hopes to dupe users into relinquishing sensitive data like credit card numbers.

HANDLING VIRTUAL DOMAINS

You can use Apache to serve Web pages for a single site, such as http://www.threeroomco.com, as described earlier in this chapter. Suppose, though, that you want to host two or more sites on one computer. Is this possible? Yes! In fact, Web hosting services use this feature extensively, to host dozens, hundreds, or more Web sites from a single Web server. The bulk of the configuration for handling these *virtual domains* is the same as for a simpler Apache configuration, but there are some special details to which you must attend.

WHY USE A VIRTUAL DOMAIN?

A virtual domain allows a Web server to respond differently depending upon the name with which it's addressed. (This requires you to point several different hostnames to the Web server computer in DNS records for one or more domains.) There are several possible uses for such a configuration, including the following:

- If you're changing your domain name (or the Web server's name within a single domain), you can have Apache display a message to that effect on the old name, then redirect to the new name. In time, most of the sites and bookmarks that link to the old name should be updated.

- If two closely related companies, or even departments within a single company, want to share a single Web server, you can configure it to respond to appropriate names for each. In some cases (particularly departments within a single company), using subdirectories may make more sense than using distinct server names, though. Physically proximal small businesses might want to use this approach to reduce their Internet expenses.

- An individual, members of a family, or roommates might register separate domain names and host them all on a single computer. This approach is most useful to individuals who have broadband Internet access with ISPs that permit running personal servers.

- You can go into the Web hosting business, and set up a Web server to handle a large number of third-party Web sites. If this is your goal, you'll need far more expertise than can be delivered by a single Linux networking book, though.

As a general rule, the capacity of Apache to handle domain hosting tasks is certainly most useful to large organizations and ISPs that might want or need to handle multiple domains. Smaller-scale uses can certainly be important for those who happen to be in appropriate situations, though.

VIRTUAL DOMAIN CONFIGURATION OPTIONS

There are two common methods of handling virtual domain hosting. One assigns different document root directories based on the requested domain name, and the other allows you to set up a collection of (possibly differing) options for each virtual domain.

Using VirtualDocumentRoot

One key virtual domain configuration option is VirtualDocumentRoot. This directive lets you specify a directory name to be used as the root of a request to the server, dependent upon the name used. To that end, you can include several variables in the directory name you give to VirtualDocumentRoot, as outlined in Table 20.1.

For instance, consider the following directive:

```
VirtualDocumentRoot /home/httpd/%0
```

This results in the server using subdirectories of /home/httpd named after the entire hostname by which the server is referenced. If a call comes in for http://www.threeroomco.com/index.html, the server looks for a file called /home/httpd/www.threeroomco.com/index.html. This approach is very useful if you want to host many sites, although it can create a large number of subdirectories directly under the base directory (/home/httpd in this exam-

Table 20.1 Variables Used to Specify Hostname-Specific Home Directories

Variable	Description
%%	A single % in the directory name
%p	The port number on which the server runs
%N.M	Select parts of a name, as separated by periods. N is a number that refers to the period-separated component, with 0 being the entire name, 1 being the first component, 2 being the second component, -1 being the last component, -2 being the next-to-last component, and so on. M is similar to N, but it refers to the characters within the name component. (You can omit M if you want to use an entire hostname component rather than a single character.)

ple). If you know you'll be serving domains of a given length, you might prefer something that further breaks up the directory structure, like this:

```
VirtualDocumentRoot /home/httpd/%-1/%-2
```

In a configuration like this, a call to retrieve http://www.threeroomco.com/ index.html causes Apache to look for /home/httpd/com/threeroomco/ index.html. Alternatively, you might want to alphabetize your virtual site directories with a configuration like this:

```
VirtualDocumentRoot /home/httpd/%-2.1/%0
```

With this configuration, a URL of http://www.threeroomco.com/index.html causes Apache to return /home/httpd/t/www.threeroomco.com/index.html, if it exists. The %-2.1 variable returns the first (.1) character of the next-to-last (-2) component of the hostname, so the directories are stored in subdirectories by their domain names' first letters.

No matter what your precise VirtualDocumentRoot directive, you should set UseCanonicalName to Off, thus:

```
UseCanonicalName Off
```

When UseCanonicalName is set to On, as is the default with most configurations, Apache uses what it believes its hostname to be when doing relative references within Web sites. For instance, if the index.html page includes a call to load products.html, Apache will try to retrieve products.html from its canonical name. With a virtual domain, this lookup will fail. Setting UseCanonicalName to Off changes Apache's behavior to use the hostname associated with the virtual domain instead.

Using <VirtualHost>

Another approach to virtual hosting is to explicitly define each virtual host. You do this by using two special directives:

- **NameVirtualHost**—This directive goes in the main Apache configuration file, and informs Apache that you want to configure virtual hosts. The value of this directive is normally either a single asterisk (*), in which case you must define virtual hosts for all the server's definitions, or an IP address associated with one interface, in which case the main server configuration handles all requests *except* those that come on the specified interface, and those are handled by the virtual host definitions.

- **<VirtualHost>**—This directive begins a specific virtual host definition block. It takes a value that should be identical to the value given to NameVirtualHost. The directive block ends with a </VirtualHost> directive. Between these two are directives to specify the hosting directory and otherwise customize the virtual host. You can include many of the same directives within this block that you might use in a configuration that doesn't use virtual hosts.

Two directives that you're likely to include within the <VirtualHosts> block are ServerName (to set the name to which the block applies) and DocumentRoot. You can also customize other features, such as enabling CGI. As an example, consider the following lines, which set up a server to handle two virtual Web sites:

```
NameVirtualHost *

<VirtualHost *>
    ServerName www.threeroomco.com
    DocumentRoot /home/httpd/threeroomco/html
    ScriptAlias /cgi-bin/ "/home/httpd/threeroomco/cgi-bin/"
</VirtualHost>

<VirtualHost *>
    ServerName www.pangaea.edu
    DocumentRoot /home/httpd/pangaea-u/html
</VirtualHost>
```

When a server so configured is accessed via the www.threeroomco.com name, it serves files stored in /home/httpd/threeroomco/html as static files, and enables CGI scripts in /home/httpd/threeroomco/cgi-bin. When the server receives a request addressed to www.pangaea.edu, on the other hand, it serves the files from /home/httpd/pangaea-u/html. This latter configuration doesn't support CGI scripts. If a request comes in using another name or the raw IP address, the first configuration takes precedence, so such requests go through the www.threeroomco.com configuration in this example.

Compared to VirtualDocumentRoot, <VirtualHost> configurations make it easy to customize virtual hosts in unique ways, or to place their files in arbitrary directories. The advantage of the VirtualDocumentRoot approach is that you don't need to reconfigure the server to add a new domain; you need only create a new directory. In practice, most sites use the <VirtualHost> approach, but you can pick whichever is more appropriate for your purposes.

PRODUCING SOMETHING WORTH SERVING

Although this chapter is concerned mainly with running and maintaining a Web server, it's important that you understand something of how the Web pages served by a Web server come into being. Some of the preceding sections have already described some types of Web pages (particularly dynamic content). The most common type of static content is HTML, which is a text-based format with formatting extensions. There are several different tools available to help you create HTML, as well as the file formats upon which HTML pages frequently rely, such as graphics file formats. Understanding how to use these tools, and how Web browsers interpret HTML, will help you create Web sites that can be handled by most Web browsers available today.

HTML AND OTHER WEB FILE FORMATS

Although there are many tools for creating Web files, as discussed in the next section, "Tools for Producing Web Pages," it helps to understand something about the various file formats that are common on static Web pages. File formats that are common on the Web include various text file formats, graphics files, and assorted data files.

Most Web pages are built around an HTML text file. This file is a plain text file that you can edit in an ordinary text editor. Listing 20.2 shows a simple HTML file as an example. Most text in an HTML file is displayed in the Web browser's window, but text enclosed in angle brackets (<>) is formatting information. Many of these codes come in pairs, with the second bearing the same name as the first but using a slash (/) to indicate it's the end of the formatted area. The opening code sometimes includes parameters that fine-tune its behavior, such as setting the size and filename of a graphic or specifying the color of text and background. Some of these codes reference other documents on the Web (both on the main document's server and on other Web servers).

Listing 20.2   A sample HTML file

```
<!DOCTYPE HTML PUBLIC "-//IETF//DTD HTML 2.0//EN">
<HTML><HEAD>
<TITLE>Sample Web Page</TITLE>
</HEAD>
<BODY BGCOLOR="#FFFFFF" TEXT="#000000">
<CENTER><H1 ALIGN="CENTER">Sample Web Page</H1></CENTER>
<IMG SRC="graphics/logo.jpg" ALT="Logo" WIDTH="197" HEIGHT="279">
<P>This is a sample Web page, including <A
HREF="http://www.threeroomco.com/anotherpage.html">a link.</A></P>
</BODY></HTML>
```

Some of the formatting codes in Listing 20.2 should be self-explanatory, but others are more obscure. A handful of the more important codes include the following:

- **<HTML>**—This code identifies the page as being HTML. Most browsers don't actually require this code, but it's best to use it in order to create proper HTML.

- **<HEAD>**—HTML pages contain both a *header* and a *body*. The header provides information that's not usually displayed in the Web page proper, such as the <TITLE> code in Listing 20.2. The body includes the bulk of the text that appears in the Web browser's window. <HEAD> identifies the header.

- **<TITLE>**—Most Web browsers display a Web page's title in the window's drag bar, and enter it as the default title if a user enters the Web page in a bookmark list.

- **<BODY>**—This code denotes the main body of the Web page. It frequently includes parameters to set text color, background color, and similar attributes.

- **<H1>**—*Headings* allow you to create text that's useful to break up a Web page into sections. They're usually displayed in a larger font than is regular text. You can create several levels of headings, starting with 1 (<H1>). <H2> is a heading below <H1>, and so on. Listing 20.2's <H1> code includes an ALIGN option to tell the Web browser to center the text. Unfortunately, not all Web browser respond to the same alignment codes, so some redundancy in this matter is required for consistent display.

- **<CENTER>**—The <H1> heading in Listing 20.2 is centered by both an option within the <H1> code and by a <CENTER> code that surrounds the <H1> code. Some browsers respond to one or the other of these codes, but not both. The <CENTER> code is usually not needed for modern browsers, but some older ones do need it.

- **<IMG>**—You can include a graphic on a Web page by using the <IMG> code, as shown in Listing 20.2. These codes usually include several parameters, including SRC (which points to the source of the image— its filename on the server or a complete URL if it's stored on another server), ALT (text that's associated with the image for those who have automatic image display disabled or for display when the user moves a mouse over the image), WIDTH, and HEIGHT (the width and height of the image, which allows the Web browser to display the text of the document before the image has loaded, or to dynamically scale an image if it's some other size).

- **<P>**—This code denotes a paragraph. A Web browser will automatically rewrap text within a paragraph to fit the window size, font size, and other characteristics of the browser's window.

- **<A HREF>**—This code denotes a link. The text or image enclosed by this code usually appears on the Web browser underlined or in a different color, and users can click the link to view the page specified by the URL within the code.

It's possible to use nothing but these codes to create a Web page, but HTML supports many more options, including the ability to format tables, specify fonts, display bulleted or numbered lists, break the document into multiple independent *frames*, and so on. It's possible to over-use advanced HTML features, though. The upcoming section, "Web Page Design Tips," includes some information on this matter.

In addition to HTML, Web servers can deliver other document types to browsers. Indeed, HTML documents often refer to these documents directly, as in the <IMG> option in Listing 20.2. You can link to plain text pages, graphics, downloadable program files, scripts, or any other type of file. One important caveat is that your Web server should have an appropriate MIME type set for your documents, usually in the mime.types file described in the earlier section, "Understanding Apache Configuration

Files." If Apache can't determine the MIME type of the file, it usually sends it as plain text, which can cause problems because the target OS may alter certain characters in the file, thus corrupting it.

Because many Web pages incorporate extensive graphics, it's important to understand something of the graphics file formats that are common on the Web. The three most common formats are as follows:

- **GIF**—The Graphics Interchange Format has been popular since the 1980s. It uses a *lossless* compression scheme, which means that it compresses data, but in a way that allows the exact input data to be displayed. GIF supports images with color depths of up to 8 bits (256 colors). One unique drawback to this format is that it uses a compression scheme that is covered by a patent (which is due to expire in 2003). Some people object to using a graphics file format that's so encumbered.
- **PNG**—The Portable Network Graphics file format is another one that uses a lossless compression scheme. It also supports greater color depth (up to 64-bit, but 24-bit is a more common depth), and hence many more colors than GIF. Its compression scheme isn't covered by patents. On the down side, some older Web browsers don't support PNG graphics. There's a Web site devoted to PNG at http://www.libpng.org/pub/png/.
- **JPEG**—The Joint Photographic Experts Group format uses a *lossy* compression scheme, meaning that it can attain greater compression than a lossless format, but the compressed image may not exactly match the original when displayed. JPEG supports true-color (up to 24-bit) images.

As a general rule, a lossless format is best for line art and cartoon-like images that use just a handful of colors. These images tend to acquire ugly-looking artifacts when converted to JPEG format. Digitized photos, by contrast, usually look best in a true-color format (PNG or JPEG), and JPEG's lossy compression scheme doesn't impact such images as much. Therefore, JPEGs are common for digitized photos displayed on the Web.

When you use JPEG, your graphics package will give you an option for a compression level. You can save your graphics file with little compression, which produces a large but good-looking image, or use a great deal of compression, which produces a much smaller file that degrades more in quality. The exact scale used to describe the level of compression varies from one package to another, but a 1–100 scale is not uncommon, with 100 representing the best quality. Most images you're likely to put on the Web look acceptable at a fairly low compression level (say, around 50), and compressing these images can help reduce the load on your Web server and cause the images to appear more quickly in your users' Web browsers. You may want to experiment with different types of graphics files to learn what compression level works best for you.

TOOLS FOR PRODUCING WEB PAGES

Although you can create Web pages by hand by editing the raw HTML in a text editor and using separate tools like The GIMP (`http://www.gimp.org`) to create or edit graphics, many Web page designers prefer to use GUI HTML design tools. These tools let you type in and edit text much as you can in a what-you-see-is-what-you-get (WYSIWYG) word processor, using buttons or special keystrokes to indicate centering, bold text, new paragraphs, and so on. This approach is certainly convenient, and Apache doesn't really care how you generate your files, so from a server operation point of view, there's no reason to avoid such tools. One exception is that Microsoft's Front Page can create Web pages that depend on special server extensions, so it's best to avoid it when using Apache.

NOTE *Creating* Web pages with a design tool isn't normally a problem for Apache, but some creation tools include interfaces to automatically upload a Web page to a Web server. These upload features might not work with Apache, at least not directly. You may need to save your Web pages in local files, then transfer them by floppy, FTP, or some other means to the Web server computer.

Examples of Web page creation tools include the following:

- **Word processors**—Many modern GUI word processors include a feature to export documents as HTML, or special HTML formatting modes. Such HTML exports may lose some formatting features if the files were generated as normal word processor documents. This can be a convenient way to generate HTML documents if you're already familiar with a word processor that supports such a feature. Linux word processors with HTML export capabilities include Applix Words, StarOffice, and WordPerfect.

- **Web browsers**—Many Web browsers, including Netscape for Linux, come with document-creation modules. As a general rule, these are more finely tuned to the needs of Web page design than are word processors, but if you're already familiar with a word processor, the browser tools represent another program to master.

- **Standalone Web page creation tools**—These tools are designed from the ground up to do nothing but create Web pages. Examples in Linux include ASHE (`http://www.cs.rpi.edu/pub/puninj/ASHE/`), August (`http://www.lls.se/~johanb/august/`), Bluefish (`http://bluefish.openoffice.nl`), and WebSphere (`http://www-4.ibm.com/software/webservers/hpbuilder/`). Some of these are very basic tools, whereas others are extremely complex.

If you use a Web page development tool, you should be aware of the limitations of these tools. Because of the nature of the Web, no two browsers are likely to display the same page in precisely the same way, but working with these tools makes it easy to overlook this fact. If the tool creates HTML that's optimized for particular browsers, your Web site's visitors may find your site difficult to read because of the assumptions your HTML editor made.

Web Page Design Tips

Some Web designers like to use HTML features to their fullest, thus creating a layout that can be almost as complex as anything that could be created on a printed page. There are drawbacks to using the more advanced HTML features, though. Specifically, it's impossible to predict precisely how a given browser will handle a code. Indeed, even the codes in Listing 20.2 aren't entirely consistent in their application—as noted in the preceding descriptions, different browsers respond differently to the various codes used to center text, for instance. Font specifications work only if the font is installed on the client's Web browser; if it's not, the usual result is a fallback to an ugly default, such as Courier. Color specifications may interact poorly with a user's own color choices. (One particularly annoying error is specifying a background color without specifying a text color. If you specify a white background color but no text color, a user who has defaults set to white text on black background will be unable to read your page. Listing 20.2 specifies background and foreground colors, but it doesn't specify link colors, which can also be important in this equation.)

Because Web browsers vary wildly, it's best to test your Web pages on multiple browsers. At the very least, you should test on both Netscape Navigator and Microsoft Internet Explorer. If possible, you should test on multiple versions of these browsers. Other browsers that are popular, particularly in the Linux community, include Mozilla (`http://www.mozilla.org`, an open source cousin to Netscape Navigator), Opera (`http://www.opera.com`), Konqueror (a part of the KDE project), and Lynx (`http://lynx.browser.org`, a text-based Web browser). Lynx is particularly important if you want your site to be accessible to all users. Because it's text-based, it will turn up problems you might not notice in a GUI browser, but that might be important to somebody who uses Lynx, or to a visually impaired person who uses a speech synthesizer with a computer. Also, keep in mind that many (perhaps most) of your Web server users won't be using Linux. On Windows, Internet Explorer is the most popular browser, but others (including many of the preceding browsers) are available. MacOS, BeOS, OS/2, and many other platforms all sport their own browsers, some of which are shared with other platforms and some of which are not.

TIP You can examine your server log files, as described shortly, to determine what types of browsers are most often used with your Web site.

ANALYZING SERVER LOG FILES

Web server log files can be an important source of information to help you manage your Web site. Log files may include information on the clients that are visiting your site, which of your documents are popular with those clients, when your files are being accessed, and so on. Unfortunately, examining raw log files can be a tedious undertaking, so various tools exist to help summarize the data in the log files. Two common tools are Analog and Webalizer.

NOTE This section describes the routine log files created by Apache, as set by the `CustomLog` directive, described earlier. Apache may also log errors, startup messages, and so on to a separate log file.

THE APACHE LOG FILE FORMAT

There are actually several different Apache log file formats, which you can set with the `CustomLog` directive, as described in "Setting Common Configuration Options." This section describes the `combined` format, which combines information into a single file. The other options provide a subset of this information.

An entry in the combined log file looks something like this:

```
192.168.1.1 - - [06/Nov/2002:16:45:49 -0500] "GET /index.html \
HTTP/1.0" 200 8597 "-" "Mozilla (X11; I; Linux 2.0.32 i586)"
```

This entry consists of several parts:

- **Client hostname or IP address**—The first field is the IP address or hostname of the client that made a request.
- **User identification**—The next two fields (both dashes in this example) provide the username of the individual who made the request. The dashes indicate that this information isn't available. If they're present, the first field is the name as identified by the identd server and the second is as identified by HTTP user authentication.
- **Date and time**—Apache logs the date and time of the transfer request. This information is recorded in local time, but the log includes the time zone (-0500 in this example, meaning five hours before GMT).
- **HTTP request**—The HTTP request code (GET /index.html HTTP/1.0 in this example) shows the command that the client used (GET), the document requested (/index.html), and the HTTP level used (1.0). You can use this information to discover which of your pages are the most popular. This field also often contains clues to attempted break-ins, because these often rely upon requests for strange documents.
- **Response code**—Apache replies to the client, in part, with a response code that provides information about the ability of the server to fulfill a request. In this example, the response code is 200, which means Apache could fulfill the request. Codes beginning in 3 are redirections, client errors are indicated by codes beginning in 4, and server errors turn up in codes beginning in 5.
- **Object size**—The 8597 entry in this example is the size of the document that Apache returned, not counting HTTP overhead.
- **Referrer**—When a user clicks a link from another page, most browsers deliver the URL of the referring page to the new page's Web server. Apache records this information in its log file. In the preceding example, the referrer is "-", indicating there was no referring page—the user typed the URL into the Web browser directly.
- **User agent**—The final field contains information that the browser sends to Apache about itself, such as its name and the OS on which it runs. (Note that Netscape reports itself as Mozilla.) This information isn't wholly reliable; Web browsers can be programmed to lie, or proxy servers may change the information.

Using this information, you can peruse your Apache log files to determine something about the popularity of your Web pages, when they're being accessed, who's accessing them, and so on. Examining these files "raw" can be tedious, though. That's where log file analysis tools come in handy.

NOTE Most Linux installations include cron jobs to automatically rotate log files, including Apache log files. Check your system's cron jobs (usually stored in /etc/cron.d, /etc/cron.interval, or a similar location) for such a log file rotation system. If your Web file logs aren't being rotated, you may want to add this feature to prevent the log files from growing to consume available disk space.

USING ANALOG

Analog (`http://www.analog.cx`) claims to be the most popular Web log file analyzer in the world. This package's output is heavily text-based, but includes some bar and pie charts. You can see an example report at `http://www.statslab.cam.ac.uk/~sret1/stats/stats.html`. Analog ships with some distributions, or you can obtain it from its Web page.

Setting Analog Options

Analog is controlled through its configuration file, `analog.cfg`, which usually resides in /etc. This file contains various options that help Analog combine data into useful chunks. For instance, SEARCHENGINE specifies search engines that might appear as referrers, so that Analog can summarize search engine links to your sites. Three options you're likely to want to set immediately are the following:

```
LOGFILE /path/to/log/file
OUTFILE /path/to/output/file
HOSTNAME "Your Organization's Name"
```

The first two of these items are critically important. If you don't specify them, Analog won't be able to locate your log file, and it will dump its output file directly to standard output. Analog's output is in the form of an HTML file with associated graphics, so you can read it with a Web browser. (You specify only the name for the main file, such as /home/httpd/html/analog/index.html; Analog creates its graphics files in the

567

same directory.) The HOSTNAME specification is purely cosmetic; Analog displays this information at the top of its report.

Unfortunately, some Analog packages are not fully functional out of the box because they make peculiar and contradictory assumptions about the locations of files. These problems can be overcome by creating a few symbolic links:

- **Configuration files**—Some Analog packages are built to assume that the analog.cfg file will be in the same directory as the Analog executable (usually /usr/bin), although the file actually resides in /etc. The /usr/bin directory is a bizarre location for a configuration file, but you can type **ln -s /etc/analog.cfg /usr/bin** to leave the file in /etc but still satisfy Analog.
- **Language files**—Analog relies upon language files to operate properly. Some packages place these in /var/lib/analog/lang, but Analog may look for them in /usr/bin/lang. Typing **ln -s /var/lib/analog/lang /usr/bin** allows Analog to function.
- **Support graphics**—Analog generates some graphics, such as pie charts, for each site it summarizes, but it also relies on other fixed graphics files. Some packages drop these files in /var/www/html/images by default, but the HTML that Analog generates looks for them in the images directory under the Analog output directory, so you may need to create another symbolic link. Change to the output directory you specified with the OUTFILE option and type **ln -s /var/www/html/images** to give Analog access to these graphics files.

Keep in mind that these adjustments may not be required for all Analog packages. (I found them to be necessary with an Analog package intended for Linux Mandrake, analog-5.01-1mdk.)

Running Analog

Analog can be run by typing its name: **analog**. The user who types this command must have read access to the Web access logs, as well as write access to the Analog output directory. If you plan your permissions appropriately, you do *not* need root access for either task.

In most cases, you'll want to run Analog from a cron job on a regular basis, such as once a month, once a week, or even once a day. Keep in mind that Analog, although not a huge process, does consume some system resources, so running it very frequently (such as once a minute) can cause a performance hit, particularly on a busy server.

Interpreting Analog Output

The Analog output is broken into several distinct reports, each of which provides information that's been processed and summarized in a different way. The specific sections are as follows:

- **General summary**—This section provides general information that may be useful to judging the overall health of your Web server, such as the average number of requests it processes per day, the average number of successful and failed requests per day, and the total and average daily data transfers.

- **Monthly report**—The monthly report summarizes the number of pages served on a monthly basis. Increasing monthly use and decreasing perceived performance could mean you need to upgrade the server or its network connections.

- **Daily summary**—This section provides information on the number of pages served by the day of week (Monday, Tuesday, and so on).

- **Hourly summary**—This section is like the daily summary, but it summarizes server use by the hour within a day (1:00, 2:00, and so on). If you're experiencing slowdowns, you may want to check this summary and use it to fine-tune your diagnostics; you might miss a problem if you look for it during a less busy time of the day.

- **Domain report**—If your server handles multiple domains, you'll see a summary of the amount of traffic each one processes.

- **Organizational report**—If you associate different organizations with different domains or pages, this report breaks traffic down by organization.

- **Operating system report**—You can see which OSs your clients report using if you use a combined Apache log format or another format that provides this information. Note that because of proxies and other reporting inaccuracies, this information may not be wholly reliable.

- **Status code report**—Analog provides a pie chart showing the number of each status code responses issued by the Web server. This can be useful in quickly spotting problems if there are a lot of 4xx or 5xx responses.

- **File size report**—This section shows the number of files of various sizes that the Web server delivers. This can be very useful in traffic management; if you see your file sizes drifting up, you might want to take steps to check this trend, such as using higher compression levels on your graphics files.

- **File type report**—You can see the types of files (JPEG files, HTML files, and so on) delivered by your Web server. This may be useful in conjunction with the file size report in controlling the expansion of your Web site.
- **Directory report**—Most Web sites are broken into multiple directories, and this report tells you which of these are most popular, by bytes delivered.
- **Request report**—This report displays the popularity of the files in the root directory on the Web site.

You can use these various reports to get a good idea of how your Web site is being used. It can be even more valuable if you maintain a record of Analog reports that spans some time, because then you can examine multiple reports for changes over time. You can do this by creating or editing a cron job to rotate the Apache log files. (Many distributions' Apache packages include such a cron job script.) When the log file rotation occurs, back up an existing Analog directory in a subdirectory. You can then create a master HTML page that links into these backup directories so that you can peruse several weeks or months worth of Analog summaries.

Although Analog is a useful tool that can produce a wealth of data, sifting through that data can sometimes be almost as intimidating as confronting the raw Apache log files. Various additional tools, such as Report Magic (`http://www.reportmagic.com`), can further summarize Analog's reports and present details in a more readable form.

USING THE WEBALIZER

The Webalizer (`http://www.webalizer.org`) is a major competitor to Analog in the Web page summary sphere. Like Analog, the Webalizer reads configuration files and creates an output HTML file and supporting graphics so that you can peruse your Web site's traffic patterns in a convenient summary form. Webalizer ships with some distributions, or you can obtain it from its Web page. You can view a sample report at `http://www.webalizer.org/sample/`.

Setting the Webalizer Options

The Webalizer is controlled through its configuration file, `webalizer.conf`, which is typically stored in `/etc`. As with Analog, you must tell the Webalizer where to find your Web server log files and where to store its output. You do this with options like the following:

```
LogFile        /path/to/log/file
OutputDir      /path/to/output/directory
```

One important difference between the Analog and Webalizer settings for these options is that Analog requires you to specify an output filename, but the Webalizer has you specify an output directory in which it stores its files. If you set the output directory to a location within your Web server area, you can browse the Webalizer output using a Web browser. If you place the output elsewhere, you can still access it with your Web browser, but only on the Web server computer itself by specifying a `file://` URL. There are a few other Webalizer configuration options you might want to adjust, including:

- **Incremental**—If set to yes, this option causes the Webalizer to store its internal state between runs so that you can process logs in chunks. For instance, you can run the Webalizer once a day and it will remember the entries it's already processed and adjust to rotated log files. This option defaults to no, which causes the Webalizer to analyze the log file fresh each time it's run.

- **HostName**—You can set the hostname used in the report title (which is set with the ReportTitle option).

- **GroupDomains**—When reporting hostnames, Webalizer normally analyzes by complete hostname. You can group hostnames within a domain by specifying a non-0 value for GroupDomains, though. The value is the number of elements, starting from the rightmost hostname element, to use as a group. For instance, GroupDomains 2 causes gingko.pangaea.edu and birch.pangaea.edu to be grouped into pangaea.edu. This option can help to unclutter some of the information that the Webalizer produces.

- **GroupSite**—This is another grouping option, but it works on individual sites. For instance, GroupSite *.abigisp.net causes all hostnames under abigisp.net to be grouped together in reports.

- **HideSite**—This option hides the sites under a given domain, which is specified as in the GroupSite option. The GroupSite and HideSite options are frequently used together to create a grouping with no reporting of the individual sites.

Webalizer configuration files are often longer and more complex than are Analog configuration files, and the preceding list covers just a handful of Webalizer options. Most of the options are documented by comments in the standard configuration file, so you can consult it for more information.

Running the Webalizer

You can run the Webalizer by typing its name: **webalizer**. Like Analog, Webalizer doesn't need to be run as root unless read access to the Web server access logs or write access to the Webalizer output directory is restricted to root. You may want to run the Webalizer in a cron job with the Incremental option set to yes in order to have the program automatically build a history of Web site access summaries.

TIP   Chances are your Apache installation created a cron job to rotate the Apache log files; if it didn't, you'll want to create such a configuration, as noted earlier. To ensure that Webalizer catches as many Web hits as possible, run Webalizer just before the rotation occurs, even if you also run Webalizer in its own cron job.

Interpreting the Webalizer Output

Webalizer presents a two-tiered report. The first overview tier shows a summary of activity over the past year. (On a newly installed system, most of those months will be empty.) This summary includes information presented in both a table and a bar chart on the number of hits, Web page downloads, kilobytes transferred, and so on for each month. You can click on the month name in the summary table to get to the second tier of the analysis, which breaks down the month's activity in more detail. This page contains several subsections:

- **Monthly statistics**—The first area presents the same information as in the first-tier analysis page, plus a bit more, such as the number of various response codes returned to clients.

- **Daily statistics**—The second area shows a bar graph and table summarizing the Web traffic for each day of the month. Summary statistics include the number of pages, number of hits, number of files, and number of kilobytes transferred.

- **Hourly statistics**—This area presents information similar to the daily statistics area, but broken down by hour of the day. You can use this to locate peak traffic times for your site, which can be important information when planning capacity or debugging capacity-related problems.

- **Top URLs**—The Webalizer presents two tables that summarize the number of hits and kilobytes associated with specific URLs. (You can use grouping options in the Webalizer configuration file to create groups of URLs to appear in this list, if you like.) One table presents the top URLs by hits, the other the top URLs by kilobytes.

- **Entry and Exit pages**—Two tables show the most popular entry and exit pages. An entry page is the first page that a user viewed when visiting your site. An exit page is the last page a user viewed when visiting your site.

- **Top sites**—The Webalizer summarizes the clients that accessed your site the most, both by number of hits and by number of kilobytes. You can group sites together in the Webalizer configuration file with options like GroupSite, described earlier.

- **Top referrers**—If your Web log files include referrer information, the Webalizer summarizes this information so you can see which sites produce the most links to yours.

- **Top search strings**—Some Web search engines, when they produce links to your site, include the search string as part of the referrer URL. The Webalizer can break this information out and regenerate the search strings, which the Webalizer then summarizes for you.

- **Top user agents**—The Webalizer summarizes the names of the Web browsers that most frequently accessed your site.

- **Top countries**—The Webalizer's final section summarizes access by what it calls countries. In reality, the Webalizer is summarizing access by top-level domain (TLD) name, so your top "countries" may include *US Commercial*, *Network*, and other domains that aren't restricted to particular countries.

If you want to compare trends in your Web server access, the overview tier can give you general trends, but you'll need to compare the monthly reports (say, in side-by-side Web browser windows) to see how specific access patterns change with time.

SUMMARY

Web servers are extremely important tools on many networks. They can be used as a means of both internal and external communication. Web servers have traditionally been used to deliver static information from the Web server to its clients, but forms and scripting are increasingly being used to enable two-way communication for online order entry, surveys, and so on. Web server features like SSL security and virtual domains make transferring data securely and running multiple sites on a single computer possible.

Although running the Web server proper is extremely important, two important tasks surround the Web server itself: creating content and interpreting its log files. Web pages can be extremely simple documents created with a text editor or very complex file collections built with the help of Web page design tools. On the other end of the Web server pipeline lie the log files that document its actions. You can use these files to track the popularity of your Web site, spot potential trouble in the form of traffic patterns that might tax your hardware or connections, and discover information on sites that might be linking to yours. Analyzing these log files can be useful in planning changes and upgrades to your site.

Running FTP Servers

The *File Transfer Protocol (FTP)* is an old and common Internet protocol. As the name implies, it's used to transfer files between computers. Clients can download files from or upload files to an FTP server, depending upon the server's configuration. In some situations, you may want to run an FTP server instead of or in addition to a Web server or a file-sharing server. In other cases, running multiple server types may be redundant. If you do decide to run an FTP server, there are several FTP server options for Linux. In most cases, these servers come with default configurations that work for certain purposes, but you may want to fine-tune the configuration. More radical changes may be required to run an *anonymous* FTP site, which allows anybody to download files from the server.

WHEN TO RUN AN FTP SERVER

On the surface, FTP servers seem to have a lot in common with both Web servers (described in Chapter 20, Running Web Servers) and file-sharing servers (described in Chapter 7, File and Printer Sharing via Samba, and Chapter 8, File Sharing via NFS). All these servers allow for the transfer of complete files between computers, and so in some situations you may be able to successfully use any of these server types. Each of these protocols does have its unique strengths and weaknesses, though, any of which may be important in certain situations. Major differences between FTP and other file transfer protocols include the following:

- **Authentication**—FTP servers require a username/password pair for access. (The upcoming section, "Setting Up an Anonymous FTP Server," describes one convention to allow users without a password to gain access to your server.) Web servers usually don't require authentication, although there are ways to add authentication to Web sites. Some file-sharing protocols require username/password authentication, but others rely on IP-based authentication.

- **Accounts**—Because of FTP's username/password system, it can be a good way to provide access to individual users' files from remote locations. NFS and Samba can also be used in this way. Although Web servers can easily provide users with access to their files, the public nature of most Web servers means that it would take more configuration changes to provide security on these accesses.

- **Encryption**—Standard FTP servers don't encrypt any data, including usernames or passwords. This makes them risky to use over the Internet at large, although anonymous mode can reduce some aspects of the risk for certain uses. There are also a few secure FTP variants available that provide encryption, such as those that ship with Kerberos (see Chapter 6, Authenticating Users via Kerberos). Web servers don't usually encrypt data, but secure variants are available. Samba can be configured to encrypt passwords, and with more work can encrypt all data transfers with a matched Samba system or a proxy server. NFS doesn't use passwords, so password encryption isn't an issue, but NFS also doesn't normally encrypt data. The scp and sftp programs, which are part of the Secure Shell (SSH) package, encrypt all data transfers, and the latter can be a good substitute for FTP in many situations.

TIP If you must use a protocol that doesn't encrypt passwords, particularly over an insecure network like the Internet, you should change your passwords on a regular basis. This will minimize the window of opportunity for any miscreant who might obtain a password.

- **Connections**—FTP, like Samba and NFS, relies upon a continuous connection. A user can log into an FTP server and, if timeout parameters are set high enough, do nothing for hours and then transfer a file. Web servers usually operate differently, performing just one or a few transfers during a session. FTP is different from most other file exchange protocols in that FTP uses two ports: one for the control signals and one for actual data transfers. The client always initiates the control connection to the server's port 21. Depending upon the mode used (active or passive), the data connection may be initiated by the client or the server. This odd arrangement can complicate the configuration of firewalls, although most firewall products include simple ways to handle the issue.

- **Direct file editing**—The file-sharing servers, such as NFS and Samba, excel at allowing individuals to edit files from a remote computer as if those files were local. For instance, a user can load a file directly from the file-sharing server into a text editor and save the file directly back to the server without having the file touch the local hard disk. Neither FTP nor HTTP was designed for this purpose; to edit a file on an FTP or Web server, you must download it to a local disk, save changes, and then transfer the file back to the server. There are tools that let some OSs treat FTP servers more like file shares, though. For instance, the Linux FTP Filesystem (http://ftpfs.sourceforge.net) enables this functionality for Linux. This is best considered a workaround, though.

- **Two-way transfers**—File-sharing servers and FTP both permit easy two-way transfers, or permit the server administrator to restrict write access to parts or all of the server. Web servers are most commonly used for one-way traffic, although it's possible to transfer files from the client to the server via HTTP.

- **Cross-platform clients**—FTP and Web servers both work well with clients that are widely available on just about any OS that supports TCP/IP, even DOS. File-sharing protocols, by contrast, are usually more platform-centric—NFS serves UNIX and Linux clients; Samba serves DOS, Windows, and OS/2 clients; and so on. These lines can often be crossed, but when crossing platforms with file-sharing clients, there are often drawbacks, such as restrictions on filenames, permissions, file attributes, and so on. You may also require unusual or commercial client software that's not necessary to interact with FTP or Web servers.

- **Ease of server configuration**—The default FTP server configuration on most Linux systems allows individuals to read and write files on the server with the same access permissions they'd have from a text-mode login. If this is what you want, FTP server configuration can be fairly straightforward. To a greater or lesser extent, NFS, Samba, and Web servers require changes or additional configuration options to provide such access. On the other hand, to provide anonymous or otherwise restricted access, you may have to slightly alter an FTP configuration, whereas another server type's default might be a better match.

577

On the whole, FTP is a good choice for two purposes:

- **Local access for local users**—If your Linux system has local users, you can run FTP to allow those users to download or upload files from other systems on your local network. This access might not be quite as convenient as file-sharing access from the client's point of view, but it may be easier for you to configure on the server. FTP's cross-platform availability is also a boon in a cross-platform network.

- **Anonymous access for remote users**—Putting up an anonymous FTP site allows remote users to easily download files from a file repository you operate, or even to upload files anonymously, if you want to accept such submissions. A Web server can make a good alternative for this function, though, particularly if you don't want to accept anonymous uploads. If you don't want to run a full Web site, the anonymous FTP solution may be just as good.

In both of these cases, you should be alert to the security implications of FTP. If you want to provide local users with access to files, you should ensure that *only* local users can reach the server; the risk of password sniffing on the Internet at large is great enough that unencrypted FTP isn't a good choice if you want to provide local users with remote file access. Indeed, even if used only locally, you may want to impose mandatory password expiration times to reduce the risk should you have a local "bad apple" who sniffs passwords. Remote anonymous access doesn't pose password risks, but you should consider disabling access for conventional users to minimize the risks of a break-in. Also, providing anonymous users with write access is potentially quite risky, particularly if that access isn't restricted to certain controlled directories. If you allow anonymous write access, you should take steps to keep files from being visible to others until you've approved them, lest your site become a meeting place for software pirates or other undesirables.

FTP SERVER OPTIONS FOR LINUX

There are several FTP servers available for Linux, but three dominate the picture:

- **BSD FTPD**—The BSD versions of UNIX ship with their own FTP servers, and various ports of these to Linux exist. Some of these are also known as *OpenBSD FTPD*. BSD FTPD ports ship with Debian and

SuSE. This server family is often regarded as more secure than other FTP servers, but it's not very popular in the Linux world.

- **ProFTPd**—This package, which is headquartered at `http://www.proftpd.org`, ships with Debian, Mandrake, Slackware, SuSE, and TurboLinux. It's the second most popular Linux FTP server, and its popularity is on the rise in 2002. Parts of its operation are modeled after Apache.

- **WU-FTPD**—The Washington University FTP Daemon (WU-FTPD) is the most readily available FTP server for Linux. Its main Web site is `http://www.wu-ftpd.org`, and it ships with Caldera, Debian, Mandrake, Red Hat, SuSE, and TurboLinux. It has a history of more security problems than other popular FTP servers.

Any of these FTP servers will handle basic or advanced FTP server duties. This chapter describes configuring ProFTPd and WU-FTPD because they're the most popular servers, and all major Linux distributions ship with at least one of these servers. ProFTPd is more flexible than WU-FTPD, and given their relative security histories, ProFTPd is probably a better choice in most situations. You might want to stick with WU-FTPD if your distribution ships with it but not ProFTPd, or if you're already familiar with WU-FTPD. If you're adventurous, you might consider BSD FTPD, but it's really a small family of servers because there are several different ports to Linux. Thus, properly documenting it is difficult.

BASIC FTP SERVER CONFIGURATION

Once you've installed an FTP server package, you'll want to get it running. As a general rule, distributions that use WU-FTPD run it from a super server, while those that use ProFTPd run it from a SysV startup script. You can change these options if you like, though. On most distributions, getting the server to run is the only configuration option to which you must attend for basic functionality, because the default configurations work well for many purposes. Specifically, the default configuration allows users with accounts on the system to log in and transfer files to and from their home directories. You may need to alter these configurations if you want to have FTP serve some other role, or if you want to adjust configuration defaults. One common FTP server configuration—anonymous FTP—is covered in the upcoming section, "Setting Up an Anonymous FTP Server." The default configuration often at least comes close to handling this role.

RUNNING THE FTP SERVER

Consult Chapter 4, Starting Servers, for detailed information about running servers from a super server, SysV startup scripts, and local startup scripts. If you're using an FTP server package that shipped with your distribution, chances are you'll need to make few or no changes to get the server to run. There are a few caveats you should consider, though:

- Some distributions that use inetd ship with an /etc/inetd.conf file that includes separate entries for the different FTP servers. You may be able to install multiple FTP servers and switch between them by commenting out the inetd.conf entry for the server you *don't* want to use and restarting inetd. If you install only one FTP server, you must be sure to uncomment *only* the entry for the appropriate server. If you uncomment the wrong entry, your FTP server won't work.

- Most distributions that use xinetd include a file in /etc/xinetd.d to start the FTP server. This file is part of the FTP server package. This file probably includes a line that reads disable = yes, which has the effect of disabling the FTP server configuration. This entry exists as a security measure; it forces you to actively change the entry to read disable = no in order to run the FTP server. (You must also restart xinetd to have this change take effect.)

- Whether run from inetd or xinetd, FTP servers can accept parameters. The standard configuration files include appropriate parameters for typical installations using the FTP servers that ship with the distribution. If you want to use a different FTP server, you may need to adjust the parameters that are passed to the server, as well as the server's filename, in your super server configuration file.

If your FTP site is extremely popular, you might want to run your FTP server via a SysV or local startup script. Doing so will produce slightly quicker responses to incoming FTP requests, but FTP servers are small enough that this effect is fairly minimal. A few installations, such as Debian's and Mandrake's ProFTPd installations, run in this way by default, perhaps because ProFTPd most easily supports anonymous FTP when it's run as a standalone server.

Before proceeding with further configuration, you may want to check that the FTP server is working for conventional authenticated logins (that is, using a username/password pair). At the very least, the server should respond with some sort of login prompt when you try to use an FTP client from a remote host. For instance, consider the following exchange, using the basic Linux ftp program:

```
$ ftp harding.threeroomco.com
ftp: connect: Connection refused
```

This indicates that the FTP server isn't running at all. If you get this response, you should check your system log files for clues about why the server isn't running. If you just installed the server, you must remember to start it running or restart your super server. Once you've gotten a response out of the server, you can continue to fine-tune its configuration.

WU-FTPD CONFIGURATION

Configuring WU-FTPD requires editing one or more of several configuration files. Using these files, you can control who may access the FTP server and what users can do with the server. Some files also set up special options that permit WU-FTPD to process files or execute advanced commands for users.

WU-FTPD Configuration Files

Most distributions that use WU-FTPD place its configuration files directly in /etc. There are several WU-FTPD configuration files, and their names all begin with ftp:

- **ftpaccess**—This is the most complex WU-FTPD configuration file, and is described in more detail shortly. It's used to set logging options, permissions used by anonymous access, low-level TCP/IP options, and so on.
- **ftpconversions**—One of the features you can activate in ftpaccess is the ability to automatically compress files or archive directories prior to transmission to the client. To use this feature, you must define file types to be archived or compressed in this file.
- **ftphosts**—You can limit the hosts and even users who may access your FTP server by using this file. Lines that begin with allow explicitly allow the specified hosts, and those that begin with deny explicitly deny the specified hosts. For instance, deny sjones prevents the user called sjones from using FTP, and deny badsite.pangaea.edu prevents all users from badsite.pangaea.edu from logging in.

- **ftpusers**—This file contains a list of local users who aren't allowed to use the WU-FTPD server. This file operates through the Pluggable Authentication Module (PAM) system; it's technically not part of WU-FTPD. Nonetheless, it can be a useful way to protect your FTP server from abuse. The default version of this file contains various system account names, such as root, nobody, and daemon. You can add more such account names if you need to create them for other servers or for special purposes.

- **ftpservers**—Normally, WU-FTPD presents the same options to all clients. You can use this file to specify an entirely separate configuration for specified hosts, though. Each line in this file is an IP address, hostname, or domain name followed by a directory name. WU-FTPD then looks to the specified directory for the normal FTP configuration files if a connection request comes from the specified client. For instance, 192.168.21.8 /etc/ftpd/trusted causes WU-FTPD to look in /etc/ftpd/trusted for other configuration files if 192.168.21.8 makes a connection. Thus, you might create a default configuration with tight controls on who may use the system, but loosen those restrictions for specified clients, such as those on your local network.

Each of these files can be important in implementing particular FTP server configurations. The most important file for most options is ftpaccess, but ftphosts, ftpusers, and ftpservers can be useful in securing your server. If you want WU-FTPD to process files it transfers, ftpconversions is the one to modify, possibly in conjunction with ftpaccess.

Common WU-FTPD Configuration Options

Many WU-FTPD configuration options are built around the concept of a user *class*. This is a logical grouping of users, similar in some ways to a Linux group. WU-FTPD classes are defined in terms of the source IP address or hostname of the client, though. You set up a class in ftpaccess by using the class option, which takes the following form:

```
class classname typelist addresslist
```

The components of this definition are as follows:

- *classname*—This is a name for the class. The default configuration for many distributions defines a class called all, but you can change or expand upon this definition.

- *typelist*—This is a comma-separated list of the types of local accounts or access types to which the class applies: real for local user accounts, guest for guest accounts, and anonymous for anonymous accounts.

- *addresslist*—This is a list of IP addresses, hostnames, or domain names that belong to the class. Preceding an entry with an exclamation mark (!) causes that entry to *not* be included in the list. An asterisk (*) stands for all clients. If you include multiple entries, they're combined with a logical OR operation. For instance, threeroomco.com,pangaea.edu creates a class for clients in either domain.

The standard ftpaccess file includes a definition similar to the following:

```
class   all   real,guest,anonymous   *
```

This entry sets up a default generic class that applies to all types of access and assigns all callers to this class. To fine-tune your configuration, you might create multiple classes, such as one for local users and one for remote users. Even if the class entries are identical except for the *addresslist*, you can use them differently in subsequent options. Some of these additional options include the following:

- **deny *addresslist messagefile*—**This option tells WU-FTPD to deny all access to the specified addresses. It's similar to a deny specification in ftphosts, but you can specify a filename that's to be sent to the host as a rejection notice so that users know why they weren't allowed in.

- **autogroup *groupname class[,class...]*—**You can have WU-FTPD perform a setgid operation to *groupname* if a member of a specified *class* logs in. You might do this to allow anonymous members of the *class* to read files for which *groupname* has read access, but for which world read access doesn't exist.

- **defumask *umask class[,class]*—**This option tells WU-FTPD to create files with the specified *umask* for members of a specified *class*, when a user uploads a file.

- **timeout *option seconds*—**You can set various timeout values with this option. The *option* value may be accept, connect, data, idle, maxidle, or rfc931.

- **noretrieve [relative|absolute] [class=*classname*] *filenames*—**This option tells WU-FTPD to disallow transfer of the specified filenames. If a specified filename is actually a directory name, the entire directory is restricted. You may optionally limit this option to a specified class. The relative and absolute parameters refer to whether the file specifications are interpreted as absolute (relative to the computer's true root directory) or relative to a chroot environment, as described in Chapter 23, Configuring a chroot Jail. By default, filenames beginning with a slash (/) are interpreted as absolute. An example of this option might be noretrieve /etc /usr, which prevents transfer of any files in the /etc or /usr directories.

TIP You may want to use noretrieve to disallow access to /etc/passwd, /etc/shadow, /etc/ftpaccess, core (in any directory), and any other sensitive site-specific files.

- **allowretrieve [relative|absolute] [class=classname] filenames**—This option is an explicit counter to noretrieve; it grants exceptions to a noretrieve rule. Its syntax is identical to that of noretrieve.

- **message filename [when] [class]**—This option lists a file to be displayed to the FTP client under certain circumstances. Specifically, if when is login, the message is displayed as soon as the user logs in. If when is cwd=dir, where dir is a particular directory, then the message is displayed when the user moves into that directory. You may optionally limit this message to certain classes of users by adding the class name to the end of the option. As an example of this option in use, consider message .message cwd=*. This causes WU-FTPD to send the contents of the .message file in a directory whenever a user changes into that directory. This allows you to create banner messages describing the contents of particular directories, or the purpose of the FTP server as a whole.

- **compress [yes|no] class[,class]**—You can enable compression using this option. If a file exists and a user requests a file of that name but with an extra filename extension that indicates compression added (such as file.gz rather than file), then WU-FTPD will compress the original file and send it to the user. The extensions that indicate compression are specified in the ftpconversions file.

- **tar [yes|no] class[,class]**—This option works much like compress, but it applies to creating tar files from directories. You can use this feature to provide a simple way for users to retrieve entire directories worth of files.

- **chmod, delete, overwrite, rename, and umask**—These options all take yes or no followed by a *typelist*, as described earlier with reference to class definition. (You can also use an existing class name.) When specified, these options permit or deny use of the named FTP command by the client. For instance, `delete no guest,anonymous` configures WU-FTPD to forbid guest and anonymous users from deleting files.

- **dns refuse_mismatch** *filename*—If a forward DNS lookup on the hostname obtained from a reverse DNS lookup on the client's IP address doesn't match the original IP address, this option causes WU-FTPD to deny the connection. First, though, it displays the specified *filename* so that the user knows something is wrong.

- **dns refuse_no_reverse** *filename*—This option causes WU-FTPD to refuse a connection if there's no reverse DNS lookup on the client's IP address. WU-FTPD sends *filename* to the offender to explain the refusal.

These are only a few of the most common and useful WU-FTPD options. Consult the `ftpaccess` man page for more. The upcoming section, "WU-FTPD Anonymous Options," describes some that are of particular interest if you want to set up an anonymous FTP site.

PROFTPD CONFIGURATION

ProFTPd's configuration style is inspired by that of Apache, so if you're familiar with Apache configuration, you'll find many of ProFTPd's option names and the general configuration style quite familiar.

ProFTPd Configuration Files

The main ProFTPd configuration file is `proftpd.conf`, and it's usually stored in /etc. You set most ProFTPd options in this file. Some lines in this file are comments, which begin with pound signs (#) and continue to the end of the line. Most noncomment lines take the following form:

```
Directive [Value]
```

A few directives accept multiple values as options. Some directives are grouped together, as indicated by surrounding directives in angle brackets (<>), such as the following grouping:

```
<Limit WRITE>
  DenyAll
  Allow from 172.21.33.
</Limit>
```

The closing directive for the group uses a slash (/) to indicate that it's the end of that block of directives.

In addition to the main configuration file, ProFTPd uses the ftpusers file. ProFTPd uses this file in the same way as WU-FTPD uses the file of the same name. Specifically, ProFTPd blocks the usernames listed in the file from being used as FTP login usernames. (More precisely, ProFTPd relies upon PAM for authentication, and PAM uses ftpusers to determine who is not allowed access to the FTP server.) Default ProFTPd installations generally include ftpusers files that list common system usernames, such as nobody, daemon, and root. You should probably add any system accounts you create for unusual servers to this list. You can also enter ordinary usernames, if those users should not have FTP access to the system.

Common ProFTPd Configuration Options

ProFTPd supports a wide range of configuration directives. These are detailed in the official ProFTPd documentation, available at http://www. proftpd.org/docs/. Chances are you don't need to use all of these options, though.

First, it's necessary to know something of the different types of directives that set up context blocks. Many directives apply only within certain context blocks, so knowing what these blocks are can be extremely important. The most common blocks are as follows:

- **<Anonymous *dirname*>**—You can create an anonymous FTP site by using this directive, in which you specify directives that apply to anonymous FTP access, distinct from normal username/password access. Anonymous users will be able to access files *only* within the specified *dirname*; ProFTPd does a chroot to this directory, as described in Chapter 23.

- **<Directory *dirname*>**—You specify a directory to which a set of directives will apply with this option. As you might expect, *dirname* is the directory name. This name must normally be specified in an absolute sense—that is, with a leading slash (/). Default ProFTPd configuration files often include a block headed by <Directory /*> to specify the default behavior for all directories.

- **<Global>**—The <Global> directive block sets options that apply globally to the main server configuration and all <VirtualHost> configurations.

- **<Limit *command-group*>**—This option specifies a set of FTP client commands whose actions are to be limited according to the directives that follow this option. The *command-group* is a set of one or more FTP commands, such as CWD, CDUP, MKD, RNFR, RNTO, DELE, RMD, RETR, and STOR. Special grouping commands include READ (all read commands), WRITE (all writing commands), DIRS (all directory-related commands), and ALL (all commands). You can also use LOGIN to limit login access.

- **<VirtualHost *address*>**—ProFTPd can apply different directives depending upon how it's addressed by using this option. You can specify an *address* as an IP address or hostname, and when ProFTPd answers calls to that address, it uses the directives included within its block.

Most directives can be used within one or more of the preceding blocks, and many can be used outside of any block as global options. If a directive appears globally and within a directive block (or in two nesting locations within nested blocks), the more nested instance overrides the more global instance when the blocking condition applies. The more common and useful directives include the following:

- **Allow [from] *network-specifier***—This directive is used within a <Limit> block to specify what clients may access the resource in question. In particular, *network-specifier* is a comma-delimited list of IP addresses, hostnames, domain names (preceded by a period), IP blocks (followed by a period), or the keywords all or none. You may include from after Allow, but its use is optional and purely cosmetic; it doesn't affect the function of the directive.

TIP

If possible, use IP addresses or IP blocks rather than hostnames or domain names. This reduces the FTP server's reliance upon the DNS server for this security function, thus making it more difficult to break into the FTP server.

- **AllowAll**—ProFTPd implicitly allows access to directories, but this behavior can be overridden in various ways. You may use AllowAll in a <Directory>, <Limit>, or <Anonymous> block to restore the default allowed access.

- **AllowGroup *group-list***—You can permit access to areas in a <Limit> block to particular groups with this directive. The *group-list* is a comma-separated list of groups, and a user must be a member of *all* the listed groups to pass this test. If a group name is preceded by an exclamation mark (!), its sense is reversed, so you can allow users who are *not* members of that group. This option is often used to override a denying directive that would otherwise block access, such as DenyAll.

587

- **AllowOverwrite [on|off]**—You can allow users to overwrite existing files with this directive. The default is off, which denies overwriting rights.

- **AllowUser** *user-list*—This directive allows you to override a denying directive in order to give a specific user or set of users access to a resource that's been explicitly denied to others. If a username is preceded by an exclamation mark (!), all users *except* that one are permitted access.

- **DefaultRoot** *dirname* **[group-list]**—You can tell ProFTPd to lock a user into a specified directory tree by specifying its name with this option. The *dirname* must begin with either a slash (/) for an absolute directory or a tilde (~) for the user's home directory. You can have this directive apply to only some users by specifying an appropriate *group-list*, which is like the list in AllowGroup.

TIP

You can prevent users from wandering into others' directories, or into system directories, by including a DefaultRoot ~ directive as a global option. When so configured, ProFTPd allows users to access *only* files within their home directories.

- **DefaultTransferMode [ascii|binary]**—FTP provides two common transfer modes. Binary transfers the file exactly as-is, but ASCII provides for conversion between text file formats. Most commonly, UNIX-, DOS-, and Macintosh-style end-of-line characters are converted in an ASCII transfer. Although ASCII transfers can be convenient for text files, they're disastrous for binary files, which are corrupted when transferred using ASCII mode. ProFTPd lets you set the default transfer mode with the DefaultTransferMode directive. This directive defaults to ascii.

- **Deny [from]** *network-specifier*—This directive is the opposite of Allow; it blocks clients from accessing a resource within a <Limit> block.

- **DenyAll**—You can use this directive within a <Limit>, <Anonymous>, or <Directory> block to deny all users access to the specified resource. You might want to follow it with some specific allow options to loosen the restrictions for particular users.

- **DenyGroup** *group-list*—This directive allows you to specify a group that's to be denied access in a <Limit> block. The *group-list* is defined the same way as in the AllowGroup directive.

- **DenyUser** *user-list*—This directive works like AllowUser, except that it blocks access to a resource specified by <Limit>, rather than enabling access.

- **DisplayConnect** *filename*—ProFTPd displays *filename* when the user connects, but before a logon is complete, if you use this directive.

- **DisplayFirstChdir** *filename*—This directive causes ProFTPd to display the contents of *filename* the first time a user moves into a directory. This often defaults to .message, which causes the .message file in the target directory to be displayed to users.

- **DisplayLogin** *filename*—This directive is much like DisplayConnect, but its message appears *after* a user has successfully logged in.

- **Group** *groupid*—When run as a standalone server, ProFTPd starts up as root, but changes identity as quickly as possible to minimize the security risk of a server running as root. You set the group to which it changes with this directive. Many default configurations set the group to nogroup, ftp, or some other low-privilege group.

- **MaxClients** *number*|none—You can limit the number of clients that may log in with this directive. If you specify a *number* (such as 30), that's the limit; none is a code that disables this feature.

- **MaxInstances** *number*—This directive is similar to MaxClients in that both limit the number of connections ProFTPd accepts. MaxInstances, though, works on *connections*, rather than successful logins as MaxClients uses. MaxInstances is ineffective if you launch ProFTPd from a super server, but super servers provide similar functionality themselves.

- **Order** allow,deny|deny,allow—When both allow and deny directives appear in a <Limit> block, ProFTPd checks all allow directives, then all deny directives by default. The result is that the allow directives take precedence, and any access that's not explicitly denied is allowed. You can use Order deny,allow to change this ordering, giving deny directives precedence and making denial the default behavior.

- **RootLogin** on|off—By default, ProFTPd denies access to root as a security measure. You can change this behavior by setting RootLogin on. (You may also need to adjust other features, such as removing root from /etc/ftpusers.)

- **ServerIdent** on|off ["*ident-string*"]—This directive tells ProFTPd whether to identify itself when users connect. If set to on, you can specify an identification string. The default configuration usually identifies the server as being ProFTPd, which may be more information than you care to make readily available, so changing this string is advisable.

- **ServerName "ident-string"**—This directive sets part of the name used by the default `ServerIdent` directive. You can override both with `ServerIdent` alone, but if you want to make a more modest change, you can alter `ServerName` alone.

- **ServerType inetd|standalone**—You *must* set this directive correctly for your configuration. If you run ProFTPd through a super server, set `ServerType` to `inetd`; if you run the server from a SysV or local startup script, use `standalone`. This tells ProFTPd whether to expect to be run as an ordinary user and service requests directly (`inetd`) or to be run as root, spawning processes to handle specific connections (`standalone`).

- **SyslogLevel emerg|alert|crit|error|warn|notice|info|debug**—This directive sets the verbosity of ProFTPd's logging information. `emerg` is least verbose, `debug` is most verbose, and the others fall in between.

- **TransferLog filename|NONE**—You can specify a log file to hold information on file transfers, or disable this feature by specifying NONE. You can set this option to create multiple log files for different purposes by using it independently in `<Anonymous>`, `<VirtualHost>`, `<Global>`, and the general (ungrouped) configuration areas.

- **Umask file-mask [directory-mask]**—This directive specifies the umask to be used when creating new files (and, if specified, directories). The default is usually `022`, which is reasonable for many systems.

- **UseFtpUsers on|off**—You can turn off ProFTPd's use of the `/etc/ftpusers` file by setting `UseFtpUsers off`. The default value is on.

- **UserAlias alias username**—ProFTPd normally uses the username provided during the login process as the username for authentication. You can create *aliases*, though, which are treated just like the specified username. For instance, `UserAlias rjones ronald` causes any login attempt as `rjones` to be authenticated against the `ronald` user account. (This configuration is common for anonymous access, which often uses the `ftp` account internally.)

These directives, and others not described here, combine to give ProFTP a great deal of configurability. Most installations create a standard login ability, so that users may log in and access their own files. There may also be a standard `<Anonymous>` section to support anonymous logins, which ignore the password and so may be used by anybody. The anonymous configuration may require a few additional changes, as well as placement of files to be accessed by anonymous users, to be useful.

SETTING UP AN ANONYMOUS FTP SERVER

One popular use for FTP servers is to provide anonymous FTP access. As noted earlier in this chapter, anonymous FTP servers partially overlap in function with Web servers, so you might prefer to use *only* a Web server. On the other hand, using only an anonymous FTP server, or even using both, might be worthwhile in some situations. For instance, you might want both anonymous file retrieval and username/password login file transfer on one system, but have no need for HTTP. Running both might make sense as a convenience to your users, some of whom might prefer or have readier access to just one type of client program.

Before setting up an anonymous FTP server, you should be aware of the special needs and security concerns that come with these servers. Indeed, these issues may be critical in your decision of whether to run an anonymous FTP server. Once you've made the decision, you'll need to dig into your FTP server's configuration files to set up the appropriate options to allow anonymous FTP access. You may also need to modify additional options on your system, such as directory permissions.

SPECIAL NEEDS OF ANONYMOUS SERVERS

The usual purpose of an anonymous FTP server is to deliver files from the server to the client. You might set up such a server to hold software, documentation files, and so on that you want to be publicly available. You can link to these files by specifying a URL in a Web page that begins with `ftp://`, such as `ftp://ftp.threeroomco.com/pub/manual.pdf`. A couple of points in this description deserve special emphasis:

- The files on an anonymous FTP site are generally transferred from the server to the client, much as in a typical Web server configuration. For this reason, anonymous FTP configurations usually disallow file uploads. There are exceptions to this rule, but these are generally accompanied by configurations that immediately hide the uploaded files from callers, to prevent the site from becoming a trading post for illicit materials. If you need to receive files from others, you may want to set up a regular FTP server and give a username and password to the individual from whom you need to receive files. You might also consider exchanging documents via e-mail.

- The files on an anonymous FTP site are publicly available. This means you should *never* place confidential material on such a server. In order to protect the server's own OS files and the files of any regular users,

591

anonymous FTP servers restrict the anonymous access to a special directory tree; everything outside of that tree is off limits. Most FTP servers use the chroot() system call to create a *chroot jail*, as described in Chapter 23, to accomplish this goal.

WARNING

Although a chroot jail can be a useful security tool, it's not foolproof. The best practice is to keep sensitive data off of the anonymous FTP server so that it won't fall into the wrong hands should a miscreant break out of the chroot jail.

Because the FTP server runs in a chroot jail, you may need to copy some system configuration files into the chroot jail directory. Many FTP server packages for Linux already include appropriate copies of the critical system files. Some servers, including ProFTPd, are able to read some of their configuration files before locking themselves in the chroot jail, so the number of files that must be copied is minimal.

Some configurations, such as those generally used with ProFTPd, work best with a chroot jail if the server is run from a SysV startup script. Other configurations, such as those generally used with WU-FTPD, permit anonymous server configurations even when the server is run from a super server. The trick is that the chroot() system call can only be used by a program that's run as root. If your super server configuration for the FTP server calls the FTP server as anything but root, it won't be able to set up the chroot jail. (The username-setting options in FTP server configuration files generally operate after the chroot() call; until that time, a server run from a SysV or local startup script runs as root.)

Anonymous FTP servers require that certain files reside in particular directories. These are described in the upcoming section, "Setting Up an Anonymous Directory Tree."

SECURITY CONCERNS OF ANONYMOUS SERVERS

Anonymous FTP servers, because they are normally accessible to the outside world, are a potential security threat. In theory, this threat need not be any greater than the threat from, say, Web or mail servers. In practice, though, anonymous FTP's risk may be somewhat greater. Part of the reason for this is that FTP servers, and WU-FTPD in particular, have a less than stellar security history. A further part of the problem is that FTP was designed for two-way file transfer, so a security flaw that allows a user to break out of the chroot jail may allow the user to overwrite critical system files, or at least arbitrary user files. A mail server, by contrast, gives an attacker less leverage, because the mail is processed in certain specified ways. (To be sure, bugs in mail servers have been discovered that can be used to acquire more power.)

On the plus side, a server that functions *only* as an anonymous FTP server doesn't pose a risk due to the transfer of usernames and passwords, as is a concern for a non-anonymous FTP server. The anonymous FTP server accepts all comers and any password, so there are no sensitive passwords to be compromised. Thus, in some respects, an anonymous server can be more secure than a non-anonymous server.

Because a single FTP server can be configured to perform both anonymous and non-anonymous operations, you run the risk of getting the worst of both worlds if you run both types of FTP server configurations on one system. Your best bet when running an anonymous FTP server is to configure it to accept *only* anonymous access, at least from the outside world. Minimize the number of user accounts on the system, and don't run unnecessary servers or store any sensitive data on the computer. These steps can help minimize the damage should your anonymous FTP server be compromised.

SETTING ANONYMOUS OPTIONS

Most FTP packages that ship with Linux distributions include operational or almost-operational anonymous FTP configurations. You may need to fine-tune these configurations to get the system truly working, though. This section describes the options in WU-FTPD and ProFTPd that accomplish this task, beginning with the creation of the directory tree that's common to both servers and moving on to server-specific configuration options.

Setting Up an Anonymous Directory Tree

The first step to creating an anonymous FTP site is creating an appropriate directory tree. A common choice for this tree's location is /home/ftp, but you can place it somewhere else if you prefer. In most cases, this tree should be owned by root or a user who is to maintain the FTP site, and have 755 (rwxr-xr-x) permissions. This allows the administrator to edit files in the directory, but it gives nobody else write access. In particular, the ftp user (or whatever username you use for anonymous access) can't write to the anonymous FTP directory. Subdirectories and files should follow the same pattern, although most files will lack the execute permission bit.

A typical anonymous FTP directory contains subdirectories as follows:

- **pub**—This is the traditional location for the files that users will access. You can structure it in whatever way you feel is appropriate and populate it with whatever files you like. Be sure that all files are world readable, or at least readable by the ftp user.
- **bin**—The FTP server may call other programs to perform some functions. These programs must be accessible in the /bin directory (relative to the root created by chroot()). Most commonly, ls is required. You may also need tar, gzip, and zcat (this being a symbolic link to gzip). In FTP packages, the directory of this name may include executables that are larger than the ones in the main computer's /bin directory, because the FTP directory's executables are built statically linked, so as to obviate the need for separate library files, as described next. Be sure that your executable programs in this directory have their execute bits set.
- **lib**—This directory contains dynamic library files that are used by the binary files in /bin. If you copy binary files from your regular /bin directory, you can use the ldd command to determine what library files you must copy to the FTP tree's lib directory to match. For instance, you can type **ldd /bin/ls** to learn what libraries ls requires.
- **etc**—The FTP server may rely upon two files from the /etc directory to do its work: passwd and group. You don't need to (and should probably not) copy your entire regular passwd and group files. The most critical entry is the one for ftp, or whatever username you use for anonymous access.

Once you've set up these directories and files, the basic directory structure should be adequate. You may need to add a few more files, or modify existing files, for particular purposes. For instance, if you add the ability to compress files using a tool other than gzip, you'll need to copy an appropriate executable to the FTP server's /bin directory.

WU-FTPD Anonymous Options

The most important anonymous FTP server configuration options for WU-FTPD appear in the /etc/ftpaccess file. Specifically, you may need to set or adjust the following options:

- **class**—You must create a class that includes anonymous access. This class may be the same as a class for other types of access.

- **compress, tar, chmod, delete, overwrite, and rename**—These options, described earlier, allow you to specify who may issue commands that involve specific types of options. You may want to exclude anonymous users from the last four of these to prevent them from changing files on the server. This setting may be redundant with filesystem controls, but redundancy can be useful in the event one type of control malfunctions or is misconfigured.
- **anonymous-root**—Set this option to the root directory for the chroot jail in which WU-FTPD will run itself.

Most WU-FTPD configurations run from a super server with root privileges. When such a system receives an anonymous login, it spawns a subprocess as ftp, so WU-FTPD can run an anonymous server even from a super server.

ProFTPd Anonymous Options

The main ProFTPd options for configuring an anonymous FTP server appear in the proftpd.conf file, along with the other major server options. A simple but workable anonymous FTP configuration in this file might resemble the following:

```
<Anonymous /home/ftp>
  User                      ftp
  Group                     ftp
  # We want clients to be able to login with "anonymous" as well as
  #"ftp"
  UserAlias                 anonymous ftp
  # Limit WRITE everywhere in the anonymous chroot
  <Limit WRITE>
    DenyAll
  </Limit>
</Anonymous>
```

Some key points about this configuration include the following:

- The <Anonymous> directive grouping is the key to the ProFTPd anonymous access configuration. When this directive is present, ProFTPd knows to handle matching logins somewhat differently than normal—namely, to create a chroot jail in the specified directory (/home/ftp in this example).
- The User and Group directives tell ProFTPd which username and group name to use for the anonymous server configuration. ProFTPd

595

launches itself and then spawns a subprocess under the appropriate username and group. You should be sure that your FTP directory configuration is accessible to the username and group you choose.

- The UserAlias directive tells ProFTPd to admit users who type **anonymous** as the username as anonymous users.

- The <Limit WRITE> grouping tells ProFTPd to deny write access to all users. If you set up your permissions appropriately in the anonymous FTP directory tree, this setting *should* be redundant. Redundant security measures are a good precaution, though; in case one setting is in error or subject to a bug, the other should provide protection.

- If you wanted to create a pseudo-anonymous server that takes an anonymous username but requires a password, you could use the AnonRequiresPassword on directive. You would then also need to set an appropriate password in /etc/passwd or /etc/shadow. (ProFTPd will authenticate the user *before* locking itself in its chroot jail, so use your system's password file, not the matching file in the chroot jail directory.)

If you want the server to function *only* as an anonymous FTP server, you should take steps to limit or eliminate FTP access to ordinary users. If possible, run the FTP server on a computer that supports just the bare minimum of administrative users, and deny them access by entering their usernames in the /etc/ftpusers file.

SUMMARY

FTP servers have historically been a very important part of the Internet, but today their function has been partially taken over by Web servers. Even so, FTP servers remain important in some situations, both as a means for authenticated file transfer (possibly in two directions) and as a means of anonymous file transfer (usually just from the server to the client). The two most popular FTP servers for Linux are WU-FTPD and ProFTPd. Both are powerful servers with many options, including support for both authenticated and anonymous transfers. Their configuration styles are very different, though. WU-FTPD uses its own system, and ProFTPd's configuration files are similar to those of Apache. Most distributions ship with FTP server configurations that work for authenticated access, and with little or no additional work, for anonymous access as well. Most of your FTP server configuration will probably involve making small changes to these default setups.

Part IV

NETWORK SECURITY AND ROUTER FUNCTIONS

General System Security

22

Linux is an extremely powerful OS for many networking functions. Unfortunately, with that power comes at least the potential for vulnerability. Most major servers have a history of bugs that allow outsiders to gain access, and even those that are without bugs may be vulnerable to abuse if an intruder has obtained a password or if the server is misconfigured. Keeping your system secure is therefore a topic that deserves careful attention; you must configure your system to be as secure as possible, and monitor security developments to ensure that you don't fall victim to a newly discovered security vulnerability.

This chapter begins an investigation of security issues with information on shutting down unnecessary servers, controlling accounts and passwords, keeping your system up to date, checking for evidence of intrusion, and locating additional security information. Some subsequent chapters expand on specific security topics. In particular, Chapter 24, Configuring a chroot Jail, describes a technique that's used by some servers to minimize the risk involved in running a server; Chapter 25, Configuring iptables, describes the Linux packet filter tool that's used to set up firewalls; and Chapter 26, Using a VPN, describes a method of extending a local network across the Internet in an encrypted fashion.

In addition to the security resources described in the upcoming section, "Keeping Abreast of Security Developments," you may want to read a book dedicated to security issues. Examples include Mann and Mitchell's

Linux System Security: The Administrator's Guide to Open Source Security Tools (Prentice Hall, 1999) and Garfinkel and Spafford's *Practical UNIX & Internet Security, 2nd Edition* (O'Reilly, 1996). There are also books dedicated to firewalls, such as Constaintine & Ziegler's *Linux Firewalls* (New Riders, 2001). If your network includes non-Linux systems, you might want to consider a book with broader scope, such as McClure, Scambray, and Kurtz's *Hacking Exposed, 3rd Edition* (McGraw-Hill, 2001).

SHUTTING DOWN UNNECESSARY SERVERS

Server programs, by design, provide access to a computer. Thus, every server that runs on a computer increases the risk that an unwanted individual will gain access to the computer. The interloper might gain access through a bug in the server, a misconfiguration of the server, or a compromised password. Whatever the exact details, one effective means of reducing this risk is to shut down unnecessary servers. The first step to doing this is locating unnecessary servers. Once located, you must decide *how* to shut the server down. Shutting down a server is normally a simple task, but some methods are more effective than others.

LOCATING UNNECESSARY SERVERS

The task of locating unnecessary servers can be broken down into two subtasks: Identifying servers that are running on your system and determining which of these servers is unnecessary to normal system operation. There are several ways to go about both of these tasks, and you may want to do so in multiple ways to improve your chances of success.

Locating Servers

Unfortunately, there is no centralized registry of running servers on a Linux system. If there were, locating servers would be a relatively straightforward process. Instead, you must piece together information from several different sources. It may be possible to overlook a server by one method, so it's best if you use several to locate your servers.

Using Package Management Systems

One tool that's useful in locating servers is your distribution's package management system. If you use the Red Hat Package Manager (RPM) or Debian packages exclusively, your database should contain a listing of every package that's installed on a computer. You can use this database to browse the installed packages, reading package descriptions to help you

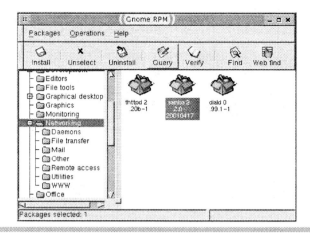

Figure 22.1   GUI package management tools let you look for installed servers.

determine whether a package contains a server, and if so, whether you need it or not. Tools that are particularly helpful for this task are GUI package management systems, such as Red Hat's GNOME RPM, SuSE's YaST, and the Storm Package Manager (part of the Storm distribution, but also useable with Debian). These tools allow you to browse the installed packages in a window, as in the GNOME RPM window shown in Figure 22.1. You can click a package and choose an option to read a description of the package. Some package managers categorize their packages so that you can more easily locate them, but these categories aren't as strictly defined as they might be, so you may need to look in all the categories to locate all your servers. This approach also will not find servers that you installed from tarballs or from source code. Finally, you can't tell whether a server is actually *running* with this approach. A server that's installed but not running poses much less risk than one that's actually running. (The main risk is that some future configuration change might accidentally start the server running, thus increasing your risk.)

Examining Server Startup Files

Another way to look for servers is to examine the common server startup files:

- **Super server configurations**—Check your /etc/inetd.conf and /etc/xinetd.conf files, and files within the /etc/xinetd.d directory. These contain references to all the servers that are started through the super server. When using inetd, server lines that begin with pound

601

signs (#) are inactive. With `xinetd`, entries that include a `disable = yes` line are inactive.

- **SysV startup scripts**—You can check your SysV startup script locations (usually `/etc/rc.d/rc?.d` or `/etc/rc?.d`, where `?` is the runlevel number) for servers started through SysV scripts. You can learn a lot from the presence of these files and their filenames. Note that some of these scripts start programs that are not servers, so you shouldn't automatically disable anything you don't recognize.

- **Local startup scripts**—Many distributions use scripts called `rc.local`, `boot.local`, or something else to run *local* programs—those that are installed in a way unique to a specific computer, rather than in a standard way for the distribution in question. You'll have to check these scripts line-by-line to determine what, if any, servers they start.

Chapter 4, Starting Servers, describes each of these server startup methods in more detail, including information such as the naming conventions for SysV startup scripts. You may also want to employ a tool such as `ntsysv` or `tksysv` to help interpret SysV startup scripts (and, on some distributions and with some tools, super server configurations). For a more console-based approach, typing **chkconfig --list** displays the status of SysV and possibly `xinetd` startup scripts on some distributions (notably Caldera, Mandrake, Red Hat, and TurboLinux).

Examining server startup methods can help you determine what servers are running, but it may not paint a complete picture of what servers are *installed*. For that, you'll need to use a package management system or examine every executable on your computer (a tedious proposition at best). As noted earlier, a package that's installed but not running poses much less of a risk than does one that's installed and running.

Examining Running Processes

Another tool that can be helpful in locating servers is `ps`. This command returns information on running processes. You can provide dozens of different options to modify the program's operation, but typing **ps ax** is a good starting point if you want to locate servers. The output is likely to be quite extensive, so you may want to redirect it to a file or pipe it through `more` or `less` so you can examine the whole of the output. If you're searching for a specific server, you can pipe the result through `grep`, as in **ps ax | grep sendmail** to locate information on any `sendmail` processes that are running. However you use it, `ps` provides information on both server and nonserver processes. Here's an edited example of its output:

```
$ ps ax
  PID TTY        STAT    TIME COMMAND
    1 ?          S       0:15 init [3]
  502 ?          S       0:05 named -u bind
  520 ?          S       0:01 cupsd
  535 ?          SW      0:00 [nfsd]
 1741 pts/4      S       0:00 /bin/bash
 4168 ?          S       0:00 httpd
```

Actual ps outputs are likely to contain dozens of lines, even on a lightly loaded system. This example has trimmed all but a few entries for demonstration purposes. The first entry, with a process ID (PID) of 1, is always init. This process sits at the root of the process tree; all others derive from it, directly or indirectly. Processes whose names (in the COM-MAND column) are in brackets, such as [nfsd], are kernel processes. You might recognize nfsd as the name of the NFS daemon—a kernel-based server. Other servers in this example are named, cupsd, and httpd, all of which are user-space servers. Two clues help identify these as servers. First, their names all end in d, for *daemon*. Second, they aren't tied to specific ttys (the TTY column contains a question mark). Many nonserver processes, such as /bin/bash in this example, are tied to specific ttys. Neither of these details indicates with certainty that a process is a server, but they're useful clues.

Once you've spotted potential servers with ps, you may want to try locating documentation for the processes in question. Type **man *name***, where *name* is the name of the process; and try locating the binary file with the name of the process, and track down its package and documentation (for instance, **rpm -qf */path/to/name*** to locate the package associated with *name* on an RPM-based system, or **dpkg -S */path/to/name*** to do the same thing on Debian).

Keep in mind when using ps that it won't locate servers that aren't running at the moment you check for them. In particular, if a server is started through a super server, you won't find it by examining a process list unless somebody is using the server at the moment you try this test. This procedure also won't locate a server that's crashed or has been temporarily taken down for maintenance.

Using netstat

One problem with the ps approach is that it's not always obvious which processes are involved in network operations, much less which are servers. One tool that you can use to help fine-tune this identification is netstat.

This program reports information on network connections, including which ports are in use. Like ps, netstat takes a large number of options that modify its behavior. To help locate servers, **netstat -lp** is a good starting point. This locates ports that are being listened to (-1), and causes netstat to print (-p) the name of the server that's doing the listening. The output also includes the port to which the server is listening, and additional information. As with ps, you'll probably want to redirect the output to a file or pipe it through less or more.

Although netstat can be a useful tool, it's got its limits. It displays the ports that are being listened to, but the program list won't be completely accurate for servers started through a super server; netstat will report the super server name rather than the name of the program that ultimately fields the request.

Using External Scanners

One of the most powerful tools for locating servers is an external scanner program, such as Nessus (http://www.nessus.org), SAINT (http://www.wwdsi.com/saint/), or Nmap (http://www.insecure.org/nmap/). These programs run on a computer other than the one you want to check, and scan the target system for running servers. Depending on the exact goals of the scanner developers, it may report additional information, such as the OS in use on the target or whether a server has any known vulnerabilities. A basic scan can often be performed very simply by typing the tool's name followed by the target system's hostname, as in **nmap gingko.threeroomco.com**. The result should be a list of open ports and associated server types.

WARNING

!

Port scanners are frequently used by crackers to help them locate vulnerable systems. Using the same tools yourself can be helpful in that you'll spot the sorts of vulnerabilities a miscreant might locate. Sadly, using these tools can also cast suspicion upon you, especially if the use of the tool is unauthorized. Before you obtain and use a port scanner, clear its use with your superiors. If you don't, you could find yourself in trouble—perhaps even enough to lose your job!

An external scan can be particularly helpful if you suspect a server may have already been compromised. A competent cracker can replace tools like ps and netstat so that any additional servers won't appear to be running. An external scan *might* discover these servers.

NOTE The media generally use the term *hacker* to refer to computer criminals. Individuals who enjoy programming or working with computers in perfectly legal and honorable ways, however, have long used this term to refer to their own activities. Indeed, many of the people who wrote Linux consider themselves to be hackers in this positive sense. For this reason, I use the term *cracker* to refer to computer criminals and miscreants.

The drawback to an external scan is that it may not spot servers if they're not accessible to the system doing the scanning. For instance, if a computer has two network interfaces, scanning one interface might turn up no servers running, when many servers are running on the other interface. Likewise, firewall tools can block access to servers based on IP addresses, so even if a computer has just one network interface, an external scanner might not detect a server if a firewall blocks the scanning system.

Determining When a Server Is Unnecessary

Once you've developed a list of servers, you must decide which ones are necessary. Unfortunately, this task isn't always easy. Unless you're intimately familiar with the operation of a Linux system, you may not understand the function of a server, and so may believe it's unnecessary, when in fact it plays some important role. The preceding chapters of this book can help you determine whether many specific servers are necessary on your system. You can also consult the server's documentation, such as its man pages, or perform a Web search to locate more information.

If you're still not sure if a server is strictly necessary, you can try shutting it down and see what happens. If the computer continues to operate normally in all respects, you can be sure that the server wasn't doing anything necessary; however, most servers *do* provide some sort of noticeable function. It's possible that the server you shut down does something necessary, but that is not immediately obvious. For instance, you can run a font server (described in Chapter 15, Providing Consistent Fonts with Font Servers) even on a computer that doesn't run X. The computer itself will continue to function if you shut down the font server, but other systems will soon begin to malfunction.

You should also be very cautious about shutting down processes related to logins. Although remote login servers, as described in Chapters 13 and 14, may not be necessary, disabling local logins can cause serious problems that would require an emergency boot floppy to correct. You should be cautious about removing login processes started from SysV startup scripts or other system startup scripts.

One fortunate fact is that no process started from a super server is vital for local operation. If you don't recognize a super server entry, you can remove it and the local computer will continue to function. As just noted, of course, *other* systems might be adversely affected, but you can remove all the super server entries and that computer will still boot and be usable from the console.

METHODS OF SHUTTING DOWN SERVERS

You can shut down servers in several different ways. As a general rule, there are two main approaches:

- You can reverse whatever process is used to start the server. For instance, you can comment out an entry in /etc/inetd.conf or rename a SysV startup script. Chapter 4 discusses these methods.
- You can uninstall the server. If the server's files aren't installed at all, it can't be run.

The first method is usually the safest one to try if you're not absolutely certain you don't need the server, because it's the easiest to reverse. If you disable a server and then find that you *do* need it, you can quickly restore its startup configuration.

TIP

When disabling a server, try doing so in a way that doesn't delete any configuration information. For instance, comment out an entry in /etc/inetd.conf rather than delete it, or rename a SysV startup script rather than delete it. This allows for easy reversal of your changes should the need arise.

Once you're convinced that the server program is completely unnecessary, removing it from the computer makes sense. Eliminating the server ensures that it won't be started accidentally in the future, and saves disk space. If you think you might want the server in the future, you might want to leave it installed; or you could remove it and back up its configuration files, if you've modified them, so that you can restore your configuration should you decide to re-install the server.

CONTROLLING ACCOUNTS AND PASSWORDS

If a server exists, it's a potential door into your computer. There are several different ways to lock this door. One is to use firewall tools like iptables (discussed in Chapter 25). Another, which works only with some servers, is to pay careful attention to user accounts and passwords on the computer. Servers that use these features can become vulnerable if the computer hosts unused accounts or if passwords fall into the wrong hands. This method of control requires a partnership between you as a system administrator and all of your users, so it's important that you communicate the risks of poor password choice, password use over unencrypted connections, and so on to your users.

ACCOUNT CREATION PROCEDURES AND POLICIES

The first step in protecting your system through account security is to develop and follow appropriate procedures and policies for the creation of accounts. To use the analogy of servers as doors, every account is a key that can open a door (often several doors). By minimizing the number of accounts on the computer, you reduce the risk that a key to enter your system will be abused. Of course, many servers *need* user accounts. Without user accounts, a file-sharing server is of limited utility, an FTP server can be used only for anonymous access, and so on. The trick is to determine when you really need to create a particular user account.

On some servers, the answer is simple: You *don't* create user accounts—at least, not for anybody but a handful of administrators (perhaps just one). Earlier chapters in this book have described the circumstances in which a server requires user accounts. Many servers, such as font, DHCP, and time servers, don't need user accounts, and so such computers can easily do without user accounts. Other server systems, such as Web and FTP servers, may or may not need user accounts, depending upon precisely how they're to be used. Remote login servers are usually run on computers that host many user accounts, so these systems always require user accounts.

Assuming a computer needs ordinary user accounts, you should have a clearly defined policy regarding use of that computer that you can use to guide when to create an account. For instance, a computer in a university's physics department might exist for use by faculty, staff, and students associated with that department, so you should have a policy to create accounts only for those individuals. Formalizing these policies can help avoid an expansion that might be undesirable from a security point of view. You can change these policies if they become too constricting, but it's easy for a system to acquire unused or unnecessary accounts if your account-creation policies are too lax or informal. This formalization is particularly important if the computer has many users.

You may also want to develop scripts or a checklist to follow when creating user accounts. One particularly important detail in this process is how you set the password. The upcoming section, "Setting Good Passwords," addresses this issue. You should also create an appropriate default permissions system for your computer. For instance, you might want to create separate project groups and assign users to specific groups, and assign permissions on home directories to restrict who may access whose files. Appropriate policies vary greatly from one environment to another, so you'll have to develop your settings with your particular needs in mind. In an open environment, loose home directory permissions such as 0755 or even 0775 may be in order, with a matching umask value for file creation; but in an environment in which intra-system security is more important, you may need to set tight 0700 home directory permissions with restrictive umasks.

MONITORING ACCOUNT USAGE

Once you've created accounts for your users, you may want to monitor those accounts to see that they aren't abused. There are two key aspects to this monitoring: Checking for inactive accounts and checking for abuses of active accounts.

Handling Inactive Accounts

User accounts are seldom permanent. Students graduate and employees move on to other jobs, for instance. Whenever an account falls into disuse, it should be disabled or removed to minimize the risk of its being abused. If you receive a notice that the user has left your organization or should no longer have an account for some other reason, you can manually disable or delete the account. You might not always receive such a notification, though. One way to help automate the process is to create accounts that automatically expire, or that have passwords that expire. You can use the usermod command to set an expiration date on an account, thus:

```
# usermod -e 2003-07-04 george
```

This command tells the system that the george account will become inactive on July 4, 2003. (You can use the -e parameter to useradd to create an account with an expiration date initially, as well.) This approach is most useful when you know that a given user will no longer need an account after a certain date, such as with student accounts and those for temporary employees.

A less drastic approach is to set up an expiring password. These require the user to change the password on a regular basis, such as once a month. You can do this with the chage command, thus:

```
# chage -M 30 -W 5 george
```

This command tells the system that george must change his password every 30 days, and to warn george of an impending deadline 5 days before the fact. If george doesn't change his password, the account will be disabled and require administrative intervention to be used again.

These automated processes can help reduce problems, but they aren't appropriate for all situations. For instance, if the account exists for some nonlogin process, such as file sharing via a Samba server or mail delivery only, users may not see password expiration messages, at least not unless you create custom cron jobs to check for impending account expirations and notify users, say by sending them e-mail about the upcoming password expirations. There are some active steps you can take to monitor account usage. For instance, the last command returns information on the last few logins, and many distributions maintain a log file called /var/log/auth in which information on authentication is stored. If you want to be very diligent, you might even set up a cron job to monitor system log files, note when users log in, and notify you if an account goes unused for more than some given period of time. You can use these tools to monitor account usage, and if an account falls into disuse, investigate further to determine if it should be deleted.

You might need to take active administrative steps to alter account availability. For instance, once an account has automatically expired, you might want to delete it if you know it won't be used again. You might want to write a script that checks for expired accounts and reports back to you if it finds any. (These accounts can be identified because the third colon-delimited field in /etc/shadow contains a smaller value than the eighth field.)

Checking for Account Abuse

A nightmare for any system administrator is a local account that's being abused. Perhaps one of your users is untrustworthy, and is using the computer to attack other systems, or even the local system itself. Another possibility is that an outsider might have hijacked a user's account in order to abuse it.

One way to check for abuse is to look for suspicious activity in your system log files, such as /var/log/messages and /var/log/secure. (Precisely what log files exist, and what information they contain, varies from one distribution to another.) System log files mostly monitor the activity of servers, though, not of clients. Therefore, you might not see any evidence of a local user abusing, say, a Telnet client to attack another system. Such evidence might turn up in a firewall's log files, though, depending on your network's configuration. You might also see suspicious activity if your system comes under attack from outside.

Unfortunately, checking for such abuses by scanning log files is tedious at best. Automated tools like the Simple Watcher (SWATCH, http://oit.ucsb.edu/~eta/swatch/) can help by scanning log files for key strings that might indicate trouble, but such tools aren't foolproof.

One potentially important step you can take in tracking, if not preventing, abuse of your system is to run the auth server (also known as identd). When a client on your system contacts an external server, that server *might* try contacting yours to find the identity of the user who makes the outgoing connection. If your user causes trouble on the remote system, that system's administrator can contact you and tell you who was causing problems, because the username will be recorded in the remote system's logs. This process only works, of course, if identd is installed and running on your system, and if it's not been compromised itself. (Most distributions ship with this server, which is very basic and so requires only minimal configuration. It's normally run from a super server.)

Ultimately, your ability to track and prevent abuse of your local systems is limited. You can be alert to suspicious local activity, such as processes that should not be running, but closely monitoring all the activity on even a single computer is far more work than a single system administrator can undertake.

SETTING GOOD PASSWORDS

In order to use passwords, computers must store them on disk. Typically, computers encrypt passwords, generally using a *hash*, or one-way encryption algorithm. In Linux, password files are usually stored in /etc/shadow (old Linux systems often used /etc/passwd). This practice makes a password file useless even if a cracker obtains it—or so it would be in a perfect world. Increasing CPU power and disk space have made it possible for crackers to encrypt entire dictionaries that span multiple languages and include many proper names and variant spellings, letter order reversals, and so on. If a cracker obtains an encrypted password file, the cracker can compare the file's entries to the encrypted results from the dictionary file. If a match results, the cracker has learned the password.

For this reason, the best passwords are random collections of letters, numbers, and any other characters the computer allows for a password. Such random strings are unlikely to appear in a cracker's password-cracking dictionary. Unfortunately, random passwords are hard to remember, so most people pick easy-to-remember—and therefore easy-to-break—passwords. A reasonable compromise is to build something that won't appear in a dictionary but that has personally memorable characteristics. This process is two-step: First, build a base, and then modify that base.

To build a base, take a pair of unrelated words and merge them together, such as *bunpen*; or use an acronym that has meaning only to you, such as *yiwttd* (for *yesterday I went to the dentist*). This base is easy for you to remember and should not appear in a dictionary. It's best if the base is as long as possible. (I used six-character bases as examples because eight is the limit on some systems, and subsequent modifications will increase the length.) Nonetheless, a cracker might stumble upon your base by combining words from a dictionary. Therefore, further modifications are necessary.

Possible modifications include:

- **Mix case**—If your system's passwords are case-sensitive, mix up the case randomly, as in *BUnPeN* or *YiWTtd*. Many systems use case-insensitive passwords, though, so this step may not help security in all situations. For instance, Windows uses case-insensitive passwords for its SMB/CIFS file sharing.
- **Add digits or punctuation**—Add two or three randomly selected digits or punctuation, creating something like *BU3nP&eN* or *Y+iWTtd2*.
- **Reverse a word**—If you used two words as your base, reverse the letter order of one of them. This might produce *BU3nNe&P*, for instance.

Further modifications are, of course, possible. The key is that, despite the random appearance of these end results, the person who produced them can regenerate the password with relative ease. Such passwords therefore need not be written down or stored unencrypted on a computer. These two practices both greatly degrade security, because the paper or computer file might fall into the wrong hands.

If you want to check that your users' passwords are good, you can use a password cracking program on them, such as Crack (http://www.users.dircon.co.uk/~crypto/). If the program delivers a password to you, you can help the user create a better password.

!

If you run a password-cracking program, do it on a computer that's *not* connected to any network to eliminate the risk that a cracker will stumble across your efforts. Also, as with port scanning, password cracking is grounds for dismissal from many employers, so if you want to do this to improve local security, be sure to obtain permission first!

In addition to creating good passwords, users should take pains to keep passwords secure. This means that users should never write down passwords or give them to other people (even friends, family members, or coworkers). You should explicitly tell your users that you will never need to know their passwords; there have been scams in the past where crackers have claimed to be system administrators and asked for passwords, and users have fallen for the ruse.

Even if users create good passwords and don't give them away, they can be discovered through various means. One is *shoulder surfing,* in which a cracker observes a user in a public area typing in the password. This is a real risk in public computer centers such as those common on university campuses, and to a lesser extent in the cubicle farms common in many companies. Another risk, which has been described elsewhere in this book, is password *sniffing,* in which a computer on a network is programmed to recover passwords sent between other computers on the network. This is a risk both on local networks and on the Internet at large. You can minimize the risk on local Ethernet networks by using switches rather than hubs; switches don't echo data to all connected devices, so the sniffer would have to be on the client or server computer itself to acquire a password. A still better approach is to use protocols that encrypt the password, rendering an intercepted password useless.

KEEPING THE SYSTEM UP TO DATE

Many compromised systems owe their inglorious compromised status to lack of appropriate maintenance. A few minutes spent checking for and installing software updates on a regular basis can save uncountable hours of work later, because updated software frequently includes fixes for security bugs. If you update buggy software quickly enough, would-be intruders will not be able to exploit security vulnerabilities.

THE IMPORTANCE OF SERVER UPDATES

Software bugs can take many forms and have many different types of effects. Bugs can corrupt data, crash the affected program, or make the program behave in some odd way. Some bugs are security-related. They may allow a person to write arbitrary files in arbitrary locations (potentially overwriting critical configuration files), or give the abuser the ability to run programs under some other username. In sum, such bugs can compromise the system, giving a normal user superuser privileges.

Servers, like any other program, can be buggy. Buggy servers are particularly important because they're potentially more accessible than are buggy local programs. If a non-network program (say, man) contains a security-related bug, only local users can exploit the bug. Assuming your users are trustworthy, and assuming a cracker hasn't gained local access to your system, such a bug won't cause harm. (Of course, those assumptions aren't always valid, so fixing such bugs is important.) Many servers, by contrast, are accessible to the world at large. If a flaw in a Web server allows any user to take control of the computer, then that Web server is vulnerable to attack from just about anybody. Thus, security bugs in servers are particularly critical, and it's vital you protect yourself against them.

The problem is exacerbated by the fact that many servers run as root. If a program (server or nonserver) that runs as an ordinary user is compromised, chances are little damage can be done with it. For instance, such a program can't ordinarily rewrite your /etc/passwd file. If a program that runs as root is compromised, though, the attacker has much greater power; if such a program can be made to write arbitrary files, changing /etc/passwd is very possible. Many servers need root privileges to function correctly. For instance, root access is needed to provide login services, or even to listen to the first 1024 ports, on which most servers run. (A super server runs as root, but can spawn a server that runs as another user, even when it serves a sub-1024 port.)

For all of these reasons, it's critical that you keep your servers up to date. You don't necessarily need to perform every server update, because many server updates exist to add features or fix nonsecurity bugs that might not affect you. You should upgrade whenever an update emerges that fixes a security bug, though.

How to Monitor for Updated Software

There are several ways to look for updated software packages:

- **Software package Web sites and mailing lists**—Most software packages, including most servers, have official Web sites, mailing lists, and occasionally newsgroups or other communication forums. You can monitor these resources on a regular basis to locate software updates. This approach can be tedious, though; a Linux system may have a dozen or more servers installed, and monitoring all the relevant forums can be difficult at best. This approach is best reserved for unusual packages—those that aren't part of your normal distribution's software mix—and perhaps for very popular servers you might be running.

- **Your distribution's Web site**—All distributions have Web pages that include information on software updates. Distribution maintainers do the work of monitoring various security resources, including the Web pages for the individual server packages included in the distribution. This provides you with a one-stop location for security and other update information. The drawback is that it may take some time for a security fix to filter down from its original source to your distribution's Web page. In a best-case scenario, the delay might be just a few minutes, but it's more likely to be a few hours or even days.

- **Generic security information sources**—The upcoming section, "Keeping Abreast of Security Developments," describes resources for information on security-related developments. These can be extremely useful and important. They usually include information on workarounds to problems, if they exist, so you may be able to take steps to minimize the risk before an official fix is available. You'll have to go back to the program maintainer or your distribution's updates page to obtain fixed software, though.

In most cases, some combination of the last two approaches is a good way to keep an eye on security developments. Reading your servers' Web sites can also be important, particularly if you're using unusual servers that aren't officially supported by your distribution. A quick check of two or three Web pages or newsgroups once a day can save untold hours of work recovering from a break-in. Even a once-a-week check is better than nothing, and a periodic comparison of installed packages against the latest versions available can help catch updates that might have slipped through the cracks, as it were.

AUTOMATIC SOFTWARE UPDATE PROCEDURES

Unfortunately, manually checking for software updates can be tedious at best. For this reason, there are several tools available to help automate the process. These include the following:

- **apt-get**—This program is a standard part of the Debian distribution and its derivatives. It's used for installing software, and it can also check for updates to already installed packages. Specifically, typing **apt-get update** followed by **apt-get dist-upgrade** will retrieve updated package information and then upgrade any packages that have newer versions. Replace the second command with **apt-get -s -u upgrade** to receive a report on new packages without actually installing them. Using apt-get in this way will only work, however, if you list at least one Debian package distribution site in the /etc/apt/sources.list file. There are also ports of apt-get (part of the larger apt package) for RPM-based systems, such as the one created by Connectiva (http://distro.conectiva.com/projetos/42) and apt4rpm (http://apt4rpm.sourceforge.net).

- **Red Hat's Update Agent**—Red Hat uses a package it calls the Update Agent to help keep systems up to date. This package requires you to register with Red Hat, and the program sends information on your computer's hardware and software to Red Hat. It can then keep your system updated. Configuration and use of the program is moderately complex, so you should consult its documentation at http://www.redhat.com/docs/manuals/RHNetwork/ref-guide/ for more information.

Automatic security updates are desirable in many ways, because they can help protect you against security breaches. They aren't without their drawbacks, though. By giving an automatic process control of your computer, you're entrusting it with a huge responsibility. Automatic updates can and do fail in various ways. For instance, an updated package might include a new bug or an incompatibility with another important package (especially if you've mixed packages from your distribution with others you build yourself or install from tarballs). It's also conceivable that a cracker could break into the automatic update site or a DNS server in order to deliver modified packages. Because Debian packages sometimes include installation scripts that require human interaction, you shouldn't run apt-get in a cron job or other automated procedure; you should run it manually, even if you plan to do so on a regular basis. (Using **apt-get -s -u upgrade** in a cron job should be safe, though.) These tools don't always differentiate between security updates and others that are less critical, but which might cause problems for your system.

On the whole, automated software updates can be quick and convenient, but I recommend using them only in a strictly supervised manner. Ideally, you should be able to authorize individual upgrades so as to head off problems due to an overzealous update agent. This is an area of active development, so it's likely that these tools will become more sophisticated and helpful in the future.

Monitoring for Intrusion Attempts

Unfortunately, even systems that are very well maintained, with good account and password policies and no unnecessary servers running, are sometimes compromised. Knowing how to spot an intrusion can be critically important to minimizing the damage from such an event. There are several intrusion-detection tools available for Linux, and there are also symptoms for which you can look to help you identify a compromised computer.

Intrusion-Detection Tools

Crackers who break into computers frequently alter the system's configuration in some way. Examples of changes include defaced Web pages, modified password files with new accounts to simplify future break-ins, modified program files that do things other than what you expect, and hidden surprises in just about any configuration or data file. Unfortunately, it's impossible to predict precisely what files a cracker will modify. This is part of what makes a successful intrusion so serious: Because you don't know precisely what was done to your system, you can't trust any of it any longer. The safest course of action is to completely delete all data on the computer and re-install it or restore it from a backup made before the compromise. (The upcoming section, "What to Do if You Discover an Intruder," covers this topic in more detail.)

The fact that intruders modify files, however, can be used as a way to detect them. The idea is to record information on critical system files, like /etc/passwd and various files in /bin, in such a way that this information can't be modified. The information might be encrypted or stored on a removable medium, for instance. You can then compare your stored information against the critical files on a regular basis. If a file that should not have changed has changed, you should suspect an intrusion. (Of course, there are also innocent explanations for some changes, such as the legitimate addition of users causing changes to /etc/passwd.)

Using Package Databases

One tool that can be used in this endeavor already exists on most Linux distributions: Your package database. The Debian package system and RPM system both store a wide variety of information about all installed packages in package database files. You can use the --verify (or -V) option to rpm to check an installed package against its original file contents, thus:

```
# rpm -V postfix
S.5....T c /etc/postfix/aliases
S.5....T c /etc/postfix/main.cf
```

This output shows the names of files that have changed in some way from their original state. The string at the start of each line of output indicates the information that no longer matches. For both of the files reported in this example, the S indicates that the file size has changed, the 5 means that the MD5 sum is different, and the T refers to an altered file modification time. In this particular case, these changes are not a problem, because both the files in question are configuration files that *should* be different than what was delivered with the original package. If the Postfix executable had changed, though, there would be cause for concern.

On Debian systems, dlocate provides similar functionality, but as of Debian 2.2, this tool isn't part of the standard system. Once you've installed it, you can issue a command like the following:

```
# dlocate -md5check postfix
```

This checks the postfix package's MD5 sums, and reports whether this sum is correct for each file in the package.

In addition to checking just one package, you can check all your installed packages on an RPM-based system by typing **rpm -Va**. The resulting output is likely to contain hundreds of lines, mostly referring to changed configuration files and other innocent alterations. You may want to redirect the output to a file or pipe it through more or less so that you can more readily examine the output.

One drawback to using rpm or dlocate in this way is that it doesn't allow you to track changes to configuration files made *after* the package was installed. Because you're likely to make such changes, package tools aren't sensitive to intruders who might modify your system's unique configuration files. Another problem is that an intruder need only add software via your package manager to hide that fact from you. For instance, if an intruder wanted to change /bin/bash on an RPM-based system, the cracker could do so by installing a new bash RPM package, and rpm -Va wouldn't detect the change. For these reasons, it's best not to rely upon a package manager as your sole intrusion-detection tool. It's worth mentioning as something you might use if you believe you have been compromised. Although you can't be certain that a system hasn't been compromised if rpm -Va doesn't turn up any problems, you can be suspicious if it turns up changes to critical binary files.

Using Tripwire

A tool that's designed to detect intruders is called Tripwire (http://www.tripwire.org). This program ships with many Linux distributions, or you can download it from its Web site. A version that ships with your distribution is far easier to set up, because it will be preconfigured for your distribution's particular mix of files and file locations. Tripwire works by storing information on various files in its database. In this respect, Tripwire is similar to RPM or Debian package management tools. Tripwire was designed as a security tool, though, so it has certain advantages over package management tools for this purpose. Most importantly, Tripwire can be configured to store information on an arbitrary set of files at some point *after* they're installed, so you can change configuration files and *then* record their information. Tripwire can also use encryption to reduce the odds of a miscreant modifying the Tripwire database. For better security, you can store the Tripwire database on a read-only or removable medium, and mount it only when you want to perform a database check or update.

Tripwire runs in one of four different modes:

- **Database generation**—The first run of Tripwire initializes its database. You do this by typing **tripwire -initialize** after editing its configuration file. This process can take some time to execute, because it must compute hashes of all the files it's to monitor. The resulting database file may be placed in the databases subdirectory under the current directory, but it should normally be moved to /usr/lib/tripwire/databases, which ideally should be a read-only filesystem after you've created the database file.

- **Database update**—If you make changes to your system, you can use the database update mode by typing **tripwire -update */path/to/file*,** where */path/to/file* is the file whose entry you want to update.

- **Interactive update**—If you make substantial changes to your system, such as adding a large package, you can type **tripwire -interactive**. This enters an interactive mode in which the program reports files that have changed and asks if you want to update the entry.

- **Integrity checking**—This is the default mode for Tripwire; you run it by typing **tripwire** with no options. This mode checks your files for changes and reports them. You might run this check on a daily basis in a cron job.

The Tripwire configuration file is /etc/tripwire/tw.config. Like many configuration files, pound signs (#) indicate comments in this file, and text after these characters is ignored. Other lines indicate directories that Tripwire is to check. The format of these lines is as follows:

```
[!|=] entry [select-flags | template]
```

The meaning of each component is as follows:

- **Inclusive prune (!)**—An entry that's preceded by an exclamation mark indicates that the specified directory or file is not to be examined. In the case of directories, all its subdirectories are ignored, as well.

- **Exclusive prune (=)**—This code is used on directories that should be checked, but whose children should not be checked. It's often used on directories like /home. When an exclusive prune is indicated, Tripwire tells you that the directory has changed if files or directories in it have been added or deleted, but Tripwire won't identify which files have been added or deleted.

- *entry*—The *entry* is the name of a file or directory that's to be checked, such as /etc or /usr. If you list a directory, all its subdirectories are scanned as well, unless they reside on separate filesystems. Thus, if /usr/local is on a different partition than /usr, you'd need to create entries for both /usr and /usr/local to scan the entire tree.

- *select-flags*—You can tell Tripwire what types of changes to report by specifying *select-flags*. These take the form [+|-] [pinugsamc123456789].... The + or - indicates that Tripwire should or should not report changes, respectively. Each subsequent character indicates an attribute to check: p for permission changes, i for inode number changes, n for number of links, u for user ID of the file's owner, g for the group ID of the file's owner, s for file size, a for access timestamp, m for modification timestamp, c for the inode creation timestamp, and 0 through 9 for various hashes and checksums.

- *template*—Instead of specifying a *select-flags* entry, you can use a shorthand *template*. The default is R, which stands for +pinugsm12-ac3456789. Other *template* entries include L (+pinug-sacm123456789), which is useful for log files; N (+pinugsamc123456789), which is very time-consuming but thorough; and E (-pinugsamc123456789), which ignores everything.

Once you've set up a Tripwire configuration file, you should run the program in database generation mode. This produces a file in the databases directory. Subsequent runs of Tripwire expect to find the file in /usr/lib/tripwire/databases. Because this file is so sensitive, you should take steps to protect it against modification. Some possibilities include the following:

- You can store the database file on a write-protected removable medium, such as a write-protected floppy (if the file will fit; it may not) or CD-ROM, and permanently mount that medium at /usr/lib/tripwire/databases. This is the safest approach, but it may be the least convenient. A variant is to leave the medium unmounted and mount it only when you run a check. If you run checks in cron jobs, this may be inconvenient.

- You can create a small partition that you mount in a read-only manner to house the Tripwire database file. There are several possible variants on this. For instance, you might use a write-protected CD-ROM disc image or a filesystem type for which Linux has read-only but no read-write support. (The latter would obviously require the intervention of another OS.) These variants can make it more difficult for an interloper to modify your Tripwire database file, but a truly competent and determined cracker could probably overcome these measures.

- Back up your Tripwire database file to a removable medium and manually compare it to the stored version every now and then. If the stored copy has changed, that may indicate a break-in. If you use this approach, you should compare the two files before you make any modifications yourself, then replace the backup with the updated database file.

- Some Tripwire packages support encryption, usually through a third-party utility. When so used, an interloper would have to know your encryption password to modify the database.

If you take reasonable precautions, you can be quite confident in your Tripwire database's veracity, and therefore in the trustworthiness of your computer. It's important to note, though, that Tripwire is best used when it's installed on a fresh Linux installation. If you install Linux, then wait a day or two, then install Tripwire, you'll learn of changes to your system made after Tripwire's installation, but if your system was invaded before that time, Tripwire won't detect that fact.

GENERAL INTRUSION DETECTION PROCEDURES

In addition to using intrusion detection tools like Tripwire, there are various actions you can take and procedures you can follow to help you detect an intrusion. These include:

- **Monitor log files**—Log files, most of which appear in the /var/log directory tree, contain a great deal of information about server activity. As described earlier, monitoring them manually can be tedious at best, but with the help of a tool like SWATCH, you may be able to spot at least some suspicious activity, such as local logins by users who you know to be on vacation thousands of miles away.

- **Monitor system health**—If a server suddenly begins behaving strangely, this *could* be a sign of an intrusion, because crackers frequently damage your configuration in making their changes. You shouldn't be *too* alarmed by a sudden malfunction, though; there are many other less sinister possible causes. The possibility of an intrusion is worth investigating, though.

- **User complaints**—Crackers sometimes break in via ordinary user accounts, and just as a cracker may damage your system's configuration, a cracker may damage a user's settings. As with general system health issues, there are other possible explanations for user complaints like "forgotten" passwords or mysteriously altered shell defaults, but you might want to check details like the change dates on configuration files and passwords to see if these might be suspicious.

- **Strange files**—You may notice peculiar files appear on your computer. These are frequently the detritus of intrusion scripts, or perhaps your original program files under new names, called by replacement scripts to help mask the replacements' presence. Intruders also sometimes delete or alter log files, so suspicious gaps in your log files can be a clue to an intrusion.

- **Unusual network traffic**—If the amount of network traffic a server sees suddenly increases, one possible explanation is that your system is under attack or is being abused. Of course, it's also possible that your system has simply jumped in popularity. For instance, a link to a small Web site on the popular Slashdot (`http://slashdot.org`) frequently swamps a small Web site. (This effect is so well known that it's spawned a word—a site so affected is said to be *Slashdotted*.) You might also notice unusual connections coming from a computer. For instance, if a Web server is used *only* as a Web server, logs on other computers on your network showing Telnet attempts from the Web server could indicate that the Web server system has been compromised.

Ultimately, it's up to you to spot unusual events. Most network intrusions are the work of *script kiddies*—crackers with little skill who work from intrusion scripts created by others. (Some people prefer not to call script kiddies crackers, reserving the latter term for more skilled computer miscreants.) The scripts that script kiddies deploy frequently leave identifiable traces behind. Unfortunately, each intrusion script leaves behind its own unique fingerprint of changes, so it's impossible to give a short list of files to watch. Security Web sites frequently include discussions of the symptoms of particular intrusion methods, so using such a site's search function can help you identify the nature of an intrusion.

It's also important not to overreact or jump to the conclusion that your system has been cracked. Hardware failures, software misconfiguration, and bugs can all produce symptoms that resemble those of intrusions.

WHAT TO DO IF YOU DISCOVER AN INTRUDER

What should you do if you detect an intruder? The general recovery steps are as follows:

1. **Disconnect the computer from the network**—A compromised computer might be used to cause problems for others or to infect other systems on your own network. If your cracked system contains sensitive data, the longer it's networked, the more likely it is your sensitive data will be stolen.

2. **Verify the nature of the compromise**—You should verify that your problem is due to a security breach. As noted earlier, many less sinister problems can be mistaken for a break-in. You should also try to identify the route that the attacker used to gain entry to your system. Even if you clean the infection, if you don't lock the door the intruder used to get in, the intruder will be able to gain entry in the same way

again. Unfortunately, identifying the specific security problem may be easier said than done, so you may have to settle for upgrading your software and increasing your security level generally.

3. **Back up vital data**—If your system isn't backed up routinely or hasn't been backed up recently, you should back up regular user data. You may also want to create a backup of the entire compromised system. You can peruse this backup later, and it might become important evidence if the break-in becomes a criminal matter.

4. **Restore a clean system**—Unfortunately, cleaning out only infected files is not safe. You might get most altered files but miss something important, thus leaving the intruder a way back in. You should wipe your hard disk clean, or at least the partitions on which Linux itself resides; you might be able to leave /home untouched. You can then re-install Linux from scratch or restore it from a backup that you're sure was made prior to the intrusion. *Do not* configure your system's network functions at this point, though; leave it disconnected from the network.

5. **Restore data files**—If you wiped out the entire hard disk in Step 4, you should restore the user data you backed up in Step 3. You should also alter your configuration to suit your needs, if you re-installed everything from scratch in Step 4.

6. **Correct the security problem**—You should correct whatever problem existed that allowed the intruder entry to your system, as identified in Step 2. You may also want to take steps to improve security generally, such as installing Tripwire if it wasn't installed already, setting up a local firewall as described in Chapter 25, and so on.

7. **Return the system to the network**—After you've recovered the system and fixed its problems, you can restore it to its normal duties.

There are other steps you can take along the way, if you like. For instance, if you can trace the intrusion back to a specific remote site, you might try contacting that site's administrator. Crackers like to use several systems as stepping-stones to their true targets, so there's a good chance that the site that launched an attack on you was itself a compromised system. If your losses due to the intrusion were substantial, you can contact the FBI or other law enforcement agencies; however, the amount of cracking activity and difficulty of obtaining convictions means that you're unlikely to see much action unless your case is very clear-cut or involves substantial losses. (In the United States in 2002, losses must exceed $5,000 before the FBI will take notice.)

KEEPING ABREAST OF SECURITY DEVELOPMENTS

Because of publication delays, a book cannot present the most up-to-date information on specific *exploits* (methods of compromising a computer), security bugs, and so on. This chapter therefore focuses on general security procedures and a few tools that are useful in fighting intrusion attempts. There are times when you need the most up-to-date information, though, such as when you're investigating a successful break-in or suspicious activity that makes you think your system might be under attack. Fortunately, there are several resources that are available to help you track developments in the security arena or locate information on specific exploits, bugs, and so on.

SECURITY WEB SITES

As with many computer-related topics, Web sites can be a very useful resource in tracking security issues. Web sites can be updated quickly with the latest information, but you must check them yourself on a regular basis if they're to do any good. Some security Web sites you might want to check on a regular basis include the following:

- **Your distribution's Web site**—All major Linux distributions have Web sites, and most include security or errata pages. As noted earlier, in the section "How to Monitor for Updated Software," these Web sites usually host information on bug fixes for specific packages included with your distribution, as well as links to updated versions of these packages built for your distribution.

- **The CERT/CC Web site**—The Computer Emergency Response Team Coordination Center (CERT/CC) is one of the leading organizations for tracking security-related bugs. Their Web site is at `http://www.cert.org`, and is well worth checking on a regular basis.

- **The CIAC Web site**—The United States Department of Energy operates an organization known as the Computer Incident Advisory Capability (CIAC), which maintains a Web page at `http://www.ciac.org/ciac/`. This site is similar to the CERT/CC site in general scope.

- **The Linux Weekly News Security Section**—The Linux Weekly News (`http://lwn.net`) is a Web-based Linux "newspaper." It includes a security section with information on exploits, including some distribution-specific comments. (Click the Security link in the column on the left of the main page; the exact URL changes from day to day.)

- **The SecurityFocus Web site**—A site maintained at `http://www.securityfocus.com` is something of a news outlet for security-related information. It focuses less on incident reports and includes more in the way of tutorials and "digested" news than the CERT/CC and CIAC sites.

These sites can all provide useful information on popular exploits, new bugs, new viruses and worms, security-related updates to major servers, and how to protect your system from various dangers. It's well worth checking at least one or two of these sites on a regular basis—say, once a day, or at least once a week.

SECURITY MAILING LISTS AND NEWSGROUPS

One of the problems with security Web sites is that they require constant monitoring. Fortunately, there are other types of resources that are more active in getting information to you. In particular, mailing lists are a means of communication that allow mail from individuals to reach an entire group of readers as quickly as the e-mail system can operate. Many security mailing lists don't allow posting from members; they exist solely to distribute information from the list maintainer. If you check your mail regularly, you can subscribe to a mailing list and learn of a new threat very soon after it is reported to that list.

TIP You can set up a Procmail filter (discussed in Chapter 19, Push Mail Protocol: SMTP) to watch for mailing list postings and run a special program to get your attention when a new alert arrives over the list. For instance, you might write a script that causes Procmail to play a sound file or pop up a special alert dialog box.

An information distribution medium that's similar to mailing lists in some ways is a security newsgroup. Like mailing lists, newsgroups are a way for a group of individuals to share information in text-based messages. Newsgroups require more active monitoring, though, so to get the most benefit from a newsgroup you must read it on a regular basis, or perhaps set up a special "robot" script to scan newsgroup postings for important keywords.

Some of the mailing lists and newsgroups that are particularly relevant to Linux security include the following:

- **The CERT/CC mailing list**—The CERT/CC runs a mailing list to which they publish their security advisories. To subscribe, send an e-mail message to `majordomo@cert.org` and include `subscribe cert-advisory` in the text of the message.

- **The CIAC mailing list**—Like CERT/CC, CIAC maintains a mailing list of its bulletins. You can subscribe by sending a message to `majordomo@ tholia.llnl.gov` and including the text `subscribe ciac-bulletin` in the body of the message.

- **The Bugtraq mailing list**—The Bugtraq mailing list is a discussion list, rather than a notification list. It can be a good way to obtain advice or learn about security issues from others in an interactive environment. You can subscribe by sending mail to `listserv@netspace.org`. The mail should include `subscribe bugtraq` in its text.

- **The `comp.security` newsgroups**—There are several newsgroups in the `comp.security` newsgroup hierarchy, including `comp.security.unix` and several related to specific products or product types, such as `comp.security.firewalls`.

- **The `comp.os.linux.security` newsgroup**—This newsgroup specializes in discussion of Linux security issues.

NOTE   Most Linux security issues are really UNIX security issues, because most Linux servers run on other UNIX-like OSs, and sometimes even non-UNIX OSs, like Microsoft Windows. Therefore, most "Linux" security discussions are broader than Linux.

SUMMARY

Maintaining a secure Linux system requires that you understand a great deal about how Linux (or UNIX generally) operates. You must be able to identify and shut down unnecessary servers, create user accounts as securely as possible, update software to fix security bugs, and keep your eyes open for successful and attempted intrusions. Because the security landscape is constantly changing, you must maintain your knowledge by monitoring security-related Web sites, mailing lists, and newsgroups. Although this sounds like a daunting task, once you're familiar with Linux you can keep yourself up to date by spending just a few minutes a day on the task. The time you take to improve your system's security will likely pay off at some point when a crack attempt is thwarted.

Chapters 23, 25, and 26 continue discussion of security themes by covering some more specific security-related topics.

Configuring a chroot Jail

Every server must be able to read certain local files, and some servers must be able to change at least some local files. If these powers can be warped to serve the needs of an attacker, that attacker can corrupt your system's configuration, gain more power, and ultimately gain complete control of your system. What, though, if that corrupted system is really just a *subset* of the real computer, and a subset with very limited abilities? This is the idea behind a chroot jail—to run a server in an environment so limited that it won't do an attacker any good if the server is compromised.

Not all servers operate well in a chroot jail, but some are designed to be used in this way. For those servers that support chroot operation, you must set up both the server's configuration options and a limited chroot environment in which the server can run.

WHAT IS A chroot JAIL?

Linux's directory system is built on a root (/) directory. All directories fall off of this one, and can be referred to relative to the root directory. A chroot jail effectively changes the root directory (hence the name) to something else, as illustrated in Figure 23.1. For instance, if you set aside /opt/chroot as a new root directory for a server, all file references made by the server will be relative to /opt/chroot rather than the true root directory. Thus, even if a server is compromised and the attacker uses it to modify, say,

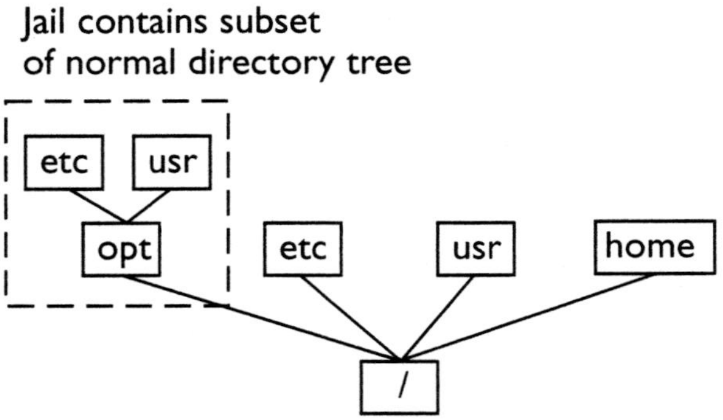

Jail contains subset
of normal directory tree

Figure 23.1 A chroot jail creates a special environment that contains only those files required for a particular server to run.

/etc/passwd, the modification will *actually* affect /opt/chroot/etc/passwd, which is not nearly as serious a matter as a change to the real /etc/passwd.

This scheme is implemented through a system call known as chroot(), often as used by a program called chroot. You can set up a chroot jail either by using a server that handles the matter itself with its own chroot() call or by using the chroot program to launch the server. These issues are described in more detail shortly, in the section "Configuring a Server to Operate in a chroot Jail."

The entire chroot jail system has several important consequences and implications:

- If a program relies on configuration files, uses dynamic libraries, accepts or delivers files, or otherwise manipulates any local files, those files *must* exist within the chroot environment. This requirement can result in a very large chroot environment directory tree if the server requires many support files. One exception is that if the server implements its own chroot() call, and if it reads the support files *before* making the chroot() call, those support files should exist outside of the chroot environment.

- A server running in a chroot jail can access only those files that reside within the same jail. This means that you should keep extraneous files within that environment to a minimum to give the jailed tool as little opportunity to do mischief as possible.

- A corollary of the preceding consequence is that if you run multiple servers in chroot jails, you should create *separate* jails for each of them.

This minimizes the chance that a bug in one server could be used to reconfigure the other server, thus giving the attacker greater access to your system.

- Because the chroot jail environment exists as a subdirectory within the normal Linux directory tree, programs that are *not* run from a chroot jail can place files within the jail. This can be a convenience or a potential security risk, depending upon your point of view. This point is further elaborated in the upcoming section, "Controlling Local Access to the chroot Environment."

Although a chroot jail sounds like a great way to minimize the risk of running servers, it's not without its drawbacks and limitations. One of these is that not all servers operate well in chroot jails. Some, such as most FTP servers using anonymous mode and some mail servers, are designed to operate partly or wholly in a chroot jail. Others, like Telnet servers, require more-or-less complete access to the normal Linux system in order to do their jobs. Thus, you can't simply set up all your servers to operate in chroot jails, although you can do this with some.

Because most chroot jails are configured by the system administrator rather than set up automatically by package management systems, it's possible to overlook the chroot server after you upgrade the server package. You must remember to recopy any changed files after any upgrade. If you don't, your chroot server may be left vulnerable.

Another limitation of chroot jails is that they aren't impenetrable. Processes run as root from within the jail can issue the chroot() call to return to the *real* root directory. (It's actually a bit more complex than issuing a single chroot() call, but not by much.) Thus, you should be very cautious about giving root privileges to any server run from within a chroot jail. Although servers are *supposed* to be well behaved, bugs and misconfigurations have been known to provide root access to undesirable outsiders in the past, and this is all but certain to happen in the future. Thus, although a chroot jail is a useful security tool, it's not a panacea.

A chroot jail can provide protection against attacks on your computer, but if a miscreant uses a server to attack other systems, a chroot jail provides little or no protection. For instance, a compromised DNS server may give false name lookups, allowing an attacker to access an NFS server that authorizes hosts by name rather than by IP address, even if the DNS server runs in a chroot jail. Similarly, a server run from a chroot jail might provide an attacker with a means to directly attack other systems from your server's IP address.

Finally, even if you run one server in a chroot jail, others may not be running in this way, and so may pose a risk. What's more, if the filesystem areas handled by these servers overlap, it may be possible to pass files between the chroot server and the conventional server, which might be risky if the files in question are configuration files or the like.

NECESSARY chroot ENVIRONMENT FILES

The first task in configuring a server to operate in a chroot jail is to prepare the jail. This means you must create an appropriate directory tree, copy system files, and copy the server's files. In some sense, you set up a miniature Linux system in the chroot jail, but this miniature system is missing most of the programs and configuration files that make up a normal Linux system.

NOTE This section describes the process of setting up the chroot environment in a relatively abstract way. The next section, "Configuring a Server to Operate in a chroot Jail," provides a more concrete look at server configuration, including an example of running BIND in a chroot jail.

PREPARING A DIRECTORY TREE

A chroot jail needs a directory to call its own. In principle, you can place this directory anywhere in the Linux filesystem tree, except for pseudo-filesystem directories like /proc. If your server needs to be able to write files, the chroot directory tree must exist on a read/write medium. The examples in this chapter use /opt/chroot as the root of the chroot jail, but this is an arbitrary placement.

Within your chroot tree, you should create directories modeled after those of the normal Linux root directory, including subdirectories. Chances are you'll need only a small subset of the directories needed in a regular Linux installation, though. Common directories you might need to create include /bin, /sbin, /usr, /lib, /etc, and /var. You may need to add to this directory list as you add server-specific files. You should *not* populate these directories with all the files that reside in their regular counterparts; much of the point of running in a chroot jail is to deprive a would-be cracker of access to the regular mix of tools available in these directories.

If you want to run multiple chroot servers, you should create a separate chroot tree for each one. For instance, you might create /opt/chroot/ftp and /opt/chroot/sendmail.

COPYING SERVER FILES

Once you've created a basic chroot jail directory tree, you need to copy files into that tree. There are actually two different conditions that may apply. First, the server may directly support chroot operations. In this case, it may not be necessary to copy the server's executable to the chroot jail. Instead, you run the server from outside the jail, but tell it where the jail is. The server then issues a chroot() command internally, and thereafter it's locked into the jail. The server might read its configuration files from outside of the jail, too, so this operation can be nearly transparent—you only need to provide the jail itself and whatever files the server needs during normal operation. FTP servers often lock themselves into chroot jails in this way, particularly when they run as anonymous FTP servers. Chapter 21, Running FTP Servers, covers anonymous FTP server operation, including setting up the necessary chroot jail directory.

The other option is to run a server that doesn't include built-in chroot support by using the chroot program. In this approach, you must copy the server executable file, its configuration files, and any files it requires during normal operation to the jail. You'll also have to copy some more general system files, as described in the next section, "Copying System Files." Tracking down the files that the server needs can be tricky, because there's no simple rule that will always find the necessary files. You may be able to find leads by checking the server's documentation and by examining the list of files that come with the distribution package. For instance, you can use tar, rpm, or dpkg to find the files in the original server package. You may not need to copy *all* of these files. For instance, you can leave documentation files outside of the chroot jail. Another trick is to use the strace program to discover what files a server opens. You can run the server with a command like **strace *serverprog*** and examine the output to discover what *serverprog* is doing, including what files it's opening.

NOTE Although I refer to *copying* files, you may ultimately want to *move* them instead. This will guarantee that your server is running from the jail, at least if your configuration files use absolute references to other files, such that they won't work except in a chroot environment. Creating hard links, if the jail is on the same partition as the main files, may also be an option. (Symbolic links won't work if they lead outside of the jail.) On the other hand, creating a chroot jail in its own partition offers some security advantages because it's then impossible to create hard links outside of the chroot environment, thus reducing the risk of a server compromise being used to modify outside files.

COPYING SYSTEM FILES

After you've copied the basic server files to the chroot jail, you must copy any general-purpose Linux system files upon which the server depends. Precisely what files are needed varies from one server to another, but some common files you might need include the following:

- **Libraries**—Many servers rely upon dynamically linked libraries. These are usually stored in /lib, or occasionally /usr/lib. You can discover what libraries a given server requires by using the ldd command, as in **ldd /usr/sbin/named**. You should copy any files listed by this command to equivalent directories in the chroot jail.

- **Support programs**—Some servers rely on support programs. For instance, a Web server that supports scripting relies upon the scripting language executable (such as /usr/bin/perl), and perhaps files that support this executable. You must copy these support programs to appropriate directories in the chroot jail. You must also locate and copy the libraries upon which the support programs rely. In some cases, such as scripting languages used by Web servers, you'll actually copy more support program files than server files into the chroot jail.

- **Device files**—Some servers may rely upon access to hardware device files. For instance, a backup server needs access to your tape device file. A few libraries and programs require access to special-purpose device files like /dev/zero or /dev/null. Device files are normally found in /dev. They can't be copied like ordinary files; instead, you should recreate them in the chroot jail by using the mknod command, as in **mknod /opt/chroot/dev/st0 c 9 0**. Note that many device files provide great power, so you shouldn't create device files in a chroot environment unless they're absolutely necessary.

- **Special filesystems**—A few servers may rely upon special filesystems or filesystem manipulation tools. In particular, some servers need access to the /proc filesystem. You can't copy this directory like most others. Instead, you must create a duplicate entry in /etc/fstab for this filesystem, but mounted within the chroot jail. *Do not* remove the original /proc filesystem, though; *duplicate* it! Other non-chroot programs still require /proc in its usual location. If you can avoid it, you shouldn't duplicate /proc in this way, because it includes pseudo-files that could give an attacker substantial power over your computer, even from within a chroot jail.

- **User database files**—Some servers require access to the /etc/passwd, /etc/group, /etc/shadow, and similar group database information files.

Servers that use the Pluggable Authentication Module (PAM) approach to authentication require the entire PAM infrastructure, including the /etc/pam.conf file, the contents of /etc/pam.d and /etc/security, and various libraries with pam in their names in /lib and /lib/security. Check your PAM package's contents for clues about what you might need to duplicate. (This package is often called libpam.)

- **Logging files**—If the server creates log files, you should create an appropriate directory for them. Some servers rely upon syslogd to do their logging, so you may need to copy this daemon and all its support files into the chroot jail. Some servers can be configured to do their own logging, even if they ordinarily rely upon syslogd.

For servers that include explicit internal chroot() support, chances are good that you'll need to copy fewer system files than for servers that don't include this support. The servers that include internal chroot() calls can often load libraries, system files, and so on before running, and so don't need files to be stored in their chroot environments, even if those files are required for ordinary operation.

TIP For best security, take a minimal approach to support files. Copy only those files you're reasonably certain the server requires, then try running the server (perhaps with a debugging option to produce extra debugging output on the console, if the server supports such an option). This should give you some clues about what extra files might be required; for instance, the server might complain that it can't find a configuration file. Add more files as necessary, and you should end up with the minimal configuration that works.

CONFIGURING A SERVER TO OPERATE IN A chroot JAIL

Once you've set up the chroot jail, you can begin using it. This involves configuring the server to operate in the jail, starting the server so that it runs in the jail, and controlling outside access to the jail. This section describes how to do these things, and it concludes with an example of running a name server in a chroot jail.

RUNNING A SERVER IN A chroot JAIL

If you're running a server with explicit chroot() support, chances are it includes one or more configuration options relating to chroot operation. For instance, ProFTPd's <Anonymous> directive automatically sets up the server to operate from the specified directory as a chroot jail. You should consult your server's documentation to learn what configuration options invoke chroot operation, and set them appropriately.

If you're configuring a server that lacks explicit chroot support, you should begin with a working configuration from the main Linux environment. Test the server outside of its jail to be sure the basic configuration works. You can then copy the configuration files to a chroot jail, and that configuration should continue working with few or no changes. Once the environment is correctly configured, you should be able to run the server by using the chroot command, which has the following syntax:

```
chroot /new/root server-name [server-options]
```

The /new/root directory is the chroot jail directory, server-name is the name of the server (complete with path, if necessary), and server-options is any options the server needs. Note that you specify the path to server-name relative to its new root. For instance, if the program file is /opt/chroot/bin/server, with /opt/chroot as the jail directory, you'd type the following to launch the server:

```
# chroot /opt/chroot /bin/server
```

If your server normally starts through a SysV startup script or a local startup script, you'll have to modify the startup script to include the chroot command, or disable the startup script and find some other way to start the server. If the server normally runs from a super server, you'll need to set up the super server within the chroot environment along with the target server, alter the super server launch command to incorporate a chroot call, or change the server startup method to use a SysV or local startup script.

CONTROLLING LOCAL ACCESS TO THE chroot ENVIRONMENT

The chroot jail sets up one-way protections—programs within the chroot jail cannot influence the system outside of the jail. You might want to limit access in the other direction, as well. For instance, you might want to set up a server in a chroot jail and use restrictive permissions on the chroot jail directories to prevent unauthorized users from reading the files in those directories. You can do this by setting the ownership on the chroot jail to root, setting the group ownership to a special group, and using 0640 (rw-r-----) permissions on the files in the directory tree. You can then run the server as a user in the special group you create for this purpose. The result is that the server can read but not write files within the chroot jail, and outside of the jail, only root can read or write files within the tree. Of course, you may need to loosen some of these permissions if the server must be able to write files.

WARNING As a general rule, you shouldn't give the server write access to all the files or directories in its jail. In the case of a server compromise, this would allow the server to rewrite critical configuration files and utilities in a way that might cause problems. If a server normally runs as root, the risk of giving it full write access to all files in the jail is no greater than the risk of running the server as root outside of the jail, but for a server that doesn't run as root, giving ownership of program files to the server can increase the risk, at least within the chroot environment.

AN EXAMPLE: RUNNING BIND IN A chroot JAIL

The preceding description may be helpful in setting up a chroot jail, but it may be even more helpful to ground the topic with a more concrete example. Therefore, this section describes the installation of the Berkeley Internet Name Domain (BIND) in a chroot jail. You may want to read, or at least skim, Chapter 18, Administering a Domain via DNS, before proceeding. This example doesn't change the default BIND configuration except to move it to a chroot jail, though, so you don't need to be familiar with the intricacies of name server configuration. This section uses a Debian 2.2 installation as an example. The procedures used will differ slightly for other distributions because of different package management systems and different default configuration files.

NOTE This example uses the chroot command to run BIND in its jail. Chapter 21, Running FTP Servers, includes an example of FTP configuration using an FTP server's built-in chroot support.

To begin the process, we need the standard BIND package installed. This can be done in many ways with Debian, but for this example, I used apt-get:

```
# apt-get install bind
```

This installs the standard Debian BIND package in the normal way. The installation script runs, and asks if you want to add the local machine as a name server to /etc/resolv.conf. For testing purposes, I did not do this, but this detail is unimportant for demonstration purposes. When done, Debian runs BIND, which you can verify as follows:

```
# ps aux | grep named
root      7656  0.0  1.5  2184 1492 ?          S    13:29    0:00 \
/usr/sbin/named
# host awl.com localhost
awl.com                   A          165.193.123.224
```

The second command serves to verify that BIND is installed and working; it calls the host command to locate the IP address of awl.com using the server on localhost. You can substitute any other hostname you like for awl.com, or use your server's true name or IP address instead of localhost. If you get a command not found error, you must install the dnsutils package in Debian to get the host program. (This program may be in a package of another name, such as bind-utils, in other distributions.)

Now that you've verified that the server is working, you can shut it down:

```
# /etc/init.d/bind stop
```

After shutting down the server, the next step is creating a chroot directory tree. This example uses /opt/chroot as the chroot jail directory. Thus, we begin by creating the jail directory tree and moving the BIND files into that tree:

```
# mkdir -p /opt/chroot/usr/sbin /opt/chroot/var/cache/bind
# mkdir /opt/chroot/lib /opt/chroot/etc
# cp /usr/sbin/named /opt/chroot/usr/sbin
# cp -rp /etc/bind/ /opt/chroot/etc
```

NOTE This procedure shows configuring BIND to run using the chroot command, but in fact BIND includes built-in chroot() support, so there is a slightly easier way to do it, as described shortly. Even if you use the easier method, though, you'll need to set up the chroot jail directory tree and copy the configuration files to it. You may omit named itself, though.

These commands set up the basics of the BIND directory tree and copy the named server and configuration files in /etc/bind to the appropriate directories in the chroot jail. If you were installing a server from scratch, you would probably have to do some investigation to learn precisely what files you'd need to copy, and you might end up creating these files and directories in a piecemeal fashion. One particularly important bit of detective work is locating the support libraries upon which the server relies. You can do this, and copy the libraries, using ldd, as follows:

```
# ldd /usr/sbin/named
        libc.so.6 => /lib/libc.so.6 (0x40017000)
        /lib/ld-linux.so.2 => /lib/ld-linux.so.2 (0x40000000)
# cp /lib/libc.so.6 /lib/ld-linux.so.2 /opt/chroot/lib
```

At this point, you can test your configuration:

```
# chroot /opt/chroot /usr/sbin/named
# host awl.com localhost
awl.com                 A       165.193.123.224
```

If this doesn't work, check that only one instance of named is running, and that you created or copied all the necessary files. You can then modify the BIND startup script (/etc/init.d/bind in Debian) to start the server via the chroot command, or disable the SysV startup script and start the server in some other way. Many SysV startup scripts use wrapper programs (such as start-stop-daemon and ndc in Debian) to do their work, and these programs may create files in still more directories, such as /var/run, so you must copy these files and directories to within the chroot jail:

```
# mkdir -p /opt/chroot/sbin /opt/chroot/var/run
# cp /usr/sbin/ndc /opt/chroot/usr/sbin
# cp /sbin/start-stop-daemon /opt/chroot/sbin
```

You can edit the SysV startup script by adding chroot /opt/chroot before every instance of both start-stop-daemon and ndc. Unfortunately, your work still isn't done, because start-stop-daemon relies on the /proc filesystem, which isn't available in the chroot directory tree. You can edit your /etc/fstab file to make it available—copy the existing line for /proc and rename it so that it mounts at /opt/chroot/proc. You must then type **mount -a** to mount the duplicate /proc within the chroot jail.

WARNING As noted earlier, the /proc filesystem is potentially very powerful, so a better approach is to edit the SysV startup script so that it doesn't use start-stop-daemon, or abandon the SysV startup script entirely and use some other method of starting the server.

At this point, you should be able to start the server using the SysV startup script and test it in its final configuration:

```
# /etc/init.d/bind start
# host awl.com localhost
awl.com                    A        165.193.123.224
```

If you want to be sure the server is running from the chroot environment, you can delete the original program file (in /usr/sbin) and its configuration files (in /etc/bind), then restart the server. If your tests still work, you can be confident that the server is running from its chroot jail.

As an alternative to running BIND with the chroot command, you can use the -t option to named, which activates named's internal chroot() call. For instance, you can launch the server in this way:

```
# /usr/sbin/named -t /opt/chroot
```

This approach is simpler than the preceding one because you don't need to copy as many files to the chroot jail directory; you can omit named and the libraries upon which it depends. You must still copy the named configuration files, though (in /etc/bind in this example), because named's -t option causes it to lock itself in its chroot jail *before* reading its configuration file. (This contrasts with the usual FTP server configuration, described in Chapter 21, which reads the configuration file first and then locks the server in the chroot jail.) Using named's -t option also has the advantage of requiring fewer changes to the SysV startup scripts; you need only pass the -t /opt/chroot option through to the server by placing this option at the end of the start-stop-daemon call, preceded by a double dash (--). There's then no need to duplicate the /proc filesystem within the chroot jail.

Of course, the exact procedures you use will be different for other servers or other distributions. Nonetheless, the basic outline should be similar to what's described here. You might also want to make some further changes to the chroot environment, such as changing the permissions on the directories or reconfiguring the server to run as a user other than root (the default for BIND under Debian).

MAINTAINING THE chroot ENVIRONMENT

A chroot jail can be a useful tool, but it requires some additional maintenance even after it's set up. Some details to which you may need to attend include the following:

- **Log rotation**—All major distributions include some mechanism for log rotation. If your server stores log files in the chroot jail, you'll have to track down your distribution's log rotation mechanisms and modify them to handle the new location for these files. Alternatively, you can use the --bind option to mount to make your log file directory available within the chroot jail. (This works only with 2.4.*x* and later kernels.) If you fail to attend to log files, they may expand uncontrollably and possibly overwhelm your available disk space.

- **Program updates**—As noted earlier, if you update your server software, you must remember to copy the updated program files to the chroot jail directories. If you fail to do this, your server will remain vulnerable to whatever problems the update fixes. You must also remember to recreate any changes you make to startup scripts, else your updated server may run from *outside* the chroot jail.

- **File availability**—If your server works with data files you make available, such as a Web server that delivers Web pages, you must maintain the data files within the chroot environment. This isn't normally a problem, because the data files should normally exist only within the chroot jail. You might want to periodically check the file permissions to be sure that new files and directories have appropriate permissions for whatever security scheme you use, though.

- **New support files**—On occasion, you may need to add new support files. For instance, if you run a Web server from within a chroot jail and decide to start using a new CGI scripting language, you must copy the new language's files to the chroot jail directory. You might also want to *delete* files that are no longer being used, to reduce the risk of security breaches that might be caused by these files.

Fortunately, these tasks shouldn't consume too much time, above and beyond routine server maintenance. Most involve setting an option once and letting automatic procedures handle the rest, or taking extra steps when updating or reconfiguring a server.

SUMMARY

Running a server within a chroot jail can be a useful security precaution for many server types, and especially for those that don't need access to most files on the computer. Setting up the server requires creating a partial duplicate of the regular Linux directory tree, possibly including the server's executable file itself. You must then either activate a server-specific configuration option to have it lock itself into the chroot jail, or run the server with the chroot command. In either case, the server then operates from within the chroot jail as if the directory you set up were the root directory of the computer, thus limiting the potential for damage the server can do if it's compromised. Doing all of this requires some digging into a server's normal requirements for support files and programs, copying files, and modifying startup procedures so that the server runs in its chroot jail whenever appropriate. You must also be sure to maintain the chroot environment so that it continues to operate as you intend.

Advanced Router Options 24

Although Linux is generally considered a general-purpose OS, it's increasingly being used in various specialized applications, such as palmtop computers (http://www.agendacomputing.com, http://www.gmate.com/english/overview.htm, and others) and digital video recorders (http://www.tivo.com). Some of these specialized applications use specialized hardware. One that does not (or at least *need* not) is using Linux as a router OS. Routers are unglamorous devices that aren't much in the public eye, but they serve the vital function of linking together the computers that form the Internet. Routers range from small and simple devices sold to individuals and small businesses that tie a handful of computers to the Internet via a broadband connection to devices that cost thousands of dollars and that link together Internet backbones. Linux can serve as a low-end router with little fuss, but if you want it to handle more than a few dozen computers, you may want to investigate Linux's advanced router options. These allow the OS to use various techniques to prioritize packet delivery and to communicate with other routers.

NOTE If you want to use Linux as a broadband router that performs network address translation (NAT), consult Chapter 25, Configuring iptables.

641

Basic router configuration in Linux is relatively straightforward, but the advanced router options can be very intricate. Thus, this chapter can present only an overview of the issues and tools involved. For more information, you should consult the documentation for specific tools, such as Malkin's *RIP: An Intra-Domain Routing Protocol* (Addison Wesley, 2000); or a general routing book such as LeBlanc et al.'s *Linux Routing* (New Riders, 2002).

WHEN TO USE ADVANCED ROUTER CONFIGURATIONS

You should first recognize that this chapter covers *advanced* router configuration. If your Linux-based router delivers so little traffic that it has no trouble keeping up with the load, and if the router's configuration is simple and static so that it doesn't need to reconfigure itself to work with other routers, then there's no point in using the options described in this chapter. You can simply enable router features by configuring two network cards and enabling routing between them by typing the following command:

```
# echo "1" > /proc/sys/net/ipv4/ip_forward
```

This command, in conjunction with an appropriate routing table configuration for multiple networks, as described in Chapter 2, TCP/IP Network Configuration, is enough to turn a Linux computer into a router. This configuration may work well enough for many networks.

NOTE   Configuring your Linux router with multiple interfaces, an appropriate routing table, and IP forwarding is all you need to do *locally*. The systems to which this computer most directly communicates, though, must recognize it as a router in order for this configuration to work. For instance, consider a Linux computer that serves as a router for a dozen computers using a Symmetrical Digital Subscriber Line (SDSL) broadband connection to the Internet. If the router doesn't perform NAT, your ISP's router, to which one network interface of the Linux router connects, must know that your Linux router is a router for your network block. If this isn't the case, network packets will get out, but your ISP's router won't know how to route return packets back in. For most router configurations, therefore, you must communicate with whoever maintains the other routers to which your router connects. You must also configure your local systems to use your Linux router as a gateway.

One type of advanced router configuration described in this chapter, in the "Advanced Kernel Options" and "Using `iproute2`" sections, relates to modifications of the way Linux decides to route packets based on some feature of the packets, such as their origins, destinations, or protocol type. These options can influence how responsive the Internet appears to be, because you might give priority to packets associated with interactive protocols, or favor traffic from certain computers. Such configurations are most often used on heavily loaded dedicated routers.

The second type of advanced router configuration described in this chapter is routing protocols. These are protocols you can use to communicate with other routers. The servers that implement these protocols allow your system to dynamically update its routing table to reflect the best path for packets to travel so that the packets can reach their destinations most quickly. Such protocols can enhance the performance of a network that uses them, but they're most useful for a router that has several network interfaces that reach the Internet. If the router has just one link to the Internet, that link can't be changed in any meaningful way, and so there's no point to running a routing protocol on the server, because the protocol will have no effect on the router's routing table.

ADVANCED KERNEL OPTIONS

The 2.4.*x* Linux kernels include several advanced routing options in the Networking Options kernel configuration menu. Many, but not all, of these options fall under the IP: Advanced Router option, so you must activate this option to activate its suboptions. You can use these options to modify how Linux routes packets—for instance, how it prioritizes the packets, responds to the priority codes in packets it receives, or handles particular types of packets. You can activate support for these options by selecting Y, or sometimes M for modular compilation, to the appropriate configuration option. Most of these options, though, also require configuration through special utilities. Some of these are fairly complex, so this section presents only an overview of these tools.

NOTE   Kernel options sometimes change names, split into multiple options, or disappear with new kernel versions. This section describes the options as they appear with the 2.4.17 kernel, but if you use a kernel that's substantially older or newer than this one, your options may differ.

POLICY ROUTING

The first advanced Linux kernel routing option is called IP: Policy Routing. This option enables three new methods of deciding how to route data:

- **Source address**—A Linux router normally uses only the destination address to determine how to route data. You can have the router use the source address as well. You might use this to pass data from low-priority hosts over a slower or less reliable connection than you'd use for data from high-priority hosts. Use this option with caution, though; if a router with this configuration interacts with routers that use regular routing criteria, inconsistent routing, or even routing loops, can result.
- **Mark filtering**—Packets can be labeled with unique data known as *mark values*. You can use these to send packets over particular network routes if you activate the IP: Use Netfilter MARK Value as Routing Key option. In order to enable this option, you must also enable the Network Packet Filtering option earlier in the menu.
- **Fast NAT**—NAT is a tool for "hiding" a network behind a single IP address, or for changing the IP address associated with a single computer by altering its packets in a router. If you want your system to function as a NAT router, you may want to activate this option; however, it's not strictly required. This option enables NAT in a way that's different from the usual method. (Chapter 25 describes NAT in more detail.)

All of these options rely upon the `iproute2` package, which communicates with the kernel to set the various advanced routing features. This package is described in the upcoming section, "Using `iproute2`."

TYPE OF SERVICE VALUES

TCP/IP supports a field type known as the *Type-of-Service (TOS)* field. You can set this field on the packets that leave clients, servers, or networks to identify the packets as requiring a particular type of handling. You might use this to give some packets access to faster or more reliable connections than you give others. To use this feature, you must activate the IP: Use TOS Value as Routing Key kernel option.

This option also uses the `iproute2` package, described shortly. Specifically, the `tos` option in the `ip` command's *selector* operates on TOS values. These values are ordinary numbers, such as 4. In addition to local software, other routers must honor the TOS requests. Most ISPs' routers ignore TOS fields, though, so this option may do you no good.

MULTIPATH ROUTING

Normally, when you specify a routing action, an incoming packet is matched against rules that determine the output path with perfect certainty. For instance, you might have a routing table rule to send packets destined to 10.201.0.0/16 over eth1. All packets with destination addresses in this range necessarily go over eth1. It's sometimes possible to specify two rules that seem to conflict. For instance, you might have another rule that tells the system to send all packets destined to 10.201.34.0/24 to ppp0. In the usual configuration, though, this second rule takes precedence over the first, because the second rule is more specific. If you provide a second path for 10.201.0.0/16 (say, sending those packets over ppp0), Linux simply uses the first matching rule it finds.

If you activate the IP: Equal Cost Multipath kernel configuration option, Linux's behavior in the event of multiple matching routing table rules changes; it picks one of the two routes randomly. You might use this as a crude form of load balancing if you've got two Internet connections. This option does not affect the case where two rules exist, but one is more specific—the more specific rule still takes precedence over the less specific rule.

ROUTER LOGGING OPTIONS

The IP: Verbose Route Monitoring kernel option activates a kernel feature that requires no further configuration: additional logging of routing information. Normally, the kernel doesn't log routine routing information, so you have little or no evidence in your logs about routing activity. This option, though, causes the kernel to log information about suspicious packets. You can then examine your system logs to discover more information about the traffic your router handles.

Verbose router logging may sound like a good security measure, and in some cases it is. On a very busy router, though, this extra information might consume a lot of system resources in terms of disk activity, disk space, and even CPU time. It can therefore degrade performance. In theory, a person who wanted to crash your server could create a denial-of-service (DoS) attack designed to get your router to log an inordinate number of packets, thus degrading performance and perhaps causing your disk to fill up. If you try this option, you should check your log sizes and router performance to be sure it's not having a negative impact, and perhaps develop a contingency plan such as having the router page you so you can deal with problems should your system come under a DoS attack related to this option.

LARGE ROUTING TABLES

The Linux kernel is optimized to deal with routing tables of about 64 entries or fewer. If your router configuration is unusually complex, it may include more than this number of entries, in which case you should activate the IP: Large Routing Tables option. This changes the kernel's configuration to work better with routing tables holding more than 64 entries.

MULTICAST ROUTING

Most Internet traffic is point-to-point—for instance, you may send a request to a Web server, which in response sends a Web page back to you. This traffic is intended for just one recipient, although as is mentioned at many points in this book, it's possible for one computer to snoop on data destined for another under certain circumstances. Another common type of network traffic is a *broadcast*. These are data packets that are addressed to all computers on a local network. Two types of broadcasts exist. First, a *local subnet* broadcast uses a recipient address of 255.255.255.255, which reaches all computers on the local subnet. A *directed subnet* broadcast is more restrictive; it uses the values for the network portion of the address followed by binary 1 values, such as 192.168.34.255 for the 192.168.34.0/24 network). DHCP clients use broadcasts when they first try to locate a DHCP server, because the DHCP clients don't know the server's address. Broadcasts can also be used by a few other protocols, such as some forms of SMB/CIFS name resolution. Broadcasts are usually restricted to just one subnet; they aren't normally routed. (Some routers do route directed subnet broadcasts, though.)

A situation in between directed traffic and broadcasts exists: *multicasts*. A multicast consists of packets that are addressed to multiple recipients simultaneously, but not all computers on a network. Multicasts are fairly uncommon, but a few tools use them, mostly for distribution of live audio or video feeds. One such system is the Multicast Backbone (MBONE; http://www.cs.columbia.edu/~hgs/internet/mbone-faq.html). This is an example of a *network-wide* multicast, which can be quite widespread in scope. A more limited type of multicast, known as *link-local*, is typically not distributed very widely and may be used by some routing protocols for router-to-router communication, as described in the upcoming section, "Using Routing Protocols."

If you want your router to support the routing of multicast packets, you must include appropriate multicast support. This is done via the IP: Multicast Routing kernel configuration option. In addition, you may need to add support for one of two suboptions—IP: PIM-SM Version 1 Support or IP: PIM-SM Version 2 Support. These are two variants of *Sparse Mode (SM)*

Protocol Independent Multicast (PIM), which is a way to support multicasts on networks with limited bandwidth compared to that of earlier multicast implementations. SM-PIM Version 1 is more common, and is the protocol supported by Cisco in its routers.

In addition to kernel options, you need special software to support multicast routing, specifically `mrouted`. This tool configures the basic Linux multicast routing capabilities. You can find it at `ftp://ftp.rge.com/pub/communications/ipmulti/beta-test/`, if it's not in your distribution, and you can read about it at `http://jukie.net/~bart/multicast/Linux-Mrouted-MiniHOWTO.html`. If you use PIM-SM Version 2, you may also need additional software, such as `pimd` (`http://netweb.usc.edu/pim/pimd/`).

QUALITY OF SERVICE

The normal procedure a Linux router follows in routing packets is to follow a first-come/first-served policy—in scheduling delivery of two packets, Linux delivers packets in the order in which it receives them. This procedure works fine when the router has plenty of bandwidth on all its ports, or when there's no need to give priority to certain types of packets. On a busy server, though, it may be desirable to use a different scheduling method—for instance, to reduce the data flow rate to certain sites or to guarantee a certain amount of bandwidth for particular users or applications. Expanding the kernel to support such advanced scheduling options is the job of the QoS and/or Fair Queueing menu, which is accessed from an option of the same name at the end of the Networking Options menu. (*QoS* stands for *Quality of Service*, which is the name applied to a particular group of scheduling algorithms on this menu.)

Activating the QoS options will not, by itself, alter your system's operation; as with many other advanced routing options, you must use tools in the `iproute2` package to activate and configure the features. If you're not sure you need these features, you can activate basic support and compile most of the options as modules. You then don't need to use the options, but they're available if you find you do need them.

WARNING

Read the help for each option before compiling it. In 2.4.17, one option, the Clark-Shenker-Zhang (CSZ) algorithm, is reported to be broken. Attempting to use a broken option will have no noticeable effect at best, and cause unreliable operation at worst.

USING iproute2

The iproute2 package ships with most Linux distributions, often under the name iproute. You can also obtain it from ftp://ftp.inr.ac.ru/ip-routing/, its official home. This package includes several commands, two of which are covered here: ip and tc.

USING ip

The iproute2 command that's used for manipulating routing tables and rules is ip. This program relies on several of the suboptions of IP: Advanced Router in the kernel configuration, as described earlier. The program is used as follows:

```
ip command [list | add | del] selector action
```

You can specify any of several commands. One of the most important of these is rule. You can use this command to add (add), delete (del), or display information on (list) specific routing rules. You specify a rule with the selector, which itself is composed of several items:

```
[from addr] [to addr] [tos TOS] [dev device-name] [pref number]
```

The from and to elements allow you to specify IP addresses, tos lets you specify a TOS value (which is a number, such as 4; this requires a kernel option that's described shortly), dev specifies the network device name (such as eth0), and pref signifies a preference number. These items collectively tell Linux how to identify packets to which a given rule applies. The ip rule command links these to an action, which has several components:

```
[table table-id] [nat address] [prohibit | reject | unreachable]
```

The table-id is a number identifying a particular routing table, nat lets you specify a new source address for the packet, and prohibit, reject, and unreachable are codes to indicate various methods of completely rejecting the packet.

Putting this all together, you might enter an ip command that resembles the following:

```
# ip rule add from 172.20.24.128 dev eth0 table 2
```

This rule tells the system to use routing table 2 for all traffic from 172.20.24.128 on eth0. What, though, is routing table 2? An ordinary Linux installation uses the route command to create the routing table, and there's precisely one routing table on such a system. The advanced routing features allow you to use multiple routing tables, which you set up with the ip route command. You can then quickly switch between different routing tables for handling different types of traffic, using other routing tools. This command is more complex than the normal route, but its features are mostly a superset of the normal route command. Thus, you can use ip route much as you would route, as described in Chapter 2. One extension is particularly important, though: You can specify the routing table number with the table *table-id* option. For instance, you might use the following command to add a route to routing table 2:

```
ip route add 10.201.0.0/16 dev eth1 table 2
```

Aside from the leading ip and the trailing table 2, this command works just like an equivalent route command. Specifically, it tells the system to pass all data for the 10.201.0.0/16 network over eth1 without sending it to another router. (In this case, eth1 should have an address on the 10.201.0.0/16 network.)

USING tc

The tc utility is what utilizes the QoS and/or Fair Queueing kernel configuration options. You can use it to manage outgoing network bandwidth, in order to prevent one class of traffic from monopolizing the available bandwidth. For instance, suppose your organization has two subnets, each corresponding to an office with a dozen users. If a user from one of these offices begins using some very bandwidth-intensive task, this action may degrade network performance for users in the other office. You can use tc to provide a partial fix by guaranteeing a certain amount of bandwidth for each subnet.

NOTE It's important to remember that a TCP/IP router (or any computer on a TCP/IP network) can only control its *outgoing* traffic. Thus, tc can only adjust outgoing bandwidth. This works in a router because a sender will slow its transmission of TCP packets when it sees that your router is saturated, even if that saturation is created through a QoS policy. (This won't work for UDP packets, though.)

The basic syntax of tc is as follows:

```
tc [options] object command
```

Each of the parameters has certain possible values:

- **options**—This can be -statistics (or -s), -details (or -d), or -raw (or -r).
- **object**—This can be qdisc, class, or filter. The qdisc sets the *queueing discipline*—a specific rule. The class defines a set of packets that fit a category (such as one of the two offices). The filter brings these together to generate a filter rule.
- **command**—The *command* is a set of parameters that define precisely what tc does with the *object*. What goes into a *command* is quite varied and *object*-specific.

To use tc, you use it to generate a series of rules that together define the networks to which the computer is connected and how the available bandwidth should be allocated among these networks. For instance, suppose you want to implement a 50/50 split of 100Mbps of outgoing bandwidth between two offices. The Internet at large is on eth0, and both offices are on eth1, although one uses the 192.168.1.0/24 IP address subnet and the other uses 192.168.2.0/24. To begin the process, use tc to initialize a queueing discipline on eth1:

```
# tc qdisc add dev eth1 root handle 10: cbq bandwidth 100Mbit \
  avpkt 1000
```

This command can be broken down into several parts:

- **add dev eth1**—This tells the system that you're adding a queueing discipline for eth1.
- **root**—Some disciplines arrange themselves in virtual trees that branch off of a "root." This parameter tells tc that you're creating a new root for the tree.
- **handle 10:**—This parameter defines a label (*handle*) for the discipline.
- **cbq**—You must tell the system which queueing method to use. The Class-Based-Queueing (CBQ) method is a common one. This entry should correspond to the name of a specific option in the QoS and/or Fair Queueing kernel configuration menu.
- **bandwidth 100Mbit**—You must tell the system how much bandwidth is available on the network. In the case of a router with differing bandwidth on its separate ports, this will normally be the lesser bandwidth value; you don't want to overschedule the bandwidth that's actually available.

- **avpkt 1000**—Network packets vary in size, but to schedule bandwidth use, the system must have some idea of what the average packet size will be. One thousand is a reasonable first guess, but it might be higher or lower on particular networks.

Now it's time to define classes for the network as a whole and for each of the subnets whose bandwidth you want to guarantee. You can do so with commands like the following:

```
# tc class add dev eth1 parent 10:0 classid 10:1 cbq \
  bandwidth 100Mbit rate 100Mbit allot 1514 weight 10Mbit \
  prio 8 maxburst 20 avpkt 1000
```

This command is very much like the previous one, but it sets up a class that defines one of the two subnets. Note that it sets up the class to use the entire 100Mbps available bandwidth, because this particular class corresponds to the root; subsequent commands subdivide this bandwidth. This command has a few extra parameters and other differences, compared to the previous tc command:

- **class**—Rather than qdisc, this command uses class to define the class.
- **parent 10:0**—You specify the parent—the root of the tree—with this parameter. Note that you add 0 to the handle specified with the previous command.
- **classid 10:1**—This is the identifier for this particular class.
- **allot 1514**—This is the MTU value (plus a few bytes overhead) for the network.
- **weight 1Mbit**—This is a tuning parameter, and may need to be adjusted for your network.
- **prio 8**—This is a priority number. The higher the priority number, the more priority the rule gets.

The rules for the individual subnets look very much like the last one:

```
# tc class add dev eth1 parent 10:1 classid 10:100 cbq \
  bandwidth 100Mbit rate 50Mbit allot 1514 weight 5Mbit \
  prio 5 maxburst 20 avpkt 1000 bounded
# tc class add dev eth1 parent 10:1 classid 10:200 cbq \
  bandwidth 100Mbit rate 50Mbit allot 1514 weight 5Mbit \
  prio 5 maxburst 20 avpkt 1000 bounded
```

These commands are nearly identical; they differ only in their classid settings. Both refer to the root class as a parent, and both set up a 50Mbps bandwidth allotment. (You can create an asymmetrical allotment if you like—say, 60Mbps and 40Mbps.) The bounded option tells Linux to not give more than the allotted bandwidth to a network class under any circumstances. This is often inefficient, because if one office isn't using its full allotment, the other can't use the unused amount. Omitting the bounded option gives Linux the flexibility to let one office "borrow" bandwidth if the other isn't using it, while enforcing a 50/50 split if both want bandwidth.

Now it's necessary to associate a queueing discipline with each of the two classes:

```
# tc qdisc add dev eth1 parent 10:100 sfq quantum 1514b \
  perturb 15
# tc qdisc add dev eth1 parent 10:200 sfq quantum 1514b \
  perturb 15
```

These commands are similar to the original queueing discipline assignment. They tell Linux to use the Stochastic Fairness Queueing (SFQ) discipline to schedule traffic *within* each office's subnet. SFQ is popular for this purpose because it requires little CPU power, but other disciplines can be used if desired.

The commands to this point haven't provided a means for the kernel to differentiate traffic from the two offices (192.168.1.0/24 and 192.168.2.0/24). The final two commands accomplish this goal:

```
# tc filter add dev eth1 parent 10:0 protocol ip prio 100 u32 \
  match ip dst 192.168.1.0/24 flowid 10:100
# tc filter add dev eth1 parent 10:0 protocol ip prio 100 u32 \
  match ip dst 192.168.2.0/24 flowid 10:200
```

These commands are similar to the preceding ones, but they set up a filter rule to move traffic destined towards (dst) each of the two networks through the appropriate classes. Each rule is given an equal priority, and is matched using the u32 algorithm, which works on IP address blocks.

The preceding rules control the flow of data from the Internet to the local systems. To be complete, you must create a similar set of rules that control data passing in the opposite direction. These rules would resemble the preceding ones, but they would refer to eth0 (the external interface) rather than eth1 (the internal interface), and the final two `filter` commands would use `src` rather than `dst` to indicate that they control traffic originating from a local source rather than a destination.

USING ROUTING PROTOCOLS

Routers have to decide how to direct traffic. For instance, there might be two paths from the router to a packet's destination. You can use tools like the `ip` program in `iproute2` to determine which route to use, but once you've configured that route, it's set and can't be changed except by running `ip` again to change it. This may be fine for a simple configuration, but there are cases when you want your router to dynamically update its routing tables to deal with changing network conditions, such as links going down or becoming available (possibly far from your own system). You might also want to be able to tell the routers that communicate with yours about changes in your own network, such as the presence of a new block of IP addresses on your network. To fulfill these needs, several routing protocols exist. Linux implements these in dedicated servers that communicate with other routers to exchange information on route availability and costs. This section covers these protocols, beginning with some background information and moving on to each of three specific protocols.

UNDERSTANDING ROUTING PROTOCOLS

Ultimately, routing is about determining what to do with specific data packets. (Technically, *routing* refers to the routing tables, while *forwarding* refers to the actual processing of packets.) Earlier sections of this chapter have described how to configure a Linux router to handle packets in ways that depend upon the packets' addresses, content, and so on. Routing protocols let you add one more component to the equation: the external network environment. This includes information on the availability of specific networks and on the *cost* to reach those hosts. In this context, cost doesn't refer directly to money; it's usually a measure of the number of network hops between hosts or some other measure of network performance. When a router has two network connections that lead elsewhere, the cost to reach a specific network can vary from one path to another. For instance, consider Figure 24.1, which illustrates a simple internet of five networks at a university. Each department's network has its own router, and each of these routers connects directly to two other routers, as well as to its local network.

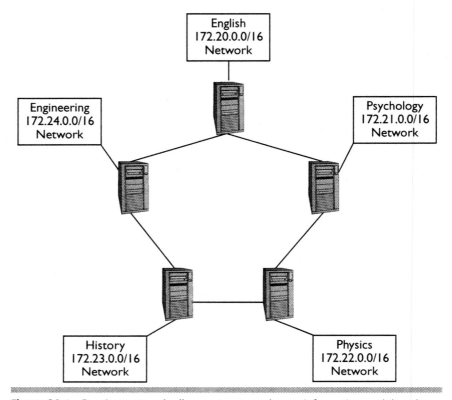

Figure 24.1 Routing protocols allow routers to exchange information, and thus determine the shortest route between two points.

NOTE This description uses a simple private internet (lowercase *i*) as an example, but the same principles apply to the Internet (uppercase *I*) as well.

Each hop on this internet increases the latency for packets sent between the networks. For instance, sending a packet from the English department's network to the physics network requires sending the packet through at least three routers. There are, though, two paths between the English and physics networks—one uses the psychology router as an intermediary, and the other uses the routers for both the engineering and history departments. The second (counterclockwise) path is longer. Ideally, you want a way to tell the English department's router about both paths. That way, if the psychology router fails, network traffic can still reach the destination via the less efficient route.

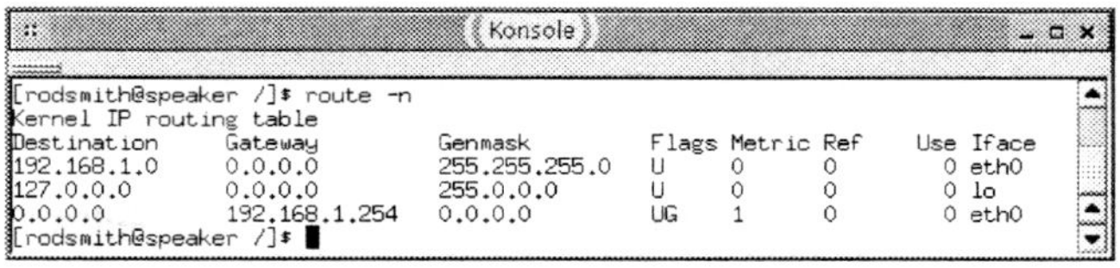

Figure 24.2   A routing table's `Metric` value specifies the cost of using a specific route.

One part of a solution is in specifying network costs. You can see these in a standard Linux routing table by using the `route` command For instance, Figure 24.2 shows the output of this command on one workstation. (A router would have a larger routing table, but the basic format would be the same.) Note in particular the `Metric` column. This shows that the number of routers involved in sending packets to the 127.0.0.0/8 (localhost) and 192.168.1.0/24 (local network) addresses is 0, but everything else requires at least one hop. This is an extremely simple example, though. In the case of a routing table for any router in Figure 24.1, there might be multiple possible paths to specific departments' networks, differing in their `Metric` values. Unfortunately, a standard Linux system ignores the metric information; you need to use a routing protocol like the ones described in this chapter to use this information.

Routing protocols work by allowing routers to exchange routing information, including metric information. In the case of Figure 24.1's network, if all the routers used a routing protocol, they would learn of each others' routes and be able to build routing tables with accurate cost information. If one router goes down, this information can propagate through the internet, allowing even distant routers to redirect traffic to avoid the outage.

Routing protocols use one of two algorithm types, which determine some key aspects of their operation:

- **Distance vector algorithms**—These algorithms track the number of routers that lie between the router and a given destination. When directing a packet to a target network, the path with the fewest number of intervening routers is chosen. The *Routing Information Protocol (RIP)* is one protocol that uses this approach.

- **Link state algorithms**—These algorithms assign a cost to each network link, and an individual router selects the route with the lowest cost to reach a destination. The cost need not correspond exactly to the number of routers, which can be useful if one router is faster or otherwise preferred over another. One protocol that uses this approach is the *Open Shortest Path First (OSPF)* protocol.

USING routed

RIP is the routing protocol that's most traditionally used on UNIX systems. In Linux, it's often implemented by a package called routed, which provides a daemon of the same name. RIP works by allowing routers to exchange RIP update packets, which contain information such as a network destination address (such as 172.22.0.0) and a metric (the number of routers between the one that sends the packet and the destination network). The metric ranges from 0 to 15; any route that takes more than 15 hops is eliminated from a system's routing table. RIP is a distance vector protocol, and its routing metric is fairly crude. RIP is most frequently used on small and mid-sized internets; it's not in common use on the Internet's backbone.

When a router receives an update packet, the router can do several things with the information. Specifically, the router can add a route to the destination, replace an existing route that has a higher metric, or delete the route if the new route metric plus 1 is greater than 15.

Using routed in Linux is relatively straightforward: You need only start the routed program, as described in Chapter 4, Starting Servers. The server relies upon a configuration file called /etc/gateways, which contains a list of starting routing information. An example line from this file resembles the following:

```
net 0.0.0.0 gateway 172.22.7.1 metric 1 active
```

This information's format is fairly straightforward. This example defines a default route (net 0.0.0.0, which matches all entries) that uses the router (gateway) at 172.22.7.1, with a metric of 1. The final option (active) indicates that RIP may update this route. If you want to keep a route permanently in the routing table, you can replace active with passive. The default /etc/gateways file is normally adequate. A computer running routed will be able to locate other RIP routers via a broadcast query, and can then communicate with them to update its configuration.

USING GATED

Although RIP is the traditional UNIX routing protocol, it's not without its limitations. One of these is the 15-hop restriction, which limits the size of networks RIP can serve. Another problem is that the protocol suffers from slow *convergence*, which is the process of settling on a stable routing table. It can take several minutes for important changes to propagate throughout your network, depending upon your network's topology. Finally, RIP doesn't provide information on network bitmasks; therefore, it can only provide routing information for networks that fall in the traditional Class A, B, or C address blocks. If your network uses, say, part of a traditional Class C address block, but if it's been carved up into smaller chunks, RIP propagates the addresses as if they were Class C addresses, which can cause problems if you need to contact another system in the same Class C address space that's really on a different network.

The RIP version 2 (RIPv2) protocol addresses the RIP lack of a network bitmask. RIPv2 adds a network bitmask field to the RIP protocols using a field that went unused in the original RIP data structures. This and other changes, though, are substantial enough that most implementations use a new daemon for RIPv2. One such server is GateD (`http://www.gated.net`). This program is controlled from its configuration file, `/etc/gated.conf`, and via the `gdc` utility, which normally ships with GateD. If you use `gdc` to reconfigure GateD, `gdc` modifies the `/etc/gated.conf` file automatically. Like `routed`, GateD normally requires little or no configuration of specific routing information; instead, it communicates with other RIP and RIPv2 systems it finds via broadcasts on all available network ports, in order to adjust the current system's routing table. Like `routed`, GateD is started like other daemons (usually through a SysV or local startup script).

In addition to handling RIP and RIPv2, GateD can handle the OSPF routing protocol. Other tools, such as Zebra, also support multiple protocols.

Using Zebra

A third routing tool for Linux is GNU Zebra (`http://www.zebra.org`). Zebra is actually a collection of several daemons that support multiple routing protocols:

- **RIP**—Zebra supports traditional RIP, the newer RIPv2, and an IPv6 version of RIP known as RIPng. The `ripd` server handles the first two, and `ripngd` handles RIPng.

- **OSPF**—Zebra includes OSPF support in its `ospfd` server, and an IPv6 variant in `ospf6d`. OSPF, like RIP, is commonly used on local internets.

- **BGP**—The *Border Gateway Protocol (BGP)* is commonly used by routers on the Internet at large, and Zebra supports it through the `bgpd` server.

- **Zebra**—The zebra program file functions as a control program for the Zebra suite as a whole, and other Zebra servers use it to update the kernel's routing table. It runs as a server to which you can connect with a normal Telnet program, as described shortly.

You can start each of the routing daemons independently, as described in Chapter 4. For instance, you can start zebra and ripd if you want to use RIP or RIPv2, but not start the others if you don't need them. Each of these servers uses its own configuration file, which normally appears in /etc or /etc/zebra and is named after the daemon in question. For instance, /etc/zebra/ospfd.conf controls ospfd. These files all have certain common elements. They all use an exclamation mark (!) or pound sign (#) as comment characters, and support several options, such as the following:

- **hostname**—This sets the router's hostname, as in hostname gw to set the hostname to gw.
- **password**—The zebra daemon itself uses passwords to control administrative access from other systems or servers. You must therefore set the password in each of the configuration files. This password grants limited access to the server.
- **enable password**—The main zebra server supports a special administrative password that you set with this option. You must enter this password before you can change a server's configuration.
- **router** *protocol*—Configuration files for most specific protocols require you to identify the routing protocol being used. In the case of ripd.conf, the line reads router rip; for ospfd.conf, it's router ospf; and for bgpd.conf, it's router bgp *as-number*, where *as-number* is your router's autonomous system (AS) number. (AS numbers must be assigned much like IP addresses. You can use an AS number between 64512 and 65535 if you're using BGP only on your local network.)

Once Zebra is running, you can configure it further by using a Telnet utility to access port 2601 on the router system. For instance:

```
$ telnet localhost 2601
```

After you enter the password, you can enter configuration commands like enable (to gain access to configuration commands), configure (to change a configuration), or show (to display information on the configuration). At any step of the way, you can type a single question mark (?) to get help on available commands or options. If you're familiar with Cisco routers, you should find Zebra's commands familiar, because they're designed to be compatible.

Summary

All networked computers, even workstations, need a routing table in order to direct network traffic to the appropriate location. Standard Linux networking tools, like `ifconfig` and `route`, are quite adequate for setting up the routing table in a workstation, a typical server, or even a low-end router. More advanced routers, though, need more sophisticated tools. Linux provides these in several forms. Because the Linux kernel is ultimately responsible for routing, some routing configuration tools require special kernel routing options to be active, so you should check your kernel configuration to be sure it has the tools you need. The `iproute2` package is a popular one for providing several advanced routing options, including the ability to manipulate multiple routing tables or set up a QoS scheme to guarantee certain users or networks a particular amount of bandwidth. Assorted routing protocols, and their associated Linux servers, give flexibility in allowing routers to communicate with each other, transferring data on the networks for which they route in order to allow a router to determine the optimal route to any given network.

Configuring iptables

The job of the TCP/IP stack in the Linux kernel is to receive data from an application, pack it up, and send it out a network port; and to receive data from the network, unpack it, and deliver it to an application. In theory, the kernel shouldn't alter or adjust the data in any but very specific ways that are permitted by the TCP/IP protocols. One particularly useful routing and security tool, though, violates this theoretical ideal. The `iptables` utility configures the Linux kernel to filter and even alter data packets based on various criteria, such as the packets' source and destination addresses. This makes `iptables` the standard utility for implementing certain network tools, most importantly packet-filter firewalls and Network Address Translation (NAT). This chapter covers these two topics and a couple of subsidiary topics: port redirection and `iptables` logging. All of these tools can be used to help secure a network, or sometimes just one computer.

This chapter's coverage of `iptables` is enough to help you implement some of the more common types of firewalls or other packet filtering tools. If you want to set up a particularly complex firewall, though, you may want to consult additional sources. Ziegler's *Linux Firewalls, 2nd Edition* (New Riders, 2001) and Sonnenreich and Yates's *Building Linux and OpenBSD Firewalls* (Wiley, 2000) are both useful resources, although the latter covers `iptables`' predecessor tool, `ipchains`, rather than `iptables`.

WHAT IS iptables?

Although the details are hidden from most networking tools, the 2.4.*x* Linux kernel uses a procedure like that outlined in Figure 25.1 to process network packets. Early on in the process, a routing decision is made: Is the packet destined for the local computer, or should it be forwarded to another computer? Depending upon the answer to that question, the packet is passed to one of two *chains*: the INPUT chain or the FORWARD chain. Each of these chains can process or modify the incoming data in various ways, but the default is not to modify the data. The INPUT chain ultimately leads to what Figure 25.1 refers to as *local processes*. These may be network clients (Netscape, telnet, and so on) or network servers (Apache, telnetd, and so on). In most cases, these processes run in user space, but they may be kernel-based, as in the kernel's Network Filesystem (NFS) support or the kHTTPd Web server. Both the local processes and the FORWARD chain eventually lead to the OUTPUT chain, which can also manipulate data packets in ways described in this chapter.

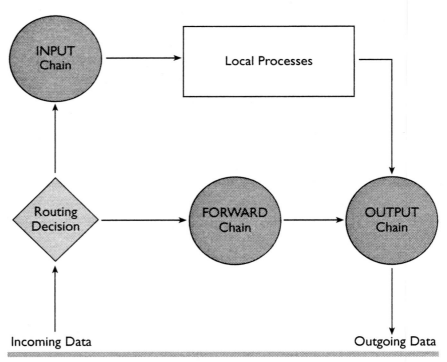

Figure 25.1 The Linux networking system provides several chains in which data packets may be manipulated.

NOTE It's possible for a data packet to not make a complete circuit in Figure 25.1. Certain chain rules can block the data packet, or the local processes might decide not to respond to a data packet. It's also possible for a transaction to *originate* with the local processes, in which case a response should arrive back as incoming data.

Each of the chains shown in Figure 25.1 provides the opportunity to manipulate data packets. A chain can filter packets based on features such as the source or destination IP address, the source or destination port, or the network interface involved in the transaction. Each chain is a collection of rules, each of which is matched in turn against the input packet. If a rule matches, the rule indicates what the kernel should do with the packet by specifying a *target* for the rule. Predefined targets include ACCEPT (accept the packet for further processing), DROP (ignore the packet), QUEUE (pass the packet to a user-space program), and RETURN (stop processing the chain and return to the chain that called the current chain). Some additional targets that require particular kernel options to be activated include REJECT (to reject the packet, telling the sender that it was rejected), MASQUERADE (used for NAT, as described in the upcoming section "Configuring NAT with iptables"), and LOG (used to log information on packet filtering).

Chains are organized into *tables*. The three chains shown in Figure 25.1 make up the filter table, which is what handles most standard traffic. Two other standard tables are nat (which is used for NAT, as described in the upcoming section "Configuring NAT with iptables") and mangle (which is used for specialized packet alterations). It's possible to place new chains within a table, and call these new chains from the existing chains. You might do this to create specialized and complex processing patterns to filter or alter data.

These network tables and chains are features of the Linux kernel, and iptables is the user-space tool you use to manipulate them. You can use iptables to add rules to any of the chains shown in Figure 25.1, or to other chains. For instance, you might add rules to the INPUT chain to block all packets directed at specific network ports, or you might add rules to the OUTPUT chain to stop packets directed at systems with which you don't want yours communicating. By manipulating these and other chains, you can implement a packet-filter firewall, NAT, or other security and routing tools.

The changes you make with iptables are transient; they disappear as soon as you reboot the computer. For this reason, you should create a script that sets your iptables rules. Some distributions, such as Red Hat and Mandrake,

Alternative Filtering Tools

The iptables program was designed for use with the 2.4.x Linux kernel. Earlier kernels, though, used different tools. Specifically, 2.2.x kernels used a tool known as ipchains, and 2.0.x kernels used ipfwadm. The changes in firewall and NAT tools reflect changes in the kernel's networking structure. The latest iptables tool can implement features in the 2.4.x kernel that didn't exist in the 2.2.x kernel, such as *stateful packet inspection*, in which packets can be tracked based on an entire multi-packet transaction with another computer, rather than as isolated entities. Stateful packet inspection greatly enhances the ability of a firewall to protect the computers it serves.

If you're using a pre-2.4.x kernel, you can continue using it with the older tools. These tools implement similar principles, but many of the details differ. This chapter doesn't cover the syntax or features of ipchains or ipfwadm, so if you want to use them, you'll have to track down appropriate documentation. If future kernels require even more sophisticated tools than iptables, you may need to locate documentation on these future tools. Chances are good that the broad outlines of these tools' operation will resemble those of iptables, though, so knowledge of iptables won't be completely useless to you.

If you have access to a firewall rule set built with ipfwadm or ipchains, you can continue to use it with a 2.4.x kernel, but you must include appropriate kernel support for the older tool. Using such a firewall rule set with a 2.4.x kernel has no disadvantages over using it with a 2.0.x or 2.2.x kernel, but you might be able to use more powerful features if you rewrite the rules for iptables.

To some extent, iptables overlaps in function with tools like TCP Wrappers, xinetd, and server-specific access control options. All of these tools allow you to restrict access to a server based on a client's IP address, for instance. As a general rule, when multiple tools are available, I recommend using two or more, so that a bug in or misconfiguration of one tool can be corrected by another tool. Compared to other tools, iptables works at a lower level and with more protocols and servers. For instance, xinetd can only protect servers that xinetd launches, whereas iptables can protect *all* servers.

include tools to help you build firewall or NAT rules. You can implement such a script yourself and call it as a SysV or local startup script.

KERNEL CONFIGURATION FOR iptables

Before you can use iptables, you must build support for it into the Linux kernel. What's more, some iptables features are only useful if you've activated appropriate iptables kernel suboptions. All of these kernel features can be found in the Networking Options menu in the 2.4.*x* kernel configuration tree, or in submenus off the Networking Options menu. Features you should check include the following:

- **Network Packet Filtering**—The Network Packet Filtering option is in the main Networking Options configuration menu.
- **Connection Tracking**—This option is available in the Netfilter Configuration menu off the Networking Options menu. It's required for NAT. (All subsequent options are in the same Netfilter Configuration menu.)
- **FTP Protocol Support**—FTP is a tricky protocol for NAT. In Linux, NAT support for FTP requires this special kernel module.
- **IP Tables Support**—This option is another that's required for NAT. A large number of suboptions become available when you select this one, corresponding to various tests you might want to perform. For best flexibility, select all of these suboptions. The Connection State Match Support option is particularly noteworthy because it's required for stateful packet inspection.
- **Packet Filtering**—Although not absolutely required for firewalls or NAT, this option enhances the range of features available to you. I recommend you enable it.
- **REJECT Target Support**—This suboption of Packet Filtering adds a rule that can be helpful in creating firewalls. It's therefore best to enable this feature.
- **Full NAT**—This option is required for many NAT features, including those described in this chapter.
- **MASQUERADE Target Support**—This suboption of the Full NAT option is required for IP masquerading—the form of NAT that is described in the upcoming section, "Configuring NAT with `iptables`." Note that the Help option for this item implies that it's only necessary if you use a dynamic external IP address, but this is incorrect; it's required for IP masquerading whether or not your external IP address is dynamic.
- **Packet Mangling**—This kernel feature is required if you want to use the `mangle` table, described earlier. I recommend you enable it.
- **LOG Target Support**—If you want to log firewall or router activity, this option allows you to do so.
- **`ipchains` (2.2-style) Support**—If you want to use an older `ipchains`-based firewall script, you need to activate this option. You'll also need the `ipchains` tool itself.

- **ipfwadm (2.0-style) Support**—If you want to use an older ipfwadm-based firewall script, you need to activate this option. You'll also need the ipfwadm tool itself.

TIP

The ipchains and ipfwadm support options are mutually exclusive, and both are incompatible with the IP Tables Support and Connection Tracking options. Therefore, you cannot compile support for both iptables and an earlier tool into the same kernel. You can, however, compile all of these tools as modules, and select which you want to use by loading the appropriate kernel module. You might want to compile your kernel this way if you currently have an older tool and want to migrate it to the newer iptables as time permits. Many distributions ship their default kernels like this.

If you compile support for features as modules, you may need to load the appropriate modules in your firewall startup script. For instance, the basic iptables functionality is in the ip_tables module, so your startup script might need the command insmod ip_tables. Check the /lib/modules/*version*/net/ipv4/netfilter directory for other modules you may need to explicitly load. To avoid manually loading modules, you can compile the support directly into the kernel, but this will increase your kernel file's size.

CHECKING YOUR iptables CONFIGURATION

Before proceeding further, you should check your current configuration. Some distributions now ship with firewall-creation tools, and it's possible these are running without your knowledge. You can check your system's current configuration by passing iptables the -L parameter. You can also add the -t *table-name* parameter to check on a particular table. (The default *table-name* is filter, but you may want to check the nat and mangle tables, as well.) This should produce output similar to the following:

```
# iptables -L -t filter
Chain INPUT (policy ACCEPT)
target     prot opt source              destination

Chain FORWARD (policy ACCEPT)
target     prot opt source              destination

Chain OUTPUT (policy ACCEPT)
target     prot opt source              destination
```

This output shows no iptables rules in the standard filter table. This is a good starting point for further modifications. If your system has firewall rules already defined, you should try to track down what script is defining them and disable it. (It may be a SysV startup script called firewall or something similar.) You can then use the -F parameter to flush the rules from a chain, thus:

```
# iptables -F INPUT -t filter
```

It's generally a good idea to begin your firewall script with this command, similar commands for other chains in the filter table, and perhaps with equivalents for other tables. This ensures that your new firewall rules aren't added to old rules, which can cause great confusion.

CONFIGURING A FIREWALL WITH iptables

The first iptables application described in this chapter is packet-filter firewall configuration. You can use these options on either a router or a nonrouter system (a workstation or server). When a router is so configured, it's often referred to as a firewall computer, but there are other types of firewall as well. Configuring a packet-filter firewall requires setting a default policy and then configuring exceptions to that policy based on port numbers, IP addresses, or other criteria.

WHAT IS A FIREWALL?

Traditionally, a firewall is a computer that sits between two networks and controls access between those networks. This function is similar to that of a router, but there are several potential differences. For one thing, a router without firewall functions doesn't control access in the same sense as a firewall; a firewall can block computers on one network from accessing particular services on the other network. For instance, a firewall can block Telnet access from the Internet to a protected internal network. Also, some types of firewall don't forward data packets in the way that a router does; these *proxy server* firewalls run special proxy server software, which partially processes requests intended for other systems, recreates the requests as coming from itself, and forwards the reply to the original system. A proxy server firewall can help protect against fairly high-level threats, such as viruses embedded in Java or JavaScript.

This section is devoted to a different type of firewall: packet-filter firewalls. These operate on a lower level of the TCP/IP stack, and are restricted to examining various types of addressing information in individual packets, or at most to tracking a transaction to ensure it's not hijacked. Although packet-filter firewalls are often implemented as part of a router, they can also be set up on a workstation or server. When so configured, the firewall works to protect the computer on which it runs, but has no effect on other computers.

Most people think of firewalls as existing to protect a local network from the Internet, as shown in Figure 25.2. Indeed, this is one of the functions of a firewall, and a very important one. Firewalls can also serve to prevent local users from attacking other systems on the Internet, though. You might use a firewall to block all but approved local protocols, and perhaps even restrict certain protocols except from particular computers. For instance, you might allow only the mail server to connect to port 25 on outside computers. (ISPs sometimes use this configuration as an anti-spam measure.) Outgoing controls provide protection against both untrustworthy individuals who have access to your local network and viruses, worms, Trojan horses and the like installed on your local computers without your knowledge. This protection most directly helps other networks, but it's ultimately important to you as well, because blocking hostile

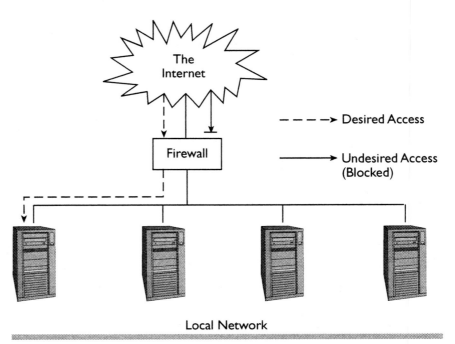

Figure 25.2   Packet filter firewalls can limit some types of access while allowing others.

actions from your own network can keep your network from being the target of investigations by your ISP or even legal action.

In some cases, you might use a firewall's rules to *redirect* connection attempts, as described in the upcoming section, "Redirecting Ports with `iptables`." This redirection causes a packet directed at one system to be sent to another. You can use this feature in conjunction with NAT to run servers on a protected network. You might also use it with external-connection restrictions to allow a connection to succeed in a way the client doesn't expect. For instance, instead of blocking outgoing SMTP connections from anything but your mail server, you might redirect such requests to your own mail server. In the case of SMTP, the result is normal mail delivery, provided the mail server is configured to relay local mail. This particular trick won't work with most other protocols, though.

Referring to Figure 25.1, a Linux packet-filter firewall operates by configuring the INPUT, FORWARD, and OUTPUT chains. Each of these chains has its role:

- The INPUT chain protects local processes. You should configure INPUT chain rules for both router firewalls and the firewalls on individual workstations or servers.
- The FORWARD chain intervenes in routing. You'd configure this chain if you want to turn a router into a packet-filter firewall.
- The OUTPUT chain blocks undesired outgoing accesses. You can use this on a standalone firewall much as you might use FORWARD or INPUT chain rules, or on a workstation or server to restrict local users' ability to contact certain hosts or use certain protocols.

A router with firewall features is most likely to use INPUT and FORWARD rules, while a workstation or server is most likely to use INPUT and OUTPUT rules. In some cases, these rules may have nearly identical effects, particularly with respect to FORWARD and OUTPUT rules on a router. The OUTPUT chain affects both forwarded and locally generated traffic, though, whereas the FORWARD chain affects only routed traffic.

SETTING A FIREWALL'S DEFAULT POLICY

The first step in firewall configuration is in setting the *default policy*. This is a statement of what the firewall is to do with packets that don't match other rules. You set the default policy with the -P option to `iptables`, thus:

```
# iptables -P INPUT DROP
# iptables -P OUTPUT DROP
# iptables -P FORWARD DROP
```

This example sets the default policy separately on each of the three standard chains in the filter table. The default policy may be any firewall target, as described earlier (ACCEPT, DROP, QUEUE, RETURN, or another policy enabled through an appropriate kernel option). The most common default policies are ACCEPT, DROP, and REJECT. The first is the default, and tells Linux to pass on all packets. DROP tells the system to ignore all packets; it's as if they don't exist. REJECT is like DROP, but instead of ignoring the packet, Linux tells the calling system that it can't accept the packet; it's similar to the way Linux responds if there's no process using the port. The most secure firewall configurations use DROP or REJECT as the default policy, because this means that any packet type you don't explicitly permit in subsequent steps is blocked. If you use ACCEPT as the default policy, you must remember to explicitly disallow all the packet types you don't want to let pass. This can be a tedious process, and it's easy to overlook something. With a default policy of DROP or REJECT, by contrast, you only need to explicitly allow certain protocol types. Most computers and even networks only use a few protocols, so this is generally a more manageable task.

CREATING FIREWALL RULES

You create firewall rules by using the --append option to iptables (-A is a shorter synonym). You follow this command by one or more criteria specifications and a --jump option (-j being a shorter synonym), which specifies a firewall target such as ACCEPT, DROP, or REJECT. In sum, the command looks something like this:

```
# iptables --append CHAIN selection-criteria --jump TARGET
```

This can be shortened by using the shorthand option names:

```
# iptables -A CHAIN selection-criteria -j TARGET
```

There are other options you can use in place of --append:

- **--delete or -D**—This option deletes the rule from the existing chain.
- **--insert or -I**—You can insert a rule in the middle of a chain with this option. You ordinarily follow this with a rule number. If you don't,

iptables inserts the rule at the top of the chain, rather than the bottom as --append does.

- **--replace or -R**—This option replaces a rule. As with --insert, you specify a rule number to replace that rule.
- **--list or -L**—This option lists the rules in the chain.

There are several additional options beyond these; consult the iptables man page for details. The following sections describe various options for the *selection-criteria* you may pass to iptables. You can include multiple criteria in one command; for instance, you can restrict access based on port number *and* IP address.

NOTE The kernel reads rules in a chain in order, and acts on the first rule that matches a packet. Thus, if you want to set up a rule with exceptions (such as denying access to the Telnet port except for local computers), you should enter the exceptions *first*, then the more general rule. In some sense, the default policy is a rule that comes at the end of a chain, and matches anything that's not already been matched.

Opening and Closing Specific Ports

One way to filter packets is to use specific source or destination ports. For instance, you might want to configure a mail server to pass packets sent to its SMTP port (25). You can do this by using the --destination-port (--dport) option. This option also relies upon the --protocol (-p) option, which sets the protocol type (tcp, udp, icmp, or all for all of them). The --source-port (--sport) option works in a similar way, but matches the port from which the packet originated. The final command might resemble the following:

```
# iptables -A INPUT -p tcp --dport 25 -j ACCEPT
# iptables -A OUTPUT -p tcp --sport 25 -j ACCEPT
```

These commands tell the kernel to accept packets directed at port 25 for its local INPUT and OUTPUT chains. The result is that, even if the default policy is set to block packets, the system will accept incoming mail and be able to send mail to others, assuming a mail server is configured appropriately. One key point is that, if you've set the default policy to DROP or REJECT, you must normally open both the input chain to the port for a particular server *and* the output chain from the same server's port. If you fail to do this, your server may be able to receive packets but not reply to them, or generate packets but not receive them. On a separate firewall computer, you might want to create --destination-port and --source-port rules on the FORWARD chain, to permit SMTP transfers to pass through the firewall. You can combine these with an IP address specification, as described in the next section, "Using Source and Destination IP Addresses," to allow SMTP transfers only to and from the mail server.

If you use a default DROP or REJECT policy, it's important to open ports to allow client programs to communicate with the outside world. There are a couple of ways you can do this:

- Open access to server ports on outside computers. This works just like the preceding example, except that -A INPUT would be paired with --source-port, and -A OUTPUT would be paired with --destination-port. On a router configured as a firewall, you'd set both --source-port and --destination-port using -A FORWARD, possibly paired with IP address specifications for your network. You must explicitly enable access for every protocol your internal clients use.
- You can open the entire unprivileged port range, 1024–65535. Instead of specifying a single port number with --source-port and --destination-port, you specify a range by separating the values with a colon, as in --source-port 1024:65535. For incoming connections, you may want to add the ! --syn option. The --syn option matches only connection initiation requests, and an exclamation mark (!) reverses the sense of a connection, so ! --syn allows return packets but not connection requests.

Using Source and Destination IP Addresses

You can match packets to source and destination IP addresses or network blocks with the --source (-s) and --destination (-d) options. For instance, if you know that the 172.24.0.0/16 network block is controlled by undesirables, you could include options like the following to block all access to and from that network block in a default ALLOW configuration:

```
# iptables -A INPUT -s 172.24.0.0/16 -j DROP
# iptables -A OUTPUT -d 172.24.0.0/16 -j DROP
```

These options are often used in conjunction with port-based connections to allow only specific computers to access certain ports, especially in a default DROP configuration. For instance, suppose you run a firewall computer that protects a network, but you want to allow external users on the 10.34.176.0/24 network to access your internal network's SSH servers (on TCP port 22). You might do this with options like the following:

```
# iptables -A FORWARD -s 10.34.176.0/24 -p tcp \
  --destination-port 22 -j ALLOW
# iptables -A FORWARD -d 10.34.176.0/24 -p tcp \
  --source-port 22 -j ALLOW
```

Because this example modifies only the FORWARD chain, it does not give any user direct access to the firewall computer's own SSH server (if it's even running one). You might want to add entries to give your local computers access to this server. Suppose your local network uses the 192.168.9.0/24 network addresses. The appropriate commands would resemble the following:

```
# iptables -A INPUT -s 192.168.9.0/24 -p tcp \
  --destination-port 22 -j ALLOW
# iptables -A OUTPUT -d 192.168.9.0/24 -p tcp \
  --source-port 22 -j ALLOW
```

Filtering by Interface

Another filtering option is to use the network interface, such as `ppp0` or `eth1`, as an identifier. This option is most useful on a router or other computer with multiple interfaces. It can help protect against address *spoofing*, in which a remote system tries to contact a router using a local address, in the hopes that the router has a more lenient configuration for local computers. For the INPUT and FORWARD chains, you specify the input interface name with the `--in-interface` (`-i`) option; for the FORWARD and OUTPUT chains, you specify the output interface with the `--out-interface` (`-o`) option. For instance, suppose your internal network uses the 192.168.9.0/24 network address space and is on the router's `eth1`, while your Internet connection is on `eth0`. You might use a generic anti-spoofing rule like the following:

```
# iptables -A INPUT -s 192.168.9.0/24 -i eth0 -j DROP
# iptables -A FORWARD -s 192.168.9.0/24 -i eth0 -j DROP
# iptables -A FORWARD -s !192.168.9.0/24 -i eth1 -j DROP
# iptables -A OUTPUT -s !192.168.9.0/24 -i eth1 -j DROP
```

The first two commands protect against packets directed at the router and internal systems from external systems (on `eth0`) that claim to be internal systems. The last two commands prevent internal systems (on eth1) from claiming to have IP addresses outside of the local network.

Performing Stateful Inspection

The latest addition to the Linux packet filtering firewall capabilities is stateful packet inspection. The options that have been described earlier in this chapter all operate on individual packets. There's no way to tell if a packet is part of an existing data stream or is an interloper inserted into an existing data stream by a clever attacker. (The --syn option allows you to check if a packet claims to be opening a new connection, but it's possible to have a computer send out packets that claim to be part of an existing data stream. Such packets can be used to "hijack" an existing TCP connection.) With stateful packet inspection, the kernel can track connections by using packet sequence numbers, source IP addresses, and so on. If you tell it to do so, you can have the kernel reject packets that contain errors that might indicate the session has been hijacked.

Stateful packet inspection requires using the --state option, preceded by the -m state option to load the stateful inspection capabilities of the kernel. You can pass this option one or more of several parameters. If you pass more than one parameter, you must separate them with commas. You can use an exclamation mark (!) prior to the --state option to reverse its meaning. The available parameters are:

- **INVALID**—The packet can't be matched to a known connection, and thus may be forged.
- **NEW**—The packet is trying to establish a new connection.
- **ESTABLISHED**—The packet is associated with an existing connection.
- **RELATED**—The packet is not part of an existing connection, but it's related, such as an ICMP error packet.

NOTE Specifying ! --state INVALID is the same as specifying --state NEW,ESTABLISHED,RELATED.

You might want to add stateful inspection to an existing rule. For instance, suppose you have a default DROP or REJECT policy on a server, but have a rule to permit connections to and from the server's HTTP port (80). You might add a stateful inspection rule to allow only new, established, or related packets to that port:

```
# iptables -A INPUT -m state -p tcp --dport 80 \
  --state NEW,ESTABLISHED,RELATED -j ACCEPT
# iptables -A OUTPUT -m state -p tcp --sport 80 \
  --state ESTABLISHED,RELATED -j ACCEPT
```

This rule permits only new, established, or related incoming connections, and only established or related outgoing connections. (New outgoing connections aren't required because the connection is always created by the client, not the server whose port these rules protect.) These rules prevent an interloper from taking over a client's existing Web server connection.

NOTE Stateful packet inspection became available in Linux with the 2.4.*x* kernel series and `iptables`; earlier kernels and packet filtering tools don't support this feature. In fact, this is one of the primary reasons you might want to upgrade an older kernel or packet filter firewall script to use `iptables`.

Using Additional Parameters

The `iptables` tool supports many additional options that may be useful in packet filter firewalls. For instance, you can create entirely new chains with the `--new-chain` (`-N`) option, create a rule that applies only to the second and subsequent fragments of a fragmented packet with the `--fragment` (`-f`) parameter, or match specific TCP flags with the `--tcp-flags` option. For more information on such parameters, consult the `iptables` man page or a book on Linux packet filter firewalls. (Be sure to get a title that covers `iptables`; some older titles cover only `ipchains`.)

Putting It All Together

It may be useful to see an entire `iptables` packet filter firewall script. Listing 25.1 presents such a script. This script is designed for a Web server computer that also supports local connections using SSH for configuring the system.

WARNING Most serious firewall scripts are much longer than Listing 25.1. This script includes just a few configuration options for the two servers the computer runs, plus a few other useful rules. For readability, Listing 25.1 calls `iptables` without a full path, which is a potential security risk should your path be modified. Listing 25.1 may serve as a core for a more complete script, but at the very best, you'll have to customize and expand it for your network.

Listing 25.1 A sample iptables firewall script

```
#!/bin/sh

iptables -F INPUT
iptables -F OUTPUT
iptables -F FORWARD

iptables -P INPUT DROP
iptables -P OUTPUT DROP
iptables -P FORWARD DROP

# Permit DNS traffic
iptables -A INPUT -p udp --sport 53 -j ACCEPT
iptables -A OUTPUT -p udp --dport 53 -j ACCEPT

# Accept local-network return traffic for clients
iptables -A INPUT -m state -p tcp --dport 1024:65535 \
  --state ESTABLISHED,RELATED -s 192.168.9.0/24 -j ACCEPT
iptables -A OUTPUT -m state -p tcp --sport 1024:65535 \
  ! --state INVALID -d 192.168.9.0/24 -j ACCEPT

# Accept all HTTP connections
iptables -A INPUT -m state -p tcp --dport 80 \
  ! --state INVALID -j ACCEPT
iptables -A OUTPUT -m state -p tcp --sport 80 \
  --state ESTABLISHED,RELATED -j ACCEPT

# Accept local (192.168.9.0/24) SSH traffic
iptables -A INPUT -m state -p tcp --dport 22 \
  ! --state INVALID -s 192.168.9.0/24 -j ACCEPT
iptables -A OUTPUT -m state -p tcp --sport 22 \
  --state ESTABLISHED,RELATED -d 192.168.9.0/24 -j ACCEPT

# Accept all local traffic on the lo interface
iptables -A INPUT -s 127.0.0.1 -i lo -j ACCEPT
iptables -A OUTPUT -d 127.0.0.1 -o lo -j ACCEPT
```

Some key features to consider about Listing 25.1 are the following:

- **Setup and default policy**—The first six iptables commands flush the existing filter set rules and set the default policy to DROP. This creates a fairly strict security setup, and subsequent commands loosen it for the desired protocols. Although the computer for which this script is intended isn't a router, this script sets the same strict default DROP policy on the FORWARD chain, just in case another interface appears (say, because of a PPP link).

- **DNS configuration**—In order to grant the computer access to a name server, the two lines following the `Permit DNS traffic` comment open the computer to connections to external DNS servers (UDP port 53). This setting is actually fairly lenient. Chances are you only need access to a couple of servers, so these commands could be expanded to include references to the DNS servers' IP addresses, or perhaps to the local network on which those servers reside.

- **Client return traffic**—The lines following the `Accept local-network return traffic for clients` comment open the server to return traffic destined for the unprivileged ports (1024–65,535). The `OUTPUT` chain specification uses stateful inspection to reject invalid connections, and the `INPUT` chain specification uses stateful inspection to reject all but established and related traffic. Note in particular that the `INPUT` chain disallows new connections, so even if the computer runs a server on an unprivileged port, other computers won't be able to connect to it. Both the `INPUT` and `OUTPUT` chain entries limit access to the local network. For a stronger firewall, you would replace these rules with more specific rules that permit traffic from unprivileged local ports to the ports used by specific protocols you might want to use from this system.

- **Web server traffic**—The computer's Web server needs to accept connections from anywhere, so the rules for this connection don't include any IP address specifications. They do use stateful inspection, though, as an anti-hijacking provision.

- **SSH server traffic**—The SSH configuration option is much like that for the Web server, but it includes an IP address restriction to ensure that only local users connect to the SSH server.

- **Loopback traffic**—Linux computers use the loopback interface (`lo`), which is associated with the 127.0.0.1 IP address, for some internal purposes. This firewall script therefore explicitly allows loopback access. This configuration doesn't use stateful inspections for this purpose, but does specify that only traffic from the `lo` interface will be accepted on the 127.0.0.1 address.

CONFIGURING NAT WITH `iptables`

A packet-filter firewall, as just described, has the capacity to deliver or stop delivery of packets based on criteria such as the source and destination IP addresses, port numbers, and so on. This is an extremely useful feature, but it's not the limit of `iptables`' capabilities. One feature of `iptables` that's particularly useful in certain situations is the ability to program the Linux kernel to perform Network Address Translation (NAT). NAT allows you to modify certain parts of a TCP/IP packet to increase the flexibility of your network addressing. Basic NAT configuration is relatively straightforward, but before you configure it, you should know what it is and what you can do with it.

WHAT IS NAT?

NAT allows a router to modify the contents of TCP/IP packets. In particular, NAT enables changes to the source and destination addresses of the packets. Why would you want to do this? There are several possibilities:

- **Internal/external translation**—You might own a block of network addresses, but you might not want to use those addresses on your internal network for some reason. For instance, you might have already configured your local network to use the private 192.168.9.0/24 network block, and you might not want to reconfigure all your systems to use public addresses. Using NAT, you can perform a one-to-one mapping of external public addresses to internal private addresses, allowing other systems on the Internet to reach your internal systems.

- **Temporary address changes**—You might use NAT in a temporary emergency situation to redirect packets to a system that's other than the normal one. For instance, if a Web server goes down, you might redirect packets for that server to another computer on your local network. There are other possible solutions to this problem, such as changing DNS server entries, but NAT can be implemented very quickly, which may be important.

- **Load balancing**—It's possible to use NAT to assign two internal computers to a single external IP address, switching between the internal systems for incoming requests. This is a crude form of load balancing that you might employ if a single server becomes overburdened. There are, however, other load balancing solutions that are more elegant than NAT.

- **IP address extension**—If you have a limited number of IP addresses, you can "hide" several computers behind a single IP address, thus making maximal use of your available IP addresses. This feature is commonly used on small networks that use PPP dial-up or broadband Internet connections, which usually give the user only one IP address. It can also be used within a larger organization to stretch available IP addresses—say, by using one IP address per department.

This final option is probably the most common use of NAT in Linux, and it's frequently referred to by another name: *IP masquerading*. For this reason, this is the use of NAT upon which this chapter focuses, but it's not the only use of NAT.

NAT requires the use of a router. This router need not be very sophisticated by router standards, but the router does need NAT support. The Linux kernel, as configured through `iptables`, is perfectly capable of filling this role. A Linux computer configured as a NAT router usually has two external network interfaces—typically two Ethernet interfaces or an Ethernet interface and a PPP interface.

NOTE Unlike a conventional router, a NAT router need not be recognized as such by the outside world. Thus, you need not reconfigure the NAT router's gateway system, as you would have to do if the NAT router were a regular router serving a public block of IP addresses.

To understand NAT, consider a network transaction through a NAT router. This transaction begins with a client on the NAT-protected network, such as a Web browser. The user tries to connect to an external site (say, at 172.18.127.45). The browser generates an HTTP request packet, addressed from its local IP address (say, 192.168.9.32). The client sends this request to its local gateway system, which is the NAT router. Upon receipt of the packets that make up this request, the NAT router examines the packets and changes the source IP address to that of the NAT router's own external address (say, 10.34.176.7) and sends the packets on their way. The Web server believes that the packets came from the NAT router, and so addresses its reply to the NAT router. When the NAT router receives this reply, it recognizes it as a reply to the request from 192.168.9.32, and so it reverses the process, changing the destination address of the reply packets and passing them on to the client. This process is illustrated in Figure 25.3. If all goes well, neither the client nor the server knows that NAT was involved, so network programs don't need to be rewritten to support NAT.

Some forms of NAT, and in particular IP masquerading, provide an added benefit: automatic firewall-like protection of the private network. Because the outside world sees just one IP address, outside systems cannot initiate normal direct connections to the internal computers. Only reply packets to connections initiated by clients within the NAT network can reach the clients. For this reason, some NAT products, particularly for home broadband users, are marketed as firewalls, but the two are slightly different.

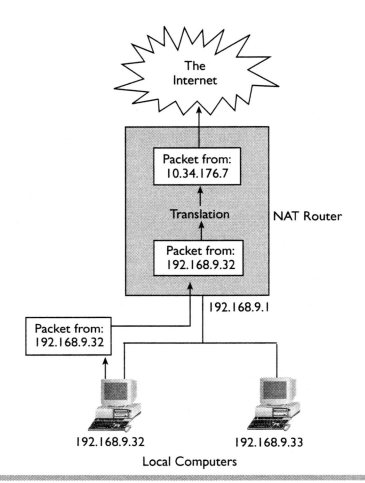

Figure 25.3 NAT involves modifying TCP/IP packets so that addresses are altered in one way or another.

NAT does have certain drawbacks, as well as advantages:

- The firewall-like protection means that you can't as easily run externally accessible servers from inside a NAT-protected network. To do so, you must use port redirection, described in the upcoming section, "Redirecting Ports with iptables."

- Not all protocols react well to NAT. Some, such as some security tools, embed information on their IP addresses within their data payloads, sometimes in an encrypted form. Others require servers at both ends of the connections. Linux's NAT implementation provides explicit support for some protocols that are tricky for NAT, but if you use videoconferencing or encryption tools, you may want to do a Web search or experiment to find out if your tools will work with Linux's NAT.

Although it's not strictly a disadvantage of NAT, you shouldn't rely upon its security features too much. A virus, worm, Trojan horse, or other local security problem can still launch attacks from within your network, or use an outgoing connection to allow an outsider access.

On the whole, NAT is a very useful tool for connecting many computers to a wider network using a single IP address, or for performing other tricks that involve the shuffling of IP addresses.

SETTING iptables NAT OPTIONS

Linux's NAT features are contained within a separate table from the filter table described in earlier sections of this chapter. In particular, NAT resides in the nat table. This table, like the filter table, consists of three chains: PREROUTING, POSTROUTING, and OUTPUT. Despite having the same name, the OUTPUT chain in the nat table is different from the OUTPUT chain in the filter table. Enabling NAT can be done by typing two commands:

```
# iptables -t nat -A POSTROUTING -o external-interface -j \
  MASQUERADE
# echo "1" > /proc/sys/net/ipv4/ip_forward
```

NOTE You may need to type **modprobe iptable_nat** before the iptables command to load the NAT module into the kernel.

In the first command, *external-interface* is the name of the external network interface, such as ppp0 or eth1. This command tells Linux to perform IP masquerading on all routed network traffic. The second command enables routing in the Linux kernel (you'd use the same command to enable non-NAT routing features).

It's common to enable firewall features, as described earlier in this chapter in the section "Configuring a Firewall with iptables," on a NAT router. Protecting computers behind the NAT router from direct attacks isn't much of an issue in this situation, but you should protect the NAT router from attacks on itself, and you should also limit external access from within your network. Even if you're the only user, it's possible that a virus, worm, or Trojan horse could try to initiate an undesirable external access, so you should limit outgoing packets. You can also use stateful inspection to block attempts to hijack connections made from inside your network. You can enter the NAT commands in the same script you use to activate your firewall features.

If at all possible, your NAT router should run no servers. If a server running on a NAT router is compromised, it can be used to compromise the rest of your network. In fact, you can install Linux on an old computer and use it as nothing but a NAT router for a small network. Even an old 80486 system should suffice.

FORWARDING PORTS WITH iptables

There are situations in which network activity directed at one computer should be handled by another computer, or possibly another port on the same computer. For these tasks, iptables lets you implement *port forwarding*, which echoes incoming network traffic to another computer.

WHEN TO FORWARD PORTS

Port forwarding can be an extremely useful tool in certain situations, including the following:

- You move a server from one computer to another, but your DNS entries have not yet been properly updated. You can also use port forwarding to *temporarily* make such a change.
- You want a server to respond to multiple ports on a single computer. You can set up the system to forward one port to another on the same system. Some servers can listen directly to multiple ports, though, which is often a simpler approach.
- You want to run an externally accessible server within a NAT-protected network. You can set up the NAT router to forward traffic directed at one of its external ports to an internal system.

This last possibility is a particularly common one when running NAT. Note that this behavior degrades the security advantages of NAT, because you're effectively exposing an internal system (or at least, one of its ports) to the outside. You can also run only one internal server of a given type on its usual port in this way, at least with the IP masquerading form of NAT. (If your NAT router has two external addresses, you can forward ports on both external addresses to different internal systems.) If you want to make two internal servers of the same type (such as two Web servers) available to the outside, you'll have to run one on a nonstandard port or obtain some other external IP address.

SETTING `iptables` PORT FORWARDING OPTIONS

There are several different ways to enable port forwarding on a Linux system that provides NAT functions. One is to do it with `iptables`, using its NAT functionality. To do so, you can type a command similar to the following:

```
# iptables -t nat -A PREROUTING -p tcp -i external-interface \
  --destination-port port-num -j DNAT --to dest-addr:port-num
```

Important features of this command include:

- The command manipulates the NAT table (`-t nat`).
- The `-A PREROUTING` parameter specifies that changes to packets are to be made prior to routing proper. The basic NAT features operate post-routing, but port forwarding happens prior to routing.
- The command forwards TCP ports (`-p tcp`).
- The rule applies to packets directed at the system's external network interface (`-i external-interface`) on the specified port (`--destination-port port-num`).
- The `-j DNAT` parameter tells the system that it's performing NAT on the destination (DNAT) rather than the source (SNAT) address.
- The final parameter, `--to dest-addr:port-num`, specifies that the packets should be directed to port port-num on dest-addr. For instance, dest-addr might be `192.168.9.33` and port-num might be `80`. Note that the port-num used with `--to` need not be the same as the port-num used with `--destination-port`.

You can enter several port forwarding commands—as many as necessary to forward any ports that handle servers you want to run internally. As with the basic NAT or firewall configuration, you can create entries in a startup script to run these commands whenever your system starts. You can then leave the configuration alone.

NOTE There are other tools that can provide port forwarding functionality. In particular, the xinetd super server includes port forwarding features. Because xinetd is a user-space program, though, it's less efficient at port forwarding than is the kernel as configured through iptables.

LOGGING iptables ACTIVITY

The iptables commands and options described to this point in this chapter operate without creating any special log entries. Sometimes, though, you want to have access attempts leave a trace in your system logs. For instance, you might want to record attempts to access sensitive ports that you've blocked, or failures related to stateful packet inspection. Such events may indicate an attempt to break into your system, so you may want to be made aware of them in order to be on the alert for other activities directed against your computer.

WARNING   Although logging firewall activities can be a useful source of information, it can also slow down your firewall's operation and provide a potential means of attack. If an attacker knows that you're logging particular types of information, the attacker can send your system packets with the goal of causing your system to write a lot of data to its log files. This degrades your firewall's performance, and in an extreme case it might cause the log file partition to run out of space, causing you further problems. For this reason, you should use these logging options with caution. If possible, place your system log files on a separate partition so that if it's overrun by an out-of-control logging process, it won't cause problems for other programs or processes.

The iptables program includes a special target, LOG, for logging information. Unlike some targets, a match to the LOG target doesn't cause the system to stop searching for matches; after matching and logging the match, the kernel continues searching the chain to which the LOG target belongs. You can use this target in several different ways:

- You can log events that may not match other explicit targets. For instance, you might include a rule to log any stateful packet inspection violation, whether your system is configured to reject such violations.

TIP

Logging events that you don't necessarily want to reject can be a useful debugging tool, because you can verify that packets are reaching your system, and automatically log some information about these packets. Other tools, such as packet sniffers, can fill a similar role, but you might find this feature useful in some situations nonetheless.

- If your system has a default DENY or REJECT policy, you can include a firewall rule for any type of activity you want to log as if you were explicitly blocking that access, but call the LOG target instead of DENY or REJECT. When the packet is logged, it will be blocked by the default policy, unless some other rule lets it through.

- If your system has a default ACCEPT policy, you can log packets you want to block by duplicating the DENY or REJECT rule for those packets and changing the *first* copy to call the LOG target. If you change the second copy to call the LOG target, the result will be ineffectual, because the ACCEPT target will exit from the chain, leaving the LOG target unused.

As an example, consider the following firewall rules on a default-ACCEPT policy firewall, which restrict access from the 172.24.0.0/16 network and log the access:

```
# iptables -A INPUT -s 172.24.0.0/16 -j LOG
# iptables -A OUTPUT -d 172.24.0.0/16 -j LOG
# iptables -A INPUT -s 172.24.0.0/16 -j DROP
# iptables -A OUTPUT -d 172.24.0.0/16 -j DROP
```

The first two commands are exact duplicates of the last two, except for the change in the target—LOG as opposed to DROP. The position of the second and third targets could easily be swapped; this detail is unimportant. You could also add other rules in-between the LOG and DROP rules, but this would make it more difficult to see that the two rules are related.

The result of a logging operation resembles the following from a /var/log/messages file:

```
Nov 18 22:13:21 teela kernel: IN=eth0 OUT=
MAC=00:05:02:a7:76:da:00:50:bf:19:7e:99:08:00 SRC=192.168.1.3
DST=192.168.1.2 LEN=40 TOS=0x10 PREC=0x00 TTL=64 ID=16023 DF
PROTO=TCP SPT=4780 DPT=22 WINDOW=32120 RES=0x00 ACK URGP=0
```

Information included in this output includes the following:

- **Date and time**—The entry begins with a timestamp showing when the packet arrived.
- **System name**—This computer is called teela.
- **Input network interface**—The IN=eth0 entry indicates that the packet in question was an incoming packet on the eth0 interface.
- **Output network interface**—The packet in question was not an outgoing packet, so the OUT= field is empty.
- **MAC addresses**—The MAC= entry includes two *media access control (MAC)* addresses. The first six fields of this entry are the local system's MAC address, and the next six fields are the remote system's MAC address. (The remote system's MAC address is not reliable for packets that have passed through a router, such as packets from the Internet at large.)
- **Source and destination IP addresses**—The SRC= and DST= entries provide the source and destination IP addresses, respectively.
- **Source and destination ports**—The SPT= and DPT= entries specify the source and destination ports, respectively.
- **Packet information**—Additional fields provide further information about the packet, such as its length (LEN=), its time-to-live (TTL) value (TTL=), and so on.

The LOG target supports several additional options that you can use to control material that goes into log entries. The most useful option is probably --log-prefix *prefix*. This option lets you specify a string of up to 29 characters to help you identify log entries, and hence the rule that caused the log entry to be made.

SUMMARY

The Linux iptables tool is extremely useful for setting up firewalls, configuring NAT, performing port forwarding, and logging low-level network access. Frequently, two or more of these features are performed together, such as firewalling a NAT router and logging at least some failed access attempts. A single iptables command sets up a single rule, but most tasks you perform with this tool require multiple rules. Therefore, chances are you'll set up an iptables firewall script that includes many iptables commands.

Using a VPN

One problem frequently faced on the Internet at large is encryption. Many common protocols, such as Telnet and FTP, were not designed with data security in mind; they send data, often including usernames and passwords, in an unencrypted form. Such practices are sometimes tolerable on a local network, where you can control access to the network hardware, but they're very risky on the Internet at large, where your data may pass through a dozen or more routers between client and server.

WARNING

Don't assume that data on your local network is safe. A cracker controlling a compromised computer or a disgruntled local user can wreak considerable havoc using local network access. Using encrypted protocols locally may be justified. The Kerberos suite (described in Chapter 6, Authenticating Users via Kerberos) can be a useful local security tool.

Users sometimes want to use local network resources from a distance—for instance, from home or when traveling. One approach to allowing such access without imposing too great a security risk is to implement a *Virtual Private Network (VPN)*. This is a way of giving remote users access to local network resources as if they were themselves local. VPNs set up virtual network interfaces in both a VPN server and a VPN client system used by the remote user, and link those interfaces across the Internet in an encrypted fashion. VPNs can be used to link individual computers or entire remote networks to a local network. This chapter describes the basics of VPN configuration and use, including two common VPN protocols, PPTP and FreeS/WAN.

WHEN TO USE A VPN

A VPN allows you to extend your local network to remote locations. Of course, if your local network is connected to the Internet, remote users may have access to the local network even without a VPN. A VPN offers two main advantages over direct non-VPN access:

- **The illusion of local access**—Many local networks include protections against unwanted outside access. These may include firewall computers or `iptables`-based firewall rules on individual computers (both covered in Chapter 25, Configuring `iptables`), restrictions implemented in TCP Wrappers or `xinetd` (described in Chapter 4, Starting Servers), or restrictions set in individual server programs. A VPN allows a remote computer to look to local computers as if it were local, thus simplifying the configuration of potentially dozens of servers. The tricky task of determining what remote systems should have access as if they were local is isolated to the VPN server.

- **Encrypting nonencrypted protocols**—The *P* in *VPN* stands for *Private*, so a VPN that doesn't include some sort of encryption to provide privacy isn't much of a VPN. By encrypting normally nonencrypted protocols like NFS and Telnet, a VPN allows you to transfer data over the Internet in a fairly straightforward way, at least from the point of view of the client and server. These clients and servers need no special security configuration, but benefit from the encryption provided by the VPN. Of course, there are encrypted protocols you might use instead of a VPN, and if you're only looking for encryption on one or two protocols, these may be easier to set up than a VPN.

One common use for a VPN is in linking multiple offices at distant locations. If your company has offices in Boston and San Francisco, you can use a VPN to tie them together, giving employees secure access to servers at one location from the other. Figure 26.1 illustrates this arrangement. The VPN routers in this figure *are* routers, much like ordinary routers, NAT routers, or firewall computers. Instead of or in addition to performing ordinary routing, though, the VPN routers set up an encrypted link over which they can transfer data destined for each other.

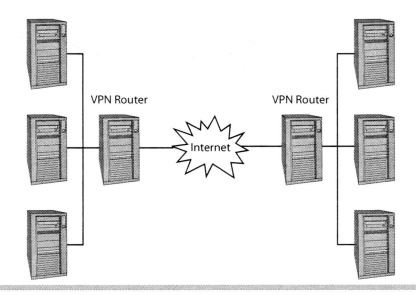

Figure 26.1 A VPN is usually implemented by routers that are capable of encrypting data destined for particular targets.

NOTE Although Figure 26.1 shows a VPN that links just two networks, that's not the limit of VPN technology. You can link three, four, or more networks via a VPN.

Another use of a VPN is to grant individual users access to a larger network. This application is common to serve telecommuters and traveling employees. An individual can link a home computer or notebook to a larger network via a broadband or even a dial-up connection to get the benefit of the main office's servers. The VPN router in this scenario communicates directly with the individual remote systems; essentially, they are VPN routers as well, but they route only their own traffic for the remote system. This situation is illustrated in Figure 26.2.

When implementing a VPN, you should carefully consider your bandwidth needs. Particularly when linking multiple remote networks to a central one, the large central network may need a great deal of external bandwidth to handle the demands from the remote sites. Many protocols that are common on local networks, such as file-sharing protocols and X, transfer vast quantities of data. These transfers may be reasonable on a 100Mbps local Ethernet connection, but over a slower Internet link, such as a 1.5Mbps T1 line, the local protocols may be unacceptably slow. If any of

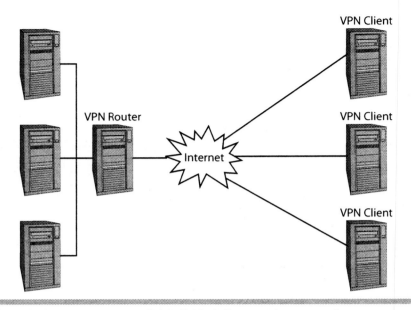

Figure 26.2 VPN systems can link individual clients to a host network.

your connections use low-end broadband connections, such as Asymmetric Digital Subscriber Line (ADSL) accounts for telecommuters, you should remember that some such accounts are asymmetric in nature. Typically, upstream bandwidth is much lower than downstream bandwidth. ADSL, for instance, frequently uses 600–1,500Kbps downstream speeds tied to 100–300Kbps upstream speeds. This may be acceptable for some VPN uses, but not for others. Worse, travelers will probably be limited to analog modem speeds of no more than 56Kbps, and often less.

VPNs are not without their drawbacks, even over fast external connections. For one thing, although they're designed as a secure way to link networks, if they're implemented improperly they can actually *degrade* your security. Consider a telecommuter who connects to a larger network via a VPN. If the larger network is protected by firewalls and similar measures, it should be fairly safe. The home computer, though, may not be very well protected against intrusion. If a cracker breaks into this system, it serves as a gaping hole through the larger network's firewall. These security risks are covered in more detail in the upcoming section, "Potential Security Risks with a VPN."

Another problem with VPNs is that they can be tedious to configure, particularly in conjunction with firewalls. If your need for linking telecommuters, traveling individuals, or remote offices is limited, you might find it simpler to use one or two secure protocols, such as SSH.

VPN OPTIONS FOR LINUX

There is no single standardized VPN tool, although there are moves toward creating VPN standards. In the meantime, organizations that want to configure VPNs need to settle on one of several tools. The three most common tools for Linux are the following:

- **PPTP**—The *Point-to-Point Tunneling Protocol (PPTP)* was developed by a consortium of companies, known collectively as the PPTP Forum. PPTP is commonly used to link telecommuters or travelers to a home office. PPTP support ships with recent versions of Windows, so it's easy to implement on Windows clients. A Linux PPTP server, PoPToP (`http://poptop.lineo.com`), is available.
- **FreeS/WAN**—The FreeS/WAN project (`http://www.freeswan.org`) builds on the Internet Key Exchange (IKE) and IPSec protocols to provide an open source VPN tool for Linux. It's quite popular for Linux-to-Linux VPNs (one or both ends may host non-Linux computers behind the VPN router, of course).
- **SSH**—The Secure Shell (SSH) protocol has the capacity to *tunnel* other protocols' connections. It's possible to use this capability to tunnel a PPP connection over an SSH link. Properly routed, the PPP interfaces on each end of the connection then provide a VPN between the two sites.

This chapter focuses on the first two approaches. PPTP is a very popular VPN approach, particularly when Windows clients must connect directly to the VPN router at a central location. There are also PPTP implementations for many other OSs, and even in dedicated hardware devices that are frequently referred to as *remote access switches*. FreeS/WAN is less popular outside of the Linux world, but it can be an excellent way to link together multiple networks using Linux VPN-enabled routers.

CONFIGURING PPTP IN LINUX

Because PPTP isn't a native Linux protocol, installing and using it on a Linux system may require jumping through some unusual hoops. The PoPToP server itself isn't very unusual, but it must communicate with pppd, the Linux PPP daemon. To provide security, the entire system must also use encryption features that aren't a standard part of pppd, so you must replace the standard pppd with an expanded one. Clients for both Linux and Windows are available, but of course they're configured and used differently.

Obtaining and Installing PoPToP

PoPToP ships with some Linux distributions, such as Debian and Mandrake, usually under the package name pptpd or pptpd-server. If your distribution ships with a PoPToP package, try using it first, because it will probably be easier to install and configure than a generic PoPToP package. If your distribution doesn't ship with a PoPToP package, you can obtain it from the main PoPToP Web site (http://poptop.lineo.com). This site hosts the software in the form of a source tarball, source RPMs, and binary RPMs for x86 systems.

Although you can install and run the PoPToP package on a standard Linux system, the default Linux and PoPToP combination provides a VPN with little in the way of security features. This is because PPTP relies on special PPP encryption features that aren't part of the standard Linux pppd. In particular, PPTP uses the *Microsoft Point-to-Point Encryption (MPPE)* protocol. In order to enable encryption, you must obtain and install MPPE encryption patches for the standard Linux pppd and for your Linux kernel. Unfortunately, this process is tedious and tricky. It's described in the upcoming section, "Enabling Encryption Features."

PoPToP Server Configuration

Once you've downloaded and installed the PoPToP package, you can activate it as follows:

1. Edit the /etc/ppp/options file. This file controls the Linux pppd program, which handles the network link between the VPN router and remote PPTP systems. The file should contain entries like the following:

```
debug
    name servername
    auth
    require-chap
    proxyarp
    192.168.1.1:192.168.1.100
```

Most of these items set critical PPTP options. The last line is optional; it sets the address used by the VPN router on its local network (*192.168.1.1*) and the address to be assigned to a VPN client

(*192.168.1.100*). If you omit this line, you can specify the IP address to be used in the VPN client's configuration. The *servername* is the hostname of the VPN server.

2. Edit the /etc/ppp/chap-secrets file to specify the username and password you intend to use for VPN logins, one entry per line. An example, specifying a username of vpn1 and a password of vpnpass, is:

```
vpn1    *    vpnpass    *
```

WARNING The passwords stored in /etc/ppp/chap-secrets are not encrypted. This file is therefore extremely sensitive and should be protected as well as is possible. Normally, root owns the file and it's readable only to root. If your PoPToP server is compromised, though, this file might be read, giving others remote access to your network. For this reason, you should run as few servers as possible on your VPN router.

3. Look for a reference to pptpd in your /etc/inittab file. If you find such a reference, disable it by adding a pound sign (#) to the start of the line, then type **telinit Q** to activate this change. This allows you to manually start **pptpd** to test its configuration changes. Once you've settled on a working configuration, you can re-enable pptpd in /etc/inittab or start it like a more conventional server, as described in Chapter 4.

4. Type **pptpd** as root to start the server.

At this point, PoPToP should be running, and you should be able to connect to the system using a PPTP client, as described in the upcoming section "PPTP Client Configuration." Without enabling encryption features, though, you may need to disable encryption on your client in order to make a connection. The next section describes enabling PoPToP encryption.

WARNING Although connecting to PoPToP without encryption is a useful first step in testing your configuration, you should not run it in this way as a routine matter. One of the primary reasons for running a VPN is to provide secure connections, and when you disable encryption, you lose these security benefits.

Additional PPTP-specific options are controlled through the pptpd.conf file, which normally resides in /etc or /etc/ppp. Some options you might want to set in this file include the following:

- **debug**—Entering this option causes PoPToP to log more data to the system log, which can be useful if you're having problems getting a connection to work.

- **localip**—PPTP works by using two IP addresses per client, one for use on the local network and one for use by the client remotely. The PPTP router responds to the local address itself, and passes data for it to the remote address. This is similar to a network address translation (NAT) setup. You can specify the local IP addresses with the `localip` option, using a comma-separated list or a range with a dash. For instance, `localip 192.168.9.7,192.168.9.100-150` assigns 192.168.9.7 and all the addresses from 192.168.9.100 to 192.168.9.150. Be sure that other computers on your local network don't use these addresses.

- **remoteip**—This option specifies the IP addresses to be used by the remote clients. They're normally addresses on a private IP address block. You specify IP addresses in the same format as for the `localip` option.

- **listen**—You can have `pptpd` listen for connections on only one interface by listing the IP address associated with that interface with this option. By default, PoPToP listens to all interfaces, which permits PPTP connections within PPTP connections.

ENABLING ENCRYPTION FEATURES

PoPToP relies on `pppd`, which in turn relies upon the kernel. In PoPToP's implementation, encryption features require support from `pppd`, and `pppd` requires that the Linux kernel include appropriate encryption features. For this reason, using encryption with PoPToP requires patching or replacing both `pppd` and your kernel.

You may need to obtain patches and packages from several different locations in order to activate PPTP encryption support with PoPToP. Precisely how you go about this depends on the specific packages you install.

The easiest approach is to use a prepatched version of `pppd` and a prepatched Linux kernel. You can obtain both of these from `http://mirror.binarix.com/ppp-mppe/`. In particular, you must download two files:

- **The Linux kernel**—Prepatched Linux kernels are available under the filenames that begin with `kernel`, such as `kernel-2.4.9-13mppe.i386.rpm`. Some of these packages are precompiled binary kernels for specific system types, and others are kernel source packages. If you download a source package, you must configure and compile it for your system.

- **The ppp package**—Prepatched `pppd` packages have filenames like `ppp-2.4.1-3mdk.i586.rpm`. You may be able to install such a package directly over your existing `pppd` package.

The `http://mirror.binarix.com/ppp-mppe/` site favors binary packages built for the Mandrake distribution, so your best chance of using these packages is if you use Mandrake. It's possible that some of these packages, and particularly the `ppp` package, can be made to work with other distributions, particularly other RPM-based distributions.

TIP If you run a distribution that doesn't use RPM, you may be able to use the `alien` utility to convert package formats. This program is a standard part of Debian, and it allows you to convert between RPM, Debian packages, and tarballs.

Another source of prepatched utilities is the PPTP-Linux site, `http://pptpclient.sourceforge.net`. This site hosts PPTP client software, as described shortly, and the `ppp-mppe` packages are `pppd` programs prepatched with MPPE support. These packages also include kernel modules with MPPE support. Consult the Web site to determine what kernel versions are supported when you download the file; the 2.4.0-4 packages available when I wrote this supported the 2.2.19 kernel on updated Red Hat 6.2 and 7.0 systems. Because 2.4.*x* kernels are now more common, this approach may not be desirable unless the files have been updated by the time you read this.

If you can't or don't want to use prebuilt binaries, you must patch both PPP and your kernel. You'll need to obtain and use at least five things:

- **The Linux kernel**—You can obtain a standard Linux kernel source package from a site like `http://www.kernel.org`. I recommend using a standard Linux kernel, rather than a kernel from a Linux distribution, because the latter have often been modified with their own patches. This can make applying new patches difficult.
- **The pppd source code**—Go to `ftp://cs.anu.edu.au/pub/software/ppp/` to obtain the original `pppd` source code.
- **OpenSSL**—The MPPE patches require that you have OpenSSL and the OpenSSL header files installed on your system. You can obtain these from `http://www.openssl.org`.

- **Linux kernel patches**—You can obtain Linux kernel patches from `http://mirror.binarix.com/ppp-mppe/`. Look for files that begin with `linux` and end with `patch.gz`, such as `linux-2.4.16-openssl-0.9.6b-mppe.patch.gz`.

- **pppd patches**—The `pppd` patches are also available from `http://mirror.binarix.com/ppp-mppe/`. These files have names that begin with `ppp` and end in `patch.gz`, such as `ppp-2.4.1-openssl-0.9.6-mppe-patch.gz`. There are variants of many of these, such as a special version for Alpha CPUs.

Unfortunately, many of these patches and utilities are very version-specific. It's best to begin with the patch files and locate the exact kernel and pppd packages they support to avoid problems caused by version changes. To patch and use these tools, you'll need to uncompress the kernel and pppd source code packages, uncompress the patch files (with **gunzip** *filename.patch.gz*), patch the source code (with **cd** *source-dir*; **patch -p1 <** *patchfile.patch*), configure the packages (with **make menuconfig** or **make xconfig** for the Linux kernel and **./configure** for pppd), compile the packages (with **make bzImage** and **make modules** for the Linux kernel and **make** for pppd), and install the packages (with **make modules_install** and LILO configuration for Linux and **make install** for pppd).

Whether you install your new encryption support from prebuilt binaries, by patching and compiling your tools yourself, or by a mixture, you'll need to reboot your computer to use the new kernel before your encryption support will be available.

PPTP CLIENT CONFIGURATION

If your PPTP clients are Windows systems, using them with a PoPToP VPN is fairly straightforward because Windows includes PPTP support. Linux clients require an extra software package. In either case, once the VPN connection is made, it's as if the VPN client is part of the local network, at least from a logical point of view. (As noted earlier, speed is likely to be well below true local network speed.)

Using Linux PoPToP Clients

PoPToP is a Linux PPTP *server*. To link a Linux system (or a Linux router) to a PoPToP or other PPTP server, you need another package: PPTP-Linux (`http://cag.lcs.mit.edu/~cananian/Projects/PPTP/` or `http://pptpclient.sourceforge.net`). The second site includes PPTP-Linux source code in tarball and RPM formats, as well as binary RPMs for *x*86 and Alpha CPUs. You should download and, if necessary, compile one of these packages, then install it.

Like PoPToP, PPTP-Linux relies upon pppd and the Linux kernel for MPPE encryption. Therefore, you must install appropriate kernel and pppd changes before you can use an encrypted connection. The preceding section, "Enabling Encryption Features," describes how to do this. The PPTP-Linux site includes appropriate tools. Specifically, the ppp-mppe package is an MPPE-patched pppd program and kernel modules (for the 2.2.19 kernel, as of ppp-mppe version 2.4.0-4).

The PPTP-Linux package includes a setup script called pptp-command. To use this tool, follow these steps:

1. Start the script by typing **pptp-command**.
2. The script displays a list of four options: start, stop, setup, and quit. Type **3** to use the setup procedures.
3. The script displays a list of nine items that you may configure. Type **2** to select Add a New CHAP secret.
4. The system asks for your local name. This is the name your system will have on your VPN-mediated network. If the VPN router is a Windows system, you must include a NetBIOS domain name. For instance, you might type **arbor\\maple** to give your system the name maple in the arbor domain.
5. The system asks for your remote name. In most cases, you can leave this at the default (an empty string). You only need to use this if your network has multiple entries with the same local name but different passwords.
6. The system asks for a password. This is the password that you entered in your PoPToP or other VPN server configuration, such as Step 2 in "PoPToP Server Configuration."
7. The script again displays the list of nine items you can set up. Select option 5, Add a NEW PPTP Tunnel.
8. The system displays a list of predefined tunnels. This will most likely be empty, including only an option called Other. If you see a tunnel that's correct for you, select it; but most likely you'll need to select Other.
9. The system prompts for assorted pieces of information related to your tunnel definition, such as the tunnel's name (use whatever you like),

the VPN server's IP address, and routing commands to be used with the tunnel. The latter are similar to those used with the `route` command (described in Chapter 2, TCP/IP Network Configuration). For instance, **add -host 172.19.87.1 gw DEF_GW** sets up the system to use 172.19.87.1 as its default gateway, and **add -net 172.19.0.0/16 TUNNEL_DEV** tells it to pass all data for the 172.19.0.0/16 network through the tunnel.

10. Once again, you see the list of nine items you can configure. Select option 7, `Configure resolv.conf`.

11. Select the tunnel configuration you created in Step 9. The system will ask you for DNS information that would ordinarily go in `/etc/resolv.conf` (as described in Chapter 2). Enter this information.

12. The 9-item list of options to configure appears again. Select option 8, `Select a default tunnel`.

13. The system asks for the name of a default tunnel. Select the one you created in Step 9 (or some other tunnel if you're creating multiple tunnels).

14. At the next appearance of the 9-item list, select option 9, `Quit`. This terminates the setup program.

At this point, PPTP-Linux is configured to use your PPTP server. You can bring up the PPTP VPN link by using the same `pptp-command` program you used to set up the link. Instead of choosing option 3 at the first prompt, though, pick option 1 (`start`). The program asks for a tunnel number. Enter it (probably 1) and `pptp-command` brings up the PPTP VPN link.

NOTE   Bringing up the VPN link requires the existence of a regular network connection. Thus, you may need to configure your system to use a regular connection, as described in Chapter 2, or bring up a dial-up PPP link, before you can activate your VPN link.

You can test your VPN link by using `route` to view your routing table, and by attempting to contact servers on the VPN system. If you can't reach your VPN servers, try pinging the VPN router. You might also try using `traceroute` to see if your packets are going over the VPN link. If `traceroute` shows packets traversing your normal (non-VPN) Internet connection, then something is wrong with your routing table. There should be a path to the VPN systems via the VPN's PPP link. If there isn't, Linux will try to route the packets to that network via its normal Internet connection.

Using Windows PPTP Clients

Frequently, PPTP clients are Windows computers belonging to frequent travelers, telecommuters, or others who need to work away from an office. Windows 9*x*/Me and Windows NT/2000/XP include PPTP clients, although they're usually not installed by default. The PPTP software works only after you have a working Internet connection, be it via a broadband ISP, a dial-up PPP ISP, or some other mechanism. The procedure for running a Windows Me PPTP client is as follows:

1. Double-click Add/Remove Programs from the Control Panel. This produces the Add/Remove Programs Properties dialog box.
2. Click the Windows Setup tab in the Add/Remove Programs Properties dialog box.
3. Double-click the Communications item in the list of component types. This brings up the Communications dialog box.
4. Check the Virtual Private Networking item in the Communications dialog box.
5. Click OK in both the Communications and Add/Remove Programs Properties dialog boxes. Windows will install the PPTP software, and will probably require you to reboot the computer. Do so.
6. After the system reboots, open the Dial-Up Networking folder in the Control Panel.
7. Double-click the Make New Connection icon. This produces the Make New Connection Wizard (shown in Figure 26.3).

Figure 26.3 Be sure to choose the Microsoft VPN Adapter when creating a VPN link, not the modem over which the connection goes.

8. Type an identifying name for the link and select the Microsoft VPN Adapter device, as shown in Figure 26.3.

9. Click Next. The Make New Connection window now provides a text entry field in which you type the hostname or IP address of the VPN server. Enter this information.

10. Click Next. The system now informs you that the new device is available. Click Finish to dismiss the Make New Connection window.

A new icon now appears in the Dial-Up Networking window. When you double-click this icon, Windows displays the Connect To dialog box shown in Figure 26.4. You should enter the username and password you use on the VPN server, and you may adjust the VPN server's name or IP address, if desired. When you click Connect, Windows initiates the connection, which may take a few seconds. Thereafter, your system has an additional IP address, corresponding to one on the VPN server's network. You can access systems on that network as if they were local, including performing actions such as browsing the network in My Network Places (Network Neighborhood in earlier versions of Windows) and using any resources that are available only to local computers. Remember, though, that the physical networking is *not* local, so you don't get the same sort of speed that you would get if your system were directly connected to the same networking medium as the VPN systems.

You can change some features of the VPN from the Connect To dialog box before initiating a connection. As shown in Figure 26.4, you can elect to have Windows remember (save) your password. If you do this, you can have Windows initiate the connection whenever it starts up by selecting Connect Automatically. Further options are available by clicking Proper-

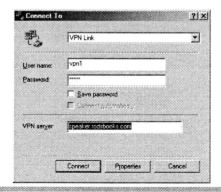

Figure 26.4   You can control a VPN link from the Connect To dialog box.

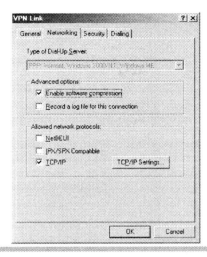

Figure 26.5   You can control many details of a PPTP VPN from the client's configuration tools.

ties. This brings up a dialog box named after your VPN connection, as shown in Figure 26.5. The most interesting options are on the Networking and Security tabs. From the Networking tab, you can control whether the system uses software compression or keeps a log of the session. You can also control what network protocols are passed through the VPN. If you click TCP/IP Settings, you can tell the system to obtain its IP address from the PPTP server or request a particular address itself, and do the same for DNS server addresses. The Security tab lets you set the username, password, and NetBIOS domain names. It also lets you enable or disable password and data encryption (both are enabled by default, and disabling them removes much of the benefit of a VPN).

CONFIGURING A LINUX FREES/WAN SERVER

FreeS/WAN is a more Linux-centric VPN solution than is PPTP, but considered broadly, both serve a similar function: linking two or more computers or networks in a secure way over an insecure network, such as the Internet. As with PPTP, the first step in running a FreeS/WAN VPN is obtaining and installing the software. You can then begin configuring the system and establishing a link between FreeS/WAN systems.

FreeS/WAN is actually a very sophisticated package, with more options than can be covered in this chapter. For more information, consult the FreeS/WAN documentation, and particularly the configuration manual,

```
http://www.freeswan.org/freeswan_trees/freeswan-1.91/doc/
config.html.
```

Obtaining and Installing FreeS/WAN

In early 2002, few Linux distributions ship with FreeS/WAN, but there are exceptions. Most notably, SuSE comes with the package, and a Mandrake package is also readily available. You should check your distribution to be sure it doesn't come with FreeS/WAN before obtaining it from the main FreeS/WAN Web site, `http://www.freeswan.org`. This site (or more precisely, the FTP site to which it links, `ftp://ftp.xs4all.nl/pub/crypto/freeswan/`) holds the software in source code form. FreeS/WAN requires explicit kernel support that's not standard in the Linux kernel, so to use it, you must recompile your kernel, as described shortly. If you install a FreeS/WAN package that came with your distribution, chances are these kernel changes are part of the kernel that came with the distribution, so your configuration task is simpler. The rest of this section assumes you're installing FreeS/WAN using its source code.

If you compile FreeS/WAN from source code, you must have several components installed on your system:

- **Standard development tools**—You must have typical development tools, such as GCC, `make`, and normal libraries and library headers. Such tools are installed on most Linux systems by default.
- **Kernel source code**—The FreeS/WAN compilation tools automatically change your Linux kernel source tree, in `/usr/src/linux`. This tree should therefore contain your *current* kernel source code. If you're using your distribution's standard kernel, you should be able to install a matching source code package. You'll later have to recompile the kernel and reboot. If you plan to change your kernel's configuration, you should do this (with **make menuconfig**, **make xconfig**, or a similar command) prior to compiling FreeS/WAN. You may want to make the kernel and test it before proceeding further.
- **GMP library**—FreeS/WAN relies upon the *GNU Multi-Precision (GMP)* library (`http://www.swox.com/gmp/`). This package is available on most distributions, so try to find it and install it from your installation CD-ROM or your distribution's main FTP or Web site.
- **Ncurses library**—Some configuration options use the ncurses library. This isn't strictly required, but it's very helpful. It's also very common, so it may already be installed.

To make and install the FreeS/WAN package, follow these steps:

1. Make sure you've got all the components described earlier, such as your kernel source code and the GMP library.

2. Uncompress the FreeS/WAN package in some convenient location, such as /usr/src. (*Do not* copy or move the freeswan-*version* directory after uncompressing it; the directory contains symbolic links that are sensitive to changes.)

3. Change into the FreeS/WAN source code directory and type a command to configure the package, patch the Linux kernel, and make the FreeS/WAN package. You can use **make oldgo** to use your existing Linux kernel configuration and default FreeS/WAN settings, **make ogo** to use the kernel's make config configure utility, **make menugo** to use the kernel's make menuconfig, or **make xgo** to use the kernel's make xconfig. The last three of these options run you through the specified kernel configuration routine so that you can change kernel options. In any event, the last line of output should report that the system was calling an errcheck script. If you don't see this line, it means that something went wrong. You can check the out.kpatch and out.kbuild files for information on the patching and building process for clues to what went wrong.

4. Type **make kinstall** to rebuild your kernel. This process builds the kernel and its modules, and uses the kernel's make modules_install process to install the new kernel modules. If there are any errors, they should appear in the out.kinstall file.

5. Reconfigure LILO, GRUB, or whatever method you're using to boot your Linux kernel to handle the new kernel. You may need to copy your new kernel file from /usr/src/linux/arch/*architecture-code*/ boot, edit /etc/lilo.conf or some other configuration file, and type **lilo** or some other boot loader command.

6. Reboot the computer. Be sure to specify the correct new FreeS/WAN-enabled kernel if you have a choice.

At this point, your system should be working with a kernel that's capable of supporting FreeS/WAN. As part of the process, FreeS/WAN should have created a file called /etc/ipsec.secrets, which contains encryption keys. You'll need to deal with this file later, so for now you should check that it exists and contains some keys (which resemble hexadecimal gibberish).

In order to be useful, you must configure FreeS/WAN on at least two computers, presumably on different networks. The installation process is the same on both. In many cases, both systems will be configured as routers, although you can install FreeS/WAN on a single system that's to connect to a remote network.

EDITING CONFIGURATION FILES

FreeS/WAN uses two configuration files: `/etc/ipsec.secrets` and `/etc/ipsec.conf`. Each is important and plays a different role. The first contains encryption keys, which the servers use to identify themselves to each other. The second controls general-purpose configuration options.

Setting Up Keys

As noted earlier, the FreeS/WAN build process should have created an `/etc/ipsec.secrets` file that contains encryption keys. If this file isn't present, or if it doesn't contain a key you want to use, you can generate a new key with the following command:

```
# ipsec rsasigkey 128 > /root/rsa.key
```

This command creates a 128-bit key and places it in the `/root/rsa.key` file. You can generate a key of some other length by specifying the desired length instead of `128` in the preceding example. The output of this command isn't quite what's needed, though. Specifically, you must add the following line to the start of the file:

```
: RSA {
```

Be sure to include the spaces around RSA. You must also add a line containing at least one space followed by a single right curly brace (`}`) to the end of the file. You can then copy the result into the existing `/etc/ipsec.secrets` file, replacing the current `: RSA {` block in that file. You should perform this step on both the FreeS/WAN VPN routers.

NOTE The output of the `ipsec rsasigkey` command includes a comment to the effect that the key is only useful for authentication, not for encryption. This is fine; FreeS/WAN uses the key in precisely this way, and uses other algorithms for encryption.

The output of the `ipsec rsasigkey` command includes a commented-out line that begins `#pubkey=`. This sets the public key that you must give to other systems with which this system must communicate. You should make note of it now, because you'll need to enter it into the /etc/ipsec.conf file of your other systems.

Editing the IPSec Settings

Most FreeS/WAN installations create a default /etc/ipsec.conf file. This file isn't terribly useful as is, but it can be used as a good template for configuring your system. The file has three basic types of setup sections: config setup, conn %default and conn *remotename*.

Adjusting Local Options

The config setup section specifies local settings. The default example section resembles the following:

```
config setup
  # THIS SETTING MUST BE CORRECT or almost nothing will work;
  # %defaultroute is okay for most simple cases.
  interfaces=%defaultroute
  # Debug-logging controls:  "none" for (almost) none, "all" for \
lots.
  klipsdebug=none
  plutodebug=none
  # Use auto= parameters in conn descriptions to control startup \
actions.
  plutoload=%search
  plutostart=%search
  # Close down old connection when new one using same ID shows up.
  uniqueids=yes
```

The most important setting in this section is the interfaces line, which tells FreeS/WAN which interfaces to use for VPN connections (that is, where it can find VPN partners). The default value of %defaultroute tells FreeS/WAN to use your default route, which normally connects to all non-local IP addresses. You might want to specify particular interfaces, though. For instance, the following option tells the system to use eth0 and ppp1:

```
interfaces="ipsec0=eth0 ipsec1=ppp1"
```

The klipsdebug and plutodebug options set the logging options for the *Kernel IP Security (KLIPS)* kernel features and for the Pluto daemon, which is a part of the FreeS/WAN package that handles key exchange. You can set these to all if you're having problems.

Pluto can load connections into memory or start them automatically when FreeS/WAN starts up. The `plutoload` and `plutostart` options tell the system with which connections it should do this. The default value works well in most cases, but if you want to specify just some connections, you can name them instead. The drawback to listing individual FreeS/WAN servers is that if one crashes, it may not come back up into the VPN automatically after restarting.

Adjusting Default Remote Options

Individual connections are defined through sections that begin with the keyword `conn`. FreeS/WAN supports a `%default` connection name for setting default connection options. Options you're likely to see in this section include the following:

- **keyingtries**—In the event of a connection failure, FreeS/WAN normally retries the connection. A default value of 0 for this option makes FreeS/WAN infinitely persistent, but if you want to limit the number of times it retries its connections, set this value lower. You might want to do this when you're first testing your setup.
- **authby**—The usual authentication method uses `authby=rsasig`, which causes the system to use RSA keys. Another method uses *shared secrets*, but this chapter only covers RSA key authentication.

In addition to these options, it's possible for various other options described in the next section, "Adjusting System-Specific Remote Options," to appear in a default connection section. If you find yourself entering the same options for several connections, you might move them all to the default configuration to reduce the chance of a typo causing problems and to shorten the configuration file.

Adjusting System-Specific Remote Options

Each connection requires some customization, which is done in a `conn` section. The connection name follows `conn`, and that connection's options follow on subsequent lines, all of which are indented at least one space. Many of the options in this section relate to network interfaces. To help understand this, consider Figure 26.6. This shows a typical FreeS/WAN network. The configuration is described from the top ("left") VPN router. You must tell FreeS/WAN about various IP addresses used in this configuration. You do so with several options:

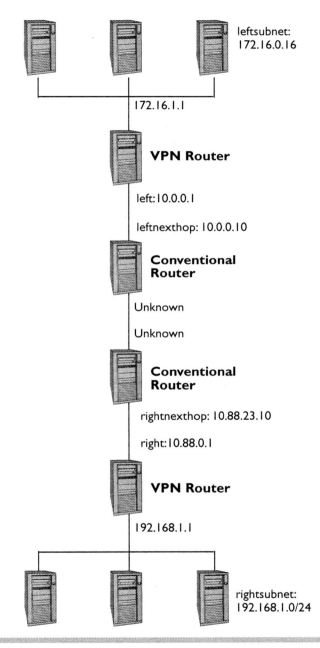

leftsubnet:
172.16.0.16

172.16.1.1

VPN Router

left:10.0.0.1

leftnexthop: 10.0.0.10

**Conventional
Router**

Unknown

Unknown

**Conventional
Router**

rightnexthop: 10.88.23.10

right:10.88.0.1

VPN Router

192.168.1.1

rightsubnet:
192.168.1.0/24

Figure 26.6 A FreeS/WAN configuration requires you to identify several computer
and network addresses involved in creating the VPN.

- **leftsubnet**—This is the local subnet to which the FreeS/WAN router is connected—172.16.0.0/16 in the case of Figure 26.6.

- **left**—This is the address associated with the VPN server's external interface. This can be set to %defaultroute in most cases, or you may want to provide an exact IP address, such as 10.0.0.1 in Figure 26.6

- **leftnexthop**—This is the IP address of the conventional router to which the VPN system connects, such as 10.0.0.10 in Figure 26.6. This information is required because KLIPS bypasses the normal kernel routing machinery and sends the data directly to the next router.

- **leftfirewall**—If the subnet that the VPN router serves uses non-routable IP addresses with NAT, or if the VPN router also functions as a firewall, set leftfirewall=yes. This adjusts the way FreeS/WAN treats packets to support firewall functionality.

- **rightnexthop**—This is the mirror of the leftnexthop entry; it's the IP address of the conventional router that delivers packets to the remote network. Note that this is the IP address of this router as seen by the remote FreeS/WAN system.

- **right**—This entry corresponds to the remote VPN router's external network interface. Unlike left, you can't leave this entry set at a default.

- **rightsubnet**—This is the IP address block of the remote network, such as 192.168.1.0/24 in Figure 26.6.

- **leftid**—This is an identifier for the left system. This can be an IP address, a domain name, a hostname preceded by an at-sign (such as @vpn.threeroomco.com) or a username and hostname (much like an e-mail address, such as emily@vpn.threeroomco.com). The hostname preceded by the at-sign indicates that the system shouldn't try to resolve the name into an IP address. As a general rule, this is the best form to use because it's reasonably memorable and won't cause problems if DNS is down.

- **rightid**—This is just like leftid, but it identifies the other side of the VPN link.

- **leftrsasigkey**—This is the RSA public key value from the /etc/ipsec.secrets file on the left VPN server. You should cut and paste this value if you're configuring the left system, or transfer the file and then copy and paste it if you're configuring the right system.

- **rightrsasigkey**—This is the RSA public key value from the /etc/ipsec.secrets file on the right VPN server.

- **auto**—This option, in conjunction with the `plutoload` and `plutostart` options in the `conn setup` section, controls which networks are loaded or started when FreeS/WAN starts up. Specifically, if `plutoload=%search` and `auto=add`, then the configuration is loaded; if `plutstart=%search` and `auto=start`, then the configuration is started. For initial setup and testing, `auto=add` is a good configuration because this allows you to manually start connections. Once you set up a production system, `auto=start` usually works better because it requires no manual intervention to start the connections.

The labeling of a system or network as `left` or `right` is arbitrary. One useful mnemonic may be to give the link a name that includes both ends, such as `boscinci` for a VPN linking Boston and Cincinnati offices. You can then call the Boston side `left` and the Cincinnati end `right`, reflecting their positions in the name. You use the same configuration on both sides of the link; FreeS/WAN figures out which end it is by examining the system's existing network connections.

ESTABLISHING A LINK

The basic procedure for establishing a link between two FreeS/WAN routers is to start the `ipsec` program as a daemon on one and to use the same program to initiate a connection from the other computer. Once you've tested the connection, it should be started automatically whenever you start the computers and run `ipsec` on both. It doesn't matter which system you use in daemon mode and which you use to manually start the connection when you do this stage of the testing; unlike PPTP, FreeS/WAN makes little distinction between clients and servers.

To start FreeS/WAN in daemon mode, type the following command:

```
# ipsec setup start
```

This starts the server and, depending upon the configuration of the `plutoload`, `plutostart`, and `auto` options described earlier, the system loads a configuration and waits for a connection or tries to initiate a connection. If you configured your systems as described earlier, with `auto=add` on both ends of the connection, you can start the server on one end and it will wait for a connection request from the other system. This will occur when you type the following command on the system that's not yet running the program:

```
# ipsec auto --up name
```

In this example, *name* should be the name of a connection link, such as boscinci. The system should attempt to start up that link. You can check to see if it was successful by typing **ipsec look**. If you receive a set of encryption information and a VPN routing table as output, then the connection was successful. You can also try using normal networking commands, like ping, traceroute, and telnet, to see if you can establish connections with systems on the remote network, and to verify that they're being routed via the VPN. Remember that, if the remote network is publicly accessible from the Internet at large, tools like ping won't verify that the connection is via the VPN. You should use protocols that are blocked from scrutiny by the general public, or from your local public addresses, to test your VPN functionality.

Once you've gotten your network up and running, you can change the configuration of auto in /etc/ipsec.conf. If you set this to start on both ends, the startup will be automatic whenever the **ipsec setup start** command is issued. You can start FreeS/WAN in this way by starting it in a SysV or local startup script, as described in Chapter 4.

POTENTIAL SECURITY RISKS WITH A VPN

VPNs are intended, in part, as a tool for increasing a network's security. They can easily become a doorway through which intruders can enter, though. VPNs are frequently explained through diagrams like Figures 26.1, 26.2, and 26.6. These show the way the various VPN components are tied together. Such figures don't emphasize strongly enough that many of the links are actually *two* links. For instance, consider a PPTP VPN in which a central network uses a VPN router to communicate in a secure way with Windows computers. Those Windows computers actually have *two* network interfaces—one for the VPN and one for their normal Internet connections. Depending upon the firewall rules on the VPN router itself, the *logical* configuration of such a network might more closely resemble that shown in Figure 26.7.

Normally, the VPN is configured to trust its VPN clients more than it trusts hosts on the Internet at large. The VPN clients, though, have their own independent links to the Internet (in fact, those links are usually the means by which the VPN connection is established). Thus, unless security on the VPN clients is quite strong, they can become a means of attack. If the VPN or any other intervening firewalls or security tools treat VPN clients as truly local, the security provided by those firewalls and other security measures

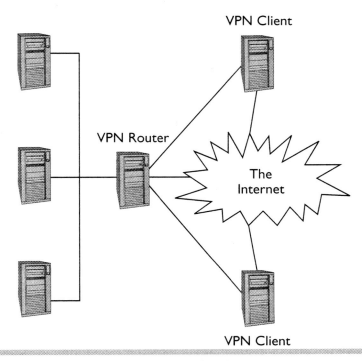

Figure 26.7   Although a VPN provides secure links between systems or networks, both sides of the VPN link normally have direct Internet connections, and those can be abused.

isn't nearly as good as it might at first appear. For instance, consider the case of an Internet worm or virus that attacks random computers. You might build protections from such attacks into your regular firewall. If a VPN client is compromised, though, and if the firewall protection doesn't apply to VPN clients, the worm or virus will quickly find its way into your allegedly protected network.

There are two approaches to restoring security in the face of potential VPN bypasses:

- **Secure both ends of the VPN**—If both ends of a VPN connection boast equivalent security, then the network as a whole remains secure. This approach is common when a VPN links entire networks; typically, both VPN routers or separate firewall systems protect all forms of entry. Such a configuration is trickier when the VPN links individual telecommuters or the like, because the number of VPN end-points can be quite high, and those systems may not be under your direct control. If an employee decides to install a potentially risky program on a home computer, there may be little you can do to stop it.

- **Don't trust VPN clients**—You might install firewall rules that deny certain types of access to the VPN clients, in effect relegating them to "second-class" status within your network's hierarchy. Taken to an extreme, this approach eliminates all benefits of the VPN, but you might use it to give your local network *some* protection. If your VPN users won't be using X, for instance, you could block the X protocols to VPN clients but not to local systems, thus reducing the chance of an X-based attack succeeding through the VPN.

In many cases, a combination of these two approaches is appropriate. You might insist that employees who use PPTP client software install firewall packages as well, and give them access only to particular local computers or protocols. You can use the Linux `iptables` command (described in Chapter 25) to configure these restrictions. When both ends of the VPN are under your complete control, you can rely more upon the first approach, because you can configure identical security measures on both Internet access points.

Summary

A VPN is a useful tool for extending the reach of a local network. You can use this tool to give individual remote users, or entire remote networks, access to nonpublic servers on your local network. This is an extremely useful tool when you want to support telecommuting or when you want to tie together two or more networks at distant locations, in order to share servers or otherwise integrate those networks. Several VPN products exist, and many of these are available for Linux. Two particularly popular protocols are PPTP, which is implemented in Linux by PoPToP and PPTP-Linux, and FreeS/WAN. PPTP is commonly used by individual remote clients to link to a central network, while FreeS/WAN is more commonly used to tie together entire networks. Both can be used in either way, though. Before you implement a VPN, you should carefully consider the security implications of doing so, paying particular attention to the fact that each VPN client is another potential entry point to your local network.

Index